Foreign Investment, International Partnerships, and Modern Business Regulation for Economic Growth

Nasser Al Harrasi
https://orcid.org/0000-0003-4456-0926
University of Technology and Applied Sciences, Oman

Badar Khalid Hakim Al-Shabibi
University of Technology and Applied Sciences, Oman

Mohd Abass Bhat
https://orcid.org/0000-0003-0705-5410
University of Technology and Applied Sciences, Oman

S. Porkodi
University of Technology and Applied Sciences, Oman

IGI Global
Scientific Publishing
Publishing Tomorrow's Research Today

Vice President of Editorial	Melissa Wagner
Director of Acquisitions	Mikaela Felty
Director of Book Development	Jocelynn Hessler
Production Manager	Mike Brehm
Cover Design	Jose Rosado

Published in the United States of America by
IGI Global Scientific Publishing
701 East Chocolate Avenue
Hershey, PA, 17033, USA
Tel: 717-533-8845 | Fax: 717-533-7115
Website: https://www.igi-global.com E-mail: cust@igi-global.com

Library of Congress Cataloging-in-Publication Data

LCCN: 2026011385 (CIP Data Pending)
ISBN13: 9798337389646
Isbn13Softcover: 9798337389653
EISBN13: 9798337389660
British Cataloguing in Publication Data
A Cataloguing in Publication record for this book is available from the British Library.

Table of Contents

Detailed Table of Contents

The impact of foreign direct investment on the economic growth of host countries has generated discussion in previous theoretical and empirical studies. This study analyzes the influence of foreign direct investment and institutions, specifically economic and political aspects, on economic growth. The research analyzed panel data from four North African countries spanning the years 2002 to 2023. The PMG/ARDL model was employed to examine the short- and long-term impacts of foreign direct investment and institutions on economic growth. The panel unit root test and the panel co-integration test were utilized to enhance the model's estimation. The empirical evidence substantiates that economic freedom and foreign direct investment function as the fundamental catalysts of growth in both the short term and the long term. Political institutional variables remain non-significant across both temporal horizons, a phenomenon attributed to the compounding structural disruptions of the Arab Spring and the COVID-19 pandemic, which introduced persistent non-linearities into the region's governance indicators. Consequently, these findings underscore the centrality of economic liberalization and enhancing institutional quality for FDI attraction as critical policy priorities for North African economies navigating post-revolutionary and post-pandemic recovery.

The chapter examines the relationship between foreign direct investment (FDI), corporate regulation, and economic growth through an integrated conceptual framework. It highlights that FDI serves not only as a source of capital inflows but also as a catalyst for technology transfer, innovation diffusion, employment generation, and integration into global value chains. The study argues that the impact of FDI on economic growth significantly depends on the quality of corporate regulation and institutional governance. Drawing on neoclassical growth theory, endogenous growth theory, institutional theory, and the Eclectic Paradigm (OLI framework), the chapter develops a multidimensional model linking FDI, regulatory quality, and economic performance. It further examines the mediating roles of human capital development, trade openness, financial development, and technological advancement, while emphasizing the moderating influence of regulatory effectiveness for sustainable economic growth. It stresses policy adaptability and governance now.

The concept of positive and negative externalities goes beyond a textbook topic in introductory economics. Developing nations with abundant natural resources often experience primarily similar negative externalities, even when they are in different regions of the world. This chapter shows that foreign direct investment (FDI) impacts the lives of real people, primarily in disruptive and negative ways in selected developing nations i.e., Ghana, Kazakhstan, and Ecuador. The objectives are to understand how to qualitatively assess the costs and benefits of natural resources for local communities, gain a deeper understanding of the true experiences of local communities that cannot be easily quantified in econometric models, systematically categorize the diverse perspectives of stakeholders, and reconceptualize the economic growth of resource-rich countries. Qualitative research methods, including reflective journaling, qualitative content analysis (QCA), and critical discourse analysis (CDA), were used to achieve these objectives.

With fintec acting as one of the catalysts, Financial Inclusion (FI) and strategy to improve FI has gained focal light in academia as well as amongst policy makers. FI has become strongest tool to enhance economic growth and reduce poverty levels. This paper analyses the drivers of FI, focusing on the MENAAP region and comparing them with the rest of the regions. It utilizes supervised machine learning, focusing on the Multi-Layer Perceptron Artificial Neural Network model with data collected from the World Bank Group's report. The findings indicate disparity among MENAAP regions in terms of penetration of FI. The low and middle-income group are low on financial access and strategic efforts but successful in consumer credit providence and penetration of owning bank accounts with underprivileged. The region is seen taking efforts focusing on leveraging technology and targeted policies to close existent gaps, particularly in Pakistan and Afghanistan. The region has been successful in setting up strong and transparent institutions to build public confidence in the financial sector.

The world of global investment has experienced significant change over the last twenty years due to convergence of regulatory reform, sustainability requirements, and institutional reconfiguration. This chapter discusses the extent to which contemporary regulatory frameworks influence global patterns of investment in a manner that promotes sustainable economic development. The chapter draws on the recent empirical literature and theoretical advances in the field of institutional economics, international investment law, and sustainable finance. It is found in the analysis that quality of regulatory institutions is the only most powerful determinant of foreign direct investment (FDI) inflows, especially in developing economies. The chapter also argues that the alignment of the private capital to the goals of sustainable development will be merely a far-fetched dream unless coherent, enforceable, and internationally harmonized regulatory frameworks are in place. Recommendations and guidelines on policy are made as well as future research directions.

This paper aims to explore how women from working class with typical local career background and privileged-defined women directors from western influenced backgrounds in combination may lead to distinct or common pathways towards women directorship experiences and trajectories. A qualitative study was undertaken of a mixed Middle Eastern sample of women directors from Egypt, Morocco, Dubai, Oman and Saudi Arabia from varied economic sectors were interviewed. Two rounds of interviews were conducted with 6-month time duration in between. Women directors from bourgeoisie social class and multi-cultural exposure in the West reflected contemporary directorship models stressing the importance of tribe's power, nepotism calculations, ease of networking, less negative feelings, and less faced obstacles, yet a smaller number of board directorships. In contrast, women directors from working class background emphasized the importance of merit and hard work, labor market reputation, and importance of work mentor in defining effective women directorship models

This paper is a systematic literature review that aims to understand how digital transformation, innovation, investment, and policy frameworks contribute to economic growth, with a special focus on Oman's Vision 2040. The study begins by explaining why digital technologies and investment have become important for modern economies. It then clearly describes how existing research papers were carefully searched, selected, and reviewed using a systematic method. The main part of the paper categorises earlier studies into key themes, including foreign direct investment, fintech, innovation ecosystems, public–private partnerships, and regulatory reforms. Finally, the paper explains the implications of these findings for Oman's economic development and highlights areas where future research is needed, thereby helping policymakers, investors, and researchers better understand the path forward.

This article investigates how strategic communication and territorial intelligence interact to support sustainable innovation trajectories and employment outcomes in family business entrepreneurship in the Middle East and North Africa (MENA). Empirically, the study relies on a cross sectional survey administered to owner managers and next generation leaders of family firms across several MENA economies, analyzed using PLS SEM with bootstrapped mediation tests. To deepen interpretation, qualitative insights from open ended responses are examined using thematic analysis. The results provide convergent evidence that strategic communication significantly predicts territorial intelligence, which partially mediates the link between communication capability and sustainable innovation, and is positively associated with job creation intentions. Moderation effects indicate that stronger governance and entrepreneurial culture intensify the conversion of territorial intelligence into innovation outcomes, whereas women's empowerment strengthens governance-related sustainability effects.

Artificial intelligence (AI) is reshaping digital transformation and sustainable investment ecosystems. However, prior studies mainly focus on firm-level AI

Preface

INTRODUCTION

In an era characterized by economic uncertainty, technological disruption, and increasing globalization, foreign investment and international partnerships have become indispensable instruments for fostering sustainable economic growth. Governments across both developed and emerging economies are continually seeking strategies to attract high-quality foreign direct investment (FDI), strengthen regulatory institutions, and create business environments that encourage innovation while maintaining economic resilience. At the same time, policymakers face the complex challenge of balancing investment promotion with social equity, environmental sustainability, and responsible governance. This volume, *Foreign Investment, International Partnerships, and Modern Business Regulation for Economic Growth*, explores these interconnected issues through multidisciplinary perspectives that bridge economics, public policy, finance, technology, management, and international business.

The contributions assembled in this edited collection demonstrate that foreign investment alone cannot guarantee long-term prosperity. Rather, the effectiveness of FDI depends upon the quality of institutions, regulatory frameworks, technological readiness, financial inclusion, and collaborative partnerships between governments, industries, and international stakeholders. As economies increasingly embrace digital transformation, artificial intelligence, sustainable finance, and knowledge-driven development, new opportunities and challenges continue to reshape the global investment landscape. Understanding these dynamics requires insights that extend beyond traditional economic theory to incorporate emerging technologies, governance innovations, and evolving business ecosystems.

A distinctive feature of this volume is its strong emphasis on regional perspectives while maintaining global relevance. Several chapters focus on North Africa, the Middle East, and Oman, offering valuable case studies that illuminate how national development strategies, particularly Oman Vision 2040, can leverage foreign investment, regulatory modernization, and technological innovation to achieve sustainable development objectives. These regional analyses are complemented by broader conceptual and empirical discussions that provide lessons applicable across diverse economic contexts. Together, the chapters illustrate how local institutional realities interact with global investment trends, producing unique opportunities for economic transformation.

This book is intended for researchers, policymakers, practitioners, graduate students, and international business professionals seeking a comprehensive understanding of the evolving relationship between foreign investment, business regulation, innovation, and economic development. By combining empirical research, conceptual modeling, systematic literature reviews, qualitative analyses, and technological applications, the volume offers readers both theoretical insights and practical recommendations for designing policies and business strategies that promote inclusive and sustainable economic growth.

OVERVIEW OF THE CHAPTERS

The volume begins by establishing the institutional foundations of foreign investment and economic development. Chapter 1 investigates how political and economic institutions influence the effectiveness of foreign direct investment in promoting long-term economic growth across North African countries. Using advanced panel data analysis, the authors demonstrate that institutional quality plays a decisive role in maximizing the developmental benefits of FDI. Complementing this perspective, Chapter 2 develops a comprehensive conceptual model linking FDI, business regulation, governance quality, human capital, technological advancement, and financial development. Drawing upon several prominent economic and institutional theories, the chapter illustrates the multidimensional relationships that shape sustainable economic growth.

Broadening the discussion beyond quantitative models, Chapter 3 examines the social and environmental implications of foreign investment in natural resource sectors through qualitative analyses of documentaries focused on Ghana, Kazakhstan, and Ecuador. The chapter highlights the lived experiences of local communities and encourages a more nuanced understanding of the externalities associated with resource-based investment. Chapter 4 shifts attention to financial inclusion, utilizing artificial neural networks to identify the key determinants of financial access across the MENAAP region. The findings emphasize how technological innovation, institutional strength, and targeted public policies contribute to broader financial participation and economic development.

Regulatory governance forms the central theme of Chapter 5, which explores how contemporary investment regulations influence global capital flows while supporting sustainable economic development. The chapter emphasizes the growing importance of harmonized regulatory systems capable of balancing investment attractiveness with environmental and social responsibility. Expanding the discussion into corporate leadership, Chapter 6 investigates the experiences of women directors across Middle Eastern countries, examining how psychological capital, gender, social class, and multicultural experiences shape leadership pathways and governance practices. Together, these chapters illustrate that institutional effectiveness encompasses not only regulatory quality but also inclusive leadership and organizational diversity.

Innovation, digital transformation, and national development strategies receive considerable attention in the next group of chapters. Chapter 7 presents a systematic review of investment, technology, fintech, innovation ecosystems, and policy frameworks supporting Oman Vision 2040. Building on these themes, Chapter 8 investigates how Generative Artificial Intelligence transforms organizational knowledge management and innovation, proposing an integrated framework that combines knowledge creation theories with technology adoption models. Chapter 9 addresses the intersection of FDI and environmental sustainability by examining Oman's transition toward renewable energy and its commitments under Vision 2040 and Net Zero 2050, providing evidence that strategically directed investment can simultaneously promote economic development and environmental stewardship.

The final section of the book explores the growing role of artificial intelligence, entrepreneurship, and digital governance in shaping modern investment ecosystems. Chapter 10 proposes an AI-driven framework for detecting fraudulent companies and suspicious commercial transactions within Oman's digital economy, strengthening investor confidence through enhanced regulatory oversight. Chapter 11 investigates how strategic communication and territorial intelligence support innovation and employment creation within family businesses across the MENA region, highlighting the importance of governance and entrepreneurial culture. Chapter 12 further explores AI-enabled digital transformation by examining how artificial intelligence enhances sustainable investment ecosystems through improved regulatory agility and institutional trust in alignment with Oman Vision 2040. Finally, Chapter 13 concludes the volume by presenting a conceptual framework for AI applications in the telecommunications industry, demonstrating how responsible AI governance, organizational readiness, and ethical implementation contribute to long-term organizational sustainability.

Collectively, these chapters offer an integrated examination of the evolving relationship between foreign investment, institutional quality, technological innovation, sustainability, and economic development. While each contribution addresses a distinct aspect of these themes, together they underscore the importance of collaborative governance, evidence-based policymaking, and responsible innovation in creating resilient economies capable of meeting the challenges of an increasingly interconnected world.

CONCLUSION

The chapters presented in this volume collectively demonstrate that sustainable economic growth is no longer driven solely by capital accumulation or market expansion. Instead, successful development increasingly depends upon the integration of effective regulatory institutions, international collaboration, technological innovation, and responsible investment practices. Throughout this book, contributors illustrate how foreign direct investment serves as a catalyst for economic transformation when supported by transparent governance, inclusive institutions, digital capabilities, and strategic public policy. These findings reinforce the notion that investment quality often matters more than investment quantity.

Another important contribution of this collection lies in its interdisciplinary perspective. By bringing together research from economics, finance, management, public policy, artificial intelligence, sustainability, and organizational studies, the volume reflects the complexity of today's global investment environment. The chapters demonstrate that issues such as financial inclusion, renewable energy, knowledge management, fraud detection, women's leadership, entrepreneurship, and AI-enabled governance should not be viewed as isolated topics. Rather, they represent interconnected components of broader economic ecosystems that collectively shape national competitiveness and long-term prosperity.

The regional emphasis on North Africa, the Middle East, and particularly Oman provides valuable practical insights while also contributing to broader international discussions. National development initiatives such as Oman Vision 2040 illustrate how governments can leverage investment policy, regulatory modernization, digital transformation, and international partnerships to diversify their economies and promote sustainable growth. Although grounded in regional case studies, the lessons presented throughout this volume possess broad relevance for policymakers, researchers, business leaders, and international organizations working across both developed and developing economies.

As editors, we hope this book serves not only as a comprehensive academic resource but also as a catalyst for continued dialogue and future research. The rapidly evolving nature of global investment, technological innovation, and regulatory governance ensures that many questions remain open for exploration. We encourage readers to build upon the ideas presented in these chapters, foster interdisciplinary collaboration, and develop innovative solutions that strengthen international partnerships while advancing inclusive, resilient, and sustainable economic development for future generations.

Nasser Al Harrasi
University of Technology and Applied Sciences, Oman

Badar Khalid Hakim Al-Shabibi
University of Technology and Applied Sciences, Oman

Mohd Abass Bhat
University of Technology and Applied Sciences, Oman

S. Porkodi
University of Technology and Applied Sciences, Oman

Chapter 1
The Effect of Institutions and Foreign Direct Investment on Economic Growth:
What Matters Most In North Africa?

Hamza Ayass
http://orcid.org/0000-0001-5395-2599
Faculty of Legal, Economic, and Social Sciences of Agdal, Mohammed V University in Rabat, Morocco

Fatima Zahra Belarbi
http://orcid.org/0009-0005-4810-2297
Faculty of Legal, Economic, and Social Sciences of Agdal, Mohammed V University in Rabat, Morocco

ABSTRACT

The impact of foreign direct investment on the economic growth of host countries has generated discussion in previous theoretical and empirical studies. This study analyzes the influence of foreign direct investment and institutions, specifically economic and political aspects, on economic growth. The research analyzed panel data from four North African countries spanning the years 2002 to 2023. The PMG/ARDL model was employed to examine the short- and long-term impacts of foreign direct investment and institutions on economic growth. The panel unit root test and the panel co-integration test were utilized to enhance the model's estimation. The empirical evidence substantiates that economic freedom and foreign direct investment

DOI: 10.4018/979-8-3373-8964-6.ch001

function as the fundamental catalysts of growth in both the short term and the long term. Political institutional variables remain non-significant across both temporal horizons, a phenomenon attributed to the compounding structural disruptions of the Arab Spring and the COVID-19 pandemic, which introduced persistent non-linearities into the region's governance indicators. Consequently, these findings underscore the centrality of economic liberalization and enhancing institutional quality for FDI attraction as critical policy priorities for North African economies navigating post-revolutionary and post-pandemic recovery.

INTRODUCTION

A wide range of studies in the economic literature has examined the contribution of foreign direct investment (FDI) to economic growth. Numerous studies have investigated the diverse transmission mechanisms, both direct and indirect, by which foreign direct investment (FDI) might promote growth in host nations. As a result, numerous international development organisations regard foreign direct investment (FDI) as an essential element in combating poverty (OECD, 2002; UNCTAD, 1999; World Bank, 2021). Consequently, they promote the adoption of policies within disadvantaged nations designed to streamline the influx of foreign capital (UNCTAD, 1999; UNCTAD, 2025a; World Bank, 2021; other FDI on the World Bank's Moroccan report). This trend accounts for why numerous countries, particularly in Africa, have either enacted or updated their regulatory frameworks concerning foreign investment (UNCTAD, 2015).

To attract increased foreign capital, nations should establish a suitable institutional framework characterized by political stability, market efficiency, and secure property rights. Insufficiently protected property rights tend to result in elevated risk premiums, while intricate compliance requirements can impede economic advancement (Kalandia, 2023).

In this sense, African development represents a major and intricate challenge. Since the 1990s, a global trend in foreign direct investment flows has developed, as indicated by the International Institute for Sustainable Development (IISD) report, which notes that the region has consistently failed to satisfy investment demand, primarily due to capital-related limitations (World Bank, 2021). Furthermore, global economic integration necessitates demands that surpass the region's existing capacities, especially in light of its poor productivity (Wang et al., 2023; Sghaier, 2023; Ilyas et al., 2023). Several research studies have focused on the effect of institutions on foreign direct investment (Were 2015; Tekin 2012; Busse and Königer 2012; Zahonogo 2016; Singh 2010), while others have reevaluated the influence of foreign direct investment on economic growth (Lee et al. 2020; Linh et al. 2019; Orbes et al. 2019).

North Africa is at a pivotal moment in its economic history, necessitating a balance between structural transformation and the progression of the global financial landscape. In the last decade, the region has exhibited resilience amid considerable global disruptions, including volatile commodity prices, regional conflicts, and the decline of international financial conditions. Notwithstanding these problems, North Africa has sustained moderate economic development, averaging 3.3% yearly from 2015 to 2021, above the continent's average (AfDB, 2024). The region recorded economic growth of 3.8% in 2023, down from 5.0% in 2022. Moreover, alongside persistent inflationary pressures, the region's significant dependence on hydrocarbons and external growth stimuli has underscored its susceptibility to external shocks, attributable to its limited economic diversification and insufficient structural reform (AfDB, 2025). North African countries must remove barriers to the growth of the private sector, particularly those associated with institutional development, regulation, and financing.

This literature review suggests that empirical research addressing the dynamic interaction between institutions, foreign direct investment (FDI), and economic growth-across both short-term and long-term horizons-remains limited within the North African context. While no consensus exists regarding the optimal method for quantifying institutional quality, various studies have operationalized this concept using indicators such as property rights protection, the rule of law, political stability, and market efficiency. Consequently, the present study examines political and economic institutions in North African nations to evaluate the dynamic effects of different institutional dimensions and FDI on economic growth. Our methodology is motivated by the hierarchy of institutions hypothesis proposed by Acemoglu & Johnson (2005). Their findings suggest that political institutions serve as the fundamental driver of growth by establishing the framework for economic institutions, which subsequently exert a more direct influence on economic growth.

This research seeks to address this gap by analyzing political and economic institutions to clarify both short-term and long-term connections. The paper is organized into three subsequent sections. We will first present the literature review, followed by the model specification and data, and finally, we will examine the acquired outcomes alongside concluding insights.

1. LITERATURE REVIEW

The investigation on the relationship among institutions, foreign direct investment, and economic growth has notably intensified in recent decades. These studies have revealed that domestic private investment significantly impacts economic growth, while there remain differences about the relationship between these factors, foreign direct investment (FDI), and institutional quality. This literature review seeks to analyse the complex relationships among institutions, foreign direct investment (FDI), and economic growth. This will analyse the empirical evidence and theoretical underpinnings of the beneficial effects of these variables on economic development.

1.1 Theoretical Background

At the turn of the 20th century, the economic analysis of institutions was characterized by developments typically categorized as heterodox, particularly within Germany and the United States. This included the German Historical School represented by Schmoller (1902) and the American institutional movement, which evolved through the contributions of. From the 1970s onward, the emergence of scholarship now recognized as New Institutional Economics (NIE) has facilitated a renewal of the field. Key works in this area include those by (North, 1990). This contemporary approach utilizes refined neoclassical methodologies to examine how institutions function in the coordination and execution of economic activities.

North (1991, 1994) posits that factors of production, including the accumulation of physical capital, human capital, knowledge, and technology, do not account for growth. This questions the assertions of neoclassical growth theory and endogenous growth theory, which contend that economic expansion facilitates the accumulation of production elements (physical capital, human capital, knowledge).

New institutional economics research has demonstrated that these determinants are inadequate since they only account for a small portion of the variation in national growth rates. These latter factors are seen as direct drivers of growth because of the direct influence that institutions have on them. Economists, including neo-institutionalists, will look to deeper variables, especially institutional variables, to explain international income disparities because these models fail to give a structural analysis of growth.

Similarly, argued that the quality of institutions contributes to the growth disparities between East Asian countries, as these disparities are intangible when traditional economic variables such as capital accumulation, technological progress, or labour supply growth are used. The researchers believe that other deep characteristics, such as institutions, openness, and geography, can structurally explain growth. According to the writers, overseas commerce has an indirect effect on a country's economic growth. It will first address the quality of institutions, which will then have an impact on economic development.

To go forward, the neo-institutionalism hypothesis criticised the neoclassical growth theory's incapacity to give a structural analysis of economic growth, as well as its lack of institutional knowledge. The latter includes the works of a number of scholars, including and other empirical studies to incorporate the quality of governance in order to explain income inequality between countries (Acemoglu & Johnson, 2005).

1.2 Empirical Literature

Nguyen (2022) attempts to measure the shocks impacting the effect of FDI on economic growth in Vietnam between 1990 and 2020, following the country's economic and political reforms in 1986. The study used the VAR model through unit root tests, Granger causality, impulse response, and variance decomposition. According to the study's conclusions, FDI has negative effects on economic growth in both the short term and the long term.

Sohail and Li (2023) study the non-linear relationship between domestic investment, financial development, FDI, and economic growth for the case of Pakistan during the period from 1970 to 2019. Using the nonlinear autoregressive distributed lag (NARDL) cointegration technique, the authors demonstrate that FDI and domestic investment have nonlinear beneficial effects that are more significant than their negative effects. According to the authors, to support the economic development of Pakistan, policymakers should strengthen their control over the channeling of FDI and ensure the implementation of adequate institutions, particularly the rule of law.

In Africa, Ayenew (2022) studies the effect of FDI on economic growth, focusing on 22 sub-Saharan African countries during the period 1988-2019. By adopting the PMG/ARDL model to capture the long-term and short-term structural shocks of FDI on economic growth. The results show that FDI has a statistically insignificant impact in the short term, but a significant and favorable impact in the long term. The results of the study indicate that sustained economic growth is favored by foreign direct investment. Therefore, Sub-Saharan African countries should focus on attracting FDI. In the same African context, Yimer (2023) uses a dynamically shared correlation effect technique for an error correction model to study the growth effects of FDI in Africa from 1990 to 2016. He employs an analytical framework to classify African economies into three groups: investment, incentive factors, and fragility. In economies driven by incentive factors or investments, FDI has a significant long-term direct effect on growth; in economies driven by factor-based or investment-based strategies, the short-term impact of FDI is negligible. In the fragile group, however, the long-term and short-term effects of FDI on growth are negligible.

By revisiting the vital role of institutions adopt a vector autoregressive model using the VAR panel for a sample of 42 countries in Latin America and the Caribbean during the period 1970 – 2019. The authors confirm that economic growth responds positively to exogenous shocks related to institutional performance, and the response to shocks in political institutions is higher in Latin America and the Caribbean.

A growing wave of empirical literature has attempted in the past decade to examine the link between institutions, FDI, and economic growth in the MENA region after the popular uprisings that the said region experienced under the name of the "Arab Spring," using factors including corruption, political stability, property rights security, political rights, and civil liberties. And even using diversified econometric methods (Hadhek, 2012; Oueslati and Labidi, 2015; Arayssi et al., 2019).

In the same vein, by applying the dynamic panel GMM estimation of focus on the issue of institutional governance and its impact on economic growth, targeting a sample of 16 countries in the MENA region, and including the World Bank database (WGI) created during the period 2005-2016. The result of their work justifies that the uprisings of the "Arab Spring" were negatively associated with economic growth. According to the researchers, the effects of the global crisis were probably secondary compared to those of the "Arab Spring," which may have exacerbated macroeconomic imbalances in some countries in the region.

Regarding the North African countries, Zghidi et al. (2016) based their analysis on foreign direct investment (FDI), the economic freedom index, and economic growth in North African countries during the period from 1980 to 2013. Using the GMM method, the researchers conclude that FDI positively impacts economic growth and that the economic freedom index seems to work in harmony with the attraction of FDI, as the effect of FDI on economic growth is more pronounced in the presence of the economic freedom variable. This means that countries that promote greater freedom of economic activities benefit more from the presence of multinational corporations (MNCs). Sidamor (2016) reached a similar result in the North African countries, highlighting that FDI inflows in the sub-region have not yet reached the expected level.

In summary, it is worth mentioning that despite significant economic growth rates in Africa over the past two decades, achieving inclusive growth remains a challenge that concerns several researchers and international organizations (AfDB 2014). Some studies have focused on the effect of institutions on FDI, while others have revisited the effect of FDI on economic growth. According to this literature review, it can be noted that very few empirical studies have been dedicated to examining the dynamic relationship between institutions, FDI, and economic growth in the short term and long term in North Africa. From this perspective, this paper attempts to fill this gap by focusing on political and economic institutions to reveal short-term and long-term relationships.

This study agenda has been identified in the literature as hierarchies of institutions. This hierarchy, founded on the interconnection between economic and political institutions, was initially theorised by Acemoglu & Johnson (2005). Their conclusion posits that political institutions are the fundamental drivers of growth, as they establish the framework within which economic institutions develop, thus influencing economic growth more directly.

As indicated in the literature, economic institutions consist of a set of policies and legal frameworks that govern economic interactions, thus facilitating the enforcement of contracts and the safeguarding of private property rights. Conversely, political institutions represent highly persistent social and constitutional arrangements that provide the basis for the evolution of economic institutions (Acemoglu & Johnson, 2005). In this context, established the concept that institutions may function at different levels in determining growth by differentiating between institutional quality and institutional flexibility. The latter enables enhancements in institutional quality in response to economic circumstances. Within the model proposed by Davis, an immediate yet temporary rise in the rate of economic growth is generated by an increase in institutional quality, which lowers market transaction costs. In contrast, an increase in institutional flexibility leads to a delayed but permanent rise in growth.

2. DATA AND METHODOLOGY

To assess the dynamic influence of foreign direct investment and institutions, particularly economic and political institutions, on economic growth in North Africa. The study utilized balanced panel data from four North African nations (Morocco, Algeria, Tunisia, and Egypt) spanning the years 2002 to 2023. In this study, GDP per capita growth is the dependent variable, while foreign direct investment and institutions are the independent variables. We opted to evaluate economic institutions with a composite index encompassing economic freedom (Economic Freedom Index from the Fraser Institute) and corruption (World Development Indicators). Concurrently, we opted to assess political institutions' impact on economic growth utilizing democratic factors from Freedom House and Political Stability indicators from the World Development Indicators (WDI). We selected this option rather than a composite index to capture the region's distinctiveness characterized by political transitions during the analyzed period. While financial development and the openness rate are control variables.

Table 1. Definition of variables and their sources

Variables	Definitions (measures)	Sources
Growth	GDP growth (annual %)	WDI
FDI	Foreign direct investment inflows (% of GDP)	UNCTAD
Economic Freedom of the World (EFW) Index	The index scores countries on a 0–10 scale across five major areas	The Fraser Institute
Political Rights	measured on a one-to-seven scale, with one representing the highest degree of Freedom and seven the lowest.	Freedom House
Civil liberties	measured on a one-to-seven scale, with one representing the highest degree of Freedom and seven the lowest.	Freedom House
Political Stability and Absence of Violence	(between –2.5 and 2.5)	WGI
Control of Corruption	(between –2.5 and 2.5)	WGI
Trade	**Exports + Imports as % of GDP**	WDI
Financial development	Domestic credit to private sector by banks (% of GDP)	WDI

Source: Autours.

To study the short-run and long-run effects of foreign direct investment (FDI) and institutions—specifically economic and political institutions—on economic growth, our method considers an empirical approach based on the panel ARDL. This type of model is based on three estimators, namely, mean group, pooled mean group (PMG) and dynamic fixed effect. Mean group (MG), dynamic fixed effect (DFE), and pooled mean group (PMG) estimators are applicable in the ARDL model. The research utilized the PMG/ARDL model as suggested by Pesaran et al. (1999). This model was selected due to its compatibility with the data set utilized in this study. The pooled mean group estimator posits that long-run coefficients are uniform while permitting variations in short-run coefficients and error variances among groups. This approach offers the practical benefit of enabling the assessment of each country's short-run dynamics, taking into account the quantity of time-series observations available for each instance.

Table 2. Descriptive Statistics on the Chronicles

Variable	Obs	Mean	Std. Dev.	Min	Max
GDP	88	1.8	2.625	-9.764	6.881
FDI	88	2.13	1.821	-.287	9.425
EFW	88	5.711	.599	4.46	6.61
CC	88	-.42	.248	-.929	.284
PR	88	5.352	1.104	3	7

continued on following page

Table 2. Continued

Variable	Obs	Mean	Std. Dev.	Min	Max
CL	88	4.807	.981	3	6
PV	88	-.745	.479	-1.754	.318
FD	88	40.949	18.677	10.187	67.615
TO	88	67.648	21.587	29.857	114.344

Source: autours.

The table above presents the statistics on all our study variables. They present the number of observations, the minimum and maximum values, the mean, as well as the standard deviation.

Table 3. Correlation Matrix of the Study Variables

Variables	(1)	(2)	(3)	(4)	(5)	(6)	(7)	(8)	(9)
(1) GDP	1.000								
(2) FDI	0.372	1.000							
(3) EFW	0.141	0.417	1.000						
(4) CC	-0.056	0.159	0.644	1.000					
(5) PR	0.217	0.101	-0.379	-0.480	1.000				
(6) CL	0.176	0.135	-0.363	-0.591	0.845	1.000			
(7) PV	0.131	0.401	0.716	0.677	-0.049	-0.230	1.000		
(8) FD	-0.053	0.303	0.852	0.658	-0.600	-0.527	0.642	1.000	
(9) TO	0.045	0.258	0.593	0.754	-0.514	-0.692	0.568	0.629	1.000

Source: Authors

The table above presents the correlation matrix of our variables. This matrix allows us to identify potential connections between the different variables of the study.

The following paragraph is dedicated to presenting the various results obtained. Finally, it will be a matter of presenting the short-term and long-term results of the ARDL model estimated using the different estimators (PMG, DFE, and MG).

3. RESULTS

a) Results of the stationarity tests

Table 4. Table of stationarity test results

Variables	Abréviations	P-value	Stationary	Order
Economic growth	GDP	0.0384	At level	I (0)
Foreign Direct Investment	FDI	0.0125	At level	I (0)
Financial development	DF	0.0277	At level	I (0)
Economic Freedom Index	EFW	0.0005	first difference	I (1)
Control of corruption	CC	0.0376	first difference	I (1)
Political stability and absence of violence	PV	0.0269	first difference	I (1)
Political rights	PR	0.0367	first difference	I (1)
Civil liberties	CL	0,0356	first difference	I (1)
Opening rate	OR	0.0071	first difference	I (1)

Tests: Levin, Lin & Chu (LLC) at level — Augmented Dickey-Fuller (ADF) in first difference | Thresholds: *** p<0.001 ** p<0.05 * p<0.01 NS = not significant | H_0: unit root present | I (0) = stationary at level I(1) = stationary in first difference | Source: Authors

The results of the unit root test reported in Table 4 reveal a mixed integration order among the variables under study. Specifically, at the 5% significance level, three variables, namely Economic Growth (GDP), Foreign Direct Investment (FDI), and Financial Development (FD), are found to be stationary in level, i.e., integrated of order zero, I(0). In contrast, the remaining six variables the Economic Freedom Index (EFI), Control of Corruption (CC), Political Stability and Absence of Violence (PV), Political Rights (PR), Civil Liberties (CL), and Openness Rate (OR) contain a unit root at level but become stationary after first differencing, classifying them as integrated of order one, I (1). This mixed integration structure, I (0)/I (1), provides the necessary condition for the application of the Panel ARDL framework and its associated Pooled Mean Group (PMG) estimator, as developed by Pesaran, Shin, and Smith (1999), which accommodates variables of different integration orders without requiring prior transformation of the data.

b) Result of the cointegration test

Table 5. Kao (1999) panel cointegration test

Statistic	P-Value
- 4.1496	0.01

Decision rule: p-value < 0.05 → reject H_0 → cointegration confirmed | Source: Authors

The residual-based panel cointegration test established by Kao (1999) yields an ADF statistic of -4.1496 and a p-value of 0.01, thereby rejecting the null hypothesis of no cointegration at the 5% significance level. This finding confirms the presence of a stable long-run equilibrium relationship among the variables under investigation, validates the Panel ARDL-PMG estimation technique, and ensures that the long-run coefficients presented in this study represent authentic structural relationships.

c) Hausman specification test: confirmation of the Panel ARDL-PMG estimator

To ascertain the best suitable estimator between the Pooled Mean Group (PMG) and the Mean Group (MG), we use the Hausman (1978) specification test. The two estimators fundamentally differ in their approach to long-run coefficients: the PMG enforces homogeneity of long-run slope parameters across nations while permitting variation in short-run dynamics, whereas the MG estimates all parameters independently for each country. Given the null hypothesis of long-run slope homogeneity, both estimators exhibit consistency, however PMG demonstrates superior efficiency; conversely, given the alternative of slope heterogeneity, only MG retains consistency while PMG incurs bias.

Table 6. Hausman specification test (PMG vs MG)

Element	**Result**
Test applied	Hausman (1978) specification test
Null hypothesis H_0	Long-run slope homogeneity across countries
Chi² statistic	$\chi^2(8)$
P-value	**0.6994** > 0.05 → fail to reject H_0
Decision	H_0 not rejected — PMG preferred
Retained estimator	Panel ARDL-PMG

Decision rule: p-value > 0.05 → fail to reject H_0 → PMG efficient and consistent | p-value < 0.05 → reject H_0 → MG preferred | Source: Authors.

The Hausman test produces a p-value of 0.6994, significantly exceeding the standard 5% significance level. Consequently, we do not reject the null hypothesis of long-run slope homogeneity among the four North African economies. This outcome entails three significant ramifications. Initially, it statistically verifies that Algeria, Egypt, Morocco, and Tunisia possess analogous long-term structural parameters, a conclusion that aligns with the generally comparable economic structures and institutional frameworks of these nations. Secondly, it corroborates the pooling constraint established by the PMG estimator, guaranteeing that the long-run coefficients presented in this study are both consistent and efficient. Third, it validates the suitability of the Panel ARDL-PMG framework as the optimal estimation strategy, consistent with the methodology established by Pesaran, Shin, and Smith (1999).

The subsequent paragraph will delineate the outcomes of the estimated ARDL model. This will be executed in two (02) phases. We will first provide the short-term findings, followed by the long-term outcomes.

- **Short-term Result**

Short-term results provide interesting information on the temporal dynamics and the various immediate impacts of the explanatory variables on the dependent variable. It is important to specify that the short-term coefficients are those of the differenced variables that appear in the model equation. The short-term results of the estimated ARDL model are recorded in the table below.

Table 7. Short-term Results of the ARDL Model

Variables	PMG estimator
Δ (Economic Freedom Index)	3.055951*(0.0353)
Δ (Control of Corruption)	-0.116396 (0.9565)
Δ(Political Rights)	0.217193 (0.8044)
Δ(Civil Liberties)	-2.299236† (0.0999)
Δ(Political Stability and Absence of Violence)	1.674506 (0.3114)
Δ(Foreign Direct Investment)	0.334031† (0.0665)
Δ(Financial Development)	0.179091** (0.0050)
Δ(Openness Rate)	-0.151647*** (0.000)

Significance: *** p<0.001 ** p<0.01 * p<0.05 † p<0.10 | Short-**run coefficients are country-specific (heterogeneous)** under PMG | **Source:** Authors.

The short-run PMG estimations indicate three statistically significant findings. Initially, financial development demonstrates the most significant beneficial short-term impact on growth ($\beta = 0.179$, $p < 0.01$), validating that credit expansion and enhanced financial intermediation swiftly direct resources towards productive investment. The economic freedom score yields a substantial positive short-term growth effect ($\beta = 3.056$, $p < 0.05$), indicating that market-oriented changes result in immediate efficiency improvements. Thirdly, trade openness demonstrates the most pronounced and significant negative short-term impact ($\beta = -0.152$, $p < 0.001$), indicative of the well-established adjustment costs linked to trade liberalisation, a phenomenon likely exacerbated by the substantial disruption of global trade flows during the COVID-19 pandemic of 2020–2021. Foreign direct investment exhibits a marginally significant positive short-term effect (β = 0.334, p 0.10), whereas the institutional variables control of corruption, political rights, and political stability are statistically non-significant, aligning with the inherently gradual transmission mechanisms of governance reforms.

Table 8. Long-term Results of the ARDL Model

Variables	PMG estimator
Economic Freedom Index	4.199018** (0.0045)
Control of Corruption	1.203680 (0.5836)
Political Rights	-0.071996 (0.9388)
Civil Liberties	1.586746 (0.2511)
Political Stability and Absence of Violence	-0.708986 (0.6601)
Foreign Direct Investment	0.298906† (0.0946)
Financial Development	-0.248070*** (0.0001)
Openness Rate	0.110220** (0.0013)

Significance: *** p<0.001 ** p<0.01 * p<0.05 † p<0.10 NS = not significant I Long-**run coefficients are homogeneous** across countries under PMG restriction (validated by Hausman test p=0.6994) I Source: Authors

The long-run PMG estimates, consistent across countries as confirmed by the Hausman test, reveal three major structural factors of growth. Economic freedom serves as the principal driver of long-term growth, exhibiting a stronger positive coefficient (β = 4.199, p < 0.01) that surpasses its short-term impact, so affirming that the benefits of liberalisation aggregate and intensify over time. Trade openness shifts from a negative short-run effect to a considerably positive long-run impact (β = 0.110, p < 0.01), aligning with the theoretical expectation that adjustment costs precede sustainable efficiency improvements from trade integration. Financial development exhibits a remarkable finding: a total and statistically significant sign reversal from positive in the short term to markedly negative in the long term (β = −0.248, p < 0.001), aligning with the 'too much finance' hypothesis proposed by Arcand, Berkes, and Panizza (2012). Foreign direct investment exerts a consistently favourable influence (β = 0.299, p < 0.10) over both time horizons, affirming its status as the most enduring growth catalyst in the model. Institutional variables remain statistically insignificant in the long term, a consequence of the cumulative structural disruptions caused by the Arab Spring (2011) and the COVID-19 pandemic (2020–2022), which established enduring non-linearities in the governance trajectories of the four countries.

CONCLUSION

The paper indicates that nations in Northern Africa should enhance efforts to attract foreign direct investment. Countries can attract foreign direct investment through subsidies, infrastructural development, and a stable political climate. These nations should recognize the obstacles to foreign direct investment and mitigate them. Furthermore, they ought to discern the beneficial spillover pathways and enhance them. This indicator enables countries to experience a favorable and substantial impact of foreign direct investment on economic growth in the short term.

Even though the country is facing significant challenges, there are promising opportunities in other areas like economic reforms, increased investment, regional integration, and technological advancements. In order to take advantage of these opportunities, the northern African countries must implement reforms, such as improving the business environment, strengthening the efficiency of the public sector, and liberalizing commerce. This could lead to increased investment, increased productivity, and stronger economic growth. Despite the persistence of several global challenges, Afrique du Nord continues to have one of the strongest rates of growth on the continent. In fact, economic growth statistics tend to show that North Africa has fared better than several other African regions in withstanding the COVID-19 pandemic.

In order for the northern African countries to obtain the accessible external financing required for their structural transformation, a comprehensive and unrestricted reform of the architecture finance mondiale (AFM) is necessary. It involves, among other things, achieving the long-term development goals (ODD) and implementing the Union of Africa's Agenda 2063. Despite a challenging global environment, including the COVID-19 pandemic and geopolitical difficulties, the northern African countries have demonstrated remarkable resilience. They achieved high scores on the ODD composite index, indicating good success in all areas of the long-term development goals. The northern African countries must strengthen their institutional capacity to mobilize sufficient internal resources to meet their development goals and revitalize their climate-related initiatives.

The limitations and spillover mechanisms of foreign direct investment were not covered in this study. This study suggests that more research be done to determine the challenges and advantageous spillover mechanisms of foreign direct investment in host countries. The institutional settings and prospects for foreign direct investment in North African and sub-Saharan African nations can be compared in another research.

REFERENCES

Acemoglu, D., & Johnson, S. (2005). Unbundling institutions. *Journal of Political Economy, 113*(5), 949–995. DOI: 10.1086/432166

Arayssi, M., Fakih, A., & Haimoun, N. (2019). Did the Arab Spring reduce MENA countries' growth? *Applied Economics Letters*, *26*(19), 1579–1585. DOI: 10.1080/13504851.2019.1588938

Ayenew, B. B. (2022). The effect of foreign direct investment on the economic growth of SubSaharan African countries: An empirical approach. *Cogent Economics & Finance*, *10*(1), 2038862. DOI: 10.1080/23322039.2022.2038862

Busse, M., & Königer, J. (2012). Trade and economic growth: A re-examination of the empirical evidence (HWWI Research Paper No. 123). Hamburg Institute of International Economics.

Hadhek, Z. (2012). Institutions, Investment and Economic Growth. *International Journal of Economics and Finance.*

Ilyas, M., et al. (2023). Relevant paper on FDI, productivity, or economic integration in Africa/developing contexts

Kalandia, A. (2023). The Role of Foreign Direct Investment (FDI) on Georgian Economy. In *The Digital Transformation of Georgia: Economics, Management, and Policy* (pp. 23-34): Springer.

Kao, C. (1999). Spurious regression and residual-based tests for cointegration in panel data. *Journal of Econometrics*, *90*(1), 1–44. DOI: 10.1016/S0304-4076(98)00023-2

Lee, C.-C., Lee, C.-C., & Cheng, C.-Y. (2020 or 2022). The impact of FDI on income inequality: Evidence from the perspective of financial development. International Journal of Finance & Economics. https://doi.org/ (or related threshold/inequality paper).DOI: 10.1002/ijfe.XXXX

Linh, D. T. H., et al. (2019). Foreign direct investment and economic growth in developing/Asian contexts; often with short- vs. long-run analysis.

Nguyen, L. T. H. (2022). Impacts of Foreign Direct Investment on Economic growth in Vietnam. *Journal of Economic and Banking Studies, 4*, 01-15.

North, D. C. (1991). Institutions. *The Journal of Economic Perspectives*, *5*(1), 97–112. DOI: 10.1257/jep.5.1.97

OECD. (2002). *Foreign Direct Investment for Development: Maximising the Benefits, Minimising the Costs*. OECD.

Orbes, et al. (2019). Paper reevaluating FDI influence on economic growth.

Oueslati, A., & Labidi, M. A. (2015). Growth, Inequality and Governance: A case of MENA countries. *SSRG International Journal of Economics and Management Studies*, *2*(4), 1–7.

Sghaier, I. M. (2023). Paper on trade openness, financial development, FDI, and economic growth in North Africa or similar.

Sidamor, Z. (2016). The Role Of Foreign Direct Investment In Spurring Economic growth In North African Countries. *ElWahat pour les Recherches et les Etudes*, *9*(1), 760–769. DOI: 10.54246/1548-009-001-020

Singh. (2010). Work on FDI, institutions, or growth in developing/African contexts.

Tekin, R. B. (2012). Economic growth, exports and foreign direct investment in least developed countries: A panel Granger causality analysis. *Economic Modelling*, *29*(3), 868–878. DOI: 10.1016/j.econmod.2011.10.013

UNCTAD. (1999). *World Investment Report 1999: Foreign Direct Investment and the Challenge of Development*. United Nations.

UNCTAD. (2015). *Investment Policy Framework for Sustainable Development*. United Nations.

UNCTAD. (2025a). World Investment Report 2025. Geneva: United Nations. (Focuses on global FDI trends, digital economy, and policy implications.)

Wang, J., Yang, J., & Yang, L. (2023). Do natural resources play a role in economic development? Role of institutional quality, trade openness, and FDI. *Resources Policy*, *81*, 103294. Advance online publication. DOI: 10.1016/j.resourpol.2023.103294

Were, M. (2015). Paper on determinants of FDI or institutional factors in Africa, e.g., West Africa drivers.

World Bank. (2021). *Harmonized bilateral FDI database or related report on Africa's FDI environment and capital flows*. World Bank Group.

Yimer, A. (2023). The effects of FDI on economic growth in Africa. *The Journal of International Trade & Economic Development*, *32*(1), 2–36. DOI: 10.1080/09638199.2022.2079709

Zahonogo, P. (2016). Paper on trade openness, FDI, and economic growth in sub-Saharan Africa.

Zghidi, N., Sghaier, I. M., & Abida, Z. (2016). Does Economic Freedom Enhance the Impact of Foreign Direct Investment on Economic Growth in North African Countries? A Panel Data Analysis [March.]. *African Development Review*, *28*(1), 64–74. DOI: 10.1111/1467-8268.12167

Chapter 2

Modeling the Relationship Between Foreign Direct Investment, Business Regulation, and Economic Growth

Rizwan Khan
http://orcid.org/0000-0002-3942-9985
Haji Taufeeq Ali Mahavidyalaya, India

Mohammad Taqi
Bahrain Polytechnic, Bahrain

ABSTRACT

The chapter examines the relationship between foreign direct investment (FDI), corporate regulation, and economic growth through an integrated conceptual framework. It highlights that FDI serves not only as a source of capital inflows but also as a catalyst for technology transfer, innovation diffusion, employment generation, and integration into global value chains. The study argues that the impact of FDI on economic growth significantly depends on the quality of corporate regulation and institutional governance. Drawing on neoclassical growth theory, endogenous growth theory, institutional theory, and the Eclectic Paradigm (OLI framework), the chapter develops a multidimensional model linking FDI, regulatory quality, and economic performance. It further examines the mediating roles of human capital

DOI: 10.4018/979-8-3373-8964-6.ch002

development, trade openness, financial development, and technological advancement, while emphasizing the moderating influence of regulatory effectiveness for sustainable economic growth. It stresses policy adaptability and governance now.

1. INTRODUCTION

1.1 FDI, Economic Growth, and the Global Investment Environment

Foreign direct investment (FDI) is widely recognised as a key driver of economic growth, structural transformation, and global economic integration. In an increasingly interconnected economy characterised by trade liberalisation, financial integration, and technological advancement, FDI contributes to capital accumulation, productivity enhancement, and industrial upgrading (Alfaro et al., 2004; Dunning, 2001). Unlike portfolio investment, FDI involves long-term commitments and facilitates the transfer of technology, managerial expertise, organisational capabilities, and access to international markets.

The relationship between FDI and economic growth has been extensively examined in the economics and international business literature. Studies suggest that FDI promotes growth through technology spillovers, human capital development, innovation diffusion, and increased market competition (Keller, 2010; Iamsiraroj, 2016). However, these benefits are not automatic and depend on host-country conditions such as institutional quality, human capital, financial development, and governance effectiveness (Li & Liu, 2005; Azman-Saini et al., 2010).

Recent developments have reshaped global investment patterns. According to UNCTAD (2024), geopolitical uncertainty, supply-chain restructuring, digitalisation, sustainability transitions, and regional integration increasingly influence FDI flows. Investment is becoming more concentrated in technology-intensive, knowledge-based, and sustainable sectors, highlighting the need to examine FDI within broader institutional and regulatory contexts rather than solely through a capital-based lens.

1.2 Business Regulation and Investment Dynamics

Business regulation forms a critical component of the institutional environment influencing investment decisions and economic performance. Regulatory frameworks establish the legal and administrative conditions under which firms operate, affecting market entry, operational efficiency, and long-term investment decisions.

Effective regulation reduces uncertainty, strengthens property rights, improves contract enforcement, and enhances investor confidence (OECD, 2023).

Empirical evidence indicates that countries with transparent and predictable regulatory systems attract more stable and productivity-enhancing forms of FDI, particularly in technology-intensive sectors (UNCTAD, 2024). Conversely, weak institutions, bureaucratic inefficiencies, and regulatory uncertainty increase transaction costs and discourage long-term investment.

Regulation therefore acts not merely as a background condition but as an active mechanism shaping the developmental impact of FDI. Well-designed regulatory frameworks facilitate knowledge transfer, innovation, and productive investment, whereas ineffective regulations can constrain entrepreneurial activity and limit investment spillovers. In addition, digitalisation has expanded the scope of regulation to areas such as digital trade, data governance, cybersecurity, and artificial intelligence, making regulatory adaptability increasingly important for investment competitiveness (Goldfarb & Tucker, 2019).

The growing emphasis on environmental, social, and governance (ESG) standards has further transformed regulatory priorities. Sustainability-oriented policies are increasingly used to attract responsible investment and support long-term development objectives, reinforcing the strategic role of regulation in contemporary investment environments.

1.3 Research Gap and Research Questions

Despite extensive research on the FDI–growth relationship, important gaps remain. Many studies analyse FDI and economic growth without adequately incorporating the institutional and regulatory environments in which investment occurs (Carkovic & Levine, 2005; Durham, 2004). Consequently, the interaction between investment, regulation, and development remains insufficiently understood.

A second limitation is the reliance on aggregate and linear approaches that overlook differences in both investment types and institutional contexts. Market-seeking, efficiency-seeking, resource-seeking, and strategic asset-seeking FDI are likely to generate different developmental outcomes under varying regulatory conditions (Dunning, 2001; Beugelsdijk et al., 2008). However, this heterogeneity is rarely integrated into existing frameworks.

Furthermore, although factors such as technology transfer, human capital, governance quality, and financial development are frequently discussed, they are seldom incorporated into a unified framework explaining how FDI contributes to growth (Alfaro et al., 2004; Li & Liu, 2005). Contemporary issues including digital regulation, ESG standards, and sustainable investment have also received limited attention in traditional conceptual models.

Accordingly, this chapter addresses the following research question:

How does regulatory quality shape the relationship between foreign direct investment and economic growth, and how can this interaction be conceptualised within an integrated analytical framework?

To address this question, the chapter examines:

- How different types of FDI influence economic growth under varying regulatory conditions.
- The mediating mechanisms through which FDI affects host economies.
- The role of regulatory quality, digital governance, and sustainability-oriented policies in shaping investment outcomes.

1.4 Contribution and Objectives

This chapter contributes to the literature by developing an integrated conceptual framework linking FDI, regulatory quality, and economic growth. Unlike studies that examine these elements separately, the proposed framework explicitly incorporates different types of FDI, mediating mechanisms, and regulatory conditions to explain heterogeneous growth outcomes.

The chapter also incorporates contemporary developments, including digital regulation, sustainability considerations, and institutional adaptability, thereby extending traditional analyses of investment-led development.

The specific objectives are:

- To examine the theoretical relationship between FDI and economic growth.
- To analyse the role of regulatory quality in shaping investment outcomes.
- To identify key mediating and moderating mechanisms influencing FDI effectiveness.
- To develop an integrated conceptual framework linking FDI, regulation, and economic growth.
- To derive policy implications for enhancing the developmental benefits of foreign investment.

1.5 Literature Review Approach and Chapter Structure

This chapter adopts a structured narrative literature review based on peer-reviewed studies and reports from international organisations including UNCTAD, the OECD, and the World Bank. The review focuses on research published between 2000 and

2025 addressing FDI, regulatory quality, institutional governance, and economic growth.

The remainder of the chapter is organised as follows. Section 2 discusses the theoretical foundations of FDI, regulation, and economic growth. Section 3 reviews the relevant literature. Section 4 develops the integrated conceptual framework. Section 5 examines the mediating and moderating mechanisms underlying the FDI–growth relationship. Section 6 discusses theoretical contributions, Section 7 presents policy implications, and Section 8 concludes with limitations and future research directions.

2. THEORETICAL FOUNDATIONS

Understanding the relationship between foreign direct investment (FDI), regulatory quality, and economic growth requires a multidisciplinary perspective. Traditional growth theories explain the role of capital accumulation, while contemporary approaches emphasise innovation, institutions, and firm-level strategic behaviour. This section examines four complimentary theoretical perspectives: neoclassical growth theory, endogenous growth theory, institutional theory, and the Eclectic Paradigm (OLI framework), which together establish the foundation for the integrated framework presented in this chapter.

2.1 Growth Theories and FDI-Led Development

Classical and neoclassical growth theories provide the earliest explanation of how FDI contributes to economic development. According to the neoclassical model, economic growth is driven by capital accumulation, labour expansion, and productivity improvements, while technological progress is treated as exogenous (Solow, 1956; Swan, 1956). Within this framework, FDI supplements domestic savings, increases investment, and enhances productive capacity. Capital flows from capital-abundant to capital-scarce economies are expected to improve resource allocation and accelerate economic growth.

Subsequent extensions of the neoclassical model incorporated international trade and economic integration, suggesting that FDI promotes growth by increasing competition, facilitating access to foreign markets, and integrating host economies into global production networks (Barro & Sala-i-Martin, 2004; De Mello, 1999). Multinational enterprises (MNEs) can also introduce superior technologies and managerial practices that enhance firm productivity and competitiveness (Javorcik, 2004; Keller, 2010).

However, neoclassical theory has limitations in explaining contemporary investment dynamics because it assumes relatively uniform effects of FDI across countries. Empirical evidence indicates that the benefits of FDI depend significantly on institutional quality, human capital, and absorptive capacity (Alfaro et al., 2004; Li & Liu, 2005).

To overcome these limitations, endogenous growth theory emphasises innovation, knowledge accumulation, and human capital formation as drivers of long-term growth (Romer, 1990). From this perspective, FDI contributes not only through capital inflows but also through technology transfer, managerial expertise, and innovation spillovers. Such spillovers occur through labour mobility, supplier linkages, demonstration effects, and competitive pressures (Javorcik, 2004; Iamsiraroj, 2016).

Endogenous growth theory further argues that the impact of FDI depends on a country's ability to absorb and utilise transferred knowledge. Human capital, technological capability, financial development, and institutional effectiveness therefore become critical determinants of investment outcomes (Hermes & Lensink, 2003; Alfaro et al., 2004). This perspective is particularly relevant in the current era, where FDI is increasingly concentrated in digital, technology-intensive, and knowledge-based industries.

2.2 Institutional Theory and Regulatory Quality

Institutional theory extends growth analysis by emphasising the role of governance structures, legal systems, and regulatory frameworks in shaping economic performance (North, 1990). Economic growth depends not only on capital and labour but also on the quality of institutions that govern economic interactions.

Effective institutions reduce uncertainty, lower transaction costs, strengthen property rights, and improve contract enforcement, thereby creating favourable conditions for investment and entrepreneurship (Acemoglu & Robinson, 2012). Within the FDI context, regulatory quality is particularly important because it influences investor confidence, operational risk, and business efficiency. Countries with transparent and predictable regulatory systems generally attract higher-quality and longer-term investments (Globerman & Shapiro, 2002; Busse & Hefeker, 2007).

Institutional theory also suggests that regulation shapes not only the volume of FDI but also its developmental impact. Strong institutions facilitate innovation, knowledge diffusion, and productive spillovers, whereas weak institutions may constrain these benefits. Consequently, regulatory quality acts as a key moderating factor in the FDI–growth relationship.

Recent developments in digitalisation and sustainability have further expanded the importance of institutions. Digital governance, data protection, cybersecurity regulations, and ESG-related standards increasingly influence investment decisions and economic competitiveness (UNCTAD, 2024).

2.3 Eclectic Paradigm (OLI Framework)

The Eclectic Paradigm, commonly known as the OLI framework, provides a firm-level explanation of foreign investment decisions (Dunning, 1988; Dunning, 2001). According to the framework, firms engage in FDI when they possess ownership (O), location (L), and internalisation (I) advantages.

Ownership advantages include technological capabilities, managerial expertise, innovation assets, and intellectual property. Location advantages relate to host-country characteristics such as market size, infrastructure, labour availability, institutional quality, and regulatory effectiveness. Internalisation advantages arise when firms prefer direct control of operations rather than relying on external market transactions.

Among these dimensions, location advantages are particularly relevant to this chapter because they incorporate institutional and regulatory conditions. Contemporary investment decisions increasingly depend on regulatory quality, digital infrastructure, innovation ecosystems, and sustainability policies rather than traditional market factors alone. Countries with efficient regulatory systems are more likely to attract technology-intensive and innovation-driven investments, whereas regulatory uncertainty may discourage long-term commitments and reduce investment quality.

The OLI framework therefore complements growth and institutional theories by explaining how firm-level investment decisions interact with national regulatory environments and influence economic development outcomes.

Table 1. Theoretical Perspectives on FDI, Regulation, and Economic Growth

Theory	Core Argument	Relevance to FDI	Role of Regulation
Neoclassical Growth Theory (Solow, 1956; Swan, 1956)	Growth results from capital accumulation and productivity improvements	FDI supplements domestic capital and investment	Improves investment efficiency and resource allocation
Endogenous Growth Theory (Romer, 1990)	Growth is driven by innovation, knowledge, and human capital	FDI facilitates technology transfer and knowledge spillovers	Supports innovation, learning, and absorptive capacity
Institutional Theory (North, 1990; Acemoglu & Robinson, 2012)	Institutions shape economic performance and investment outcomes	FDI effectiveness depends on governance quality	Reduces uncertainty and transaction costs
Eclectic Paradigm (Dunning, 1988; 2001)	FDI is driven by ownership, location, and internalisation advantages	Explains firm-level investment decisions	Regulatory quality constitutes a key location advantage

Source: Developed by the author based on the cited literature.

2.4 Theoretical Synthesis

The theories discussed above provide complementary explanations of the relationship between FDI, regulatory quality, and economic growth. Neoclassical theory highlights the role of capital accumulation, endogenous growth theory emphasises innovation and knowledge spillovers, institutional theory focuses on governance and regulatory effectiveness, and the OLI framework explains firm-level investment decisions.

While each perspective contributes important insights, none independently captures the complexity of contemporary investment dynamics. Collectively, however, they suggest that the developmental impact of FDI depends on the interaction between capital flows, innovation capabilities, institutional quality, and firm strategy. A common theme across all theories is the importance of regulatory quality, which influences investment attraction, knowledge transfer, resource allocation, and long-term economic performance.

Accordingly, this chapter conceptualises regulatory quality as a central moderating factor linking FDI and economic growth. This theoretical synthesis provides the foundation for the integrated conceptual framework developed in Section 4 and supports the analysis of mediating and moderating mechanisms discussed later in the chapter.

3. LITERATURE REVIEW: FDI, REGULATION, AND ECONOMIC GROWTH NEXUS

3.1 FDI and Economic Growth: Empirical Evidence

The relationship between foreign direct investment (FDI) and economic growth has been extensively examined in the development and international economics literature. While many studies identify FDI as a significant driver of economic growth, the evidence suggests that its effects are conditional rather than universally positive.

Early empirical research generally supported the growth-enhancing role of FDI. Borensztein et al. (1998) argued that FDI contributes more effectively to growth than domestic investment because it facilitates technology transfer and human capital development. Similarly, De Mello (1999) found that foreign investment improves productivity through knowledge diffusion and capital accumulation. A comprehensive review by Iamsiraroj (2016) further concluded that FDI generally promotes economic growth, although the magnitude of its impact varies considerably across countries.

At the firm level, multinational enterprises (MNEs) play a critical role in technological upgrading and organisational innovation. Javorcik (2004) demonstrated that domestic firms benefit from productivity spillovers through supplier linkages with foreign investors, while Keller (2010) highlighted international knowledge diffusion as a major channel through which FDI contributes to economic development.

However, subsequent research has shown that the benefits of FDI depend heavily on host-country conditions. Human capital, financial market development, institutional quality, and technological capability significantly influence the extent to which countries can absorb and utilise foreign investment effectively (Hermes & Lensink, 2003; Alfaro et al., 2004; Li & Liu, 2005). Consequently, FDI should be viewed not as an independent engine of growth but as a catalyst whose effectiveness depends on complementary domestic factors.

A contrasting stream of literature questions the assumption that FDI is inherently beneficial. Aitken and Harrison (1999) found evidence of crowding-out effects on domestic firms, while Carkovic and Levine (2005) reported that FDI may not exert a significant independent effect on growth once broader institutional and macroeconomic conditions are considered. These findings suggest that FDI outcomes differ across sectors, regions, and institutional environments.

Recent developments have further transformed the nature of FDI. Investment is increasingly concentrated in digital technologies, advanced manufacturing, renewable energy, and knowledge-intensive sectors. Consequently, the quality and composition of FDI have become as important as the volume of inflows, reinforcing the need for analytical frameworks that incorporate institutional quality, sectoral heterogeneity, and technological change (UNCTAD, 2024; OECD, 2023).

Table 2. Global FDI Inflows and Economic Growth Trends (2018–2024)

Year	Global FDI Inflows (USD Trillion)	Global GDP Growth (%)	Major Global Development
2018	1.48	3.6	Stable global expansion
2019	1.50	2.9	Trade tensions and uncertainty
2020	1.00	-3.1	COVID-19 pandemic shock
2021	1.58	6.0	Post-pandemic recovery
2022	1.29	3.0	Inflation and geopolitical disruptions
2023	1.33	3.1	Gradual stabilisation
2024*	1.40 (estimated)	3.2 (estimated)	Digital and sustainability-driven investment recovery

Source: UNCTAD World Investment Report (2024); World Bank Global Economic Prospects (2024).

Table 2 illustrates the sensitivity of global FDI flows to major economic shocks and policy responses. The post-pandemic recovery also highlights the growing importance of technology-oriented and sustainability-related investments, suggesting that investment quality increasingly shapes economic outcomes.

3.2 Business Regulation and the Investment Climate

Business regulation is a central component of the institutional environment influencing investment decisions. Regulatory systems affect market entry, operational costs, competition, investor protection, and contract enforcement, thereby shaping both the quantity and quality of foreign investment.

Research consistently demonstrates that transparent and predictable regulatory frameworks improve investment attractiveness by reducing uncertainty and transaction costs (La Porta et al., 1998; Djankov et al., 2002). Globerman and Shapiro (2002) found that governance quality significantly influences international investment decisions, while Busse and Hefeker (2007) identified regulatory quality and political stability as important determinants of FDI inflows.

Beyond attracting investment, regulation also shapes developmental outcomes. Effective regulatory systems support innovation, competition, technology transfer, and efficient resource allocation. Conversely, weak governance structures often attract short-term or resource-seeking investments that generate limited spillovers for domestic firms and industries.

Importantly, regulation performs both enabling and constraining functions. Insufficient regulation may lead to market failures and governance challenges, whereas excessive regulation can increase compliance costs and discourage investment. Consequently, regulatory effectiveness depends on achieving an appropriate balance between market efficiency and institutional oversight.

Recent studies further highlight the growing importance of digital governance. Regulatory frameworks governing data protection, cybersecurity, digital trade, and artificial intelligence increasingly influence investment decisions, particularly in technology-intensive sectors (OECD, 2023; UNCTAD, 2024). As investment patterns evolve, regulatory adaptability has become a key component of investment competitiveness.

3.3 Regulation as a Moderating Factor in the FDI–Growth Nexus

A growing body of literature conceptualises regulatory quality as a moderating factor that influences the effectiveness of foreign direct investment. Rather than affecting growth independently, regulation shapes the conditions under which FDI generates productivity gains, technology transfer, and structural transformation.

Studies indicate that countries with stronger institutional frameworks are more likely to attract efficiency-seeking and innovation-driven investments that generate substantial spillovers (Alfaro et al., 2004; Li & Liu, 2005). Effective regulatory systems improve resource allocation, encourage innovation, and strengthen linkages between foreign and domestic firms.

Conversely, weak institutional environments often attract resource-seeking or short-term investments characterised by limited integration with local production systems (Campos & Kinoshita, 2003). Although such investments may contribute to capital accumulation, they frequently generate weaker technological and developmental benefits.

Institutional effectiveness also depends on implementation capacity. Regulatory frameworks may fail to achieve intended outcomes when governance systems are affected by corruption, administrative inefficiency, or policy inconsistency (Acemoglu & Robinson, 2012). Therefore, regulatory quality should be understood as a multidimensional concept encompassing transparency, enforcement capability, policy stability, and institutional credibility.

The literature thus suggests that regulation influences not only the attraction of FDI but also the extent to which foreign investment contributes to sustainable economic development.

3.4 Emerging Trends and Comparative Evidence

Recent literature highlights significant changes in global investment patterns driven by sustainability concerns and technological transformation. Environmental, Social, and Governance (ESG) considerations increasingly shape investment decisions and government policy frameworks. Investors are placing greater emphasis on environmental sustainability, corporate governance, and social responsibility when evaluating investment destinations.

A related development is the growing importance of green FDI, which supports renewable energy, resource efficiency, sustainable infrastructure, and low-carbon development. International organisations increasingly view green investment as a critical mechanism for achieving sustainable development and climate objectives (UNCTAD, 2024; World Bank, 2024).

Digitalisation has also transformed international investment. The expansion of digital platforms, artificial intelligence, cloud computing, fintech, and data-driven business models has increased the importance of digital infrastructure and regulatory adaptability. Countries with effective digital governance systems are better positioned to attract knowledge-intensive and innovation-driven investments.

Comparative evidence further reveals substantial variation between developed and emerging economies. Developed economies generally possess stronger institutions, advanced technological capabilities, and highly skilled labour forces, enabling them to capture greater benefits from knowledge-intensive FDI. Emerging economies often face institutional and infrastructural constraints but can significantly improve investment outcomes through regulatory reforms, human capital development, and digital transformation initiatives.

Recent experience demonstrates that several emerging economies have successfully attracted investment in advanced services, digital technologies, and innovation-intensive industries. These developments highlight the importance of adaptive regulatory frameworks and context-specific policy approaches rather than uniform investment strategies.

3.5 Literature Synthesis and Research Gap

Table 3. Literature Synthesis on FDI, Regulation, and Economic Growth

Study	Focus Area	Key Findings	Limitation
Borensztein et al. (1998)	FDI and growth	FDI promotes growth through technology transfer	Human capital threshold effects not fully explored
Aitken & Harrison (1999)	Spillover effects	Mixed evidence on productivity spillovers	Limited country coverage
De Mello (1999)	FDI and productivity	Positive long-run contribution of FDI	Limited institutional analysis
Javorcik (2004)	Firm-level spillovers	Vertical linkages generate productivity gains	Focus on manufacturing sectors
Alfaro et al. (2004)	Financial markets and FDI	Financial development enhances FDI benefits	Limited regulatory focus
Li & Liu (2005)	FDI and growth	Institutional factors condition growth outcomes	Limited sectoral differentiation
Iamsiraroj (2016)	Meta-review	Positive but heterogeneous FDI effects	Limited attention to ESG and digitalisation
Goldfarb & Tucker (2019)	Digital economy	Regulation increasingly shapes digital activity	Not focused specifically on FDI

Source: Developed by the author based on the cited literature.

The literature reveals four important gaps. First, existing studies often analyse FDI, regulation, and economic growth separately rather than within an integrated framework. Second, limited attention has been given to how regulatory quality interacts with different forms of FDI to influence growth outcomes. Third, contemporary issues such as digital regulation, ESG standards, and green investment remain insufficiently incorporated into traditional FDI–growth models. Finally, existing studies provide limited explanation of how mediating and moderating mechanisms jointly shape investment outcomes across different institutional contexts.

Addressing these gaps, this chapter develops an integrated conceptual framework that links FDI, regulatory quality, and economic growth through a system of direct, indirect, and interaction effects. The framework explicitly incorporates mediating channels, moderating mechanisms, and contemporary developments in digitalisation and sustainability, providing a more comprehensive understanding of investment-led development.

4. CONCEPTUAL FRAMEWORK DEVELOPMENT

4.1 Rationale for an Integrated Framework

The literature reviewed in previous sections indicates that the relationship between foreign direct investment (FDI), business regulation, and economic growth is complex, multidimensional, and context dependent. While extensive research has examined the growth effects of FDI, most studies analyse investment, institutions, and economic performance separately rather than as interconnected components of a broader development system (Borensztein et al., 1998; Carkovic & Levine, 2005; Acemoglu & Robinson, 2012).

A consistent finding across the literature is that the developmental impact of FDI depends on host-country characteristics such as institutional quality, governance effectiveness, human capital, and technological capability (Alfaro et al., 2004; Li & Liu, 2005). However, these factors are often treated independently, limiting understanding of the mechanisms through which FDI contributes to economic growth.

Recent changes in the global economy further reinforce the need for an integrated perspective. Contemporary FDI increasingly targets digital industries, innovation-intensive sectors, renewable energy projects, and knowledge-based activities. At the same time, governments are strengthening regulatory frameworks related to digital governance, sustainability, environmental standards, and data protection. Consequently, traditional linear models of FDI-led growth are insufficient for explaining current investment dynamics.

To address these limitations, this chapter proposes an integrated conceptual framework that combines insights from growth theory, institutional economics, and international business. The framework views economic growth as the outcome of interactions among foreign investment, regulatory quality, and several mediating mechanisms through which investment effects are transmitted. It also incorporates dynamic feedback effects, recognising that growth, institutions, and investment continuously influence one another.

4.2 Core Constructs and Causal Relationships

The framework is built around three core constructs: foreign direct investment, regulatory quality, and economic growth.

Foreign Direct Investment (FDI) refers to long-term cross-border investment through which multinational enterprises establish a lasting interest and managerial influence in host-country operations (Dunning, 2001). Beyond financial capital, FDI facilitates technology transfer, managerial expertise, organisational learning, innovation capabilities, and access to international production networks. Recognising the heterogeneity of investment, the framework differentiates between market-seeking, efficiency-seeking, resource-seeking, and strategic asset-seeking FDI, each generating distinct developmental outcomes.

Regulatory Quality refers to the effectiveness of institutional arrangements governing economic activity. It includes transparency, policy consistency, enforcement effectiveness, and adaptability to technological and environmental change (North, 1990; Acemoglu & Robinson, 2012). Within the framework, regulatory quality functions both as a direct determinant of economic performance and as a moderating factor shaping the effectiveness of FDI.

Economic Growth is viewed broadly as sustained improvement in productive capacity, productivity, technological capability, competitiveness, and structural transformation rather than merely increases in output (Barro & Sala-i-Martin, 2004).

The framework proposes two direct relationships. First, FDI contributes to growth through capital accumulation, employment generation, technological upgrading, and integration into global markets (De Mello, 1999; Javorcik, 2004). Second, regulatory quality promotes growth by improving market efficiency, reducing transaction costs, strengthening contract enforcement, and supporting entrepreneurship and innovation (North, 1990).

A central feature of the framework is the identification of mediating mechanisms through which FDI influences growth. These mechanisms include:

- **Technology Transfer and Innovation:** Foreign firms introduce advanced technologies, production methods, and innovation practices that enhance productivity and competitiveness.
- **Human Capital Development:** Training, knowledge transfer, and managerial learning improve workforce skills and absorptive capacity.

- **Global Value Chain (GVC) Integration:** Participation in international production networks increases export opportunities, productivity, and access to global markets.
- **Organisational and Managerial Upgrading:** Exposure to advanced management systems and governance practices improves firm performance and operational efficiency.

Together, these mechanisms explain how foreign investment translates into broader development outcomes rather than assuming a direct and automatic relationship.

The framework further identifies **regulatory quality as a moderating factor**. High-quality regulatory environments strengthen investment spillovers by reducing uncertainty, facilitating innovation, and encouraging productive linkages between multinational enterprises and domestic firms. In contrast, weak institutions may limit knowledge diffusion, increase transaction costs, and reduce the developmental impact of FDI. This moderating role helps explain why countries receiving similar levels of FDI often experience different growth outcomes.

Table 4. Key Components of the Proposed Conceptual Framework

Component	Role in Framework	Expected Contribution to Growth
Foreign Direct Investment	Primary input variable	Capital formation, productivity enhancement, technology transfer
Regulatory Quality	Direct determinant and moderator	Institutional efficiency, investment effectiveness
Technology Transfer	Mediating mechanism	Innovation and productivity gains
Human Capital Development	Mediating mechanism	Improved absorptive capacity and skills
Global Value Chain Integration	Mediating mechanism	Export competitiveness and market access
Organisational Upgrading	Mediating mechanism	Managerial and operational efficiency
ESG and Green FDI	Emerging dimension	Sustainable and inclusive growth
Digital Regulation	Institutional enabler	Innovation and digital investment facilitation
Economic Growth	Outcome variable	Structural transformation and development

Source: Developed by the author.

4.3 Emerging Dimensions: ESG, Green FDI, and Digital Regulation

Recent developments in international investment have expanded the scope of the FDI–growth relationship. Environmental, Social, and Governance (ESG) considerations increasingly influence investment decisions, with multinational enterprises placing greater emphasis on sustainability, responsible business conduct, and governance standards (UNCTAD, 2024; OECD, 2024).

Similarly, **Green FDI** has emerged as an important component of sustainable development strategies. Investments in renewable energy, clean technologies, low-carbon infrastructure, and environmentally responsible production contribute not only to economic growth but also to broader sustainability objectives.

Digital transformation has created additional regulatory challenges and opportunities. Data governance, cyber security, digital trade regulations, and artificial intelligence policies increasingly affect investment attractiveness and innovation performance. Countries capable of developing adaptive digital regulatory systems are more likely to attract knowledge-intensive and innovation-driven investment.

The inclusion of ESG considerations, Green FDI, and digital regulation enhances the contemporary relevance of the framework and reflects emerging trends in global investment patterns.

4.4 Dynamic Feedback Effects and Theoretical Propositions

Unlike traditional static models, the proposed framework incorporates feedback relationships among investment, regulation, and growth. Economic growth can strengthen institutional capacity by increasing government resources and administrative effectiveness. Improved institutions subsequently attract additional foreign investment, creating a self-reinforcing development cycle.

Based on these relationships, the following propositions are advanced:

P1: Foreign direct investment positively influences economic growth through capital accumulation, productivity enhancement, and technological upgrading.

P2: Regulatory quality positively influences economic growth by improving institutional efficiency and reducing transaction costs.

P3: Regulatory quality positively moderates the relationship between FDI and economic growth, such that the growth effects of FDI are stronger in economies characterised by higher regulatory quality.

P4: The relationship between FDI and economic growth is mediated by technology transfer, human capital development, organisational upgrading, and global value chain integration.

P5: Different forms of FDI generate distinct growth outcomes depending on host-country regulatory conditions and institutional capabilities.

P6: ESG-oriented regulation, Green FDI, and digital governance frameworks strengthen the long-term developmental impact of foreign direct investment.

4.5 Conceptual Interpretation and Research Implications

The proposed framework conceptualises economic growth as the outcome of interactions among foreign direct investment, regulatory quality, and several mediating development mechanisms. FDI serves as the primary input, regulatory quality functions as the enabling and moderating environment, and economic growth represents the developmental outcome.

By integrating direct effects, mediating mechanisms, moderation effects, and feedback relationships, the framework provides a more comprehensive explanation of investment-led development than conventional linear approaches. The incorporation of ESG considerations, Green FDI, and digital regulation further improves its relevance to contemporary economic realities.

The framework also provides a foundation for future empirical research using panel-data analysis, structural equation modelling, moderation–mediation techniques, and comparative cross-country studies. Consequently, it offers a theoretically grounded and policy-relevant basis for understanding the evolving relationship between foreign direct investment, business regulation, and economic growth.

Figure 1. Conceptual Framework Linking Foreign Direct Investment, Business Regulation, and Economic Growth

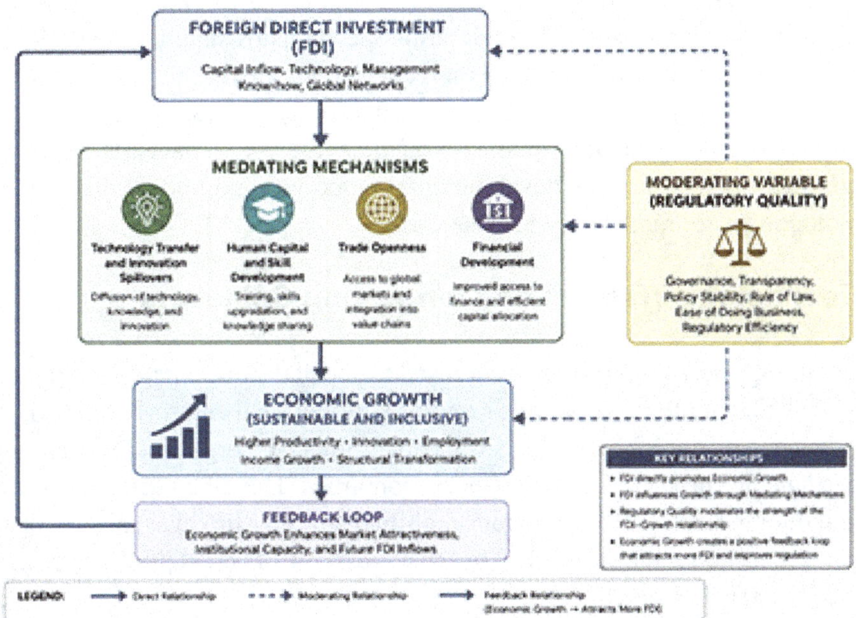

Source: *Developed by the author based on OECD (2023), World Bank (2023), Khan et al. (2021, 2025), and related literature.*

The conceptual model (Figure 1) illustrates that:

- FDI influences growth both directly and indirectly
- Mediating channels determine how spillovers occur
- Regulatory quality determines whether spillovers materialize effectively
- Feedback loops create a self-reinforcing development cycle

This mechanism-based and interaction-driven approach represents a clear advancement over prior literature that treated FDI, regulation, and growth as independent or linear relationships.

5. MEDIATING AND MODERATING MECHANISMS

The relationship between foreign direct investment (FDI) and economic growth cannot be fully explained through direct causal links alone. Although FDI contributes to capital accumulation, productivity enhancement, and employment generation, its developmental impact varies considerably across countries and sectors. This variation suggests that FDI influences economic performance through a set of intermediate mechanisms whose effectiveness depends on institutional and structural conditions.

Building upon the conceptual framework developed in Section 4, this section examines the key mediating and moderating mechanisms shaping the FDI–growth relationship. Specifically, it focuses on technology transfer, human capital development, trade openness and global value chain (GVC) integration, financial market development, and regulatory quality. Together, these mechanisms explain how foreign investment generates developmental outcomes and under what conditions those outcomes are most likely to materialise.

5.1 Technology Transfer and Innovation Spillovers

Technology transfer is widely recognised as one of the principal channels through which FDI contributes to economic growth. Multinational enterprises (MNEs) possess advanced technologies, managerial capabilities, and organisational knowledge that can enhance productivity within host economies. These benefits are transmitted through demonstration effects, labour mobility, supplier linkages, and competitive pressures that encourage domestic firms to adopt more efficient production methods (Javorcik, 2004; Keller, 2010).

Beyond productivity gains, foreign firms introduce new production processes, quality standards, digital technologies, and innovation practices that strengthen domestic technological capabilities. Such spillovers facilitate industrial upgrading and support participation in higher-value economic activities. However, these benefits are not automatic. Their magnitude depends on the absorptive capacity of host economies, including educational attainment, innovation systems, research infrastructure, and institutional quality (Hermes & Lensink, 2003).

In the contemporary digital economy, technology-intensive investments increasingly generate value through knowledge creation and innovation rather than physical capital accumulation alone (OECD, 2023; UNCTAD, 2024). Consequently, technology transfer remains a central mechanism linking FDI to long-term economic growth.

Link to Proposition 4: Technology transfer mediates the relationship between FDI and economic growth by enhancing productivity, innovation, and technological upgrading.

5.2 Human Capital Development

Human capital represents another critical channel through which FDI influences economic performance. According to human capital theory, education, skills, and workforce capabilities improve productivity and facilitate the adoption of new technologies (Lucas, 1988; Barro, 1991).

Foreign investors contribute to human capital formation through employee training, managerial learning, technical skill development, and exposure to international production standards. These activities strengthen the absorptive capacity required to benefit from technology transfer and innovation spillovers. Empirical studies consistently show that economies with higher levels of human capital derive greater developmental benefits from FDI (Borensztein et al., 1998; Iamsiraroj, 2016).

The importance of human capital has become even more pronounced in digital and knowledge-intensive industries, where innovation, technological competence, and entrepreneurial capabilities determine competitiveness (World Bank, 2024). Human capital therefore functions as a fundamental prerequisite for maximising the growth-enhancing effects of foreign investment.

Link to Proposition 4: Human capital development mediates the relationship between FDI and growth by facilitating knowledge absorption, productivity improvement, and technological adaptation.

5.3 Trade Openness, Global Value Chain Integration, and Financial Market Development

Trade openness and financial market development serve as important enabling mechanisms that strengthen the developmental impact of FDI.

Open economies generally attract greater foreign investment because lower trade barriers facilitate market access, international production, and economic integration.

Through FDI, domestic firms become integrated into global value chains (GVCs), gaining access to international markets, specialised knowledge, advanced technologies, and production networks. Such participation enhances productivity, export competitiveness, and structural transformation (Baldwin, 2016; UNCTAD, 2024).

At the same time, financial market development influences the ability of domestic firms to respond to opportunities created by foreign investment. Efficient financial systems improve resource allocation, facilitate capital mobilisation, and support entrepreneurial activity (Levine, 2005). Research suggests that countries with more developed financial sectors experience stronger growth effects from FDI because domestic firms are better positioned to innovate, expand operations, and establish productive linkages with multinational enterprises (Alfaro et al., 2004).

However, the benefits of trade openness and financial development depend on complementary institutional and productive capabilities. Weak financial systems and limited competitiveness may constrain the diffusion of FDI-related benefits across the broader economy.

Link to Proposition 4: Trade openness, GVC integration, and financial market development facilitate the transmission of FDI spillovers into productivity growth, export expansion, and structural transformation.

5.4 Regulatory Quality as a Moderating Mechanism

Regulatory quality represents the central moderating variable within the proposed framework. While mediating mechanisms explain how FDI contributes to growth, regulatory quality explains when and under what conditions these benefits materialise.

High-quality regulatory systems characterised by transparency, predictability, accountability, and effective enforcement create an environment conducive to productive investment. Such systems reduce uncertainty, lower transaction costs, strengthen property rights, and encourage long-term business planning (La Porta et al., 1998; Acemoglu & Robinson, 2012).

Strong regulatory environments enhance the effectiveness of technology transfer, human capital development, financial intermediation, and global value chain participation. Consequently, countries with stronger institutions are generally more successful in converting foreign investment into sustained economic growth.

Conversely, weak regulatory systems may increase uncertainty, discourage innovation, limit domestic linkages, and attract lower-quality investments with weaker spillover potential. Regulatory quality therefore influences not only the magnitude of FDI effects but also the composition of foreign investment itself.

Link to Proposition 3: Regulatory quality moderates the relationship between FDI and economic growth by determining the extent to which investment-generated spillovers are effectively transmitted throughout the economy.

5.5 Emerging Moderators: ESG Standards, Green FDI, and Digital Regulation

Recent developments suggest that traditional institutional variables alone are insufficient for understanding contemporary investment dynamics. Three emerging factors increasingly influence the developmental impact of FDI.

ESG Standards: Environmental, Social, and Governance (ESG) frameworks influence investment location decisions and corporate behaviour. Strong ESG standards improve transparency, accountability, and sustainability, thereby attracting higher-quality and longer-term investments.

Green FDI: Green FDI includes investments directed towards renewable energy, clean technologies, environmental innovation, and sustainable production systems. Such investments contribute simultaneously to economic growth and sustainability objectives.

Digital Regulation: The growing importance of digital trade, artificial intelligence, cybersecurity, and data governance has increased the significance of digital regulation. Effective digital governance frameworks encourage innovation while reducing uncertainty associated with digital economic activities (Goldfarb & Tucker, 2019; World Bank, 2024).

These emerging factors broaden the traditional understanding of regulatory quality and provide additional channels through which institutions influence investment outcomes.

Theoretical Implications

The analysis demonstrates that the relationship between FDI and economic growth is fundamentally conditional rather than automatic. Mediating mechanisms explain how foreign investment generates developmental outcomes, whereas moderating mechanisms determine the circumstances under which these outcomes occur. Accordingly, the impact of FDI should be understood as the result of an interconnected system involving investment flows, institutional quality, technological capability, human capital, and broader structural conditions. This mechanism-based perspective provides a stronger theoretical foundation for explaining the heterogeneous growth effects observed across countries and supports the integrated framework proposed in this chapter.

6. DISCUSSION AND THEORETICAL CONTRIBUTIONS

This chapter develops an integrated framework explaining how foreign direct investment (FDI), regulatory quality, and economic growth interact within a dynamic and institutionally conditioned system. Building upon insights from growth theory, institutional economics, and international business, the framework moves beyond traditional linear interpretations of the FDI–growth relationship and offers a more comprehensive explanation of why investment outcomes differ across countries and contexts.

6.1 Reinterpreting the FDI–Growth Relationship

A central insight emerging from the proposed framework is that foreign direct investment (FDI) should not be viewed as an automatic driver of economic growth. While FDI provides capital, technology, managerial expertise, and access to international markets, its developmental impact depends on the mechanisms through which these resources are transmitted and absorbed within the host economy.

The framework demonstrates that FDI contributes to economic growth through several mediating channels, including technology transfer, human capital development, financial market development, and integration into global value chains. These mechanisms facilitate productivity enhancement, innovation, and structural transformation. However, the effectiveness of these channels depends significantly on institutional conditions, particularly regulatory quality.

This interpretation helps explain why countries receiving similar levels of foreign investment often experience different economic outcomes. The findings therefore support the view that the FDI–growth relationship is conditional, heterogeneous, and context-dependent rather than universally positive.

An additional contribution of the framework is the incorporation of feedback effects. Economic growth is conceptualised not only as an outcome of investment and regulation but also as a factor influencing future investment attractiveness and institutional development. This dynamic perspective captures the co-evolutionary relationship among investment flows, regulatory systems, and economic performance.

6.2 Theoretical Contributions

The chapter makes four key contributions to the literature.

Integration of Disparate Research Streams

Previous studies have frequently examined foreign investment, institutional quality, and economic growth as separate areas of inquiry. This chapter integrates these perspectives within a unified analytical framework, offering a more comprehensive explanation of investment-led development.

Regulatory Quality as a Central Moderating Variable

A major contribution of the framework is the explicit conceptualisation of regulatory quality as a moderating mechanism. While existing studies recognise the importance of institutions, relatively few explain systematically how regulatory quality shapes the effectiveness of foreign investment. The framework demonstrates that institutions influence not only investment attraction but also the extent to which FDI-generated spillovers contribute to long-term growth.

Identification of Mediating Mechanisms

The framework advances the literature by highlighting key channels through which FDI affects economic performance, including technology transfer, human capital development, financial market development, and global value chain integration. This mechanism-based perspective clarifies how investment contributes to development and helps explain inconsistencies in previous empirical findings.

Extension to Contemporary Investment Dynamics

Unlike traditional FDI–growth models, the proposed framework incorporates emerging dimensions of international investment, including ESG considerations, green FDI, and digital regulation. These factors increasingly influence investment decisions and economic competitiveness, enhancing the contemporary relevance of the framework.

6.3 Implications for Theory Development

The framework generates several implications for future theoretical research.

First, the findings highlight the need to move beyond single-theory explanations towards integrated approaches that combine economic, institutional, technological, and organisational perspectives. Contemporary investment dynamics cannot be adequately explained through capital accumulation or institutional quality alone.

Second, future research should adopt dynamic approaches capable of capturing feedback relationships among investment, regulation, and economic growth. Longitudinal and system-oriented analyses may provide a more realistic understanding of development processes than static models.

Third, institutional variables should be incorporated more explicitly into growth frameworks. The evidence presented in this chapter suggests that regulatory quality is not merely a background condition but an active determinant of investment effectiveness and economic performance (North, 1990; Acemoglu & Robinson, 2012).

Finally, increasing digitalisation and sustainability concerns require an expansion of traditional FDI theories. Future conceptual models should incorporate digital governance, innovation ecosystems, ESG standards, and green investment strategies as integral components of development analysis.

6.4 Concluding Reflection

The discussion reinforces the central argument of this chapter: the developmental impact of foreign direct investment depends not only on the volume of investment received but also on the institutional environment within which investment operates. Regulatory quality shapes the effectiveness of technology transfer, human capital development, financial intermediation, and global value chain participation, thereby influencing whether foreign investment contributes to sustained economic growth.

By integrating mediating mechanisms, moderating effects, emerging investment dimensions, and dynamic feedback relationships, the proposed framework offers a more comprehensive explanation of the FDI–regulation–growth nexus. It therefore contributes to theory development by providing a mechanism-driven and institutionally grounded perspective on investment-led growth in an increasingly digital and sustainability-oriented global economy.

7. POLICY IMPLICATIONS AND STRATEGIC INSIGHTS

The framework developed in this chapter demonstrates that the developmental impact of foreign direct investment (FDI) depends not only on the volume of investment received but also on the institutional and structural environment within which investment operates. Regulatory quality, human capital, technological capability, financial development, and integration into global value chains collectively determine whether FDI generates sustained economic growth.

Accordingly, policy should move beyond attracting FDI toward maximising its developmental impact. The following implications emerge from the proposed framework.

7.1 Enhancing Regulatory Quality and Investment Attractiveness

Regulatory quality is a key determinant of both investment attraction and investment effectiveness. Governments should prioritise reforms that improve transparency, predictability, accountability, and enforcement effectiveness.

Key priorities include:

- Simplifying business registration and licensing procedures.
- Strengthening contract enforcement and dispute-resolution systems.
- Protecting property rights and investor confidence.
- Reducing regulatory uncertainty and policy inconsistency.
- Improving administrative efficiency through regulatory modernisation.

The objective should not be limited to increasing FDI inflows but to attracting high-value investments that generate technology transfer, innovation, and productivity spillovers. Effective regulation should therefore be adaptive, balancing investment facilitation with governance, environmental, and social objectives.

7.2 Strengthening Human Capital and Technological Capability

Human capital and technology transfer are central channels through which FDI contributes to economic growth. Governments should therefore invest in education, skills development, and innovation systems to strengthen absorptive capacity.

Policy priorities include:

- Investment in education and vocational training.
- Development of STEM capabilities.
- Industry–academia collaboration and research partnerships.
- Workforce upskilling in digital technologies.
- Support for innovation ecosystems and research infrastructure.

Such initiatives enable domestic firms and workers to benefit more effectively from foreign investment and technological spillovers.

7.3 Deepening Financial Markets and Domestic Linkages

Financial development enhances the ability of domestic firms to participate in investment-led growth. Well-functioning financial systems facilitate capital mobilisation, innovation, and business expansion.

Governments should focus on:

- Expanding access to finance for SMEs.
- Strengthening financial institutions and capital markets.
- Promoting venture capital and innovation financing.
- Enhancing financial inclusion.
- Encouraging partnerships between domestic and foreign firms.

Stronger domestic linkages ensure that FDI contributes to broad-based development rather than operating as an isolated source of growth.

7.4 Promoting Global Value Chain Integration

Trade openness and participation in global value chains (GVCs) strengthen the developmental impact of FDI by improving productivity, competitiveness, and market access.

Policy measures include:

- Trade facilitation and logistics reforms.
- Export promotion initiatives.
- Investment in transport and digital infrastructure.
- Development of industrial clusters and special economic zones.
- Supplier-development programmes linking domestic firms with multinational enterprises.

While global integration creates growth opportunities, it should also support domestic capability development and long-term competitiveness.

7.5 Advancing ESG-Oriented and Green Investment Strategies

The growing importance of sustainability has transformed international investment patterns. Governments increasingly compete for investments that contribute to both economic growth and sustainable development.

Key priorities include:

- Establishing ESG governance frameworks.
- Incentivising renewable energy and clean technology investment.
- Supporting sustainable infrastructure projects.
- Promoting responsible business conduct and transparency.
- Aligning investment policies with sustainability objectives.

Green FDI can simultaneously support productivity growth, environmental protection, and long-term economic resilience.

7.6 Developing Effective Digital Regulatory Frameworks

Digital transformation has become a major determinant of investment attractiveness. Increasingly, multinational enterprises evaluate countries based on digital infrastructure and regulatory readiness.

Governments should prioritise:

- Expansion of digital infrastructure and connectivity.
- Data governance and cybersecurity regulations.
- Facilitation of digital trade and cross-border transactions.
- Support for digital entrepreneurship and innovation ecosystems.
- Adaptive regulation for emerging technologies.

Effective digital regulation reduces uncertainty, promotes innovation, and attracts technology-intensive investment.

7.7 Strategic Priorities for Developing and Emerging Economies

For developing and emerging economies, FDI promotion should be embedded within broader development strategies. Attracting investment without strengthening institutions and absorptive capacity is unlikely to generate sustained growth benefits.

Strategic priorities include:

- Institutional strengthening and governance reforms.
- Human capital development and workforce upgrading.
- Technology adoption and innovation capacity building.
- Promotion of sustainable and green investment.
- Digital transformation and regulatory modernisation.

Such measures enable countries to use foreign investment as a catalyst for structural transformation and long-term competitiveness.

Concluding Policy Perspective

The principal policy message emerging from this chapter is that FDI-led development is not an automatic consequence of capital inflows. Its effectiveness depends on the broader ecosystem within which investment operates, including regulatory quality, institutional capacity, technological readiness, financial development, and global market integration.

Consequently, governments should focus not only on attracting foreign investment but also on creating the conditions necessary for investment-generated spillovers to occur. Policies that strengthen institutions, enhance absorptive capacity, support innovation, and promote sustainable development are more likely to transform FDI into a durable source of economic growth and structural transformation.

8. CONCLUSION, LIMITATIONS, AND FUTURE RESEARCH

8.1 Key Findings

This chapter examined the relationship between foreign direct investment (FDI), regulatory quality, and economic growth through an integrated conceptual framework. The analysis shows that while FDI can contribute significantly to economic development, its effects are neither automatic nor uniform across countries.

The framework identifies technology transfer, human capital development, financial market development, and global value chain integration as the principal mechanisms through which FDI influences economic growth. At the same time, regulatory quality emerges as a critical moderating factor that determines the extent to which these benefits materialise. Economies characterised by transparent, predictable, and effective regulatory systems are generally better positioned to attract high-quality investment and translate FDI inflows into sustainable development outcomes.

The chapter further demonstrates that the FDI–growth relationship is dynamic and context dependent. Economic growth can strengthen institutional capacity and investment attractiveness, creating feedback effects that reinforce long-term development. These findings suggest that investment-led growth is best understood through an institutional and mechanism-based perspective rather than a narrow focus on capital inflows.

8.2 Contributions of the Chapter

This chapter contributes to the literature in four ways.

First, it develops an integrated conceptual framework linking FDI, regulatory quality, and economic growth within a unified analytical structure.

Second, it advances a mechanism-based explanation by identifying key mediating channels through which foreign investment affects economic performance.

Third, it positions regulatory quality as a central moderating variable, helping explain why the developmental impact of FDI varies across countries and institutional contexts.

Finally, the framework incorporates contemporary dimensions of investment, including digital transformation, sustainability considerations, and global value chain participation, thereby enhancing its relevance to current development challenges.

Collectively, these contributions provide a more comprehensive understanding of the FDI–regulation–growth nexus and establish a foundation for future theoretical and empirical research.

8.3 Limitations

Despite its contributions, the chapter has several limitations.

First, the study is conceptual in nature and does not empirically test the proposed framework. The relationships identified should therefore be regarded as theoretically grounded propositions requiring empirical validation.

Second, the framework adopts a broad perspective and may not fully capture country-specific institutional, political, and economic conditions that influence investment outcomes.

Third, the analysis focuses primarily on macro-level relationships and provides limited attention to firm-level behaviour, sectoral heterogeneity, and regional disparities that may affect the developmental impact of FDI.

These limitations provide opportunities for future research and refinement of the framework.

8.4 Future Research Directions

Several avenues exist for extending this research.

Future studies should empirically test the proposed framework using panel data techniques, structural equation modelling (SEM), and moderation–mediation analysis. Comparative studies across developed and developing economies would further clarify how institutional differences shape the effectiveness of foreign investment.

Additional research is also needed on the role of digital transformation, innovation ecosystems, ESG frameworks, and sustainability-oriented investment in influencing contemporary FDI patterns. Furthermore, firm-level and sector-specific investigations could provide deeper insights into the mechanisms through which investment spillovers occur.

Finally, interdisciplinary approaches combining economics, international business, management, and public policy perspectives may contribute to a more comprehensive understanding of investment-led development.

Concluding Remarks

The central argument of this chapter is that foreign direct investment does not generate economic growth automatically. Its developmental impact depends on the institutional and regulatory environment within which investment operates. Regulatory quality shapes the effectiveness of technology transfer, human capital development, financial intermediation, and global value chain integration, thereby influencing whether FDI contributes to sustained economic progress.

By integrating mediating mechanisms, moderating effects, and dynamic feedback relationships, the proposed framework offers a comprehensive explanation of the FDI–regulation–growth nexus. As economies navigate digital transformation, sustainability challenges, and increasing global uncertainty, understanding these interactions will remain essential for both researchers and policymakers seeking to promote inclusive and long-term economic development.

REFERENCES

Acemoglu, D., & Robinson, J. A. (2012). *Why nations fail: The origins of power, prosperity, and poverty*. Crown Publishers.

Aitken, B. J., & Harrison, A. E. (1999). Do domestic firms benefit from direct foreign investment? Evidence from Venezuela. *The American Economic Review, 89*(3), 605–618. DOI: 10.1257/aer.89.3.605

Alfaro, L., Chanda, A., Kalemli-Ozcan, S., & Sayek, S. (2004). FDI and economic growth: The role of local financial markets. *Journal of International Economics, 64*(1), 89–112. DOI: 10.1016/S0022-1996(03)00081-3

Baldwin, R. (2016). *The great convergence: Information technology and the new globalization*. Harvard University Press. DOI: 10.2307/j.ctv24w655w

Barro, R. J. (1991). Economic growth in a cross section of countries. *The Quarterly Journal of Economics, 106*(2), 407–443. DOI: 10.2307/2937943

Barro, R. J., & Sala-i-Martin, X. (2004). *Economic growth* (2nd ed.). MIT Press.

Beugelsdijk, S., Smeets, R., & Zwinkels, R. (2008). The impact of horizontal and vertical FDI spillovers on local productivity. *International Business Review, 17*(4), 452–472. DOI: 10.1016/j.ibusrev.2008.02.004

Borensztein, E., De Gregorio, J., & Lee, J. W. (1998). How does foreign direct investment affect economic growth? *Journal of International Economics, 45*(1), 115–135. DOI: 10.1016/S0022-1996(97)00033-0

Busse, M., & Hefeker, C. (2007). Political risk, institutions and foreign direct investment. *European Journal of Political Economy, 23*(2), 397–415. DOI: 10.1016/j.ejpoleco.2006.02.003

Campos, N. F., & Kinoshita, Y. (2003). Why does FDI go where it goes? New evidence from the transition economies. IMF Working Paper No. 03/228.

Carkovic, M., & Levine, R. (2005). Does foreign direct investment accelerate economic growth? In T. Moran, E. Graham, & M. Blomström (Eds.), Does foreign direct investment promote development? (pp. 195–220). Institute for International Economics.

De Mello, L. R. (1999). Foreign direct investment-led growth: Evidence from time series and panel data. *Oxford Economic Papers, 51*(1), 133–151. DOI: 10.1093/oep/51.1.133

Djankov, S., La Porta, R., Lopez-de-Silanes, F., & Shleifer, A. (2002). The regulation of entry. *The Quarterly Journal of Economics, 117*(1), 1–37. DOI: 10.1162/003355302753399436

Dunning, J. H. (1988). The eclectic paradigm of international production: A restatement and some possible extensions. *Journal of International Business Studies, 19*(1), 1–31. DOI: 10.1057/palgrave.jibs.8490372

Dunning, J. H. (2001). The eclectic (OLI) paradigm of international production: Past, present and future. *International Journal of the Economics of Business, 8*(2), 173–190. DOI: 10.1080/13571510110051441

Globerman, S., & Shapiro, D. (2002). Global foreign direct investment flows: The role of governance infrastructure. *World Development, 30*(11), 1899–1919. DOI: 10.1016/S0305-750X(02)00110-9

Goldfarb, A., & Tucker, C. (2019). Digital economics. *Journal of Economic Literature, 57*(1), 3–43. DOI: 10.1257/jel.20171452

Hermes, N., & Lensink, R. (2003). Foreign direct investment, financial development and economic growth. *The Journal of Development Studies, 40*(1), 142–163. DOI: 10.1080/00220380412331293707

Iamsiraroj, S. (2016). The foreign direct investment–economic growth nexus. *International Review of Economics & Finance, 42*, 116–133. DOI: 10.1016/j.iref.2015.10.044

Javorcik, B. S. (2004). Does foreign direct investment increase the productivity of domestic firms? *The American Economic Review, 94*(3), 605–627. DOI: 10.1257/0002828041464605

Keller, W. (2010). International trade, foreign direct investment, and technology spillovers. Handbook of the Economics of Innovation, 2, 793–829.

La Porta, R., Lopez-de-Silanes, F., Shleifer, A., & Vishny, R. W. (1998). Law and finance. *Journal of Political Economy, 106*(6), 1113–1155. DOI: 10.1086/250042

Levine, R. (2005). Finance and growth: Theory and evidence. In P. Aghion & S. Durlauf (Eds.), Handbook of Economic Growth (Vol. 1A, pp. 865–934). Elsevier.

Lucas, R. E.Jr. (1988). On the mechanics of economic development. *Journal of Monetary Economics, 22*(1), 3–42. DOI: 10.1016/0304-3932(88)90168-7

North, D. C. (1990). *Institutions, institutional change and economic performance*. Cambridge University Press. DOI: 10.1017/CBO9780511808678

Organisation for Economic Co-operation and Development (OECD). (2023). *OECD international direct investment statistics 2023*. OECD Publishing.

Organisation for Economic Co-operation and Development (OECD). (2023). *FDI in figures*. OECD Publishing.

Romer, P. M. (1990). Endogenous technological change. *Journal of Political Economy*, *98*(5), S71–S102. DOI: 10.1086/261725

Solow, R. M. (1956). A contribution to the theory of economic growth. *The Quarterly Journal of Economics*, *70*(1), 65–94. DOI: 10.2307/1884513

Swan, T. W. (1956). Economic growth and capital accumulation. *The Economic Record*, *32*(2), 334–361. DOI: 10.1111/j.1475-4932.1956.tb00434.x

UNCTAD. (2023). World Investment Report 2023: Investing in Sustainable Energy for All.

UNCTAD. (2024). World Investment Report 2024: Investment Facilitation and Digital Transformation.

United Nations Conference on Trade and Development (UNCTAD). (2023). World investment report 2023: Investing in sustainable energy for all. United Nations.

United Nations Conference on Trade and Development (UNCTAD). (2024). World investment report 2024: Investment facilitation and digital economy. United Nations. OECD. (2023). FDI Qualities Policy Toolkit. OECD. (2023). International Direct Investment Statistics.

World Bank. (2023). Worldwide Governance Indicators.

World Bank. (2024). Global Economic Prospects. IMF. (2024). *World Economic Outlook*.

Chapter 3
Framing Foreign Direct Investment:
A Discourse and Content Analysis of Documentaries on Natural Resources in Developing Nations

Ibrahim Niftiyev
http://orcid.org/0000-0003-3437-9824
Azerbaijan State University of Economics (UNEC), Azerbaijan

ABSTRACT

The concept of positive and negative externalities goes beyond a textbook topic in introductory economics. Developing nations with abundant natural resources often experience primarily similar negative externalities, even when they are in different regions of the world. This chapter shows that foreign direct investment (FDI) impacts the lives of real people, primarily in disruptive and negative ways in selected developing nations i.e., Ghana, Kazakhstan, and Ecuador. The objectives are to understand how to qualitatively assess the costs and benefits of natural resources for local communities, gain a deeper understanding of the true experiences of local communities that cannot be easily quantified in econometric models, systematically categorize the diverse perspectives of stakeholders, and reconceptualize the economic growth of resource-rich countries. Qualitative research methods, including reflective journaling, qualitative content analysis (QCA), and critical discourse analysis (CDA), were used to achieve these objectives.

DOI: 10.4018/979-8-3373-8964-6.ch003

1. INTRODUCTION

Developing nations hold a distinct position in economic sciences, which development economics explores. Most have considerable economic potential due to rapidly growing populations and abundant natural resources (Bloom & Williamson, 1998; Meetei et al., 2024). Some have shown strong economic performance, particularly newly industrialized economies, while many remain low-income and poverty-stricken—a phenomenon often called "divergence" (Pritchett, 1997; Ahmadov, 2025). Over the past 40 years, economic literature has debated whether these resources foster development or become a curse rather than a blessing. This has prompted extensive research on natural resources and the "resource curse" (Sachs & Warner, 1995), as well as its economic explanation, "Dutch disease" (Corden & Neary, 1982). These theories provide explanations for current challenges and problems (Udemba & Yalçıntaş, 2022), but the central question remains: can developing economies catch up with developed nations in terms of sustainable economic growth and development within a reasonable time frame in the near future (Rodrik, 2013)?

The question above is unlikely to serve as a viable research question for the current chapter, but it encourages continued research in this area to further clarify possible answers. Although the answers will likely remain vague and uncertain, each new attempt enriches our understanding of developing resource-rich countries. Selecting special economic channels such as FDI to track potential failures or success stories appears to be an effective research strategy. FDI can play an important role in achieving rapid economic growth in developing countries by enhancing knowledge spillover and significantly affecting the growth rate of a country's GDP (Mottaleb, 2007). FDI bridges the gap between domestic investment and savings, aiming to improve capital, technology, and knowledge in developing countries to boost their development. In the economic literature, FDI has been conceptualized as instrumental for economic growth (Chaudhuri & Mukhopadhyay, 2014) and improves employment opportunities to a certain extent (Sinha et al., 2023).

The importance and positive impacts of FDI, especially in developing countries, cannot be overlooked given the empirical evidence in recent publications. Emako et al. (2022) argued that the savings-investment gap can be effectively bypassed through FDI, which serves as a valuable external source for ensuring output growth. Similarly, Ghosh and Saha (2025) demonstrated that a high inflow of FDI leads to economic growth. The main purpose of FDI in developing countries is to accumulate physical capital and develop infrastructure, resulting in higher employment levels and capital formation (Pamantung, 2026). This also applies to resource-rich countries, even if they are prone to the natural resource curse (Manasseh et al., 2023). However, without domestic capacity to manage FDI effectively, positive outcomes are not guaranteed. Ultimately, results depend on institutional quality and the readiness of the financial system to receive high levels of FDI (Gosh & Saha, 2025; Acquah & Ibrahim, 2020; Scalamonti, 2026).

The motivation for this chapter is multifaceted. First, the author has conducted extensive research on natural resource abundance and dependence, thoroughly analyzing de-industrialization and industrial policies (Niftiyev, 2021; Czech and Niftiyev, 2021). Second, economic sciences have become heavily reliant on quantitative methods such as econometrics and statistics, often neglecting additional data sources like expert interviews, surveys, and documentary films that could generate original ideas for classical problems in development economics. Qualitative methods deserve greater attention in economics to illuminate economic issues and matters of economic theory. Third, the interests of a broad readership in economics are rarely considered when addressing complex questions such as, "Is it possible for developing economies to catch up with developed nations in terms of sustainable economic growth and development within a reasonable time frame in the near future?" This motivates the author to make the chapter accessible to readers who may not have expertise in econometrics or related fields, enabling them to understand crucial economic aspects of resource-rich nations. Finally, the lack of a context that bridges social, political, and economic aspects of natural resource utilization for economic development can be addressed by qualitative methods. These methods help contextualize ongoing narratives and dynamics from the perspectives of multiple stakeholders, including locals, journalists, politicians, economists, and domestic suppliers.

This chapter addresses four objectives: primary, secondary, methodological, and practical. The primary objective is to explore the potential of using documentary films to understand the narratives behind FDI as a driver of economic growth, focusing on developing countries as case studies. The resource curse framework will be tested to achieve this goal. The secondary objective is to systematically categorize the diverse perspectives of stakeholders who express their views on FDI in resource-rich countries, capturing the richness and context of these perspectives, which quantitative methods often overlook. The methodological objective is to validate the use of authored documentaries as a rigorous secondary data source for International Political Economy research, particularly for understanding non-quantifiable sentiment and social context. The practical objective is to propose a framework for conceptualizing FDI, economic growth, and international partnerships among resource-rich countries in a methodological way.

Two sets of research questions have been developed to guide the chapter:

Option A: Focus on Perception & Narrative (Social Constructivist Approach)

- RQ1: How do authored documentaries frame the narrative of FDI in resource-rich developing nations?

- RQ2: In what ways do the perspectives of marginalized stakeholders (local communities, domestic laborers) regarding natural resource extraction differ from official state and corporate narratives?
- RQ3: How does the "visual rhetoric" of documentaries reveal the social and political side effects of the Dutch disease that quantitative data overlooks?

Option B: Focus on International Partnerships & Policy (Political Economy Approach)

- RQ1: What barriers to "interactive investment" are revealed through the discourse analysis of stakeholder conflicts in extractive industries?
- RQ2: How does the perception of FDI among local populations influence the long-term sustainability of international economic partnerships?
- RQ3: Can qualitative insights from documentaries provide early warning signals for political instability that traditional economic indicators fail to capture?

The main research gap addressed in this study concerns the typical top-down approach in most research on FDI and the resource curse. Prioritizing state-level institutional data or corporate reports has led to neglect of the discursive mechanisms that sustain and resist extractive enclaves. This chapter addresses this gap by employing a critical discourse analysis of bottom-up narratives, using mediatized data from three distinct geographical contexts: Kazakhstan, Ecuador, and Ghana. Special attention is given to the negative externalities caused by FDI in these countries.

The main research methodology combines three qualitative methods: reflective journaling, qualitative content analysis of the journaling results, and critical discourse analysis (CDA). This approach aligns with the rapidly expanding use of qualitative research methods in economics (Pereira et al., 2026). The results show that, despite their different geographical locations, various developing countries exhibit clear signs of failing FDI within the framework of resource curse theory. Unfortunately, the most feared outcome has occurred and continues to occur in developing countries: FDI is predatory, benefiting large multinational companies (MNCs) and serving the interests of major geoeconomic powers. This further complicates the well-being of the locals and native people, making them more vulnerable to ongoing economic shifts (Godoy et al., 2026; Agarwal et al., 2026). Hence, the primary contribution of this research is twofold. Theoretically, it links New Institutional Economics with Fairclough's sociolinguistic framework to demonstrate how regulatory capture is reflected in the linguistic strategies of multinational entities. Empirically, it identifies the "Bio-Economic Trap" as a universal feature of extractive FDI, providing a cross-continental synthesis of how industrial toxicity undermines local livelihoods.

This study goes beyond macroeconomic trends to offer a detailed understanding of the human and ecological externalities that traditional FDI models often overlook.

2. LITERATURE REVIEW

The chapter's broad scope requires reviewing various studies to clarify conceptual units and operationalize research variables to achieve the research objectives. The review will cover scholarly work on natural resource curse theory and the use of documentary films in qualitative research.

2.1. The Importance of the Natural Resources for the Developing Nations

Since the 1970s, the problematic role of natural resources in economic growth and development among low-income or developing countries have been widely debated (Di John, 2010). The main reason is that natural resources can be either a curse or a blessing for the nations that possess them. As a result, economists have different and often conflicting views regarding the benefits of available resources in developing nations. Barbier (2003) notes that economically efficient and sustainable resource management are critical policy objectives to ensure that natural resources contribute to economic prosperity. Recent empirical studies by Badeeb et al. (2016), Yu (2023), and Khan et al. (2023) support this claim, but also warns about the fragile line between natural resources being a curse or a blessing in developing countries, especially when institutional quality is weak.

Economic growth can be driven by foreign exchange generated through employment and export channels (OECD, 2008; Di John, 2010). Extraction, processing, and export of natural resources such as minerals, oil, and timber can quickly boost a country's GDP (OECD, 2008). Infrastructure and social well-being issues can be addressed through FDI and its multiplier effects (OECD, 2008). Many countries have significantly benefited from abundant natural resources to reduce poverty and transition to market-based economies, including former Soviet Union countries.

Natural resources are significantly related to economic growth in developing countries (Hasanli et al., 2026), but these countries should maintain high trade elasticity to benefit from their resource wealth and potential FDI (Hasanli et al., 2025a). Moreover, ongoing or past structural changes in economic architecture must support future economic output driven by FDI (Hasanli et al., 2025b).

While it is possible to recognize that both positive and negative outcomes can result from resource booms in resource-rich countries, a comparative and critical approach reveals important details for understanding the significance of natural resources in any context. For example, through effective revenue management and a dedicated sovereign wealth fund (i.e., government pension fund), Norway is considered a successful case of using resource wealth to achieve developed country status in the world economy (Holden, 2013; Sanders & Sandvik, 2015). In Latin America, Chile succeeded with its vast copper resources due to the Copper Stabilization Fund, which helped overcome volatility in resource earnings and spending (Yi-Chong & Leiva, 2021).

Other examples of countries where the benefits of natural resources are evident through successful institutional measures and policy decisions include Indonesia, the Democratic Republic of Congo, Botswana, and Saudi Arabia. Rosser (2007) attributes Indonesia's success in overcoming the resource curse to rational economic policy choices, the political victory of counter-revolutionary forces, and the country's strategic Cold War location. The Democratic Republic of Congo overcame its economic recession in 2018 due to its abundance of copper (Elmi, 2020). Botswana and Saudi Arabia are similar cases, where natural resources enabled economic independence and capital accumulation (Elmi, 2020). In these countries, economic issues such as unemployment, regional development, infrastructure, and organization have been addressed (Elmi, 2020).

The significance of natural resources in developing nations can be seen from both positive and negative perspectives. Depending on factors such as institutional and governance quality, natural resources may be either a blessing or a curse, particularly in managing scarce but economically dynamic sectors. In the early stages of development, these nations should adopt innovative solutions to address challenges in natural resource management. Examples include applying AI to resource management (Jones et al., 2024), using resource rents to promote entrepreneurial opportunities in non-resource sectors (Regmi et al., 2023), joining regional organizations like BRICS (Brazil, Russia, Indonesia, China, South Africa) to leverage intergovernmental economic cooperation and overcome the resource curse (Yadav et al., 2024), and increasing trade openness (Guo et al., 2023). This brief list of creative approaches to issues such as the role of natural resources in economic growth and development underscores the unchanged ultimate goal: achieving sustainable economic growth and development based on natural resources. However, pessimistic views persist, supported by real-world data and governance failures. This can be systematically explained by the natural resource curse theory.

2.2. A Brief Overview of the Resource Curse Theory

While common sense and some narratives in scientific economic literature and broader investigations suggest that natural resource abundance should lead to improved economic growth and development, a rapidly growing academic perspective argues otherwise. Specifically, resource curse theory examines how and why political, institutional, and governance problems emerge after large-scale natural resource exports.

Di John (2010) argued that natural resources generally do not lead to extraordinary instances of corruption, rent-seeking, or other negative associations typically discussed in this context. He claimed that, in most cases, negative developments such as corruption coincide with cycles of growth and stagnation among resource-dependent or resource-abundant countries. In other words, the structure of resource ownership and institutional foundations are the true determinants of whether a nation benefits from natural resource abundance. However, several empirical studies still contend that there is a cause-and-effect relationship between high natural resource rents and institutional problems such as corruption, poor selection of government officials, restrictions on media freedom, and a negative culture in public services (Henri, 2019; Sedighi, 2024; Razmi et al., 2016).

Sachs and Warner (1997, 1998, 1999, 2001) empirically analyzed the inverse relationship between GDP growth rates and resource abundance and dependence in cross-country studies, systematizing the argument for the natural resource curse. These studies supported the thesis that resource-rich countries do not exhibit higher growth rates compared to non-resource-rich countries and tend to have lower per capita income levels (Auty, 2001). Welsch (2008) argued that resource-richness leads to low knowledge accumulation, even when some capital accumulation occurs. All these outcomes occur through the economic channel of resource curse theory, which is often accompanied by political, governance, and institutional dimensions of resource abundance and dependence. Recent studies indicate that the resource curse may also occur via environmental channels (Hasanov et al., 2025). Negative externalities remain significant market failures that can lead to human capital deterioration (Hasanov et al., 2024).

2.3. Dutch Disease as an Economic Explanation of the Resource Curse Theory

Dutch disease is a primary explanation for the natural resource curse, where natural resource extraction fails to promote economic development over time. The term was introduced by The Economist (1977), with the first modeling by Corden and Neary (1982, 1984). The model identifies several economic symptoms that must be considered if natural resources do not enhance national welfare, including an overvalued national currency, increased government spending, and reduced non-resource manufacturing output (Humphreys et al., 2007). Following a resource boom, governments often increase spending. While this is not inherently negative, it frequently results in a loss of competitiveness for the domestic economy compared to international trading partners. Unsustainable financial mechanisms caused by natural resource abundance and institutional mismanagement are key initial conditions for Dutch disease to develop (Eerd, 2010). Politicians' tendency to consume and spend resource revenue often leads to accountability problems, resulting in high inflation, labor market issues, external balance problems, industrial structure challenges, and social policy issues (Ciuriak, 2014).

Dutch disease is one of the most controversial theories in economics. While it is a useful model for understanding how sectoral changes occur due to macroeconomic events such as technological improvements or resource discoveries, some researchers have found no statistically significant impact of resource prices on political decisions or the loss of national competitiveness (see Waczirag, 2012). Nonetheless, the Australian gold rushes in the 19th century and the gold and silver extraction activities of Spanish and Portuguese colonial powers demonstrate that long-term economic problems can arise from the rapid injection of resource revenue into economies (Humphreys et al., 2007).

Dutch disease manifests through the resource movement effect and the spending effect, as modeled by Corden and Neary (1982; 1984). The resource movement effect describes how economically attractive sectors draw capital and labor away from non-resource sectors, often resulting in de-industrialization. De-industrialization of productive sectors typically leads to unemployment and related social problems. The spending effect refers to government spending directed toward financing imports. During this process, real appreciation of the national currency occurs, creating additional challenges for domestic manufacturers competing in international markets. Both effects can lead to de-industrialization and the collapse of established economic systems.

Although this chapter does not aim to detail every aspect of how Dutch disease arises during resource booms and discoveries, one point is clear: the phenomenon primarily shows that a nation benefits from resource abundance and exports only in the short term, and even these benefits are unequally distributed. This economic explanation of natural resources is a powerful tool for systematically analyzing macroeconomic signals and symptoms of deep structural and political challenges in developing and low-income societies. Adopting FDI further operationalizes the key variables needed to apply the necessary theoretical frameworks.

2.4. How FDI is Relevant for the Developing Resource-rich Countries?

Mallampally and Sauvant (1999) argued that, beginning in the 1990s, FDI flows into developing countries increased, resulting in a greater presence of multinational companies in low- and middle-income countries which had not previously experienced such large capital flows. Higher FDI flows are linked to greater natural resource endowments (Ogbonna et al., 2022), which can increase domestic economic output and trade openness. Individual country studies indicate that FDI is associated with both short- and long-term positive effects on economic growth (Kanval et al., 2024). However, some assessments are less optimistic. For example, Amirahmadi and Wu (1994) noted the unequal distribution of FDI, which leads to chronic trade imbalances, exchange shortages, and dependence, mainly on imported raw materials and capital goods that developing countries, especially low-income ones, cannot supply domestically.

The economic literature examines how to attract more FDI into national economies through policy choices such as capital account liberalization, stable political environments, and liberal macroeconomic policies (Amirahmadi & Wu, 1994). Increased FDI can lead to technology transfer, employment opportunities, job training, and entrepreneurship stimulation (Amirahmadi & Wu, 1994). Foreign policy also leverages FDI to deter external political interventions (Amirahmadi & Wu, 1994). However, challenges and risks associated with FDI remain relevant to the main research objectives and questions of this chapter, as summarized by Amirahmadi and Wu (1994) and Chaudhuri and Mukhopadhyay (2014).

First, FDI may become an enclave. If sectors receiving FDI lack multiplier effects, the sector becomes the sole leading sector, creating dependence and structural problems (Andreoni, 2022). This can worsen unemployment and distort labor markets. Second, during economic recessions, MNCs are likely to repatriate earnings without reinvesting in local development, as they often compete with local companies. Over time, negative externalities such as pollution and spillovers from one industry can outweigh the benefits of FDI. Third, MNCs, through dominant FDI, may take control of the country's economic policies. Disputes over special economic zones and agricultural lands are clear examples. As shown, FDI and its macroeconomic impacts have complex relationships, and without proper economic coordination and institutional mechanisms, FDI will fail to deliver tangible and positive outcomes.

This chapter focuses on developing countries, where various country-specific factors influence FDI outcomes. Amirahmadi and Wu (1994) note that the nature of non-traded goods, factor endowments, technology, and institutions play a role. Lesteri et al. (2022) found that financial development positively affects FDI flows, but institutional aspects such as corruption may not be significant when considered individually. However, Lesteri et al. (2022) argue that when financial development is accompanied by increased corruption, FDI declines in developing countries.

Although FDI increases industrial activity in developing countries (Desbordes & Wei, 2017), its multiplier effect, mediated by institutional mechanisms, is significant for long-term prosperity. FDI directed toward the natural resources sector plays an important role in economic development, but this often results in a few

MNCs controlling valuable resources (Wang et al., 2021; 2023). While FDI boosts industrial activity, developing countries often base their strategies on market prices for natural resources, creating challenges for sustainable growth. If MNCs value domestic institutional quality and human capital, FDI flows can lead to stable growth dynamics. Recent studies show that institutional quality has mixed effects on FDI depending on the region (Ren et al., 2022; Khan et al., 2024). To benefit from the direction indicated in the academic literature, researchers should adopt a solid and well-defined theoretical and conceptual framework.

2.5. Theoretical and Conceptual Frameworks of the Current Study

This chapter builds on the theoretical framework of the natural resource curse. This theory does not explain why developing nations may fail to benefit from their natural resources, although it has sparked several debates.

According to the framework, natural resource abundance or dependence leads to capital accumulation through high levels of resource exports and FDI flows into productive sectors such as oil (see Figure 1). However, if rent-seeking behavior or political mismanagement occurs, low political and institutional quality prevents the creation of an environment that enables positive spillovers among sectors. In other words, the multiplicative effects of resource revenues and FDI will be limited. When FDI increases, economic growth follows, but in the second scenario, economic growth is threatened by an unstable macroeconomic environment.

Figure 1. Theoretical framework of the current study based on the natural resource curse theory.

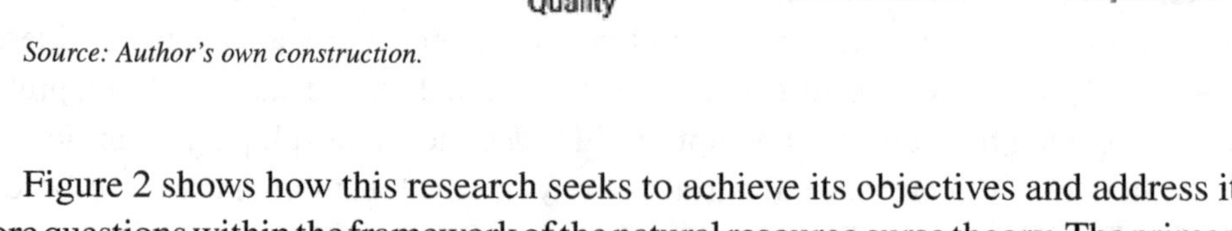

Source: Author's own construction.

Figure 2 shows how this research seeks to achieve its objectives and address its core questions within the framework of the natural resource curse theory. The primary motivation for this study comes from daily observations of economic realities in several oil-exporting countries, especially those in Africa. Various stakeholders—

including agricultural workers, service sector employees, journalists, independent think tanks, and citizens—observe and assess the ongoing impacts of FDI in resource sectors. Their perspectives are crucial for contrasting lived experiences with traditional theories that rely on physical data and quantitative methods to debate whether a society suffers from resource dependence and industrial imbalance. By using the methodological strengths of discourse analysis and qualitative content analysis, this study examines the underlying nuances and linguistic patterns these stakeholders use to express their realities and expectations. The research will provide qualitative evidence, based on secondary data, to determine how the natural resource curse appears in relation to FDI in developing countries.

Figure 2. Conceptual/research framework of the current chapter.

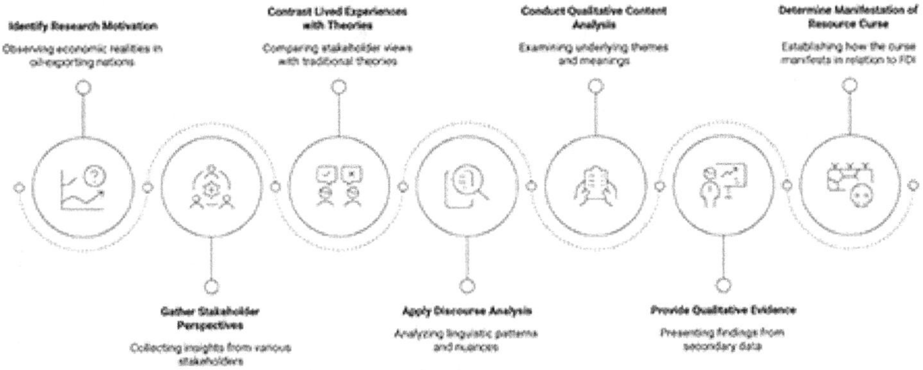

Source: Author's own construction.

2.6. Literature Review on Discourse and Qualitative Content Analysis

One of the most revolutionary developments in qualitative research is discourse analysis. According to the core philosophy of this methodology, the language people use is not merely a medium of communication; it also constructs social reality and reflects power dynamics (Gee, 2014). Discourse analysis can reveal institutional structures (Gee, 2014). It examines both spoken and written language in relation to social, cultural, and political contexts. By doing so, discourse analysis identifies why something is said and how it is said, distinguishing it from related methods such as thematic analysis or grounded theory. In other words, discourse analysis goes beyond simply summarizing qualitative data obtained through various means. This makes it suitable for analyzing how FDI is perceived among different stakeholders. However, before discussing the research methodology and results, it is important to clarify what discourse analysis is and is not, to reduce the possibility of malpractice and confusion.

There are various approaches to discourse analysis, but two remain popular among researchers. When discourse analysis focuses on the relationship among language, power, and ideology, it is mainly referred to as CDA, developed by Fairclough (2013). Fairclough's CDA primarily examines the linguistic choices made by stakeholders who reproduce or address social inequalities or dominance. CDA involves three main levels: textual (focus on grammar, metaphors, and specific vocabulary), discursive practice (how the text is produced, distributed, and consumed), and social practice (broader context, either macroeconomic or political).

Foucauldian Discourse Analysis (FDA) is a major form of discourse analysis. It draws on Michel Foucault's philosophy and adopts a macro-level approach, linking the concept of truth to the historical period and established ways of thinking and talking about a topic (Jørgensen & Phillips, 2002; Khan & MacEachen, 2021). FDA is particularly useful for examining how state systems, governance, and institutional frameworks maintain authority. FDA contends that dominant power structures and specific realities are reflected through thought processes and language (Arribas-Ayllon & Walkerdine, 2017).

Discourse analysis is increasingly popular in economics. Although many studies exist in this field, this chapter focuses on institutional aspects of resource wealth in relation to different stakeholders, including ordinary citizens, producers, independent thinkers, journalists, and others. For example, Yefimov (2011) used discourse analysis to examine institutional economics and regulatory aspects, specifically how socially constructed rules are memorized through language, conversation, and storytelling by economic actors. This approach revealed more knowledge than typical quantitative methods, as it included qualitative data that helped to understand aspects of economics not easily analyzed with statistical or econometric models. Salihu (2026), in their recent study on Nigeria's extractive industry, focused on government reports and academic scholarship to conceptualize the resource curse, which aligns with the main focus of this chapter. This enables an understanding of how political elites, ecological stakeholders, and the exclusion of the public have been conceptualized through the language used in government reports and academic scholarship.

Kelsey et al. (2019) examined the public finance aspect of economics, analyzing how political rhetoric and financial reporting influence ongoing and widespread realities. This source discusses how austerity measures, state budget allocations, and policy arguments emerge after periods of economic crisis. Maeße (2015) used discourse analysis to explore expert knowledge, demonstrating that it can sometimes function as an ideological tool. Maeße (2015) also investigated how academic environments, institutions, and related power dynamics interpret and evaluate government rules for macroeconomic policy during crisis management.

Another method used in this chapter is QCA. The purpose of content analysis is to develop a qualitative model that conceptually describes a phenomenon (Elo & Kyngäs, 2008). Its main function is to systematically analyze text, revealing aspects of the data that cannot be examined with quantitative methods, including econometrics (Mayring, 2021). This method is popular among researchers who use mixed methods approaches (Mayring, 2021). Data sources such as interviews, documents, or video transcripts can be analyzed with QCA to investigate underlying meanings and reach general research conclusions (Campos & Turato, 2009; Hsieh & Shannon, 2005). QCA is accessible and applicable to a wide range of data types, which contributes to its popularity among researchers in economics.

For example, Haapanen and Tapio (2016) used QCA to critique and examine economic growth and growth institutions, considering central themes such as phenomenon, institution, and ideology. Their message is clear: simple GDP growth rate analysis is insufficient without additional analytical dimensions to fully understand sustainable long-term economic growth. In another study, Kahveci and Odabaş (2016) examined the tone of monetary policy statements, focusing on the certainty, optimism, and realism expressed by central banks over time, using QCA. Similarly, Voloshchenko-Holda and Niedziółka (2024) applied textual analysis, primarily using QCA techniques, to study the communication of the National Bank of Poland regarding its COVID-crisis response package. The study revealed risky inconsistencies in the central bank's communication that could potentially undermine policy actions during crisis periods. Izadi et al. (2023) analyzed how national policy documents relate to cultural-social, political, and economic structural changes in Iran. As these examples show, non-standard research problems require carefully tailored approaches to reveal novel insights, which can be achieved through a range of qualitative methods. For this reason, documentary movies can serve as qualitative data sources based on the principles and methods of qualitative research.

2.7. Documentary Movies as Qualitative Data Sources

In academia, the importance and popularity of using documentaries as a methodological approach for qualitative inquiry are increasing (Borish et al., 2021). Documentary films provide valuable insights as secondary data for qualitative research on social issues (Daniel et al., 2025). High-quality, research-oriented documentaries serve as reliable means of data collection, analysis, and dissemination (Borish et al., 2021). Borish et al. (2021) stated that video interviews collected through the documentary film process are data that can be analyzed using qualitative procedures.

Bohnsack et al. (2010) explained that applying the documentary method to interpret pictures and videos provides qualitative data sources.

The main motivation for using documentary films in qualitative research is that they provide empirical evidence for theoretical considerations by scholars who cannot conduct experiments. In the social sciences, especially economics, natural experiments are well-known sources of empirical data for methodological application. Producing a documentary film is a research process that presents original data for researchers to use in methodological exercises (Fitzgerald & Lowe, 2020). Documentaries allow researchers to collect different viewpoints, facilitating the exploration of the phenomenon at hand (Morgan et al., 2019). Gbambu et al. (2023) argued that documentary films can enhance academic work by offering a compelling and engaging medium for exploring complex issues and promoting critical thinking. Therefore, economic analysis of developing countries on topics already well investigated by mainstream methods should be open to new and innovative approaches.

3. DATA AND METHODOLOGY

The primary data source for this chapter is documentary films that examine the potential impacts of natural resource abundance. The documentaries were selected using keyword searches on open-access platforms such as YouTube. This chapter employs a qualitative multi-case study design, using purposive sampling to select three feature-length documentaries: The Other Side of Oil (2020), Crude (2009), and Ghana: The Oil Curse (see Table 1). Selection was based on four strict criteria: (1) focus on the petroleum sector, (2) representation of diverse Global South regions (Central Asia, Latin America, and Africa), (3) presence of clear state-investor-community conflict, and (4) sufficient documentary length for in-depth CDA. These criteria enabled a purposeful and systematic approach to the main research objectives of communicating negative externalities arising from FDI in resource-rich economies.

Table 1. The documentary movies and their key characteristics.

N	Title	Director(s)	Length	Link	Country
1.	Oil promises—how oil changed a country	Elke Sasse and Andrea Stäritz	104 min 52 sec	https://www.youtube.com/watch?v=b58b-BvWEpo&t=34s	Ghana
2.	Crude: The real price of oil	Joe Berlinger	104 min 28 sec	https://vimeo.com/ondemand/crude	Ecuador
3.	The other side of oil	Lukpan Akhmedyarov and Raul Uporov	36 min 10 sec	https://www.youtube.com/watch?v=EonJhzr6Pn4&t=1689s	Kazakhstan

Although the sample is limited to three documentaries (or cases), it allows Fairclough's Three-Dimensional Model to be applied to analyze discursive practices and social power structures. Due to time and resource constraints, three documentaries were considered sufficient, as a larger sample would have resulted in only surface-level descriptions. To mitigate selection bias, the researcher triangulated perspectives by comparing the activist-led narratives in the films with official corporate defenses and peer-reviewed economic literature.

The first methodological step was reflective journaling, as described by Edwards (2023). This technique is used for knowledge acquisition in qualitative research, although it is primarily supplemental to other methods (Edwards, 2023). Its main purpose in this chapter was to track progress while watching the documentaries and maintaining field notes, which transcription, discourse analysis, and QCA did not allow. This approach documented the evolution of the research through personal notes on emotions and critical analyses by the researchers, thereby increasing the credibility of the research as a systematic process (Mertens, 2005; Ortlipp, 2008, as cited in Edwards, 2023). In other words, the author's prior knowledge of the natural resource curse theory and new insights from the documentaries were reflectively journaled using question prompts, intuition, and assessment. Each reflective journal entry was completed for each documentary and followed a flexible structure. All methodological considerations regarding reflective journaling were addressed according to Edwards (2023), including the strengths and weaknesses of this approach.

Forman and Damschroder (2007) defined QCA as a generic, atheoretical set of techniques used in qualitative inquiry. When the informational content of textual data is relevant, QCA contrasts with methods that focus on theoretical perspectives. Through close reading, data are inductively analyzed to systematize contextual information. QCA enables in-depth exploration of a particular phenomenon to understand it (Forman & Damschroder, 2007). Although QCA may involve quantitative elements, its main purpose is to assign categories to specific qualitative data excerpts to conduct a rule-guided research process (Mayring, 2014). QCA aims to build a model describing a phenomenon in conceptual form (Elo & Kyngäs, 2008). These features made it possible to use QCA in this research to achieve the research objectives.

CDA is designed to reveal how power dynamics and ideology are embedded in language and visuals. Because this research bridges International Political Economy (IPE) and Social Constructivism, applying CDA requires a multi-layered approach, often called Fairclough's Three-Dimensional Model.

In the first phase, textual analysis focused on the micro level of content, including semiotic and linguistic elements. Special attention was given to the depiction of FDI and related issues in resource-rich countries. Vocabulary, framing, and visual rhetoric were analyzed. Silence in the documentary films was also monitored to gather information about what is not being said.

In the second phase, intertextuality and interconnectedness were examined. How do these documentaries interact with other texts? Do they quote government white papers or echo the slogans of local activist movements? This helps categorize stakeholder perspectives (Secondary Aim). Audience reception was also considered, guided by questions such as: How does the narrative shape the viewer's perception of the "resource curse"? Does it present the curse as an inevitable "natural" law or as the result of specific political choices?

At the macro level, social practice was conceptualized. The main aim in this phase was to connect findings from the primary aim (the Resource Curse framework) and the practical aim (the FDI framework). The analysis of how the discourse maintains or challenges the "status quo" reflected the power relations among stakeholders surrounding natural resources. If the documentary frames local resistance as an "obstacle to growth," it reinforces the power of FDI. If it frames resistance as "legitimate sovereignty," it challenges it.

In the final stage, using the "Dutch Disease" concept to explain why certain economic realities are rendered invisible became an integral part of CDA. The following question guided the methodological rigor of this phase: Does the discourse prioritize the "macro" (e.g., national currency, exports, export-led growth) over the "micro" (e.g., local food security)?

4. RESULTS

This section presents the results of a qualitative analysis of three documentaries. Filmmakers Elke Sasse and Andrea Stäritz spent ten years documenting the emotional decline in three Ghanaian villages following a rapid influx of domestic and foreign investments. Their film serves as a formal case study on the hollow promises of investors and politicians. It raises a painful question: is this simply history repeating itself, with profits disappearing overseas while fishermen are left to deal with the debris of a ruined ecosystem? The documentary examines globalization and encourages a reconceptualization of FDI in developing, resource-rich countries.

The second documentary, by Joe Berlinger, depicts the heartbreaking story of native Amazonians in Ecuador. It captures diverse perspectives from stakeholders involved in the judicial process between local communities and Chevron, which was accused of systematically contaminating the Amazon jungle. The film demonstrates how FDI can lead to environmental disasters that cannot be resolved solely by corporate goodwill. It addresses individual human rights, large-scale societal changes, political will, and corporate power.

The third documentary focuses on Kazakhstan. Although Kazakhstan is often viewed as a successful post-Soviet country benefiting from its vast energy resources, some local communities experience widespread disease and the loss of traditional economic activities. Most importantly, these communities lose their quality of life and their connection to the land that has sustained them for generations. Once again, the influx of FDI without proper institutional regulation demonstrates that the country suffers from negative externalities, and resource curse theory may partially explain this phenomenon.

4.1. Oil Promises—How Oil Changed a Country | DW Documentary

Filmed over a decade by Elke Sasse, "Oil Promises—How Oil Changed a Country" examines how the discovery of oil transformed a coastal Ghanaian village that previously relied on fishing and rubber cultivation. The two-part documentary investigates whether "black gold" brought the promised progress or instead brought the "oil curse" often linked to extractive globalization. Artistic contributions from Nigerian animator Ebele Okoye offer a comparative perspective, drawing on her country's history to critique the socio-economic and environmental changes in the region. The documentary provides valuable insight into the real human experiences shaped by extractive industries and both local and foreign investments.

4.1.1. The Results of the Reflective Journaling

Reflective journaling produced twenty structured notes based on direct observation of the documentary. The documentary illustrates how initial optimism about oil-driven development and investments, including FDI, has devolved into a "resource curse." Significant negative externalities and unfulfilled promises of employment and infrastructure modernization have been identified as the main channels for the resource curse. Community trust was built through promises made by various stakeholders, such as investors and politicians, but the reality has been the disruption of traditional fishing and agricultural ecosystems. The marginalization of local labor and a return to neo-colonial economic patterns followed the disruption of the natural socioeconomic equilibrium in local village communities. Consequently, the failure of these investments to generate positive multiplier effects has replaced hope with growing civil unrest and a demand for more equitable resource governance.

4.1.2. QCA Results

QCA enables systematic categorization of information observed or collected from secondary data sources. Both the transcript and journaling notes were coded and synthesized into specific themes using a coding matrix. QCA reveals patterns in the data, increasing validity and reliability. As a result, four themes were constructed based on qualitative analysis.

Theme 1: Unreal promises and expectations (Notes 2, 3, 4, 8). In this theme, the media focused exclusively on optimistic aspects of potential investment flows into Ghana. For example, vocational training in carpentry and welding was promised to local communities if they supported oil extraction activities. Local communities were expected to be trained and improved by investors and politicians to adapt their skills to ongoing economic growth and development. However, industrial jobs were never realized for the local population.

Theme 2: The parasitic nature of FDI and investments (Notes 14, 15, 18) shows that the multiplier effect from potential investments was nearly zero. Analysis of the Sinopec project confirms this. The investment model favored "enclave development," where foreign companies brought their own labor and infrastructure, leaving the local community with "White Elephants" (tarred roads with no cars, rusted water tanks). This is the mechanical core of the Resource Curse: high-value extraction with zero local integration.

Theme 3: Disruption of the ecological equilibrium (Notes 6, 11, 17, 20) indicates that a functional, sustainable subsistence equilibrium existed before 2007. QCA identifies a Substitutive Failure: the oil sector did not simply add to the economy; it actively destroyed the artisanal fishing sector through negative externalities such as algal blooms and sargassum. Compensation was inadequate because it failed to quantify the intrinsic value of the lost ecosystem.

Theme 4: Neocolonial cycles and the "Goliath" Complex (Notes 5, 19) found consensus among local stakeholders (the Assemblyman, Teacher Matthew, and Chiefs) that the current "Oil Era" mirrors the 1683 gold and ivory trade. This aspect of the documentary clearly shows that local communities are aware of the true nature of investor behavior in Ghana. QCA codes this as Historical Parallelism. The exchange of "Oil for Seaweed" (meaning oil drilling caused a seaweed outbreak that destroyed local fishing and threatened food security for local communities) is viewed as the 21st-century equivalent of "Gold for Schnapps," reinforcing the perception that domestic investments and FDI, without strong institutional oversight, continue to function as extractive colonial tools.

4.1.3. CDA Results

Applying Fairclough's Three-Dimensional Model to the documentary "Oil Promises— How Oil Changed a Country" enables a systematic exploration of how the narrative of development is constructed, contested, and ultimately dismantled over a ten-year period.

At the micro level, the textual analysis (Description) stage focuses on the formal properties of the language and visuals used in the film. The discourse is saturated with transformative metaphors. Early in the documentary, oil is described as a "shot in the arm" and a catalyst to turn Ghana into an "African tiger." These medical and predatory metaphors frame oil as an external, life-saving force. Conversely, local stakeholders use metaphors of consumption—"a piece of the big pie" or "crumbs of the master's table"—reflecting a perceived lack of agency and dependency on external "largesse." From the outset, the importance and role of investments for economic growth are emphasized.

Contrasting modality is another aspect of the analysis. There is a sharp divide between the high-certainty modality of the "Ghana News" reports (e.g., "will bring much-needed... will be transformed") and the conditional or aspirational modality of the villagers. Francis and Matthew speak in terms of "hopes" and "dreams" (e.g., "my dream is going tall every day"), underscoring the power imbalance between those who dictate reality and those who wait for it.

Visual semiotics further contrast the high-tech, metallic world of helicopters and oil rigs with the organic, deteriorating world of the fishing villages. The constant sound of helicopters acts as a persistent auditory reminder of a global industry that operates physically above, yet remains socially detached from, the local community.

At the meso level, the discursive practice or Interpretation stage examines how the text is produced, distributed, and consumed, as well as its intertextual links. The documentary deliberately connects modern oil extraction to colonial history by referencing the 1683 German gold and ivory trade and the "Door of No Return." It frames the current FDI influx as a continuation of a centuries-old pattern of extraction. This intertextual link suggests that the "resource curse" is not a new phenomenon but a modern iteration of historical exploitation.

The "Nigeria" reference acts as a discursive shield throughout the documentary for both politicians and journalists. They use Nigeria as a "counter-narrative" (e.g., "not like Nigeria"). By framing Nigeria as the ultimate "disaster" or "paradox,"

Ghanaian authorities use this comparison to validate their own policies, creating a false sense of security that masks identical structural failings.

Production context reveals that, as a DW Documentary, it is produced for a global audience. It adopts a "narrative of disillusionment," where the filmmaker's "doubts" serve as the guiding thread, leading viewers to critique the neoliberal promises of "shared prosperity."

At the macro level, the Social Practice (Explanation) stage connects the discourse to broader social, political, and economic structures, specifically the "Resource Curse" and "Dutch Disease." Institutional friction and power dynamics are portrayed indirectly and carefully. The presence of the Chinese company Sinopec reveals a critical failure in "local content" institutions. The discourse of "training" and "empowerment" for locals like Gifty and Francis is shown as a performative gesture. When actual work begins, the local workforce is bypassed for international laborers, demonstrating that the "rules of the game" are dictated by global capital rather than domestic social contracts.

The documentary provides evidence of the manifestation of Dutch Disease at the linguistic level. Dutch Disease is shown not just as a currency phenomenon, but as a social one. The "algae infestation" and "oil slicks" that destroy fishing nets represent the "industrial lopsidedness" where the extractive sector actively cannibalizes traditional livelihoods. The discourse shifts from "oil as a blessing" to "oil as a curse" as the fishing economy becomes non-viable. This is why the final parts of the documentary introduce the concept of "White Elephants—tarred streets in villages where no one owns a car. This represents the ultimate discursive failure: the state provides symbols of development (infrastructure) without the substance of economic formalization or public trust.

4.2. The Documentary "Crude"

Crude is an epic documentary by Joe Berlinger about the Amazon disaster caused by FDI in Ecuador. The film follows 30,000 indigenous Ecuadorians in a high-stakes legal battle against Chevron, accusing the oil giant of systematic contamination that transformed a biodiverse paradise into a "death zone" plagued by cancer and birth defects. The documentary features 600 hours of footage collected over three years. This provocative drama balances complex legal issues with the raw human suffering at the core of a global struggle for environmental justice and corporate responsibility. The documentary aligns with the main research questions and objectives of the current chapter.

4.2.1. The Results of the Reflective Journaling

The documentary Crude chronicles the landmark legal battle between 30,000 indigenous Ecuadorians and Chevron over systematic environmental contamination; a crisis aptly termed the "Amazon Chernobyl." Throughout the struggle, the corporation employs a calculated strategy of blame-shifting and financial attrition, offloading liability onto a structurally weak local government while effectively exhausting the opposition's resources. This creates a harrowing bio-economic trap for residents, whose health and subsistence farming are decimated by the very industrial toxicity that produces their mounting medical bills. To bridge this power gap, legal teams and global activists mobilize transnational advocacy networks and celebrity influence, forcing a localized tragedy into the international spotlight. The emergence of a supportive political administration under Rafael Correa provided a temporary institutional shield, yet the core conflict remains a sobering example of how multinational profit can bypass communal survival. Ultimately, the film highlights the profound FDI paradox where the economic necessity of foreign investment frequently collides with the fundamental rights of those living in extraction sacrifice zones. Overall, 16 structured notes have been taken during the process.

4.2.2. QCA Results

Theme 1: The "Enclave" of Impunity and Blame-Shifting (Notes 2, 6, 7, 8): The data shows that extraction sites functioned as "legal enclaves," separating corporate responsibility from modern standards. Chevron's defense relies on a historical "blame-shifting" narrative, asserting that legacy licenses from the 1960s absolve them of current ecological obligations. By attributing health crises to pre-existing poverty rather than petrochemical exposure, the corporation attempts to erase the causal link between industrial activity and biological decline.

Theme 2: The Bio-Economic Trap and Stationary Populations (Notes 9, 10, 12, 13): A central finding is the "Vicious Cycle of Contamination," which creates an inescapable economic trap. The capital needed for survival—especially for treating cancers and birth defects—is tied to subsistence farming rendered unproductive by industrial toxicity. This results in a stationary population, unable to relocate due to lack of capital, yet continually exposed to lethal environmental conditions. Violence and suppression of dissent further reinforce this trap through physical intimidation.

Theme 3: Glocalized Justice and Transnational Advocacy (Notes 3, 4, 5, 14, 15): Because the local administrative apparatus is often "captured" or institutionally unequipped, the struggle bypasses national structures. This analysis shows a shift from local grievance to global discourse. By leveraging "celebrity shields" and stylized media such as animated satire, activists translate indigenous suffering into a universal language of human rights. This "glocalization" compels the multinational entity to defend its reputation in international markets, not just in local courtrooms.

Theme 4 (Notes 1, 2, 6, 9, 16): Critical Interpretation: The IPE Perspective: From an International Political Economy perspective, this case demonstrates a profound Multiplier Failure. Instead of the expected "spillover" effects of wealth and technology, FDI in this region produced a "negative multiplier," where one industry (petroleum) destroyed the viability of others (agriculture). The corporation maintains "Strategic Opacity" by contesting independent research and using its own experts to validate a narrative of safety. Ultimately, the "Crude" case study shows that without robust institutional filters and transparency, FDI can shift from a developmental asset to a parasitic force that cannibalizes the host's natural and human capital.

4.2.3. CDA Results

Textual Analysis: The Micro Level (Description): At the textual level, the data reveal a sharp linguistic divide between the "Multinational Giant" and the "Indigenous Population." The narrative uses high-impact metaphors, such as "Amazon Chernobyl" and "David vs. Goliath," to frame the conflict as an epochal struggle for justice rather than a civil dispute. A critical linguistic feature identified in the notes is the "deflective narrative" used by Chevron. By attributing health crises to "pre-existing poverty" and "lack of sanitation" instead of "industrial toxicity," the corporation uses language to disconnect its activities from the biological decay affecting the locals. This choice of words erases causality and rebrands an environmental disaster as a developmental deficiency.

Discursive Practice: The Meso Level (Interpretation): The discursive practice dimension examines how this narrative is produced and consumed. The notes highlight a shift from "cold academic debate" to "creative engagement" through animated satire and media-friendly "packaging." Because local institutional channels were compromised by "regulatory capture," the discourse had to be reproduced for a global audience. This involved intertextuality—connecting the local struggle to the influence of international celebrities like Sting and mainstream media outlets. By packaging indigenous suffering into a universal language of human rights, activists bypassed local censorship to reach the "court of public opinion" in the United States, forcing the MNC to defend its reputation on a global stage.

Social Practice: The Macro Level (Explanation): On the macro scale, these discourses reflect the "FDI Paradox" and structural power imbalances of global capitalism. The analysis explains the "Necropolitics" at play: a social reality where the logic of capital accumulation accepts the "slow death" of a community as an externality for shareholder profit. The notes show that the discourse is shaped by broader political shifts, such as the rise of a "socialist, anti-U.S." administration under Rafael Correa, which provided a temporary ideological alliance for the activists. Ultimately, this level reveals that the "Resource Curse" is not just an economic condition but a political one, where "asymmetric attrition" and "predatory litigation" maintain a globalized supply chain that prioritizes raw commodity export over the biological survival of the host population.

This CDA suggests that the legal struggle in Ecuador is a battle over the power to define reality. Chevron seeks to define reality through "historical licenses" and "scientific contests," while activists attempt to redefine it through "human rights" and "ecological survival." The documentary itself serves as a discursive tool that shifts the power balance by making the "invisible" externalities of FDI visible to the global consumer.

4.3. The Documentary "The Other Side of Oil"

The documentary "The Other Side of Oil" offers a raw, unfiltered look at life for ordinary people living atop Western Kazakhstan's massive oil fields. It is an impressive short film. By combining hauntingly beautiful landscape shots with heart-wrenching interviews, the film compels viewers to confront the harsh reality of environmental destruction and the systemic poverty that persists in the shadow of extreme wealth.

This project was created by Lukpan Akhmedyarov and Raul Uporov of Uralskaya Nedelya. As one of the few remaining independent news outlets in Kazakhstan, they have the freedom to tell stories that state-run media may overlook.

The crew traveled through three key regions—Aktyubinsk, Mangystau, and Atyrau—all magnets for international investment because of their vast natural resources. Most of the operations featured in the film are managed by subsidiaries of the China National Petroleum Corporation (CNPC) and the Korea National Oil Corporation (KNOC). Thus, CNPC and KNOC are the main FDI actors in this analysis.

The filmmakers attempted to present the other side of the story by reaching out to the corporations for comment. They were met with silence. Every request for information was systematically ignored, leaving the grievances of the local community unaddressed.

4.3.1. The Results of the Reflective Journaling

Reflective journaling indicates that the documentary demonstrates how FDI-driven oil extraction in Kazakhstan has caused severe negative externalities, including environmental toxicity and the deterioration of public infrastructure. This results in increased mortality and pediatric morbidity. Industrial expansion has prioritized corporate hydrological needs and resource export over local subsistence, leading to regulatory capture, where state institutions favor investor interests over communal health. Reflective journaling enables us to conceptualize FDI as a privileged economic event that outweighs the needs of local communities in an opaque manner. Ultimately, resource depletion triggers involuntary migration and state withdrawal, illustrating a predatory model of governance in which infrastructure and care depend solely on the presence of extractable wealth.

4.3.2. QCA Results

Three themes were identified through reflective journaling and the qualitative coding matrix.

Theme 1: The "Transient State" and Institutional Retreat (Notes 5, 9, 11): The data indicate a model of Resource-Dependent Governance. In this framework, the state acts as a "temporary landlord" rather than a permanent provider. The relocation of the Baishonas population demonstrates that state interest is strictly geographical and tied to extractable wealth. Once the wealth is depleted, the "institutional infrastructure" (schools, hospitals) disappears, revealing these were never intended as long-term developmental pillars.

Theme 2: Parasitic Integration and the Hydrological Crisis (Notes 3, 6, 12): A critical insight from the notes is the Hydrological Dependency Model. By consuming large amounts of potable water for well maintenance, the industry creates artificial scarcity. The subsequent corporate-led water delivery becomes a "trap," forcing the community into dependency on the very entities that depleted their resources. This is further compounded by the marginalization of local shell rock mining, suggesting that the presence of FDI actively de-industrializes or "crowds out" local secondary markets.

Theme 3: Lay Epidemiology vs. Strategic Opacity (Notes 1, 4, 7, 8): There is a significant clash between official discourse and the lived reality of residents. While the state-investor alignment omits environmental costs, the community develops "Lay Epidemiology"—a bottom-up logic linking industrial intensification to pediatric morbidity and mortality. The failure to provide detection equipment for poisonous gases is not simply an oversight; it is a deliberate tool of information asymmetry used to prevent the formalization of environmental claims.

4.3.3. CDA Results

This analysis applies Fairclough's Three-Dimensional Model to the documentary's depiction of the oil industry in Western Kazakhstan. Along with reflective journaling and QCA, CDA uncovers details ranging from specific linguistic choices to broader socio-political structures in the region.

The textual analysis reveals a deliberate linguistic tension centered on a binary between "Big Oil" (in Russian: большая нефть) and the "Small People" (in Russian: маленькие люди) who inhabit the periphery of extraction zones. This choice of adjectives naturalizes the industry as an overwhelming, quasi-environmental force, while simultaneously diminishing the agency and visibility of local citizens. This power imbalance is most poignantly captured in the subversion of domestic imagery: the traditional "smell of home" is redefined not by safety or comfort, but by the toxic presence of industrial emissions—literally becoming the air the next generation breathes from birth. By utilizing post-apocalyptic cultural references like Mad Max, the narrative frames these regions as lawless "extraction frontiers" rather than integrated parts of a modern state.

At the level of discursive practice, the documentary functions as a robust counter-narrative that systematically deconstructs state propaganda. By intertextually juxtaposing archival footage of presidential promises from the late 1990s with contemporary scenes of abandoned schools and "rainbow-colored" water, the film exposes the informational opacity sustaining the current power structure. The documentary highlights a clear historical path dependency: the transition from the Soviet era—where the word "ecology" was functionally absent from the public lexicon—to a modern era of FDI has not changed the underlying logic of resource extraction. Instead, knowledge production remains strictly controlled; by withholding data on emissions and water toxicity, the state maintains exclusive authority to define what constitutes a "safe" environment.

On a macro scale, these discourses reflect the systemic reality the narrator calls the "gas station country" (in Russian: страна-бензоколонка). This social practice reveals an ideology in which the "stability of the investor" is prioritized over the biological and economic survival of the population. In this framework, public health and environmental integrity are treated as externalities which are acceptable costs for maintaining national rent-seeking. The ultimate outcome of this socio-economic logic is exemplified by the ghost town of Baishonas. The community's existence depends entirely on the resource; once the oil is depleted, the social contract is voided and the community disappears. This demonstrates a terminal stage of the resource curse, where the land retains value only as long as it can be emptied of its contents.

When viewed alongside similar cases in Africa or other transition economies, a shared discursive template emerges: "The Myth of the 'Tiger'"—using predatory metaphors to justify rapid FDI; "Industrial Lopsidedness"—framing traditional livelihoods (herding or fishing) as "obsolete" compared to the high-tech, yet detached, oil sector; and "Institutional Voids—using international "benchmarks" to distract from domestic failures in regulation and public trust. Thus, this CDA suggests that the "Resource Curse" is as much a narrative phenomenon as an economic one, sustained by the systematic marginalization of local voices in favor of global capital.

5. CONCLUDING REMARKS

History seems to be repeating itself: developing countries lacking the resources to grow sustainably and defend themselves from predatory actions by larger, stronger nations continue to face significant challenges. Although colonialism in its literal sense has ended, a new form has emerged over the past 50–70 years. Instead of direct involvement, countries such as the United States and China use private corporations to extract valuable natural resources and promise FDI to local governments to stimulate economic growth and development. This trend has generated an unprecedented volume of scientific literature on FDI and its effects across economies. While these studies have produced mixed results, academia generally promotes a positive view of FDI. However, this perspective is often disconnected from real life and local communities, where natural resource extraction becomes an irresponsible activity driven solely by profit maximization by large corporations. This issue is more complex than a simple economic optimization problem for both firms and local communities; it requires a more nuanced mindset and a paradigm shift toward environmental and human rights protection. The approach in this chapter demonstrates that the complexity and multilayered nature of these topics can only be analyzed with qualitative research methods.

Reflective journaling and QCA revealed that Ghana experienced labor decoupling, infrastructure asymmetry, and negative environmental externalities due to the inflow of both domestic and foreign investments. Imported labor was favored over trained locals, who lacked basic water and electricity amenities, while engineers and businessmen enjoyed much higher quality facilities. Reflective journaling in Kazakhstan presents a similar picture to Ghana, but in Ecuador, there is a power struggle between local communities and large FDI entities. These results clearly show that FDI can be used as a predatory economic tool to reduce production costs of valuable natural resources in developing countries and maximize profits without considering negative externalities at various levels.

Across the three case studies, discourse analysis reveals a consistent "enclave" model of development, where multinational capital systematically externalizes social and ecological costs. In Kazakhstan, the "transient state" narrative illustrates how governance becomes contingent on extractable wealth, while the Ecuadorian case exposes how predatory litigation and blame-shifting are used to silence the human toll of the "Amazon Chernobyl." In Ghana, the analysis highlights the "modernization myth," where the promised developmental benefits of oil discovery failed to materialize, instead disrupting traditional livelihoods and entrenching the resource curse. Collectively, these cases demonstrate that without robust institutional mechanisms, FDI operates as a parasitic rather than catalytic force, prioritizing global shareholder profit over the biological and economic survival of host communities.

The qualitative analysis generally exposes a parasitic "enclave" model, where industrial toxicity and systemic health crises undermine local subsistence economies, trapping indigenous populations in a cycle of ecological and financial decline. These findings underscore how institutional blame-shifting and predatory litigation exacerbate the resource curse, forcing marginalized communities to bypass captured state mechanisms in favor of transnational advocacy and global media intervention.

The overall message of this chapter is more intuitive than mainstream economics, which often regresses a few economic variables to deliver a straightforward message about some econometric association. Instead of simply stating that FDI promotes economic growth, a more granular view is needed to objectively weigh the costs and benefits for local communities and their environments. On a macro level, the impact may be positive, but on a micro level, it can be quite the opposite. This is why qualitative methods should be promoted in economics, although this is not currently the norm. Most economists and practitioners prefer quantitative methods because they do not require direct communication with economic agents; collecting data from secondary sources addresses many challenges related to publication and reporting. However, quality research requires much more effort and direct involvement, which may not be favored by many authors and practitioners.

The main empirical and methodological innovations of this chapter should be compared with the existing literature. Extensive cross-country panel data studies (e.g., Fajrian et al., 2023) typically regress FDI inflows on GDP per capita, generally concluding that FDI promotes economic growth, although this effect may be weaker in resource-abundant countries. Thus, a granular, community-level approach is needed to complement econometric models for a realistic evaluation of FDI's impact in developing countries. Furthermore, building on Alfaro's (2017) ideas, many argue that FDI benefits local economies through economic spillovers such as technological diffusion, infrastructure development, and forward and backward supply chain linkages. However, these spillovers can also result in ecological decline. The framework presented in this chapter compels the discipline to recognize that FDI spillovers can be strongly negative, trapping populations in financial decline rather than lifting them through technological transfer. Similarly, qualitative political ecology often examines how resource extraction leads to violent conflict between the state and indigenous groups. In addition to Svampa (2019), the formulation of the "Bio-Economic Trap" in this chapter is a highly original economic concept that demonstrates how industrial toxicity specifically destroys the alternative capital (farming and fishing) needed to address the health crises caused by industry. This represents a more sophisticated understanding of poverty than the standard political ecology narrative.

Nevertheless, some limitations of the current approach in this chapter and suggestions for future research should be included as the final component of the conclusions section. First, documentary films provide valuable qualitative insights, but they are inherently created and mediated over technical and longitudinal economic data. Second, this chapter used qualitative data analysis techniques, which are interpretive by nature. This creates methodological subjectivity, posing a significant challenge in objectively demonstrating that the author's interpretation is valid and reliable. Third, the sample size and geographical scope were limited, as only three countries were discussed, leading to issues with generalizability. Different institutional settings and cultural endowments naturally result in differences in the management of FDI. Lastly, there is a "snapshot constraint" in this research. The negative externalities and harmful effects of FDI on local communities cannot be comprehensively analyzed based on data covering only a few years. Therefore, future research should focus on low ordinal data using a mixed methods approach. A specific approach should also be based on industrial policy and diversification, as different developing countries rapidly experience economic shifts in growth and development that must be accounted for. Additionally, it is recommended that success stories be contrasted with failures among developing countries to conceptualize FDI iteratively.

REFERENCES

Acquah, A. M., & Ibrahim, M. (2020). Foreign direct investment, economic growth and financial sector development in Africa. *Journal of Sustainable Finance & Investment, 10*(4), 315–334. DOI: 10.1080/20430795.2019.1683504

Agarwal, B., Roy, S. N., & Sharma, S. C. (2026). Can indigenous political representation improve forest conservation? India's experience. *World Development, 201*, 107295. DOI: 10.1016/j.worlddev.2025.107295

Ahmadov, V. (2025). Technological capabilities and economic growth in Visegrad countries. *Regional Statistics, 15*(6), 1103–1123. DOI: 10.15196/RS150603

Alfaro, L. (2017). Gains from foreign direct investment: Macro and micro approaches. *The World Bank Economic Review, 30*(Supplement_1), S2–S15.

Amirahmadi, H., & Wu, W. (1994). Foreign direct investment in developing countries. *Journal of Developing Areas, 28*(2), 167–190.

Andreoni, A. (2022). Compressed development and the political economy of developmentalism. *Development and Change, 53*(5), 1103–1120. DOI: 10.1111/dech.12729

Arribas-Ayllon, M., & Walkerdine, V. (2017). Foucauldian discourse analysis. In Carla W. & Wendy (Eds), *The Sage handbook of qualitative research in psychology* (pp. 91–108). Sage. DOI: 10.4135/9781526405555.n7

Auty, R. (2001). *Resource abundance and economic development*. Oxford University Press.

Badeeb, R., Lean, H. H., & Clark, J. (2016). The evolution of the natural resource curse thesis: A critical literature survey. *Resources Policy*, 51, 123–134.

Barbier, E. B. (2003). The role of natural resources in economic development. *Australian Economic Papers, 42*(2), 253–272. DOI: 10.1111/1467-8454.00198

Bloom, D. E., & Williamson, J. G. (1998). Demographic transitions and economic miracles in emerging Asia. *The World Bank Economic Review, 12*(3), 419–455. DOI: 10.1093/wber/12.3.419

Borish, D., Cunsolo, A., Mauro, I., Dewey, C., & Harper, S. L. (2021). Moving images, moving methods: Advancing documentary film for qualitative research. *International Journal of Qualitative Methods, 20*, 16094069211013646. DOI: 10.1177/16094069211013646

Campos, C. J. G., & Turato, E. R. (2009). Content analysis in studies using the clinical-qualitative method: Application and perspectives. *Revista Latino-Americana de Enfermagem, 17*(2), 259–264. DOI: 10.1590/S0104-11692009000200019 PMID: 19551282

Chaudhuri, S., & Mukhopadhyay, U. (2014). *Foreign direct investment in developing countries. A Theoretical Evaluation*. Springer India. DOI: 10.1007/978-81-322-1898-2

Ciuriak, D. (2014). *Diagnosing Dutch Disease*. Available at *SSRN* 2540108.

Corden, W. M. (1984). Booming sector and Dutch disease economics: Survey and consolidation. *Oxford Economic Papers, 36*(3), 359–380. DOI: 10.1093/oxfordjournals.oep.a041643

Corden, W. M., & Neary, J. P. (1982). Booming sector and de-industrialisation in a small open economy. *Economic Journal (London), 92*(368), 825–848. DOI: 10.2307/2232670

Czech, K., & Niftiyev, I. (2021). The impact of oil price shocks on oil-dependent countries' currencies: The case of Azerbaijan and Kazakhstan. *Journal of Risk and Financial Management, 14*(9), 431. DOI: 10.3390/jrfm14090431

Daniel, M., Bergstøl, I. K. G., & Hansen, M. (2025). Fools rush in… exploring the use of documentary films as qualitative data. *Qualitative Research,* •••, 14687941251377256. DOI: 10.1177/14687941251377256

Desbordes, R., & Wei, S. J. (2017). Foreign direct investment and external financing conditions: Evidence from normal and crisis times. *The Scandinavian Journal of Economics, 119*(4), 1129-1166. DOI: 10.1111/sjoe.12192

Di John, J. (2010). *The 'resource curse': Theory and evidence (ARI)*. School of Oriental and African Studies (SOAS), University of London.

Edwards, S. (2023). Reflective journaling. In *Varieties of qualitative research methods: Selected contextual perspectives* (pp. 419–424). Springer International Publishing. DOI: 10.1007/978-3-031-04394-9_65

Elmi, L. (2020). Developing countries with natural resources. https://borgenproject.org/developing-countries-that-benefit-from-natural-resources/

Elo, S., & Kyngäs, H. (2008). The qualitative content analysis process. *Journal of Advanced Nursing, 62*(1), 107–115. DOI: 10.1111/j.1365-2648.2007.04569.x PMID: 18352969

Emako, E., Nuru, S., & Menza, M. (2022). The effect of foreign direct investment on economic growth in developing countries. *Transnational Corporations Review, 14*(4), 382–401. DOI: 10.1080/19186444.2022.2146967

Fairclough, N. (2013). *Critical discourse analysis: The critical study of language* (2nd ed.). Routledge. DOI: 10.4324/9781315834368

Fajrian, M. A., Achsani, N. A., & Widyastutik, W. (2023). Foreign direct investment (FDI), abundance of natural resources, and economic growth. *Signifikan: Jurnal Ilmu Ekonomi, 12*(1), 11–26. DOI: 10.15408/sjie.v12i1.29975

Fitzgerald, A., & Lowe, M. (2020). Acknowledging documentary filmmaking as not only an output but a research process: A case for quality research practice. *International Journal of Qualitative Methods, 19*, 1609406920957462. DOI: 10.1177/1609406920957462

Forman, J., & Damschroder, L. (2007). Qualitative content analysis. In L. Jacoby & L. A. Siminoff (Eds.), *Empirical methods for bioethics: A primer* (Advances in Bioethics, Vol. 11, pp. 39–62). Emerald Group Publishing Limited. DOI: 10.1016/S1479-3709(07)11003-7

Gbambu, A. R., Dramani, J. S., & Adekunle, M. O. (2023). A contextual analysis of documentary film as a product and tool for academic exercise. *European Journal of Communication and Media Studies, 2*(4), 25–35. DOI: 10.24018/ejmedia.2023.2.4.22

Gee, J. P. (2014). *An introduction to discourse analysis: Theory and method* (4th ed.). Routledge. DOI: 10.4324/9781315819679

Ghosh, S., & Saha, S. K. (2025). Impact of foreign direct investment on economic growth in developing countries: The role of institutional quality. *Sustainable Economies, 3*(1), 389. DOI: 10.62617/se389

Godoy, R., Bauchet, J., Reyes-García, V., & Undurraga, E. A. (2026). Economic convergence, intragenerational economic mobility, and inequality in a native Amazonian small-scale society of Indigenous People in Bolivia. *World Development, 199*, 107237. DOI: 10.1016/j.worlddev.2025.107237

Guo, X., Meng, X., Luan, Q., & Wang, Y. (2023). Trade openness, globalization, and natural resources management: The moderating role of economic complexity in newly industrialized countries. *Resources Policy, 85*, 103757. DOI: 10.1016/j.resourpol.2023.103757

Haapanen, L., & Tapio, P. (2016). Economic growth as phenomenon, institution and ideology: A qualitative content analysis of the 21st century growth critique. *Journal of Cleaner Production, 112*, 3492–3503. DOI: 10.1016/j.jclepro.2015.10.024

Hasanli, Y., Musayeva, J., & Musayeva, F. (2026). How do oil and gas reserves affect the economic growth of the CIS countries: Evidence from panel data. In *Digitalisation and Artificial Intelligence Using Mathematical and Computational Approaches: FAI-DAIRBM 2024*, Baku, Azerbaijan, April 18–20, 291.

Hasanli, Y., Rahimli, G., Ibişov, E., & Rzayev, R. (2025b). Inter-Sectoral Linkages and Structural Change in Azerbaijan: Insights from the Transport Sector. In *4th International Conference on Problems of Logistics, Management and Operation in the East-West Transport Corridor (PLMO 2025).*

Hasanli, Y., Rahimli, G., Quliyev, F., & Ferrari, M. (2025a). Evaluation of sectoral foreign trade elasticities of Azerbaijan. *Journal of Economic Sciences Theory and Practice*, *82*(2), 117–137.

Hasanov, R. I., Giyasova, Z., Azizova, R., Huseynova, S., & Zemri, B. E. (2024). Long-term dynamics between human development and environmental sustainability: An empirical analysis of CO_2 emissions in Azerbaijan. *Challenges in Sustainability*, *12*(4), 273–280. DOI: 10.56578/cis120403

Hasanov, R. I., Giyasova, Z., Mahmudova, I., Marchwiński, J., & Karimova, N. (2025). Examining the relationship between manufacturing value added and environmental impact in Azerbaijan. *International Journal of Energy Economics and Policy, 15.*

Henri, P. A. O. (2019). Natural resources curse: A reality in Africa. *Resources Policy*, *63*, 101406. DOI: 10.1016/j.resourpol.2019.101406

Holden, S. (2013). Avoiding the resource curse the case Norway. *Energy Policy*, *63*, 870–876. DOI: 10.1016/j.enpol.2013.09.010

Hsieh, H. F., & Shannon, S. E. (2005). Three approaches to qualitative content analysis. *Qualitative Health Research*, *15*(9), 1277–1288. DOI: 10.1177/1049732305276687 PMID: 16204405

Humphreys, M., Sachs, J. D., & Stiglitz, J. E. (2007). Introduction: What is the problem with natural resource wealth. In Humphreys, M., Sachs, J. D., & Stiglitz, J. E. (Eds.), *Escaping the Resource Curse* (pp. 1–20). Columbia University Press.

Izadi, R., Bahrami, M. A., Sarikhani, Y., & Bastani, P. (2023). Qualitative document analysis on Iranian contents and trends of population policies: Lessons learned and avenues for future. *Heliyon*, *9*(6), e17377. DOI: 10.1016/j.heliyon.2023.e17377 PMID: 37408904

Jones, J., Harris, E., Febriansah, Y., Adiwijaya, A., & Hikam, I. N. (2024). AI for sustainable development: Applications in natural resource management, agriculture, and waste management. *International Transactions on Artificial Intelligence*, *2*(2), 143–149. DOI: 10.33050/italic.v2i2.549

Jørgensen, M., & Phillips, L. J. (2002). *Discourse analysis as theory and method.* Sage Publications. DOI: 10.4135/9781849208871

Kahveci, E., & Odabaş, A. (2016). Central banks' communication strategy and content analysis of monetary policy statements: The case of Fed, ECB and CBRT. *Procedia: Social and Behavioral Sciences*, *235*, 618–629. DOI: 10.1016/j.sbspro.2016.11.039

Kanval, N., Ihsan, H., Irum, S., & Ambreen, I. (2024). Human capital formation, foreign direct investment inflows, and economic growth: A way forward to achieve sustainable development. *Journal of Management Practices. Humanities and Social Sciences*, *8*(3), 48–61.

Kelsey, D., Mueller, F., Whittle, A., & KhosraviNik, M. (Eds.). (2019). *The discourse of financial crisis and austerity: Critical analyses of business and economics across disciplines*. Routledge.

Khan, H., Dong, Y., Bibi, R., & Khan, I. (2024). Institutional quality and foreign direct investment: Global evidence. *Journal of the Knowledge Economy*, *15*(3), 10547–10591. DOI: 10.1007/s13132-023-01508-1

Khan, T. H., & MacEachen, E. (2021). Foucauldian discourse analysis: Moving beyond a social constructionist analytic. *International Journal of Qualitative Methods*, *20*, 16094069211018009. DOI: 10.1177/16094069211018009

Maeße, J. (2015). Crisis management policy: How discourses shape academic-political actors. *On the Horizon*, *23*(3), 231–244. DOI: 10.1108/OTH-05-2015-0016

Mallampally, P., & Sauvant, K. P. (1999). Foreign direct investment in developing countries. *Finance & Development*, *36*(1), 34.

Manasseh, C. O., Nwakoby, I. C., Okanya, O. C., Ifediora, C. U., & Nzidee, W. A. (2023). The impact of foreign direct investment and oil revenue on economic growth in Nigeria. *Studia Universitatis Vasile Goldi Arad. Seria tiin e Economice*, *33*(3), 61–85.

Mayring, P. (2021). Qualitative content analysis: A step-by-step guide. *Sage (Atlanta, Ga.).*

Meetei, L. A., Bhattacharjya, B. R., & Bhowmick, B. (2024). The role of universities in the innovation systems in the developing countries. *Foresight and STI Governance, 18*(1), 58–67. DOI: 10.17323/2500-2597.2024.1.58.67

Mertens, D. M. (2005). *Research and evaluation in education and Psychology: Integrating diversity with quantitative, qualitative, and mixed methods* (2nd ed.). SAGE Publications.

Morgan, R., Game, A. M., & Slutskaya, N. (2019). Qualitative research through documentary filmmaking: Questions and possibilities. In Cassell, C., Cunliffe, A., & Grandy, G. (Eds.), *The Sage handbook of qualitative business and management research methods: Methods and challenges* (pp. 329–344). Sage.

Mottaleb, K. A. (2007). *Determinants of foreign direct investment and its impact on economic growth in developing countries*. MPRA Paper, No. 9457.

Niftiyev, I. (2021). Dutch disease effects in the Azerbaijan economy: Results of multivariate linear ordinary least squares (OLS) estimations. *HSE Economic Journal, 25*(2), 309–346. DOI: 10.17323/1813-8691-2021-25-2-309-346

OECD-Organisation for Economic Co-operation and Development. (2008). *Natural resources and pro-poor growth: The economics and politics*. Organisation for Economic Cooperation and Development, DAC Guidelines and Reference Series, A Good Practice Paper.

Ogbonna, O. E., Ogbuabor, J. E., Manasseh, C. O., & Ekeocha, D. O. (2022). Global uncertainty, economic governance institutions and foreign direct investment inflow in Africa. *Economic Change and Restructuring, 55*(4), 2111–2136. DOI: 10.1007/s10644-021-09378-w

Ortlipp, M. (2008). Keeping and using reflective journals in the qualitative research process. *The Qualitative Report, 13*(4), 695–705.

Pamantung, R. (2026). The role of foreign direct investment in driving economic growth: Evidence from developing countries. Available at *SSRN* 6595701. DOI: 10.2139/ssrn.6595701

Pereira, M., Silva, G. M., & Coelho, F. (2026). A fuzzy-set QCA approach exploring the role of public and private debt in shaping environmental performance. *World Development, 198*, 107213. DOI: 10.1016/j.worlddev.2025.107213

Pritchett, L. (1997). Divergence, big time. *The Journal of Economic Perspectives, 11*(3), 3–17. DOI: 10.1257/jep.11.3.3

(2010). Qualitative analysis and documentary method. InBohnsack, R., Pfaff, N., & Weller, W. (Eds.), *International educational research*. Barbara Budrich.

Razmi, M. J., Sedighi, S., & Rezaeian, S. (2016). Essential requirements of good governance for achieving human development. *Journal of Public Administration, 10*(1), 1–30.

Regmi, R., Zhang, Z., & Zhang, H. (2023). Entrepreneurship strategy, natural resources management and sustainable performance: A study of an emerging market. *Resources Policy, 86*, 104202. DOI: 10.1016/j.resourpol.2023.104202

Rodrik, D. (2013). Unconditional convergence in manufacturing. *The Quarterly Journal of Economics, 128*(1), 165–204. DOI: 10.1093/qje/qjs047

Rosser, A. (2007). Escaping the resource curse: The case of Indonesia. *Journal of Contemporary Asia, 37*(1), 38–58. DOI: 10.1080/00472330601104557

Sachs, J. D., & Warner, A. (1999). Natural resource intensity and economic growth. In Mayer, J., Chambers, B., & Farooq, A. (Eds.), *Development policies in natural resource economies* (pp. 13–38). Edward Elgar Publishing. DOI: 10.4337/9781782541295.00011

Sachs, J. D. & Warner, A. M. (1995). *Natural resource abundance and economic growth*. NBER Working Paper Series, No. 5398.

Sachs, J. D., & Warner, A. M. (1999). The big push, natural resource booms and growth. *Journal of Development Economics, 59*(1), 43–76. DOI: 10.1016/S0304-3878(99)00005-X

Sachs, J. D., & Warner, A. M. (2001). The curse of natural resources. *European Economic Review, 45*(4-6), 827–838. DOI: 10.1016/S0014-2921(01)00125-8

Salihu, O. (2026). Natural resource governance and conflict in Nigeria's extractive frontiers: A scoping review. *Preprints*. https://www.preprints.org/manuscript/202601.0443

Sanders, A. R. D., & Sandvik, P. T. (2015). Avoiding the resource curse?: Democracy and natural resources in Norway since 1900. In Badia-Miro, M. Pinilla, V. & Willebald, H. (Eds.) *Natural Resources and Economic Growth* (pp. 313–338). Routledge.

Scalamonti, F. (2026). The impact of FDI on economic growth in emerging and developing economies: The role of institutional quality and technology diffusion. *Transnational Supply Chain Research, 2*(1), 24–45. DOI: 10.65773/tscr.2.1.92

Sedighi, S. (2024). Rents, financial development, and economic growth in MENA countries, 2000–2020. *Regional Statistics, 14*(03), 589–608. DOI: 10.15196/RS140308

Sinha, M., Tirtosuharto, D., Ray Chaudhury, A., & Basu, P. (2023). FDI, digitalization and employment: Empirical evidence from developing economies. *Studies in Economics and Finance, 40*(4), 740–756. DOI: 10.1108/SEF-10-2021-0450

Smith, S. K., Mountain, G. A., & Hawkins, R. J. (2016). A scoping review to identify the techniques frequently used when analysing qualitative visual data. *International Journal of Social Research Methodology, 19*(6), 693–715. DOI: 10.1080/13645579.2015.1087141

Svampa, M. (2019). *Neo-extractivism in Latin America: Socio-environmental conflicts, the territorial turn, and new political narratives.* Cambridge University Press. DOI: 10.1017/9781108752589

The Economist. (1977). The Dutch disease. *The Economist*, 26, 82–83.

Udemba, E. N., & Yalçıntaş, S. (2022). Unveiling the symptoms of Dutch disease: A comparative and sustainable analysis of two oil-rich countries. *Resources Policy, 79*, 102949. DOI: 10.1016/j.resourpol.2022.102949

van Eerd, R. (2010). Of Dutch disease and other ailments. *Bologna Center Journal of International Affairs, 13*, 99–112.

Voloshchenko-Holda, L., & Niedziółka, P. (2024). Central bank communication in unconventional times: Some evidence from a textual analysis of the National Bank of Poland communication during the COVID-crisis. *Economics and Business Review, 10*(1), 101–124. DOI: 10.18559/ebr.2024.1.1039

Wacziarg, R. (2012). The first law of petropolitics. *Economica, 79*(316), 641–657. DOI: 10.1111/j.1468-0335.2011.00902.x

Wang, J., Yang, J., & Yang, L. (2023). Do natural resources play a role in economic development? Role of institutional quality, trade openness, and FDI. *Resources Policy, 81*, 103294. DOI: 10.1016/j.resourpol.2023.103294

Wang, R., Tan, J., & Yao, S. (2021). Are natural resources a blessing or a curse for economic development? The importance of energy innovations. *Resources Policy, 72*, 102042. DOI: 10.1016/j.resourpol.2021.102042

Welsch, H. (2008). Resource dependence, knowledge creation, and growth: Revisiting the natural resource curse. *Journal of Economic Development, 33*(1), 45–70. DOI: 10.35866/caujed.2008.33.1.003

Yadav, S., Samadhiya, A., Kumar, A., Luthra, S., & Pandey, K. K. (2024). Nexus between fintech, green finance and natural resources management: Transition of BRICS nation industries from resource curse to resource blessed sustainable economies. *Resources Policy*, *91*, 104903. DOI: 10.1016/j.resourpol.2024.104903

Yefimov, V. (2011). *Discourse analysis in economics: Methodology and history of economics reconsidered.* Munich Personal RePEc Archive.

Yi-chong, X., & Leiva, D. (2021). Chile: A Successful Story in Latin America? In Okpanachi, E., Chowdhari Tremblay, R. (Eds.), *The Political Economy of Natural Resource Funds* (pp. 87–115). International Political Economy Series. Palgrave Macmillan

Yu, Y. (2023). Role of Natural resources rent on economic growth: Fresh empirical insight from selected developing economies. *Resources Policy*, *81*, 103326. DOI: 10.1016/j.resourpol.2023.103326

Chapter 4
Predicting Financial Inclusion:
Leveraging Neural Networks for MENAAP and Beyond

Vidya Suresh
http://orcid.org/0000-0001-7356-8228
College of Banking and Financial Studies, Oman

Muneer Shaik
http://orcid.org/0000-0002-3508-1096
Mahindra University, Hyderabad, India

Medhansh Bairaria
Mahindra University, Hyderabad, India

ABSTRACT

With fintec acting as one of the catalysts, Financial Inclusion (FI) and strategy to improve FI has gained focal light in academia as well as amongst policy makers. FI has become strongest tool to enhance economic growth and reduce poverty levels. This paper analyses the drivers of FI, focusing on the MENAAP region and comparing them with the rest of the regions. It utilizes supervised machine learning, focusing on the Multi-Layer Perceptron Artificial Neural Network model with data collected from the World Bank Group's report. The findings indicate disparity among MENAAP regions in terms of penetration of FI. The low and middle-income group are low on financial access and strategic efforts but successful in consumer credit providence and penetration of owning bank accounts with underprivileged. The region is seen taking efforts focusing on leveraging technology and targeted

DOI: 10.4018/979-8-3373-8964-6.ch004

policies to close existent gaps, particularly in Pakistan and Afghanistan. The region has been successful in setting up strong and transparent institutions to build public confidence in the financial sector.

1. INTRODUCTION

Financial inclusion (FI) plays a central role in generating employment, fostering entrepreneurial activity, and enhancing households' capacity to absorb economic shocks (Suresh & Maity, 2022). In economically vulnerable regions, improvements in financial inclusion have been associated with sustained increases in household income and the gradual accumulation of productive assets (Sarma & Pais, 2011). Accordingly, the emphasis on the enhancement of financial inclusions is particularly very important for the MENAAP region. The World Bank clearly defines the concept of FI as follows: "Financial inclusion is the access to appropriate, affordable, timely, and readily usable financial products and services needed by all individuals, firms, and communities in the economy, and which are accessible at all times in a responsible and sustainable manner that is environmentally friendly and socially viable" (World Bank Group, 2013). FI provide access to formal bank accounts, credit, payments, savings, pensions, and insurance services for the individuals in the economy. Likewise, access to the above opportunities is necessarily very crucial for firms, as it assists them in investment decisions, grasping prospective market opportunities, and supporting the cultivation of innovation. Additionally, FI helps in management of liquidity, costs and the mitigation of risks for the firms in the economy. The MENAAP designation stands for Middle East, North Africa, Afghanistan, and Pakistan. The aforesaid expansion of regional grouping was introduced by the World Bank for its fiscal year 2026 shifting Pakistan and Afghanistan out of the traditional South Asia cluster (World Integrated Trade Solution, n.d.). Countries included in the MENAAP region are Afghanistan, United Arab Emirates, Bahrain, Djibouti, Algeria, Egypt Arab Republic, Iran Islamic Republic, Iraq, Israel, Jordan, Kuwait, Lebanon, Libya, Morocco, Malta, Oman, Pakistan, Qatar, Saudi Arabia, Syrian Arab Republic, Tunisia and Yemen.

There are approximately 166 Islamic banks in the MENAAP region, out of which 45 are among the top 100 in the world. However, this is unequally distributed, as the majority lie in the Middle East. In Pakistan, there are only 21 such banks, while for Afghanistan, it is one institution. Overall, these 45 banks have assets of more than half a trillion US dollars and represent approximately 18% of total banking assets within the Middle East and North Africa region. This enormity therefore underlines the suitability of the region as a representative context to Islamic finance. In the era of digital technology, financial inclusion depends on technology to achieve economies of scale in including more people into the fold of financial services and the usage of artificial intelligence and machine learning to speed up this process (De Mariz, 2022). Financial technology combines innovative financial models with digital technologies to improve the accessibility, efficiency, and inclusivity of financial services (Arner et al., 2015). Applications encompass alternative credit-scoring algorithms, AI-driven back-office systems, mobile payments, blockchain-based transfers, and robot-advisory platforms. The use of the internet is becoming more and more visible at microeconomic levels households, small, and medium-sized businesses. as well as in the macroeconomic levels (financial systems of countries). The worldwide financial technology industry has recorded rapid growth during the last ten years. By 2027, there are more than 30,000 fintech firms globally, with projected revenues surpassing USD 200 billion. National fintech strategies are essential in directing this growth. Effectively crafted plans can promote innovation, enhance regulatory frameworks, broaden financial inclusion, and reduce consumer risks (Shewale, 2024).

Current research offers significant insights into factors influencing FI like fintech adoption, existence of strategy for fintech and financial inclusion at national level in policy making. In the year 2012, the World Bank initiated its financial inclusion support framework, which is meant to support countries in formulating national strategies. The countries benefitted through this program are Haiti, Indonesia, Paraguay, Pakistan, Russia, and Rwanda (Fernando et al., 2018). Apart from the above-mentioned drivers of FI, the variables that could possibly impact the growth and penetration of FI would be consumer credit providers, availability of electronic money, existence of microfinance, digital finance and financial literacy strategies at national level. For strategy to be developed at the national level, leadership becomes crucial. However, more important is how these institutions organize themselves in order to develop a national strategy. Evidence suggests that these institutions organize themselves in extremely diverse ways. A new trend in the methods used in the process of consultation during the formulation of strategy is the utilization of technical and thematic working groups. This is done to acquire different views in relation to the industry, the barriers to financial inclusion, potential strategies to circumvent the barriers and other aspects (Chitimira & Warikandwa, 2023). Nations such as Bhutan, Fiji, Pakistan, the Philippines, Nigeria, and Tanzania applied this method.

Financial inclusion is shaped by multiple interacting dimensions, which makes linear or additive empirical approaches insufficient for capturing its underlying structure. Addressing this complexity requires analytical frameworks capable of learning non-linear interactions among institutional, regulatory, and policy-related determinants. In this context, machine learning methods offer a distinct advantage. Of these, Multi-Layer Perceptron Artificial Neural Networks (MLP-ANNs) have proven useful in their ability to handle high-dimensional input data. ANN also supports to identify implicit relationships in the data and evaluate the relative importance of the predictors without any parametric assumptions.

Research based on measuring traditional financial inclusion relies heavily on linear regression models like Ordinary Least Square models, Logit or Probit. These conventional models are highly reliable and used for their interpretability, simplicity and wide range of applicability in multiple fields. However, these econometric models come with certain assumptions which make them static. Machine learning techniques like Artificial Neural Network relaxes some of these assumptions allowing more efficient modeling (Setianto et al., 2025). The database that needs to be analysed through conventional models needs to be converted to linear or log linear. In reality, real- time survey data are highly complex and non- linear. For example, variables like financial access, socioeconomic factors, types of barriers to banking activities are non- linear in nature (Benkraiem & Zopounidis, 2021). ANN uses functions like ReLU or Sigmoid activation function which are non-linear. This gives a free hand to researchers to take the data as it is without getting into the need for any conversion (Intam et al., 2024). Another issue that comes with traditional models is variable interaction. Here, the researcher is required to manually indicate the interaction terms like 'income with wealth'. Either the researcher suggests the interaction variables based on previous studies or uses his or her past learning. If it is not suggested, the model misses it. Either way, the specification error or bias is created. ANN has hidden layers that automatically dig out deep and complex interactions between variables along with patterns (Hoxha, 2023). Global State of Financial Inclusion and Consumer Protection (FICP) data surveyed by World Bank Group are multi-dimensional with binary responses. These responses typically include access to banks, lending facilities, non- bank access, fintech awareness and readiness to use and the likes (Ortiz et al., 2023). Conventional models may not be able to capture multi-dimensional and highly correlated variables simultaneously without getting into the problem of multi-collinearity. While studying the impact factors of fintech usage and strategy, it is critical to understand nuances of vulnerable populations. A machine learning technique like ANN is useful in capturing localized threshold impact points like where a non- bank loan transitions a household from poverty to financial accessibility (Pinelis & Ruppert, 2021). Thus, ANN allows the variables to map complicated, real-world baselines where a minimum change in input like mobile phone ownership, opening a bank account triggers a massive leap in financial inclusion. Thus, ANNs stand out at processing enormous, complicated data sets, including unconventional data sources like mobile wallet transaction histories, social media footprints and satellite imagery of bank branches (Sathupadi et al., 2025 and Xu, 2025). Conventional models struggle in analyzing such unstructured data. These advantages also allow for hyper-targeted policymaking by Governments as well as corporations. Following these techniques, this research adopts the MLP-

ANN approach with a broad data set used across the countries, based on the World Bank's Global State of Financial Inclusion and Consumer Protection survey. The objectives of this study are the following:

1. Identify the major determinants of global financial inclusion
2. Identify the factors influencing the adoption of financial inclusion strategies across various regions
3. Compare MENAAP region with regions of rest of the world with respect to financial inclusion indicators.
4. Offer evidence-based guidance for policymakers to harmonize financial inclusion and consumer protection.

The structure of the paper is as follows: section 2 is for overviewing the literature, and then section 3 presents the method, followed by section 4, where the results and discussions are placed, and finally, section 5 concludes the paper.

2. LITERATURE REVIEW

2.1 Financial inclusion and its significance

Inclusive financial strategy or a system achieves credit risk effectively, improves banking performance, and lowers risk concentration (Zamore et al., 2019). It also supports economic growth and stability by addressing financial imbalances caused by internal or external shocks. However, FI also carries risks due to increased access to credit for less secure borrowers. This may lead to non-performing loans over a period of time (Khan, 2011; Sahay et al., 2015). In the recent past, academicians and policymakers have begun to highlight the importance of the expansion of financial systems and services with technology. It is also referred to as a "component of FI." The purpose is to understand FI as a catalyst for reducing poverty, improving the quality and flow of financial services, and enhancing the quality of life in a micro-level economic scenario. In a national economic scenario, it is associated with economic development (Pal & Bandyopadhyay, 2022). As a result, many countries have implemented formal FI strategies at national level to not only to implement but also to measure its reach (Tay et al., 2022).

The World Bank emphasizes financial inclusion as a key policy instrument for poverty reduction (The World Bank, 2022). This is in agreement with the finance-led growth hypothesis, where financial inclusion enables economic growth through capital accumulation. This in turn leads to more output and higher income. Higher economic growth levels would in turn support financial inclusion through increased demand for financial services. In parallel, global policy consensus has strengthened around this agenda. Notably, the G20 Finance Ministers and Central Bank Governors formally committed to advancing financial inclusion worldwide at the 2017 summit in Germany, under the framework of the Global Partnership for Financial Inclusion (GPFI, n.d.). On the one hand, the notion of the finance-led growth hypothesis affirms that FI has an opportunity to improve financial growth in terms of an increase in capital formation, while, on the contrary, there is an increase in GDP that is expected to enhance financial inclusion through an increase in access to financial services. On the other hand, the G20 Finance Ministers and Central Bank Governors vowed to promote FI all over the world, as exemplified by the G20 Summit held in Germany in the year 2017 (The Global Partnership for Financial Inclusion (GPFI), n.d.). Yorulmaz (2018) studied the relationship between FI and growth for MENA countries and finds that FI is measured by the number of ATMs, number of depositors, number of borrowers, number of accounts and credit as percentage of GDP. All these variables were found to have a positive impact on GDP. In a recent study Cama & Emara (2021)FI in MENA region was found to be positively associated with the size of gross capital formation in industries with low research and development expenditures. Yaltaa & Yaltab (2022) analyzed the causality between economic growth and a large number of FI indicators in MENA countries by adopting the recently developed nonlinear and nonparametric Kernel Causality Approach. Their research also revealed that FI is enhanced when the number of women with accounts, number of adults with primary education and accounts, and adults with mobile accounts increased. The research linked main barriers to FI with GDP, where affordability of funds or lack of funds was linked to growth in GDP.

In Pakistan, financial transactions continue to rely heavily on informal networks, with only about 21 percent of adults holding either a bank account or an account with a mobile money provider. Financial exclusion is particularly pronounced among women, who are approximately half as likely as men to access formal financial services. Despite these structural gaps, financial inclusion in Pakistan expanded sharply by 127 percent between 2019 and 2024. Notwithstanding, much work still has to be done since almost two-fifths of the adult population still do not have formal financial services, illustrating the importance of elaborating a national financial inclusion strategy (Development Asia, 2025). Financial exclusion is particularly felt in Afghanistan, which is recognized as a country faced with the highest rates of exclusion. Currently, about 85 percent of the total Afghan population remains outside the overall system of finance, a situation that is more vibrant compared to the overall low-income economy. This has been attributed to a number of factors, including high transactional costs, limited access points compared to the overall population. Also, added to the list are limited linkages of existing financial products to meet the demands of low-income populations. Security-related issues, religious issues, lack of trust in financial entities, and low levels of financial literacy have also been identified as potential issues facing the attainment of comprehensive financial inclusion in Afghanistan (World Bank Afghanistan, 2020).

2.2 Regulatory and Institutional Frameworks

One of the drivers of sustained growth in the FI is regulatory clarity. FI might be impacted by the regulations regarding activities carried out in the banking sector. Such regulations could be improved upon by improving the quality of institutions. For instance, improving the quality of laws could limit bank activities in correlated risks during situations of financial inclusion (Setianto et al., 2025). Rau (2017) finds that licensing frameworks are significantly enhanced with clear regulations in the laws of law, leading to confidence among customers. Frost et al., (2020) show that permitting non-banking business organizations to issue e-money under a regulated environment boosts adoption significantly, especially in sub-Saharan Africa or Southeast Asia. An institutional setting with sufficient stability encourages financial institutions with great stability that are successful in running intermediary services (Ho & Michaely, 1988). This minimizes errors, costs of transactions, as well as asymmetry of information which was a major challenge in channeling funds to the borrower (Cohen et al., 1983; Jude & Levieuge, 2016). Quality regulations and monitoring in the institutional supervision encourage a strong risk culture within banks in the financial and banking sectors (Canh et al., 2019). However, studies conducted by Ahamed and Mallick (2019) found evidence that institutions have little impact on the influencing variables of FI on financial stability. The reach of FI can be significant only in the case when the quality of supervision within the institutional reaches up to a certain level (Su et al., 2019).

2.3 National Strategies for FI

National strategies rank as one of the significant institutional drivers of financial inclusion (FI). Literature highlights the enablers as well as the barriers associated with national strategy implementation. An important example worth citing is the Philippines, which launched its national strategy on FI in 2015. The strategy envisaged an inclusive vision, strategic objectives, as well as several guiding principles to achieve the goals of financial inclusion in the country. FI still lacks prioritization in the national agenda in the MENA region. In this regard, the levels of engagement among the regulators of the respective countries rank as the lowest, with the exception of high-income economies due to naturally low levels of financial exclusion. Nevertheless, certain countries, including Iran, Kuwait, Egypt, Morocco, and Oman, have introduced measures to enhance their inclusive growth strategies.

This includes moving government-to-person payments into bank accounts and leveraging branchless banking through agent networks. Afghanistan is a special case where the Da Afghanistan Bank (DAB), along with other stakeholders, launched and implemented the country's first-ever National Financial Inclusion Strategy for the period of 2020-2024. The key objective of this strategy was to reduce financial exclusion by a minimum of 10 percent while enhancing access to finance for individuals and Micro, Small, and Medium Enterprises (MSMEs). Additionally, focus was on strengthening access to finance to key sectors such as the agricultural sector, improving consumer protection, and leveraging technology to enhance outreach. However, progress is being achieved at a sluggish rate due to security risks and political instability in the country, along with a thin level of financial depth, thereby requiring a gradual and adaptive approach to enhance financial inclusion in the country (Da Afghanistan Bank, 2020).

Financial inclusion has been a major focus area for Pakistan, as reflected through a cohesive effort by the Government of Pakistan (GoP) and the State Bank of Pakistan (SBP) through a series of National Financial Inclusion Strategies introduced since 2015. These initiatives have resulted in a considerable increase in account ownership, from 16 percent in 2015 to 64 percent in 2023. Additionally, the strategy has harnessed conducive regulations, technology, and public-private partnerships, with initiatives such as *Asaan Mobile Accounts, Raast, and Asaan Digital Accounts* being successful in streamlining access to financial services. With regard to gender-based initiatives, a positive result has been seen following the 'banking on equality policy' formulation by SBP. It recorded an increase in the number of adult women with at least one bank account from 13 million in 2018 to 31 million in 2023. With these developments in financial services, the NFIS 2024 - 2028 aims to remove the remaining barriers. It also has targeted to increase digitalization, strengthen secure digital financial services, improve finance terms to priority sectors, and expand the range of capabilities of financial institutions and consumers, as encapsulated in the State Bank of Pakistan (2024) report. However, the persistent culture of cash usage remains a challenge, impeding progress in digitalizing financial services for underbanked consumers.

2.4 Digital Financial Strategies and FI

Digital Financial Strategies (DFS) has been defined as a concept of union or integration of new financial models and technologies to improve the efficiency, access, and inclusiveness of new financial innovations. Fintech-related services cover mobile-based payment solutions, digital technologies for direct matches between borrowers and lenders. Also, data-driven technologies for assessing borrowers' creditworthiness, and investment advice with the use of artificial intelligence technologies.

Additionally, it covers remittance products with distributed ledger technology support. Due to the development and advancement of mobile connections, distributed ledger technology, and big data analytics technology, fintech has gone global (Jihane & Aziz, 2022). According to the World Bank (2022), there are currently 64 percent of the world's customers using at least one fintech service with clients' adoption rates exceeding 80 percent in some of these markets. This comes with an overall fintech industry value of $226 billion as of 2023 and some 30,000 fintech startups showcasing the pace of innovation. In China, the adoption rate of fintech reached 90 percent of citizens. Amongst fintech businesses, the ranking is controlled by Visa, with a market capitalization of $500 billion, followed by Mastercard at 389 billion (Market Research Report, 2025). In emerging economies, adoption of fintech services is often higher than traditional banking services, enabling more people to access financial services, even those considered marginalized (Risman et al., 2023). Enhanced financial literacy enables consumers to efficiently utilize fintech products, arguing that well-knowledgeable consumers are better positioned to manage threats like fraudulence and exploitation of data (Go et al., 2020). In a study by Grohmann et al. (2018), researchers sought to determine a relationship between heightened financial comprehension and utilization of formal financial services. Therefore, digital literacy programs being a part of the nationwide inclusion programs have been highly beneficial. As indicated in the World Bank Global Findex database 2022, it is evident that countries which include fintech education as a part of their overall legislation regulations register a higher usage rate of advanced financial instruments such as crowdfunding or mobile wallets.

3. METHODS

3.1 Dataset

This study is based on the data collected from the Global State of Financial Inclusion and Consumer Protection (FICP), which is derived from the large-scale survey carried out by the World Bank Group in the year 2022. The survey report and the data used are openly accessible through the World Bank's public data repository, as mentioned in the World Bank report (World Bank, 2025). It was asserted by the World Bank that such surveys are the only source of information that offer evidence on financial inclusion and the national financial strategies, as well as the consumer protection systems, from a comparative and longitudinal viewpoint. The objectives of the survey are to collect information on the institutional and policy aspects, including national financial strategies, financial inclusion initiatives, consumer protection systems, and the related factors that are responsible for the development of fintech in the respective nations. In order to accommodate the changed priorities in policy and the environment, the survey questionnaire is upgraded in each new iteration of the research, thereby including the data collection based on the point-in-time and overtime trends. In the year 2022, the survey received responses from the financial sector regulatory authorities from almost 130 nations.

With respect to regional concentration, the highest concentration of participating economies was from the European and Central Asia regions, which comprised 41 economies. Next in the list were Latin America and Caribbean, Sub-Saharan African, MENAAP, East Asia and Pacific, South Asia, and North America regions, which comprised 26, 19, 14, 12, 5, and 2 economies respectively. In terms of size, the highest concentration of participating economies comprised of more than one-third of the economies from the high-income and upper-middle-income categories. Lower-middle-income economies comprised 27 percent of the sample, while low-income economies were represented by five countries, corresponding to approximately four percent of total respondents. Consistent with established empirical practice, twelve economies were excluded from the analysis due to missing information exceeding 80 percent across key model variables (Chowdhury et al., 2024). After data screening and missing-value treatment, the final analytical sample consists of 118 countries and sixteen variables. Detailed definitions, measurement scales, and functional roles of all variables are reported in Table 1, while descriptive statistics are presented in Table 2. For all binary indicators used in the empirical model, a value of "1" denotes the presence of a given attribute at the country level, whereas a value of "0" indicates its absence. Except for 'Digital Financial Inclusion Strategy' as dependent variable all the other variables are classified as independent.

Table 1. List of variables used in the model with their functions

Sl. No	Variable Name	Variable Type and level
1	Country	Nominal
2	Region	Nominal
3	Income Group	Ordinal 1. Low Income Group 2. Lower middle-income group 3. Upper middle-income group 4. High income group
4	Regulated Institutional Framework	Scale
5	Regulated Consumer Credit Providers	Scale
6	Regulated E-Money	Binary

continued on following page

Table 1. Continued

Sl. No	Variable Name	Variable Type and level
7	E-Money issued by non-Banks	Binary
8	Existence of National Financial Inclusion Strategy	Binary
9	Financial Sector Development Strategy with a Financial Inclusion Component Exists	Binary
10	National Development Strategy with a Financial Inclusion Component Exists	Binary
11	Microfinance Strategy	Binary
12	Financial Literacy Strategy	Binary
13	Digital Financial Inclusion Strategy	Binary
14	Fintech Strategy (Digital Financial Strategy)	Binary
15	Policies to Promote Financial Inclusion	Binary
16	Is Financial Inclusion Measured?	Binary

Source: Prepared by authors based on "The Global State of Financial Inclusion and Consumer Protection (FICP) Report" 2022 (World Bank, 2025)

Table 2. Descriptive statistics

	N	Minimum	Maximum	Mean	Std. Deviation
Income Group	118	1	4	3.0	0.9
Regulated Institutional Framework	118	0	1	0.7	0.2
Regulated Consumer Credit Providers	118	0	1	0.8	0.2
Regulated E-Money	118	0	1	0.8	0.4
E-Money issued by non-banks	118	0	1	0.8	0.4
Existence of National Financial Inclusion Strategy	118	0	1	0.5	0.5
Financial Sector Development Strategy with a Financial Inclusion Component Exists	118	0	1	0.3	0.5
National Development Strategy with a Financial Inclusion Component Exists	118	0	1	0.3	0.4
Microfinance Strategy	118	0	1	0.1	0.4
Financial Literacy Strategy	118	0	1	0.5	0.5
Digital Financial Inclusion Strategy	118	0	1	0.3	0.5
Fintech Strategy (Digital Financial Strategy)	118	0	1	0.4	0.5
Policies to Promote Financial Inclusion	118	0	1	0.9	0.3
Is Financial Inclusion Measured?	118	0	1	0.7	0.2

Source: Prepared by authors

3.2 Artificial Neural Networks

Artificial Neural Network (ANN) is also one of the machine learning algorithms. Machine learning algorithms have been used in modeling nonlinear relationships within supervised variables data sets. ANN, according to the functionality of the human brain, could also be an efficient tool in modeling the data sets, especially in cases whereby information concerning the data sets' relationship is limited. It has the ability to recognize and learn data sets' relationship and patterns between data sets' input values and their corresponding target values (Lishner & Shtub, 2022). In other words, it can be described as a computer program or structure that is designed based on the natural process of networks of biological neurons of the brain (Angela et al., 2011). Overall, the structure of the ANN consists of many layers, particularly hidden and activated functions. The entire processing done by a neural network is related to calculation, where it has to be trained with sets of representative data. There are also outputs and inputs of data sets in this processing. Between these two values, there are hidden layers (Permanasari et al., 2013). It has many simple computing elements known as neurons, which have a high level of connectivity between them. The exact count of hidden neurons as well as hidden layers is empirically decided to improve the network and achieve a better result. The fundamental element of the ANN architecture is the artificial neuron. An artificial neuron is a mathematical construct in which the values enter separately in the weighting function, which is summed up by the transfer function to relate the outputs. In the artificial neurons, the values that are entered are the vector of figures. This neuron receives the figures of the input vector and another figure named weight. The neurons then compute their values by weighing the product of the input vector and another figure named bias. These are connected by a nonlinear function that standardizes all the values that the artificial neurons can compute into the values that are predicted for the output values. A series of artificial neurons that function in the same way is referred to as an artificial neural network. Thus, an ANN is said to be defined by having input artificial neurons connected to the input values, with the number of artificial neurons in the input layer equal to the number of values in the data. In other words, ANN is said to be defined by having one or more additional layers of artificial neurons, which can be several or few, and an output layer for the output values. The number of output variables determines the number of artificial neurons in this layer. Figure 1 illustrates the generic structure of an ANN. However, the number of hidden layers and the number of neurons per layer also need to be carefully specified as it impacts the prediction outcome. An insufficient number of hidden-layer neurons typically leads to underfitting, where the network lacks the representational capacity needed to extract signal from complex data (Seifipour & Mehrabian, 2025). Conversely, an excessive number of neurons can induce overfitting, as model capacity becomes disproportionate to the informational content of the training set, resulting in learning patterns that do not generalize beyond the sample. Accordingly, the appropriate hidden-layer width is intrinsically linked to the sample size and feature dimensionality.

The study estimated MLP architectures with one and two hidden layers to benchmark model strength. The two-hidden-layer configuration delivered superior predictive performance and is therefore retained for subsequent analysis. Raw survey data cannot be inputted directly into an ANN because machine algorithms for neural networks are massive matrix multiplication programmed. It scales all types of data into standard normal distribution or fits them between 0 and 1. The data pipeline prepares the data into binary columns with (1 or 0). For example, a 'country' variable with 120 countries becomes 120 separate columns where only one column contains a (1) per row. Data imputation is carried out with specific instructions like replacement with mean or median of series or mean of nearby data points. Alternatively, missing values are also predicted using a secondary algorithm so that the mathematical matrices of the network remain complete (Rytov, 2025).

Validation is the process of demonstrating that the network can perform accurate predictions on a new set of data, specifically, data, the machine has never encountered before. The model automates this process using a strict internal partitioning system. ANN divides the dataset into three parts training set that takes 70% of the entire data. It teaches patterns and adjusts weights. Validation set that takes 15% of the data and is responsible for turning the network. After every cycle called an Epoch, the network runs the updated weights against the validation. Finally, testing set takes remaining 15% of the data to provide final un-biased report card. Here, the system calculates the validation error. If the error is reduced, the network understands it is learning general patterns. However, if the training errors are reduced but the validation error starts to increase, the network signal that it is starting to memorize data rather than learn (Seffahlou et al., 2025).

Once an ANN is trained, they have the ability to forecast the outcome of the independent input data provided to them. The learning process of the brain is mimicked, and they are able to learn non-linear and complicated data even when such data fed to them is imprecise and noisy. ANNs have attracted considerable attention, especially because of their applicability and the ease with which complex problems are handled. They are networks of parallel computational units that are densely interconnected, known as Adaptive Processing Units. The networks have fine-grained parallelism and relate to the modeling of nonlinear static or dynamic systems. This unique feature is associated with ANN, whereby "learning by examples" replaces "programming" with the objective of solving problems. This makes it highly attractive for use in situations or problem domains where there is little or no awareness of the situation under consideration and yet there exists relevant examples or training data associated with the problem. ANNs are now being increasingly recognized in the area of classification and prediction, where regression models and other related statistical techniques have traditionally been employed (Devi et al., 2012). The core issue in ANN is finding that trade- off between an underfitting and overfitting model. This becomes the main reason for neural network models sometimes failing to make accurate predictions. Underfitting means when a model is too simple to extract the underlying patterns from the data. Its performance is poor both in training data and unseen data. The reasons for underfitting could be a researcher using a linear model to solve a complex, non-linear problem. Insufficient data for training and validation and lack of sufficient training provided to the model (Zlobin & Bazylevych, 2025). Overfitting happens when ANN learns the training data very well such that it has memorized the random noise and outliers instead of the actual patterns and trends in the dataset. It does perform perfectly with the training data but somehow does not perform well on completely new data. This would be visible when a model comes out with very low errors on training data but high errors on validation dataset. Therefore, the researcher would not be able to use the model for prediction or estimation. The reason for overfitting could be the model being too complex for the size of the dataset. In other words, the researcher provides a massive neural network with training data on only 100 rows and less than 10 variables (Maharana, 2025).

Figure 1. General Structure of an ANN

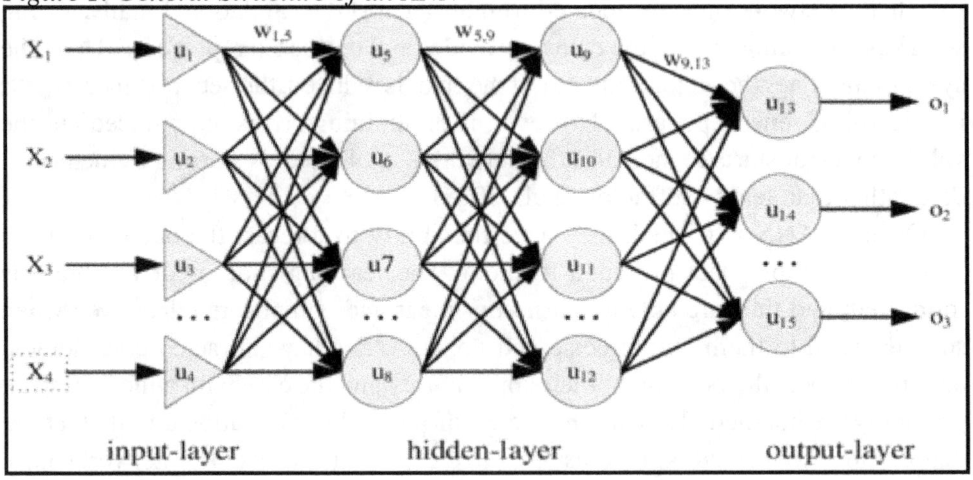

Source: Permanasari et al. (2013)

4. RESULTS AND DISCUSSION

The objective of training the ANN is to arrive at a point of generalization whereby it becomes possible to make correct inferences about the data the system does not know. This section explains and describes the results obtained from the MLP in order to ascertain the major factors in FI, which are fully functional around the world. MS Excel and SPSS were used to obtain the outputs that are discussed in this section. In the following section, the intention lies in capturing the use of these kinds of policies and determining the major differences in the tools used by various policymakers across the financial sector for the purpose of financial inclusion.

Table 3. Income Group Comparison of Mean Values for Institutional Framework and Consumer Credit Providers.

		Regulated Institutional Framework	Regulated Consumer Credit Providers
Region	East Asia & Pacific	0.81	0.85
	Europe & Central Asia	0.71	0.86
	Latin America & Caribbean	0.77	0.60
	MENAAP	0.58	0.88
	North America	0.84	1.00
	South Asia	0.83	0.71
	Sub-Saharan Africa	0.85	0.85

Source: Prepared by authors

Table 3 depicts that in establishing institutional framework MENAAP region lags behind the rest of the regions in the world. Europe and North America have a better supervisory framework that places them in a better economic position. However, the results in Table 4 indicate that that high and Upper middle-income group MENAAP region countries have indicated well-functioning intuitional framework. So, the scope for establishment of regulated institutional framework lies with low-income group countries like Afghanistan and Pakistan. The same holds good for institutions functional for consumer credit provision. In fact, MENAAP region has better reach even amongst the lower middle income group countries like, Egypt, Ghana, Pakistan and West Bank and Gaza.

Table 4. Mean of Income group comparison on institutional framework and consumer credit providers

Income Group	Region	Regulated Institutional Framework	Regulated Consumer Credit Providers
Low Income Group	East Asia & Pacific	**	**
	Europe & Central Asia	**	**
	Latin America & Caribbean	0.83	0.33
	MENAAP	**	**
	North America	**	**
	South Asia	**	**
	Sub-Saharan Africa	0.92	0.87
Lower Middle-Income Group	East Asia & Pacific	0.8	0.83
	Europe & Central Asia	0.6	0.9
	Latin America & Caribbean	0.77	0.47
	MENAAP	0.57	0.8
	North America	**	**
	South Asia	0.94	0.78
	Sub-Saharan Africa	0.83	0.79
Upper Middle-Income Group	East Asia & Pacific	0.83	0.72
	Europe & Central Asia	0.79	0.79
	Latin America & Caribbean	0.81	0.67
	MENAAP	0.44	0.83
	North America	**	**
	South Asia	0.5	0.5
	Sub-Saharan Africa	0.86	0.9

continued on following page

Table 4. Continued

Income Group	Region	Regulated Institutional Framework	Regulated Consumer Credit Providers
High Income Group	East Asia & Pacific	0.79	0.96
	Europe & Central Asia	0.7	0.88
	Latin America & Caribbean	0.66	0.57
	MENAAP	0.67	0.97
	North America	0.84	1
	South Asia	**	**
	Sub-Saharan Africa	0.67	1

Source: Prepared by authors

Note:**' indicates the regions where data is not available to calculate the mean values.

Figure 2. Regional comparison on Digital Financial Inclusion Strategy

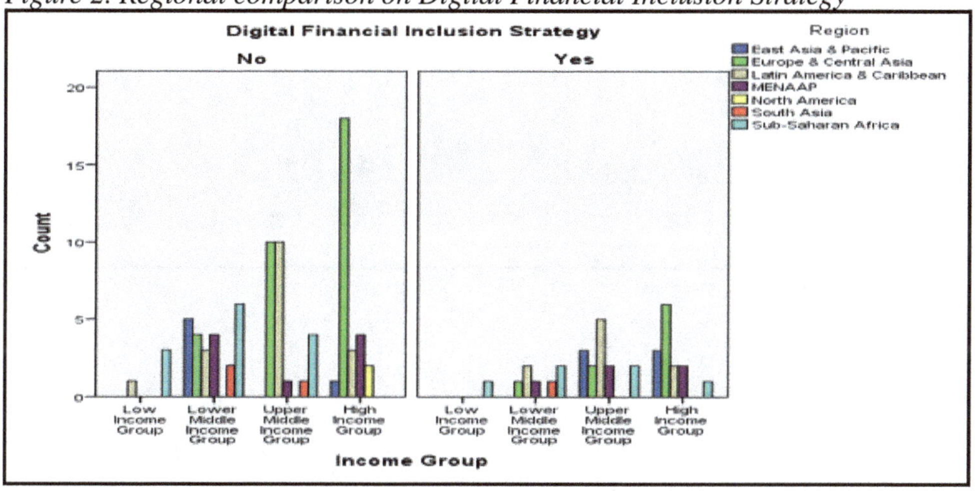

Source: Prepared by authors

Figure 2, 3, and 4, as shown in the MENAAP region, clearly indicates the presence of Digital Financial Inclusion Strategy (DFIS) in high and upper middle group income countries including but not limited to Libya, Lebanon, Jordan, United Arab Emirates, Bahrain, Israel, Kuwait, Malta, and Saudi Arabia. Formulation of policies to promote financial inclusion as well as impact analysis pertaining to the implementation of FI prevailed in the lower middle income group region in the MENAAP region including Egypt, Morocco, Pakistan, and West Bank and Gaza. The above-mentioned countries were observed to have adopted different approaches and instruments to ensure integration with digital financial strategies as a standalone national financial inclusion strategy among others. Sixty-three countries were observed to be in possession of financial inclusion strategy or in the process of developing one. The regions which were not observed to attain a seventy percent mark with regards to financial inclusion strategy were the Middle East and North Africa region, Europe and Central Asia region, and North America region. The Europe and Central Asia and North America regions belong to the category of high-income countries as per the World Bank (2025).

Figure 3. Regional comparison on availability of policies to promote Financial Inclusion

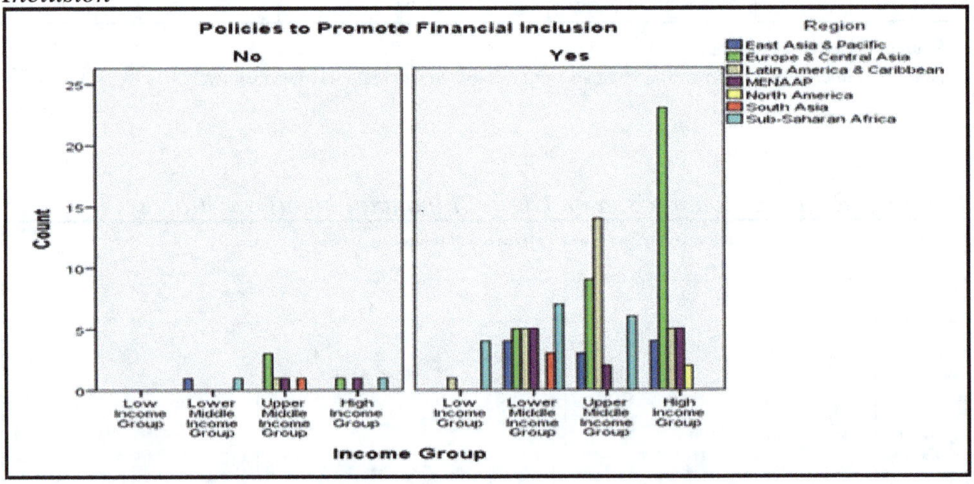

Source: Prepared by authors

Figure 4. **Regional comparison on existence of financial inclusion measurement**

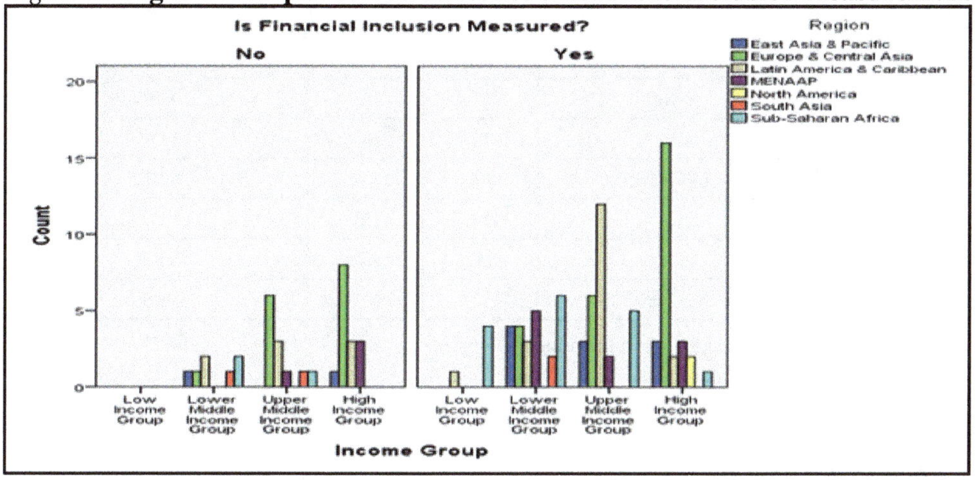

Source: Prepared by authors

Table 5. Case processing summary of MLP-ANN model

Data design		**N**	**Percent**
Sample	Training	88	74.6%
	Testing	30	25.4%
Valid		118	100.0%
Excluded		0	
Total		118	

Table 6. Comparative model summary

Training	Cross Entropy Error	38.696
	Percent Incorrect Predictions	19.3%
	Stopping Rule Used	1 consecutive step(s) with no decrease in error[a]
	Training Time	0:00:00.02
Testing	Cross Entropy Error	14.956
	Percent Incorrect Predictions	20.0%

Dependent Variable: Digital Financial Inclusion Strategy
a. Error computations are based on the testing sample.

Table 7. Model summary classification

Sample	Observed	Predicted		
		No	Yes	Percent Correct
Training	No	57	5	91.9%
	Yes	12	14	53.8%
	Overall Percent	78.4%	21.6%	80.7%
Testing	No	18	2	90.0%
	Yes	4	6	60.0%
	Overall Percent	73.3%	26.7%	80.0%

Dependent Variable: Digital Financial Inclusion Strategy

Figure 5. ROC curve

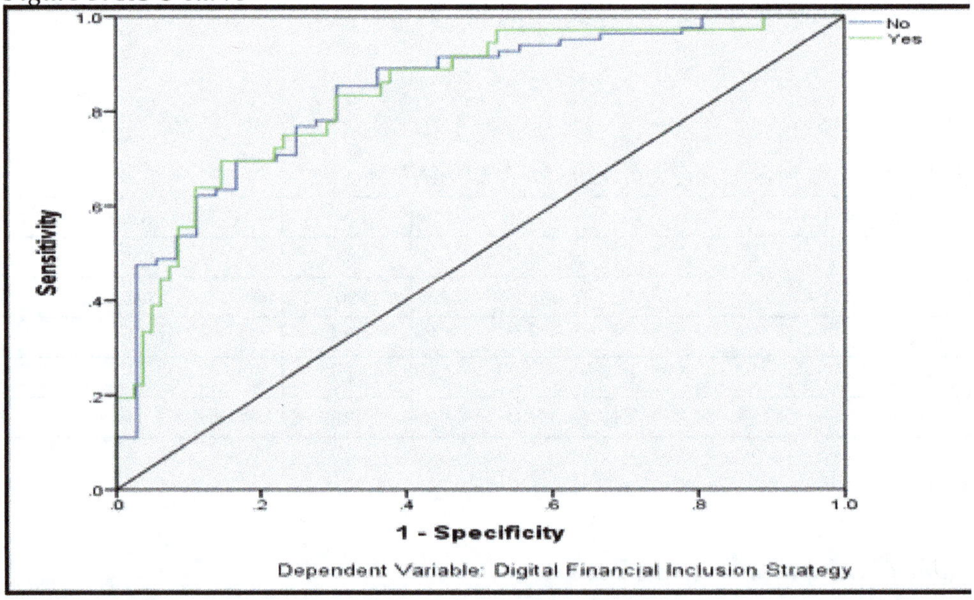

Source: Prepared by authors

Table 8. Area under the curve

Area under curve		Area
Digital Financial Inclusion Strategy	No	0.838
	Yes	0.838

Table 9. Independent Variable Importance

Variables		Normalized Importance
Income Group	0.081	36.1%
Regulated E-Money	0.076	33.8%
E-Money issued by non-Banks	0.057	25.4%
Existence of National Financial Inclusion Strategy	0.029	12.8%
Financial Sector Development Strategy with a Financial Inclusion Component Exists	0.082	36.7%
National Development Strategy with a Financial Inclusion Component Exists	0.039	17.3%
Microfinance Strategy	0.004	1.9%
Financial Literacy Strategy	0.225	100.0%
Fintech Strategy (Digital Financial Strategy)	0.213	94.7%
Policies to Promote Financial Inclusion	0.008	3.3%
Is Financial Inclusion Measured?	0.062	27.7%
Regulated Institutional Framework	0.053	23.5%
Regulated Consumer Credit Providers	0.071	31.3%

Figure 6. Independent Variable Importance

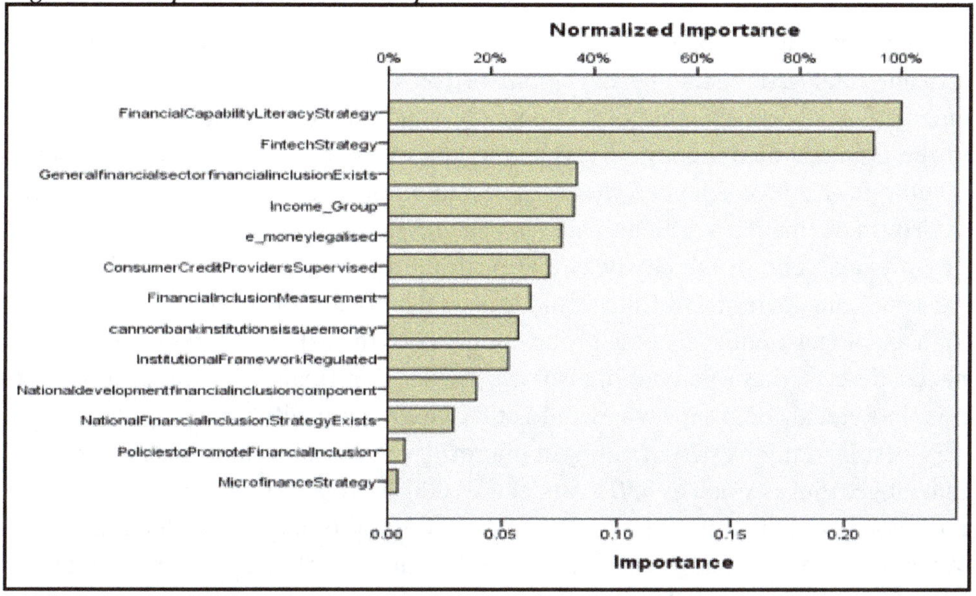

Source: Prepared by authors

Table 9 and Figure 6 summarize the key factors driving financial inclusion and rank them according to their relative influence. One of the most influential variables is electronic money (e-money), which refers to monetary value stored electronically within banking systems to facilitate digital transactions. E-money is a fiat-backed medium of exchange, classified as both convertible into physical form and transferable across international borders between individuals and businesses, facilitated by digital applications (Bloomenthal, 2026). The results suggest that all 118 sampled countries allow for the issue of commercial bank-issued e-money. Among banking entities, 39 countries permit other banking institutions, 34 authorize financial co-operatives, while only 21 permit other regulated entities to issue e-money. Furthermore, in relation to regional adoption, it is prominent that Europe and Central Asian countries have emerged as the early adopters of formal recognition of the legality of e-money systems. With reference to income, lower-middle-income economies have been found to be relatively more progressive in formally adopting and integrating incentives for the recognition of e-money systems in their respective legislations. Meanwhile, others have been adopting national-level financial inclusion strategies for enhancing their access to digital financial inclusion strategies. To complement government-led initiatives, regulatory frameworks in the surveyed regions permit 80 to 90 percent of commercial banks to deploy third-party retail agents, leverage agent banking models, and issue e-money. Consequently, these institutional arrangements solidify e-money as a primary driver of financial inclusion across diverse economic contexts.

The fact that non-banks have been allowed to issue e-money has been a significant catalyst for strategy development (Staschen & Meagher, 2018). Ghana emerged as a good example of a country in which the participation of non-banks in the issuance of e-money served as the key to the explosion of mobile money (Demirguc-Kunt & Klapper, 2012). The most important variables that emerged as drivers of financial inclusion are fintech and financial literacy strategy. Income group is also one of the catalysts that push the FI. As observed from the results existence and operation of fintech and financial literacy strategies is more visible in high and upper-middle-income group countries of the MENAAP regions. Microfinance, described as microcredit also, is a service that financial institutions offer to poor individuals or groups who would otherwise remain without access to financial services. Institutions participating in microfinance most often provide microloans that range from as small as \$50 to under \$50,000 (European Commission, 2022). In most countries, the Finance Ministry and the Central Banks are the leading actors. When it comes to microfinance and fintech strategies, they are the most likely to be leading the process. Regardless of who leads the process, the most important factor that influences success is the level of commitment and the level to which the leadership is empowered.

5. CONCLUSION

Financial inclusion (FI) has been one of the prime drivers of economic growth; by focusing on strategies related to FI, countries are making their economic growth faster. The MENAAP region depicts a complex combination of socio-economic factors, institutional reforms, political instability, and digital innovation. While the low- and middle-income group MENAAP has lagged global averages in financial access and strategic efforts, they are, however, more successful in consumer credit provision and penetration of bank accounts with the underprivileged. Overall, MENAAP are taking efforts focusing on leveraging technology and targeted policies to close persistent gaps, particularly for vulnerable populations in the region of Pakistan and Afghanistan.

Accordingly, economies within the MENAAP region that fall into the higher-income brackets—namely Jordan, Lebanon, Libya, the United Arab Emirates, Bahrain, Israel, Kuwait, Malta, and Saudi Arabia have formulated national financial inclusion strategies and are implementing them through fintech adoption, financial capability programs, microcredit initiatives, and technological advancement. Financial technologies, also known as fintech, and digital financial services are the points of focus that help in advancing financial inclusion in the countries. The MENAAP region has been able to provide solid and transparent financial institutions which build the confidence of the people in the financial system, including aspects like governing quality-rule of law, regulatory quality, and control of corruption.

REFERENCES

Ahamed, M. M., & Mallick, S. K. (2019). Is financial inclusion good for bank stability? International evidence. *Journal of Economic Behavior & Organization, 157*, 403–427. DOI: 10.1016/j.jebo.2017.07.027

Angela, K., Taddeo, S., & James, M. (2011). Predicting Global Solar Radiation Using an Artificial Neural Network Single-Parameter Model. *Advances in Artificial Neural Systems, 2011*(1), 1–7. DOI: 10.1155/2011/751908

Arner, D. W., Barberis, J. N., & Buckley, R. P. (2015, October 1). *The Evolution of Fintech: A New Post-Crisis Paradigm?* Papers.*ssrn*.com. https://ssrn.com/abstract =2676553 DOI: 10.2139/ssrn.2676553

Benkraiem, R., & Zopounidis, C. (2021). Preface: Regression methods based on OR techniques and computational aspects in management, economics and finance. *Annals of Operations Research, 306*(1-2), 1–6. DOI: 10.1007/s10479-021-04306-7

Bloomenthal, A. (2026, June 17). *Understanding eMoney: A Guide to Electronic Transactions and Benefits*. Investopedia. https://www.investopedia.com/terms/e/electronic-money.asp

Cama, F. A. R., & Emara, N. (2021). Financial inclusion and gross capital formation: A sectoral analysis approach for the MENA region and EMs. *International Review of Financial Analysis, 101993*. Advance online publication. DOI: 10.1016/j.irfa.2021.101993

Canh, N. P., Schinckus, C., & Thanh, S. D. (2019). Do economic openness and institutional quality influence patents? Evidence from GMM systems estimates. *Inter Economics, 157*, 134–169. DOI: 10.1016/j.inteco.2018.10.002

Chitimira, H., & Warikandwa, T. (2023). *Financial Inclusion Regulatory Practices in SADC*. Taylor & Francis. DOI: 10.4324/9781003369400

Chowdhury, M. S., Nabi, N., Rana, M. N. U., Shaima, M., Esa, H., Mitra, A., Mozumder, M. A. S., Liza, I. A., Sweet, M. M. R., & Naznin, R. (2024). Deep Learning Models for Stock Market Forecasting: A Comprehensive Comparative Analysis. *Journal of Business and Management Studies, 6*(2), 95–99. DOI: 10.32996/jbms.2024.6.2.9

Cohen, K. J., Hawawini, G. A., Maier, S. F., Schwartz, R. A., & Whitcomb, D. K. (1983). Friction in the trading process and the estimation of systematic risk. *Journal of Financial Economics, 12*(2), 263–278. DOI: 10.1016/0304-405X(83)90038-7

Da Afghanistan Bank. (2020). *National Financial Inclusion Strategy 2020–2024*. https://www.dab.gov.af/sites/default/files/2020-06/National%20Financial%20 Inclusion%20Strategy%20for%20Afghanistanfinal.pdf

De Mariz, F. (2022). *Finance With a Purpose: Fintech, Development and Financial Inclusion in The Global Economy*. World Scientific. DOI: 10.1142/q0359

Demirguc-Kunt, A., & Klapper, L. (2012). Measuring Financial Inclusion: The Global Findex Database. In *Policy Research Working Papers*. The World Bank. DOI: 10.1596/1813-9450-6025

Development Asia. (2025, March 24). *From Cash to Digital: Advancing Financial Inclusion in Pakistan*. Development Asia. https://development.asia/insight/cash-digital-advancing-financial-inclusion-pakistan

Devi, G., Sarma, K. K., Datta, P., & Mahanta, A. K. (2012). Prediction of high energy particle shower sizes and core location using artificial neural networks. *Indian Journal of Physics and Proceedings of the Indian Association for the Cultivation of Science*, *86*(1), 77–84. DOI: 10.1007/s12648-012-0007-4

Emara, N., & El Said, A. (2021). Financial inclusion and economic growth: The role of governance in selected MENA countries. *International Review of Economics & Finance*, *75*, 34–54. DOI: 10.1016/j.iref.2021.03.014

European Commission. (2022, July). *Microfinance and Social Enterprise Finance*. Employment, Social Affairs and Inclusion. https://employment-social-affairs.ec.europa.eu/policies-and-activities/funding/microfinance-and-social-enterprise-finance_en

Fernando, N., Newnham, R., Jemila Zahari, M., Marwa, C., & Wong, T. (2018). *National financial inclusion strategies: Current state of practice*. Natinal Financial Inclusion Strategy (FIS) Peer Learning Group. https://sdgs.un.org/sites/default/files/publications/2679National_Financial_Inclusion_Strategies.pdf

Frost, J., Gambacorta, L., Huang, Y., Shin, H. S., & Zbinden, P. (2020). BigTech and the Changing Structure of Financial Intermediation. *Economic Policy*, *34*(100), 761–799. Advance online publication. DOI: 10.1093/epolic/eiaa003

Go, E. J., Moon, J., & Kim, J. (2020). Analysis of the Current and Future of Artificial Intelligence in Financial Industry with Big Data Techniques. *Global Business Finance Review*, *25*(1), 102–117. DOI: 10.17549/gbfr.2020.25.1.102

Grohmann, A., Klühs, T., & Menkhoff, L. (2018). Does financial literacy improve financial inclusion? Cross country evidence. *World Development*, *111*, 84–96. DOI: 10.1016/j.worlddev.2018.06.020

Ho, T. S. Y., & Michaely, R. (1988). Information Quality and Market Efficiency. *Journal of Financial and Quantitative Analysis*, *23*(1), 53. DOI: 10.2307/2331024

Hoxha, V. (2023). Exploring the predictive power of ANN and traditional regression models in real estate pricing: Evidence from Prishtina. *Journal of Property Investment & Finance. Journal of Property Investment & Finance*, *42*(2), 134–150. DOI: 10.1108/JPIF-06-2023-0051

Intam, R. N. J., Raihan, A., Alfajri, M., Kaswar, A. B., & Andayani, D. D., & Asnidar. (. (2024). Sistem Klasifikasi Jenis Sampah Berdasarkan Kombinasi Fitur Warnac Tekstur Menggunakan Artifical Neural Network Berbasis Pengolahan Citra Digital. *Jurnal Teknologi Informasi Dan Ilmu Komputer*, *11*(2), 411–420. DOI: 10.25126/jtiik.20241128330

Jihane, T., & Aziz, M. (2022). Banks and FinTech Relationship in a Digital Transformation Context. *European Scientific Journal*, *18*(12), 106. DOI: 10.19044/esj.2022.v18n12p106

Jude, C., & Levieuge, G. (2016). Growth Effect of Foreign Direct Investment in Developing Economies: The Role of Institutional Quality. *World Economy*, *40*(4), 715–742. DOI: 10.1111/twec.12402

Khan, S. H. R. (2011). *Financial inclusion and financial stability: are they two sides of the same coin?* BIS Central Bankers' speeches, Indian Bankers Association and Indian Overseas Bank. https://www.bis.org/review/r111229f.pdf

Lishner, I., & Shtub, A. (2022). Using an Artificial Neural Network for Improving the Prediction of Project Duration. *Mathematics*, *10*(22), 4189. DOI: 10.3390/math10224189

Maharana, K. (2025). A Review: Data Overfitting and Underfitting Techniques. *Journal of Information Systems Engineering & Management*, *10*(13s), 387–405. DOI: 10.52783/jisem.v10i13s.2072

Market Research Report. (2025, January 10). *FinTech Industry Market*. Market.us. https://market.us/report/fintech-industry-market/

NSFI 2022-2028. (2024). *National Strategy for Financial Inclusion 2022-2028*. Bsp.gov.ph. https://www.bsp.gov.ph/Pages/InclusiveFinance/NSFI-2022-2028.pdf

Ortiz, R., Contreras, M., & Mellado, C. (2023). Regression, multicollinearity and Markowitz. *Finance Research Letters*, *58*, 104550–104550. DOI: 10.1016/j.frl.2023.104550

Pal, S., & Bandyopadhyay, I. (2022). Impact of financial inclusion on economic growth, financial development, financial efficiency, financial stability, and profitability: International evidence. *SN Business & Economics*, *2*(9), 139. Advance online publication. DOI: 10.1007/s43546-022-00313-3

Permanasari, A. E., Chamsudin, A., & Wahyunggoro, O. (2013, August 25). *Utilization of Neural Network for Disease Forecasting*. ResearchGate; ResearchGate. https://www.researchgate.net/publication/265784353_Utilization_of_Neural_Network_for_Disease_Forecasting

Pinelis, M., & Ruppert, D. (2021). Machine Learning Portfolio Allocation. *The Journal of Financial Data Science*, *8*, 35–54. DOI: 10.1016/j.jfds.2021.12.001

Rau, P. R. (2017). Law, Trust, and the Development of Crowdfunding. SSRN *Electronic Journal*. DOI: 10.2139/ssrn.2989056

Risman, A., Ali, A. J., Soelton, M., & Siswanti, I. (2023). The behavioral finance of MSMEs in the advancement of financial inclusion and financial technology (Fintech). *The Indonesian Accounting Review*, *13*(1), 91–101. DOI: 10.14414/tiar.v13i1.3213

Rytov, R. (2025). Artificial Neural Network for Downward Continuation of Anomalous Magnetic Fields. *Russian Journal of Earth Sciences*, *1–5*, 1–5. Advance online publication. DOI: 10.2205/2025ES000996

Sahay, R., Cihak, M., N'Diaye, P., Barajas, A., Mitra, S., Kyobe, A., Mooi, Y., & Yousefi, R. (2015). Financial Inclusion: Can it Meet Multiple Macroeconomic Goals? *Staff Discussion Notes*, *15*(17), 1. DOI: 10.5089/9781513585154.006

Sarma, M., & Pais, J. (2011). Financial Inclusion and Development. *Journal of International Development*, *23*(5), 613–628. DOI: 10.1002/jid.1698

Sathupadi, K., Achar, S., Bhaskaran, S. V., Faruqui, N., & Uddin, J. (2025). BankNet: Real-Time Big Data Analytics for Secure Internet Banking. *Big Data and Cognitive Computing*, *9*(2), 24. DOI: 10.3390/bdcc9020024

Seffahlou, H., Boudriche, Z., & Djelloul, C. (2025). Using Artificial Intelligence Models To Predict Bitcoin Prices: Artificial Neural Network Model. داصتقالا ةلجم ةيرشبلا ةيمنتلاو, 189. DOI: 10.35658/1445-016-002-013

Seifipour, R., & Mehrabian, A. (2025). Application of Artificial Neural Networks in Economic and Financial Sciences. *IntechOpen EBooks*. DOI: 10.5772/intechopen.1007604

Setianto, R. H., Azman-Saini, W. N. W., & Law, S. H. (2025). Threshold effects of institutional quality on the financial inclusion and stability nexus: International evidence. *Borsa Istanbul Review*, *25*(2), 388–399. DOI: 10.1016/j.bir.2025.01.015

Shewale, R. (2024, January 1). *43 Fintech Statistics For 2024 (Startups, Financials & Trends)*. DemandSage. https://www.demandsage.com/fintech-statistics/

Staschen, S., & Meagher, P. (2018). Basic Regulatory Enablers for Digital Financial Services. In *World Bank, Washington, DC eBooks*. World Bank. DOI: 10.1596/30275

State Bank of Pakistan. (2024). *National Financial Inclusion Strategy 2024-28*. https://www.sbp.org.pk/nfis/nfis2024-28.pdf

Su, D. T., Nguyen, P. C., & Schinckus, C. (2019). Impact of foreign direct investment, trade openness and economic institutions on growth in emerging countries: The case of Vietnam. *Journal of International Students*, *12*(3), 243–264. DOI: 10.14254/2071-8330.2019/12-3/20

Suresh, V., & Maity, B. (2022). Exploratory research on bank-based financial inclusion for sustainable economic growth. *Finance India, 36*(1), 105–115. https://financeindia.org/data/2022/FI361/FI-361-Art05.pdf

Tay, L.-Y., Tai, H.-T., & Tan, G.-S. (2022). Digital Financial inclusion: a Gateway to Sustainable Development. *Heliyon, 8*(6), e09766. ScienceDirect. DOI: 10.1016/j.heliyon.2022.e09766

The Global Partnership for Financial Inclusion (GPFI). (n.d.). *About GPFI | GPFI*. Www.gpfi.org. Retrieved September 7, 2025, from https://www.gpfi.org/about-gpfi

The World Bank. (2022, March 29). *Financial Inclusion*. World Bank. https://www.worldbank.org/en/topic/financialinclusion/overview#1

World Bank. (2025). *The Global State of Financial Inclusion and Consumer Protection*. World Bank. https://documents.worldbank.org/en/publication/documents-reports/documentdetail/099013124180517721

World Bank Afganisthan. (2020, February 19). *A pathway to financial inclusion in Afghanistan*. World Bank Blogs. https://blogs.worldbank.org/en/endpovertyinsouthasia/pathway-financial-inclusion-afghanistan

World Bank Group. (2013, November 11). *Global Financial Development Report 2014: Financial Inclusion*. World Bank. https://documents.worldbank.org/curated/en/225251468330270218

World Integrated Trade Solution. (n.d.). *Countries in Middle East & North Africa.* [online] wits.worldbank.org. Available at: https://wits.worldbank.org/chatbot/SearchItem.aspx?RegionId=MEA [Accessed 20 Jun. 2026].

Xu, K.-L. (2025). A revisit to bias-adjusted predictive regression. *Journal of Empirical Finance, 80*, 101578. DOI: 10.1016/j.jempfin.2024.101578

Yaltaa, A. T., & Yaltab, A. Y. (2022, December 14). The Effects of Financial Inclusion on the Economic Development of MENA Countries. *ERF 29th Annual Conference*. ERF 29th Annual conference, Egypt.

Yorulmaz, R. (2018). An analysis of constructing global financial inclusion indices. *Borsa Istanbul Review, 18*(3), 248–258. DOI: 10.1016/j.bir.2018.05.001

Zamore, S., Beisland, L. A., & Mersland, R. (2019). Geographic diversification and credit risk in microfinance. *Journal of Banking & Finance, 109*, 105665. DOI: 10.1016/j.jbankfin.2019.105665

Zhang, X., Xue, T., & Eugene Stanley, H. (2019). Comparison of Econometric Models and Artificial Neural Networks Algorithms for the Prediction of Baltic Dry Index. *IEEE Access : Practical Innovations, Open Solutions, 7*, 1647–1657. DOI: 10.1109/ACCESS.2018.2884877

Zlobin, M., & Bazylevych, V. (2025). A Data-Driven Approach for Balancing Overfitting and Underfitting in Decision Tree Models. *Central Ukrainian Scientific Bulletin. Technical Sciences, 1*(11(42)), 14–26. DOI: 10.32515/2664-262X.2025.11(42).1.14-26

Chapter 5
Modern Regulatory Frameworks Shaping Global Investment Dynamics for Sustainable Economic Growth

Adarsh Kumar
http://orcid.org/0009-0002-3988-5961
Institute of Technology and Management, Gwalior, India

ABSTRACT

The world of global investment has experienced significant change over the last twenty years due to convergence of regulatory reform, sustainability requirements, and institutional reconfiguration. This chapter discusses the extent to which contemporary regulatory frameworks influence global patterns of investment in a manner that promotes sustainable economic development. The chapter draws on the recent empirical literature and theoretical advances in the field of institutional economics, international investment law, and sustainable finance. It is found in the analysis that quality of regulatory institutions is the only most powerful determinant of foreign direct investment (FDI) inflows, especially in developing economies. The chapter also argues that the alignment of the private capital to the goals of sustainable development will be merely a far-fetched dream unless coherent, enforceable, and internationally harmonized regulatory frameworks are in place. Recommendations and guidelines on policy are made as well as future research directions.

DOI: 10.4018/979-8-3373-8964-6.ch005

1. INTRODUCTION

Cross-border investment has experienced a dramatic shift in its institutional framework in the last seventy years. The history of investment law, from the post-war Bretton Woods consensus that favoured capital controls and state-led industrialisation, to the liberalisation wave of the 1980s and 1990s that led to over 3,000 bilateral investment treaties (BITs) based on the protection of investor rights, and to the present day, when environmental, social and governance (ESG) principles are being systematically integrated into investment law, is marked by a recurring tension between market efficiency and public interest goals (UNCTAD, 2023; Sornarajah, 2021; Muchlinski, 2021). A qualitative change in this trend occurred in 2015, when the international community set up the United Nations Sustainable Development Goals (SDGs) and the Paris Agreement on Climate Change, which for the first time provided binding and measurable sustainability benchmarks to which public policy and private capital allocation could be measured (United Nations, 2015; UNFCCC, 2015).

This post-2015 architecture has made investment regulation a more broad-based legal-technical discipline and a vital instrument in the global development agenda, and has introduced new challenges to the design of regulation and new areas of research.

The analysis is based on three concepts. Investment regulation refers to the rules, norms and institutional frameworks that range from international treaties, national laws and soft law that regulate the conditions of investment entry, operation and exit to a host economy (Salacuse, 2015; Dolzer et al., 2022). Sustainable investment is defined as investment that takes into account environmental, social and governance (ESG) factors and is directed towards creating long-term value without harming the environment (OECD, 2020; Eccles & Klimenko, 2019). The financial instruments, market infrastructure and regulatory requirements that aim to channel private capital towards sustainability goals at scale, such as green bonds, disclosure requirements on environmental, social and governance (ESG) principles, and green taxonomies, are sustainable finance in its systemic context (European Commission, 2018; Popescu et al., 2021). The institutional backbone of investment regulation is the institutional framework that either enables or hinders the implementation of sustainable finance aspirations (Sulehri et al., 2024; Munif and Wahrudin, 2025).

In this conceptual context, a basic regulatory trilemma has come to the fore as the central issue in the literature. Host states need policy space to implement environmental and social policies without being held liable under investment protection standards; investors need legal predictability and protection from discriminatory and arbitrary state action; and the international community needs institutional frameworks to facilitate private investment in public goods like climate change mitigation and infrastructure development in developing economies (Bjorklund,

2019; Van Harten, 2007; Schill, 2018). In documented cases, first generation BITs have chilled host state regulatory action through the chilling effect of investor-state dispute settlement, and overly broad regulatory reservations risk to undermine the legal certainty that is the basis for long-term capital commitment (Cotula, 2014; Tienhaara, 2011; Salacuse, 2015). The question of how current regulatory systems address this trilemma and what institutional conditions enable them to do so effectively, is an open and important question for scholarship and policy (Sulehri et al., 2024; Munif and Wahrudin, 2025).

The question is not just a specialist investment law question. The post-2015 sustainability agenda has led to an increasing number of regulatory instruments, such as ESG disclosure requirements in the EU SFDR and ISSB frameworks, green finance taxonomies and the revised investment treaty models with sustainability provisions and right-to-regulate clauses (European Commission, 2020; ISSB, 2023; Johnson & Sachs, 2019). These are all signs of a general recognition that a free market approach to capital flows is not a solution to the systemic issues of climate change and inequality (Sachs et al., 2019). However, the empirical evidence is not as consistent as the normative consensus: the effectiveness of instruments is highly dependent on the institutional quality of the regulatory environment in which these instruments are applied (Wu, 2024; Hilbrich et al., 2025).

The institutional coherence thesis is used as the main organising argument in this chapter. The idea is that the effectiveness of sustainable investment regulation does not depend on the sophistication of any single instrument, whether it's an investment treaty, an ESG disclosure requirement or a green taxonomy, but on the coherence of the institutional system in which they are embedded and applied. How has international investment law and treaty design evolved to include sustainability objectives and what are the remaining conflicts to be addressed? (ii) What are the key strengths and weaknesses of the current law and treaties, and how can they be improved? (iii) What are the future challenges and opportunities for international investment law and treaty design, and how can they be addressed? (ii) How do the ESG disclosure requirements, green taxonomies and sustainable finance regulatory frameworks affect capital allocation decisions and when do they achieve real reallocation or greenwashing? (iii) How does institutional quality (rule of law, capacity of regulatory enforcement, transparency and accountability) affect the ability of sustainable investment instruments to fulfil their goals, especially in developing and emerging market economies? To answer these questions, the chapter draws on a variety of empirical and conceptual research that has been conducted in the fields of investment law, finance, political economy and development economics.

Section 2 describes the literature review methodology. Section 3 establishes the theoretical foundations. Sections 4 through 8 analyse the four regulatory domains: international investment law, ESG disclosure mandates, green finance taxonomies, institutional quality and foreign direct investment, and greenwashing regulation. Sections 9 through 11 synthesise the findings and develop theoretical, practical, and policy implications. Sections 12 through 14 address limitations, future research directions, and the conclusion. The institutional coherence thesis is applied throughout as a diagnostic framework.

2. LITERATURE REVIEW METHODOLOGY

The chapter is based on a systematic narrative literature review that was performed in several academic databases and institutional repositories. The search strategy, inclusion and exclusion criteria and analytical approach used are detailed below.

Literature search: The literature search was done in Scopus, Web of Science, Google Scholar, SSRN and UNCTAD digital library. The keywords used were: sustainable investment regulation, ESG disclosure, green finance taxonomy, bilateral investment treaties, investor-state dispute settlement, institutional quality FDI, greenwashing regulation, and sustainable finance developing economies. Boolean operators (AND, OR) were used to broaden or narrow the search results as necessary. The search was limited to studies published between 2018 and 2025, which is the timeframe of the current regulatory environment, and also included basic theoretical studies, irrespective of their publication date.

The inclusion criteria: (i) were published in peer-reviewed journals, edited academic volumes or authoritative institutional reports (UNCTAD, World Bank, IMF, IOSCO); (ii) covered one or more of the four regulatory areas covered in the chapter: international investment law, ESG disclosure, green finance taxonomies, and anti-greenwashing regulation; and (iii) included empirical evidence, theoretical frameworks, or systematic policy analysis relevant to the link between regulatory quality and investment outcomes.

Exclusion criteria: Studies were excluded if published in journals not indexed or predatory journals due to limited language skills of the research team (see Limitations section); or if it was descriptive commentary without analytical contribution.

Screening and analytical approach: Titles and abstracts of the retrieved studies were screened for relevance and short-listed studies were then reviewed in full text. A range of methodological techniques were kept, such as panel-data econometric studies, automated text analysis of treaties, difference-in-differences event studies and semi-structured interview-based case studies. The literature was synthesized thematically, by the four regulatory domains that structure the chapter. In cases where the results of the studies were ambiguous, such as in the institutional quality and FDI literature, the chapter provides analytical reconciliation, but does not leave the tension unresolved (see Section 3.1). The cross-study syntheses in Tables 1 and 4 are interpretive, and not scores from a formal meta-analysis.

3. THEORETICAL FOUNDATIONS: INSTITUTIONS, REGULATION, AND INVESTMENT

This section sets the theoretical context for the analysis in this chapter. Three complementary approaches are used: institutional economics (North, 1990), the Ownership-Location-Internalization paradigm (Dunning, 1977) and regulatory legitimacy theory (Beetham, 1991; Suchman, 1995). The frameworks chosen are those that focus on different aspects of the link between regulatory quality and investment behaviour, and that together offer the analytical underpinning of the institutional coherence thesis presented in this chapter.

The analytical starting point for this chapter is institutional economics, but other approaches to the analysis of the treaty, such as transaction cost economics, game-theoretic models of regulatory competition and political economy models of treaty design, offer complementary perspectives (Williamson, 1985; Neumayer, 2007). The most notorious argument that was put forward by North (1990) was that the long-run economic performance is mainly determined by the institutions, the formal rules, informal norms, and enforcement mechanisms that define human interaction. This is because investment is a potential activity, which is legally and socially contracted, and is particularly vulnerable to the institutional conditions. Uncertainty over the enforcement of contracts, poor property rights, and lack of transparency in the regulatory environment all raise the risk premium that investors would face in investing in a jurisdiction, or the distortion in their sector allocation of capital.

A second analytical lens is the Ownership-Location-Internalization (OLI) paradigm of Dunning (1977). Multinationals make investment decisions on the basis of locational advantages which are not just the cost of factors and the size of markets, but also the institutional and regulatory setting. In a study of 189 economies, Contractor et al. (2020) find that better contract enforcement and more efficient trade regulations are associated with a much larger increase in FDI inflows, and that targeted improvements in specific dimensions of the institutions can make a difference in investment decisions at the margin without necessitating a wholesale overhaul of the regulatory framework.

A third analytical dimension is added by the theory of regulatory legitimacy (Beetham, 1991; Suchman, 1995; Black, 2008) which has been developed in the organisational sociology literature and applied to regulatory contexts. Regulations create productive investment behaviour not only because they are enforced or incentivized, but because they are perceived as legitimate, that is, they are believed to be suitable, fairly applied and reliably enforced by the actors who are regulated. It is important to make sure that the regulations are not seen as barriers, but as enablers to investments, by the actors for which the regulations are intended. Thus, legitimacy is based on the transparency, procedural fairness, and credibility of enforcement. This is particularly applicable to sustainable finance regulation, wherein the ESG disclosure requirements and the green taxonomy systems must convince the investors that the systems are rightly signalling true sustainability as opposed to being a means of political signalling or regulatory arbitrage.

The three theories have a common analytical thread: the quality of the regulatory framework is a key factor in shaping the location of capital, and whether or not it helps to achieve sustainable outcomes. Even if the instruments are well designed, weak enforcement is a problem, as North's institutional theory suggests. Dunning's OLI framework places regulatory quality as a location advantage, which is a mediator of investment decisions. The theory of regulatory legitimacy helps to understand why instruments that are not credible result in symbolic compliance. These frameworks provide the analytical support for the empirical parts that follow: each part examines whether the regulatory instruments examined fulfill the institutional prerequisites that theory has identified as essential for effectiveness.

3.1 The Political Economy of Regulatory Quality

Regulatory quality is one of six dimensions of governance measured by the World Bank Worldwide Governance Indicators (Kaufmann et al., 2011) and is the ability of a government to create and enforce effective policies and regulations that allow and encourage the private sector to develop. Using panel data, Saha et al. (2022) conducted a study on 28 lower-middle income countries and concluded that regulatory quality is the most important of all institutional measures among the factors affecting FDI inflows. The results remained unchanged when GDP per capita was controlled for. The results of the threshold analysis also showed that the positive impact of regulatory quality on FDI inflows was significantly increased after reaching a certain threshold of per capita income. This suggests a stratified relationship: regulatory quality matters for investment across all income groups, but the returns to regulatory reform are disproportionately high as economies move out of the low-income category.

This analysis was extended to 189 countries across the world from 2002 to 2019 by Khan et al. (2024). In some model specifications, regulatory quality is the only institutional indicator that has a positive association with FDI inflows, while other institutional factors (government effectiveness, political stability) have a negative association with FDI inflows. The apparent paradox is explained by Sabir et al. (2019): In developing-country settings, where investors have long taken advantage of regulatory forbearance, new regulations could have a dampening effect on FDI in the short-term while increasing regulation costs, but over the longer-term would increase the credibility of regulation. Khan et al. (2024) does not contradict, but rather contextualises, the positive findings of Saha et al. (2022) and Sabir et al. (2019) because the effect of regulatory quality on FDI is positive, but this is moderated by the income level, enforcement capacity and initial state of regulation from where regulatory reforms are implemented. Combined, these three studies suggest a non-linear, context-dependent effect, rather than a simple positive monotone effect. The dangers of policy prescriptions that are one-size-fits-all are highlighted by such heterogeneity of results.

Table 1. Institutional Quality Dimensions and Their Effect on FDI Inflows by Country Income Group

Institutional Dimension	Low-Income Countries	Middle-Income Countries	High-Income Countries	Global Panel
Regulatory Quality	Mixed	Positive*	Positive*	Positive*
Control of Corruption	Positive	Positive*	Negative	Mixed
Government Effectiveness	Neutral	Positive	Neutral	Negative
Rule of Law	Neutral	Negative	Positive	Neutral
Political Stability	Positive*	Positive*	Neutral	Negative
Voice & Accountability	Positive	Positive*	Neutral	Negative

Note. Synthesized from Saha et al. (2022), Khan et al. (2024), and Sabir et al. (2019). *Statistically significant at $p < 0.05$. Mixed = context-dependent. Effectiveness ratings (Positive, Negative, Neutral, Mixed) represent the predominant direction of statistically reported effects across the reviewed studies. Positive indicates a statistically significant positive association with FDI inflows in the majority of model specifications. Negative indicates a significant inverse association. Neutral indicates no statistically significant association. Mixed indicates results that are positive in some specifications and negative or null in others, typically varying by income group or time period.

Table 1 reveals a consistent but heterogeneous pattern. Regulatory quality is the most consistently positive institutional determinant of FDI inflows across income groups, with statistically significant positive associations in middle-income and high-income country panels and mixed results in low-income settings. This heterogeneity carries a direct implication for regulatory strategy: the sequencing and prioritisation of institutional reforms should reflect the income context of the host economy, with early-stage reforms in low-income settings focused on the dimensions that generate the highest marginal returns to investment attractiveness.

The main policy implication is that institutional reform should be strategically sequenced, that is, reforms that are most strongly linked to FDI attraction in each income context should be prioritized, followed by multi-dimensional reforms as institutional capacity and enforcement infrastructure develop.

4. THE EVOLVING ARCHITECTURE OF INTERNATIONAL INVESTMENT LAW

The section looks at the development of international investment law (IIL) as the legal framework on which the regulation of sustainable investment is built. The purpose of IIL has been traditionally to protect foreign investors from arbitrary or discriminatory treatment by the host government, around which thousands of bilateral investment treaties (BITs), regional trade agreements and investor-state dispute settlement (ISDS) mechanisms have been built. It was a successful legal system for its intended purpose. The world for which it was created, however, is no longer. The treaty drafters of the 1960s and 1970s were not able to foresee the current era of global climate emergency, growing international human rights framework and increased focus on corporate governance.

Kriebaum (2022) has traced the gradual inclusion of sustainable development terms in investment treaties. Through a jurisprudential analysis of arbitral tribunals, Kriebaum concludes that the jurisprudence of the expropriation and fair and equitable treatment provisions has developed to provide more flexibility for the host state to regulate for environmental and social reasons, while still providing the legal certainty that investors need. This jurisprudential evolution was slow and uneven in the various treaties; but it is a significant change from the previous practice where virtually any measure that would impact on an investor's profits could trigger an ISDS claim.

Dotzauer et al. (2024) added a quantitative twist to this development, carrying out automated text analysis of 2,083 bilateral investment treaties and 374 other agreements containing investment provisions. The results of their research are impressive: over the last several years, the number of sustainability references in investment treaties has increased dramatically. The level of democracy among the treaty parties and the experience of being sued in the past were both found to be great motivators to this trend. States that have borne the financial and reputational costs of ISDS litigation have proved more willing to incorporate sustainability provisions in subsequent treaty negotiations, suggesting that the reform of international investment law is, at least in part, a learning process driven by adverse litigation experience.

This transformation is very large in scale, as well. The UNCTAD (2024) notes that as of the end of 2023, there were more than 2,800 active BITs in the world, with the proportion of new BITs signed with specific sustainable development provisions increasing from below 10 per cent before 2010 to more than 65 per cent after 2020.

At the same time, UNCTAD noted more than 1,300 known cases of treaty-based ISDS by 2024, making compounding legal and financial risks for states that are going on signing unreformed treaties. The pressure on treaty design is compounded: states are the ones that are being pressured by investors seeking legal certainty, while civil society is pressuring states for regulatory autonomy for climate governance.

4.1 The Tension Between Investor Protection and Regulatory Autonomy

The fundamental contradiction in IIL has been that right of the investor to legal protection is in conflict with the right of the state to regulate in the common good. Choudhury (2026) argued powerfully that the form and meaning of investment agreements, with their broad definitions, expansively-worded standards of treatment, and mechanisms of ISDS, have often limited the autonomy of states in their regulatory functions, especially in the context of sustainable development goals. The outcome, she argued, is that IIL has in many cases worked as a tool that hinders, as opposed to facilitating, sustainable development, despite the rhetoric of FDI as a tool to achieve the SDGs.

According to Zagel (2021), although traditional IIAs generate what the literature terms the regulatory chill effect the deterrent impact of investor-state dispute settlement mechanisms on host governments' willingness to enact environmental, labour, or social regulation several reform approaches are currently under active consideration. Right-to-regulate clauses, sustainability carve-outs and investor obligation provisions are all minor changes that are slowly giving states greater flexibility. Munif and Wahrudin (2025) cite the EU-Vietnam Investment Protection agreement and reforms in the UNCITRAL and ICSID as a case study of slow yet significant progress toward establishing a balance between the rights of investors and the responsibilities of the state as well as the development goals of the whole world.

The African experience illustrates these reform dynamics. Qumba (2024) finds that African states are incorporating sustainable development principles into IIAs not as aspirational soft law but as binding treaty obligations, drawing on the New Delhi Declaration of the International Law Association. Xiang and Maïnkade (2023) confirm that a human rights-based approach is gaining traction in African BIT practice, though practical impact remains limited by the scope of intra-African treaty coverage. Table 2 presents the principal sustainability provisions now found in modern investment treaties, drawing on Dotzauer et al. (2024), Munif and Wahrudin (2025), Kriebaum (2022), and Choudhury (2026).

Table 2. Key Provisions in Modern Investment Treaties Supporting Sustainable Development

Treaty Provision	Purpose	Example Treaties	Effectiveness
Right-to-Regulate Clauses	Preserves host state policy space	EU-Vietnam IPA, CPTPP	Moderate–High
Environmental Carve-outs	Exempts green regulations from ISDS claims	USMCA, RCEP	Moderate
Investor Obligations	Imposes CSR and human rights duties on investors	African BITs (post-2017)	Low–Moderate
Labour Standards Provisions	Prevents social dumping via low labour costs	EU trade agreements	Moderate
Sustainable Development Preambles	Sets interpretive context for tribunals	SADC Model BIT	Low (soft)
Investment Facilitation Provisions	Reduces bureaucratic barriers while embedding sustainability	WTO Investment Facilitation Agreement	Emerging

Note. Synthesized from Dotzauer et al. (2024), Munif and Wahrudin (2025), Kriebaum (2022), and Choudhury (2026). The effectiveness ratings are based on the general trend of empirical and legal evaluations found in the literature cited. Moderate-High means that the provision has been documented to have a significant effect on reducing ISDS exposure or increasing the space available for host state regulation in a moderate to high number of cases. Low-Moderate means that the provision is included in the treaties, but its enforceability by interpretation is not clear. Emerging means that the provision is a relatively new development and there is not enough case law or empirical evidence to evaluate the effectiveness of the provision.

Table 2 shows that provisions that are legally binding and have been interpreted in the past have higher effectiveness ratings than aspirational preamble language, and that right-to-regulate clauses and environmental carve-outs have higher effectiveness ratings than the other provisions. This imbalance between formal commitment and enforceable obligation is a recurring issue in the law of sustainable investment, and is a direct driver of the institutional coherence argument: normative text without infrastructure leads to symbolic change.

The evidence in this section demonstrates that international investment law is on the substantive transition. Both the quantitative evidence of Dotzauer et al. (2024) and the jurisprudential analysis of Kriebaum (2022) show that sustainability provisions are increasingly a part of the design of modern treaties, both because of the normative commitment and because of the rational calculations of states that want to reduce future exposure to ISDS. However, it is not a full change. First-generation treaties remain in force, reform is proceeding at different speeds across regions, and the enforceability of investor obligation provisions and sustainability carve-outs through arbitral interpretation remains uncertain. The legal architecture reviewed here provides the formal framework within which the more targeted sustainable finance instruments examined in subsequent sections operate.

5. ESG DISCLOSURE MANDATES AND CAPITAL MARKET DYNAMICS

This section examines mandatory Environmental, Social, and Governance (ESG) disclosure as the second major regulatory instrument analysed in this chapter. ESG disclosure mandates operate at the capital market level, seeking to correct the information asymmetries that prevent investors from accurately pricing sustainability risks and opportunities. The section proceeds as follows: the global expansion of mandatory ESG disclosure is documented; the theoretical mechanisms through which disclosure affects investor behaviour are examined; and the empirical evidence on capital market effects is reviewed, with particular attention to the conditions under which disclosure effectiveness varies across institutional contexts.

The Environmental, Social, and Governance criteria are no longer voluntary reporting standards such as the Global Reporting Initiative which was launched in 1997; now, they are quasi-obligatory, in a variety of major markets. The European Union Sustainable Finance Disclosure Regulation (SFDR), the Securities and Exchange Board of India Business Responsibility and Sustainability Report (BRSR) framework and the proposed climate disclosure rules by the U.S. Securities and Exchange Commission all represent this trend.

In June 2023, the International Sustainability Standards Board (ISSB) published IFRS S1 and IFRS S2, building on the TCFD framework to establish the most comprehensive global baseline for sustainability reporting to date. As of end-2024, more than twenty jurisdictions had announced pathways to adopt or reference the ISSB standards. These standards directly address the standardisation and materiality gaps identified by Moktar et al. (2023) as limiting ESG disclosure effectiveness in emerging markets. Whether adoption translates into credible enforcement remains to be determined as implementation progresses.

The most comprehensive multi-country study of this development is Krueger et al. (2024), who compile a novel global dataset on mandatory ESG disclosure and analyse its effect on stock market liquidity. The paper records that there is a positive impact of the ESG disclosure requirements on the stock liquidity of firms, with the effects being strongest where the requirements are enforced by government institutions, on a mandatory as opposed to a comply-or-explain basis, and with strong informal enforcement institutions. The benefits of mandatory disclosure are largest for firms operating in environments characterised by high information asymmetry precisely the conditions prevailing in many emerging markets. Paramaiah et al. (2025) confirm that ESG investing has become a major trend in the global financial market, influencing both investment strategies and long-term financial stability assessments.

5.1 Information Asymmetry, Signalling, and Investor Confidence

The theoretical reasoning of the ESG disclosure regulation relies on two fairly developed theories information asymmetry theory and signalling theory. The Information asymmetry theory is based on the premise that when the sellers (who in this case are companies) have more information about the real quality of their products (in this case their sustainability performance) than the buyers (investors), markets can fail to help in the efficient allocation of resources. Mandatory disclosure is a remedy to this issue since it compels companies to disclose information they would otherwise hide. Signalling theory is the view that observationally feasible actions of better-informed agents could credibly transmit private information to less-informed counterparties, as long as the action is sufficiently costly that only high-quality actors can credibly send the signal.

Both of the frameworks are empirically supported. Moussa and Elmarzouky (2024) discovered that ESG disclosure has a significant negative effect on market uncertainty among non-financial U.K. companies listed in the Financial Times Stock Exchange (FTSE) All-Share index, with a disclosure of carbon having a greater negative impact on this uncertainty. The study expanded Information Asymmetry as well Signalling Theories, with the role of ESG reporting in reducing the cost of capital, increasing firm value, and enhancing investor confidence. Meng-tao et al. (2023) also revealed similar effects in the Chinese stock market, which proved that high ESG disclosure increased stock liquidity, both through an institutional investor preference channel and a risk alleviation channel.

However, the evidence is more nuanced than a simple positive relationship would suggest. Moktar et al. (2023) discovered that in the Malaysian stock market, higher ESG disclosure in fact increases investor uncertainty regarding what the true value of firms is, as opposed to reducing it. This apparently contradictory finding can be viewed as an indication of a situation in which the regulatory regime of ESG reporting is not sufficiently standardized, and thus it is not easy to interpret the disclosures of the firms in a similar way. The discovery highlights that the regulation of disclosure is not a magic bullet; the effectiveness of the regulation depends crucially on the other infrastructure which is composed of standards, verification, as well as enforcement.Khan et al. (2024) confirms this contextualisation across 189 economies: the effect of regulatory quality on FDI is consistently positive but moderated by income level, enforcement capacity, and the initial regulatory baseline, indicating a non-linear rather than a simple monotone relationship and cautioning against one-size-fits-all policy prescriptions.

5.2 The EU Sustainable Finance Disclosure Regulation: A Case Study

The most ambitious compulsory ESG disclosure framework, which is currently under operation, is the SFDR by the European Union. The regulation aimed to establish a plausible signal hierarchy in sustainable finance markets by classifying investment funds into three tiers, namely: Article 6 (no sustainability claim), Article 8 (funds promoting environmental or social characteristics) and Article 9 (funds with explicit sustainable investment objectives). Abouarab et al. (2025) studied whether the SFDR has indeed decreased the greenwashing effort of equity mutual funds, using a Greenwashing Index derived based on the decarbonisation effort of a fund relative to its flows. Their difference-in-differences analysis discovered that Article 9 funds do experience a lower greenwashing following the enactment of SFDR, although Article 8 funds do not. This imbalanced outcome implies that the most powerful impact of the regulation is at the high sustainability level.

Partiti (2024) has found the essential flaws of the design of the SFDR. The regulation does not oblige fund managers to end or remedy the major adverse effects of their investments; instead, it requires them to disclose the effects. It is not an insignificant difference: the disclosure of the harm is not identical to the prevention of the harm. The definitions of sustainable investment and do no significant harm are so open-ended that funds can even include oil and coal investments and be regarded as Article 8 or even Article 9 funds. The article suggested the shift towards a labelling regime, the one that is analogous to food nutrition labels and which offers investors standardization and benchmarked sustainability scores as opposed to open-ended policy descriptions.

The EU has partially addressed the SFDR's design limitations through the Corporate Sustainability Reporting Directive (CSRD), applicable from January 2023. It differs from previous frameworks in three ways: it moves from investor-level disclosure to company-level disclosure, filling the information gap that can't be addressed by fund-level SFDR disclosure; it introduces double materiality reporting, which means that sustainability risks to the company and impacts of the company on the environment are both reported; and its extraterritorial scope extends to non-EU companies with significant revenues in the EU, making it a de facto global standard for multinational reporting (European Commission, 2023).

In Section 7, the greenwashing risks raised by the SFDR Article 8/9 divergence are explored in detail, as anti-greenwashing regulation is a specific regulatory field. The regulatory response to greenwashing is discussed separately in this section, to maintain analytical clarity across the discussion, while the disclosure design implications are discussed here. Figure 1 Illustrates the pathway from ESG regulatory architecture to investment outcomes, integrating the relationships between disclosure stringency, institutional quality, investor behaviour, and capital allocation discussed in this section.

Figure 1. Relationship Between ESG Disclosure Strength, Regulatory Quality, and Investment Outcomes

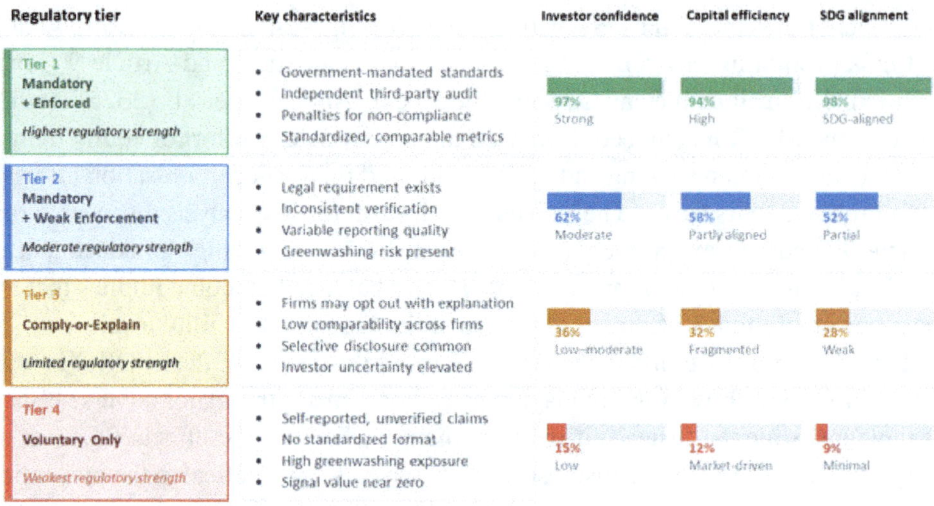

Figure 1. *Authors' synthesis based on Krueger et al. (2024), Moussa and Elmarzouky (2024), and Abouarab et al. (2025). The direction of the relationships indicated are those of the effects reported in the literature cited. The composite indicators (investor confidence, capital efficiency, SDG alignment) are qualitative synthesis of the evidence reviewed and are not cardinal measurement scores. They are shown to indicate the direction of relationships, rather than the size of the relationships.*

The connection between ESG regulatory architecture and investment outcomes is not linear as shown in Figure 1. This relationship is mediated by the investor decision framework: investors do not react to the intent of the regulations, but to the credibility of the disclosure signals, which is influenced by the verification and enforcement framework of the investor decision framework. This mediated pathway explains the finding of Moktar et al. (2023) that disclosure can raise uncertainty rather than reduce it in contexts of low standardisation and reinforces the central argument that institutional coherence is the critical determinant of regulatory effectiveness.

The evidence reviewed in this section reinforces the central argument of the theoretical framework: ESG disclosure frameworks cannot be evaluated in isolation from the institutional context in which they are embedded. Where institutional quality is high, mandatory disclosure frameworks reduce information asymmetry, improve stock liquidity, and lower the cost of capital. Where institutional quality is low, even technically well-designed disclosure requirements generate inconsistent outcomes. The next level of regulatory ambition beyond disclosure is the classification of economic activities as environmentally sustainable or otherwise the function of green finance taxonomies, examined in the following section.

6. GREEN FINANCE TAXONOMIES AND THE REDIRECTION OF CAPITAL

This section examines green finance taxonomies classification systems that define which economic activities qualify as environmentally sustainable as the most technically ambitious instrument for redirecting capital examined in this chapter. Unlike ESG disclosure, which asks companies to report on what they are doing, taxonomies define what counts as green in the first place.

investment strategy, and both regulatory and market-based environmental policies exert substantial influence on sustainable development outcomes. The critical precondition, as both reviews emphasise, is institutional quality precisely the condition identified throughout this chapter as determinative of instrument effectiveness.

6.1 The EU Taxonomy and Global Diffusion

The most technologically advanced green taxonomy that is currently operative is the EU Taxonomy Regulation that came into force in 2020. It implements six environmental objectives, such as: climate change mitigation, climate change adaptation, sustainable use of water, circular economy, pollution prevention and biodiversity protection; and provides that activities should do no significant harm to any of the six and that the activity must make a substantial contribution to or at least one of the six. In a survey of the global picture in the development of taxonomies, Pavani and Fernandes (2025) have found significant regional differences: the EU framework is aimed at a net-zero level of emissions by 2050, the taxonomy of China is oriented towards achieving the national economic goals, the taxonomies of India and ASEAN emphasize the need to develop local approaches to taxonomies that correspond to different socioeconomic realities.

The implementation challenges facing technically competent taxonomies are starkly illustrated by Hilbrich et al. (2025), whose case study of the South African Green Finance Taxonomy draws on 44 semi-structured interviews with financial sector stakeholders. The study reveals that after one year of publication, the taxonomy was hardly used in practice. The three identified institutional barriers were: (i) the advisory nature of the taxonomy, rather than it being a legal requirement, meant that there was no compliance obligation attached to using the taxonomy; (ii) the taxonomy was not recognised by the European Union, which is a key consideration for South African companies seeking to access European capital markets;

and (iii) path dependencies in the domestic financial system, which is dominated by the fossil fuel industry, meant that there was structural resistance to investing in taxonomy-consistent projects. The case illustrates that a technically adequate taxonomy, without compulsory regulatory embedding and institutional linkage, does not provide enough signal to beat market inertia.

In the context of Qatar, Ahmad et al. (2026) also concludes that the investment in green finance needs to be supported by a consistent legal framework that provides transparency in the market and integrates climate policy into a wider institutional framework.

The ASEAN Taxonomy for Sustainable Finance (Version 2, 2023) for ten economies with varying energy mixes, includes a traffic-light classification that explicitly includes transition activities that the EU Taxonomy would not include. This split creates a double reporting burden and legal uncertainty for investors investing in both the EU and ASEAN markets. It reflects a larger point: if there are no interoperability standards, there will be a proliferation of taxonomies, which will lead to fragmentation and unequal compliance costs for cross-border sustainable capital flows.

The international evidence reviewed here suggests that green finance taxonomies are powerful in principle but fragile in practice. Their effectiveness is conditional on three institutional preconditions: mandatory regulatory embedding that creates compliance obligations; mutual recognition arrangements that extend the taxonomy's signalling value across international capital markets; and institutional capacity within financial sector supervisory agencies to monitor, enforce, and update taxonomy classifications as climate science and technology evolve. Where these preconditions are absent, as in South Africa and much of ASEAN, taxonomies function as policy aspirations rather than market-shaping instruments.

6.2 Green Finance and the Climate Investment Trap in Developing Economies

Ameli et al. (2021) refers to such a phenomenon as the climate investment trap in developing economies. Its modelling work demonstrated that the higher cost of capital in developing countries - because of premiums on political risk, currency risk, and reduced institutional credibility - disproportionately increases the cost of green investments as compared to fossil fuel alternatives. The 2°C pathway modelling, using regionally specific weighted average cost of capital (WACC) values, indicated that Africa would produce only one-third of the green electricity projected under standard models that do not account for regional cost-of-capital differentials, rather than what the standard models assume. This implies that, despite developing economies adopting sound regulatory green frameworks, there could be a systemic under-investment in clean energy by the developing economies, unless there are explicit policy interventions to specifically target the cost of capital.

Bylo (2025) followed the development of green finance in emerging markets between 2000 and the present and was able to identify structural challenges throughout: data and regulatory fragmentation, significant financing gaps especially in relation to nature-based solutions, institutional misalignment, and poor integration of social dimensions. Based on this analysis, to scale green finance in emerging economies, harmonized green taxonomies with compulsory climate-related financial reporting, and cross-border cooperation beyond voluntary commitments is needed.

Blended finance, which is the strategic use of development finance and philanthropic funds to mobilise additional private finance for developing country investment (OECD, 2018), has been identified as a bridge to overcome the climate investment trap. Based on the experiences of India and Brazil, Sakyi et al. (2024) conclude that green bonds and ESG investments in emerging markets need to be supported by specific policies and public-private partnerships to achieve their potential. Their case-study analysis also suggests that financial literacy development and regulatory capacity building are necessary to get these mechanisms going with domestic investors, which is in line with the institutional coherence thesis presented in this chapter.

The green finance regulatory landscape is compared across selected economies as of 2020–2024 in Table 3, which is based mainly on Bylo (2025) and Hilbrich et al. (2025), and uses publicly available data from the Climate Bonds Initiative, UNCTAD and national regulatory authorities.

Table 3. Green Finance Landscape - Selected Economies (2020–2024)

Country/ Region	Taxonomy Status	Green Bond Market Size	Primary Regulatory Body	Key Challenge
European Union	Mandatory (EU Taxonomy Reg.)	~€500bn cumulative	European Commission / ESMA	Greenwashing; political resistance
China	Mandatory (aligned w/ national plan)	~$90bn annual issuance	People's Bank of China	Divergence from intl. standards
India	Quasi-mandatory (BRSR)	~$55.9bn GSS+ debt	SEBI	Capacity constraints; market depth
South Africa	Advisory (Green Finance Taxonomy)	Limited issuance	National Treasury / FSCA	Low adoption; fossil-fuel path dependency
Indonesia	Regulatory framework (OJK)	Nascent market	Financial Services Authority (OJK)	Regulatory fragmentation; greenwashing
United States	Proposed (SEC Climate Disclosure)	~$80bn annual	SEC	Political uncertainty; litigation risk

continued on following page

Table 3. Continued

Country/ Region	Taxonomy Status	Green Bond Market Size	Primary Regulatory Body	Key Challenge
Qatar	Framework in development	Emerging	Qatar Financial Centre	Hydrocarbon dependency; limited capacity
ASEAN	Traffic-light (Version 2, 2023)	Emerging	ASEAN Finance Ministers	Taxonomy-EU divergence; interoperability

Note. Synthesized from Bylo (2025), and Hilbrich et al. (2025). Market size figures are approximate and sourced from cited literature. The figures for EU green bonds are cumulative, while the figures for China and US are approximate annual issuance and cannot be directly compared with each other. The data currency, the maturity of the taxonomies and the definitions of the regulations differ significantly between the economies listed and cross-country comparisons should be treated with caution.

The cross-jurisdictional differences in taxonomy maturity, green bond market development and the stringency of the regulatory framework highlighted in this section are confirmed in Table 3. The EU and China are the two most developed green finance regulatory regimes in terms of market size and depth of mandatory regime, while the South Africa, Qatar and ASEAN economies show the implementation challenges of developing and transition economies. This is an analytically important variation because it shows that the effectiveness of green finance taxonomies is not only dependent on the technical design of the taxonomy, but also on the regulatory ecosystem in which it is situated.

7. INSTITUTIONAL QUALITY, FDI, AND GREEN ECONOMIC GROWTH

This section examines how institutional quality encompassing regulatory quality, rule of law, control of corruption, and government effectiveness mediates the volume and environmental character of foreign direct investment. The evidence presented complements the cross-instrument analysis in Table 4 by establishing the macro-level institutional conditions under which sustainable investment regulatory frameworks generate their strongest effects. One of the primary channels through which host economies gain access to capital, technology, management capabilities, and global value chains is foreign direct investment. The question of what makes FDI inflows is thus a key question in development policy. The regulatory and institutional quality have been identified in evidence repeatedly as among the most significant determinants although the exact relationship is more complex than simple advocacy of deregulation would have suggested.

Sabir et al. (2019) who used panel data of low, lower-middle, upper-middle, and high-income countries between 1996 and 2016 found that institutional quality has a positive effect on FDI in all groups of countries. Nonetheless, coefficient size of dimensions like, control of corruption, government effectiveness, political stability, regulatory quality, rule of law and voice and accountability is always larger in developed countries compared to developing countries. This finding carries significant implications for policy: the institutional dimensions most strongly associated with attracting investment are precisely those most difficult to strengthen in developing-country contexts. This does not counsel against institutional reform quite the contrary but it suggests that developing economies may need to rely on bilateral investment treaties, tax incentives, and other compensating instruments in the interim while institutional capacity is being built.

7.1 FDI, Regulatory Quality, and Green Economic Growth

There is an increasing volume of literature that explores the environmental pathway of FDI's impact on sustainable development outcomes, especially the role of the rigor and structure of regulatory regimes. Hunjra et al. (2024) did find some support of the dynamics of the Environmental Kuznets Curve: as developing economies grow; they do eventually turn to clean technologies and practices. But they also discovered that there is a positive relationship between FDI and carbon emissions at lower levels of income which indicates that the nature of investment and the regulation structures should be taken into consideration. When economic growth, presence of natural resources and high FDI are coupled, there is more environmental degradation.

Xiao et al. (2023) added a more granular view of this question, investigating how the moderating effect of environmental regulation on the impact of FDI on the growth of a green economy is embodied in 30 Chinese provinces between 2004 and 2019. Their results indicated that FDI played a significant role in promoting green economic growth in China and this was carried out through independent innovation but moderated both positively and negatively by the intensity of environmental regulations. Increased regulation of the environment, in other words, can influence the direction in which FDI leads to growth, and induce firms to pursue genuine innovation, rather than imitative methods of catching up.

Meanwhile, Rao et al. (2024) discovered that the contribution of FDI to local innovation in host countries is conditional on both regulatory quality and protection of property rights: in countries with higher standards of regulation quality, FDI and domestic innovation complement each other, whereas in countries with lower standards of regulatory quality, FDI can in fact crowd out local innovation.

Table 4 presents an original cross-instrument, cross-income-group synthesis of regulatory effectiveness, developed by the author on the basis of the literature reviewed in Sections 3 through 7. It is the principal analytical contribution of this chapter. The term regulatory chill, as used in Table 4, refers to the deterrent effect that investor-state dispute settlement mechanisms can exert on host governments' willingness to adopt environmental, labour, or social regulation, documented by Tienhaara (2011) and Choudhury (2026). Effectiveness ratings (Positive, Moderate, Weak, Absent) represent the predominant direction and approximate magnitude of effects reported across the reviewed studies, as described in the table note.

Table 4. Comparative Effectiveness of Regulatory Instruments Across Country Income Groups

Regulatory Instrument	High-Income Economies	Middle-Income Economies	Low-Income Economies	Key Moderating Condition	Evidence Strength
IIL / BITs	Positive (investor confidence); negative (regulatory chill)	Positive (FDI attraction); mixed (sustainability)	Weakly positive (depends on treaty quality)	Democratic governance; past ISDS exposure	Moderate
ESG Disclosure Mandates	Strong positive (capital market liquidity, cost of capital)	Moderate positive (varies by enforcement)	Weak (capacity and standardisation constraints)	Mandatory vs comply-or-explain; enforcement infrastructure	Strong
Green Finance Taxonomies	Positive where mandatory; minimal where advisory	Mixed (adoption barriers; fossil-fuel path dependencies)	Weak / absent (South Africa; WACC trap)	Regulatory embedding; EU recognition; blended finance	Moderate
Anti-Greenwashing Regulation	Mixed (unintended crowding-out; SFDR Article 8 gap)	Weak-Moderate (China pilot zone paradox)	Absent / minimal	Third-party verification; enforcement credibility	Moderate-Weak
Institutional Coherence (all instruments)	Highest effectiveness across all dimensions	Moderate effectiveness; returns to sequencing	Lowest absolute effectiveness; highest returns to reform	All four instruments in coherent ecosystem	Emerging

Note: Original synthesis by the authors. Effectiveness ratings (Positive, Moderate, Weak, Absent) represent the predominant direction and magnitude of effects reported across studies reviewed. Evidence Strength reflects: (i) volume number of independent studies; (ii) methodological consistency degree to which different research designs converge; and (iii) geographic breadth range of country contexts represented. These ratings are interpretive assessments, not formal meta-analytic scores.

Table 4 is an original contribution of this chapter because it is a cross-instrument cross-income-group synthesis not included in any of the studies that were reviewed. Note. Evidence Strength is a measure of the quantity, consistency and geographic scope of the literature that supports the concept. The last row Institutional Coherence is the most important analytical contribution of the chapter as a whole; no single-instrument row of the table generates consistently good results across income groups, while coherent multi-instrument deployment combined with institutional quality yields the most consistent positive results.

Table 4 reveals four cross-cutting patterns. First, mandatory and institutionalised ESG disclosure delivers the most consistent capital market effects across all income groups and should be the first component deployed in any sustainable finance architecture. Second, green finance taxonomies are the most technically demanding instrument and correspondingly the most dependent on institutional preconditions that low-income economies typically lack. Third, anti-greenwashing regulation exhibits a paradox: unintended consequences appear in both high-income and middle-income settings, suggesting that enforcement design matters more than regulatory ambition. Fourth, no single instrument dominates across all income groups the empirical foundation for the institutional coherence thesis.

8. GREENWASHING: THE INTEGRITY CHALLENGE OF SUSTAINABLE FINANCE REGULATION

Greenwashing defined as the practice of making misleading or unsubstantiated claims about the environmental credentials of investments, products, or corporate practices represents the fundamental integrity challenge of sustainable finance regulation. Its forms are varied: Dempere et al. (2024) document ambiguous language, irrelevant environmental claims, selective disclosure, and deliberate obfuscation through complexity (opacity). This section examines how existing regulatory frameworks address greenwashing, where they fall short, and what design principles the evidence suggests are necessary for effective anti-greenwashing regulation. Greenwashing risk has already been identified in the ESG disclosure context (Section 5.2); this section focuses specifically on regulatory responses and unintended consequences. The evidence reviewed below suggests that existing regulatory frameworks have achieved only partial effectiveness in containing greenwashing, with unintended consequences documented in both high-income and middle-income regulatory contexts.

8.1 Regulatory Responses to Greenwashing

Greenwashing has been most regulated in the European Union. Buttigieg & Pulis, (2024) analysed a report of IOSCO (December 2023) on the topic of supervisory practices regarding greenwashing, and the regulatory framework of the EU, and argued that more international harmonisation, proportionate regulation and effective enforcement are needed to maintain the credibility of sustainable finance. They cited fragmented regulations, convoluted disclosure regulations and the burgeoning growth of ESG investing as contributors to greenwashing despite regulation efforts.

A counterintuitive finding from China complicates this picture.Wu (2024) investigated the impact of the creation of Green Finance Pilot Zones in China on corporate greenwashing behavior, by using data on Chinese listed companies. The mechanism identified by Wu (2024) operates through financial pressure: as environmental subsidies associated with pilot zone membership expire, and as debt levels constrain firms' ability to make genuine sustainability investments, firms substitute symbolic disclosure improvements for substantive environmental performance improvements. The pilot zones thus inadvertently create an environment in which greenwashing is financially rational. The researchers discovered that these pilot zones in fact enhance greenwashing: they do not change the disclosure practices of companies, but instead decrease their actual disclosure performance. The impact is more acute in firms with a larger debt ratio, and when environmental subsidies run out- pointing to the fact that financial pressures would push firms towards symbolic rather than substantive sustainability commitments. This can be alleviated by the stricter government regulation, but the underlying finding that despite well-intentioned green finance reform, it may inadvertently encourage greenwashing is a significant warning to policymakers.

Li et al. (2023) reports their research on 735 Chinese listed companies in 21 industries and found that greenwashing positively influences the corporate financial performance in the context of high information asymmetry, as the stakeholders are not able to easily identify the deceptive practices. But this information asymmetry is mitigated by the local environmental regulation and negative media coverage, and thus the detection and punishment of greenwashing is simplified. The main policy takeaway from this finding is that there is a need for proactive monitoring capacity, investigative infrastructure and credible enforcement threats in addition to disclosure requirements to be effective in regulating against greenwashing.

Mukherjee (2025) used the changing regulatory environment in India regarding ESG practices as a prism through which the environment is viewed and which leads to the conclusion that the interplay of the securities law, consumer protection, competition law, environmental regulation and constitutional principles will result into a successful ESG regulation in India. The BRSR framework that SEBI has put forward has catapulted India into voluntary to quasi-mandatory reporting on ESGs, but the threat of greenwashing remains since legal enforcement mechanisms are poorly developed and judicial precedent on green issues in reporting remains thin. The article points out that disclosure regulation in the absence of an enforcement infrastructure is at best, a signalling exercise and, at worst, a legitimizing cover to further unsustainable practices.

8.2 Unintended Consequences of Anti-Greenwashing Regulation

Even carefully designed regulatory interventions may generate unintended consequences, as the following evidence demonstrates. Shui et al. (2025) examined the impact of the 2020 New Securities Act in China, which increased personal liability of independent directors, on corporate behavior with regard to greenwashing. The research discovered that increased director liability in fact increased greenwashing as directors diverted their efforts towards financial oversight in the face of increased liability at the expense of firms strategically switching to symbolic environmental commitments. The crowding-out effect in which the goal of one regulatory requirement aggravates the performance of another regulatory requirement is a familiar problem in multi-objective regulatory frameworks.

The implications of multi-objective regulatory interaction have wider implications than merely for the Chinese context. The stringency and specificity of sustainability requirements are important: vague sustainability requirements can be complied with in a symbolic manner as shown by Abouarab et al. (2025) in the comparison of the effectiveness of Article 9 SFDR funds and Article 8 funds in curtailing greenwashing. Likewise, Dempere et al. (2024) suggest that there are structural conditions that allow greenwashing to make sense when sustainability requirements are not sufficiently monitored and are not mandatory, as opposed to self-reported sustainability disclosure. The results of this study are convergent on a practical design principle for multi-objective sustainable finance regulation: minimise space for symbolic compliance by having clear performance thresholds, clear sanctions for failure to meet thresholds, and independent third-party verification systems, together with real time monitoring systems. The ISSB's new standards for assurance of sustainability reporting are a hopeful step in this direction, but they still need to be translated into binding frameworks of jurisdictions.

8.3 Digital Finance, Regulatory Technology, and the Future of ESG Verification

The governance of sustainable finance is also being transformed by digital technology in ways that fall partially outside the scope of this review but merit acknowledgement. Regulatory technology (RegTech) tools using machine learning are increasingly capable of auditing sustainability claims at scale, cross-referencing corporate disclosures with satellite imagery, supply-chain records, and environmental sensor data (Ehrentraud et al., 2020; Macchiavello & Siri, 2022). These tools have potential to shift the enforcement paradigm from ex ante declaration to ex post verification. Concurrently, the use of AI in ESG ratings introduces new information asymmetries through non-transparent algorithmic methodologies. The governance of ESG rating methodologies will need to be incorporated into future regulatory architecture alongside the disclosure frameworks this chapter has examined.

9. DISCUSSION

The evidence reviewed across the preceding sections converges on a single overarching finding: the effectiveness of any regulatory instrument for sustainable investment is not determined primarily by the sophistication of the instrument itself, but by the quality and coherence of the institutional environment in which it is deployed. This chapter builds on this finding, and proposes the institutional coherence thesis, which states that regulatory instruments for sustainable investment are complementary rather than mutually exclusive, and that their effectiveness depends on the capacity to enforce them, the infrastructure to verify them, and the legitimacy of the regulatory regime.

This is well reflected in international investment law. The evolution of investor protection-oriented BITs to those that include right-to-regulate clauses, sustainability carve-outs and investor obligations is a real step forward in terms of norms. But, as Dotzauer et al. (2024) show, the motivation for reform has been more reactive, in response to the financial and reputational risks of ISDS litigation, than proactive sustainability planning. The outcome is an investment law framework that is undergoing change, but not yet changed.

The four instruments reviewed offer the strongest cross-country evidence of disclosure regulation for ESG, with the strongest evidence being found in ESG disclosure regulation. When properly implemented, mandatory disclosure decreases information asymmetry, enhances stock liquidity and reduces the cost of capital (Krueger et al., 2024; Moussa and Elmarzouky (2024). However, the Malaysian study by Moktar et al. (2023) shows that disclosure regulation is not automatic –

in under-standardised markets, greater disclosure can lead to greater uncertainty for investors. It is as effective as the institutional infrastructure that it is supposed to complement, and its effectiveness relies on the same standards of institutional infrastructure, verification and enforcement.

Green finance taxonomies are the most technically advanced regulatory tool examined, and as such the most reliant on the institutional prerequisites. The South African case (Hilbrich et al., 2025) is illustrative: a technically well-designed taxonomy that is not required to be regulated, mutually recognised by the EU and aligned with the realities of the domestic financial system results in little capital reallocation.

The unintended consequences of regulatory reform is another complexity that is revealed by anti-greenwashing regulation. The study by Wu (2024) that China's Green Finance Pilot Zones led to an increase in greenwashing, and the study by Shui et al. (2025) that director liability reform drove out real sustainability effort are both examples of this. The Article 8 gap in the EU SFDR is a classic case of the lack of coherence at the instrument level.

These findings collectively suggest a sequencing implication for policy: In developing economies, institutional capacity development should come before, not after, the implementation of sophisticated regulatory instruments. This is not an argument against regulatory ambition. It is an argument that regulatory ambition without institutional foundations produces symbolic compliance rather than genuine capital reallocation.

10. THEORETICAL AND PRACTICAL IMPLICATIONS

10.1 Theoretical Implications

The results also expand North's (1990) institutional theory, which was limited to the enforcement of property rights and contracts, to show that the credibility of enforcement and the capacity to verify are important factors in the effectiveness of environmental regulatory instruments. The institutional coherence thesis presented here adds to the literature on the effectiveness of regulation by suggesting that the effect of individual pieces of regulation is enhanced by the coherence of the regulatory system as a whole.

The evidence reviewed is used to provide a contextual qualification of Dunning (1977) OLI paradigm. The empirical evidence indicates that the sensitivity of investors from various countries to regulatory quality dimensions differs: European and North American investors are more sensitive to regulatory quality dimensions, whereas emerging-economy multinationals are more sensitive to market size and labour cost (Yuan & Ji, 2025). The implications of this heterogeneity for the design of regulatory strategies have not been explored to any great extent.

The results confirm the signalling theory prediction that mandatory signals that are verifiable are more credible than voluntary signals. In all regulatory areas examined, the evidence clearly indicates that mandatory schemes with independent verification are more effective than comply-or-explain schemes. Signals are believed only if they are costly enough to prevent mimicry.

10.2 Practical Implications

The main practical take-away for developing economy policy makers is sequencing. Governments should build the enforcement and verification system that will ensure that complex regulatory measures like green finance taxonomies and mandatory ESG disclosure frameworks drive real capital reallocation or symbolic compliance.

The consequences of regulatory fragmentation are great for investors and financial intermediaries. The EU Taxonomy and ASEAN Taxonomy have some differences, resulting in a double reporting burden and legal uncertainty for cross-border investors. In the absence of taxonomy interoperability standards, investors in EU-ASEAN markets will have to pay a compliance complexity premium.

The EU SFDR experience is a warning to regulators in developed markets that there is a disconnect between the instrument and the instrument effect. The Article 8/9 divergence highlighted by Abouarab et al. (2025) indicates that the effectiveness of anti-greenwashing regulation needs to be achieved at the instrument level, rather than just the framework level.

11. CHALLENGES, OPPORTUNITIES, AND RECOMMENDATIONS

11.1 Key Challenges

The issue of regulatory fragmentation is the most prevalent issue identified in all four areas. The growing number of frameworks that differ from one another (e.g., the EU-ASEAN taxonomy divergence) and the number of frameworks that exist side by side (e.g., ISSB, TCFD, GRI and national disclosure frameworks) increases the complexity of compliance for smaller companies and regulators in developing countries. Enforcement capacity constraints are especially high in developing economies. Where disclosure requirements are in place, there is a lack of trained supervisory staff, independent verification systems and effective sanctions regimes, resulting in compliance being largely nominal. This institutional gap is one of the causes of the climate investment trap identified by Ameli et al. (2021): investors in developing economies have a higher risk premium due to their doubts about the credibility of regulatory signals.

Greenwashing is a systemic risk that is ongoing. In all four regulatory areas examined, greenwashing in different forms, such as lack of clarity in labelling, selective disclosure and opacity, has a negative impact on the informational integrity of sustainable finance markets.

11.2 Key Opportunities

The ISSB is an important step towards global ESG disclosure harmonisation, as it is being adopted by over 20 jurisdictions. If the pace of ISSB adoption remains as it is and the ISSB incorporates credible assurance requirements, it could significantly narrow the standardisation and materiality gaps which have plagued ESG disclosure effectiveness in emerging markets in the past.

Digital regulatory technology (RegTech) has the potential to transform the enforcement process. Machine learning tools that can be used to compare corporate disclosures with satellite data, supply chain data and outputs from environmental sensors can change the enforcement paradigm from ex ante declaration to ex post verification.

Blended finance mechanisms that combine public guarantees, multilateral development bank concessional capital and private investment are a targeted instrument to overcome the climate investment trap. De-risking interventions can create a more attractive cost of capital for green investments in developing economies, which cannot be achieved through sound domestic regulation alone (Sakyi et al., 2024; Ameli et al., 2021).

11.3 Policy Recommendations

First, the governments that want to attract sustainable FDI should focus on regulatory quality as the foundational institutional condition as it has been consistently and statistically significantly positively associated with FDI inflows across income groups (Saha et al., 2022; Khan et al., 2024).

Second, international organisations need to speed up the process of harmonising green taxonomy standards, while maintaining provisions for localisation to enable developing economies to include transition activities and local economic realities (Bylo, 2025; Pavani and Fernandes, 2025).

Third, ESG disclosure frameworks should move from comply-or-explain to mandatory disclosure regimes that are institutionally enforced and have meaningful sanctions for misrepresentation, because the evidence is clear that mandatory, institutionally enforced disclosure regimes have stronger capital market effects (Krueger et al., 2024).

Fourth, investment treaty reform should systematically include right-to-regulate clauses, investor obligation provisions and sustainable development preambles, and not be limited to the investor-protection paradigm that creates regulatory chill, which is the effect on governments' willingness to enact environmental, labour or social regulation (Choudhury, 2026; Zagel, 2021).

Fifth, there is a need to scale up blended finance mechanisms and offer capacity building support to regulatory agencies in developing economies, acknowledging that robust domestic regulation is essential but not enough to address the structural cost-of-capital disadvantage identified by Ameli et al. (2021).

12. FUTURE RESEARCH DIRECTIONS

There are a number of areas of the literature that need to be explored further. First, the distributional effects of sustainable finance regulation, specifically who benefits and who will have to bear the costs of transition to a green economy, have not been sufficiently researched, especially in developing countries where the risks of transition are borne by the fossil fuel dependent communities and informal sector workers.

Second, the long-term impact of the mandatory ESG disclosure on the behaviour of the firms rather than on the performance of the capital market should be systematically studied. The question of whether mandatory disclosure leads to substantive changes in corporate environmental performance, or disclosure performance is an empirically open question with important policy implications.

Third, the political economy of regulatory reform, as some countries manage to establish sustainable finance frameworks that are credible, and others do not, necessitates interdisciplinary research that combines political science, legal scholarship, development sociology, economics and finance.

Fourth, the governance aspects of AI in ESG rating and disclosure verification are a new field of research. Theoretical and empirical research will be needed to address issues of algorithmic transparency, regulatory control, and the emergence of new information asymmetries.

Fifth, the interaction effects of regulatory instruments, specifically whether combinations of ESG disclosure, green taxonomy and anti-greenwashing enforcement are superadditive have not been systematically studied. The institutional coherence thesis presented in this chapter suggests these interaction effects, but empirical tests will need to rely on longitudinal panel data that correlates the adoption of regulatory instruments with outcome measures of investments in all four regulatory domains examined in this chapter.

13. LIMITATIONS

First, the search was conducted in English-language databases specifically Scopus, Web of Science, Google Scholar, SSRN, and the UNCTAD digital library and therefore may not be representative of regulatory developments documented in Chinese, Portuguese, French, and Arabic-language scholarship, particularly regarding reforms currently underway in China, Brazil, West Africa, and the MENA region.

Second, the results from the main studies are not directly commensurable, as they use methodologically diverse techniques: panel data econometrics, automated treaty text analysis, difference-in-differences event studies, and semi-structured interview case studies. The cross-study comparisons presented in Table 4 do not constitute a formal meta-analysis; they represent interpretive assessments of the balance of evidence across the reviewed literature.

Third, this chapter recaps association and mechanism reports from the observation and quasi-experimental literature. Causal claims are allowed only for natural experiments and difference in differences designs, as indicated in the text. Positive relationships between regulatory quality and FDI, as well as mandatory ESG disclosure and stock liquidity, should not be taken as causal relationships without considering the identification strategies used in the original studies.

Fourth, a form of publication bias is likely present. Jurisdictions with more developed regulatory systems and stronger data infrastructure generate more academic studies and are therefore over-represented in the evidence base. Specifically, the EU, China, and the United States account for a disproportionate share of the empirical literature on ESG disclosure and green finance, while low-income and lower-middle-income country experiences are under-represented relative to their importance for the global sustainable investment agenda. This bias may mean that the chapter underestimates the severity of implementation challenges in developing economies.

14. CONCLUSION

This chapter has discussed the way the modern systems of regulation influence global investment relationships towards sustainable economic growth. The evidence reviewed in this chapter demonstrates that regulation need not be and at its best is not an inhibitory architecture that frustrates the legitimate expectations of investors. On the contrary, well-designed regulatory frameworks that direct capital towards socially productive purposes can simultaneously enhance long-run investor confidence. The question facing policymakers is how to develop regulatory frameworks that are both credible to investors, equitable towards host populations, effective against greenwashing, and able to navigate the tensions brought about by international investment law.

'The principal contribution of this chapter is the consolidation and cross-instrument synthesis of the empirical literature on sustainable investment regulation into a single analytical framework: the institutional coherence thesis. Across all four regulatory domains examined, and drawing on methodologically diverse evidence from panel econometric studies, treaty text analyses, difference-in-differences event studies, and case study research, the evidence consistently supports the thesis that the effectiveness of any regulatory instrument is conditional on the institutional quality of the system in which it is deployed. There is limited impact of the EU Taxonomy in South Africa where the taxonomy is not embedded into institutions. This is because there is no verification at Article 8 level in the SFDR, which creates greenwashing risk. But the regulatory chill on sustainable development is inherent in the design of BITs which allows for enforcement asymmetry. The instrument is never the limiting factor in each case, it is institutional coherence that is. In developing economies, the logical reform sequence is therefore to build enforcement and verification capacity first, then layer sophisticated regulatory instruments onto that institutional foundation not the reverse.

REFERENCES

Abouarab, R., Mishra, T., & Wolfe, S. (2025). Does the EU sustainable finance disclosure regulation mitigate greenwashing? *European Journal of Finance*, *31*(8), 957–989. DOI: 10.1080/1351847X.2025.2457944

Ahmad, F., Boumaiza, A., Sanfilippo, A., & Al-Fagih, L. (2026). Towards Net-Zero Energy Transition: A Detailed Climate Change Integrated Green Finance Policy Investment Framework for Qatar. *Sustainable Development (Bradford)*, •••, 1–35. DOI: 10.1002/sd.70657

Ameli, N., Dessens, O., Winning, M., Cronin, J., Chenet, H., Drummond, P., Calzadilla, A., Anandarajah, G., & Grubb, M. (2021). Higher cost of finance exacerbates a climate investment trap in developing economies. *Nature Communications*, *12*(1), 4046. DOI: 10.1038/s41467-021-24305-3 PMID: 34193868

ASEAN Taxonomy Board. (2023). ASEAN Taxonomy for Sustainable Finance, Version 2. ASEAN Finance Ministers and Central Bank Governors' Meeting. Https://www.theacmf.org/images/downloads/pdf/ASEAN-Taxonomy-Version-2.pdf?Utm

Beetham, D. (1991). The legitimation of power. Macmillan Education. Https://psi412.cankaya.edu.tr/uploads/files/Beetham%20-%20The%20Legitimation%20of%20Power%20(1991).pdf

Bjorklund, A. K. (2019). Sustainable development and international investment law. In *Research handbook on environment and investment law* (pp. 38–68). Edward Elgar Publishing., DOI: 10.4337/9781784714635.00008

Black, J. (2008). Constructing and contesting legitimacy and accountability in polycentric regulatory regimes. *Regulation & Governance*, *2*(2), 137–164. DOI: 10.1111/j.1748-5991.2008.00034.x

Buttigieg, C. P., & Pulis, S. (2024, September). Strategic initiatives to address greenwashing. In ERA Forum (Vol. 25, No. 3, pp. 327-337). Berlin/Heidelberg: Springer Berlin Heidelberg. DOI: 10.1007/s12027-024-00815-7

Bylo, A. (2025). Assessing the impact of green finance on sustainability in emerging markets: Trends, challenges, and future prospects (2000–Present). *International Scientific Journal Monte*, *10*(1), 8–18. DOI: 10.33807/monte.20253288

Choudhury, B. (2026). International Investment Law and Sustainable Development – Friend or Foe? *Law and Development Review*, *19*(2), 717–755. Advance online publication. DOI: 10.1515/ldr-2025-0094

Contractor, F. J., Dangol, R., Nuruzzaman, N., & Raghunath, S. (2020). How do country regulations and business environment impact foreign direct investment (FDI) inflows? *International Business Review*, *29*(2), 101640. DOI: 10.1016/j.ibusrev.2019.101640

Cotula, L. (2014). *Foreign investment, law and sustainable development: A handbook on agriculture and extractive industries*. International Institute for Environment and Development (IIED). https://pubs.iied.org/pdfs/17513IIED.pdf

Dempere, J., Alamash, E., & Mattos, P. (2024). Unveiling the truth: Greenwashing in sustainable finance. *Frontiers in Sustainability*, *5*, 1362051. DOI: 10.3389/frsus.2024.1362051

Dolzer, R., Kriebaum, U., & Schreuer, C. (2022). *Principles of international investment law*. Oxford University Press., Https://files.pca-cpa.org/pcadocs/bi-c/1.%20Investors/4.%20Legal%20Authorities/CA199.pdf

Dotzauer, M., Biber-Freudenberger, L., & Dietz, T. (2024). The rise of sustainability provisions in international investment agreements. *Global Environmental Politics*, *24*(4), 10–36. DOI: 10.1162/glep_a_00759

Dunning, J. H. (1977). Trade, location of economic activity and the MNE: A search for an eclectic approach. In The international allocation of economic activity: proceedings of a Nobel Symposium held at Stockholm (pp. 395-418). London: Palgrave Macmillan UK. DOI: 10.1007/978-1-349-03196-2_38

Eccles, R. G., & Klimenko, S. (2019). The investor revolution. [Harvard Business Review Article]. *Harvard Business Review*, *97*(3), 106–116.

Ehrentraud, J., Ocampo, D. G., & Vega, C. Q. (2020). *Regulating fintech financing: digital banks and fintech platforms*. Bank for International Settlements, Financial Stability Institute. Https://www.bis.org/fsi/publ/insights27.pdf?Utm

European Commission. (2018). Action plan: Financing sustainable growth (COM (2018) 97 final). European Commission. European Commission Action Plan: Financing Sustainable Growth. Https://eur-lex.europa.eu/legal-content/EN/TXT/?Uri=CELEX%3A52018DC0097&utm

European Commission. (2020). Regulation (EU) 2020/852 of the European Parliament and of the Council of 18 June 2020 on the establishment of a framework to facilitate sustainable investment, and amending Regulation (EU) 2019/2088 (Taxonomy Regulation). *Official Journal of the European Union, L, 198*, 13–43. Https://eur-lex.europa.eu/eli/reg/2020/852/oj?Utm

European Commission. (2023). Corporate Sustainability Reporting Directive (CSRD). Official Journal of the European Union. Https://eur-lex.europa.eu/eli/dir/2022/2464/oj?Utm

Hilbrich, S., Berensmann, K., Artmann, G., Ashman, S., Herbold, T., Lötters-Viehof, S., Monti, A., Paffhausen, F., Roigk, S., & Steenkamp, L. A. (2025). Implementing sustainability taxonomies to redirect capital flows: The case of South Africa. *Climate Policy*, *25*(5), 741–755. DOI: 10.1080/14693062.2024.2415382

Hunjra, A. I., Bouri, E., Azam, M., Azam, R. I., & Dai, J. (2024). Economic growth and environmental sustainability in developing economies. *Research in International Business and Finance*, *70*, 102341. DOI: 10.1016/j.ribaf.2024.102341

ISSB. (2023). IFRS S1 general requirements for disclosure of sustainability-related financial information and IFRS S2 climate-related disclosures. International Sustainability Standards Board. Https://www.ifrs.org/sustainability/knowledge-hub/introduction-to-issb-and-ifrs-sustainability-disclosure-standards/?Utm

Johnson, L., & Sachs, L. E. (2019). Investment Treaties, Investor-State Dispute Settlement, and Inequality: How International Investment Treaties Exacerbate Domestic Disparities. Https://scholarship.law.columbia.edu/cgi/viewcontent.cgi?Article=1105&context=sustainable_investment_staffpubs

Kaufmann, D., Kraay, A., & Mastruzzi, M. (2011). The Worldwide Governance Indicators: Methodology and Analytical Issues. *Hague Journal on the Rule of Law*, *3*(2), 220–246. DOI: 10.1017/S1876404511200046

Khan, H., Dong, Y., Bibi, R., & Khan, I. (2024). Institutional quality and foreign direct investment: Global evidence. *Journal of the Knowledge Economy*, *15*(3), 10547–10591. DOI: 10.1007/s13132-023-01508-1

Kriebaum, U. (2022). International Investment Law and Sustainable Development. Siobhan mcinerney-Langford/Robert mccorquodale: The Role of International Law in Development. DOI: 10.2139/ssrn.4298374

Krueger, P., Sautner, Z., Tang, D. Y., & Zhong, R. (2024). The effects of mandatory ESG disclosure around the world. *Journal of Accounting Research*, *62*(5), 1795–1847. DOI: 10.1111/1475-679X.12548

Li, W., Li, W., Seppänen, V., & Koivumäki, T. (2023). Effects of greenwashing on financial performance: Moderation through local environmental regulation and media coverage. *Business Strategy and the Environment*, *32*(1), 820–841. DOI: 10.1002/bse.3177

Macchiavello, E., & Siri, M. (2022). Sustainable Finance and Fintech: Can Technology Contribute to Achieving Environmental Goals? A Preliminary Assessment of 'Green Fintech' and 'Sustainable Digital Finance'. *European Company and Financial Law Review*, *19*(1), 128–174. DOI: 10.1515/ecfr-2022-0005

Meng-tao, C., Da-peng, Y., Wei-qi, Z., & Qi-jun, W. (2023). How does ESG disclosure improve stock liquidity for enterprises—Empirical evidence from China. *Environmental Impact Assessment Review*, *98*, 106926. DOI: 10.1016/j.eiar.2022.106926

Moktar, N., Mat Deli, M., Abdul Rauf, U. A., Idris, F., & Purwati, A. A. (2023). ESG disclosure: The extent of investors' confidence in stock market. *International Journal of Academic Research in Progressive Education and Development*, *12*(3), 1008–1027. DOI: 10.6007/IJARPED/v12-i3/18989

Moussa, A. S., & Elmarzouky, M. (2024). Sustainability reporting and market uncertainty: The moderating effect of carbon disclosure. *Sustainability (Basel)*, *16*(13), 5290. Advance online publication. DOI: 10.3390/su16135290

Muchlinski, P. T. (2021). *Multinational enterprises and the law* (3rd ed.). Oxford University Press., DOI: 10.1093/law/9780198824138.001.0001

Mukherjee, S.Dr. Subholaxmi Mukherjee. (2025). Regulating ESG disclosures in India: Greenwashing and legal accountability. *International Journal of Leading Research Publication*, *6*(2), 1–14. DOI: 10.70528/IJLRP.v6.i12.1880

Munif, M., & Wahrudin, B. (2025). Transnational Legal Cooperation And Global Trade: Rethinking International Investment Law In The Era Of Sustainable Development. Journal of Law. *Policy and Global Development*, *1*(1), 64–77. DOI: 10.71305/jlpgd.v1i1.336

Neumayer, E. (2007). Do double taxation treaties increase foreign direct investment to developing countries? *The Journal of Development Studies*, *43*(8), 1501–1519. DOI: 10.1080/00220380701611535

North, D. C. (1990). *Institutions, institutional change and economic performance*. Cambridge Univ Pr., DOI: 10.1017/CBO9780511808678

OECD. (2018). *Making blended finance work for the Sustainable Development Goals*. OECD Publishing., DOI: 10.1787/9789264288768-

OECD. (2020). *Developing sustainable finance definitions and taxonomies*. OECD Publishing., DOI: 10.1787/134a2dbe-

Paramaiah, C., Verma, V., Radhakrishnan, G. V., Pal, S., & Wagh, V. W. (2025). The influence of ESG investing on financial markets and economic growth. *Journal of Information Systems Engineering & Management, 10*(22s). Advance online publication. DOI: 10.52783/jisem.v10i22s.3527

Partiti, E. (2024). Addressing the flaws of the sustainable finance disclosure regulation: Moving from disclosures to labelling and sustainability due diligence. *European Business Organization Law Review, 25*(2), 299–332. DOI: 10.1007/s40804-024-00317-6

Pavani, N., & Fernandes, J. (2025). Catalyzing Climate Action: The Role of Green Taxonomy and the Green Climate Fund in Sustainable Development [IJIREM]. *International Journal of Innovative Research in Engineering and Management, 12*(2), 76–83. DOI: 10.55524/ijirem.2025.12.2.13

Popescu, I.-S., Hitaj, C., & Benetto, E. (2021). Measuring the sustainability of investment funds: A critical review of methods and frameworks in sustainable finance. *Journal of Cleaner Production, 314*, 128016. DOI: 10.1016/j.jclepro.2021.128016

Qumba, M. F. (2024). Incorporating Sustainable Development Principles in Africa's Investment Treaty-Making. *Journal of Comparative Law in Africa, 11*(2), 43–79. Https://hdl.handle.net/10520/ejc-jlc_jcla_v11_n2_a2. DOI: 10.47348/JCLA/v11/i2a2

Rao, A., Ali, M., & Smith, J. M. (2024). Foreign direct investment and domestic innovation: Roles of absorptive capacity, quality of regulations and property rights. *PLoS One, 19*(3), e0298913. DOI: 10.1371/journal.pone.0298913 PMID: 38457448

Sabir, S., Rafique, A., & Abbas, K. (2019). Institutions and FDI: Evidence from developed and developing countries. *Financial Innovation, 5*(1), 1–20. DOI: 10.1186/s40854-019-0123-7

Sachs, J. D., Schmidt-Traub, G., Mazzucato, M., Messner, D., Nakicenovic, N., & Rockström, J. (2019). Six Transformations to achieve the Sustainable Development Goals. *Nature Sustainability, 2*(9), 805–814. DOI: 10.1038/s41893-019-0352-9

Saha, S., Sadekin, M. N., & Saha, S. K. (2022). Effects of institutional quality on foreign direct investment inflow in lower-middle income countries. *Heliyon, 8*(10), e10828. Advance online publication. DOI: 10.1016/j.heliyon.2022.e10828 PMID: 36217489

Sakyi, J. K., Eboseremen, B. O., Adebayo, A. O., Essien, I. A., Okojie, J. S., & Soneye, O. M. (2024). Designing a sustainable financing model for emerging economies: Addressing climate goals through green bonds and ESG investments. *International Journal of Multidisciplinary Futuristic Development*, *5*(1), 20–33. DOI: 10.54660/IJMFD.2024.5.1.20-33

Salacuse, J. W. (2015). *The law of investment treaties* (2nd ed.). Oxford University Press., Https://files.pca-cpa.org/pcadocs/bi-c/1.%20Investors/4.%20Legal%20 Authorities/CA115.pdf DOI: 10.1093/law/9780198703976.001.0001

Schill, S. W. (2017). Reforming investor-state dispute settlement: A (comparative and international) constitutional law framework. *Journal of International Economic Law*, *20*(3), 649–672. DOI: 10.1093/jiel/jgx023

Shui, Z. L., Wang, H., Xin, C. K., & Xue, R. (2025). Unintended societal outcome of investor protection: Independent director liability and greenwashing. *Journal of Accounting Literature*, •••, 1–34. DOI: 10.1108/JAL-06-2025-0310

Sornarajah, M. (2021). The international law on foreign investment. Cambridge university press. Https://tamilnation.org/conflictresolution/Tamileelam/norway/sornarajah.pdf

Suchman, M. C. (1995). Managing legitimacy: Strategic and institutional approaches. *Academy of Management Review*, *20*(3), 571–610. DOI: 10.2307/258788

Sulehri, F. A., Ali, A., & Alam, M. (2024). Assessing the pathways of sustainable development: A structural equation modeling investigation of regulatory framework, innovation, and economic indicators. *Journal of Asian Development Studies*, *13*(1), 970–982. DOI: 10.62345/jads.2024.13.1.80

Tienhaara, K. (2011). Regulatory chill and the threat of arbitration: a view from political science. Evolution in Investment Treaty Law and Arbitration, Chester Brown, Kate Miles, eds., Cambridge University Press. Https://ssrn.com/abstract=2065706

UNCTAD. (2023). World investment report 2023: Investing in sustainable energy for all. United Nations Conference on Trade and Development. Https://unctad.org/publication/world-investment-report-2023

UNCTAD. (2024). World Investment Report 2024. United Nations Conference on Trade and Development, https://unctad.org/wir2024

UNFCCC. (2015). Paris agreement. United Nations Framework Convention on Climate Change. Https://unfccc.int/process-and-meetings/the-paris-agreement

United Nations. (2015). Transforming our world: The 2030 agenda for sustainable development (A/RES/70/1). United Nations General Assembly. Https://docs.un.org/en/A/RES/70/1

Van Harten, G. (2007). *Investment treaty arbitration and public law*. Oxford University Press., Https://global.oup.com/academic/product/investment-treaty-arbitration-and-public-law-9780199217892?Cc=in&lang=en&utm

Williamson, O. E. (1985). The economic institutions of capitalism. Firms, markets, relational contracting. In *Das Summa Summarum des Management: Die 25 wichtigsten Werke für Strategie, Führung und Veränderung* (pp. 61-75). Wiesbaden: Gabler. Https://link.springer.com/chapter/10.1007/978-3-8349-9320-5_6

Wu, T. (2024). Green finance reform policy increases corporate hypocritical business strategies: Evidence from the greenwashing behavior. *Mitigation and Adaptation Strategies for Global Change*, *29*(7), 63. DOI: 10.1007/s11027-024-10162-0

. Xiang, M. J., & Maïnkade, B. F. (2023). The human rights-based approach to sustainable development: Lessons from recent African investment treaty practice. Heliyon, 9(8). . 2023.e18578DOI: <ALIGNMENT.qj></ALIGNMENT>10.1016/j.heliyon

Xiao, D., Gao, L., Xu, L., Wang, Z., & Wei, W. (2023). Revisiting the green growth effect of foreign direct investment from the perspective of environmental regulation: Evidence from China. *International Journal of Environmental Research and Public Health*, *20*(3), 2655. DOI: 10.3390/ijerph20032655 PMID: 36768017

Yuan, L., & Ji, P. (2025). Motives of Chinese foreign direct investment in Africa: With regulation effects of institutional quality. *PLoS One*, *20*(6), e0326970. DOI: 10.1371/journal.pone.0326970 PMID: 40561167

Zagel, G. M. (2021). Achieving Sustainable Development Objectives in International Investment Law. In Handbook of International Investment Law and Policy (pp. 1933-1985). Singapore: Springer Singapore. DOI: 10.1007/978-981-13-3615-7_57

Chapter 6
Psychological Capital Gender and Social Class Intersections in MENA Women's Directorship Experiences: A Multi-Cultural Perspective

Lujain El-Maghraby
Muscat College, Oman

Nabila Al Macki
Majan University College, Oman

Venkoba Rao
Majan University College, Oman

Kishan Kanchralapalli
Majan University College, Oman

Hussein Ibrahim
Majan University Colloge, Oman

Fatma Al Ajami
http://orcid.org/0009-0008-6446-4097
Majan University College, Oman

Abdullah M. Al-Ansi
http://orcid.org/0000-0002-1682-3154
Dhofar University, Oman

ABSTRACT

This paper aims to explore how women from working class with typical local career background and privileged-defined women directors from western influenced backgrounds in combination may lead to distinct or common pathways towards women directorship experiences and trajectories. A qualitative study was undertaken of a mixed Middle Eastern sample of women directors from Egypt, Morocco, Dubai, Oman and Saudi Arabia from varied economic sectors were interviewed.

DOI: 10.4018/979-8-3373-8964-6.ch006

Two rounds of interviews were conducted with 6-month time duration in between. Women directors from bourgeoisie social class and multi-cultural exposure in the West reflected contemporary directorship models stressing the importance of tribe's power, nepotism calculations, ease of networking, less negative feelings, and less faced obstacles, yet a smaller number of board directorships. In contrast, women directors from working class background emphasized the importance of merit and hard work, labor market reputation, and importance of work mentor in defining effective women directorship models

1. INTRODUCTION

Female directorship research frequently overlooks the critical interplay between gender, social class, and psychological capital. This article addresses that gap by using an intersectional framework to examine how differing class and cultural backgrounds shape distinct or shared pathways to the boardroom. Business organizations are microcosms of the communities within which they are fabricated, and how real business is executed cannot be understood if the overall context of the socio-cultural environment in which it is embedded is not accurately considered (Badghish et al., 2023). Institutional mechanisms and dynamics spanning across industrial sectors, both within the private and public spheres, typically reflect communities' structural makeup, values and challenges, including distinctive outcomes for persons centered around (but not limited to) specific social class and gender categories with possible roots in self-identity and perception (Markoczy et al., 2020). Accordingly, business hierarchies are frequently viewed as being 'gendered', 'self-viewed' and 'classed' (Phoenix, 2023). This is predominantly at upper managerial levels (Snaggs-Wilson, 2021). Females and in particular women of working class and limited career exposure face less networking opportunities, more negative stereotypes and a 'glass ceiling' at the upper echelons in the corporate sector in the Middle East (Moghadam, 2005). The power elite being in military, legislative and corporate arenas in the Middle East is still constituted principally of bourgeoisie heterosexual men with multi-cultural exposure in the West (Keddie, 2012).

The pattern observed in the West (in US and European Union countries) is replicated in the Middle East. For example, the Spencer Stuart Report stated that a minority of 29% of FTSE 10 companies report that they are 'compliant' or 'non-compliant' with the Parker Review target of 'One by 21' (Stephenson, 2022). Along the same lines, a newspaper article in the Middle East reported a research study on women representation in corporate boardrooms in MENAT (Middle East, North Africa and Turkey) which indicates that females assume a minority of only 8.6% of board positions in 1,148 in the 16 countries located in the MENAT region (Khan,

2023). The figures are less obvious when we relate the women director experiences with their social classes. Yet, reportedly, only about 70% of these women directors are defined as "self-made women" who started from scratch. The researchers in this article argue that this may have its roots to how labor market views the merit of working-class versus bourgeoisie women directors and resulting opportunities with every type of women director. For example, one powerful asset a woman director from bourgeoisie class may bring to the board room is social capital that may have been inherited across long family generations. Whilst women directors from working class may have developed equally important social capital, their key merit remains the quality of thought and expertise built up across extensive years of successful hard work (Basuthakur, 2022).

Although the proportion of women board directors has increased because of the recently introduced gender quotas in Egypt, UAE and Morocco (Khan, 2023), there is a disparity between the number of women directors and their male counterparts in the Middle East. This gap may signal to the fact that the problem will not be sufficiently addressed by more numbers of females moving up the career ladder and finding their ways into the board rooms, but that rather the females' progression within the corporate sector may still not be welcomed by many. With empirical evidence concluding that biological sex differences in financial and environmental corporate performance (or subjective and objective aspects of corporate performance) exist (Birindelli et al., 2019; El Marghi et al., 2019; El-Caarami et al., 2019; Salloum et al., 2019). The efforts of many scholars and academicians to pinpoint the reasons behind board gender disparity have emphasized instead the Middle Eastern women's household demands that may significantly compete with females seeking the highest managerial positons, including board job titles. Accordingly, in the Middle East and the West, across different sectors, gendered directorship and power are dominated by a homogeneous gender and social class group: wealthy men.

Literature on psychological capital—comprising hope, efficacy, resilience, and optimism and challenges for women directors in the MENA region reveals a strategic integration opportunity to address persistent barriers (Dorsaf, 2025). Psychological capital (PsyCap) is an individual's positive psychological state of development, characterized by having the internal mental resources to manage tough situations, improve well-being, and drive performance. Psychological capital enhances women's leadership effectiveness by mitigating cultural norms confining roles to domestic spheres, family pressures, work-life conflicts, and exclusion from male-dominated networks, while countering structural issues like weak gender quotas, biases blocking career pipelines, family firm dominance, and low representation (e.g., 8.6% MENAT-wide, 5.2% GCC average, with over 55% of firms lacking female directors) (El Jadidi et al., 2022; Farah et al., 2021). Theoretically, Psychological capital aligns with agency theory for resilient oversight, resource dependence for diverse networking, and social role theory to overcome role incongruity, as evidenced in Saudi, Jordanian, and Bedouin studies linking it to empowerment and performance amid governance reforms in UAE, Oman, and beyond (Abed et al., 2025). This synthesis positions psychological capital as a trainable resource to boost board contributions and equity in the region.

Given the aforementioned disparities, our chapter objective in this article is to shed the light under driving factors towards directorship for diversity. This qualitative study explores gendered directorship by analyzing the experiences of 20 Middle Eastern women directors across the wide social class continuum and how they self-define themselves. Our sample comes from 5 key countries in the Middle East, namely: Egypt, Morocco, UAE, Oman and Saudi Arabia with either Western-influenced or local career backgrounds. Social class distinctions are the hierarchical divisions in a society based on economic, social, and cultural differences. These divisions create unequal access to resources, power, and opportunities. We also present an intersectional conceptual framework, which emphasizes the importance of simultaneous consideration of various identities for accurately understanding individuals' experiences at the directorship level. The different identities are: gender, social class and psychological capital. The article contributes to understanding women directorship as lived through by under-examined women groups: working class women directors with local career background. The results show how gender, psychological capital, cultural and class differentially shape bourgeoisie and working-class women's directorship constructions, self-definitions and experience. The results also provide pathways into alternative and new types of women directorships that may be fruitful for supporting our contemporary diverse workplaces and organizations. Figure 1 illustrates the framework of this study.

Figure 1. Research Framework

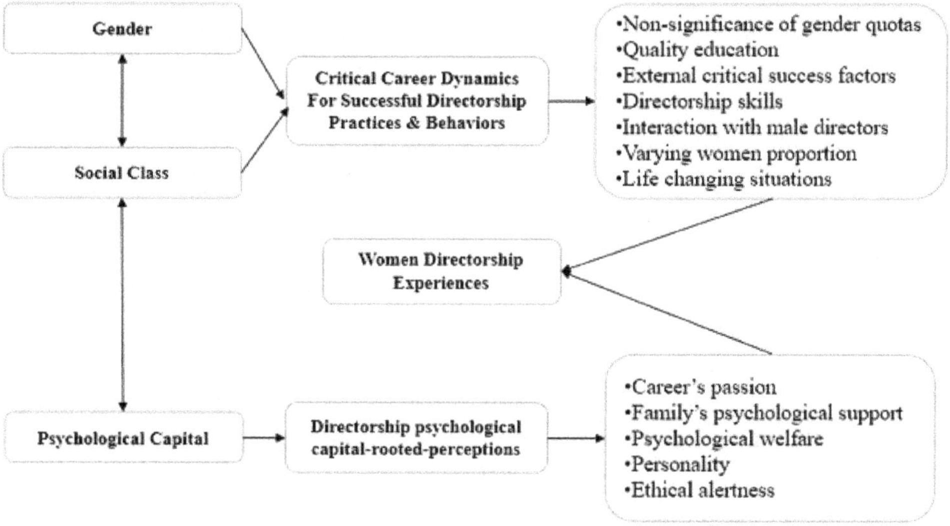

2. LITERATURE REVIEW

2.1 Study Context: Social Classes in Middle East

It is difficult to define the Middle East in terms of geography. However, scholars concur that the region from the southeast corner of Europe to the Indian Ocean, which includes the Muslim nations of Middle Asia (roughly the Amur Darya Valley or the Oxus River), is what is meant to be understood as the Middle East. Western Asia also refers to the Muslim nations of Asia, which are commonly referred to as the region known as the Near East and more precisely the Asian Continent. Following World War II, the US is credited with popularising the phrase "Middle East" (Ediyono et al., 2020). The Middle East has long been believed to be at the intersection of the Old World and Afro-Eurasia. As a result, the region is additionally referred to by a variety of titles, including "land of the seven seas" and "land of the birth of celestial religions." Because this is a nation with a long history of advanced civilisation, invasions—both internal and external—occur frequently in the area. New dialects, faiths, and races were introduced by the invaders. Because of this, an extensive collection of mosaics—a dynamic museum composed of many physical manifestations of cultural backgrounds, languages, faith systems and hierarchical classes rose (Ediyono et al., 2020). Within this hierarchical structure is the social class which describes the differences that exist in society according to social and economic position. Individuals belonging to the same socioeconomic class generally possess comparable wealth, levels of education, work types, and incomes. Social class is flexible, though, and most people concur that within the past 20 years, a social stratum has emerged with limited opportunities for working full-time (Thompson, 2022). Like in other parts of the world, social class in the Middle East is a more comprehensive notion that takes into account social and cultural aspects in addition to economic ones. It takes into account elements including social standing, education, and cultural value. Regional differences, religious identification, and tribal affinities can all have an impact on socioeconomic status in several Middle Eastern civilizations. A complex system of social classes might arise from the junction of several ethnicities. Marxists believe that the way people act varies depending on social class, with people in socialist economies having more altruistic views and capitalists trying to maximise their personal interests by exploiting the staff if required (Saif, 2011).

2.2 Diverse Directorship

Gender and class identities are jointly paramount to our self-concepts (Bullough et al., 2022), yet in academia the three aforementioned identities (gender, class and self) often viewed independently as the shaping aspect of individuals' experiences, in remoteness from other identity threads. Past directorship research on diversity often concentrates on single elements or aspects, fencing our understanding of the richness and depth of women individuals' directorship experiences (Brieger et al., 2019). Yet, debatably, directing the general public to perceive experiences from one-category perspective (e.g. gender) to the exclusion of the other (e.g. social class) is an invalid theorization of reality when belonging to both categories can be confounded in female individuals (Pullen & Vacchani, 2023). Such 'essentialism' classifies women directors' deep psychological capital, hearts, cognition, mindsets, characters and experiences with regards to single identity classifications (such as gender) without taking into consideration how other factors (such as broader cultural context, self-identities, and corporate norms) shape these. The aforementioned essentialist conventions constitute previously-discussed criticisms of gender universalism in gender directorship research (Reddy & Jadhav, 2019).

One potential remedy to essentialist issues is adopting an intersectional conceptual framework. Intersectionality refers to utilizing various category classifications and, in this article, the theoretical implications for diverse directorship. Intersectionality can be defined as the: 'idea that social identities such as race, class, and gender interact to form qualitatively different meanings and experiences' (Warner & Schmincke, 2008). The jargon is originally attributed to Crenshaw (1991), who highlighted the fact of the African American women's hiddenness stemmed from their social status in cultural and gender scholarship. As a result, lower-social-class women have been associated with categories that did not precisely mirror their capabilities, views and experiences. In the 32 years since Crenshaw's scholarly works, management scholars have increasingly embraced intersectionality to understand how various identity categories like social class, sexual orientation and culture shape women's directorship and employment experiences all over the world. Intersectional insights meld social, feminist and multiculturalist angles in order to understand females' directorship experiences from a more solid standpoint (Asad & Georgakakis, 2023). They focus on how all identity dimensions interrelate with each other for definitions and importance. Intersectionality hence can be related to "self-identity" as the basic "cell" forming the "gendered classed" organizational hierarchy (Clark, 2020). The interrelatedness between gender, class and psychological capital is often ignored in female directorship research [see Bell et al. (1990) and McIntosh (1992)] for exceptions]. Accordingly, this paper aims to contribute to the directorship literature by embracing an intersectional conceptual framework to explore how women from working class with typical local career background and privileged-defined women directors typically from western influenced backgrounds in combination may lead to distinct or common pathways towards women directorship experiences and trajectories.

2.3 Conceptualizing Intersectional Directorship Theories

Directorship and socio-demographic identities are diligently interrelated (Ubaradka et al., 2023). According to research by Volkan (2019) directors' social makeup relevant to their subordinates shaped their success and the degree to which they think they can enact their director identity. Other research suggests prototypical directors (typical or exemplary members of a group) are favored more and have stronger relationships with staff and colleagues. This boosts the probability that employees will follow requests, further strengthening director–follower relationships (Volkan, 2019). The directorship perceptions that staff hold of less-status category members may be less powerful since they do not so easily match the cognitive representations held by persons of these roles. For instance, misalignment between women stereotypical elements and the largely masculine nature at the top managerial levels of many firms may add to pervasive 'glass ceiling' repercussions witnessed by multiple female directors (Domínguez et al., 2019).

Despite the fact of females' non-proportional representation at the top signals to gender bias implications, directorship scholars can go beyond the 'counting' milestone, to directly assessing the universalist norms of diverse directorship studies (Nayak, 2022). Recent literature increasingly critiques the traditional treatment of "MENA women" as a monolith, highlighting that elite networks and high socioeconomic status heavily skew board representation, while early-career "broken rungs" cause severe talent attrition among lower-class women. Furthermore, with the surging emphasis on ESG compliance and corporate sustainability across GCC states, contemporary research is intensely debating whether female board appointments serve as authentic drivers of intellectual capital or mere progressive optics. Our study directly advances these debates by using longitudinal, intersectional data to prove how social class drastically alters a woman's directorship journey and psychological coping mechanisms, thereby answering the regional call to dismantle superficial "men vs. women" metrics in Arab management research.

This paper seeks to explore how underprivileged women directors' respondents' retrospect their own directorship experiences. It is an exploratory research of an under-examined sample's directorship insights, targeting the contribution of developing more conclusive theories of diverse directorship for the corporate and governmental institutions. The research was conducted with a constructivism–interpretivism approach, in which knowledge is co-developed and no one known 'truth' targeted. A qualitative methodology constituting interviews was used with working class, high social class women in directorship positions. This will build upon and add to the current body of knowledge in women diversity and gendered leadership literature, with extra focus on information of female directorships with practical implications for a flourishing diverse directorship and enacting various directorship styles.

While institutional theorists argue that female board representation linearly boosts corporate ESG compliance and intellectual capital across the GCC, critical governance scholars expose a harsher reality: token appointments often serve purely as progressive optics to satisfy state mandates. Our research directly intervenes in this tension. By leveraging longitudinal data, we demonstrate whether a female director's Psychological Capital (PsyCap) allows her to authentically drive strategic governance, or if intersecting socio-economic vulnerabilities reduce her presence to compliance tokenism. A fierce contradiction exists between neo-liberal corporate narratives in the MENA region—which champion meritocracy and individualized resilience (PsyCap)—and the deeply entrenched structural patriarchy analyzed by post-colonial feminists. Our study challenges the Western-centric, neo-liberal assumption that individual psychological resources alone can overcome institutional barriers. By introducing an intersectional lens, we highlight the contradiction that while elite, highly networked women may successfully navigate the corporate ladder, lower-class women face an entirely different institutional reality where PsyCap is systematically depleted by localized structural hurdles rather than rewarded by merit.

This paper discusses how interrelated social, gender and self-identities influenced Middle Eastern privileged and working-class women's enactment and construction of director identities. An intersectional conceptual framework permitted interpretation of working class and bourgeoisie identities emerging from the parallel positioning of directorship with lower-status gender and self-perceived identities. Intersectionality also drew the attention towards possible western-influenced multi-cultural (or cultural relative) versus patriotic local-dominated (or ethnocentric) identities that arouse from data collection.

3. RESEARCH DESIGN

3.1 Participants

A varied group of 20 women directors participated (Egyptian, Moroccan, Emirati, Omani and Saudi), 10 of privileged social class with Western shaped background, and 10 of working class with local background. Participants were aged between 25 and 60, with educational qualifications ranging from bachelor's to master's degrees and marital status spanning from being married to being divorced or widowed. They self-defined themselves as women leaders in their local society or corporate sector, or as entrepreneurs working in a directorship role. Because of the study's exploratory nature, female directors from varied business disciplines were targeted. Participants included female directors in multiple fields such as: business, engineering, law and mental health. This 'maximum variation' sampling technique (a type of purposeful sampling) is suitable for capturing and describing central themes that cut across a wide group of participants (Patton, 1990). Their international experience was related to a number of global economic centers in the world, like: France, Australia, UAE, Switzerland, Spain, Australia, UK and USA. This 'maximum variation' sampling technique (one kind of purposeful sampling) is appropriate for picking up and depicting main themes that run across a diverse group of interviewees.

3.2 Research Procedures

Semi-structured interview guides were used to explore multiple dimensions and dynamics of identity and directorship. The guide involved a number of open questions based on our focus areas of theoretical interest. In specific, interviewees were asked questions around three key areas: (1) their personal conceptions of directorship related to their mindset, psychological capital and hearts; (2) the relationship between their social (i.e. gender/social class) and director identities and (3) their career journey and quota perceptions to gender directorships, including when they first discovered their proclivities towards assuming leader and director positions and driving and restraining factors in this journey.

The main aim of this kind of study was to offer deep contextualized information of this sample. In keeping with the paper's exploratory nature and its constructivist– interpretivism orientation, questions were asked to initiate deliberations and open further pathways towards quality thought and followed up with extensive investigation and a 2nd round of interviews six months after the first round. This enabled rich varied answers rather than a typical, traditional list. Ethics were taken into consideration by complying to the "British Educational Research Association" guidance. Pseudonyms were used as a way to upkeep anonymity to the interviewees. All interviews were given the opportunity of opting out of our research during and after their interview participation.

Invitations for the international women directors in our research on 'identity and directorship' were distributed via email to their office managers or themselves directly. Females who expressed interest were informed of a guaranteed anonymous response. In addition, 1 participant from Morocco was interviewed through snowball sampling, having recruited from another director who participated in the study.

The first author allocated respondents to different interview sessions either face-to-face or via Zoom based on their preferred timings and dates. In the first round of interviews, five interview sessions were conducted face-to-face in Muscat in Oman and 15 sessions were conducted online. All second-round interviews were conducted online. In each round, interviewees were classified as originating from either privileged or working social classes. There were 10 women per each social class.

There were some differences in the age composition across the geographical regions represented. In the Gulf Cooperation Council (GCC) countries (participants from UAE, Oman and Saudi Arabia), most participants (90%) were less than 35 years, comprising primarily bourgeoisie social class (who primarily is part of a family business or has a C-suit executive as a first line relative). Outside GCC (Egypt and Morocco), leadership experiences were gleaned from more self-made backgrounds and older age groups. These demographics reflect the extra hard work accumulated and needed outside the wealthy GCC region to ascend the career ladder rather than relying only on powerful tribe power present in Saudi Arabia, Oman and UAE.

Each interview session lasted from 40 minutes to 90 minutes. Considering interview time restrictions, the first author utilized social and interviewing skills and open, probing questioning style to make sure all interviewees were fully involved and truly represent reality in the discussion. Finally, all interviewees were invited to communicate with the first author if they think they had more details to share after the interview session.

After six months, a second and final interview round was conducted with 10 participants for further in-depth examination and validation of original findings.

These women were approached via the same business networking connections of the first author. It was clarified to them that a research project was being undertaken on intersectional identity and directorship on a regional scale. Interviews took place face-to-face in private offices or via online platforms, like: Microsoft Teams and Zoom. The second-round interviews lasted about half an hour.

Table 1. Participants Profile

Social Class	**Number**	**Percentage**
Social Class with western shaped background	10	50 per cent
Working Class with local background	10	50 per cent
First Round of Interviews		
Face to Face Interviews	5	25 per cent
Online Interviews	15	75 per cent
Total	20	100 per cent
Second Round of Interviews		
Online	10	100 per cent
Total	10	100 per cent

3.3 Thematic Analysis

Interview answers were recorded and fully transcribed. Data were then interpreted thematically via NVivo analysis, in pursuit of clarifying and identifying the meanings and structures of the answers given by the interviewees. Despite it might be inferred that women directors stemming from working classes would reveal certain hurdles and obstacles in enacting needful directorship behaviors, which is in lines with the exploratory and constructivist orientation. Instead, the objective was to ground results in the information given by the interviewees. The research question directing our study was, 'How do psychological capital, social class and gender identities shape privileged and working-class women's directorship on a regional level?'.

To ensure a transparent thematic analysis, the study followed a systematic coding procedure within NVivo, beginning with a hybrid deductive and inductive approach to codebook development based on the research questions and initial data immersion. Transcripts were uploaded to NVivo, where primary codes were meticulously assigned to raw text segments and iteratively refined through continuous comparison to ensure conceptual clarity. These codes were then clustered into broader, hierarchically organized themes that directly captured the core patterns of the participants' experiences. Quality assurance was rigorously maintained throughout this process by establishing an audit trail of all coding decisions, conducting peer debriefing sessions, and calculating inter-coder reliability to guarantee analytical consistency, trustworthiness, and minimization of researcher bias.

Interpretation and coding were performed in a constant and iterative comparative manner. The first author started with open coding (classifying and breaking down). At this point, noticeable and meaningful insights regarding the intersectionality of directorship and other social aspects were coded straightforward from the data collected. Relationships between codes were taken into consideration and classified into higher order themes. It is noteworthy to mention that the first author embraced 'intersectional sensibilities' (Crenshaw, 1991) while analyzing the interviewees' quotes. This means considering when and how social class, gender and inner psychological capital and any other identities became relevant in shaping the interviewees' experiences of directorship.

Table 2. Percentage of Board Seats Held by Women

Country	Percentage of Board Seats Held by Women	Percentage Change (2018)
Egypt	10.0 percent	NA
Morocco	8.7 percent	3.3 per cent
Saudi Arabia	1.7 percent	1.0 per cent
UAE	5.3 percent	1.6 per cent
Oman	2.3 percent	N/A

Egypt

Quotas empowered women to exhibit their qualities and skills by opening doors for them. Additionally, voluntary goals rather than mandated quotas would probably be more effective in achieving company-wide gender equality. Establishing goals would assist in levelling the playing field and grant women the same opportunities as their male counterparts. The women will acquire knowledge and experience as they advance through the levels of the organization, preparing them for promotion to board roles as in the International Finance Corporation (IFC).

Morocco

Although it did not garner much notice, the change that the Moroccan Parliament approved was a significant step towards closing the disparity between men and women in the nation. In order to encourage equitable representation of men and women in business governance organizations, a new revised law on publicly traded companies was implemented (law 19.20 amending and completing laws 17-95 linked to publicly limited organizations). It established required gender quotas for public company boards, with a goal of not less than 30 per cent female representation by 2024 and 40 per cent by 2027 (Mouline et al, 2022).

Saudi Arabia

Gender quotas are required for two primary reasons, preferably in the short term. One is attempting to rectify and dissuade current biases and stereotypes about women. The second objective is to interpret and acknowledge the crucial and vital role that women can play in a nation's political, economic, and social growth. One could not ensure equitable representation if every official, legislator, and corporation were composed of men. Recognizing that gender quotas will be ineffective if they persist in reflecting and exacerbating the pay gap between men and women is also essential.

United Arab Emirates (UAE)

It is now required that UAE Public Joint Stock Companies (PJSCs) listed on the Dubai Financial Market (DFM) or the Abu Dhabi Securities Exchange (ADX) possess a minimum of one female board of directors as of March 14, 2021. This comes after the Securities and Commodities Authority (SCA) of the UAE announced a number of judgements during its board conference.

4. RESEARCH FINDINGS

Analyses revealed two broad areas in which gender, social class and other identities became salient in the women's directorship reflections. These were directorship psychological capital-rooted-perceptions and the career dynamics through which they enacted directorship practices and behaviors.

4.1 First Area: Career Dynamics Critical for Successful Directorship Practices and Behaviors

Career dynamics critical for successful directorship practices and behaviors encompass the strategic accumulation of diverse professional experiences, continuous leadership development, and the intentional navigation of socio-cultural networks. Successful directors rely on these shifting career trajectories to build strong human capital, shape their executive identities, and refine essential board behaviors such as strategic vision, emotional intelligence, and stakeholder engagement. Rather than following a single linear path, navigating these dynamics effectively allows aspiring leaders to transition successfully from executive management into active governance, directly correlating positive career progression with improved corporate oversight and long-term organizational success.

One obvious pathway towards women directorship is to get appointed through gender quotas. That is why, 'The interview guide included questions on quota perceptions because quotas are a recognized pathway to board representation. The majority of female board directors interviewed were against gender quotas. They preferred to get a directorship position because of their competence, qualifications and reputations rather than being imposed on the board table. Yet, most of them also claimed that it can be a quick strategy to boost number of females on board tables.

For example, K.J. from Morocco revealed: "*I am convinced that the aim of gender quota is to promote diversity and create equal; equal opportunities for women. But I am not proud of it because it means we are in the board because we have to fulfill a quota and not because we are able to do it and it is normal to be there.*"

Indeed, the interviewees from quota countries (Egypt, UAE and Morocco) have revealed that the quota did not influence much their career trajectories simply because the quota legislations were recently introduced (the earliest was introduced in UAE in 2021). They also added that because of the absence of the non-quotas in the past and the typical cultural stereotypes that women are less qualified than men, they were challenged and motivated to put double the effort to reach their current board positions, something that would not have been done in the presence of a quota.

In this regard, A.L. from Egypt whereby it is obligatory for companies to appoint 2 women directors at least said: "*I do not think quotas have impacted my career personally. Yet, it might in the future because I think I have built up a certain experience and reputation that allows me to stand on my own merit.*"

M.H. opinion was very similar: "*So the number of female ministers in the government or the number of female directors on the board, it gets implemented in a very naive way. So I generally feel very negative about quotas, but I have to admit that eventually, they do work. Because even if the implementation starts off by just needing to tick the box, it does raise awareness about the subject. And eventually, you try to find qualified members who would really do a good job, whether they are male or female*"

Typical career challenges faced by directors especially coming from working class included: building up business networks which are typically dominated by men, feelings of awareness to speak up own mind amid a table domineered by males, family commitments, political behavior and jealousy behaviors displayed by both men and women, and superior behavior displayed sometimes by their male counterparts in boardroom. The typical advantages were: boosted confidence, financial security, increased social capital, developed leadership skills and talent, and continuous self-assessment.

It is also noteworthy to mention here that women directors who come from high social class (those who are directors because of their family background) have emphasized that they did not face any sort of significant challenges to become a woman director.

Most of the interviewees also claimed that a gender board quota is not a matter of interest internally amongst employees. The royalty B.A. from Oman claimed that: "*We don't care. We care about our clients and who we are getting and how many clients*".

Additionally, the majority of the interviewees said that the ideal women director's proportion is never a fixed percentage. It depends eventually on the business situation at hand, company's characteristics, company's needs, qualifications and managerial talent of woman director herself who should match the company's idiosyncrasies. One may hire one hundred women directors, but if they are not matching the company's needs and idiosyncrasies, they will be useless. Royalty B.A. said: "*I think we should not put a percentage. We should put who is working, who is giving back, who is doing it. I mean it is about your work*".

As for being the sole woman director, feelings ranged from being normal (that is no difference between being amid men directors and women directors) to feelings of challenge to prove herself to feelings of awkwardness and anxiety to get challenged by men directors especially during debates and disputes. Yet, women directors coming from high social classes have expressed fewer negative feelings to be the sole woman in boardroom compared to women directors coming from professional and working classes.

Women directors from bourgeoisie social classes revealed no considerable challenges in their careers. Women directors coming from working and professional social classes have emphasized the significant policies and strategies adopted by their governments to enhance women conditions in recent years. Yet, the first author believes that non-openness to answer question related to challenges can be rooted to the norms or values of not criticizing any issue related to the country's political decisions or actions.

While some women directors have explicitly revealed that it is much easier to become a woman director in the West given the strong gender egalitarianism values there, the others (especially with strong multicultural exposure!) have expressed that there is no significant gap between efforts exerted and possible challenges faced by a typical woman director in the west versus the Middle East. One final group of women directors did not have a multicultural exposure and hence refrained from answering this question.

S.F. said: "*Surprisingly, because I dealt with a lot of multinational banks and institutions in Egypt, women are especially in the banking sector, they are given a lot of positions more than women in France, for example, whether they are directors, whether they are in managerial positions in banks. So we cannot claim that women are not heard or are not given good positions. And you should, I mean, definitely, I'm not sure whether when you were living in Egypt, but you could see even in the president and the parliament and how he really supported women in the, in even the cabinet in the parliament, in the ministries*".

As for life changing situations that enthused the women directors' interest towards directorship and leadership positions, these ranged from giving a theater play at school, to an education opportunity in the West, to a foreign work assignment, to a mentor behavior that encouraged them to give their best, to loss of a husband or father or moving from home country to a foreign country as a new domicile or receiving a lifetime internship.

For instance, R.M. told us about the incidence of getting divorced and how did this influence her pathway towards a directorship: "*what changed my life also is I divorced, all right? So I had to take care of myself. I had to take care of my children. This was also one of the things that changed me from a very spoiled shy child to a strong woman. It was the only way I could survive is to show men that I'm as strong as they are and to continue because it's not easy being a mother. It's not easy being a mother to five children, divorced, all right, with single-handed. And yet you are the mother, you are the boss. You take all the decisions for yourself and your family*".

Moreover, the majority of interviewees coming from working or professional social classes emphasized confidence, hard work and reputation. As for the women directors coming from upper class, they stressed the importance of their family background in securing a seat on board. In addition, even other companies may invite them to their own boards to get this security and sense of power and influence of such women's families, for example: the social power of a tribe.

R.Z. from a very privileged social class in Oman said: "*We come from a tribal mentality, and this Western approach is relatively new. While I am a third-generation individual, in the West, they may be ten or twelve generations deep into this mindset. For us, it's still relatively new. It's a tribal mentality, and even though we are educated, this mentality persists. You need to know who's who, who their parents are, and what their family history is to establish trust and credibility*".

More importantly, women from professional backgrounds have mentioned that they received immense support from their work mentor (the "superman" or "hero" typically during early career years), family and husband. As for women directors from high social classes, they emphasized very much family including husband.

Interestingly, it was claimed that as long as a woman director is the boss, they receive no discrimination, harm or any negative feelings from their male subordinates. *This is contrary to the situation when men are colleagues or superiors on boards. I believe that this may root back to the high scores of power distance as a cultural value in the Middle East. R. Z. said.*

Most interviewees have expressed that their personalities and work styles have evolved considerably across the years. Most of them have told us that they are initially assertive by nature to the degree that they can become aggressive and confrontational many times. Yet, this has changed by experience and across time. They used to learn diplmacy skills, political skills and how to handle a conflict in a wise manner such that they reach out a win-win outcome.

As for developing strong networking connections in the industry, answers by working class and bourgeoisie directors were largely the same. A very difficult experience was faced by both types of directors primarily because of social norms in the Middle East that prevent a woman from having friendships with men or sipping coffee cup with them in a café to finding an indifference between striking friendships and social connections between men and women. *The relatively indifference attitude was more prevalent amongst directors with stronger multicultural exposure compared to women directors with local experience only.*

The majority of interviewees have also expressed they planned very carefully for their careers before reaching to where they are now. N.T from Saudi Arabia said: *"I make sure that I've read all the documents and prepare for topics that might require input from my team. Sometimes I need to check with my team, and I might need to check with teams in the companies that are submitting specific work. I ensure that I'm well-prepared and that the agenda is sufficiently prepared. These are routine expectations of a board member".*

While women directors with only-local exposure found our questions about internationalization importance as irrelevant, the women directors with past international experience have applauded the international expertise they witnessed and have emphasized its considerable value adding impact on shaping their ambitious, flexible and extrovert personalities and work styles and quality. Some of them also reported that some key benefits were improved English language proficiency and enhanced communication skills.

Moreover, women directors from high social classes revealed they were appointed actually on the board tables because of their family power which the company typically waits to benefit from. This may signal to the significance of nepotism calculations. As for directors coming from working classes, they were selected primarily because of their merit and reputation amid celebrations by investors and their male colleagues.

Women directors who built themselves or are coming from professional classes have emphasized the *interrelatedness* of their networks that eventually they cannot contribute their social capital and the benefits they get from it to one source only. It is typically a combination of university colleagues, business associations, friends, colleagues, mangers, and family. Yet, again the women directors from high level background have emphasized that family is the most important source of networking and that people deal with them on the basis of their line of blood.

The vast majority have revealed that their ties with men colleagues are very healthy with a minority of women directors who have claimed that it becomes very much stressful during debates and disputes. *The surprising finding here is that women directors coming from high social class have revealed more stress feelings compared to women directors from professional classes. This may signal to the fact that women directors who are selected because of their merit not because of their families may have stronger social skills to cope and handle with stressful situations that women directors coming from family background.*

All women directors have emphasized they prepare very well before board meetings and may sometimes ask for extra materials for clarification to be able to do their homework before entering the boardroom and engage in discussions. They are very detail oriented. The most featured critical success factors to reach directorship positions were: mastering knowledge related to the field, confidence, and communication skills to be able to express her mind and defend her argument in persuasive way and more importantly to be able to debate with men in case of conflict of opinion.

Not all women directors interviewed hold multiple directorships. However, the ones who do from working class have revealed that it stimulated a sort of challenge feelings to prove themselves on all boards. This is first to preserve their reputation in the market and second not to let down those who nominated them across boards. For women coming from high social classes, they serve on one board only. Figure 2 illustrates the first and second order codes related to career dynamic.

Figure 2. **First and second order codes related to career dynamics**

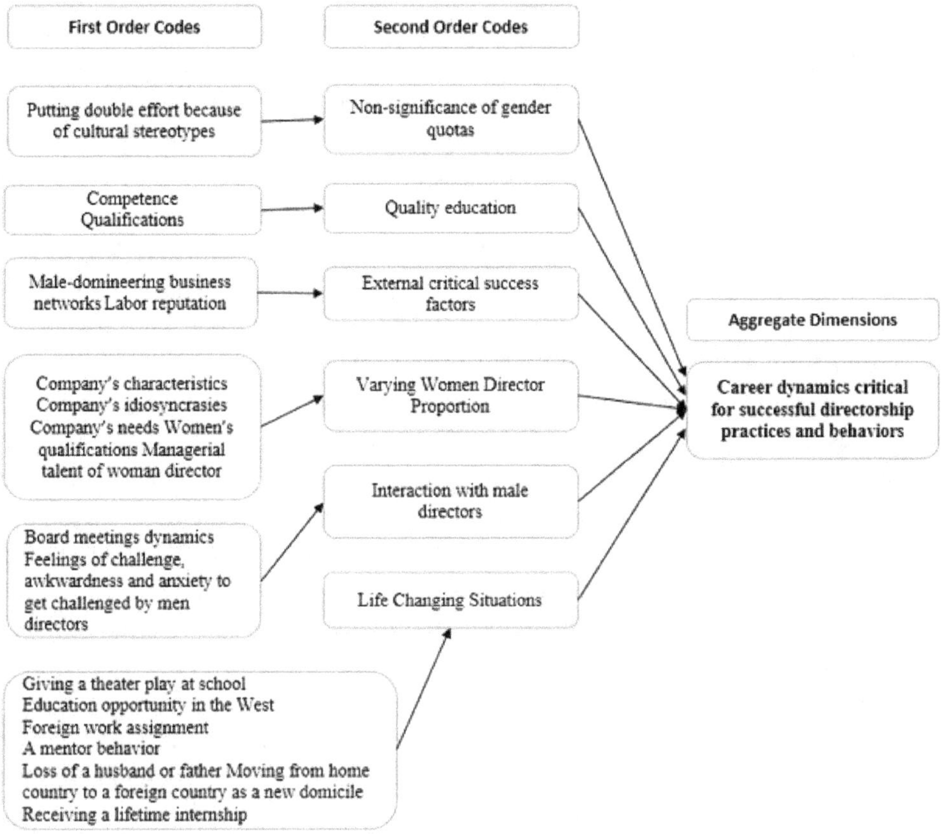

4.2 The Second Area: Directorship Psychological Capital-Rooted-Perceptions

Most women directors interviewed have expressed that they are nowhere close to a "typical" woman in their societies and if they would have been so, they would never have reached to their current level of success. They are more confrontational, achievement oriented and career ambitious compared a typical woman.

N.S. said: "*I don't know what's the typical woman in Egypt or Germany, for example, or Switzerland, the country. I'm just me. And everyone has very different experiences. And now I'm 60, and the way I am now has been influenced by, first of all, my family history, my work, my colleagues, my mentors. So, I can't tell you how typical I am or not. So, I don't want to be different, but I'm just saying, I don't know what exactly a typical woman is. I mean, if a typical woman is to stay at home, mom, I'm not a typical woman*".

One exception was N.J. who serves as a director at Abu Dhabi ports: she revealed that one Emirati senior royalty is her role model that acts as an inspirational model to learn from. But she also added that she is nowhere close to her greatness.

Moreover, most women directors have expressed high difficulty in balancing between home and work demands, especially during early years of their kids. M.H. shared with us here experience by saying: "*Because it does remain a challenge to balance family, motherhood, and a full-blown career. House chores, I have a very supportive husband. But despite that, house chores are not equally split. Men, whatever we do, will not be the ones who will be bearing children. They will not be the ones nursing children. They will not be the ones who might have difficult pregnancies that might require them to lie on their back for nine months, for example* ".

The vast majority, being women from professional or high social classes, have emphasized the importance of the family's role in helping them grow. Sources of power that a family typically gives include: sense of security, encouragement to pursue education and pushing the ambition boundaries of their daughters fueled by the desire that they want them a better version of themselves. *This may have roots in the cultures of the Middle East which overemphasizes the importance of family ties and collectivism.*

N.J talked about the outstanding support her father gave her: *"He used to be an army person working for UAE Army. And he is a person who does not differentiate between women and men, by the way. He used to take us every summer into our farm and he asked everyone to participate by hand because he felt like this is yours and you need really to show. And he's one of the biggest supports for me."*

As for the first situation that developed their current critical thinking and questioning mindset, these mainly revolved around a novel idea that erupted during childhood, being: a hobby, an activity, task or innovation on a family and friend's scale. Later on, this was typically translated into proclivities towards curiosity, questioning mindset, the urge to critically think issues and ways of doing things on boards.

In addition, the most frequently mentioned traits necessary to excel in directorship positions were reported to be confidence, hardworking and non-traditionalism. Figure 3 illustrates the Career ambition and passion related to psychological capital.

Figure 3. **Career ambition and passion related to psychological capital**

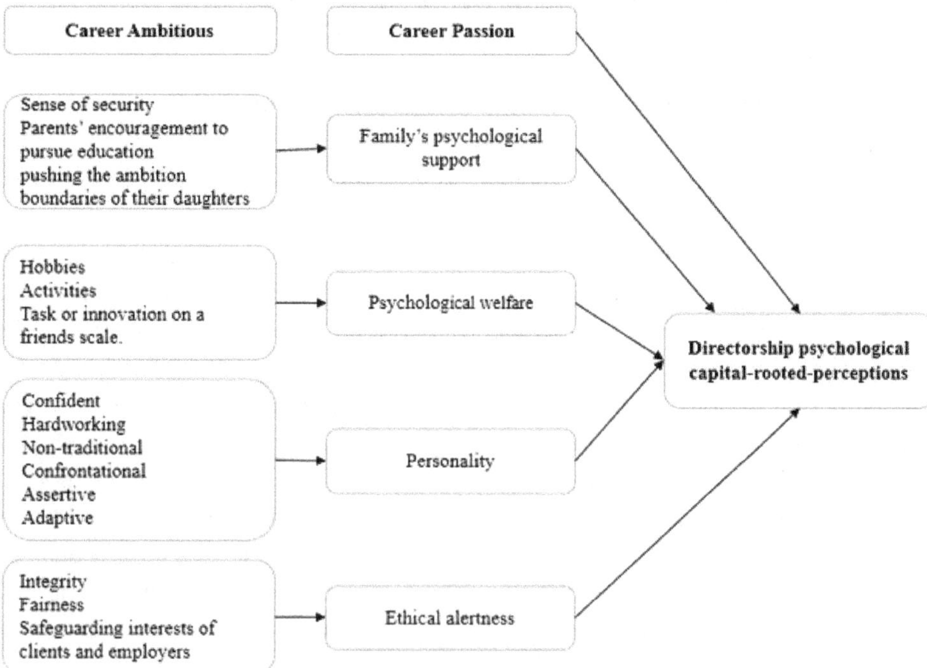

Finally, the top three ethical values reported were integrity, fairness and safeguarding interests of clients and employers. The majority of interviewees attributed these values to Islam roots in their cultures which emphasized these norms and enshrined them as red lines.

A.I. from Oman said: *"We have a comprehensive values system in Oman, and I'm striving to instill the same Islamic values in my new generations. It's ultimately about human values".*

5. DISCUSSION

This qualitative research embraced an intersectional perspective to study the women directors' experiences of two different social classes. An intersectional perspective, which adopts that multiple social identities may work differently to shape women directors' experiences, revealed how social class, psychological capital and social class identities played out in Middle Eastern women directors from upper and working social classes and how in return these have shaped their directorship constructions and execution of women leadership in board rooms.

Past literature critiques the limited consideration of intersectionality in the significant area of gendered corporate governance (Asad & Georgakakis, 2023). Women directors from bourgeoisie social class and multi-cultural exposure in the West reflected contemporary directorship models and leadership definitions involving power of tribe importance, nepotism calculations, ease of networking, less negative feelings, and less faced obstacles, yet a smaller number of board directorships. In contrast, women directors from working class background and more local career background have emphasized the importance of merit and hard work, labor market reputation, and importance of work mentor in defining effective women directorship models using primarily demographic-cultural lenses. With regards to shrining women director identities, both women directors from upper and working classes described some common critical success factors to enacting effective women directorship experiences barriers linked to: (1) their family identity, (2) cultural identity in that they do not resemble a" typical women" in their own communities, (3) ethical alertness and (4) their personal traits with a focus on confidence and non- traditionalism. This orientation parallels both situational leadership and traits leadership models. The director or leader is situation-centric with some traits that distinguish him/her from "average" or "non-leader" people, like: optimism, confidence and integrity (Zaccaro et al., 2018).

However, the working-class directors' heightened attention to merit and qualifications suggests that level 5 leadership is operationalized as well. That is, women directors emphasize level 1 of 5 levels of leadership by being reliable and committed on the individual level before leading groups, departments and even societies at more advanced levels of leadership (Sengupta, 2021). At the core of level 5 leadership lie ethical values and norms in the process of leading individuals and groups. This conceptualization of directorship also strongly matches with the authentic leadership theories especially when there is a fit between the director's career dynamics (external force) and psychological capital (internal force). Authentic leadership by Avolio and Gardner (2005) refers to increasing one's self-awareness, controlling their behavior and being as a positive model, leaders will foster authenticity amongst followers. Authenticity means achieving consistency between one's internal feelings and thoughts and one's external actions and decisions. From this stance, attention can be drawn to any possible misalignments between career dynamics and psychological capital considerations and how directors from different social closes can manage them differently.

This research advances theory by shifting psychological capital (PsyCap) from an individual trait to a context-dependent, intersectional phenomenon. By examining MENA women's directorships longitudinally, the study differs from Western-centric assumptions in organizational behavior, demonstrating that PsyCap resources (hope, efficacy, resilience, and optimism) are not static but fluctuate based on intersecting gender and social class structures over time. It introduces a dynamic framework showing how cultural and structural barriers either deplete or catalyze psychological resources, providing a blueprint for future researchers to move away from static, single-axis diversity studies. Furthermore, it opens new research directions by prompting scholars to investigate how systemic inequality shapes psychological coping mechanisms in other emerging economies and non-Western corporate governance models.

5.1 Research Limitations

Our research was qualitative exploratory of an under-examined sample, undertaken with a constructivist–interpretivism approach. The degree to which the results can be generalized to the wider population are hence restricted. Indeed, the interviewees were self-defined as directors. While no standardized proxy measure of director effectiveness was adopted, the research targeted examining self-conceptions of directorship instead of validating against directorship outcomes. Another limitation is that because of the purposeful (not random) sampling method selected, the results could include sampling bias. We purposefully divided the sample into two equal groups of 10 per each type of social class: 10 participants per social group in the first round of in interviews and 5 participants per social class in the second round. More importantly, the absence of data triangulation and depending largely on interviews may have limited quality thought regarding how and which other identity intersections shaped directorship identity and execution for these Middle Eastern women.

Despite the design of mixed "demographic" profile of interviewees which allowed rich data on regional experiences of directorships in this sample, it limited the opportunity to interpret answers by social class and/or cultural sub-groups. Furthermore, our participants were recruited from a diverse range of economic sectors and accordingly we cannot infer on how every associated distinctive organizational context, sectors and multiple professions recall a certain type of directorship practice. Comparative data analysis across diverse industrial sectors and with a multitude of professional classifications could offer further interesting understanding into the themes that arouse from this research.

To address these limitations, future research should transition from exploratory qualitative inquiry to larger-scale quantitative or mixed-methods designs, utilizing random or stratified sampling to minimize bias and enhance the generalizability of the findings across wider populations. Prospective studies are encouraged to introduce objective proxy measures of board performance to validate how these self-conceptions of directorship correlate with actual corporate outcomes. Furthermore, researchers can implement data triangulation—such as combining interviews with behavioral observations or 360-degree feedback—and apply a deeper intersectional lens to examine how variables like age, industry, and education interact with social class to shape directorship execution. Finally, cross-cultural comparative studies and longitudinal tracking would help determine the regional specificity and long-term evolution of these identity dynamics among Middle Eastern female leaders.

5.2 Practical Implications

Although this research has some limitations, it offers a myriad of practical implications for organizations and academics. It grounds its results on the differing social group's real experiences of directorship. One possible implication is that there may be merit in customizing directors' development programs not just to gender, but potentially for different social classes as one important dimension. These will pave the way towards meaningful identity spaces for females to reveal how gender, social class, and cultural intersections may shape career progression dynamics, directorship norms and actions. The apparent borders between the privileged and working-class women's experiences and conceptions of what constitutes effective directorship implies there is a room for women of multiple backgrounds to participate in collaborative dialogue and collectively retrospect on their self-strengths to debate and change current stubborn universalist women leadership assumptions.

To elevate this research into an impactful, multi-dimensional toolkit for both academia and industry, the longitudinal, multi-cultural findings have been explained as actionable blueprints for systemic corporate and regulatory change across the MENA region. In terms of policy and governance, we used the intersectional data on gender and social class to help policymakers design smarter, nuanced board diversity mandates and regional ESG disclosure frameworks that move past binary gender metrics and align with national economic visions. For corporate practice, the insights on Psychological Capital into concrete human resource strategies have been translated by redesigning executive recruitment matrices to evaluate psychological resilience over elitist socioeconomic networks, implementing cross-cultural leadership training, and developing customized corporate sponsorship pipelines that actively dismantle the unique structural barriers faced by lower-class women.

6. CONCLUSION

This research showed how identity intersections operationalize in working class and privileged Middle Eastern female directors' experiences on a regional scale and longitudinally. Identities and dynamics emerged from of social class, cultural, gender, and religion had considerable effects on how the women related to 'directorship'. The primary contribution of this research was the embracing of intersectional identities to report the females' significant variation in conceptualizing and practicing directorship task and duties. Compared to privileged women directors, women from working class classes showed greater and more rational links between psychological capital, gender and social identities, and involved more challenging obstacles to execute their director identities across a variety of economic sectors of employment in the Middle East. This exploratory research has suggested many avenues for future research on the nuances and idiosyncrasies of interrelated identities in under-examined categories.

REFERENCES

Abed, A., Al-Najjar, B., & Salama, A. (2025). Breaking down barriers: How board composition drives sustainability in GCC countries. *International Journal of Human Resource Management, 36*(4), 513–547. DOI: 10.1080/09585192.2025.2452971

Asad, S., & Georgakakis, D. 2023. Diversity on corporate boards and shareholder activism: an intersectionality approach. In *Research Handbook on Diversity and Corporate Governance* (pp. 113-123). Camberly: Edward Elgar Publishing. https://doi.org/DOI: 10.4337/9781800377783.00019

Avolio, B. J., & Gardner, W. L. (2005). Authentic leadership development: Getting to the root of positive forms of leadership. *The Leadership Quarterly, 16*(3), 315–338. DOI: 10.1016/j.leaqua.2005.03.001

Badghish, S., Ali, I., Ali, M., Yaqub, M. Z., & Dhir, A. 2023. How socio-cultural transition helps to improve entrepreneurial intentions among women? *Journal of Intellectual Capital, 24*(4), 900-928. https://doi.org/DOI: 10.1108/JIC-06-2021-0158

Basuthakur, Y. 2022. Battle of the Classes. Social Class and Work Status in Determining Women Director Appointments. In *Academy of Management Proceedings*, No. 1, p. 12511. https://doi.org/DOI: 10.5465/AMBPP.2022.12511abstract

Bell, El. (1990). The bicultural life experience of career-oriented black women. *Journal of Organizational Behavior, 11*(6), 459–477. DOI: 10.1002/job.4030110607

Birindelli, G., Iannuzzi, A. P., & Savioli, M. (2019). The impact of women leaders on environmental performance: Evidence on gender diversity in banks. *Corporate Social Responsibility and Environmental Management, 26*(6), 1485–1499. DOI: 10.1002/csr.1762

Brieger, S. A., Francoeur, C., Welzel, C., & Ben-Amar, W. 2019. Empowering women: The role of emancipative forces in board gender diversity. *Journal of Business Ethics, 155*, 495-511. https://doi.org/DOI: 10.1007/s10551-017-3489-3

Bullough, A., Guelich, U., Manolova, T. S., & Schjoedt, L. 2022. Women's entrepreneurship and culture: gender role expectations and identities, societal culture, and the entrepreneurial environment. *Small Business Economics, 58*(2), 985-996. https://doi.org/DOI: 10.1007/s11187-020-00429-6

Clark, A. W. 2020. A Moment Defined: Corporate Board Composition and Intersectionality, the Broadening Conceptualization of Gender-only to Gender and Race (Doctoral dissertation).

Crenshaw, K. (1991). Mapping the margins: Intersectionality, identity politics, and violence against women of color. *Stanford Law Review*, *43*(6), 1241–1299. DOI: 10.2307/1229039

Delloitte (2 February 2022). Progress at a snail's pace Women in the boardroom: A global perspective. (7th Edition). file:///C:/Users/Prachi%20Avinashi/Downloads/gx-women-in-the-boardroom-seventh-edition.pdf

Domínguez, M. B., Rivo-López, E., & Villanueva-Villar, M. 2019. 'The glass ceiling'. *Organizational Dynamics, 48*, 100706. https://doi.org/DOI: 10.1016/j.orgdyn.2019.02.008

Dorsaf, B. (2025). Breaking glass ceilings or boardroom gridlock? Gender, independence and the new rules of MENA banking resilience. *Journal of Economic Studies (Glasgow, Scotland)*, •••, 1–21. DOI: 10.1108/JES-06-2025-0440

Ediyono, S., Istadiyantha, I., Farhah, E., Malik, A., & Jazuli, A. (2020, October). The Study of Socio-Cultural Changes in the Middle Eastern Community's Thoughts. In *Proceedings of the First International Conference on Communication, Language, Literature, and Culture, ICCoLLiC 2020,* 8-9 September 2020, Surakarta, Central Java, Indonesia. https://doi.org/DOI: 10.4108/eai.8-9-2020.2301440

El Jadidi, J., Arsi, S., & Ghoneim, H. (2020). Struggles to break the corporate board ceiling: the case of women in North Africa. In *Struggles and Successes in the Pursuit of Sustainable Development* (pp. 123–138). Routledge., DOI: 10.4324/9781351140560-14

Farah, B., Elias, R., Aguilera, R., & Abi Saad, E. (2021). Corporate governance in the Middle East and North Africa: A systematic review of current trends and opportunities for future research. *Corporate Governance*, *29*(6), 630–660. DOI: 10.1111/corg.12377

IFC. Women on Board in Egypt. https://documents1.worldbank.org/curated/en/612601567750997033/pdf/Women-on-Board-in-Egypt-How-Gender-Diverse-Boards-Bring-Value-to-Egyptian-Companies.pdf

Keddie, N. R. (2012). *Women in the Middle East: past and present* (1st ed.). Princeton University Press., DOI: 10.2307/j.cttq94c5

Khan, S. (2023, May 05). '"Women vastly underrepresented in region's corporate boardrooms, report says". *The National News: UAE Edition.* https://www.thenationalnews.com/business/2023/05/05/women-vastly-underrepresented-in-menat-region-corporate-boardrooms-report-says/

Markoczy, L., Sun, S. L., & Zhu, J. 2020. Few women on boards: what's identity got to do with it? *Journal of business ethics, 165*, 311-327. https://doi.org/DOI: 10.1007/s10551-019-04104-z

Maróczy, G. (2020). *Die französische Partie* (Vol. 8). Walter de Gruyter GmbH & Co KG., DOI: 10.1007/978-3-8349-9305-2_1

McIntosh, P. (1992) White privilege. *Creation Spirituality,* 33–35.

Moghadam, V. M. (2005). Women's economic participation in the Middle East: What difference has the neoliberal policy turn made? *Journal of Middle East Women's Studies, 1*(1), 110-146. https://doi.org/DOI: 10.2979/MEW.2005.1.1.110

Mouline, S., Ozlu, O., & Herzog, L. (January 19, 2022). A big step forward for women's leadership in Morocco. https://blogs.worldbank.org/arabvoices/big-step-forward-womens-leadership-morocco

Patton, M. Q. (1990). *Qualitative Evaluation and Research Methods*. Sage.

Phoenix, A. (2023). *Boys and Schooling. Routledge Handbook on Men, Masculinities and Organizations: Theories*. Practices and Futures of Organizing., DOI: 10.4324/9781003193579-26

Pullen, A., & Vachhani, S. (2023). Feminist ethics and women leaders: From difference to intercorporeality. In *Leadership, Gender, and Organization* (pp. 63–81). Springer International Publishing., DOI: 10.1007/978-3-031-24445-2_4

Reddy, S., & Jadhav, A. M. 2019. Gender diversity in boardrooms–A literature review. *Cogent Economics & Finance, 7*(1), 1644703. https://doi.org/DOI: 10.1080/23322039.2019.1644703

Saif, I. (November 02, 2011). The Middle Class and Transformations in the Arab World. https://carnegie-mec.org/2011/11/02/middle-class-and-transformations-in-arab-world-pub-45895

Salloum, C., Jabbour, G., & Mercier-Suissa, C. 2019. Democracy across gender diversity and ethnicity of Middle Eastern SMEs: how does performance differ?. Journal of Small Business Management, 57(1), 255-267. https://doi.org/DOI: 10.1111/jsbm.12336

Sengupta, S. S. (2021). Level-5 Integral Leadership Styles: Transcendence of Mind. *IUP Journal of Organizational Behavior, 20*(2).

Snaggs-Wilson, S. E. (2021). *Black Women in Leadership–Dominant Discourses that Construct, Maintain and Legitimize Gender, Race Class Bias in Top Canadian Corporations* (Doctoral dissertation).

Stephenson, L. (2022, February). Boardroom Diversity: Slow Progress. *The Financial Times Board Director Programme*. https://www.bdp.ft.com/newsletter-blogs-2022/february-2022

Thompson, K. (December 13, 2022). Social Class – An Introduction to the Concept. https://revisesociology.com/2016/08/04/social-class-definition-introduction/

Ubaradka, A., Bapu, V., Siby, A., & Chandra, S. (2023). The Allegory of the Glass Ceiling and Reverberance of Woman Leadership in Politics: The Case of Arya Rajendran. In *From Industry 4.0 to Industry 5.0: Mapping the Transitions* (pp. 183-189). Cham: Springer Nature Switzerland. https://doi.org/DOI: 10.1007/978-3-031-28314-7_16

Volkan, V. D. 2019. Large-group identity, who are we now? Leader–follower relationships and societal–political divisions. *The American Journal of Psychoanalysis, 79*, 139-155. https://doi.org/DOI: 10.1057/s11231-019-09186-2

Warner, C., & Schmincke, D. (2008). *High Altitude Leadership: What the World's Most Forbidding Peaks Teach Us About Success*. John Wiley & Sons., DOI: 10.1111/j.1744-6570.2009.01160_4.x

Zaccaro, S. J., Green, J. P., Dubrow, S., & Kolze, M. (2018). Leader individual differences, situational parameters, and leadership outcomes: A comprehensive review and integration. *The Leadership Quarterly, 29*(1), 2-43. https://doi.org/DOI: 10.1016/j.leaqua.2017.10.003

Chapter 7
A Systematic Review: Investment, Technology, and Innovation Pathways in Oman Vision 2040

R. Kavya
http://orcid.org/0000-0001-6062-4470
Dayananda Sagar College of Arts, Science, and Commerce, India

Mythili Kolluru
http://orcid.org/0000-0002-4464-5164
College of Banking and Financial Studies, Oman

Roohi Kursheed Khan
http://orcid.org/0000-0002-0731-4868
Dayananda Sagar University, India

ABSTRACT

This paper is a systematic literature review that aims to understand how digital transformation, innovation, investment, and policy frameworks contribute to economic growth, with a special focus on Oman's Vision 2040. The study begins by explaining why digital technologies and investment have become important for modern economies. It then clearly describes how existing research papers were carefully searched, selected, and reviewed using a systematic method. The main part of the paper categorises earlier studies into key themes, including foreign direct investment, fintech, innovation ecosystems, public–private partnerships, and regulatory reforms. Finally, the paper explains the implications of these findings for Oman's economic development and highlights areas where future research is needed, thereby helping policymakers, investors, and researchers better understand the path forward.

DOI: 10.4018/979-8-3373-8964-6.ch007

INTRODUCTION

There is a remarkable transformation taking place within the current global economy. This is brought about by fast-paced technological innovations, increasing digitalization trends, and the challenges posed by climate change and an imbalanced demographic profile. Automation and AI are transforming the world of work at an extremely rapid pace; however, their positive impacts have not been evenly shared. According to the (IMF, 2026), global growth will stand at 3.3% for 2026 and 3.4% for 2027, backed by strong performance of the private sector, the balancing effects of widespread adoption of AI technology, and industry policies adopted by governments.

The Sultanate of Oman has undergone a remarkable transformation over the years within the broader Middle Eastern context. Oman has adopted a policy of noninvolvement in regional disputes. It maintains a strategic ambivalence, coupled with a stable, balanced domestic and foreign policy, reflecting the foundations of Oman's economy. According to Transparency International Defense & Security (2020), the approach of political and economic neutrality positions itself to compete effectively with powerful regional neighbors such as the United Arab Emirates (UAE) and Saudi Arabia (SA). Within this evolving global landscape, Oman has articulated its own long-term response. Under the Royal Directives of His Majesty the late Sultan Qaboos bin Said, a master economic and social blueprint, Oman Vision 2040, was crafted for the nation's future and is currently being steered and implemented under the leadership of His Majesty Sultan Haitham bin Tarik.

Over multiple years, national foresight, technical studies, and extensive dialogue across sectors of society, including youth, the private sector, and civil society, were conducted to craft the Vision 2040. It is referred to as the supreme doctrine for economic and social planning for 2021–2040. The vision was strategically designed to steer Oman through a post-oil, knowledge-based development path. Oman Vision 2040 provides a comprehensive framework for overcoming structural challenges, maintaining peace and stability amid regional and global volatility, seizing opportunities to foster economic competitiveness and social well-being, stimulating growth, and building confidence across the economic, social, and developmental spheres nationwide (Oman Vision 2040). One of the key pillars of Oman Vision 2040 is the digital economy, anchored in digital growth, in-country value creation, and strategic partnership with the private sector. The digital economy is projected to contribute approximately 10 percent of GDP by 2040. It aims to create opportunities for micro, small, and medium-sized enterprises (MSMEs) while supporting cloud computing, artificial intelligence, cybersecurity, and fourth industrial revolution technologies. In doing so, it seeks to provide new opportunities, accelerate growth, and attract foreign direct investment to Oman, with a particular focus on machine learning and data science. Amid a rapidly transforming, fast-paced economy. There are four main pillars of the vision: People and Society, Economy and Development, Governance and Institutional Performance, and Environment.

The research problem in this context is that while there is a more literature on Oman Vision 2040, the current academic body is still fragmented in three different ways. First, conceptually, most of the current research studies deal with separate topics like renewable energy, e-government, and development of small businesses and lack a comprehensive conceptualization where investment, technological advances, and innovations are connected to the overall vision of Oman Vision 2040. Secondly, methodologically, the majority of current literature on the topic includes qualitative research methods, with few longitudinal or mixed-methods studies that could measure long-term impacts. Lastly, Sectorally, most of the research studies cover only energy, government, and digitization sectors. To address this research problem, the study aims to answer the following interrelated research questions: (1) Which studies have examined technology and investment in the context of Oman Vision 2040, and what are their findings? (2) Does the available literature establish any linkage between the global economic transformation and Oman Vision 2024? (3) Are there any conceptual, methodological, or sectoral gaps based on technology, investment, and innovation-driven transformations in the Sultanate of Oman? and (4) What are the future directions that can strengthen investment, technology, and innovation pathways to substantially contribute to realizing Vision 2040's purpose? The resolution of the research problem will be achieved by using a Systematic Literature Review (SLR) guided by PRISMA (Preferred Reporting Items for Systematic Reviews and Meta-Analyses). This approach is well-suited to the research problem, as it ensures that valid and relevant empirical evidence on investment, technology, and innovation in the context of Oman Vision 2040 is identified, filtered, and synthesized transparently. Unlike the narrative approach, the Systematic Review Approach provides a structured, replicable method for synthesizing relevant studies on the formulated research question. The structured and rigorous PRISMA approach will provide integrated, evidence-based guidance on investment, technology, and innovation pathways that will accelerate and support the realization of Vision 2040 priorities and the transition to a knowledge-based, innovation-driven economy.

This article first reviews prior literature on systematic reviews in national development contexts, followed by a detailed account of the methodology, including the PRISMA protocol, search strategy, inclusion and exclusion criteria, data extraction, and quality assessment. The thematic results from the 24 selected studies are then presented, followed by a discussion of the findings against the four pillars of Oman Vision 2040. The article concludes with directions for future research.

LITERATURE REVIEW

There is sufficient literature available on Investments, Technology and Innovation in terms of national development strategy have seen a significant rise in the past two decades, especially in rapidly evolving countries that are trying to minimize their dependence on natural resources. The research focus has shifted to the ways through which developing countries are taking good advantage of digital transformation and innovation ecosystems (IMF, 2026; World Bank, 2020)Within the Gulf Cooperation Council (GCC) region, this body of knowledge has taken on added significance as member states pursue ambitious long-term national visions aimed at transitioning toward knowledge-based, diversified economies (Khalifa Alhabsi et al., 2022; OECD, 2025)Vision 2040 is one such example that offers an encompassing strategy. Although there has been an increasing body of research on this issue, the current literature about Vision 2040 appears to be disconnected. Researches about the vision appear to be Sectorally bound without any holistic analysis. The upcoming discussion will attempt to synthesize research on five key themes pertinent to Vision 2040.

Strategic investment has gained widespread recognition as a significant catalyst in diversifying resource-based economies. Strategic investment approaches by the government and the private sector are necessary for sustainable development and reduced dependence on hydrocarbon exports (Al-Badi et al., 2011). Regulatory policies and governance mechanisms are highlighted as crucial facilitators for foreign direct investment in manufacturing and logistics (Khalifa Alhabsi et al., 2022). Transport and logistics investments can increase the efficiency and competitiveness of the regions (Salim Ba Awain et al., 2021). Additionally, the improvement of institutional performance and governance measures enhances investors' confidence (World Bank, 2020).

Digital transformation has become a significant facilitator of economic modernization. Several studies suggest that the introduction of e-government practices can increase the efficiency of management, improve service delivery, and ensure greater transparency in governmental organizations (Al-Busaidy & Weerakkody, 2011). Utilization of the technology of Industry 4.0 can make operations within the private sector more efficient through automation and data analysis but faces obstacles related to the scarcity of competent employees and insufficient level of digital readiness (Negi et al., 2026).

Innovation ecosystems make substantial contributions to knowledge-driven economic growth. The triple helix, characterized by the collaboration between governments, academic institutions, and industries, is noted as the best approach in promoting innovation and enhancing national innovation capacity (Nikolaou, 2022; Vernyuy Wirba, 2017). Funding innovation through investment in research and development enhances national innovation and productivity performance (IMF, 2026; Omar, 2019).

The development of human capital serves as the basis that helps enable all transformation paths. The skills development and talent management, along with education reform, were highlighted as major contributors to the effective adoption of new technologies (S. H. Aldulaimi & Abdeldayem, 2022; Shannaq & Al Shamsi, 2024). The digital skills deficit remains one of the biggest obstacles to implementing innovations across industries (Park et al., 2023). On the firm side, small firms are seen as major engines of employment and diversification, where finance and a regulatory environment would be key instruments of stimulating innovation in small businesses (Akram et al., 2024; Palalic et al., 2026; World Economic Forum, 2024).

Green investment and innovation towards sustainability have become key elements in the national development agenda. Green investment and technologies that involve renewables are critical not only for ensuring environmental sustainability but also for the diversification of economies (S. H. Aldulaimi & Abdeldayem, 2022; Leal-Arcas et al., 2025). Innovation in digital health is an example of how innovation can contribute to enhancing the resilience and accessibility of the system. Policy coherence is deemed necessary within all three dimensions for achieving national development integration (Ousmane Dione; Khamis Bin Saif Al Jabri, 2025).

METHODOLOGY

This paper follows a Systematic Literature Review (SLR) approach to review the existing empirical studies and policy-oriented studies on investment, technology and innovation pathways in the context of Oman Vision 2040. A traditional narrative review is believed to be less rigorous than an SLR because it adheres to a systematic and transparent way of identifying, assessing and synthesizing the previous research evidence (Thorpe et al., 2005; Tranfield et al., 2003). This kind of strategy is mainly applicable to amalgamation of disaggregated knowledge and research gaps in developing and interdisciplinary fields of research.

Figure 1 presents the conceptual framework synthesized from the thematic findings, mapping the five identified thematic clusters against the four pillars of Oman Vision 2040 and illustrating the directional relationships between investment, technology, innovation.

Figure 1. Conceptual Framework of Investment, Technology, and Innovation Pathways Aligned with Oman Vision 2040 Pillars and sustainable development.

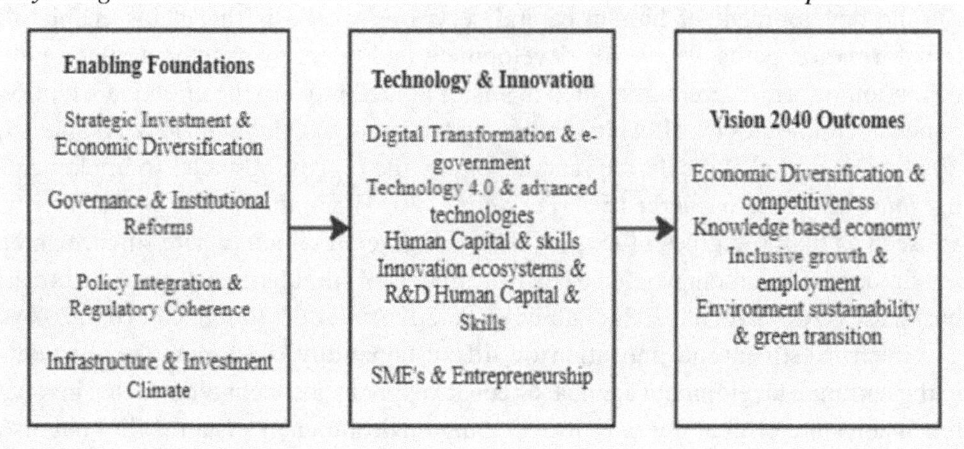

Source: (Created by Authors)

The methodological rigor and transparency principles require that this review is based on the Preferred Reporting Items of Systematic Reviews and Meta-Analyses (PRISMA) 2020 guidelines (Page et al., 2021). PRISMA is commonly accepted as a powerful methodology to report and critically review evidence-based reports in any field, such as management, policy, and social sciences (Grant & Booth, 2009). Application of the PRISMA protocol improves the replication and the credibility of the review through the systematic documentation of search, screening, and selection.

REVIEW PROTOCOL AND RESEARCH DESIGN

The search was restricted to studies published between 2010 and 2026, capturing scholarship relevant to both the formulation and early implementation phases of Oman Vision 2040. Before the literature search, a review protocol was prepared in order to state the aim, search strategy, inclusion criteria, exclusion criteria and the methodology of analysis. It is advisable to develop a priori protocol to reduce bias and increase the level of transparency in systematic reviews (Petticrew & Roberts, 2008).

The following objectives were the design of the review:

(i) to trace the literature connecting global economic transformation and Oman Vision 2040;
(ii) to discuss prevailing themes of investment, digitalization and innovation;

(iii) to establish conceptual, methodological and sectoral research gaps.

The analysis of results was conducted using a content analysis method, which involved systematization of the results, by coding and synthesizing the findings of the chosen studies. The qualitative method applied in systematic reviews is content analysis, which helps to systematize and interpret the textual information using a structured classification method (Elo & Kyngäs, 2008).

DATA SOURCES AND SEARCH STRATEGY

Four large academic databases were searched through an extensive literature search, and they included Scopus, Web of science, ScienceDirect, and Emerald Insight databases. The reason behind the choice of these databases is because they have a vast coverage of peer-reviewed journals in economic, management, innovation, and policy domains.

In the search strategy, Boolean operators have been used on titles, abstracts and key words in order to capture more and narrow the search. The search keywords were developed through a pilot search and review of prior SLRs. Boolean operators (AND, OR) were applied across titles, abstracts, and keywords. The primary search strings were: ("Oman Vision 2040" AND "investment"); ("Oman" AND "digital transformation" OR "e-government"); ("Oman" AND "innovation" OR "technology"); ("GCC" AND "economic diversification" AND "knowledge economy"); and ("green investment" OR "renewable energy" AND "Oman")

INCLUSION AND EXCLUSION CRITERIA

To ensure relevance and quality, predefined inclusion and exclusion criteria were applied.

Table 1. Inclusion& Exclusion Criteria

Inclusion criteria	Exclusion criteria
• Peer-reviewed journal articles • Conceptual, empirical, or policy-oriented studies • Research addressing investment, technology, innovation, or economic transformation • Studies explicitly focused on Oman or comparable GCC contexts	• Conference papers, editorials, book chapters, and non-peer-reviewed sources • Studies unrelated to Oman Vision 2040 or national development strategies • Duplicate records and articles without full-text availability

Source: created by the authors

Establishing explicit selection criteria is consistent with best practices in systematic review methodology (Petticrew & Roberts, 2008).

SCREENING AND SELECTION PROCESS

The initial screening and selection of studies was done in three stages as suggested by the PRISMA framework (Page et al., 2021). To start with, reference management software was used to export all the records retrieved, and eliminate any duplicates. Second, titles and abstracts were filtered to exclude studies that did not support the aim of the review. Third, eligibility of full-text articles was evaluated using the set inclusion criteria.

Any inconsistency in the screening exercise was addressed via a discussion to make decisions on selection consistent. The qualitative synthesis was also done to include the last group of articles. Overall selection process is described with the help of a PRISMA flow diagram that indicates the figure of records identified, screened, excluded, and included at every step.

In accordance with PRISMA 2020 guidelines, a flow diagram (Figure 2) illustrating the complete screening and selection process is presented alongside the tabular summary below. This transparent reporting ensures methodological reproducibility and is consistent with PRISMA 2020 guidelines (Page et al., 2021).

The screening and selection of studies was conducted in three stages as prescribed by the PRISMA 2020 framework (Page et al., 2021). In the first stage, all 312 records retrieved from the four databases were exported into reference management software, yielding 245 unique records after the removal of 67 duplicates. In the second stage, these 245 records were screened based on titles and abstracts; 181 records were excluded at this stage because they were unrelated to Oman Vision 2040, did not address investment, technology, or innovation themes, or were not peer-reviewed. This resulted in 64 records proceeding to full-text retrieval, of which 7 were inaccessible due to restricted database access or unavailability of full text. In the third stage, the remaining 57 full-text articles were assessed for eligibility against the predefined inclusion and exclusion criteria. A total of 33 articles were excluded at this stage: 14 were sector-specific without a clear linkage to Vision 2040; 11 exhibited insufficient relevance or conceptual overlap with the review themes; and 8 were excluded due to methodological limitations that did not meet the quality threshold for synthesis. The final sample comprised 24 studies retained for qualitative thematic synthesis. Any inconsistency in the screening exercise was addressed through discussion to ensure consistency in selection decisions. The complete record of this process, including the count and justification at each stage, is presented in Table 2 and illustrated in Figure 2 (PRISMA Flow Diagram).

Table 2. PRISMA Stage-by-Stage Record of Screening and Selection

Stage	Action Taken	Records (n)	Justification
Identification	Records retrieved from databases	312	Scopus (n=128), Web of Science (n=74), ScienceDirect (n=63), Emerald Insight (n=47) were selected for their comprehensive coverage of peer-reviewed management, economics, and policy journals
Deduplication	Duplicate records removed	67	Same records appearing across multiple databases were identified using reference management software and removed to avoid redundancy
Screening	Records screened (titles & abstracts)	245	Titles and abstracts were reviewed against the inclusion criteria; studies unrelated to Oman, Vision 2040, investment, technology, or innovation were excluded
Excluded screening	Records excluded	181	Studies excluded for being unrelated to Oman or GCC development context, not addressing investment/technology/ innovation themes, or being non-peer-reviewed sources
Full-text retrieval	Reports sought for retrieval	64	Studies that passed title/abstract screening were retrieved in full text for detailed eligibility assessment
Not retrieved	Full texts inaccessible	7	Full texts were unavailable in the selected databases or access was restricted
Eligibility assessment	Full texts assessed for eligibility	57	Full texts were evaluated against all predefined inclusion and exclusion criteria
Excluded eligibility	Reports excluded with reasons	33	Sector-specific without Vision 2040 linkage (n=14); insufficient relevance or conceptual overlap (n=11); methodological limitations (n=8)
Included	Studies included in final synthesis	24	Studies met all inclusion criteria and contributed substantively to the themes of investment, technology, and innovation in the context of Oman Vision 2040

Source: Created by the authors following PRISMA 2020 guidelines

Figure 2. PRISMA 2020

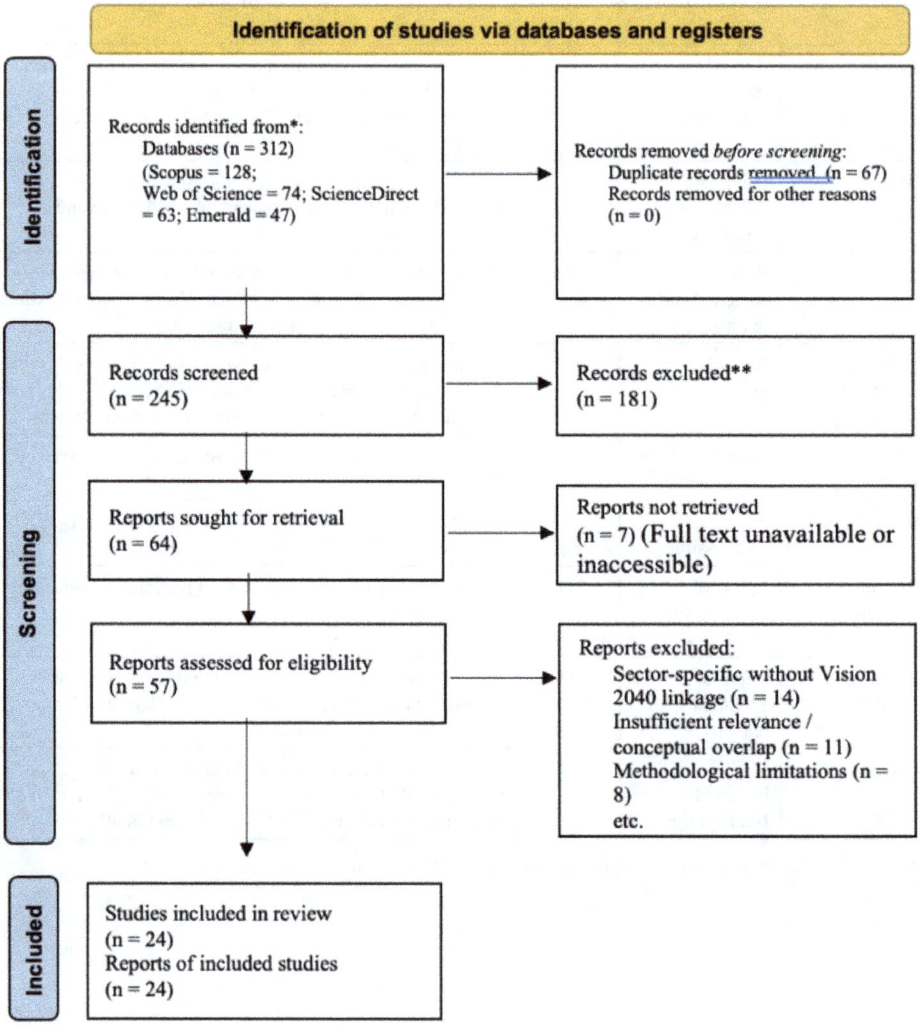

Source: (Created by Authors following the PRISMA 2020 Diagram)

DATA EXTRACTION AND QUALITY ASSESSMENT

Data extraction was performed using a structured Microsoft Excel template, with references managed in Mendeley. Data were extracted from each study using a structured spreadsheet template developed in Microsoft Excel. Fields captured included: author(s), year of publication, research focus, methodology, sectoral context, and key findings. Two reviewers independently extracted data; any discrepancies were resolved through discussion and consensus. This kind of organized data handling helps to ease synthesis and comparison of studies (Elo & Kyngäs, 2008). The qualitative quality analysis was conducted through the evaluation of clarity of the research objectives, research methodological rigor, relevance to Oman vision 2040, and advancement of the theory or policy. Studies were assessed on three criteria: clarity of research objectives, methodological rigor, and relevance to Vision 2040. Each was rated 1–3 (weak/moderate/strong), giving a maximum score of 9. Studies scoring below 5 were excluded from the synthesis.

RESULTS AND THEMATIC FINDINGS

After the screening process using the PRISMA, This analysis followed the four phases described below. Phase 1 (Open Coding): The key concepts, results, and findings identified from each of the 24 articles were coded using Microsoft Excel. At this stage, 48 initial codes emerged. Phase 2 (Code Consolidation): The codes that were similar in meaning were then consolidated, leaving only 24 codes which corresponded with the scope of the review. Phase 3 (Theme Development): From the 24 codes obtained above, 12 sub-themes were then developed. This is outlined in Table 3. Phase 4 (Theme Consolidation): Finally, the 12 sub-themes were consolidated into five themes. Each of the themes is associated with one of the five pillars of Oman Vision 2040 and is outlined in Table 4. Throughout this process of coding, inter-coder reliability was achieved by having both of the reviewers independently code each article according to all the four phases above.

OVERVIEW OF SELECTED STUDIES

The chosen articles date between 2010 and 2026, which indicates the growing interest of scholars in relation to the adoption of Oman Vision 2040. The articles reviewed are methodologically conceptual analysis articles, empirical articles, policy articles, and comparative GCC-based articles. Sectoral coverage is wide, which includes energy, manufacturing, logistics, tourism, SMEs, digital governance, healthcare, and green technologies.

All in all, the literature is characterised by a high policy-driven focus, and the majority of the studies focus on the ability of investment structures and technological capacity to help Oman shift into a diversified, knowledge-based, and innovation-oriented economy.

Table 3. Key findings of the selected review articles

Sl. No.	Author(s) & Year	Journal	Research Design	Focus Area	Key Findings	Sector	Country
1	Al-Badi et al. (2011)	Renewable and Sustainable Energy Reviews	Empirical quantitative	Strategic investment and economic diversification	Coordinated public and private investment is essential for economic diversification and long-term sustainability	Energy and national economy	Oman
2	Khalifa Alhabsi et al. (2022)	Journal of Research in Humanities and Social Science	Empirical quantitative	Foreign direct investment and regulatory reform	Regulatory reforms and targeted incentives improve FDI inflows aligned with Vision 2040 priorities	Manufacturing and logistics	Oman
3	World Bank (2020)	World Bank Group Report	Policy report	Investment climate and governance reform	Institutional quality and governance reforms strengthen investor confidence and competitiveness	Cross-sectoral	Global / GCC
4	Salim Ba Awain et al. (2021a)	International Business Research	Empirical quantitative	Infrastructure investment and logistics	Infrastructure-led growth enhances productivity and regional economic integration	Transport and logistics	Oman
5	Al-Busaidy & Weerakkody (2011)	Electronic Government	Empirical qualitative	Digital governance and e-government	E-government initiatives improve service efficiency, transparency, and administrative effectiveness	Public administration	Oman

continued on following page

Table 3. Continued

Sl. No.	Author(s) & Year	Journal	Research Design	Focus Area	Key Findings	Sector	Country
6	Negi et al. (2026)	SAGE Open	Empirical qualitative	Industry 4.0 and workforce development	Advanced digital technologies enhance operational efficiency but require skilled human capital	Manufacturing and education	Oman
7	OECD (2025)	OECD Policy Report	Policy report	Digital governance and policy coherence	Policy coherence and digital regulation support national innovation ecosystems	National policy	OECD / GCC
8	Nurunnabi (2020)	Book Chapter — Routledge	Conceptual analysis	Knowledge-based economy and smart cities	Smart infrastructure investment facilitates sustainable and inclusive urban development	Urban development	Saudi Arabia / GCC
9	Nikolaou (2022)	Higher Education Evaluation and Development	Empirical qualitative	Innovation ecosystems and triple-helix collaboration	Triple-helix collaboration between government, academia, and industry drives innovation outcomes	Higher education and innovation	Oman
10	Vernyuy Wirba (2017)	European Journal of Business and Management	Conceptual analysis	Knowledge economy and R&D investment	Institutional support and R&D investment positively influence innovation capacity	Knowledge economy	GCC

continued on following page

Table 3. Continued

Sl. No.	Author(s) & Year	Journal	Research Design	Focus Area	Key Findings	Sector	Country
11	IMF (2026)	IMF World Economic Outlook	Policy report	Macroeconomic growth and technological innovation	Technological innovation enhances productivity growth and economic resilience	Macroeconomic	Global
12	Omar (2019)	Review of Economics and Political Science	Empirical quantitative	R&D investment and innovation performance	Increased R&D expenditure strengthens national innovation performance	Science and technology	MENA
13	S. Aldulaimi et al. (2020)	IEEE Conference Proceedings	Empirical quantitative	Human capital and knowledge economy	Skills development is critical for technology absorption and innovation diffusion	Education and labour market	GCC
14	Shannaq & Al Shamsi (2024)	Studies in Systems, Decision and Control	Empirical qualitative	Digital transformation and competitiveness	Digital skills gaps constrain effective implementation of Vision 2040 initiatives	Workforce and digital economy	Oman
15	Park et al. (2023)	International Journal of Innovative Research and Scientific Studies	Mixed method	Education reform and sustainable development	Education reform supports innovation-led and inclusive economic growth	Education sector	International / SDG context
16	Palalic et al. (2026)	Book Chapter — Springer	Conceptual analysis	SME development and entrepreneurship	SMEs play a vital role in innovation, diversification, and employment generation	SMEs	Oman

continued on following page

Table 3. Continued

Sl. No.	Author(s) & Year	Journal	Research Design	Focus Area	Key Findings	Sector	Country
17	Akram et al. (2024)	Book Chapter — Emerald	Empirical qualitative	Entrepreneurial ecosystems and access to finance	Access to finance and policy support enhance SME innovation capabilities	Entrepreneurship	Oman
18	World Economic Forum (2024)	WEF Annual Report	Policy report	Startup ecosystems and digital innovation	Startups accelerate digital and green innovation pathways	Innovation ecosystems	Global
19	Azhar & Romero-Castro (2025)	International Journal of Professional Business Review	Empirical quantitative	Green investment and sustainable economy	Investment in green technologies supports sustainable economic transformation	Energy and environment	Oman
20	S. H. Aldulaimi & Abdeldayem (2022)	International Journal of Engineering Business Management	Empirical quantitative	Renewable energy and sustainability	Renewable energy investment aligns with Vision 2040 sustainability and energy diversification goals	Energy sector	MENA / Oman
21	Leal-Arcas et al. (2025)	Energies	Empirical qualitative	Energy policy and decarbonization	Clean energy adoption improves environmental performance and economic efficiency	Energy transition	Oman
22	Salmi et al. (2025)	Eastern Mediterranean Health Journal	Mixed method	Digital health and system sustainability	Digital health adoption enhances service accessibility and system efficiency	Healthcare	Oman

continued on following page

Table 3. Continued

Sl. No.	Author(s) & Year	Journal	Research Design	Focus Area	Key Findings	Sector	Country
23	WHO (2021)	WHO Global Strategy Report	Policy report	Health technology and innovation	Health technology innovation strengthens system resilience and service delivery	Public health	Global
24	Ousmane Dione & Al Jabri (2025)	World Bank Blog — MENA Perspectives	Policy report	Policy integration and Vision 2040 implementation	Policy coherence across investment, technology, and innovation strengthens Vision 2040 implementation	National policy	Oman

To enhance conceptual clarity and address the interconnected nature of the identified themes, Table 4 reorganizes the twelve thematic factors into five consolidated main themes, each comprising related sub-themes. This hierarchical organization reflects the logical clustering of sub-themes based on shared policy orientation and sectoral focus. Further, each main theme is aligned with the corresponding pillar of Oman Vision 2040 to demonstrate how the synthesized evidence directly supports the national strategic framework.

Table 4. Consolidated Thematic Framework: Main Themes, Sub-themes, and Strategic Alignment with Oman Vision 2040 Pillars

Main Theme	Sub-themes (from Table 3)	Supporting Studies	Oman Vision 2040 Pillar
1. Investment-Led Economic Diversification	Strategic investment and economic diversification; Infrastructure and logistics development; SME development and entrepreneurship	(Akram et al., 2024a; Al-Badi et al., 2011a; Khalifa Alhabsi et al., 2022a; Palalic et al., 2026a; Salim Ba Awain et al., 2021a; World Bank, 2020a)	Economy and Development
2. Digital Transformation and Governance	Digital transformation and e-government; Governance and institutional reforms; Policy integration and cross-sectoral alignment	(Al-Busaidy & Weerakkody, 2011; OECD, 2025; Ousmane Dione; Khamis Bin Saif Al Jabri, 2025; Shannaq & Al Shamsi, 2024; World Bank, 2020)	Governance and Institutional Performance
3. Innovation Ecosystems and Knowledge Economy	Innovation ecosystems and R&D investment; Industry 4.0 and advanced technologies; Digital society and inclusion	(IMF, 2026; Negi et al., 2026; Nikolaou, 2022; Omar, 2019; World Economic Forum, 2024)	Economy and Development
4. Human Capital and Social Development	Human capital development and skills; Digital society and inclusion; SME development and entrepreneurship	(S. H. Aldulaimi & Abdeldayem, 2022; Negi et al., 2026; Park et al., 2023; Shannaq & Al Shamsi, 2024)	People and Society
5. Green Investment and Sustainable Innovation	Green investment and sustainability; Renewable energy and energy transition	(S. H. Aldulaimi & Abdeldayem, 2022; Azhar 2025; Leal-Arcas et al., 2025; Salmi et al., 2025)	Environment

Source: Created by Authors

The five main themes that emerge from this consolidated structure are not arbitrarily selected; rather, they represent the dominant policy clusters that recur across the 24 reviewed studies. Each main theme subsumes its related sub-themes, ensuring that all twelve thematic factors identified in Table 4 are systematically accounted for. The alignment with Vision 2040 pillars further confirms the strategic coherence of the reviewed literature and provides a structured basis for the thematic discussion that follows.

INVESTMENT-LED ECONOMIC DIVERSIFICATION

One of the most common themes in the reviewed studies is that strategic investment plays a central role in economic diversification and eliminating the reliance on hydrocarbon revenues. A number of studies point out that the constant frameworks of both public and private investments are necessary to promote sustainable development and long-term economic stability (Al-Badi et al., 2011). Specifically, the regulation reforms, good governance practices, and investment-friendly policies are identified to increase investor confidence and foreign direct investment in accordance with Vision 2040 priorities (Khalifa Alhabsi et al., 2022).

Infrastructure investments, particularly logistics and transport investments and industrial zones, are the identified catalysts of productivity increase and regional competitiveness numerous times over (Salim Ba Awain et al., 2021). All these together mean that diversification with investment focus is not only a financial tool but also a structural change tool that can help Oman in its overarching development policy.

DIGITAL TRANSFORMATION AND TECHNOLOGICAL ADOPTION

The second key theme is on the importance of digital transformation as an enabling factor in economic modernization as part of Oman Vision 2040. Research on e-government and digital governance documents efficiency, quality, and transparency in the administration, which further substantiates the position of technology in reforming the government (Al-Busaidy & Weerakkody, 2011; OECD, 2025). The implementation of Industry 4.0 technologies, including automation, data analytics, and smart manufacturing, has also been proven to improve operational efficiency and competitiveness in the private sector, especially in the manufacturing and industrial industries (Negi et al., 2026). Nevertheless, there are also implementation challenges identified in the literature, such as the shortage of skills and the disproportionate digital preparedness, implying that the overall investments in human capital and institutional capacity are required to be made.

INNOVATION ECOSYSTEMS AND KNOWLEDGE-BASED DEVELOPMENT

The significance of innovation ecosystems and knowledge-based development has a large amount of literature highlighting the importance of these concepts in realizing Vision 2040 goals. In promoting the spread of innovation and diffusing technology faster, studies emphasize the importance of the collaboration networks between the government, academia, and industry (Negi et al., 2026; Panteli et al., 2019)

Enhanced national innovation performance and growth in productivity is always related to investment in research and development (R&D), as well as institutional support on innovation (IMF, 2026; Omar, 2019) Such observations indicate that innovation-related growth demands, besides funding, robust system of governance and coordination at the ecosystem levels.

HUMAN CAPITAL, SMEs, AND ENTREPRENEURIAL DEVELOPMENT

One necessary enabling theme that comes out among various studies is human capital development. It is stated in the literature, that the development of skills, talent management, and education reform are the keys to the successful technology absorption and diffusion of innovations (S. Aldulaimi et al., 2020; Shannaq & Al Shamsi, 2024b) Continuous digital skills gaps are, however, mentioned as limitations that can restrict the successful process of implementing the initiatives of the Vision 2040.

Simultaneously, the role of SMEs and entrepreneurial ecosystems as the primary force behind innovation, job generation, and diversification of economies is identified. The literature shows that the availability of finance, favourable regulatory environments, and start-up ecosystems play a vital role in maximizing SME innovation abilities and competitiveness (Palalic et al., 2026b; World Economic Forum, 2024). This underscores the strategic position of inclusive entrepreneurship in the transformation pathway in Oman.

GREEN INVESTMENT AND SUSTAINABLE INNOVATION

The last topic indicates the increased focus on green investment and innovation with the orientation toward sustainability in accordance with Oman Vision 2040. Research work dedicated to renewable energy and green technologies identifies that an investment in clean energy can be aligned with both the goals of environmental sustainability and economic diversification (Azhar, 2025). The indications also indicate that the initiation of energy transition can improve environmental performance and create an economic resilience and long-term efficiency (Azhar, 2025). In addition to energy, medical and social services innovation is demonstrated to enhance the resilience of the system and access to services, which demonstrates the significance of cross-sectoral sustainable growth and technology facilitation (WHO, 2021).

SYNTHESIS OF FINDINGS

Three overarching findings of major analytical significance are obtained from the thematic analysis and are found within all five dominant themes.

Starting with the dominant themes, strategic investments and digital transformations emerge as the two most prominent themes in the analyzed 24 articles, with occurrence rates of 18 and 17 respectively (see Table 5 below). It is evident that both financial investments and digitalization are key mechanisms to facilitate the realization of Vision 2040. On the other hand, innovation ecosystems and human resource development have been identified as the next most prominent themes, which signifies the importance of the absorptive and managerial capacity to utilize the financial and technical inputs effectively.

The four gaps highlighted in the review include the following. First, there is a lack of longitudinal research, which could help analyze how investments and innovations influence productivity and employment growth in Oman in the long run. The second gap is that of cross-sectoral integration of policies for achieving innovation and technological development. It was stated by numerous scholars to be among the priorities in relation to Vision 2040 and its pillars. The third issue, which is under researched, concerns the socioeconomic aspects of the transition to green economy and includes the effects on employment opportunities in Oman, as well as regional equity and adaptation challenges. Lastly, the digitalisation of SMEs and green jobs have not been thoroughly researched yet.

From a policy perspective in relation to Oman Vision 2040, there are four recommendations based on the evidence synthesis. To start with, investment policy needs to shift towards quality rather than quantity by focusing on investments that contribute to innovation spillovers, skills development, and export diversification in addition to building infrastructure. Secondly, digital policy needs to evolve beyond individual project implementation to cross-sectoral coordination policies. Thirdly, human capital policy needs to consider not only education reform, but also digital skills training and labor market integration as interrelated policies. Finally, green investment needs to be developed as a cross-sectoral strategy rather than just an energy sector one, taking into consideration health technology and green employment opportunities in the process.

DISCUSSIONS

The purpose of this systematic review was to synthesise the available empirical and policy-based literature on investment, technology, and innovation pathways in the frame of Oman Vision 2040. The discussion could be interpreted as explaining the findings of the four pillars of the Vision 2040 Economic Development, Governance and Institutional Performance, Social and Human Capital Development, and Environmental Sustainability pillars, in order to show how the reviewed evidence would support the strategic ambitions of the national vision, extend it, or, in certain ways, challenge it.

Table 5. Key thematic factors identified in the systematic review (n = 24)

No.	Thematic Factors (CSFs)	Author(s) (Year)	Occurrence
1	Strategic investment and economic diversification	(Al-Badi et al., 2011; IMF, 2026; Khalifa Alhabsi et al., 2022; Salim Ba Awain et al., 2021; World Bank, 2020)	18
2	Digital transformation and e-government	(Al-Busaidy & Weerakkody, 2011; Negi et al., 2026; OECD, 2025)	17
3	Innovation ecosystems and R&D investment	(Nikolaou, 2022; Omar, 2019; Vernyuy Wirba, 2017; World Economic Forum, 2024)	16
4	Governance and institutional reforms	(OECD, 2025; Ousmane Dione; Khamis Bin Saif Al Jabri, 2025; World Bank, 2020)	15
5	Human capital development and skills	(S. Aldulaimi et al., 2020; Park et al., 2023; Shannaq & Al Shamsi, 2024)	15
6	SME development and entrepreneurship	(Akram et al., 2024; Palalic et al., 2026b; World Economic Forum, 2024b)	14
7	Industry 4.0 and advanced technologies	(IMF, 2026b; Negi et al., 2026b; OECD, 2025b)	13
8	Green investment and sustainability	(S. H. Aldulaimi & Abdeldayem, 2022b; Azhar & https://dialnet.unirioja.es/servlet/autor?codigo=6853671, 2025b; Leal-Arcas et al., 2025b)	13
9	Renewable energy and energy transition	(S. H. Aldulaimi & Abdeldayem, 2022b; Leal-Arcas et al., 2025b)	12
10	Infrastructure and logistics development	(Salim Ba Awain et al., 2021c; World Bank, 2020b)	12
11	Digital society and inclusion	(Al-Busaidy & Weerakkody, 2011b; OECD, 2025b; Park et al., 2023b)	11
12	Policy integration and cross-sectoral alignment	(Ousmane Dione; Khamis Bin Saif Al Jabri, 2025b; World Bank, 2020b)	11

Note: "Occurrence" refers to the number of studies in the final sample (n=24) that explicitly addressed each thematic factor as a central focus or substantive sub-theme.

ECONOMIC DEVELOPMENT AND DIVERSIFICATION PILLAR

The results are very supportive of the key issue of diversification of the economy through investments that is the core issue in the Oman Vision 2040 economic development pillar. The studies examined indicate consistently that strategic public and private investments, especially in infrastructure, manufacturing, logistics and tourism is a key element towards lessening the reliance in hydrocarbons and more towards productivity-led growth. This works in line with the focus of Vision 2040 in developing a competitive, diversified and knowledge based economy.

Nevertheless, as much as the idea of investment flows has been discussed, literature has been found to emphasize on sectoral performance instead of structural transformation in the long-term. It implies that further studies are necessary on understanding the relationship between investment policies and their ability to convert into long term competitiveness, degree of innovation and diversification of exports. The review therefore expands the pillar of economic development by pointing to the quality of investments and strategic fit, as opposed to the volume of investments. Governance and Institutional Performance Pillar

Oman Vision 2040 governance pillar focuses on effective institutions, policy coherence and digital governance. The findings of the review qualify as a strong argument in support of this pillar especially the available evidence on e-government, regulatory reforms, and digital public services. Research has shown that digital governance projects can increase transparency, service performance, and investor trust, which improve institutional performance.

However, it is also found that there is fragmentation in the policy application in the areas of investment, technology and innovation. Although individual reforms are successful, there is a lack of cross-sectoral coordination that limits a systemic impact. This implies that the governance reforms of Vision 2040 should cease to focus on individual digital projects and instead adopt the principles of comprehensive policy frameworks to be able to harmonize regulatory, investment, and innovation strategies.

The development of human capital is one of the most important enablers of Oman Vision 2040, and the literature under consideration justifies this focus. Research findings keep pointing at the importance of skills development, education reform, and talent management as the key factors in successful technology adoption and innovation diffusion. Digital skills gaps occur, however, as a common limitation across sectors.

These results indicate that although the Vision 2040 acknowledges human capital as the strategy, current studies are insufficiently considered to capture the full complexity. This highlights the importance of lifelong upskilling, academia-industry liaison and dynamic learning systems. The social pillar is therefore strengthened by the review as it goes further to show how unsustainable the growth through technology can be unless the human capabilities are equally invested.

INNOVATION AND KNOWLEDGE ECONOMY INTEGRATION

Oman Vision 2040 cuts across various pillars with innovation and knowledge-based development being key to economic and social development. The review provides solid findings that innovation ecosystems, R&D investment, and triple-helix collaboration have a significant impact on improving national innovation performance. Nevertheless, the literature is still disjointed to investigate the functioning of these ecosystems as a whole in the Omani context.

This gap recommends that innovation within the framework of the Vision 2040 be considered as not only a technological product but also a process of institutions and cultures. There is a need to pay more attention to the ecosystem governance, absorptive capacity, and long-term innovation metrics. This discussion also expands the innovation agenda of Vision 2040 by requiring systemic views as opposed to solitary innovation projects.Environmental Sustainability and Green Transition Pillar

The green investment, renewable energy, and sustainable innovation literature clearly demonstrate the presence of the environmental sustainability pillar of Oman Vision 2040. The results show that investments in clean energy and green technologies can serve both as a part of the environmental goals and as an element of economic diversification, which proves the integrated character of the growth in connection with the sustainability concept.

Although this is the case, the review shows that there is a paucity of empirical data on the socio-economic effects of green transitions especially on the employment, skills adjustment and regional equity. This implies that the next generation of research and policy formulation in the Vision 2040 must take a just transition approach, by making sure that the environmental sustainability is consistent with the inclusive economic performance.Integrated Interpretation Across Vision 2040 Pillars

The findings, when compared, imply that the pillars of Oman Vision 2040 are not independent but instead interconnected. The quality of governance is a prerequisite to investment effectiveness; the willingness to adopt technology is contingent on the preparedness of human capital; the technological adoption to drive growth can never be made without the factor of sustainability. This review therefore justifies a holistic understanding of Vision 2040, in which institutional coordination and policy integration are just as essential as sectoral investments.

The synthesisation of the evidence in these dimensions allows the given study to contribute to the literature, providing an integrated framework of how investment, technology, and innovation pathways can all be used to support the long-term transformation agenda in Oman.

ALIGNMENT WITH OMAN VISION 2040 PILLARS

The results and suggested framework is more or less in line with the four pillars of the Oman Vision 2040. Economy and Development pillar is helped by strategic investment, SME development, ecosystems of innovation, and digitalisation towards diversification and competitiveness. The Governance and Institutional Performance pillar is supported with evidence about regulatory reforms, digital governance, and policy integration as drivers of change. The pillar of People and Society is discussed in terms of the development of human capital, growth of skills, inclusive entrepreneurship and digital inclusion. Lastly, the pillar of the Environment can be seen in the increased focus on green investment, renewable energy, and sustainability-focused innovation.

Such consistency proves that investment, technology and innovation have not been isolated priorities, but rather interrelated drivers which in combination propel the overall development agenda of Vision 2040.

CONCLUSION AND FUTURE SCOPE OF RESEARCH

This research paper aimed to synthesise the disjointed literature on the study of investment, technology and innovation pathways with respect to Oman Vision 2040. Following a PRISMA-based systematic literature review, 24 peer-reviewed and policy-oriented articles have been analysed to determine prioritised themes, success factors that are critical to the process and gaps in the literature that influenced the long-term transformation agenda in Oman.

The results demonstrate that strategic investment, digital transformation, the system of innovations, the quality of governance, and human capital development form the main pillars in the context of transitioning Oman into a diversified, knowledge-based economy. The review has shown that expertise has a high level of academic agreement over the significance of investment-driven diversification and digitalisation, but it has also reflected the increased role of innovation ecosystems, SMEs, and sustainability-focused activities. Nevertheless, the literature is still disproportionate in its coverage and there is a shortage of integration across policy areas and a lack of empirical analysis of long-term consequences.

This study adds value to the existing literature by presenting cross-sectoral evidence in the following three eminent ways. First, it offers a systematic themed review of the research of investment, technology, and innovation in regard to the Vision 2040. Second, it determines the critical success factors (CSFs) that reveal the process of operationalisation of the Vision 2040 objectives in the economic, institutional, social, and environmental realms. Third, it provides the integrated analytical lens to assist policymakers, practitioners, and scholars in realizing the interdependences of the investment, technology, and innovation in national development strategies. Despite the growing body of work on Oman Vision 2040, several future research opportunities emerge from this review.

Future research should move beyond restrictive sector-specific approaches of addressing sectors and embrace systemic models that examine interactions among the investment policy, digital transformation, innovation ecosystems, and sustainability. Vision 2040 needs to be conceptualised as a process of systemic transformation, and not a series of discrete initiatives.

Methodologically speaking, the literature is mostly dominated by qualitative and descriptive studies. Longitudinal study, mixed-method, and impact analysis that will determine the effects of investment and technology adoption on productivity, employment, innovation capacity, and social inclusion with time would be beneficial in future research. It also could be beneficial to compare GCC and emerging economies to get some benchmarking insights.

Sectorally, energy, governance and digitalisation are heavily looked at although other sectors, including tourism, logistics, healthcare innovation, SME digitalisation, and green jobs are not well explored. Also, there is no extensive empirical research on policy integration and cross-sectoral coordination, which is of utmost importance to fulfil the holistic goals of Vision 2040.

Lastly, the next generation of research must be more focused on outcomes of inclusive and sustainable development, specifically in the impact of digital transformation and green transitions on workforce adaptation, the equity of regions, and their social resilience.

REFERENCES

Akram, H. W., Dana, L. P., Abbas, H., & Ciddikie, M. D. (2024). Family Start-up in Oman: Entrepreneurship Ecosystem Perspective. *Entrepreneurial Behaviour of Family Firms: Perspectives on Emerging Economies*, 43–58. DOI: 10.1108/978-1-83753-934-520241003

Al-Badi, A. H., Malik, A., & Gastli, A. (2011). Sustainable energy usage in Oman - Opportunities and barriers. *Renewable & Sustainable Energy Reviews, 15*(8), 3780–3788. DOI: 10.1016/j.rser.2011.06.007

Al-Busaidy, M., & Weerakkody, V. (2011). E-government services in Oman: An employee's perspective. *Electronic Government, 8*(2–3), 185–207. DOI: 10.1504/EG.2011.039836

Al Salmi, S. A., Rafiq, M., Al Salmi, Q., Al-Alawi, B. T. S., Al Jabri, S. S., Al Jabri, A., & Al Maniri, A. A. N. (2025). Progress, challenges and opportunities in building a sustainable digital health system in Oman. *Eastern Mediterranean Health Journal, 31*(9–10), 574–580. DOI: 10.26719/2025.31.10.574 PMID: 41451744

Aldulaimi, S., Kharabsheh, R., Al Shishany, A., & Alazzawi, A. (2020). Investment in Human Capital to Promote Knowledge-Based Economy: Data Analysis in the GCC. *2020 International Conference on Data Analytics for Business and Industry: Way Towards a Sustainable Economy, ICDABI 2020*. DOI: 10.1109/ICDABI51230.2020.9325675

Aldulaimi, S. H., & Abdeldayem, M. M. (2022). Examining the impact of renewable energy technologies on sustainability development in the middle east and north Africa region. *International Journal of Engineering Business Management, 14*, 18479790221110835. Advance online publication. DOI: 10.1177/18479790221110835

Azhar, A. I. M., & https://dialnet.unirioja.es/servlet/autor?codigo=6853671. (2025). The impact of sustainable environment on the development of the green economy in oman. *International Journal of Professional Business Review: Int. J. Prof.Bus. Rev., ISSN 2525-3654, ISSN-e 2525-3654, Vol. 10, Nº. 4, 2025 (Ejemplar Dedicado a: Continuous Publication; E05444), 10*(4), 5. DOI: 10.26668/businessreview/2025.v10i4.5444

Dione, O., & Jabri, K. B. S. A. (2025, May 28). *Oman Vision 2040: A Blueprint for Sustainable Growth and Global Integration*. Perspectives: MENA, Afghanistan. https://blogs.worldbank.org/en/arabvoices/oman-vision-2040-a-blueprint-for-sustainable-growth-and-global-integration

Elo, S., & Kyngäs, H. (2008). The qualitative content analysis process. *Journal of Advanced Nursing*, *62*(1), 107–115. DOI: 10.1111/j.1365-2648.2007.04569.x PMID: 18352969

Grant, M. J., & Booth, A. (2009). A typology of reviews: An analysis of 14 review types and associated methodologies. *Health Information and Libraries Journal*, *26*(2), 91–108. DOI: 10.1111/j.1471-1842.2009.00848.x PMID: 19490148

IMF. (2026). *World Economic Outlook Update, January 2026: Global Economy: Steady amid Divergent Forces*. World Economic Outlook Update. https://www.imf.org/en/publications/weo/issues/2026/01/19/world-economic-outlook-update-january-2026

Khalifa Alhabsi, S., Salim Alamri, S., Mubarak, A., & Mohammed, E. (2022). A Study on the Role of Small and Medium Enterprises (SME) in the Economic Growth of Oman Student at Oman college of management & technology-Department of administrative and financial sciences. *Quest Journals Journal of Research in Humanities and Social Science*, *10*(6), 2321–9467.

Leal-Arcas, R., Almashloum, S., Jazzar, R., Saleh, N. Bin, & Almunifi, R. (2025). Energy Policy of Oman: Pursuing Decarbonization. *Energies 2025, Vol. 18, Page 1270, 18*(5), 1270. DOI: 10.3390/en18051270

Negi, S., Karyamsetty, H. J., & Fida, B. A. (2026). Developing Graduates for the Fourth Industrial Revolution and Oman Vision 2040: The Role of Business Schools in Shaping the Future Workforce. *SAGE Open*, *16*(1), 21582440251410308. Advance online publication. DOI: 10.1177/21582440251410308

Nikolaou, P. (2022). Sustainable development: A developmental evaluation of logistics higher education in the Sultanate of Oman based on two innovation approaches (the triple helix of innovation and innovation competencies). *Higher Education Evaluation and Development*, *16*(2), 102–120. DOI: 10.1108/HEED-07-2021-0056

Nurunnabi, M. (2020). Knowledge-based economy in Saudi Arabia and Vision 2030. *Research, Innovation and Entrepreneurship in Saudi Arabia*, 84–103. DOI: 10.4324/9781351040020-4

OECD. (2025, December 9). *The Organisation for Economic Co-operation and Development | OECD*. https://www.oecd.org/

Oman Vision 2040. (2022). *Oman Vision 2040 Implementation Follow-up Unit*. https://www.oman2040.om/?lang=en

Omar, N. S. (2019). Innovation and economic performance in MENA region. *Review of Economics and Political Science*, *4*(2), 158–175. DOI: 10.1108/REPS-12-2018-0042

Page, M. J., McKenzie, J. E., Bossuyt, P. M., Boutron, I., Hoffmann, T. C., Mulrow, C. D., Shamseer, L., Tetzlaff, J. M., Akl, E. A., Brennan, S. E., Chou, R., Glanville, J., Grimshaw, J. M., Hróbjartsson, A., Lalu, M. M., Li, T., Loder, E. W., Mayo-Wilson, E., McDonald, S., . . . Moher, D. (2021a). The PRISMA 2020 statement: an updated guideline for reporting systematic reviews. *BMJ (Clinical Research Ed.), 372*. DOI: 10.1136/bmj.n71

Page, M. J., McKenzie, J. E., Bossuyt, P. M., Boutron, I., Hoffmann, T. C., Mulrow, C. D., Shamseer, L., Tetzlaff, J. M., Akl, E. A., Brennan, S. E., Chou, R., Glanville, J., Grimshaw, J. M., Hróbjartsson, A., Lalu, M. M., Li, T., Loder, E. W., Mayo-Wilson, E., McDonald, S., . . . Moher, D. (2021b). The PRISMA 2020 statement: An updated guideline for reporting systematic reviews. In *The BMJ* (Vol. 372). BMJ Publishing Group. DOI: 10.1136/bmj.n71

Page, M. J., McKenzie, J. E., Bossuyt, P. M., Boutron, I., Hoffmann, T. C., Mulrow, C. D., Shamseer, L., Tetzlaff, J. M., Akl, E. A., Brennan, S. E., Chou, R., Glanville, J., Grimshaw, J. M., Hróbjartsson, A., Lalu, M. M., Li, T., Loder, E. W., Mayo-Wilson, E., McDonald, S., . . . Moher, D. (2021c). The PRISMA 2020 statement: An updated guideline for reporting systematic reviews. In *The BMJ* (Vol. 372). BMJ Publishing Group. DOI: 10.1136/bmj.n71

Palalic, R., Al Riyami, S., & Umrani, W. (2026). *Small and Medium Enterprises (SMEs) Development in Oman: Current Trends, Challenges, Opportunities and Future Prospects*. 327–342. DOI: 10.1007/978-3-032-04214-9_21

Panteli, N., Yalabik, Z. Y., & Rapti, A. (2019). Fostering work engagement in geographically-dispersed and asynchronous virtual teams. *Information Technology & People*, *32*(1), 2–17. DOI: 10.1108/ITP-04-2017-0133

Park, K. H., Liu, Q., & Li, H. (2023). UNESCO practices under the SDG4 and COVID-19 response framework: Topic modeling from 2003 to 2021. *International Journal of Innovative Research and Scientific Studies*, *6*(2), 322–329. DOI: 10.53894/ijirss.v6i2.1407

Petticrew, M., & Roberts, H. (2008). Systematic Reviews in the Social Sciences: A Practical Guide. *Systematic Reviews in the Social Sciences: A Practical Guide*, 1–336. DOI: 10.1002/9780470754887

Salim Ba Awain, A. M., Jantan, M. D., & Sukati, I. (2021a). Assessing the Effect of Integration in Logistics Sector on Economic Growth: Evidence from Sultanate of Oman. *International Business Research*, *15*(1), 35. DOI: 10.5539/ibr.v15n1p35

Salim Ba Awain, A. M., Jantan, M. D., & Sukati, I. (2021b). Assessing the Effect of Integration in Logistics Sector on Economic Growth: Evidence from Sultanate of Oman. *International Business Research, 15*(1), 35. DOI: 10.5539/ibr.v15n1p35

Shannaq, B., & Al Shamsi, I. (2024). Integrating Digital Transformation: Analyzing New Technological Processes for Competitiveness and Growth Opportunities in the Oman Economy. *Studies in Systems. Decision and Control, 525*, 443–454. DOI: 10.1007/978-3-031-54383-8_34

Thorpe, R., Holt, R., Macpherson, A., & Pittaway, L. (2005). Using knowledge within small and medium-sized firms: A systematic review of the evidence. *International Journal of Management Reviews, 7*(4), 257–281. DOI: 10.1111/j.1468-2370.2005.00116.x

Tranfield, D., Denyer, D., & Smart, P. (2003). Towards a Methodology for Developing Evidence-Informed Management Knowledge by Means of Systematic Review. *British Journal of Management, 14*(3), 207–222. DOI: 10.1111/1467-8551.00375

Vernyuy Wirba, A. (2017). The role of research in knowledge economy within GCC countries. *European Journal of Business and Management* Www.Iiste.Org *ISSN, 9*(3).

WHO (2021). *Global strategy on digital health 2020-2025.*

World Bank. (2020). *Comparing Business Regulation in 190 Economies.*

World Economic Forum. (2024). *Annual Report 2023-2024.*

Chapter 8
Transforming Knowledge Dynamics: A Mixed-Methods Investigation of Generative AI-Enabled Knowledge Management for Organizational Innovation

Veena Tewari
http://orcid.org/0000-0003-4025-9909
University of Technology and Applied Sciences, Oman

Amal Sulaiman Al Alawi
University of Technology and Applied Sciences, Oman

Shaik Mastanvali
University of Technology and Applied Sciences, Oman

Swapnil Morande
http://orcid.org/0000-0003-4720-2980
University of Naples, Italy

ABSTRACT

This study investigates the transformative role of Generative Artificial Intelligence (GenAI) in reshaping organizational knowledge management (KM) processes and their subsequent impact on innovation outcomes. Adopting an explanatory sequential mixed-methods design, data were collected from 247 knowledge-intensive organizations across manufacturing, financial services, and technology sectors through semi-structured interviews (n=32) and a structured questionnaire survey. Building

DOI: 10.4018/979-8-3373-8964-6.ch008

upon Nonaka's SECI framework and the Technology-Organization-Environment (TOE) model, this research proposes an integrated conceptual framework examining GenAI-enabled knowledge creation, transfer, and application mechanisms. Organizations with higher GenAI-KM integration reported a 34.2% higher mean perceived innovation score than lower-integration organizations; this represents a cross-sectional association rather than an objective or causal performance effect. Theoretical implications extend the SECI model by incorporating AI-mediated knowledge transformation, while practical recommendations address implementation challenges.

1. INTRODUCTION

Knowledge-intensive organizations now compete on how quickly they create, transfer and apply knowledge across distributed work systems (Alavi et al., 2024; Nonaka & Takeuchi, 1995). Generative Artificial Intelligence (GenAI), expressed through large language models (LLMs) and multimodal generative systems, changes how that knowledge work is performed (Benbya et al., 2024; O'Leary, 2024). GenAI does not only automate routine tasks. It supports and shapes cognitive work, drafting, summarizing and connecting material that knowledge workers previously assembled by hand.

Despite fast enterprise adoption, the mechanisms through which GenAI reshapes knowledge creation, transfer and application are still under-examined (Kirchner, 2025; Nakash & Bolisani, 2024). Industry surveys estimate that a large majority of enterprises have launched at least one GenAI pilot (Deloitte, 2024), yet peer-reviewed evidence linking GenAI-enabled KM practices to measurable innovation outcomes is still limited and weighted toward conceptual treatment (Mariani & Dwivedi, 2024; Muzzio & Gama, 2024; Nakash & Bolisani, 2024). The gap matters in practice. Decisions on workforce reskilling, governance and data infrastructure are being made before the evidence on returns is in.

Three theoretical tensions motivate the study. First, the SECI framework was developed in a pre-AI setting (Nonaka, 1994), and whether GenAI alters its four conversion modes is contested, with some proposing wholesale revision (Böhm & Durst, 2025; Matsumoto et al., 2025) and others arguing for incremental adaptation (Richter & Richter, 2024). Second, the TOE lens (Tornatzky & Fleischer, 1990) has been applied to AI adoption but rarely to AI-mediated knowledge processes. Third, socio-technical systems theory (Trist, 1981) and dynamic capabilities (Teece, 2007) offer explanatory power that has been largely absent from the GenAI-KM literature. For practitioners these tensions are not academic. They decide whether a firm treats

GenAI as a documentation tool, a collaboration partner or a governance liability, and that framing drives where money and training go.

The aim is concise. The study examines how GenAI-enabled KM practices relate to differentiated innovation outcomes and which contextual conditions strengthen or weaken that relationship. Those contextual conditions are operationalized through three named moderators: organizational readiness, technological complexity and environmental dynamism. Four research questions follow:

- RQ1: How does GenAI integration relate to each of the four SECI knowledge processes in knowledge-intensive organizations?
- RQ2: To what extent do GenAI-enabled KM practices predict product, process and organizational innovation outcomes?
- RQ3: Which technological, organizational and environmental factors moderate the GenAI-KM-innovation relationship?
- RQ4: What mechanisms explain the differential effects of GenAI across SECI dimensions and across sectors?

The chapter makes four signposted contributions. **Empirically**, it supplies large-sample evidence on a relationship that has been theorized but not validated at scale. **Theoretically**, it refines the SECI lens by specifying where GenAI helps and where it does not and integrates TOE moderators with socio-technical and dynamic-capabilities reasoning into a multi-level model. **Methodologically**, it demonstrates an explanatory sequential design in which survey results directly drove interview sampling and protocol. **Practically**, it engages the harder side of GenAI knowledge work, including hallucination, cognitive offloading and erosion of tacit expertise (Kirchner, 2025; Sumbal & Amber, 2024), and converts the findings into a deployment checklist.

A note on framing is warranted. This is a human-centric study. The technology is examined not as an autonomous force but as a tool whose value depends on the human and organizational substrate around it. Workforce evolution is treated as a central concern, and it enters the empirical model directly through the AI-literacy component of organizational readiness and through the human-AI collaboration mechanism surfaced in the qualitative phase. Expertise preservation and ethical deployment are likewise treated as design requirements rather than afterthoughts. This framing is consistent with calls for socio-technical balance in AI research (Pasmore et al., 2019; Sarker et al., 2019; Trist, 1981) and with practitioner experience that purely techno-centric rollouts often disappoint (Jarrahi et al., 2023). The remainder proceeds as follows. Section 2 reviews the literature and develops the framework. Section 3 details the methodology. Section 4 reports findings. Section

5 interprets them. Section 6 discusses implications. Section 7 states limitations and future research. Section 8 concludes.

2. LITERATURE REVIEW AND CONCEPTUAL FRAMEWORK

This section synthesizes literature across overlapping streams and closes with a comparative positioning of the proposed framework against existing AI-SECI extensions. The review is organized to surface unresolved tensions rather than to catalog prior work.

2.1 Background

Knowledge management studies how organizations create, store, transfer and apply knowledge to improve performance. The field carries two enduring commitments that frame this chapter. Knowledge is partly tacit and resists full codification (Polanyi, 1966), and knowledge value is realized through social and technical arrangements rather than storage alone (Trist, 1981). GenAI intersects both commitments. It lowers the cost of codifying and recombining explicit knowledge, while raising new questions about what counts as reliable organizational knowledge once machine-generated content enters the repository. This background motivates the theoretical choices that follow.

2.2 Theoretical Foundations of Knowledge Management

The SECI model has shaped the field substantially (Nonaka, 1994; Nonaka & Takeuchi, 1995). It conceptualizes organizational knowledge as oscillating between tacit and explicit forms through four conversion modes: socialization (tacit to tacit), externalization (tacit to explicit), combination (explicit to explicit) and internalization (explicit to tacit). Polanyi's (1966) tacit-explicit distinction supplies the epistemological base, while Nonaka and Konno's (1998) notion of 'Ba' supplies the contextual layer where conversions occur.

Later scholarship is broadly approving but flags real limits. Some argue the model overstates the convertibility of tacit knowledge (Gourlay, 2006). Others note its Japan-centric origins and call for culturally pluralistic extensions (Glisby & Holden, 2003). A recent systematic review of KM and innovation (Muzzio & Gama, 2024) concludes that established KM frameworks remain analytically useful but need updating for digitally mediated work; the review treats KM and innovation broadly rather than SECI in AI contexts specifically, and the present study draws on it for that broader gap. Recent KM-and-AI reviews reinforce the point that empirical, theory-linked evidence remains thin (Nakash & Bolisani, 2024; Sumbal & Amber, 2024). SECI is therefore treated here as a starting heuristic to be tested against AI-mediated practice, not as a fixed template.

2.3 Generative AI and Organizational Innovation: Promise and Peril

GenAI differs from earlier AI. It produces novel content rather than only classifying or predicting (Mariani & Dwivedi, 2024). It interacts in natural language. It shows emergent reasoning behaviors at scale (Chang et al., 2024). One distinction is central to KM quality and is kept explicit throughout this chapter. GenAI produces candidate content; that content becomes validated organizational knowledge only after human verification and provenance checks. Treating the two as equivalent is the root of several risks discussed below.

Empirical evidence on innovation effects is suggestive but uneven. Doshi and Hauser (2024) report that GenAI lifts individual creativity yet narrows collective diversity. Singh et al. (2024) find positive effects on exploration and exploitation, mediated by user expertise. Kernan Freire et al. (2024) document productivity gains in manufacturing knowledge sharing through LLM-powered tools. These studies sit mostly at the individual or task level. Aggregating them to organizational hypotheses is defensible because KM theory treats organizational knowledge creation as the accumulation of individual conversions within shared contexts (Nonaka & Konno, 1998); individual and task-level gains plausibly scale into organizational outcomes when supported by routines and culture. The relationship is therefore contingent on user, task and organizational characteristics rather than unidirectional.

A growing critical literature pushes against techno-optimist framing. Bender et al. (2021) caution that LLMs are stochastic mimics rather than understanders. Weidinger et al. (2022) catalog harms including misinformation, exclusion and dependency. Bommasani et al. (2022) raise concerns about homogenization across users of foundation models. For KM systems specifically, these risks translate into polluted repositories and over-trusted summaries (Alavi et al., 2024; Sumbal & Amber, 2024). These critiques are central, not peripheral, to any examination of GenAI-enabled KM.

2.4 Critical Perspectives: Hallucination, Epistemic Reliability and Tacit Erosion

Three critical strands inform the study. First, hallucination. LLMs generate confident outputs that are not grounded in source material (Ji et al., 2023). In KM contexts, hallucinated content can pollute repositories and propagate through downstream decisions (Alavi et al., 2024). Second, epistemic reliability. AI-generated content can appear authoritative while lacking provenance, undermining the verifiability on which scholarly and managerial knowledge depends (Floridi, 2023). Third, tacit erosion. When workers offload reasoning to AI, opportunities for expertise development through deliberate practice may diminish (Carr, 2020).

These risks are not arguments against adoption. They are arguments for designed deployment, governance scaffolding and preserved human judgment loops. The framework reflects this by treating organizational readiness as a moderator that captures, among other elements, governance maturity and AI literacy of the workforce.

A further nuance is worth surfacing. Critical AI scholarship sometimes treats hallucination as a property of the model alone. It is more accurately a property of the model-task-organization interaction. The same LLM produces very different reliability when paired with retrieval-augmented generation, provenance metadata and human verification loops, versus when deployed naively (Lewis et al., 2020). Treating hallucination as a socio-technical phenomenon, rather than a glitch awaiting a better model, shifts attention from waiting for stronger models to building stronger workflows around current ones.

2.5 SECI in the AI Era: A Comparative Synthesis of Recent Extensions

Four recent contributions warrant explicit comparison. Böhm and Durst (2025) propose the GRAI (Generative AI-Augmented Innovation) framework, which respecifies each SECI mode in light of GenAI capabilities; the treatment is conceptual and offers no empirical validation. Matsumoto et al. (2025) advance the Human-AI-Collaboration SECI (HAC-SECI) model with a dual-loop architecture; the contribution is theoretically rich but illustrated through a single case. Liu (2024) presents empirical results focused on product innovation efficiency but does not differentiate across innovation types or sectors. Richter and Richter (2024) argue a more conservative position in which SECI survives GenAI with modest adjustment rather than radical reconception.

The present framework differs in three respects. It is empirically grounded in a multi-sector sample of 247 organizations rather than conceptual or single-case. It differentiates innovation into product, process and organizational categories rather than treating innovation as a monolith. And it integrates TOE moderators with socio-technical constructs, producing a contingency model rather than a universal one. Table 1 sets these differences out directly across constructs, empirical basis, moderators and outcomes. The objective is not to displace prior contributions but to add empirical specificity and contextual range.

Table 1. Comparative Synthesis of AI-Era SECI Extensions Against the Present Framework

Dimension	GRAI (Böhm & Durst, 2025)	HAC-SECI (Matsumoto et al., 2025)	Liu (2024)	Richter & Richter (2024)	Present framework
Evidence base	Conceptual	Single case	Empirical, single outcome	Conceptual / position	Empirical, 247 firms + 32 interviews
SECI treatment	Respecifies all four modes	Dual-loop human-AI	SECI as antecedent	SECI largely retained	Differential effects per mode
Innovation outcome	Innovation (general)	Knowledge creation	Product efficiency	Not central	Product, process, organizational
Moderators	None modeled	None modeled	None modeled	None modeled	Readiness, complexity, dynamism
Critical / risk lens	Limited	Limited	Absent	Partial	Hallucination, tacit erosion, power
Sector range	None	One context	One context	None	Manufacturing, finance, technology

Note. All entries reflect the cited works as represented in this chapter. 'None modeled' indicates moderators were not tested empirically in that source.

2.6 The Technology-Organization-Environment Framework

The TOE framework (Tornatzky & Fleischer, 1990) holds that adoption outcomes are shaped by technological factors (capability, complexity, compatibility), organizational factors (size, structure, culture, slack) and environmental factors (industry pressure, regulation, competitive intensity). Applied to GenAI, recent work identifies technological complexity, organizational readiness and environmental dynamism as the most predictive (Alsheibani et al., 2018; Cubric, 2020). One step in the logic deserves to be made explicit. TOE was developed to explain whether organizations adopt a technology. Here the same factors are used to explain how effectively adopted GenAI translates into KM and innovation value. The bridge is that the conditions enabling adoption, such as governance maturity, AI literacy and slack for experimentation, are the same conditions that let an adopted tool be used well rather than superficially. The present model therefore positions these three factors as moderators of effectiveness, not only predictors of adoption likelihood, and tests them empirically.

2.7 Socio-Technical Systems Theory and Dynamic Capabilities as Background Lenses

Two complementary lenses extend the explanatory range and are used as background framing rather than as separately measured constructs. Socio-technical systems theory (Pasmore et al., 2019; Trist, 1981) posits joint optimization of technical and social subsystems as the condition for sustained performance; in GenAI deployments this implies that technical capability alone is insufficient, and that workforce involvement, task redesign and trust building matter equally. Dynamic capabilities theory (Teece, 2007) describes the firm's capacity to sense, seize and reconfigure resources as environments change; GenAI adoption can be read as a sensing-seizing-reconfiguring sequence in which organizations continuously update KM practices as model capabilities evolve. Neither lens is operationalized as a survey construct in this study. Each is used to interpret why human-AI collaboration design and temporal adaptation shape outcomes, and each is flagged for explicit measurement in future work.

Together the lenses supply a multi-level account. SECI describes the micro-process of knowledge conversion. TOE specifies the adoption contingencies. Socio-technical theory clarifies why collaboration design matters. Dynamic capabilities explains the temporal evolution of organizational responses.

2.8 Sector-Specific Evidence: Manufacturing, Financial Services and Technology

Manufacturing studies report gains in shop-floor knowledge capture and cross-shift handover quality through LLM-powered tools (Kernan Freire et al., 2024), set within broader human-centric smart-manufacturing frameworks that stress the human-cyber-physical interface rather than GenAI alone (Wang et al., 2024). Financial services research highlights compliance-related knowledge synthesis, risk modeling and customer-facing retrieval (Cao, 2022; Goldstein et al., 2023). Technology-sector studies focus on code documentation, internal developer Q&A and AI-assisted research workflows (Kirchner, 2025). These signals suggest plausible heterogeneity in GenAI-KM effects, examined here through multi-group comparison.

2.9 Research Gap, Conceptual Framework and Hypotheses

Synthesizing the literature reveals a sharp residual gap. After GRAI and HAC-SECI, the field has conceptual models of how GenAI might change each SECI mode but no large-sample test of whether those changes translate into differentiated innovation outcomes, and no specification of the contextual conditions under which they do. Prior empirical work (Liu, 2024) treats innovation as a single construct and omits moderators. What remains unknown, therefore, is the shape of the effect across SECI modes, its split across innovation types and the conditions that switch it on or off. This chapter addresses that gap with an explanatory sequential design that first estimates the differentiated effects and moderators at scale, then uses interviews to explain the mechanisms behind them. The conceptual framework (Figure 1) connects four GenAI-enabled SECI processes to product, process and organizational innovation, with organizational readiness, technological complexity and environmental dynamism as moderators. Six hypotheses follow:

- H1: GenAI-enabled SECI practices are positively associated with innovation outcomes.
- H2: The effect of GenAI on externalization and combination is stronger than its effect on socialization and internalization.
- H3: Organizational readiness positively moderates the GenAI-KM to innovation relationship.
- H4: Technological complexity negatively moderates the GenAI-KM to innovation relationship.
- H5: Environmental dynamism positively moderates the GenAI-KM to innovation relationship.
- H6: GenAI-KM effects on innovation differ significantly across manufacturing, financial services and technology sectors.

Figure 1. Integrated Conceptual Framework: GenAI-Enabled SECI for Differentiated Innovation Outcomes (Moderated by TOE and Socio-Technical Conditions)

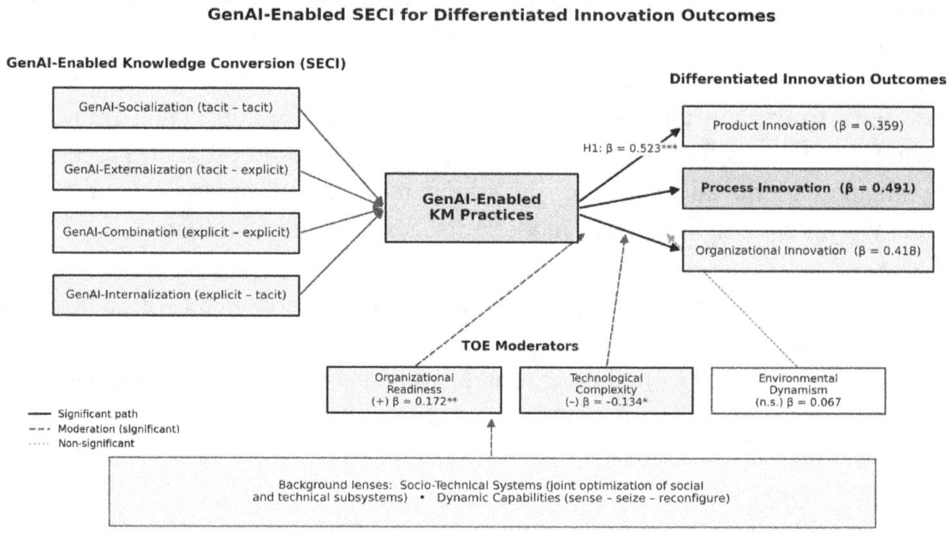

3. RESEARCH METHODOLOGY

3.1 Research Design and Philosophical Orientation

An explanatory sequential mixed-methods design was used (Creswell & Plano Clark, 2017) within a pragmatist paradigm (Morgan, 2014). The design unfolded in two phases. Phase 1 generated quantitative breadth through a structured survey. Phase 2 supplied qualitative depth through semi-structured interviews. The sequencing was deliberate and the linkage between phases was concrete rather than nominal. Survey results produced a composite GenAI-KM integration score and an innovation-outcome score for each organization; these scores then drove interview sampling and shaped the interview protocol, as detailed in Section 3.3.1. The pragmatist orientation permits methodological pluralism in service of the research questions rather than allegiance to a single epistemology.

3.2 Phase 1: Quantitative Study

3.2.1 Sampling, Unit of Analysis and Recruitment

The target population comprised knowledge-intensive organizations operating in manufacturing, financial services and technology. The unit of analysis was the organization, and a single key informant represented each organization: the most senior person responsible for KM or innovation (chief knowledge officer, chief information officer, innovation director or equivalent senior manager). The 247 usable responses therefore correspond to 247 distinct organizations and 247 respondents, one per organization. Key-informant designs are standard in organization-level KM research where the construct of interest is a firm-level practice rather than an individual attitude.

Inclusion criteria required (a) a minimum of 50 employees, (b) operational presence in at least one target sector and (c) some level of GenAI adoption activity, whether pilot or production. Sampling was stratified by sector and organization-size band, using industry-association membership directories as the sampling frame. Stratification ensured each sector and size band was represented in proportion to the frame. The frame is acknowledged as a limitation, since association membership skews toward more formally organized firms; this boundary is revisited in Section 7. Distribution was electronic, with invitations addressed to the named key informant in each organization.

Of 480 organizations invited, 247 returned usable questionnaires after two reminder waves between February and May 2024, a response rate of 51.5%. The rate is acceptable for senior-level organizational research (Baruch & Holtom, 2008). Non-response bias was assessed by comparing early and late respondents on the principal constructs using independent-samples t-tests; no significant differences were observed (all $p > .10$). Diagnostic detail is reported in Appendix C.

Respondents were drawn from organizations operating in multiple countries. Because stratification was by sector and size rather than geography, the resulting geographic concentration is treated as a boundary condition rather than a representativeness claim, and generalization across regions is addressed in Section 7.

3.2.2 Instrument Development and Validation (Procedures)

The instrument was developed through a six-step process. Step 1 generated items from established scales: SECI items adapted from Farnese et al. (2019); innovation items from Wang and Ahmed (2004) and Jiménez-Jiménez and Sanz-Valle (2011); TOE moderators from Alsheibani et al. (2018) and Cubric (2020). Step 2 contextualized items to the GenAI setting through targeted rewording while holding the underlying construct meaning constant, a point illustrated in Section 3.2.3 and Appendix A. Step 3 submitted an initial pool of 34 candidate items to five domain experts for content validation: three academic specialists in KM and two senior GenAI implementation practitioners. Among the retained items, I-CVI values ranged from 0.80 to 1.00; three candidate items scoring below 0.78 were removed, and four retained items were reworded. Step 4 piloted the instrument with 28 organizations to check clarity, reliability and response patterns. Step 5 refined items using pilot findings and exploratory factor analysis. Step 6 finalized 52 multi-item indicators: 21 SECI items, 12 innovation items, 14 moderator items and 5 pre-existing KM-infrastructure items, supplemented by organization size, sector and adoption-maturity controls. Reliability and validity outcomes from the main study are reported with the results in Section 4.2, keeping Section 3 to procedures.

3.2.3 Measurement Constructs and Measurement Model Type

Four GenAI-enabled SECI dimensions were measured with 21 items (socialization 5, externalization 6, combination 5, internalization 5) on seven-point Likert scales. Innovation outcomes used 12 items across product (4), process (4) and organizational (4) innovation. Moderators were technological complexity (4 items), organizational readiness (6 items, spanning governance maturity and workforce AI literacy as explicit sub-facets) and environmental dynamism (4 items). Controls were organization size (natural log of employee count), industry sector (categorical), GenAI adoption maturity (four-stage scale, defined in Section 4.1) and pre-existing KM infrastructure (5 items).

All multi-item latent variables were specified as reflective. This judgement rests on the conceptual interchangeability of items within each construct and their expected covariation, which is the standard condition for reflective measurement (Hair et al., 2022). Reflective specification is what licenses the reliability, AVE and HTMT evaluation reported in Section 4.2. Sample items for each SECI dimension and the GenAI rewording applied to each are listed in Appendix A.

3.2.4 Statistical Analysis

Variance-based Partial Least Squares Structural Equation Modeling (PLS-SEM) was performed in SmartPLS 4.0. PLS-SEM was chosen for its suitability with complex models, its predictive orientation and its tolerance of moderate sub-group sizes (Hair et al., 2022). Because PLS-SEM is variance-based rather than covariance-based, model assessment followed PLS conventions: indicator reliability and loadings, internal consistency, convergent and discriminant validity, standardized root mean square residual (SRMR) as the available approximate fit index, collinearity (VIF), structural path significance via bootstrapping with 5,000 resamples, effect sizes (f^2) and predictive relevance (Q^2). Covariance-based fit indices such as CFI, TLI and RMSEA were not estimated, since they are not applicable to variance-based PLS-SEM. Multi-group analysis (MGA) tested sectoral differences, and moderation used the product-indicator approach for continuous moderators.

3.3 Phase 2: Qualitative Study

3.3.1 Participant Selection, Linkage to Survey Results and Protocol

Thirty-two interviews were conducted with senior practitioners drawn from 24 surveyed organizations. Selection was driven directly by the Phase 1 results. Each organization's standardized composite innovation-outcome score was paired with its GenAI-KM integration score, and organizations were sorted into those that converted comparable GenAI investment into high versus low innovation outcomes. Purposive extreme-case sampling then selected 18 informants from high-converting organizations and 14 from low-converting organizations, so that the interviews would explain the variance the survey had measured rather than describe GenAI use in general. The protocol was also shaped by the survey: blocks were written to probe the specific paths that the model estimated, including the strong externalization and combination effects, the readiness moderation and the negative complexity moderation. The five thematic blocks covered implementation approach, perceived effects on each knowledge process, organizational frictions, governance and risk, and forward-looking adaptation. Interviews ran 45 to 75 minutes by secure video conferencing between June and August 2024. The protocol was piloted with two practitioners not in the final sample.

3.3.2 Data Analysis

Analysis used codebook thematic analysis in the structured, reliability-oriented tradition rather than reflexive thematic analysis, because the study used two coders and an a priori coding structure aligned to the survey constructs. The six-phase sequence of Braun and Clarke (2006) organized the work. Audio recordings were transcribed verbatim. Two researchers coded independently in NVivo 14 against the shared codebook. Inter-coder reliability, assessed via Cohen's kappa on a randomly selected 20% subset, reached 0.87. Disagreements were resolved through discussion, and codes were organized into themes through constant comparison.

3.4 Ethical Considerations

The study involved human participants through surveys and interviews. Ethical clearance was obtained from the institutional research ethics committee before data collection (approval reference anonymized for review and available from the corresponding author on request). All participants received an information sheet covering purpose, voluntary participation, anonymity, data handling and the right to withdraw. Written informed consent was obtained from every respondent and interviewee. Interviews were recorded only after explicit verbal and written consent. Personal and organizational identifiers were removed from transcripts and reporting. Data were held on encrypted institutional servers with access restricted to the research team. Processing complied with applicable data-protection regulation, including the General Data Protection Regulation (GDPR) where relevant, and with institutional data-handling policy.

AI tools were used during manuscript preparation only for grammar and language refinement. No AI tool generated research data, analytical results or interpretive content. The authors take full responsibility for all conceptual, methodological and interpretive choices. This disclosure is stated once here and not repeated in the declarations, to avoid duplication.

3.5 Mixed-Methods Integration Strategy

Integration occurred at three points. At the design stage, qualitative inquiry was sequenced to follow and build on quantitative results. At the analysis stage, joint displays compared statistical patterns with thematic findings (Guetterman et al., 2015). At the interpretation stage, quantitative-qualitative correspondence was evaluated for confirmation, expansion and discordance, with attention to discordant signals as a source of theoretical insight rather than something to be smoothed away.

4. DATA ANALYSIS AND FINDINGS

This section reports quantitative results, qualitative themes and the integrated synthesis, following the explanatory sequential logic: numbers first, then meaning.

4.1 Sample Characteristics and Adoption-Maturity Scale

Table 2 summarizes the 247 respondent organizations. Sectoral representation was balanced: manufacturing 37.2%, financial services 31.6% and technology 31.2%. Size ranged across small-medium (22.7%, < 250 employees), mid-sized (25.5%,

250 to 1,000), large (23.5%, 1,000 to 5,000) and very large (28.3%, > 5,000). The four-stage GenAI adoption-maturity scale was anchored as follows: Stage 1 Exploration (assessing use cases, no deployment), Stage 2 Piloting (limited pilots in one or two functions), Stage 3 Operational (integrated into specific workflows) and Stage 4 Scaled (governed enterprise-wide deployment). The sample mean of 2.4 (SD = 0.87) places most organizations between piloting and operational stages.

Table 2. Demographic Profile of Respondent Organizations (n = 247)

Characteristic	Frequency	Percentage
Industry sector		
Manufacturing	92	37.2%
Financial services	78	31.6%
Technology	77	31.2%
Organization size		
< 250 employees	56	22.7%
250 – 1,000 employees	63	25.5%
1,000 – 5,000 employees	58	23.5%
> 5,000 employees	70	28.3%
GenAI adoption maturity	**M = 2.4**	**SD = 0.87**

4.2 Measurement Model Evaluation

Measurement evaluation followed PLS-SEM conventions. Standardized indicator loadings ranged from 0.67 to 0.89, the large majority above 0.70. One externalization indicator loaded at 0.67; it was retained because its construct's composite reliability (0.93) and AVE (0.69) remained well above thresholds and the item carried distinct content coverage, so removal would have narrowed construct breadth without reliability gain (Hair et al., 2022). The full loading matrix with item-level VIF is reported in Appendix B. Internal consistency, convergent validity and discriminant validity all met accepted thresholds, summarized in Table 3. The standardized root mean square residual was 0.052, below the 0.08 guideline, indicating acceptable approximate fit for a variance-based model. Discriminant validity held on both the Fornell-Larcker criterion and the HTMT ratio (all HTMT < 0.85).

Table 3. Reliability and Convergent Validity of Latent Constructs

Construct	Items	α	CR	AVE
GenAI-Socialization	5	0.81	0.87	0.58
GenAI-Externalization	6	0.91	0.93	0.69
GenAI-Combination	5	0.88	0.91	0.67
GenAI-Internalization	5	0.79	0.86	0.55
Product Innovation	4	0.85	0.89	0.66
Process Innovation	4	0.86	0.90	0.68
Organizational Innovation	4	0.83	0.88	0.64
Organizational Readiness	6	0.89	0.92	0.65
Technological Complexity	4	0.82	0.88	0.65
Environmental Dynamism	4	0.80	0.86	0.61

Note. α = Cronbach's alpha; CR = composite reliability; AVE = average variance extracted. All CR > 0.70 and all AVE > 0.50.

Common method bias was assessed three ways. Harman's single-factor test returned a largest factor accounting for 28.4% of variance, below the 50% threshold. Because the single-factor test alone is widely regarded as insufficient, a marker-variable check was added using a theoretically unrelated marker; method-adjusted path estimates were materially unchanged. A full collinearity assessment returned inner-model VIF values from 1.34 to 2.71, all below the 3.3 conservative ceiling for common-method concern (Kock, 2015). The combined evidence indicates common method variance is not a substantive concern. Diagnostic detail appears in Appendix C.

4.3 Structural Model and Hypothesis Testing

Two structural specifications were estimated. Model 1 used GenAI-enabled KM as a higher-order construct to test H1 and explained 47% of the variance in composite innovation outcomes ($R^2 = 0.47$; $Q^2 = 0.31$); its path to innovation was positive and significant ($\beta = 0.523$, $p < .001$). Model 2 entered socialization, externalization, combination and internalization as separate predictors to compare their differentiated associations with innovation. The previously reported R^2 and Q^2 values for "KM effectiveness" were removed because no distinct endogenous KM-effectiveness construct was specified.

Examining individual SECI dimensions surfaced the differentiated pattern central to the study. GenAI-assisted externalization showed the strongest standardized effect ($\beta = 0.412$, $p < .001$, $f^2 = 0.18$), followed by combination ($\beta = 0.387$, $p < .001$, $f^2 = 0.15$), internalization ($\beta = 0.298$, $p < .01$, $f^2 = 0.08$) and socialization (β

$= 0.214$, $p < .05$, $f^2 = 0.04$). Table 4 reports the full path results with significance, effect sizes and collinearity.

Table 4. Structural Model Results: Paths, Significance, Effect Size and Collinearity

Path	β	t	p	f^2	VIF
GenAI-KM → Innovation (H1)	0.523	9.81	< .001	0.41	–
Externalization → Innovation	0.412	7.42	< .001	0.18	2.41
Combination → Innovation	0.387	6.88	< .001	0.15	2.71
Internalization → Innovation	0.298	4.36	< .01	0.08	1.96
Socialization → Innovation	0.214	2.55	< .05	0.04	1.34
Org. Readiness × KM (H3)	0.172	3.01	< .01	0.05	–
Tech. Complexity × KM (H4)	–0.134	2.28	< .05	0.03	–
Env. Dynamism × KM (H5)	0.067	1.23	.218	0.01	–

Note. Bootstrapping with 5,000 resamples. Inner-model VIF for predictors confirmed no collinearity threat.

To test H2 directly rather than by rank order alone, pairwise path-coefficient differences were evaluated using bootstrap confidence intervals (Table 5). Externalization and combination each exceeded socialization at $p < .01$, and externalization exceeded internalization at $p < .05$. The combination-internalization difference did not reach significance ($p = .074$). H2 is therefore supported in its main claim, that the explicit-oriented modes outperform socialization, with the externalization advantage over internalization confirmed and the combination advantage over internalization not statistically distinguishable.

Table 5. Pairwise Path-Coefficient Difference Tests for H2

Comparison	Δβ	p
Externalization vs Socialization	0.198	< .01
Externalization vs Internalization	0.114	< .05
Combination vs Socialization	0.173	< .01
Combination vs Internalization	0.089	.074 (n.s.)

Note. Δβ = difference in standardized path coefficients, bootstrap-based. n.s. = not significant.

4.4 Moderation and Multi-Group Analysis

Moderation returned a mixed picture. Organizational readiness positively moderated the GenAI-KM to innovation relationship ($\beta = 0.172$, $p < .01$), supporting H3.

Technological complexity moderated it negatively ($\beta = -0.134$, $p < .05$), supporting H4. Environmental dynamism did not reach significance ($\beta = 0.067$, $p = .218$), so H5 was not supported; this null result is reflected in the abstract to avoid implying that all moderators held.

Multi-group analysis across sectors returned significant differences ($\Delta\beta$ tech-mfg = 0.21, $p = .014$; $\Delta\beta$ tech-fin = 0.13, $p = .041$), supporting H6, with technology showing the strongest path, then financial services, then manufacturing. The MGA used the standard PLS-MGA permutation procedure, which assumes configural and compositional measurement invariance; invariance was checked via the MICOM procedure and held for the compared groups. Sector sub-samples were modest (manufacturing 92, financial services 78, technology 77), so sectoral coefficients are read as indicative rather than definitive, and Section 5.2 keeps the interpretation cautious on this point.

A median split on the composite GenAI-KM integration score produced higher- and lower-integration groups. The higher-integration group reported a mean perceived innovation score of 5.42 (SD = 0.94), compared with 4.04 (SD = 1.12) for the lower-integration group. The relative mean difference was 34.2%, calculated as (5.42 – 4.04) / 4.04. Inferential test statistics were omitted pending verification against the raw group sizes and underlying observations; the result should therefore be interpreted descriptively rather than causally.

4.5 Differentiated Innovation Outcomes

Disaggregating innovation into product, process and organizational sub-dimensions returned a finer pattern (Table 6). GenAI-enabled KM practices were most strongly associated with process innovation ($\beta = 0.491$, $p < .001$), then organizational innovation ($\beta = 0.418$, $p < .001$) and product innovation ($\beta = 0.359$, $p < .001$). One reading, advanced cautiously because the design is cross-sectional, is that GenAI's most immediate contribution may lie in reshaping how knowledge work is organized internally before it surfaces in market-facing product novelty. The disaggregation itself addresses a gap in prior work that has tended to treat innovation as a single construct.

Table 6. Differentiated Innovation Outcomes by SECI Process (Standardized Path Coefficients)

SECI dimension	Product (β)	Process (β)	Organizational (β)
GenAI-Socialization	0.18*	0.21*	0.24*
GenAI-Externalization	0.36***	0.45***	0.41***
GenAI-Combination	0.34***	0.43***	0.38***
GenAI-Internalization	0.26**	0.32**	0.29**
Composite β	**0.359*** **	**0.491*** **	**0.418*** **

Note. p < .05; p < .01; **p < .001.

Figure 2. PLS-SEM Path Model Results: Standardized Coefficients, Effect Sizes and R2 Across SECI Processes and Innovation Sub-Dimensions

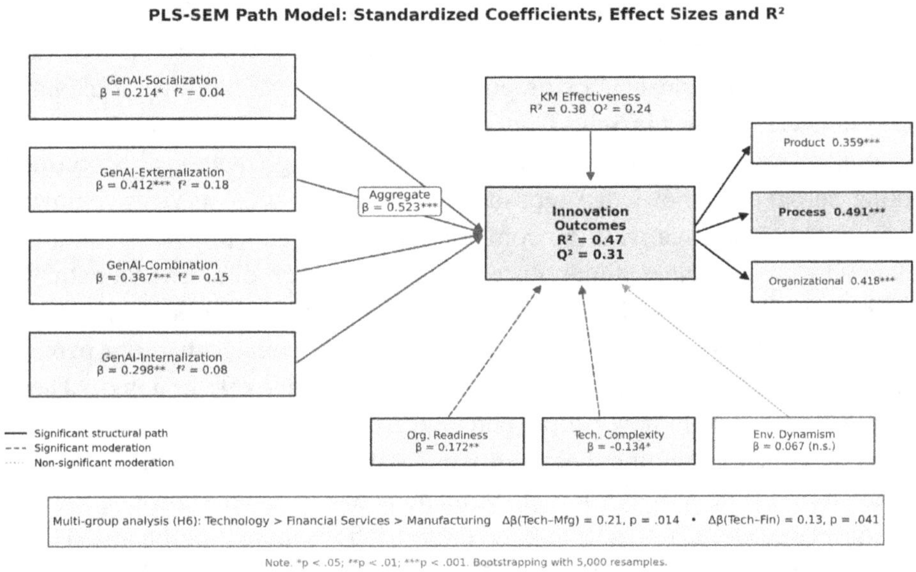

4.6 Qualitative Findings

Thematic analysis of the 32 interviews surfaced five themes that contextualize the quantitative results. Participants are identified by code, sector and role to preserve anonymity while signaling source diversity. Counts indicate how many of the 32 informants raised each theme.

Theme 1: Enhanced knowledge articulation and codification (26 of 32 informants). Participants described GenAI as lowering the cognitive cost of converting tacit expertise into written form through structured prompts, summarization and template generation. One senior knowledge manager observed: 'We have seen a dramatic lift in documentation quality and completeness since rolling out GenAI assistants. People who previously struggled to articulate their expertise are now producing comprehensive knowledge artifacts with AI support' (P04, technology, knowledge manager). The theme corresponds to the strong externalization coefficient. A caution is warranted, raised by several informants and retained here: AI-assisted text captures articulable expertise, not the full tacit substrate behind it. The codified artifact is a partial trace, not the expertise itself, so externalization gains should not be read as complete tacit capture.

Theme 2: Accelerated knowledge integration and synthesis (24 of 32 informants). Combination effects were attributed to pattern-recognition and semantic synthesis across previously siloed repositories. An innovation director explained: 'The system can connect insights from our engineering teams with market research that would otherwise have remained siloed. It is like having a meta-analyst constantly working across our knowledge repositories' (P11, financial services, innovation director). This resonates with the combination coefficient ($\beta = 0.387$) and helps explain why process innovation registered the highest sub-dimensional path.

Theme 3: Cultural and trust frictions (21 of 32 informants). Cultural resistance was the most consistently reported barrier, centered on AI reliability, perceived threat to expert status and data privacy. A chief knowledge officer noted: 'There is a generational divide in how people perceive AI assistance. Senior experts sometimes view it as undermining their hard-won knowledge, while younger employees embrace it as a productivity tool' (P19, manufacturing, chief knowledge officer). Low-converting organizations exhibited these frictions more prominently. The pattern maps directly onto the positive readiness moderation in Section 4.4, and is read here as the mechanism behind that statistical moderation: readiness works partly by defusing the trust friction that otherwise blocks adoption value.

Theme 4: Data quality, governance and hallucination risk (23 of 32 informants). A recurring concern was the dependence of GenAI utility on underlying data quality, with hallucination named as a specific risk. An IT director cautioned: 'Garbage in, garbage out – but with AI it is sophisticated-sounding garbage, which is almost worse' (P07, technology, IT director). Several informants described confidently inaccurate AI output that required time-intensive validation. Organizations with mature data governance reported markedly better outcomes. The theme expands the negative complexity moderation and points to a concrete remedy:

retrieval grounding, provenance metadata and human verification (Lewis et al., 2020), discussed in Section 6.2.

Theme 5: Human-AI collaboration dynamics (27 of 32 informants). High-converting organizations consistently described GenAI as augmentation of human work rather than replacement, preserving human judgment loops for contextual evaluation and creative direction. An innovation manager described it as: 'We have found the sweet spot is using AI for the heavy lifting of information synthesis while humans provide contextual judgment and creative direction' (P23, technology, innovation manager). The theme aligns with the symbiotic human-AI perspective of Matsumoto et al. (2025) and supports a socio-technical reading. It is also where the workforce thread is clearest: the separating variable between high and low performers was not the model but the human capability and process around it.

4.7 Mixed-Methods Synthesis: Joint Display

Table 7 links quantitative paths, qualitative themes and a concrete meta-inference for each, following Guetterman et al. (2015). Three correspondence types appeared: confirmation, expansion and contextualization. Discordance was assessed by searching for themes that contradicted a measured path or that held only in one performance group; no major discordant patterns were identified, though the partial, performance-conditioned nature of theme 3 is noted rather than smoothed over.

Table 7. Joint Display: Quantitative-Qualitative Integration with Meta-Inferences

Quantitative path	Result	Theme	Meta-inference
GenAI-KM → Innovation	$\beta = 0.523^{***}$	Themes 1, 2, 5	Value is realized through articulation, synthesis and preserved human judgment acting together, not through the tool alone.
Externalization differential	$\beta = 0.412^{***}$	Theme 1	GenAI mainly accelerates the tacit-to-explicit step, but the codified output is a partial trace of expertise.
Combination differential	$\beta = 0.387^{***}$	Theme 2	Cross-repository synthesis is where GenAI feeds internal process redesign first.
Org. readiness moderation	$\beta = 0.172^{**}$	Theme 3	Readiness works by defusing trust friction; identical investment yields different returns by readiness profile.
Tech. complexity moderation	$\beta = -0.134^{*}$	Theme 4	Opaque, provenance-poor stacks erode value; governance and retrieval grounding buffer the loss.
Sectoral MGA	Tech > Fin > Mfg	Themes 2, 4, 5	Explicit, code-mediated environments convert GenAI faster; tacit, regulated work converts slower.

Note. p < .05; p < .01; **p < .001.

5. DISCUSSION

Findings are interpreted in four parts: the differential SECI pattern, sector-specific variation, risks and boundary conditions, and comparative positioning. Throughout, interpretation is kept cautious where the cross-sectional design limits causal or temporal claims, and the outcomes are read as perceived organizational innovation rather than objective performance.

5.1 Theoretical Interpretation of Differential SECI Effects

The strongest effect on externalization is consistent with a cognitive-economy reading. Tacit-to-explicit conversion is among the most cognitively demanding operations a knowledge worker performs (Nonaka & Konno, 1998; Polanyi, 1966), and GenAI lowers its cost by supplying scaffolding, prompts and intermediate drafts. The combination effect follows similar logic, since synthesis across heterogeneous sources is a task at which current LLMs are comparatively capable (Wei et al., 2022). The weaker effects on socialization and internalization warrant care. Socialization requires shared experiential contexts that resist mediation. Internalization, the conversion of explicit knowledge into embodied skill, depends on practice loops that AI can support but not replace. The pattern refines rather than overturns the SECI lens: GenAI is well-matched to the explicit-heavy halves of the cycle and only partly helpful for the tacit-heavy halves.

An alternative interpretation deserves consideration. The differential might reflect not inherent task-AI fit but the maturity of current tooling. Externalization-oriented tools such as writing assistants and summarizers are more developed than socialization-oriented tools such as collaborative reasoning environments. As capabilities evolve toward sustained multi-party dialogue and richer experiential simulation, the gap may narrow. The present findings are therefore a contemporary snapshot rather than a permanent theoretical claim, which is exactly the kind of temporal contingency the dynamic-capabilities lens anticipates and which Section 7 flags for longitudinal follow-up.

5.2 Sector-Specific Variation

The technology sector showed the strongest associations, financial services an intermediate position and manufacturing the weakest. Several explanations fit the data, offered with the caution that sector sub-samples are modest. Technology firms operate in largely explicit, code-mediated and fast-moving knowledge environments, with higher workforce AI literacy and lower marginal cost of deploying new tools (Kirchner, 2025). Financial services show moderate gains constrained by regulatory complexity and the need for verifiable provenance (Goldstein et al., 2023). Manufacturing carries large proportions of tacit operational knowledge embedded in physical practice, which current models mediate less well (Wang et al., 2024). The relationship is context-conditioned rather than universal, and generalization should be measured.

Two qualitative nuances add texture. Financial services informants repeatedly flagged the tension between rapid synthesis and audit-trail requirements; GenAI summarization of regulatory documents was valued only when paired with source-tracking and human sign-off. Manufacturing informants described a layered pattern in which GenAI helped documentation and shift handover but added little where embodied tacit skill was central, such as fault diagnosis on equipment with idiosyncratic histories.

5.3 Critical Examination: Risks, Tensions and Boundary Conditions

Four risk-side considerations deserve explicit treatment. First, hallucination. The expansion-type integration of theme 4 with the negative complexity moderation suggests GenAI value declines as systems become more opaque and provenance-poor; mature governance buffers this, its absence exposes it. Second, cognitive offloading and tacit erosion. If externalization becomes too easy, the deliberate practice that builds expertise may be short-circuited, a concern several manufacturing informants raised directly. Third, homogenization. Doshi and Hauser (2024) report that GenAI lifts individual creativity while narrowing collective diversity; whether this holds at the organizational level is an open empirical question the present data cannot settle.

Fourth, power dynamics, which the data touch only lightly and which therefore receive measured treatment here and a dedicated place in future research. AI-mediated knowledge flows can concentrate interpretive authority in those who control prompt design, fine-tuning and deployment, so workers further from these levers may experience reduced epistemic agency even as nominal access to knowledge improves. Two informants described a quiet shift in who decides which knowledge is canonical. The point connects to socio-technical research on technology and organizational power (Pasmore et al., 2019), but the present design was not built to measure it, so it is advanced as a hypothesis for dedicated study rather than a finding.

These risks define the boundary conditions of the findings. The model holds well where data quality is high, governance is mature and human-AI collaboration is designed deliberately. Where those conditions are absent, GenAI may produce sophisticated-looking content with weak epistemic foundations, and apparent innovation effects may be illusory or short-lived.

5.4 Comparative Positioning Against Prior Literature

The findings reinforce GRAI's conceptual reading that GenAI alters each SECI mode (Böhm & Durst, 2025) while supplying the empirical specificity the original conceptual treatment lacked. The HAC-SECI dual-loop architecture (Matsumoto et al., 2025) is supported by theme 5, and the present model adds the moderators that explain when the dual loop works and when it stalls. Liu's (2024) empirical results converge with the differential pattern here, while the present study extends scope by separating innovation sub-types and adding multi-sector analysis. Richter and Richter's (2024) conservative reading of SECI survival is partly supported: the model survives, but in a modified form that gives moderation explicit prominence and acknowledges differential effects across modes. Table 1 sets these positions out side by side.

6. IMPLICATIONS FOR THEORY AND PRACTICE

6.1 Theoretical Contributions

Four contributions follow, kept distinct for clarity. First and empirically, the study supplies large-sample evidence for differential SECI effects in GenAI-mediated KM, refining the conceptual extensions of Böhm and Durst (2025) and Matsumoto et al. (2025). Second, it extends the KM-innovation pathway by disaggregating innovation into product, process and organizational sub-dimensions, with process innovation the most responsive. Third, it builds a multi-theoretical model connecting SECI to TOE moderators, with socio-technical and dynamic-capabilities reasoning as interpretive lenses. Fourth, it broadens the AI-KM conversation to engage hallucination, epistemic reliability and tacit erosion alongside the dominant techno-optimist literature.

A further point of specificity is worth surfacing. By treating organizational readiness as a moderator rather than a mere antecedent, the model captures contingent value generation. Two organizations with identical GenAI investments can produce very different innovation outcomes depending on their readiness profile. This contingent reading is consistent with strategic-management traditions linking technology returns to absorptive capacity and dynamic capabilities (Teece, 2007), and it offers a partial answer to the practitioner puzzle of why some GenAI deployments underdeliver despite strong technical execution.

6.2 Practical and Managerial Implications

For practitioners, four recommendations follow, each calibrated to the strength of the evidence behind it. The externalization and combination guidance rests on the strongest paths in the model and is offered with corresponding confidence. The readiness and collaboration guidance rests on a combination of a significant but modest moderation and consistent qualitative signal, and is offered as well-supported but not deterministic.

1. Prioritize GenAI applications that target externalization and combination. Documentation assistants, semantic search across repositories and synthesis tools offer the strongest near-term returns.
2. Invest in organizational readiness before scaling. Cultural preparation, AI-literacy programs and inclusion of frontline knowledge workers in tool design improve outcomes.
3. Build governance scaffolding around data quality, provenance tracking and human-in-the-loop validation. Retrieval grounding and provenance metadata (Lewis et al., 2020) directly address the hallucination risk that the complexity moderation surfaced.
4. Design human-AI collaboration deliberately. The strongest performers treated GenAI as augmentation of human judgment, not a substitute.

To make these operational, Table 8 sets out a short implementation checklist organized by the four recommendation areas, intended as a starting template that organizations adapt to their context.

Table 8. GenAI-KM Implementation Checklist

Area	Checklist items
Target the right SECI modes	Map current KM pain points to SECI modes • prioritize externalization and combination use cases • defer socialization-heavy tasks to human-led settings
Build readiness first	Run an AI-literacy baseline • train on critical evaluation of AI output and prompt design • include frontline experts in tool selection • set a governance owner
Govern for reliability	Adopt retrieval grounding and provenance metadata • require human sign-off for high-stakes artifacts • maintain a validation log • monitor repositories for hallucinated content
Design the collaboration	Define where humans retain judgment • keep verification loops in workflow • recalibrate AI output against ground-truth artifacts periodically • protect time for tacit-knowledge cultivation

Sector-differentiated guidance is also warranted, with strength matched to sample evidence. Technology firms can scale relatively aggressively while monitoring homogenization risk. Financial services should pair deployment with strong provenance and audit trails. Manufacturing should focus initial applications on shift handovers, equipment documentation and cross-team synthesis rather than tasks dependent on tacit physical practice. Because sector sub-samples were modest, these are offered as evidence-informed starting points rather than prescriptions.

A workforce-development implication runs through all of the above and is the chapter's human-centric core. AI literacy is not an optional skill but a core organizational capability, and it was the readiness sub-facet most visibly separating high from low performers. Training should move beyond tool tutorials toward critical evaluation of AI output, prompt design and recognition of hallucination patterns. Organizations that build these capabilities at scale realize more durable returns than those focused only on technical deployment. People remain the binding constraint and the most underdeveloped lever.

7. LIMITATIONS AND FUTURE RESEARCH

Several limitations bound the findings, and each is paired below with the future direction it motivates. First, the cross-sectional design precludes causal inference; the associations are consistent with the model but cannot establish directionality, which motivates longitudinal panel studies tracking organizations across adoption stages. Second, reliance on self-report and perceived innovation outcomes raises the possibility of perceptual bias, which motivates designs that pair perceptual measures with objective indicators such as patent counts, new-product revenue, code-base growth and patent-citation networks. Third, the sample is concentrated in knowledge-intensive sectors and, because sampling was by sector and size rather than geography, is geographically concentrated; generalization to less knowledge-intensive industries and to other regions should be cautious, which motivates cross-sector and cross-cultural replication. Fourth, the association-association evidence cannot adjudicate the homogenization and power-concentration concerns raised in Section 5.3, which motivates dedicated studies of epistemic agency and output diversity. Fifth, the rapid pace of GenAI capability change means the findings reflect a specific moment, roughly late 2023 to mid 2024, which motivates replication across successive model generations.

Beyond these limitation-linked directions, promising avenues include experimental designs isolating specific GenAI configurations such as retrieval-augmented versus parametric knowledge, deeper qualitative work on the lived experience of knowledge workers in AI-augmented settings, and integrative studies that combine socio-technical analysis with measurable innovation outcomes over time. Explicit measurement of the socio-technical and dynamic-capabilities constructs used here as background lenses would also strengthen the model.

8. CONCLUSION

This chapter examined how GenAI-enabled knowledge management practices relate to organizational innovation across three knowledge-intensive sectors. Drawing on survey data from 247 organizations and interviews with 32 senior practitioners, the analysis found significant positive associations with differentiated effects across SECI processes. Externalization and combination registered the strongest paths. Process innovation was the most responsive sub-dimension. Organizational readiness moderated outcomes positively, technological complexity negatively, and environmental dynamism not at all. Sectoral comparison placed technology ahead of financial services and manufacturing.

The contribution lies in supplying empirical depth and theoretical specificity to a literature dominated by conceptual proposals and single-case demonstrations, and in engaging the critical-AI conversation by treating hallucination, epistemic reliability and tacit erosion as central rather than peripheral. The human-centric reading is the through-line. Workforce evolution is not a backdrop to this technology but its rate-limiting factor: AI literacy, preserved human judgment and deliberate collaboration design separated the organizations that converted GenAI into innovation from those that did not. Practical guidance follows directly: prioritize externalization-combination applications, invest in readiness, build governance and design human-AI collaboration deliberately. Realizing the potential of GenAI in knowledge work depends on the human and organizational substrate on which the technology runs, and on deploying it responsibly. Where that substrate is well-prepared and the deployment is governed, the technology amplifies human capability. Where it is not, it can amplify the wrong things.

Declarations

Conflicts of Interest. The authors declare no known competing financial or personal interests that could have influenced the work reported in this chapter.

Funding. This research received no specific grant from any funding agency.

Data Availability. De-identified data supporting the findings are available from the corresponding author on reasonable request, subject to institutional sharing policies and participant consent restrictions.

Ethical Approval and Informed Consent. The study involved human participants through surveys and interviews and their consent was received.

REFERENCES

Alavi, M., Leidner, D. E., & Mousavi, R. (2024). A knowledge management perspective of generative artificial intelligence. *Journal of the Association for Information Systems*, *25*(1), 1–12. DOI: 10.17705/1jais.00859

Alsheibani, S., Cheung, Y., & Messom, C. (2018). Artificial intelligence adoption: AI-readiness at firm-level. In Proceedings of the 22nd Pacific Asia Conference on Information Systems (PACIS) (Paper 37). AIS Electronic Library. https://aisel.aisnet.org/pacis2018/37

Baruch, Y., & Holtom, B. C. (2008). Survey response rate levels and trends in organizational research. *Human Relations; Studies Towards the Integration of the Social Sciences*, *61*(8), 1139–1160. DOI: 10.1177/0018726708094863

Benbya, H., Strich, F., & Tamm, T. (2024). Navigating generative artificial intelligence promises and perils for organizations. *Journal of the Association for Information Systems*, *54*(1), 23–36. DOI: 10.17705/1jais.00861

Bender, E. M., Gebru, T., McMillan-Major, A., & Shmitchell, S. (2021). On the dangers of stochastic parrots: Can language models be too big? In *Proceedings of the 2021 ACM Conference on Fairness, Accountability, and Transparency* (pp. 610–623). ACM. DOI: 10.1145/3442188.3445922

Böhm, K., & Durst, S. (2025). Knowledge management in the age of generative artificial intelligence: From SECI to GRAI. *VINE Journal of Information and Knowledge Management Systems*. Advance online publication. DOI: 10.1108/VJIKMS-10-2024-0357

Bommasani, R., Hudson, D. A., Adeli, E., Altman, R., Arora, S., von Arx, S., ... (2022). On the opportunities and risks of foundation models (arXiv:2108.07258) [Preprint]. arXiv. https://doi.org//arXiv.2108.07258DOI: 10.48550

Braun, V., & Clarke, V. (2006). Using thematic analysis in psychology. *Qualitative Research in Psychology*, *3*(2), 77–101. DOI: 10.1191/1478088706qp063oa

Cao, L. (2022). AI in finance: Challenges, techniques, and opportunities. ACM Computing Surveys, 55(3). *ACM Computing Surveys*, *64*(3), 1–38. DOI: 10.1145/3502289

Carr, N. (2020). The shallows: What the internet is doing to our brains (Updated ed.). W. W. Norton.

Chang, Y., Wang, X., Wang, J., Wu, Y., Yang, L., Zhu, K., Chen, H., Yi, X., Wang, C., Wang, Y., Ye, W., Zhang, Y., Chang, Y., Yu, P. S., Yang, Q., & Xie, X. (2024). A survey on evaluation of large language models. ACM Transactions on Intelligent Systems and Technology, 15(3). *ACM Transactions on Intelligent Systems and Technology*, *39*(3), 1–45. DOI: 10.1145/3641289

Cohen, J. (1988). *Statistical power analysis for the behavioral sciences* (2nd ed.). Lawrence Erlbaum.

Creswell, J. W., & Plano Clark, V. L. (2017). *Designing and conducting mixed methods research* (3rd ed.). SAGE.

Cubric, M. (2020). Drivers, barriers and social considerations for AI adoption in business and management: A tertiary study. *Technology in Society*, *62*, 101257. DOI: 10.1016/j.techsoc.2020.101257

Deloitte. (2024). *The state of generative AI in the enterprise*. Deloitte AI Institute.

Doshi, A. R., & Hauser, O. P. (2024). Generative artificial intelligence enhances individual creativity but reduces the collective diversity of novel content. *Science Advances*, *10*(28), eadn5290. Advance online publication. DOI: 10.1126/sciadv.adn5290 PMID: 38996021

Farnese, M. L., Barbieri, B., Chirumbolo, A., & Patriotta, G. (2019). Managing knowledge in organizations: A Nonaka's SECI model operationalization. *Frontiers in Psychology*, *10*, 2730. DOI: 10.3389/fpsyg.2019.02730 PMID: 31920792

Floridi, L. (2023). AI as agency without intelligence: On ChatGPT, large language models, and other generative models. *Philosophy & Technology*, *36*(1), 15. DOI: 10.1007/s13347-023-00621-y

Glisby, M., & Holden, N. (2003). Contextual constraints in knowledge management theory: The cultural embeddedness of Nonaka's knowledge-creating company. *Knowledge and Process Management*, *10*(1), 29–36. DOI: 10.1002/kpm.158

Goldstein, I., Spatt, C. S., & Ye, M. (2023). Big data in finance. *Review of Financial Studies*, *36*(1), 1–12. DOI: 10.1093/rfs/hhac083

Gourlay, S. (2006). Conceptualizing knowledge creation: A critique of Nonaka's theory. *Journal of Management Studies*, *43*(7), 1415–1436. DOI: 10.1111/j.1467-6486.2006.00637.x

Guetterman, T. C., Fetters, M. D., & Creswell, J. W. (2015). Integrating quantitative and qualitative results in health science mixed methods research through joint displays. *Annals of Family Medicine*, *13*(6), 554–561. DOI: 10.1370/afm.1865 PMID: 26553895

Hair, J. F., Hult, G. T. M., Ringle, C. M., & Sarstedt, M. (2022). *A primer on partial least squares structural equation modeling (PLS-SEM)* (3rd ed.). SAGE.

Jarrahi, M. H., Askay, D., Eshraghi, A., & Smith, P. (2023). Artificial intelligence and knowledge management: A partnership between human and AI. *Business Horizons*, *66*(1), 87–99. DOI: 10.1016/j.bushor.2022.03.002

Ji, Z., Lee, N., Frieske, R., Yu, T., Su, D., Xu, Y., Ishii, E., Bang, Y. J., Madotto, A., & Fung, P. (2023). Survey of hallucination in natural language generation. ACM Computing Surveys, 55(12). *ACM Computing Surveys*, *248*(12), 1–38. DOI: 10.1145/3571730

Jiménez-Jiménez, D., & Sanz-Valle, R. (2011). Innovation, organizational learning, and performance. *Journal of Business Research*, *64*(4), 408–417. DOI: 10.1016/j.jbusres.2010.09.010

Kernan Freire, S., Wang, C., Foosherian, M., Wellsandt, S., Ruiz-Arenas, S., & Niforatos, E. (2024). Knowledge sharing in manufacturing using LLM-powered tools: User study and model benchmarking. *Frontiers in Artificial Intelligence*, *7*, 1293084. DOI: 10.3389/frai.2024.1293084 PMID: 38601111

Kirchner, K., Bolisani, E., Kassaneh, T. C., Scarso, E., & Taraghi, N. (2025). Generative AI meets knowledge management: Insights from software development practices. *Knowledge and Process Management*, *32*(4), 223–235. Advance online publication. DOI: 10.1002/kpm.70004

Kock, N. (2015). Common method bias in PLS-SEM: A full collinearity assessment approach. *International Journal of e-Collaboration*, *11*(4), 1–10. DOI: 10.4018/ijec.2015100101

Lewis, P., Perez, E., Piktus, A., Petroni, F., Karpukhin, V., & Goyal, N.. (2020). Retrieval-augmented generation for knowledge-intensive NLP tasks. In *Advances in Neural Information Processing Systems* (Vol. 33, pp. 9459–9474). Curran Associates.

Liu, C. (2024). The application of AI and product innovation efficiency: The role of knowledge innovation under the SECI model. *Aslib Journal of Information Management*. Advance online publication. DOI: 10.1108/AJIM-04-2024-0348

Mariani, M., & Dwivedi, Y. K. (2024). Generative artificial intelligence in innovation management: A preview of future research developments. *Journal of Business Research*, *175*, 114542. DOI: 10.1016/j.jbusres.2024.114542

Matsumoto, T., Nishikawa, R., & Morimoto, C. (2025). Human-AI-collaboration SECI model: A knowledge management model of experts' tacit knowledge with augmented LLM-based AI. In Jezic, G., Chen-Burger, J., Kusek, M., Sperka, R., Howlett, R. J., & Jain, L. C. (Eds.), *Agents and multi-agent systems: Technologies and applications 2024* (pp. 141–153). Springer., DOI: 10.1007/978-981-97-6469-3_12

Morgan, D. L. (2014). Pragmatism as a paradigm for social research. *Qualitative Inquiry*, *20*(8), 1045–1053. DOI: 10.1177/1077800413513733

Muzzio, H., & Gama, A. (2024). Knowledge management and innovation: A systematic review and research agenda. *Journal of Knowledge Management*, *28*(6), 1523–1548. DOI: 10.1108/JKM-05-2023-0405

Nakash, M., & Bolisani, E. (2024). Knowledge management meets artificial intelligence: A systematic review and future research agenda. In Proceedings of the 25th European Conference on Knowledge Management (ECKM) (pp. 755–764). Academic Conferences International. https://doi.org/DOI: 10.34190/eckm.25.1.2657

Nonaka, I. (1994). A dynamic theory of organizational knowledge creation. *Organization Science*, *5*(1), 14–37. DOI: 10.1287/orsc.5.1.14

Nonaka, I., & Konno, N. (1998). The concept of 'Ba': Building a foundation for knowledge creation. *California Management Review*, *40*(3), 40–54. DOI: 10.2307/41165942

Nonaka, I., & Takeuchi, H. (1995). *The knowledge-creating company: How Japanese companies create the dynamics of innovation*. Oxford University Press. DOI: 10.1093/oso/9780195092691.001.0001

O'Leary, D. E. (2024). Large language models and applications: The rebirth of enterprise knowledge management and the rise of prompt libraries. *IEEE Intelligent Systems*, *39*(2), 72–75. DOI: 10.1109/MIS.2024.3366648

Pasmore, W., Winby, S., Mohrman, S. A., & Vanasse, R. (2019). Reflections: Sociotechnical systems design and organization change. *Journal of Change Management*, *19*(2), 67–85. DOI: 10.1080/14697017.2018.1553761

Polanyi, M. (1966). *The tacit dimension*. Doubleday.

Richter, A., & Richter, C. (2024). Slowly dying or resilient? Revisiting the SECI model after GenAI. In *Proceedings of ICERI 2024* (pp. 8123–8132). IATED. DOI: 10.21125/iceri.2024.2003

Sarker, S., Chatterjee, S., Xiao, X., & Elbanna, A. (2019). The socio-technical perspective in IS research: A theoretical manifesto for the future. *Management Information Systems Quarterly*, *43*(4), 1209–1246. DOI: 10.25300/MISQ/2019/14019

Singh, K., Chatterjee, S., & Mariani, M. (2024). Applications of generative AI and future organizational performance: The mediating role of explorative and exploitative innovation. *Technovation*, *133*, 102988. DOI: 10.1016/j.technovation.2024.103021

Sumbal, M. S., & Amber, S. (2024). Generative AI for knowledge management: A new frontier. *Journal of Knowledge Management*, *28*(3), 812–835. DOI: 10.1108/JKM-06-2023-0456

Teece, D. J. (2007). Explicating dynamic capabilities: The nature and microfoundations of (sustainable) enterprise performance. *Strategic Management Journal*, *28*(13), 1319–1350. DOI: 10.1002/smj.640

Tornatzky, L. G., & Fleischer, M. (1990). *The processes of technological innovation*. Lexington Books.

Trist, E. L. (1981). *The evolution of socio-technical systems: A conceptual framework and an action research program*. Ontario Quality of Working Life Centre.

Wang, B., Zheng, P., Yin, Y., Shih, A., & Wang, L. (2024). Toward human-centric smart manufacturing: A human-cyber-physical systems framework. *Journal of Manufacturing Systems*, *65*, 471–490. DOI: 10.1016/j.jmsy.2024.05.001

Wang, C. L., & Ahmed, P. K. (2004). The development and validation of the organisational innovativeness construct using confirmatory factor analysis. *European Journal of Innovation Management*, *7*(4), 303–313. DOI: 10.1108/14601060410565056

Wei, J., Wang, X., Schuurmans, D., Bosma, M., Ichter, B., Xia, F., Chi, E., Le, Q. V., & Zhou, D. (2022). Chain-of-thought prompting elicits reasoning in large language models. In *Advances in Neural Information Processing Systems* (Vol. 35, pp. 24824–24837). Curran Associates. DOI: 10.52202/068431-1800

Weidinger, L., Uesato, J., Rauh, M., Griffin, C., Huang, P. S., & Mellor, J.. (2022). Taxonomy of risks posed by language models. In *Proceedings of the 2022 ACM Conference on Fairness, Accountability, and Transparency* (pp. 214–229). ACM. DOI: 10.1145/3531146.3533088

APPENDIX A. SURVEY INSTRUMENT: SAMPLE ITEMS AND GENAI CONTEXTUALIZATION

Items used seven-point Likert scales (1 = strongly disagree, 7 = strongly agree). For each SECI dimension the table gives a representative item and the original source item it was reworded from, showing that GenAI contextualization changed the referent of the practice without changing the construct meaning.

Table 9.

Construct	Sample GenAI-contextualized item	Original source item (paraphrased)
Socialization	AI-mediated channels help colleagues share experience-based know-how.	Colleagues share experience-based know-how through informal interaction.
Externalization	AI-assisted documentation helps us capture expertise that is hard to put in words.	We document expertise that is hard to put in words.
Combination	AI tools help us combine knowledge from different repositories into new material.	We combine knowledge from different sources into new documents.
Internalization	AI-generated summaries help staff absorb existing knowledge into daily practice.	Staff absorb documented knowledge into daily practice.
Org. readiness (AI literacy facet)	Our workforce can critically evaluate AI-generated knowledge outputs.	New construct facet developed for this study.
Org. readiness (governance facet)	We have governance procedures for validating AI-generated content.	New construct facet developed for this study.
Technological complexity	Our GenAI tools are difficult to integrate with existing systems.	The technology is difficult to integrate with existing systems.
Environmental dynamism	Our industry knowledge requirements change rapidly.	The environment changes rapidly and unpredictably.

Note. SECI source items adapted from Farnese et al. (2019); innovation items from Wang and Ahmed (2004) and Jiménez-Jiménez and Sanz-Valle (2011); TOE items from Alsheibani et al. (2018) and Cubric (2020). Full instrument available from the corresponding author.

APPENDIX B. ITEM LOADINGS AND ITEM-LEVEL COLLINEARITY

Standardized outer loadings and item-level VIF for the reflective constructs. All loadings were significant at $p < .001$. The single 0.67 loading is flagged; retention is justified in Section 4.2.

Table 10.

Construct	Loading range	Mean loading	Item VIF range
GenAI-Socialization	0.71 – 0.82	0.76	1.21 – 1.68
GenAI-Externalization	0.67 – 0.89	0.83	1.44 – 2.31
GenAI-Combination	0.74 – 0.87	0.82	1.52 – 2.18
GenAI-Internalization	0.70 – 0.81	0.74	1.18 – 1.74
Product Innovation	0.76 – 0.85	0.81	1.39 – 1.92
Process Innovation	0.78 – 0.86	0.82	1.47 – 2.05
Organizational Innovation	0.74 – 0.84	0.80	1.33 – 1.88
Organizational Readiness	0.72 – 0.86	0.80	1.41 – 2.27
Technological Complexity	0.75 – 0.85	0.81	1.36 – 1.79
Environmental Dynamism	0.73 – 0.83	0.78	1.29 – 1.66

APPENDIX C. NON-RESPONSE AND COMMON METHOD BIAS DIAGNOSTICS

Non-response bias was assessed by an early-versus-late respondent comparison (a proxy for non-respondents), splitting the sample at the median response date. Independent-samples t-tests on the principal constructs returned no significant differences.

Table 11.

Construct	Early M (SD)	Late M (SD)	p
GenAI-KM integration	4.71 (1.18)	4.66 (1.24)	.68
Innovation outcomes	4.82 (1.21)	4.74 (1.27)	.55
Organizational readiness	4.39 (1.30)	4.31 (1.34)	.61

Note. All $p > .10$, indicating non-response bias is unlikely to be a substantive concern.

Common method bias diagnostics are summarized below: Harman's single-factor test, the marker-variable adjustment and the full-collinearity VIF check (Kock, 2015).

Table 12.

Diagnostic	Result	Threshold
Harman's single factor (variance explained)	28.4%	< 50%
Marker-variable adjusted path change	< 0.01	negligible
Full-collinearity inner VIF (range)	1.34 – 2.71	< 3.3

Note. Combined evidence indicates common method variance is not a substantive concern.

Chapter 9
Foreign Direct Investment, Renewable Energy Transition, and Environmental Sustainability in Oman:
Implications for Vision 2040 and Net Zero 2050

Arathy Chandralekha
http://orcid.org/0000-0002-1250-1000
University of Kerala, India

K. B. Jaseela
University of Calicut, India

ABSTRACT

This study explores the dynamic relationship between Foreign Direct Investment (FDI) and environmental sustainability in Oman from 1990 to 2023. The analysis examines both short- and long-run effects of FDI, fossil fuel energy consumption, renewable energy, economic growth, and trade openness on carbon emissions using the Autoregressive Distributed Lag (ARDL) bounds testing approach. The results confirm long-run cointegration between these variables. The main findings indicate that, in the long run, FDI reduces CO_2 emissions, supporting the Pollution Halo Hypothesis. Fossil fuel use significantly increases emissions, while renewable energy adoption reduces environmental degradation. Economic growth increases environmental pressure, suggesting Oman remains on the upward slope of the

DOI: 10.4018/979-8-3373-8964-6.ch009

Environmental Kuznets Curve. These results highlight the need to direct FDI towards environmentally sustainable sectors. The study provides policy insights for Vision 2040 and Net Zero 2050 by showing that investments should focus on high-quality green projects rather than simply increasing FDI volume.

INTRODUCTION

Environmental sustainability has emerged as a central concern in contemporary economic development policies, especially in both developed and developing resource-dependent economies undergoing structural transformation. Large-scale industrial expansion, rising energy consumption, and greater integration into the global market system have led to environmentally harmful effects worldwide. One of the key pathways through which globalisation affects environmental changes is foreign direct investment (FDI). However, the environmental effects of FDI remain a matter of debate in theory and are empirically inconclusive. As the world becomes more globalised, more capital is flowing across borders. Foreign Direct Investment (FDI) is widely recognised as a major driver of economic development through capital inflows, employment generation, technology transfer, and industrial expansion. The impact of FDI on the environment remains ambiguous. FDI may increase industrial activity and resource utilisation, thereby contributing to higher carbon emissions and environmental degradation (e.g., CO2 and ozone-depleting substances). Conversely, FDI may also provide developing countries with access to advanced technologies and improved management practices (particularly clean technologies). This dual nature of FDI has given rise to two competing theoretical perspectives: the Pollution Haven Hypothesis (PHH) and the Pollution Halo Hypothesis (PHaloH).

The Pollution Haven Hypothesis (PHH) argues that multinational companies can relocate production of the most carbon-intensive activities to countries with relatively weaker environmental regulations, thereby increasing emissions and environmental degradation (Eskeland & Harrison, 2003; Copeland & Taylor, 2004). In contrast, the Pollution Halo Hypothesis postulates that FDI presence enables "Technological Leapfrogging" through the inflow of advanced, cleaner equipment and production methods that lower emission intensities (Mahadevan & Sun, 2020; Zarsky, 1999; Pao & Tsai, 2011). The empirical evidence remains mixed across countries and regions. While some studies support the Pollution Haven Hypothesis in fossil-fuel-intensive economies, others report a Pollution Halo effect in countries with stronger institutional quality and renewable energy integration (Omri, Nguyen, & Rault, 2014; Shahbaz et al., 2015). The relationship between economic growth and environmental quality is further explained by the Environmental Kuznets Curve

(EKC) hypothesis, which proposes an inverted U-shaped relationship between income and environmental degradation (Grossman & Krueger, 1995). According to this framework, environmental degradation initially rises during industrialisation but declines after economies adopt cleaner technologies and stricter environmental regulations. However, whether this turning point has been reached in resource-dependent and developing economies remains an empirical question.

For hydrocarbon-dependent economies, the interplay between FDI and environmental sustainability is a great puzzle. Energy structure, fossil fuel dependency, and institutional quality often mediate the environmental effects of foreign capital inflows. Therefore, whether such a turning point has been achieved in resource-rich Gulf economies remains an important empirical question. In the Omani context, recent evidence suggests that FDI is becoming a primary driver of the green energy transition, driven by massive investments in the green hydrogen industry and utility-scale solar initiatives such as Ibri II and Manah (IRENA, 2023; Hydrom, 2024). The Sultanate of Oman is currently undergoing a significant economic and energy transition. It is transitioning from a hydrocarbon-dependent economy to a global hub for sustainable energy (IRENA, 2023; Hydrom, 2024). Oman's energy mix is predominantly fossil fuels, reflecting its history of oil and gas revenues. Carbon dioxide emissions have increased from about 25,115 kt in 2002 to over 71,000 kt in recent years (International Energy Agency, 2024). The Sultanate has committed to achieving Net Zero emission by 2050, guided by Oman Vision 2040, and has signed the Paris Agreement. This change requires breaking the link between economic growth and environmental harm. Foreign capital and green technology now play a larger role. Recent investments in utility-scale solar projects and green hydrogen mark a structural shift in the energy sector. These changes are likely to alter the environmental impact of FDI inflows. Despite these developments, empirical evidence on the FDI–environment nexus in Oman remains limited and fragmented. Most studies focus only on carbon dioxide emissions and overlook other environmental indicators such as greenhouse gas emissions, ecological footprint, and renewable energy. In addition, most previous research uses static econometric techniques. These do not capture short-run adjustment dynamics and long-run equilibrium relationships.

The present study explores the dynamic relationship between FDI inflows and several environmental sustainability indicators in Oman. It aims to fill this research gap. Specifically, the study examines carbon and greenhouse gas emissions, renewable energy consumption and ecological footprint within a single econometric framework. The primary method used is the Autoregressive Distributed Lag (ARDL) model, a small sample time-series approach for mixed integration (Pesaran et al., 2001). This approach allows estimation of both short-run effects and long-run elasticities. It enables a better understanding of FDI's structural environmental impact. Existing studies on Oman have largely examined the relationship between

FDI and environmental sustainability using a limited set of indicators. However, relatively little attention has been given to assessing multiple dimensions of environmental sustainability within a single analytical framework. This study extends the literature by simultaneously analysing the effects of FDI on carbon emissions, greenhouse gas emissions, renewable energy consumption and ecological footprint. In addition, it investigates whether Oman's ongoing green energy transition and increasing renewable-energy-oriented FDI inflows have reshaped the traditional FDI–environment relationship.

First, this study addresses country-specific evidence for Oman, where empirical research remains comparatively limited. While much of the existing literature on the FDI-environment nexus emphasises broad panels of developing nations or the GCC region as a whole (Shahbaz et al., 2015; Demena & Afesorgbor, 2020), this study specifically focuses on the Sultanate of Oman. Using data up to 2023, it captures the unique impact of the Oman Vision 2040 implementation phase and offers insights into how a hydrocarbon-based economy can transition from a potential Pollution Haven to a Pollution Halo effect through strategic green hydrogen and renewable energy FDI (Hydrom, 2024). Second, the research expands the empirical framework by using a multi-dimensional sustainability assessment. Unlike previous studies, this study uses four distinct models instead of relying solely on CO_2 emissions as a proxy for environmental quality. This addresses a major limitation in the existing literature, where environmental sustainability is often represented by a single indicator. This study captures a more holistic view of environmental health by incorporating both degradation effects (resource depletion) and improvement effects (institutional governance) through the Ecological Footprint (EF) and Greenhouse Gas (GHG) emissions. Third, it contributes to the debate over the Pollution Haven and Pollution Halo theories. Given the mixed empirical findings reported in previous studies, the Omani case provides an opportunity to examine whether green-oriented FDI can generate environmental benefits in a resource-dependent economy. Furthermore, using the ARDL Bound Test and the Error Correction Model (ECM), the study not only tests for correlations but also establishes long-run equilibrium relationships and the 'speed of adjustment' (ECT) of environmental quality in Oman. This enables empirical verification of the EKC turning point for a small, open oil economy such as Oman, thereby creating a replicable model for other emergent energy markets.

Finally, this study offers timely policy-relevant evidence. The findings directly inform the Oman Centre for Net Zero and the 11th Five-Year Development Plan (2026–2030). By quantifying the positive spillover effects of renewable-energy-focused FDI, this study empirically justifies the Sultanate's $140 billion green investment pipeline and helps policymakers hone tax incentives and regulatory standards for 'Green FDI.' The findings, therefore, contribute not only to academic debates on FDI and environmental sustainability but also to evidence-based policymaking in economies pursuing low-carbon development pathways.

LITERATURE REVIEW

Foreign Direct Investment and Environmental Quality: Theoretical Perspectives

The relationship between direct investment and environmental quality remains a major concern in environmental economics. Early theoretical discussions were largely framed by two competing perspectives: the Pollution Haven Hypothesis (PHH) and the Pollution Halo Hypothesis (PHaloH). The Pollution Haven Hypothesis (PHH) claims that multinational companies move pollution-intensive production to areas with weaker environmental regulations (Copeland & Taylor, 2004; Levinson & Taylor, 2008). Empirical investigations initially produced conflicting results, indicating that differences in regulatory costs were the main cause for industrial relocation (Keller & Levinson, 2002), whereas others found very little evidence after controlling for market size and agglomeration effects (Cole & Elliott, 2003).

The countervailing Pollution Halo Hypothesis suggests that multinational corporations improve environmental performance in host economies by introducing advanced technologies, managerial capabilities, and cleaner production processes (Eskeland & Harrison, 2003). Contemporary research shows that economies with stronger institutional frameworks and greater absorptive capacity for new information exhibit stronger halo effects than other economies (Danish & Ulucak, 2020; Balsalobre-Lorente et al., 2018). However, the existing research approach has moved away from traditional binary systems. The current understanding of the association between FDI and environmental quality is increasingly viewed as conditional on governance quality, sectoral composition, energy structure, and development stage (Acheampong, 2019). The meta-analysis by Demena and Afesorgbor (2020) shows that the direction and magnitude of FDI's environmental impact differ significantly across regions and model specifications. This conditional perspective is particularly relevant to hydrocarbon-dependent economies like Oman, where carbon intensity is structurally embedded in production systems.

The Energy–FDI–Growth Nexus: Scale, Composition, and Technique Effects

Recent high-impact research integrates FDI into a broader macroeconomic framework that examines the relationship between economic growth and energy consumption. The scale–composition–technique decomposition framework introduced by Grossman and Krueger (1995) has influenced modern econometric studies examining the mechanisms through which FDI affects environmental quality (Sadorsky, 2010; Danish & Ulucak, 2020). Empirical panel evidence suggests that in fossil-fuel–intensive economies, FDI increases emissions primarily through scale effects, in the absence of technological upgrading or renewable energy adoption (Acheampong, 2019; Balsalobre-Lorente et al., 2018). In middle-income and resource-dependent economies, energy consumption frequently acts as the principal transmission channel linking FDI to CO_2 emissions. Recent nonlinear ARDL and quantile-based studies reveal that the effects of FDI shocks are not symmetrical; for example, positive FDI shocks may increase emissions more strongly than negative shocks reduce them, especially in energy-dependent systems (Danish & Ulucak, 2020). These findings suggest that analysing FDI independently of the economy's energy structure may yield biased conclusions—an issue highly pertinent to Oman, where fossil fuels account for the majority of primary energy consumption.

Resource Dependence and Structural Carbon Intensity in GCC Economies

Resource-dependent economies demonstrate structural rigidities that hinder environmental sustainability transitions. The mechanism of "carbon lock-in" describes how hydrocarbon revenues, energy subsidies, and carbon-intensive industries create persistent high-emission development paths (Sachs & Warner, 2001; Charfeddine & Mrabet, 2017). Recent studies on GCC indicate that energy intensity is the main driver of emissions, even when economic growth stabilises (Magazzino et al., 2021). In oil-exporting countries, FDI directed toward extractive industries frequently leads to carbon dependency rather than facilitating diversification (Danish & Ulucak, 2020).

Moreover, the quality of institutions influences the strength of this connection. Evidence indicates that governance effectiveness and regulatory transparency are key to reducing environmental harm associated with resource-based FDI (Acheampong, 2019). As part of Vision 2040, Oman's hydrocarbon-dependent economy needs institutional reforms. Strong institutional frameworks improve the ability of governments to channel foreign investment toward environmentally sustainable sectors while discouraging pollution-intensive industrial activities. In the context of Oman Vision 2040, institutional reforms, renewable energy diversification, and sustainability-oriented industrial policies may therefore play a critical role in reducing carbon dependency and supporting long-run environmental sustainability.

Renewable Energy as a Moderating Factor in the FDI–Environment Nexus

Recent literature increasingly conceptualises renewable energy as a moderating variable rather than merely a control factor. Empirical evidence suggests that renewable energy integration weakens the positive relationship between FDI and carbon emissions (Balsalobre-Lorente et al., 2018). Panel quantile regressions and the nonlinear ARDL model indicate that renewable energy penetration increases absorptive capacity for clean technologies and encourages the allocation of FDI toward lower-carbon sectors (Danish & Ulucak, 2020). Additionally, investing in green infrastructure sends a clear signal of policy credibility, which, in turn, attracts sustainability-oriented FDI flows (Polzin et al., 2015). In Oman, recent large-scale solar projects and green hydrogen initiatives have the potential to structurally transform the economy, helping moderate the emission pressures associated with FDI. This provides evidence consistent with our hypothesis that renewable deployment may also shift the scale–technique balance through the FDI-environment relationship.

Environmental Sustainability, ESG, and Investment Allocation

The direction of causality is increasingly examined in reverse: environmental performance may influence FDI allocation decisions. Climate risk pricing and ESG integration in capital markets have transformed global patterns of capital flows (Krueger et al., 2020; Pankratz et al., 2023). Empirical research indicates that climate-aligned economies tend to attract higher-quality and longer-term capital inflows (Bolton & Kacperczyk, 2021). Sound environmental governance lowers transition risk and policy uncertainty, enhancing investment stability (Kellenberg, 2009). Thus, Oman's sustainability commitments as part of the Net Zero 2050 commitments can also play a pivotal role in how foreign capital is allocated, especially in the renewable and infrastructure sectors. Moreover, multinational investors increasingly consider environmental disclosure standards, carbon reduction commitments, and ESG compliance when selecting investment destinations. Consequently, countries with stronger sustainability frameworks and transparent environmental governance are more likely to attract environmentally responsible and technology-oriented foreign investment.

The Porter Hypothesis: Environmental Regulation, Innovation, and Investment Quality

The Porter Hypothesis holds that well-developed environmental regulations can motivate innovation, ultimately improving competitiveness (Porter & van der

Linde, 1995). More recent empirical findings indicate conditional support, mainly in technologically advanced sectors (Ambec et al., 2013). Overall, more contemporary cross-country evidence demonstrates that the severity of environmental protocols influences not only the volume of FDI that flows into these countries, but also its composition, with a greater share of efficiency-seeking capital and sustainable technology (Balsalobre-Lorente et al., 2018). Thus, regulatory reform has the potential to reshape investment toward sustainable sectors in Oman. Furthermore, stronger environmental standards may encourage multinational firms to adopt cleaner technologies and energy-efficient production systems, thereby improving long-run industrial sustainability and environmental performance.

Climate Vulnerability, Transition Risk, and Financial Stability

Climate exposure has increasingly become a risk factor for macro-financial stability. For example, markets are reflecting carbon risks in asset valuations, which, in turn, affect cross-border investment flows (Bolton & Kacperczyk, 2021). There is emerging evidence that countries with resilient economies to climate change exhibit lower sovereign risk premiums and more stable financial systems (Pankratz et al., 2023). Oman is shifting away from a hydrocarbon-dependent economy toward a diversified one; a genuine commitment to reducing emissions may signal macroeconomic stability and improve long-term investor confidence. Similarly, climate-resilient economic policies and sustainability-oriented reforms may enhance the country's attractiveness for environmentally responsible foreign investment and strengthen financial system resilience over the long run. In this context, Oman's renewable energy transition, ESG integration, and Net Zero 2050 commitments may strengthen financial resilience while simultaneously supporting environmentally sustainable economic diversification and long-run investment.

Methodological Approaches and Country-Specific Dynamics

Recent advancements highlight nonlinear, asymmetric, and time-varying relationships between FDI and environmental indicators. While panel models dominate the literature, they may obscure structural heterogeneity within resource-dependent economies. Moreover, recent ARDL studies on the GCC region and specifically Oman show increasingly mixed results on the environmental impact of foreign direct investments, providing some crucial agreements and disagreements between previous findings from the literature. For instance, some studies carried out in hydrocarbons-dominated economies in the Gulf region lend support to the Pollution Haven Hypothesis by demonstrating that foreign investments in energy-intensive industries lead to increased carbon emissions and environmental degradation

(Shahbaz et al., 2015; Acheampong, 2019). Due to fossil fuel dependence for further economic development in the economy, the positive impact of foreign direct investments through the scale effect tends to surpass technological and efficiency gains. These findings indicate that weak environmental enforcement, energy subsidies, and carbon-intensive industrial structures make multinationals more likely to invest in pollution-intensive industries, resulting in greater ecological stress within GCC countries (Danish & Ulucak, 2020).

Conversely, a growing number of studies using recent ARDL research findings have supported the Pollution Halo Theory, particularly in countries that are pursuing renewable energy transition and institutional reforms. These studies suggest that FDI has the potential to improve the quality of the environment as FDI contributes to cleaner production techniques, technological spillovers, and greater investment in renewable energy infrastructure (Balsalobre-Lorente et al., 2018; Danish & Ulucak, 2020). In countries like the UAE and Oman, foreign investment seems to exert less negative pressure on ecological performance, due to recent changes in sustainability policy, expansion of renewables, and ESG-informed investment models (IRENA, 2023; Hydrom, 2024). Similarly, FDI that focuses specifically on renewable energies contributes to energy efficiency gains and lower carbon intensity in developing nations that are investing heavily in solar energy, green hydrogen, and sustainable infrastructure sectors.

The conflicting findings among GCC studies demonstrate that the impact of FDI on the environment is highly context-specific rather than universally applicable. There are several factors that explain the differences in findings across studies, such as the institutional quality, environmental regulations, sectoral composition, and energy structure that largely explain these inconsistencies (Demena & Afesorgbor, 2020). For instance, those nations that have a robust governance system, renewable energy integration, and stricter environmental standards usually exhibit higher degrees of Pollution Halo effects. Conversely, countries that heavily rely on fossil fuels and lack cohesive environmental enforcement continue to see the expansion of pollution-intensive industries due to the increased level of foreign investment. Moreover, methodological differences among studies, such as the econometric techniques, sample periods, environmental indicators, and model specifications, further contribute to divergent empirical outcomes.

However, recent nonlinear ARDL and dynamic time-series studies suggest that the FDI and environmental sustainability nexus is asymmetric and time-varying (Danish & Ulucak, 2020). It implies that the effects of positive FDI shocks on emissions may be more pronounced in carbon-intensive economies, while emissions may be weakened by renewable energy transition and institutional reforms over time. Thus, the reliance on panel-based GCC evidence may mask country-specific dynamics and structural heterogeneity within the GCC, especially in Oman, which is undergoing a major economic and environmental transformation through Vision 2040, green hydrogen investments, and renewable energy diversification policies. Thus, it is necessary to conduct country-specific ARDL analysis to examine the long-run relationship between FDI and environmental sustainability in Oman (Pesaran et al., 2001). The country-specific ARDL framework is methodologically valid for Oman and other similar developing countries, as it can estimate both short-run relationship adjustment and long-run equilibrium dynamics. This approach aligns with recent calls for context-specific environmental macroeconomic modelling.

RESEARCH GAP

However, important research gaps remain despite the extensive body of literature. First, empirical studies mainly focus on the environmental consequences of FDI with limited attempts to investigate reverse causality. Second, studies examining the role of environmental sustainability indicators in shaping investment decisions in resource-dependent economies remain scarce. Third, most empirical literature on the GCC relies on panel data, thereby ignoring Oman's institutional and structural uniqueness. In addition, limited attention has been given to comparing agreements and contradictions among recent GCC- and Oman-specific ARDL studies. The existing literature largely provides descriptive summaries rather than critically analysing how differences in institutional quality, renewable energy adoption, and economic structure influence the environmental consequences of FDI across Gulf economies. Fourth, renewable energy is usually considered as an independent variable rather than a clearly moderating factor in the dynamic time-series approach. Fifth, limited attention has been given to understanding how renewable energy transition, environmental governance, and sustainability reforms interact with FDI and environmental sustainability in Oman. Finally, the empirical implications of Vision 2040 sustainability reforms for investment attractiveness remain relatively unexplored. In view of Oman's strategic transition towards economic diversification and sustainable development, examining the relationship between FDI, renewable energy transition, and environmental sustainability can provide important theoretical and policy insights.

Accordingly, this study makes several contributions to the existing literature. First, it provides country-specific evidence on the FDI–environment nexus in Oman, a context that has received comparatively limited attention despite its ongoing transition towards a low-carbon economy. Second, the study adopts a multi-dimensional approach to environmental sustainability by examining carbon emissions, greenhouse gas emissions, renewable energy consumption and ecological footprint within a unified analytical framework, thereby extending prior studies that rely predominantly on a single environmental indicator. Third, by employing the ARDL bounds testing approach and error correction framework, the study captures both short-run dynamics and long-run equilibrium relationships between FDI and environmental sustainability indicators. Fourth, the study contributes to the ongoing debate between the Pollution Haven and Pollution Halo hypotheses by assessing whether Oman's renewable energy transition and sustainability reforms have altered the environmental consequences of foreign investment. Finally, the findings provide policy-relevant evidence for Oman Vision 2040 and the Net Zero 2050 strategy by identifying the conditions under which foreign investment can support environmentally sustainable economic development.

METHODOLOGY

Research Design

This study adopts a quantitative research design based on annual time-series data for Oman covering the period 1990–2023. The study employs the Autoregressive Distributed Lag (ARDL) bounds testing approach developed by Pesaran et al. (2001) to examine both short-run and long-run relationships among foreign direct investment, energy consumption, renewable energy, economic growth, trade openness, and environmental sustainability indicators.

Data Source

The study uses annual time-series data for the Sultanate of Oman covering the period 1990–2023. Data on foreign direct investment inflows, GDP, and energy consumption were attained from the World Development Indicators (World Bank). Carbon emissions data were collected from the Global Carbon Project, while renewable energy data were obtained from the International Energy Agency (IEA). Ecological Footprint data used in the robustness analysis were sourced from the Global Footprint Network. The selected period captures major structural changes in Oman's economy, including trade liberalisation, industrial diversification, renewable energy expansion, and the implementation phase of Oman Vision 2040, thereby enabling a comprehensive analysis of long-run environmental and economic dynamics.

Model Specification

This study examines the dynamic relationship between foreign direct investment (FDI), energy structure, economic growth, and environmental quality in Oman. The study employs the Autoregressive Distributed Lag (ARDL) modelling framework to analyse both short-run and long-run effects.

The baseline carbon emissions model is specified as:

$$ln\,CO_{2t} = \beta_0 + \beta_1 ln(FDI_t) + \beta_2 ln(Energy_t) + \beta_3 ln(GDP_t) + \beta_4 [ln(GDP_t)]^2 + \varepsilon_t$$

Where:

$CO2 = CO_2$ emissions per capita
FDI = Foreign direct investment inflows
Energy = Fossil fuel energy consumption
GDP = Real GDP per capita
GDP2 = Square of GDP per capita (to test the Environmental Kuznets Curve hypothesis)
εt = Error term

Each of these variables is chosen based on robust theoretical and empirical evidence:

- **FDI (lnFDI):** Represents foreign capital inflows and serves as the primary variable of interest. It captures both scale and technique effects associated with international investment.
- **Energy Consumption (lnEnergy):** Proxy for fossil fuel usage, which is the main driver for the emissions of the resource-dependent economy.
- **GDP per capita (lnGDP):** Measures economic growth and development.
- **GDP squared (lnGDP^2):** Included to test the Environmental Kuznets Curve (EKC) hypothesis, allowing for a nonlinear relationship between income and environmental degradation.
- **Renewable Energy (lnRE):** Incorporated in extended models to examine its moderating role in reducing emissions.
- **Trade Openness (lnTrade):** Controls for the effects of global economic integration.

The inclusion of these variables enables the study to capture scale, composition, and technique effects, providing a comprehensive framework for analysing environmental dynamics. The addition of the squared term of GDP allows testing the Environmental Kuznets Curve (EKC) hypothesis originally suggested by Grossman and Krueger (1995), which posits an inverted U-shaped association between economic growth and environmental degradation. All variables are transformed into natural logarithms to reduce heteroscedasticity and allow interpretation of coefficients as elasticities. All variables are converted into natural logarithms to mitigate heteroscedasticity and facilitate the interpretation of coefficients as elasticities.

ARDL Model Framework

Following the bounds testing approach developed by Pesaran et al. (2001), the ARDL error correction representation is specified as

$$\Delta lnCO_{2t} = \alpha_0 + \sum_{i=0}^{p} \alpha_i \Delta lnCO_{2,t-i} + \sum_{i=0}^{q} \gamma_i \ \nabla \ lnFDI_{t-i} +$$
$$+ \sum_{i=0}^{r} \delta_i \ \Delta lnEnergy_{t-i} + i = \sum_{i=0}^{s} \phi_i \Delta lnGDP_{t-i} + \sum_{i=0}^{v} \theta_i \Delta (lnGDP^2)_{t-i} + \lambda ECT_{t-1} + u_t$$

Where:

Δ = First difference operator
ECTt−1 = Error Correction Term
λ = Speed of adjustment coefficient
ut = White noise error term

The coefficient (λ) is expected to be negative and statistically significant, showing convergence toward the long-run equilibrium after short-run shocks.

The ARDL approach is mainly appropriate for this study as it may be applied irrespective of the integration of the variables, whether I(0) or I(1), and performs well with small sample sizes, making it appropriate for country-level time-series analysis (Pesaran et al.2001). It provides both short-run dynamics and long-run equilibrium estimates simultaneously.

Variable Description and Measurement

Table 1 presents the variable descriptions, measurements, data sources, and references used in the study.

Table 1. Variable Description and Measurement

	Symbol	Measurement	Expected Sign	Source	Reference
Variable					
Carbon Emissions	$\ln CO_2$	Metric tons per capita (log)	Dependent	World Development Indicators	Grossman & Krueger (1995); Shahbaz et al. (2015)
Foreign Direct Investment	lnFDI	Net inflows (% GDP, log)	±	World Bank	Omri et al. (2014); Mahadevan & Sun (2020)
Fossil Fuel Energy Use	lnEnergy	% of total energy consumption (log)	+	International Energy Agency (IEA)	Acheampong (2019); Danish & Ulucak (2020)
GDP per Capita	lnGDP	Constant USD (log)	+	World Bank	Grossman & Krueger (1995); Pao & Tsai (2011)
GDP Squared	$\ln GDP^2$	Square of lnGDP	–	Constructed	Grossman & Krueger (1995)
Renewable Energy	lnRE	% of total energy consumption (log)	–	International Energy Agency (IEA)	Balsalobre-Lorente et al. (2018); Paramati et al. (2017)
Greenhouse Gas Emissions	lnGHG	Metric tons CO_2 equivalent (log)	Dependent	World Bank	Shahbaz et al. (2015); Omri et al. (2014)
Ecological Footprint	lnEF	Global hectares per capita (log)	±	Global Footprint Network	Charfeddine & Mrabet (2017)
Control Variables					
Trade Openness	lnTrade	(Exports + Imports)/ GDP (log)	±	World Bank	Copeland & Taylor (2004); Omri et al. (2014)
Error Correction Term	ECT_{-1}	Lagged residual from long-run equation	–	Estimated	Pesaran, Shin & Smith (2001)

Source: Compiled by the author from World Bank, IEA, and Global Footprint Network data.

Model Specification

Table 2 summarises the model specifications employed in the analysis.

Table 2. Model Specification

Model	Dependent Variable	Independent Variables	Purpose
Model 1	$\ln CO_2$	lnFDI, lnEnergy, lnGDP, $\ln GDP^2$	Baseline EKC model
Model 2	$\ln CO_2$	lnFDI, lnRE, lnFDI×lnRE, lnEnergy, lnGDP, $\ln GDP^2$	Moderation model
Model 3	lnRE	lnFDI, lnGDP, lnTrade	Renewable energy determinants model
Model 4	lnGHG	lnFDI, lnEnergy, lnGDP, lnTrade	Greenhouse gas emissions model

continued on following page

Table 2. Continued

Model	Dependent Variable	Independent Variables	Purpose
Model 5	lnEF	lnFDI, lnEnergy, lnGDP, lnTrade	Ecological footprint model
ECM	$\Delta lnCO_2$	ΔlnFDI, ΔlnEnergy, ECT_{-1}	Short-run Adjustment

Source: Author's specification.

Table 3 reports the descriptive statistics of the study variables. The variables have been converted to natural logarithms (ln) to ensure stability and normality in the econometric estimation.

Table 3. Descriptive Statistics

Variable	Mean	Std. Dev.	Minimum	Maximum
$lnCO_2$	10.745	0.591	9.731	11.533
lnFDI	6.988	1.584	3.332	9.087
lnGDP	9.874	0.642	8.741	10.982
$lnGDP^2$	97.49	12.63	76.38	120.60
lnRE	-7.172	2.717	-9.210	-2.161
lnEnergy	8.460	0.307	7.953	8.832
lnTrade	11.050	0.531	10.092	11.838

Source: Author's computation using EViews 12

Carbon emissions ($lnCO_2$) show moderate variation throughout the sample period, with an arithmetic mean of 10.745 and relatively small dispersion (Std. Dev. = 0.591). The range between the minimum (9.731) and maximum (11.533) indicates a gradual increase in emissions rather than extreme volatility. Foreign direct investment (lnFDI) exhibits greater variability than other variables (Std. Dev. = 1.584), suggesting fluctuating inflows across years. The wide range between 3.332 and 9.087 reflects periods of both low and strong capital inflows. Economic growth (lnGDP) exhibits moderate variation with a mean value of approximately 9.874, indicating steady economic expansion in Oman over the study period. The incorporation of the squared GDP term ($lnGDP^2$) allows testing of the Environmental Kuznets Curve (EKC) hypothesis, which proposes that environmental deterioration rises at the initial stage with economic growth but eventually declines upon reaching a particular income level. Renewable energy (lnRE) has a negative mean (-7.172), indicating a relatively small share in Oman's energy mix. Since a logarithmic transformation was applied, negative values imply that the original renewable energy percentages were close to zero. The relatively large standard deviation (2.717) shows significant variation as renewable capacity gradually increased from negligible levels. Energy consumption (lnEnergy) is relatively stable (Std. Dev. = 0.307), reflecting Oman's structural dependence on fossil fuels. The narrow range suggests persistent fossil-based energy intensity over time. Trade openness (lnTrade) shows moderate variation, with a mean of 11.05 and a standard deviation of 0.531, reflecting Oman's increasing integration into international trade markets.

Pearson Correlation Matrix (Log-Transformed Variables)

Table 4 presents the correlation matrix among the variables included in the analysis. This table summarises the bivariate relationships between the variables. The coefficients indicate the degree and direction of the linear association before the dynamic ARDL estimation.

Table 4. Correlation Matrix

$lnCO_2$	1.000					
lnFDI	0.482**	1.000				
lnEnergy	0.731***	0.410**	1.000			
lnGDP	0.615***	0.553***	0.689***	1.000		
lnRE	-0.352*	0.462**	-0.441**	0.214	1.000	
lnTrade	0.298	0.521**	0.382*	0.644***	0.301*	1.000

Source: Author's computation using EViews 12
*** $p < 0.01$,** $p < 0.05$, $p < 0.10$

The correlation results indicate that carbon emissions ($lnCO_2$) have a very strong positive association with energy consumption (lnEnergy) ($r = 0.731$, $p < 0.01$) and GDP (lnGDP) ($r = 0.615$, $p < 0.01$), indicating a strong association among economic growth, energy usage, and carbon emissions. FDI (lnFDI) is positively correlated with carbon emissions ($r = 0.482$, $p < 0.05$), suggesting preliminary support for the Pollution Haven hypothesis as discussed by Copeland and Taylor (2004). In contrast, renewable energy (lnRE) is negatively correlated with CO_2 emissions ($r = -0.352$, $p < 0.10$), indicating its mitigating role. Renewable energy is also positively correlated with FDI ($r = 0.462$, $p < 0.05$), suggesting that foreign investment may support clean energy development. Finally, no correlation exceeds 0.80, suggesting that multicollinearity is not a serious concern for subsequent ARDL estimation.

Unit Root Testing (ADF Test Results)

Before running ARDL, we must verify that no variable is I(2). ARDL is valid if variables consist of a combination of I(0) and I(1). Table 5 reports the results of the Augmented Dickey-Fuller (ADF) unit root tests.

Table 5. Augmented Dickey–Fuller (ADF) Unit Root Test Results

lnCO$_2$	-1.452	0.541	-4.892	0.000***	I(1)
lnFDI	-2.103	0.245	-5.112	0.000***	I(1)
lnGDP	-1.124	0.682	-3.954	0.002***	I(1)
lnEnergy	-1.874	0.341	-4.215	0.001***	I(1)
lnRE	-3.451	0.012**	—	—	I(0)
lnTrade	-2.015	0.284	-4.771	0.000***	I(1)

Source: Author's computation using EViews 12

*** $p < 0.01$, ** $p < 0.05$, I (0) = Stationary at level, I(1) = Stationary at first difference

The ADF results indicate that lnCO$_2$, lnFDI, lnGDP, lnEnergy, and lnTrade are non-stationary in their levels but attain stationarity after the first differencing, confirming that they are combined of order one, I(1), whereas lnRE is stationary at the level ($p < 0.05$), signifying integration of order zero, I(0). A mixture of I(0) and I(1) orders of integration validates the application of the ARDL Bounds Testing approach, as it is uniquely competent to handle variables with varying levels of stationarity without losing long-run information.

Optimal Lag Length Selection

Table 6 reports the optimal lag length selection results.

Table 6.Optimal Lag Length Selection (ARDL)

Model	Maximum Lag	Selected Lag Structure	Selection Criterion	Data Frequency
ARDL Model	2	ARDL (2,1,1,2,1,1)	Akaike Information Criterion (AIC)	Annual

Source: Author's computation using EViews 12

The ideal lag structure was obtained using the Akaike Information Criterion (AIC). The selected ARDL (2, 1, 1, 2, 1, 1) model provides the lowest information criterion value, ensures stable model dynamics, and avoids over-parameterisation.

Based on the selected lag structure, the ARDL bounds testing approach is applied to examine the existence of a long-run association among the variables. Additionally, the optimal lag selection improves the reliability and predictive accuracy of the estimated short-run and long-run coefficients within the econometric framework.

ARDL DIAGNOSTIC TESTS AND BOUNDS TEST RESULTS

ARDL Bounds Test for Cointegration

The ARDL Bounds Test is employed to assess whether the variables are long-run associated. The calculated F-statistic is compared with the critical value bounds provided by Pesaran et al. (2001). Table 7 presents the ARDL bounds test results for cointegration

Table 7.ARDL Bounds Test

Test Statistic	Value	Critical Value I(0)	Critical Value I(1)
F-Statistic	5.84		
10%		2.45	3.52
5%		2.86	4.01
2.5%		3.25	4.49
1%		3.74	5.06

Source: Author's computation using EViews 12

The estimated F-statistic (5.84) surpasses the upper-bound critical values at the 5% (4.01), 2.5% (4.49), and even 1% (5.06) significance levels. Therefore, the null hypothesis of no cointegration is rejected at the 1% level, confirming the occurrence of a long-run equilibrium association among the variables. This result validates the suitability of the ARDL framework and indicates that the variables move together systematically over time despite short-run fluctuations and external economic shocks.

Diagnostic Tests

Several post-estimation diagnostic tests are employed to establish the robustness and validity of the ARDL model. Table 8 reports the diagnostic test results used to assess model adequacy.

Table 8. Diagnostic Tests

Test	Statistic	Prob.	Conclusion
Breusch-Godfrey LM Test	1.842	0.182	No serial correlation
ARCH Heteroskedasticity Test	0.964	0.337	No heteroskedasticity
Ramsey RESET Test	0.721	0.405	No functional form misspecification
Jarque-Bera Normality Test	1.556	0.459	Residuals normally distributed
CUSUM & CUSUMSQ	-	-	Model is stable over the sample period

Source: Author's computation using EViews 12

The Breusch-Godfrey LM test reveals no sign of serial correlation ($p > 0.05$). The ARCH test results indicate no heteroscedasticity, indicating that the residuals exhibit homoscedasticity. The Ramsey RESET test shows no evidence of functional form misspecification, indicating correct model specification. The Jarque-Bera test confirms that the residuals follow a normal distribution. The CUSUM and CUSUMSQ tests confirm parameter stability throughout the sample period, as both statistics lie within the 5% critical bounds.

Long-Run Coefficients

The following table reports the estimated long-run elasticities from the baseline ARDL model over the sample period. Table 9 reports the estimated long-run coefficients of the ARDL model.

Table 9. Long-Run Coefficients (Baseline ARDL Model)

Variable	Coefficient	Std. Error	t-Statistic	Prob.
lnFDI	-0.085	0.032	-2.656	0.014**
lnGDP	0.412	0.115	3.582	0.001***
$lnGDP^2$	-0.176	0.072	-2.43	0.021**
lnEnergy	0.654	0.140	4.671	0.000***
lnRE	-0.124	0.045	-2.755	0.012**
lnTrade	0.092	0.051	1.803	0.082*
Constant	2.145	0.521	4.117	0.000***

Source: Author's computation using EViews 12
*** $p < 0.01$; ** $p < 0.05$; * $p < 0.10$

The long-run ARDL results reveal that FDI has a statistically significant negative effect on CO_2 emissions ($\beta = -0.085$, $p < 0.05$), supporting the Pollution Halo Hypothesis. These findings suggest that foreign investment may enable the adoption of cleaner technologies and environmentally efficient production processes. Economic growth (GDP) has a positive and highly significant influence on CO_2 emissions ($\beta = 0.412$, $p < 0.01$), indicating that economic expansion continues to exert environmental pressure. This suggests that Oman may still be operating in the rising part of the Environmental Kuznets Curve (EKC). Energy consumption shows the robust positive influence on emissions ($\beta = 0.654$, $p < 0.01$), confirming that fossil fuel dependency remains the dominant driver of carbon emissions in Oman. Renewable energy consumption significantly decreases CO_2 emissions ($\beta = -0.124$, $p < 0.05$), demonstrating that clean energy transition policies are environmentally effective. Trade openness has a positive but weakly significant impact ($p < 0.10$), signifying that trade expansion may slightly increase emissions, possibly due to energy-intensive exports.

Short-Run Error Correction Model

Table 10 presents the short-run error correction model (ECM) results.

Table 10. Short-Run Error Correction Model (ECM)

Variable	Coefficient	Std Error	t-Statistic	Prob
ΔlnFDI	-0.031	0.014	-2.18	0.037**
ΔlnEnergy	0.421	0.118	3.56	0.001***
ΔlnGDP	0.213	0.087	2.44	0.021**
$\Delta lnGDP^2$	-0.098	0.041	-2.36	0.025**
ΔlnRE	-0.063	0.029	-2.17	0.038**
ΔlnTrade	0.044	0.021	2.09	0.045**
ECT(-1)	-0.237	0.071	-3.34	0.002***

Source: Author's computation using EViews 12
*** p < 0.01
** p < 0.05*p < 0.10

The error correction term (ECT−1) is statistically significant and negative ($\beta = -0.237$, $p < 0.01$), validating the presence of long-run cointegration between the variables. The magnitude implies that approximately 23.7% of short-run disequilibrium adjusts toward long-run equilibrium each year. This moderate speed of adjustment indicates that deviations from equilibrium are gradually corrected over time, reflecting the stability and long-run consistency of the estimated environmental model.

ARDL Regression & Robustness Analysis

Table 11 presents alternative model specifications using different environmental indicators (CO_2, GHG, Renewable Energy, and Ecological Footprint) to assess robustness. These models differ from the baseline ARDL long-run estimates (Table 9).

Table 11. ARDL Regression & Robustness Models

Variables	Model 1 (CO_2)	Model 2 (GHG)	Model 3 (RE)	Model 4 (EF)
FDI	-0.085**	-0.071*	0.748	0.010
Energy Consumption	0.654***	0.612***	2.495	0.314***
R^2	0.910	0.974	0.486	0.950
ECT(-1)	-0.237***	-0.309**	-0.033	-0.094

Source: Author's computation using EViews 12
*** $p < 0.01$, ** $p < 0.05$, * $p < 0.10$

- CO_2 = Carbon Emissions
- GHG = Greenhouse Gas Emissions
- RE = Renewable Energy
- EF = Ecological Footprint

The Table 11 results are robust, as alternative ARDL models were estimated using different environmental assessment indicators: carbon dioxide emissions (CO_2), greenhouse gas emissions (GHG), consumption of renewable energy (RE), and ecological footprint (EF). The purpose of these robustness analyses is to determine the consistency of the correlation between Foreign Direct Investment (FDI) and Energy Consumption with respect to environmental sustainability across different model specifications.

Model 1 (CO_2 Emissions)

In Model 1 with CO_2 emissions as the dependent variable, FDI has a negative and significant (β= -0.085, $p < 0.05$) influence on the dependent variable CO_2. The result confirms the Pollution Halo Hypothesis, which holds that foreign investment improves the environment by introducing cleaner technologies and more efficient production processes. Energy consumption has a strong, highly significant positive coefficient ($\beta = 0.654$, $p < 0.01$), indicating that Oman's heavy reliance on fossil fuels remains the primary source of carbon emissions. The negative and significant error-correction term ($\beta = -0.237$) provides evidence of a stable long-run equilibrium, denoting that about 23.7% of short-run deviations are adjusted back to equilibrium each year.

Model 2 (GHG Emissions)

In Model 2, which uses greenhouse gas (GHG) emissions as the dependent variable, the results remain mostly consistent. FDI keeps a negative relationship with emissions (β = -0.071), significant at the 10% level, indicating that foreign investment may help reduce broader greenhouse gas emissions through technological spillovers and improved environmental management practices. Energy consumption remains strongly positive and significant ($\beta = 0.612$, $p < 0.01$), substantiating that fossil fuel use endures as the primary source of environmental pressure in the Omani economy. The error correction coefficient (β = -0.309) suggests a faster adjustment speed, meaning nearly 30.9% of short-run disequilibrium gets corrected every year.

Model 3 (Renewable Energy)

In Model 3, renewable energy is taken as a dependent variable; the coefficient for FDI is positive ($\beta = 0.748$) but statistically insignificant, indicating that foreign investment has not yet played a key role in enhancing renewable energy capacity in Oman. Just like this, the energy variable is also positive but insignificant, and low explanatory power ($R^2 = 0.486$) indicates that growth in renewable energy is mostly due to government policy and strategic investments rather than market-driven foreign capital inflow. The ECT is small and insignificant, implying weak long-run equilibrium dynamics.

Model 4 (Ecological Footprint)

In Model 4, the ecological footprint is employed as an alternative parameter of environmental pressure. The results show that energy consumption has a positive, statistically significant influence ($\beta = 0.314$, $p < .01$), indicating that increased fossil fuel use contributes to ecological degradation beyond carbon emissions. The coefficient for FDI is small and statistically insignificant, implying that the environmental impact of foreign investment may rely on sectoral allocation and technological characteristics. The ECT is negative but weak, indicating slow adjustment toward equilibrium. The R^2 values indicate that Models 1, 2, and 4 exhibit high explanatory power (above 0.90), suggesting that the selected variable combinations explain a significant portion of the variation in environmental indicators. Model 3 has a lower explanatory power, suggesting that renewable energy dynamics depend on additional factors not included in the model.

The Error Correction Term (ECT) is negative throughout all models, which indicates convergence toward the long-run equilibrium. In Models 1 and 2, the ECT coefficients (−0.237 and −0.309, respectively) are statistically significant, suggesting that approximately 23.7% to 30.9% of short-run disequilibrium is corrected each year, confirming stable long-run relationships among the variables. Overall, the robustness analysis confirms that energy consumption is the primary driver of environmental deterioration in Oman. Meanwhile, FDI tends to have a neutral or even positive environmental effect. These findings reinforce the baseline ARDL results and emphasise the need to boost renewable energy use and steer foreign investment toward environmentally sustainable sectors. The differences between the baseline ARDL long-run estimates (Table 9) and the robustness models (Table 11) stem from alternative environmental indicators and model specifications, which may affect the magnitudes and statistical significance

DISCUSSION

The empirical results support the Pollution Halo Hypothesis in Oman ($\beta = -0.085$, $p < 0.05$), challenging the conventional "pollution haven" narrative commonly associated with resource-dependent economies. This result is consistent with the Pollution Halo Hypothesis, which holds that multinational corporations bring cleaner technologies and better management practices to host economies (Eskeland & Harrison, 2003). Foreign firms facilitate the dissemination of cleaner technologies and advanced environmental management practices in Special Economic Zones like Duqm, which enables them to achieve technological leapfrogging (Mahadevan & Sun, 2020). The results show a positive association between foreign direct investment and renewable energy adoption ($r = 0.462$), suggesting that foreign investment may support the expansion of solar power and green hydrogen projects in Oman (IRENA, 2023; Hydrom, 2024).

The findings offer support for the Pollution Halo Hypothesis, indicating that foreign direct investment contributes to environmental improvement through technological spillovers and improved production efficiency. Energy has a strong positive effect on emissions ($\beta = 0.654$, $p < 0.01$). Oman appears to be at a transitional stage of the Environmental Kuznets Curve (EKC) because foreign direct investment, together with renewable energy, significantly reduces emissions ($\beta = -0.124$, $p < 0.05$), thereby creating a "Technique Effect" which decreases carbon intensity while industrial growth adds pollution to the national environmental footprint (Grossman & Krueger, 1995; Balsalobre-Lorente et al., 2018). The need for 2030 and 2040 energy transition targets arises from the requirement to sustain the EKC downward slope through aggressive energy transition targets. Moreover, the Error Correction Term is negative and statistically significant, validating the presence of an enduring long-run equilibrium relationship among the variables. The coefficient suggests that approximately 15–30% of short-run disequilibrium is corrected each year, indicating a modest speed of adjustment leading to long-run environmental equilibrium (Pesaran et al., 2001). Institutional strength is reflected in Oman Vision 2040's environmental regulations, which require ESG criteria to be integrated into national investment policies. The findings imply that achieving the 2050 Net Zero target requires an end to government-wide FDI promotion and a shift toward "targeted green investment" to address fossil fuel dependence in manufacturing and desalination operations (UNCTAD, 2024; Bolton & Kacperczyk, 2021).

The results also show that the environmental effect of foreign direct investment (FDI) in Oman continues to be determined by shifts in the types of capital that flow into the country and broader sustainable development goals. This structural change in foreign capital inflows from hydrocarbon investment to renewable energy, sustainable infrastructure, logistics, and green industrial projects may explain why FDI appears to contribute positively to environmental sustainability, rather than worsening environmental degradation. For example, investments in green hydrogen, solar energy, and low-carbon industrial development show how foreign investment can support economic diversification and environmental goals at the same time. The results also imply that renewable energy has a moderating effect on the FDI–environment nexus, which implies that as renewable energy penetration rises, the negative environmental impacts of industrialization may be reduced. This indicates that Oman's increased use of renewable energy will not only decrease its overall carbon emissions but also improve the environmental sustainability of foreign investment. These effects appear stronger in economies actively pursuing sustainability reforms and cleaner energy policies. In this context, findings are consistent with recent GCC studies suggesting that the environmental impact of FDI is contingent on institutional quality, governance effectiveness, and energy structure, rather than on FDI itself.

Furthermore, the results reveal the significance of policy coherence and long-term environmental planning. The combination of Oman Vision 2040, renewable energy diversification strategies, and Net Zero 2050 goals will result in a more favourable investment environment for sustainability-oriented capital inflows. It can boost investor confidence while also motivating multinational companies to implement sustainable systems of production. Therefore, the transition toward renewable energy and sustainable policies will enable Oman to attract higher-quality foreign investment that will promote long-run environmental sustainability and low-carbon economic development. Overall, the findings suggest that Oman's transition toward renewable energy and sustainable industrial policies has the potential to transform foreign direct investment into a driver of environmental sustainability rather than a source of ecological degradation.

THEORETICAL CONTRIBUTIONS

This study contributes significantly to the literature on the FDI–environment nexus by integrating the Environmental Kuznets Curve (EKC) hypothesis and Ecological Modernisation Theory within a resource-dependent emerging economy. First, the study provides robust evidence of the relevance of the Pollution Halo Hypothesis to Oman's experience. The findings indicate that foreign direct investment (FDI) can facilitate technology transfer and cleaner production processes, thereby challenging the conventional view of the Pollution Haven Hypothesis. The Pollution Haven Hypothesis proposes that developing economies are mainly attractive to pollution and emission-intensive industries due to less rigorous environmental regulations.

Second, the study reinforces empirical support for the Environmental Kuznets Curve (EKC), which suggests that a non-linear relationship exists between economic growth and the environment. The results demonstrate that FDI plays a pivotal role in accelerating the diffusion of technology, enabling economies to adopt cleaner technologies as income levels rise. This highlights the dynamic interaction between international investment and environmental transition, thus extending the applicability of EKC theory to resource-driven countries undergoing structural transformation. Third, the study further contributes by adopting a multidimensional approach to environmental sustainability. Instead of a single proxy for the environment, both carbon emissions and ecological footprint were analysed. The persistence of the results across alternative proxies proved the robustness of the research findings. Moreover, the research provides a clear theoretical linkage with Ecological Modernisation Theory, demonstrating that renewable energy is central to the long-run sustainability of the environment. The findings reveal that renewable energy has a longer-lasting, more significant influence on reducing environmental degradation than FDI alone, suggesting that developing energy transition policies will be vital for achieving sustainable development.

Moreover, this study contributes to the literature on sustainable development in resource-dependent economies by showing that the adverse environmental effects associated with foreign investment depend on a number of factors, including the nature of energy structure, quality of institutions, and sustainability-oriented policy reforms. In contrast to traditional theoretical perspectives, which indicate that FDI has a universally negative effect on the environment in developing economies, these findings suggest that with the development of renewable energy, along with strong environmental governance and management, foreign investment can result in positive environmental outcomes. This supports the emerging argument within Ecological Modernisation Theory that technological innovation and cleaner production systems, as well as institutional reform, can jointly promote economic growth and environmental sustainability. This study contributes to the developing literature by providing country-specific evidence from Oman, which remains a relatively underexplored context within the FDI–environment nexus. While much of the previous empirical literature relies on panel regression models that often overlook structural heterogeneity among GCC economies, the country-specific ARDL framework employed in this study captures both short-run adjustment dynamics and long-run equilibrium relationships within Oman's economic and environmental transition process. The findings demonstrate that the environmental effects of FDI vary considerably depending on governance quality, renewable energy penetration, institutional reforms, and industrial composition.

In addition, the study expands the theoretical understanding of the interaction between renewable energy and foreign investment. The results suggest that renewable energy not only directly reduces environmental degradation but also moderates the environmental impact of FDI by facilitating cleaner technological adoption and reducing dependence on fossil-fuel-intensive production systems. This demonstrates that sustainable energy transition policies can strengthen the positive spillover effects of foreign capital inflows. Therefore, the study contributes to the broader sustainability literature by illustrating how green investment strategies and renewable energy development can collectively support low-carbon economic transformation in emerging economies. Finally, the study proposed new insights on the significance of institutional quality and policy frameworks as determinants of the FDI–environment relationship. The findings demonstrate that the impact of FDI on the environment is not the same across the board; rather, it depends on the nature of governance structures, the effectiveness of regulatory systems, and strategically oriented environmental policies. These findings reinforce the emerging view that the FDI–environment relationship is context-dependent and conditional, rather than generally applicable. Overall, the current research adds to existing theoretical frameworks by merging the Pollution Halo Hypothesis, Environmental Kuznets Curve, and Ecological Modernisation Theory into a single empirical framework to provide a more detailed perspective on the link between foreign investment and environmental sustainability in developing economies that depend on natural resources.

PRACTICAL IMPLICATIONS FOR POLICY

The empirical findings provide policymakers with actionable insights as they implement the **11th Five-Year Development Plan (2026–2030)** and advance the objectives of **Oman Vision 2040**. The results indicate that foreign direct investment (FDI) is accompanied by lower carbon emissions. This highlights the importance of shifting from quantity-based approaches to a quality-oriented strategy. The Ministry of Commerce, Industry, and Investment Promotion (MOCIIP) should prioritise attracting capital contributions to environmental sustainability, particularly in renewable energy, green hydrogen, and low-carbon sectors. Operationalising this shift requires selectively granting tax incentives and investment privileges to firms demonstrating measurable benefits. The adoption of carbon capture, energy-efficient production, or active participation in clean energy value chains should determine these incentives. This ensures inflows align with national sustainability goals rather than merely increasing capital volume.

Energy consumption remains the most significant driver of carbon emissions, reflecting a continued reliance on oil and gas. While energy use contributes to economic growth, it simultaneously intensifies environmental pressure through the scale effect. Policymakers must adopt a balanced approach by gradually phasing out industrial energy subsidies, which often encourage inefficient use, while simultaneously promoting cleaner production technologies. This transition incentivises domestic and foreign firms to adopt sustainable practices. Government leaders should accelerate investments in renewable infrastructure, as results confirm its role in reducing emissions. Strengthening support for solar, wind, and green hydrogen projects will mitigate degradation and enhance appeal for environmentally responsible investors. Another critical policy recommendation is the implementation of a National Carbon Credit trading system, which is one of the most economically viable policy responses, considering the importance of a more mature carbon market in turning Oman into a net absorber and remover of emissions from a relatively renewable - based emerging economy with a view to attaining Net Zero 2050. The market-based approach can significantly contribute to attaining Oman's Net Zero 2050 target and facilitate Oman's integration into the global carbon market. Therefore, it is essential that the government continually improve institutional quality, regulatory transparency, and the integration of ESG principles to maximise the positive influence of FDI on environmental sustainability, especially by means of the implementation of consistent policies to attract environmentally responsible investors, thereby providing long-term environmental and economic benefits.

Also, Oman's sustainability transition requires stronger integration between foreign investment policy, environmental governance, and long-term industrial diversification strategies. Policymakers should increasingly encourage foreign investors to participate in sectors that provide economic and environmental value, including renewable energy manufacturing, sustainable logistics, smart infrastructure, water-efficient technologies, and green hydrogen production. This approach would reduce environmental degradation while building economic resilience by decreasing dependence on hydrocarbon revenues. In addition, the government should also develop clearer ESG-based investment criteria and sustainability reporting standards for domestic and foreign firms in environmentally sensitive industries. Increasing the strength of environmental disclosure standards can increase transparency, build investor confidence, and encourage multinational companies to adopt cleaner production systems. Similarly, integrating sustainability-oriented environmental standards into investment approval mechanisms can help ensure that future FDI inflows align more closely with Oman's climate commitments, Net Zero 2050 targets, and broader sustainable development goals.

The findings also suggest the need to expand green finance channels to promote environmentally friendly investment. Long-term capital could be redirected to low-carbon infrastructure projects through the issuance of green bonds, sustainability-linked financing instruments, and renewable energy investment funds. Additionally, greater collaboration between public institutions, private investors, and international development agencies can speed up technology transfer and deployment of renewable energy in strategic sectors of the economy. Another policy implication is human capital development and technological capacity building. Attracting foreign investments that promote sustainable development requires combining workforce skill building, research and technological collaboration partnerships, and innovative policies that enhance domestic innovation absorption capacity. Moreover, increasing local technical capabilities will enable Oman to maximise the environmental and economic benefits in future periods of foreign direct investment and renewable energy transition. Overall, the findings emphasise that aligning foreign investment policies with environmental objectives is crucial for achieving sustainable development in Oman. A strategic focus on green, technology-driven, and policy-supported FDI can transform foreign investment into a key driver of environmental sustainability.

LIMITATIONS AND FUTURE RESEARCH DIRECTIONS

Despite the robust econometric findings of this study, some limitations must be recognised. First, the study uses aggregate (FDI) data. The results confirm the Pollution Halo Hypothesis, but the lack of sector-specific FDI data (including oil-extracting and manufacturing FDI) prevents researchers from determining which industries lead technological advancement in Oman. Future studies should use disaggregated data to identify the most environmentally sustainable investment paths in the Omani economy. Secondly, the ARDL model effectively identifies long-run cointegration, yet it assumes linear relationships among the variables. Future research could apply the nonlinear ARDL model (NARDL) or threshold regression models to examine how FDI affects changes in carbon emissions once the Sultanate reaches a specific level of renewable energy penetration or income per capita during the structural transition toward Oman Vision 2040. This process may provide stronger empirical validation of the EKC turning point through a more active validation method. Thirdly, the study does not explicitly incorporate institutional quality indicators, which may influence the environmental outcomes of foreign investment. Future research could integrate governance indicators to better explain the interaction between environmental regulation and foreign capital inflows. Lastly, the research focuses solely on the Sultanate of Oman. Oman serves as a regional model of diversification, yet the study's results cannot be applied to other GCC countries because they have different institutional systems and energy characteristics. The research should use comparative panel data analysis to examine the GCC and MENA regions, to determine whether the "Pollution Halo" effect in Oman results from regional patterns or Omani policy interventions. The use of Institutional Quality or Digital Transformation indicators will help to explain how foreign capital decreases environmental damage in the Middle East.

CONCLUSION

This study examined the association between foreign direct investment (FDI), renewable energy, energy consumption, and environmental sustainability in Oman using a dynamic ARDL framework. The empirical results highlight a long-run equilibrium relationship among the variables. The findings confirm the Pollution Halo Hypothesis, indicating that FDI contributes to environmental improvement rather than environmental degradation in Oman. The negative, statistically significant coefficient for FDI implies that foreign investment encourages the host country to deploy cleaner technologies and environmentally efficient production systems. Meanwhile, outcomes underscore the significant environmental impact of energy consumption on environmental pressure, thereby confirming that industrial and economic development are coupled with a scale effect. Conversely, renewable energy can reduce the harmful effects of carbon emissions and enhance sustainability, thereby serving as a mitigating factor. In short, these results show that the environmental consequences of economic growth in Oman depend heavily on how energy supply is organised and on how quickly the country transitions to a new energy system.

In policy terms, the findings emphasise the need to shift the focus of FDI promotion from merely increasing quantity to implementing green, quality-oriented, environmentally friendly investment strategies. It will be essential to synchronise foreign investment policies with the expansion of renewable energy, initiatives to reduce carbon emissions, and the sustainability goals outlined in Oman Vision 2040 to meet long-term environmental targets. Moreover, the current research aligns with the global sustainability agenda, specifically SDG 7 (Affordable and Clean Energy) and SDG 13 (Climate Action), by showing how the adoption of renewable energy and sustainable investment policies can together support environmental sustainability. Furthermore, the findings demonstrate that environmental sustainability and economic diversification should not necessarily be viewed as conflicting policy objectives in resource-dependent economies. As Oman advances toward renewable energy transition, sustainable industrialisation, and green investment policies, it demonstrates that economic growth and long-term environmental objectives can become more closely aligned.

These findings indicate that the environmental effect of foreign direct investment is not only related to the scale of capital inflows but also to the sectoral composition of investment, institutional quality, and the effectiveness of sustainability-oriented policy frameworks. In this regard, strengthening renewable energy infrastructure, environmental governance, and ESG integration will be critical to maximising the long-term environmental benefits of foreign investment. Oman may also offer important policy lessons for other GCC economies as they navigate the intersection of economic diversification, climate commitments, and industrial transformation in the wider context of global energy transition. Overall, this paper enriches the literature on the environmental implications of foreign investment in resource-dependent economies. The findings provide evidence that the simultaneous pursuit of sustainable investment policies and the adoption of renewable energy can transform FDI into a new market driver for improving environmental quality in developing economies.

REFERENCES

Acheampong, A. O. (2019). Modelling for insight: Does financial development improve environmental quality? *Energy Economics*, *83*, 156–179. DOI: 10.1016/j.eneco.2019.06.025

Ambec, S., Cohen, M. A., Elgie, S., & Lanoie, P. (2013). The Porter hypothesis at 20: Can environmental regulation enhance innovation and competitiveness? *Review of Environmental Economics and Policy*, *7*(1), 2–22. DOI: 10.1093/reep/res016

Balsalobre-Lorente, D., Shahbaz, M., Roubaud, D., & Farhani, S. (2018). How economic growth, renewable electricity, and natural resources contribute to CO_2 emissions. *Energy Policy*, *113*, 356–367. DOI: 10.1016/j.enpol.2017.10.050

Bolton, P., & Kacperczyk, M. (2021). Do investors care about carbon risk? *Journal of Financial Economics*, *142*(2), 517–549. DOI: 10.1016/j.jfineco.2021.05.008

Charfeddine, L., & Mrabet, Z. (2017). The impact of economic development and social-political factors on ecological footprint: A panel data analysis for 15 MENA countries. *Renewable & Sustainable Energy Reviews*, *76*, 138–154. DOI: 10.1016/j.rser.2017.03.031

Cole, M. A., & Elliott, R. J. R. (2003). Determining the trade–environment composition effect: The role of capital, labour and environmental regulations. *Journal of Environmental Economics and Management*, *46*(3), 363–383. DOI: 10.1016/S0095-0696(03)00021-4

Copeland, B. R., & Taylor, M. S. (2004). Trade, growth, and the environment. *Journal of Economic Literature*, *42*(1), 7–71. DOI: 10.1257/.42.1.7

Danish, & Ulucak, R. (2020). How do environmental technologies affect green growth? Evidence from BRICS economies. *Science of the Total Environment*, *712*, 136504. https://doi.org/DOI: 10.1016/j.scitotenv.2020.136504

Demena, B. A., & Afesorgbor, S. K. (2020). The effect of FDI on environmental emissions: Evidence from a meta-analysis. *Energy Policy*, *138*, 111192. DOI: 10.1016/j.enpol.2019.111192

Eskeland, G. S., & Harrison, A. E. (2003). Moving to greener pastures? Multinationals and the pollution haven hypothesis. *Journal of Development Economics*, *70*(1), 1–23. DOI: 10.1016/S0304-3878(02)00084-6

Grossman, G. M., & Krueger, A. B. (1995). Economic growth and the environment. *The Quarterly Journal of Economics*, *110*(2), 353–377. DOI: 10.2307/2118443

Hydrom. (2024). *Green hydrogen developments in Oman: Project overview and investment outlook*. Muscat, Oman: Hydrom. Retrieved May 20, 2026, from https://hydrom.om/projects

International Energy Agency (IEA). (2024). *Data and statistics*. Paris, France: International Energy Agency. Retrieved January 15, 2025, from https://www.iea.org/data-and-statistics

International Renewable Energy Agency (IRENA). (2023). *Renewable energy market analysis: GCC region*. IRENA.

Kellenberg, D. K. (2009). An empirical investigation of the pollution haven effect with strategic environment and trade policy. *Journal of International Economics*, *78*(2), 242–255. DOI: 10.1016/j.jinteco.2009.04.004

Keller, W., & Levinson, A. (2002). Pollution abatement costs and foreign direct investment inflows to U.S. states. *The Review of Economics and Statistics*, *84*(4), 691–703. DOI: 10.1162/003465302760556503

Krueger, P., Sautner, Z., & Starks, L. T. (2020). The importance of climate risks for institutional investors. *Review of Financial Studies*, *33*(3), 1067–1111. DOI: 10.1093/rfs/hhz137

Levinson, A., & Taylor, M. S. (2008). Unmasking the pollution haven effect. *International Economic Review*, *49*(1), 223–254. DOI: 10.1111/j.1468-2354.2008.00478.x

Magazzino, C., Mele, M., & Schneider, N. (2021). A machine learning approach on the relationship among solar and wind energy production, coal consumption, GDP, and CO_2 emissions. *Renewable Energy*, *167*, 99–115. DOI: 10.1016/j.renene.2020.11.050

Mahadevan, R., & Sun, Y. (2020). Effects of foreign direct investment on carbon emissions: Evidence from developing countries. *Journal of Environmental Management*, *276*, 111321. DOI: 10.1016/j.jenvman.2020.111321 PMID: 32896824

Omri, A., Nguyen, D. K., & Rault, C. (2014). Causal interactions between CO_2 emissions, FDI, and economic growth: Evidence from dynamic simultaneous-equation models. *Economic Modelling*, *42*, 382–389. DOI: 10.1016/j.econmod.2014.07.026

Pankratz, N., Bauer, R., & Derwall, J. (2023). Climate change, firm performance, and investor expectations. *Management Science*, *69*(12), 7352–7398. DOI: 10.1287/mnsc.2023.4685

Pao, H. T., & Tsai, C. M. (2011). Multivariate Granger causality between CO_2 emissions, energy consumption, FDI, and GDP. *Energy*, *36*(1), 685–693. DOI: 10.1016/j.energy.2010.09.041

Paramati, S. R., Alam, M. S., & Apergis, N. (2017). The role of stock markets and renewable energy in environmental degradation. *Emerging Markets Review, 35*, 183–200. DOI: 10.1016/j.ememar.2017.12.004

Pesaran, M. H., Shin, Y., & Smith, R. J. (2001). Bounds testing approaches to the analysis of level relationships. *Journal of Applied Econometrics, 16*(3), 289–326. DOI: 10.1002/jae.616

Polzin, F., Migendt, M., Täube, F. A., & von Flotow, P. (2015). Public policy influence on renewable energy investments—A panel data study across OECD countries. *Energy Policy, 80*, 98–111. DOI: 10.1016/j.enpol.2015.01.026

Sachs, J. D., & Warner, A. M. (2001). The curse of natural resources. *European Economic Review, 45*(4–6), 827–838. DOI: 10.1016/S0014-2921(01)00125-8

Sadorsky, P. (2010). The impact of financial development on energy consumption in emerging economies. *Energy Policy, 38*(5), 2528–2535. DOI: 10.1016/j.enpol.2009.12.048

Shahbaz, M., Nasreen, S., Abbas, F., & Anis, O. (2015). Does foreign direct investment impede environmental quality? *Energy Economics, 51*, 275–287. DOI: 10.1016/j.eneco.2015.06.014

UNCTAD. (2024). *World investment report 2024: Investment facilitation and digital government. United Nations Conference on Trade and Development.* DOI: 10.18356/9789210031349

World Bank. (2023). *World development indicators*. Washington, DC: World Bank. https://databank.worldbank.org/source/world-development-indicators

Zarsky, L. (1999). *Havens, halos and spaghetti: Untangling the evidence about foreign direct investment and the environment.* In *Foreign direct investment and the environment* (pp. 47–74). Paris: Organisation for Economic Co-operation and Development (OECD).

KEY TERMS AND DEFINITIONS

Autoregressive Distributed Lag (ARDL) Model: The model used in analyzing the relationship between various variables in short-run and long-run time series analysis.

Carbon Emissions: The emission of carbon dioxide in the air is caused by the use of fossil fuels and industrial production, along with transportation activities.

Ecological Footprint: The measure that indicates how much of the biologically productive land and water is needed to produce the goods and services consumed.

Environmental Kuznets Curve: The hypothesis states that environmental degradation increases initially during economic development but decreases when the threshold level of income is achieved.

Environmental Sustainability: The use of natural resources in an effective manner while making sure that such use is not detrimental to the environment for the future.

Foreign Direct Investment (FDI): Investments made by an entity in a different country in the form of business investments that involve ownership and economic interest in such ventures.

Pollution Halo Hypothesis: The hypothesis suggests that foreign direct investments will be able to help in improving the quality of the environment through better technologies.

Pollution Haven Hypothesis: The hypothesis in which firms move pollution-intensive operations to countries that have weaker environmental regulations to reduce operational costs.

Renewable Energy: Energy produced through natural renewable resources, such as the sun, wind, water, and plants, causes comparatively less environmental damage.

Trade Openness: Indicates the level at which the country engages in trading practices, usually measured as the ratio between export/import and the GDP of the country.

Chapter 10
Detect Fake Companies and Transactions Using Effective Artificial Intelligence Applications in Oman's Commercial Sector

Gouri Kiran Kumar S.
http://orcid.org/0009-0000-4565-257X
Department of Computing and Information Sciences, University of Technology and Applied Sciences, Muscat, Oman

Thirupathi Regula
http://orcid.org/0000-0002-2939-3552
Department of Computing and Information Sciences, College of Computing and Information Sciences, University of Technology and Applied Sciences, Muscat, Oman

Manisha Gupta
Department of Supporting Requirements, University of Technology and Applied Sciences, Muscat, Oman

Uzma Jahan
http://orcid.org/0009-0006-8830-5985
Department of Economics and Business Administration, University of Technology and Applied Sciences, Muscat, Oman

Jyoti. M. Sadamate
College of Engineering, Bharati Vidyapeeth (Deemed to be University), Maharashtra, India

Ponna Bhaskar
http://orcid.org/0009-0005-0408-5915
University of Technology and Applied Sciences, Muscat, Oman

DOI: 10.4018/979-8-3373-8964-6.ch010

ABSTRACT

Digitalization in Oman's commercial sector has improved business operations but also increased risks such as fraudulent company registrations, fake financial records, and unauthorized activities. Traditional verification systems often fail to detect complex and evolving fraud patterns. This paper proposes an AI-based framework to identify counterfeit firms and suspicious transactions in Oman's business environment. The model combines Isolation Forest and Autoencoder techniques to analyze large-scale business, licensing, and financial data in real time. It supports automated identity verification, risk scoring, anomaly detection, and transaction monitoring. The framework also includes secure authentication and regulatory compliance checks aligned with Oman's commercial laws and investment policies. Experimental results show improved fraud detection, reduced false alerts, and greater trust in digital business processes, offering a scalable solution for safer commercial operations.

INTRODUCTION

The rapid digitalization of business ecosystems has significantly transformed the way commercial activities are conducted across the world. Companies can now complete registration procedures quickly, manage transactions through online platforms, and access financial services with greater convenience. These technological advancements have improved operational efficiency, reduced paperwork, minimized delays, and supported the growth of digital commerce. Digital platforms also enable businesses to expand their market reach, improve customer service, and make faster financial decisions. However, along with these benefits, digitalization has introduced serious challenges (Sarna et al. 2025). The increasing use of online systems has created opportunities for fake companies, fraudulent registrations, false financial records, identity misuse, and unauthorized transactions. Such activities can damage trust, affect financial stability, and create risks for government agencies, financial institutions, and customers. Therefore, strong verification systems, secure digital platforms, and effective fraud detection mechanisms are essential to ensure safe, transparent, and reliable business operations.

Fraudulent organizations may misuse digital platforms to create counterfeit business identities, submit misleading documents, perform illegal financial activities, and avoid regulatory control. Such practices can create major risks for data security, financial stability, and investor confidence. In a rapidly developing digital economy, even a small weakness in verification or monitoring systems can be exploited by fraudsters. Therefore, it is essential to develop intelligent systems that can identify suspicious activities at an early stage and b support safer business operations (None Tamanna et al. 2024).

Existing verification and monitoring methods are often not sufficient to detect modern fraud patterns. These systems also depend on manual checking, fixed rules, and document-based verification (Marripudugala 2024). Although these methods are useful, they may not be able to process large volumes of data quickly or identify complex and changing fraud behavior. Fraudulent activities are becoming more advanced, and rule-based systems may fail when fraudsters change their methods. This creates the need for automated and intelligent solutions that can learn from data and detect unusual patterns in real time.

Artificial Intelligence (AI) has emerged as a powerful technology to address these challenges. AI-based systems can analyze large amounts of business, licensing, and financial data to identify hidden patterns, abnormal behavior, and inconsistencies. Techniques such as machine learning, anomaly detection, and deep learning can be used to distinguish between genuine and suspicious activities. For example, AI can help verify company identities, compare submitted documents with official records, monitor transaction patterns, and assign risk scores to companies or transactions (Smita Rani Parija et al. 2025).

One effective approach is the use of anomaly detection models, such as Isolation Forest and Autoencoder techniques. Isolation Forest can identify unusual data points that differ from normal business behavior, while Autoencoders can learn normal transaction patterns and detect deviations. When these methods are combined, they can improve the accuracy of fraud detection and reduce false alerts. This helps regulatory authorities focus on high-risk cases and take timely action (Heru Supriyanto. 2026).

The proposed AI-based framework can be integrated with digital business portals, company registration systems, licensing platforms, and financial transaction databases. It can support real-time monitoring by continuously analyzing incoming data and identifying suspicious activities. The system can also include secure authentication procedures, automated identity verification, compliance checks, and risk assessment tools (Narasapuram et al. 2026). These features can strengthen transparency and ensure that business activities follow commercial laws and investment policies.

In the context of Oman, such a framework can play an important role in supporting a secure and investor-friendly business environment (Ali 2025). As Oman continues to strengthen its digital economy, the protection of commercial systems becomes highly important. AI-based fraud detection can assist government authorities, financial institutions, and regulatory bodies in identifying fake companies, preventing suspicious transactions, and improving trust in digital services (Banu et al. 2024).

Overall, the integration of Artificial Intelligence into business verification and fraud monitoring systems offers a scalable, efficient, and reliable solution (Trivedi et al. 2024). It reduces dependence on manual processes, improves detection accuracy, and supports faster decision-making. By adopting AI-driven fraud detection mechanisms, Oman can enhance the safety, transparency, and reliability of its commercial sector, while encouraging sustainable economic growth and stronger investor confidence (Moturi Swathi et al. 2024).

LITERATURE REVIEW

In this section, various models are discussed based on the fraud transactions belongs to fake companies.

A. Various ML Algorithms Used to Detect Fraud Transactions

Patil et al. (2025) the increasing prevalence of online recruitment platforms has created new opportunities for both job seekers and employers. However, it has also led to a rise in fraudulent job postings, where malicious actors publish fake advertisements to exploit applicants. To address this challenge, a hybrid solution integrating Natural Language Processing (NLP) and Machine Learning (ML) is proposed for the effective detection of fake job listings.

The suggested framework focuses on analyzing textual content such as job advertisements, job descriptions, and company-related information. It identifies patterns commonly associated with fraudulent postings by applying advanced text analysis techniques. The process begins with preprocessing steps, including text cleaning, tokenization, and normalization, to ensure the quality and consistency of the input data. These steps remove noise, standardize formats, and prepare the text for further analysis.

Following preprocessing, feature extraction techniques such as Term Frequency–Inverse Document Frequency (TF-IDF) and word embeddings are employed to capture both statistical and semantic information from the text. While TF-IDF highlights important keywords, word embeddings provide contextual meaning, enabling the system to better understand the nuances of job descriptions. These features are then used as inputs for machine learning models that classify job postings as genuine or fraudulent.

To enhance detection accuracy, the proposed approach integrates rule-based indicators with contextual analysis. Rule-based methods can capture explicit warning signs such as unrealistic salaries, vague job requirements, or suspicious contact details, while ML models identify deeper hidden patterns. This hybrid combination improves classification performance and reduces false positives, making the system more reliable.

Ampumuza et al. (2026) presented a comprehensive review of AI-based methods for detecting irregularities in financial transactions, particularly within Savings and Credit Cooperative Organizations (SACCOs). SACCO is the organization formed by various employees which can manage the money transactions. Their study highlights the application of various AI techniques, including machine learning, deep learning, anomaly detection, and graph-based approaches, for fraud detection. The review evaluates key methodologies such as classification models, clustering algorithms, neural networks, and hybrid frameworks, all of which contribute to improved detection accuracy.

Furthermore, the study identifies critical challenges in implementing AI-based fraud detection systems, including data imbalance, the lack of labeled datasets, model interpretability, and privacy concerns. Addressing these issues is essential for developing robust and trustworthy systems.

Overall, the proposed NLP and ML-based hybrid framework provides an effective and scalable solution for detecting fake job postings. By combining linguistic analysis with intelligent classification, it enhances recruitment platform security and protects job seekers from fraudulent activities.

Ragini Mokkapati et al. (2023) offers an extensive overview of the major domains and applications of Artificial Intelligence (AI), Machine Learning (ML), Deep Learning (DL), and Data Science, highlighting their growing importance in solving complex real-world problems across various industries. These technologies have become fundamental in sectors such as healthcare, finance, education, transportation, manufacturing, and smart governance, where large volumes of data are generated continuously. AI and ML enable intelligent decision-making by identifying patterns, predicting outcomes, and automating processes, while DL further enhances this capability through advanced neural network architectures that can process high-dimensional and unstructured data such as images, text, and speech.

Data Science plays a central role by integrating statistical analysis, data preprocessing, and visualization techniques to extract meaningful insights from large and complex datasets. Through data cleaning, transformation, and exploratory analysis, organizations can better understand trends, behaviors, and risks. Visualization tools help present these insights in an interpretable form, supporting informed decision-making. The combination of these technologies allows organizations to improve efficiency, optimize operations, and enhance innovation in digital ecosystems.

However, the study also highlights several critical challenges associated with the adoption of AI-driven technologies. One major issue is poor data quality, which can significantly affect model performance and lead to inaccurate predictions. Incomplete, inconsistent, or noisy data can reduce the reliability of AI systems. Another important concern is model interpretability, particularly in deep learning models, which often function as "black boxes." This lack of transparency can create difficulties in understanding how decisions are made, especially in sensitive domains such as finance and healthcare. Additionally, computational complexity remains a challenge, as advanced AI models require significant processing power, storage, and time for training and deployment.

Ethical considerations also play a crucial role in the responsible use of AI and Data Science. Issues such as data privacy, bias in algorithms, fairness, and accountability must be carefully addressed to ensure that AI systems are trustworthy and socially acceptable. The study emphasizes the importance of developing frameworks and policies that promote ethical AI practices.

Seify et al. (2022) proposed a ML-based fraud detection model for supply chain systems to identify abnormalities and suspicious activities across supply chain operations. The suggested approach uses data-driven techniques by analyzing historical transaction records, supplier information, logistics data, and financial details to train ML models capable of distinguishing between fraudulent and legitimate activities. By learning patterns from past data, the model can detect irregular behaviors such as unusual supplier activity, false invoices, abnormal delivery records, and suspicious financial transactions. The research highlights the importance of intelligent analytics in improving supply chain transparency, strengthening monitoring processes, and supporting early fraud detection. It also demonstrates how machine learning can reduce financial losses, improve decision-making, and enhance the overall security and efficiency of supply chain management. Overall, the proposed model provides a practical and scalable solution for building safer, more reliable, and fraud-resistant supply chain systems.

B. Fraud Transactions in Various Organizations and Government Companies

Chen et al. (2025) examines the role of deep learning techniques in financial fraud detection and highlights recent developments and practical applications. Models such as CNNs, RNNs, LSTM, and Autoencoders are effective in detecting complex fraud patterns from large financial datasets. CNNs identify important transaction features, while RNNs and LSTMs analyze sequential transaction behavior. Autoencoders support anomaly detection by identifying deviations from normal patterns. The study also discusses challenges including data imbalance, limited labeled data, interpretability issues, computational complexity, privacy concerns, and real-time processing requirements for reliable and secure fraud detection systems.

Fatrizia et al. (2025) considers the importance of Good Corporate Governance in preventing financial statement fraud and money laundering by strengthening organizational control, transparency, and accountability. It highlights key governance mechanisms such as board oversight, internal auditing, risk management, and regulatory compliance as essential tools for detecting and reducing fraudulent activities. Effective governance structures help create a strong control environment where ethical behavior, responsible decision-making, and accurate financial reporting are encouraged. The paper emphasizes that governance principles such as transparency, accountability, fairness, and responsibility play a major role in reducing opportunities for fraud and improving organizational integrity. Board oversight ensures that management actions are properly monitored, while internal auditing helps examine financial records, operational processes, and compliance practices. Risk management systems support the early identification of potential fraud risks, and regulatory compliance ensures that the organization follows relevant laws, standards, and reporting requirements. The study also discusses the role of audit committees and independent directors in strengthening fraud prevention. Audit committees review financial statements, monitor internal controls, and coordinate with auditors to identify irregularities. Independent directors provide objective judgment and reduce the possibility of biased decision-making. Compliance systems further support organizations by tracking suspicious activities, enforcing policies, and ensuring adherence to anti-money laundering regulations. Overall, the study shows that Good Corporate Governance is a vital framework for preventing financial anomalies, protecting stakeholders, and building trust in corporate operations.

Karairia (2026) provides an empirical examination of the relationship between corporate governance practices and fraud prevention in Indian corporations. It focuses on key governance mechanisms, including board structure, audit committees, internal control systems, and regulatory compliance frameworks, and evaluates their role in reducing corporate fraud. The research specifically investigates how these governance elements influence the occurrence of fraudulent financial reporting and other forms of corporate misconduct.

Arsad et al. (2025) presented a literature review of fraud in corporate companies. It is very difficult to detect fraud in corporate companies due to their multi-functional operations across various branches. This work mainly focused on the working of forensic accounting practices and informant techniques. These techniques help audit fraud more effectively. Based on the detection of fraud, the proposed technique shows greater potential for identifying these frauds.

Alarfaj et al. (2024) the study proposed a smart fraud detection approach that combines GNNs, Autoencoders and DL techniques to efficiently and instantly determine fraudulent credit card transactions. To efficiently detect suspicious transaction behaviour in complex financial networks, he proposed a framework based on Graph Neural Networks (GNNs), which is capable of modelling hidden relationships and transaction connectivity patterns among users, merchants, devices and banking activities. It also uses autoencoders to learn what a normal transaction looks like then if the transaction deviates from that pattern the transactions get flagged as potentially fraudulent. The system incorporates pre-processing, feature extraction, Graph-based representation learning, anomaly scoring and deep classification approaches to enhance accuracy of fraudulent identification in addition to reducing false positive rates. This work demonstrates the potential of leveraging graph-based deep learning with anomaly-aware representation learning to build intelligent, scalable and secure banking fraud detection systems that are essential in modern financial ecosystems.

Hashemi et al. (2022), study presented the intelligent data driven techniques to enhance accuracy of fraud detection and minimize false transactions. The framework is based on applying ML algorithms via a banking transaction dataset to classify transactions into either a legitimate or fraudulent. This system applies additional preprocessing, important feature selection, detailed anomaly analysis including latent factor-based and report generation along with whitening adaption mechanisms to evolve existing machine learning techniques for efficient automatic fraud detection of financial datasets.

Eyad Btoush et al. (2021), study presented the survey which is conduct on various credit card fraud detection techniques in the area of cyber security frameworks. The research study also analyzes anomaly detection methods, transaction pattern analysis, behavioral analytics, and real-time fraud monitoring systems used to identify suspicious banking activities. In addition, the study explains the benefits, drawbacks, performance metrics and implementation challenges associated with available fraud detection models including class imbalance, false positive rates, data privacy issues and real-time processing constraints.

Balajee Asish Brahmandam et al. [2025] proposed an approach for intelligent fraud prevention that combines blockchain technology with deep learning approaches, providing secure and transparent transactions while reducing fraudulent detection errors in banking systems. The framework provided in this study, reinforces secure transactions and enhances their integrity using Blockchain technology as a decentralized ledger to ensure transparency of financial records in the banking environment. Also, SRNN have been used for sequential transaction characteristics and temporal dependencies analysis as well as abnormal financial behavior to accurate detection of frauds/fraud classification. It involves preprocessing, extracting features about credit transactions and validating them using blockchain for transaction security, identifying anomalies in the features gained through deep learning models-based sequence.

Bao et al. (2020) discuss fraud detection using various ML algorithms. This study mainly focused on fraud, which raises research questions with multiple stakeholders in real life. Here, real life represents accounting fraud in various companies. The main drawback of this model is that it lacks the ability to accurately detect fraud.

Liu et al. (2023) proposed an innovative approach to banking transaction data modeling by casting it as a graph structure - nodes representing entities (customers, banks, accounts, devices) and edges reflecting the relationship between those nodes as well as interactions. The GNN with hierarchical attention mechanisms enables multi-level graph structure and selective focus on transaction patterns, suspicious relationships across agents (abnormal behavioral dependencies) along various pathways. It has a preprocessing graph construction for various types of anomalies and features extraction, attention-based representation learning, anomaly analysis and finally fraud classification mechanism all together to provide enhanced capability for detecting the frauds while minimizing the number of false positives. Experimental analysis proves that the proposed hierarchical attention-based GNN framework achieves promising real-time fraud detection performance improvement over conventional machine learning and the traditional graph learning approach. Our work demonstrates the order of magnitude improvement in performance that can be obtained by correctly and practically deploying graph-based DL and attention-driven relational analysis techniques, for the purpose of enabling high throughput, where fraud detection is one of (but indeed not limited only to) intelligent, scalable and secure financial cyber security applications.

Bharath Maneel et al. (2025) study presents four ML algorithms for detecting anomalous transactions on metaverse platforms. All these transactions belong to the Kaggle dataset that contains 78,600 transactions. Among all the algorithms, RF achieved the highest precision (0.96), accuracy (0.94), recall (0.97), and F1-Score (0.96). This study mainly lacks novelty. Saynam Inthavixay et al. (2024) proposed an intelligent anomaly detection framework by implementing ML algorithms to detect suspicious and aberrant activities in banking transactions environment. Ensemble Learning Models for Transaction Behaviour Analysis and Real-time Anomaly Detectors. It conducts pre-processing, feature extraction, behavioural analysis, anomaly scoring and an intelligent classification of genuine transactions against suspicious ones. It is used to identify deviations in banking behaviours and fraudulent activities through features related to transactions like transaction amount, transaction frequency, geographical location, account behaviour entropy and temporal patterns. Experimental analysis shows that the anomal detection framework proposed in this paper enables real-time monitoring capability; and it significantly outperforms traditional banking fraud detections methods. The study emphasises the need for smart systems in detecting anomalies to boost banking cyber security, reduce risks of financial fraud and strengthen secure digital financial transaction environments of Lao banking entities. In addition to these developments, financial frauds, unauthorized transactions, money laundering and abnormal banking activities are increasingly becoming a leading cyber security threat for the financial organizations. The vast and evolving nature of transaction data makes it difficult for conventional fraud detection and transaction monitoring systems to uncover unseen but emerging patterns of anomalies in real-time.

Narayanan et al. (2025) proposed an intelligent fraud detection framework combining DL-based anomaly representation learning with ML-based outlier detection for real-time detection of fraud cases. The Autoencoder based framework consists of two major components: (1) The autoencoder networks and (2) Isolation forest algorithms that can be used to augment the anomaly detection capability on large-scale datasets from banking transactions. An Autoencoder reconstructs pattern of genuine transaction in order to learn normal behavior and thus it can recognize abnormal activities by analyzing the reconstruction error. Two algorithms that are used to improve anomaly detection from the previous steps we have seen, one is based on isolation of balance transaction instances which aims to identify abnormal ones. The Isolation Forest uses random partitioning and outlier analysis mechanisms through ensemble learning (165). Preprocessing, feature extraction, anomaly scoring, hybrid decision fusion and fraud classification are actual contributions to the system that shall identify fraudulent transactions from genuine banking activities in an efficient manner.

ROLE OF CONVOLUTIONAL NEURAL NETWORKS (CNN) FOR DETECTING FAKE TRANSACTIONS

The CNN is the DL based model that automatically discovers the underlying hidden patterns, behavioral relationships and abnormal transaction characteristics from large scale banking datasets is detecting fraud or fake financial transactions from E-commerce developed organizations (Xie et al 2023). Originally engineered to work with image-processing tasks, CNNs perform remarkably well in handling structured and sequential financial transaction information because of their powerful feature extraction ability. For fake transaction detection system, CNN model conduct analysis on various aspects of a transaction including its amount and frequency, the behavior of user (which includes geolocation), time patterns like day/week/month/years of detection, details pertaining to merchants transacting with users, device specifications etc. CNNs are able to automatically identify rich feature representations from historical transaction data, and traditional rule-based fraud detection systems may not be able to detect complex and evolving fraud patterns. This makes CNNs an excellent choice for real-time application areas, like banking fraud detection and cyber security.

The CNN architecture includes a number of layers, including convolutional depths, pooling depressions, activation functions, and fully connected dense layers that collaborate to discover useful features in transactions and classify them as real or fraudulent (Cai 2026). To learn the local feature patterns transaction feature matrices are aggregated together and convolutions are applied over these matrices in order to obtain filters that identify hidden fraud behaviours or abnormal activity/ pattern behaviour. Since pooling layers decrease computational complexity, it is able to help to keep only the most important features related to fraud and reduce noise and non-significant data. Activation functions like ReLU are installed in the model to add non-linearity, which helps CNNs prepare complex fraud patterns and nonlinear relationship features inside banks datasets. Finally fit for the signature and classification layers such as Softmax or Sigmoid do the final prediction problems, classify transactions into genuine vs fake transaction classes. This process hierarchical learning helps CNNs in detecting and also reducing sophisticated fraud attempts to be misclassified as legitimate transactions (Shaik Rehana Banu et al. 2024).

The CNN-based fake transaction detection systems have many advantages over traditional machine learning and statistical fraud detection methods. One of them is the other automatic feature extraction because the model learns important fraud indicators by itself without the need for extensive manual feature engineering. Since CNNs work well on image data for large-scale banking transaction datasets, they can aid in discovering patterns of fraud that would otherwise be lost in conventional systems. Moreover, CNN models achieve excellent detection quality along with speed and optimized scalability for real-time transaction monitoring in real-life scenarios of digital banking. With DL, the system can learn from previously seen transactions and evolve with changing fraud strategies and new types of cyber attacks. Further, CNN-based models can be incorporated in ensemble learning frameworks and attention mechanisms for improving fraud prevention performance and lowering false positive rates in banking.

Another crucial aspect of CNNs in the identification of fake transactions is their capacity to detect spatial and temporal correlations between transaction features. Fraudulent transactions tend to have irregular behavioral sequences, repetitive patterns, or feature hidden dependencies between users, devices, merchants and banking activities. Through learning feature correlations between multiple dimensions of transaction data, these complex relationships captured by CNNs. Convolutional feature learning mechanisms can detect anomalies such as if the same person is transacting in various locations, creates a sudden change in his/her spending behavior, fails to log in more than 2 times or transact too much too quickly. This ability allows getting better detection of Identity Theft, Account Takeover attacks, Phishing-based frauds and unauthorized financial transactions. They are also useful in real-time systems for fraud detection, as the time of transaction analysis and decision must happen in a few milliseconds to mitigate financial losses and prevent cyber-criminals from activity on customer accounts.

ROLE OF ALEXNET FOR DETECTING FAKE TRANSACTIONS

The system of detecting if a financial transaction is fake or fraudulent uses AlexNet based approach: deep learning-based feature extraction and intelligent classification (Mytnyk et al. 2023). Although AlexNet was initially designed for image recognition tasks, the network is now widely used in fraud detection tasks because it can automatically learn complex patterns from large-scale datasets. In banking and finance systems, deceitful transactions are frequently comprised of concealed abnormal behaviours, atypical expenditure patterns, dubious transaction sequences, and unauthorized activities that cannot be easily detected by traditional machine learning paradigms. AlexNet analyzes transaction details including transaction amount, account activity information, location data of the corresponding locations where transactions take place; types and frequencies of transactions allowed on one device and other user behaviors to detect fraudulent activities accurately. AlexNet Extracts Deep Feature Representations from Historical Transactions Datasets, thus Enhance the Detection of Cyber fraud, Identity theft, Phishing-Transactions and Unauthorized Banking Operations in Real Time Financial Environments.

One of the major advantages of AlexNet in fake transaction detection problems is its automatic extracting features were further converted into image-like matrices using normalized feature values to create a 2-D representation. In our case, we encoded each single transaction as feature map, whose pixel intensities were proportional to the normalized value of attributes. This allowed AlexNet to first automatically learn the relationships between transaction features and second, to derive high level characteristics of transactions related to whether they are fraudulent or not. With the help of AlexNet, manual feature engineering was previously useful since its deep convolutional layers could extract features automatically and thus outperform other algorithms in terms of fraud detection. In addition, AlexNet enables high-dimensional transaction analysis without compromising performance or accuracy on large-scale financial datasets. It also allows us to perform better fraud prevention by lowering the false-positive rate and increasing real-time transaction monitoring capability to cater for modern digital banking systems.

Real-time banking cyber security also plays a key role with AlexNet predicting abnormal transaction patterns as well as hidden fraud connections over multiple transaction attributes! Fraudulent transactions can exhibit unusual temporal patterns, abnormal transaction frequency, fast geographical switching between different locations of the world, suspicious merchant activities, or irregular user behavior sequence. These hidden relationships are learnt by AlexNet through mechanisms of deep convolutional feature extraction and pattern recognition. This ability aids to identify credit card fraud, account takeover attacks and transactions that are not authorized in promises. Furthermore, AlexNet can be incorporated into the anomaly detection systems, ensemble learning frameworks, GNNs and Autoencoders for more efficient fraud classification capability and intelligent threat analysis in financial systems. AlexNet is a good fit for secure banking applications as a framework because of its combination of deep feature extraction and real-time prediction capabilities.

However, although the AlexNet-based fraud detection systems has its merits, there are still some practical challenges to be addressed in bank settings. Deep learning models require a balanced dataset to be trained effectively, and the financial transaction datasets often exist in skewness, genuine transactions far exceed the fraudulent ones. Deep neural networks models like AlexNet come with some key challenges such as (i) Overfitting; (ii) Computational complexity; (iii) High memory numbers and (iv) Data Privacy. Various data balancing techniques, dropout regularization (DR), transfer learning (TL), data augmentation methods (DA), ensemble learning, and feature optimization are embedded within the fraud detection framework to tackle these challenges. AlexNet is also applied in conjunction with the latest deep learning architectures like Transformers, Autoencoders and RNNs by researchers to increase contextual learning and fraud detection capability. As a result, AlexNet not only lends itself as a highly useful and versatile deep learning model but enables proactive, scalable, adaptable and real-time detection of fake transactions for intelligent fraud prevention systems used in contemporary digital banking and financial cyber security.

METHODOLOGY

This study proposes an Artificial Intelligence based fraud detection system to identify fake businesses and fraudulent transactions in the Oman business environment. The proposed methodology follows a multi-stage pipeline consisting of data acquisition, preprocessing, feature engineering, hybrid anomaly detection, and decision-making.

In the first stage, data is collected from digital business portals, licensing authorities, and financial transaction systems. The collected data includes company registration details, ownership information, transaction logs, compliance records, and other business-related documents. This wide range of data helps create a complete profile of each company and its activities.

The acquired data then undergoes preprocessing to improve its quality and consistency. This includes data cleaning, normalization, handling missing values, and encoding categorical variables. These steps ensure that the data is suitable for AI-based analysis and reduces errors caused by incomplete or inconsistent records.

After preprocessing, feature engineering is performed to extract meaningful indicators for fraud detection. Important features include transaction frequency, abnormal financial behavior, company linkage patterns, ownership relationships, compliance history, and identity-related attributes as shown in Figure 1. These features help the system identify unusual patterns that may indicate suspicious business activities.

Figure 1. Features obtained by Feature Engineering

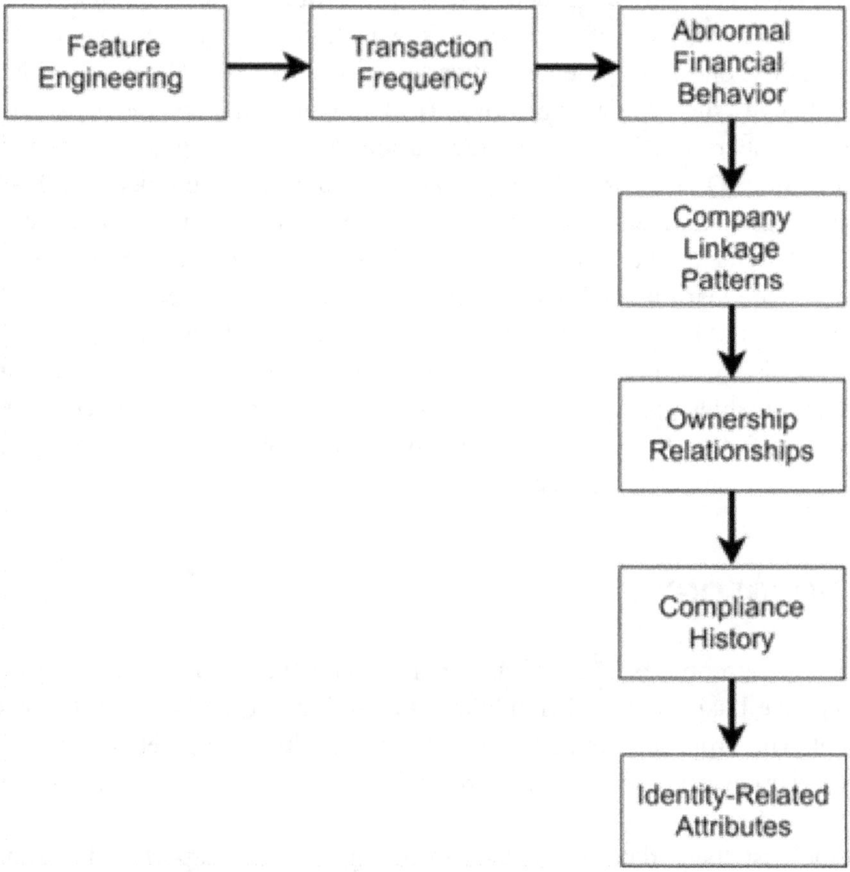

The proposed framework applies a hybrid anomaly detection approach using AI techniques such as Isolation Forest and Autoencoder models. Isolation Forest detects unusual records by isolating abnormal data points, while the Autoencoder learns normal business behavior and identifies deviations. The combination of both models improves detection accuracy and reduces false alarms.

Finally, the system generates risk scores and supports decision-making by classifying businesses or transactions as normal, suspicious, or high-risk. This enables regulatory bodies and financial institutions to take timely action. Overall, the proposed AI-based system provides a scalable, efficient, and reliable solution for strengthening fraud detection, improving transparency, and supporting a secure digital business environment in Oman.

The main idea of the suggested system is the hybrid model of AI based on the combination of Isolation Forest and Autoencoder that are aimed at identifying anomalies in the mass of business data. The Isolation Forest algorithm isolates the rare and suspicious cases, using the preparation of random decision trees and essentially finding the outliers like fake companies or abnormal transactions. At the same time, the Autoencoder, which is a deep learning-based model, obtains the normal behavioral patterns of business operations and reconstructs the input information; the large reconstruction errors are a sign of fraud. The results of the two models are combined to enhance the accuracy of detection and control false positives. Beyond that, the structure introduces identity checks implemented through artificial intelligence (AI) and risk rating algorithms and ongoing monitoring of transactions to expand real-time fraud detection applications. Each entity or transaction is assigned a risk score based on a number of weighted factors which allow a prioritization of high-risk cases.

To achieve strength and realistic usability, the system contains safe authentication frameworks, role based access management, and encryption frameworks in order to safeguard delicate business information (Gaidosch et al. 2026). Moreover, the regulatory compliance checks are integrated into the framework to correspond to the Oman Foreign Capital Investment Law, Bankruptcy Law, and anti-fraud regulations so that all anomalies could be reviewed on the basis of laws. The suggested methodology will enhance real-time processing and scalability, which will be applicable to large-scale implementation in the digital governance system. The results of the performance evaluation are measured according to the accuracy, precision, recall, F1-score, and false positive rate, which proves that the offered AI-based solution proves efficient in transparency, the decrease of fraud risks, and the increase in confidence in the Oman commercial sphere.

ENSEMBLE APPROACH: ISOLATION FOREST + AUTOENCODER (PROPOSED APPROACH)

The Isolation Forest and Autoencoder ensemble method is a powerful hybrid approach for detecting anomalies such as fake companies and fraudulent activities in large-scale financial and commercial datasets. This method combines the strengths of two effective anomaly detection techniques: Isolation Forest, which is a tree-based unsupervised learning model, and Autoencoder, which is a deep learning-based neural network model.

Isolation Forest works by randomly splitting data points using decision trees. The main idea is that abnormal data points are easier to isolate than normal data points. Therefore, suspicious records usually require fewer splits and have shorter path lengths in the tree structure. These anomalies may represent unusual transaction patterns, abnormal company registration details, irregular ownership structures, or inconsistent financial behavior. Since Isolation Forest is computationally efficient and scalable, it is suitable for processing large volumes of structured business and financial data in near real time.

On the other hand, an Autoencoder is designed to learn the normal behavior of data through an encoder-decoder architecture. The encoder compresses the input data into a lower-dimensional representation, while the decoder reconstructs the original input from this compressed form. The model is trained mainly on normal or non-fraudulent records so that it can reconstruct genuine business patterns with minimal error. When abnormal or fraudulent data is introduced, the Autoencoder produces a higher reconstruction error because it is unfamiliar with such unusual patterns. This reconstruction error becomes an important indicator for anomaly detection.

By combining Isolation Forest and Autoencoder, the proposed ensemble method improves the reliability and accuracy of fraud detection. Isolation Forest is effective in identifying outliers in structured numerical data, while the Autoencoder captures complex and hidden nonlinear patterns. The outputs from both models can be combined through a scoring mechanism, where records with high anomaly scores are classified as suspicious or high-risk.

This hybrid framework is particularly useful in detecting fake companies, suspicious financial transactions, and unauthorized commercial activities. It reduces dependence on manual verification, improves early fraud identification, and supports faster decision-making by regulatory authorities. Overall, the Isolation Forest and Autoencoder ensemble provides a scalable, intelligent, and efficient solution for strengthening fraud detection systems in modern digital business environments.

This property enables the Autoencoder to find complex and non-linear anomalies that could not be found using conventional means. It comes in handy especially when one wants to extract concealed patterns in high dimensional data like transaction logs, company behavior and financial activities.

The ensemble technique combines Isolation Forest and Autoencoder models to improve the accuracy, reliability, and strength of fraud detection in digital business environments. In this approach, both models independently analyze business and financial data and generate anomaly scores that indicate the possibility of suspicious behavior. These scores are then integrated using methods such as weighted averaging, score normalization, or threshold-based decision rules to produce a final fraud risk score. Specifically, a normalized weighted averaging method was applied to aggregate the anomaly scores given by the Isolation Forest and Autoencoder models. Normalize the individual scores to a common scale and combine them with pre-defined weights to yield an aggregated fraud risk score. Any company or transaction that went beyond this limit was labeled as suspicious. To increase transparency and reproducibility, we have included a detailed description of our scoring methodology (score computation, normalization, weight assignment, and threshold selection) in the Methodology section. Isolation Forest is a fast and scalable tree-based model that detects unusual records by isolating abnormal data points more quickly than normal ones. It is highly suitable for structured datasets such as company registration details, ownership records, compliance history, and financial transactions. In contrast, the Autoencoder is a deep learning model that learns normal business behavior through an encoder-decoder structure. When fraudulent or abnormal data is introduced, it produces a high reconstruction error, indicating a possible anomaly. By combining these two methods, the ensemble framework benefits from both statistical outlier detection and deep feature learning. This makes the system more effective in identifying fake company registrations, suspicious transaction patterns, abnormal financial behavior, irregular ownership links, and non-compliance indicators. If both models produce high anomaly scores for the same company or transaction, the system can classify it as suspicious or high-risk, thereby reducing false positives and improving decision-making reliability. In the context of Oman's commercial sector, this hybrid approach provides a practical and scalable solution for strengthening fraud detection in large-scale digital ecosystems. It supports automated risk scoring, real-time monitoring, early fraud identification, and regulatory decision-making. Overall, the Isolation Forest and Autoencoder ensemble method enhances transparency, improves trust in digital business processes, and contributes to a safer, more secure, and investment-friendly commercial environment.

DATASET DESCRIPTION: SYNTHETIC FINANCIAL DATASET FOR FRAUD DETECTION (PAYSIM)

The Synthetic Financial Dataset for Fraud Detection is a widely used dataset generated using the PaySim mobile money simulator, which models realistic financial transaction behavior based on mobile payment systems. It is designed to simulate different types of mobile money activities, including deposits, withdrawals, transfers, and payments, allowing researchers to study fraud detection in a controlled yet realistic environment. Since real financial datasets are often difficult to access due to privacy, security, and confidentiality concerns, PaySim provides a synthetic but behaviorally meaningful alternative. The dataset reflects both legitimate and fraudulent transaction patterns, making it suitable for developing and evaluating machine learning and deep learning models. It is particularly useful for testing anomaly detection techniques, classification algorithms, and fraud prediction frameworks. By using this dataset, researchers can analyze transaction behavior, identify suspicious activities, and improve the accuracy of fraud detection systems without exposing sensitive customer information. Its structured format and realistic transaction flow make it valuable for experiments involving risk scoring, pattern recognition, and financial crime detection. Overall, the Synthetic Financial Dataset on Fraud Detection supports the development of intelligent, secure, and scalable fraud detection solutions for modern digital financial systems.

Publicly available datasets on company registration anomalies and fraudulent financial transactions are not available for Oman, therefore this study integrates attributes on company registration with transaction-level information from the PaySim dataset. This combines company-level features (company age, number of employees, changes in directors and same-address companies) with transaction behavior features to produce a unified fraud detection platform which can detect both fraudulent company registrations as well as suspicious financial transactions. The important attributes are the type of transaction (e.g. CASH-IN, CASH-OUT, TRANSFER, PAYMENT), transaction amount, pre- and post-balances of the sending and receiving account, and the flags which indicate the fraudulent nature of a transaction such as isFraud and isFlaggedFraud. The incidents of fraud in this dataset can be grouped into two categories which are suspicious transfer and cash-out operations, which are real-life fraud cases such as unauthorized transfer of funds. It offers a very well-performing dataset in isolating forest, random forest, LSTM, and autoencoders, which means that this dataset is well-suited to be applied in a research on financial fraud detection, anomaly detection, and AI-based transaction monitoring systems.

Figure 2. Dataset records from Kaggle

	A	B	C	D	E	F	G	H	I	J	K
1	step	type	amount	nameOrig	oldbalanc	newbalan	nameDest	oldbalanc	newbalan	isFraud	isFlaggedFraud
2	1	PAYMENT	9839.64	C1231006	170136	160296.4	M1979787	0	0	0	0
3	1	PAYMENT	1864.28	C1666544	21249	19384.72	M2044282	0	0	0	0
4	1	TRANSFER	181	C1305486	181	0	C5532640	0	0	1	0
5	1	CASH_OU	181	C8400836	181	0	C3899701	21182	0	1	0
6	1	PAYMENT	11668.14	C2048537	41554	29885.86	M1230701	0	0	0	0
7	1	PAYMENT	7817.71	C9004563	53860	46042.29	M5734872	0	0	0	0
8	1	PAYMENT	7107.77	C1549888	183195	176087.2	M4080691	0	0	0	0
9	1	PAYMENT	7861.64	C1912850	176087.2	168225.6	M6333263	0	0	0	0
10	1	PAYMENT	4024.36	C1265012	2671	0	M1176932	0	0	0	0
11	1	DEBIT	5337.77	C7124101	41720	36382.23	C1956008	41898	40348.79	0	0
12	1	DEBIT	9644.94	C1900366	4465	0	C9976083	10845	157982.1	0	0
13	1	PAYMENT	3099.97	C2491775	20771	17671.03	M2096539	0	0	0	0
14	1	PAYMENT	2560.74	C1648232	5070	2509.26	M9728652	0	0	0	0
15	1	PAYMENT	11633.76	C1716932	10127	0	M8015691	0	0	0	0
16	1	PAYMENT	4098.78	C1026483	503264	499165.2	M1635378	0	0	0	0
17	1	CASH_OU	229133.9	C9050804	15325	0	C4764022	5083	51513.44	0	0
18	1	PAYMENT	1563.82	C7617507	450	0	M1731217	0	0	0	0
19	1	PAYMENT	1157.86	C1237762	21156	19998.14	M1877062	0	0	0	0
20	1	PAYMENT	671.64	C2033524	15123	14451.36	M4730532	0	0	0	0
21	1	TRANSFER	215310.3	C1670993	705	0	C1100439	22425	0	0	0
22	1	PAYMENT	1373.43	C2080460	13854	12480.57	M1344519	0	0	0	0
23	1	DEBIT	9302.79	C1566511	11299	1996.21	C1973538	29832	16896.7	0	0
24	1	DEBIT	1065.41	C1959239	1817	751.59	C5151329	10330	0	0	0
25	1	PAYMENT	3876.41	C5043364	67852	63975.59	M1404932	0	0	0	0

PERFORMANCE METRICS

The performance of the proposed fraud detection system based on the Isolation Forest and Autoencoder ensemble method is evaluated using standard classification and anomaly detection metrics to ensure that the model is accurate, reliable, and suitable for real-world financial and commercial applications. Since fraud detection usually involves highly imbalanced datasets, where genuine transactions are much higher than fraudulent ones, a single evaluation measure is not sufficient to judge the effectiveness of the system. Therefore, multiple performance indicators such as Accuracy, Precision, Recall, F1-score, AUC-ROC, False Positive Rate, and False Negative Rate are used to provide a complete assessment of the model.

Accuracy measures the overall correctness of the model by calculating the proportion of correctly classified normal and fraudulent cases. However, in fraud detection, accuracy alone may be misleading because a model can achieve high accuracy by classifying most transactions as normal. Therefore, Precision is used to measure how many transactions predicted as fraudulent are actually fraudulent. High precision indicates that the system produces fewer false alarms, which is important for reducing unnecessary investigations.

$$\text{Accuracy (ACC)} = \frac{\text{TP} + \text{TN}}{\text{TP} + \text{TN} + \text{FP} + \text{FN}}$$

Recall, also known as Sensitivity, measures the ability of the system to identify actual fraud cases. A high recall value means that the model successfully detects most fraudulent activities and reduces the chance of missing real fraud. This is especially important in financial fraud detection because undetected fraud can result in financial loss, legal issues, and reduced trust in digital systems.

$$\text{Recall (Re)} = \frac{\text{TP}}{\text{TP} + \text{FN}}$$

$$\text{Specificity (Spc)} = \frac{\text{No of TN}}{\text{No of TN} + \text{No of FP}}$$

The F1-score provides a balanced measure between Precision and Recall. It is particularly useful when the dataset is imbalanced, as it considers both false positives and false negatives. A high F1-score indicates that the model performs well in detecting fraud while maintaining a reasonable level of accuracy in its predictions.

$$\text{Precision (Pre)} = \frac{\text{TP}}{\text{TP} + \text{FP}}$$

$$\text{F1} - \text{Score (F1S)} = 2 * \frac{(\text{Precision*Recall})}{(\text{Precision} + \text{Recall})}$$

The Area Under the Receiver Operating Characteristic Curve, known as AUC-ROC, is used to evaluate the model's ability to distinguish between normal and fraudulent transactions at different threshold levels. A higher AUC value indicates better separation between genuine and suspicious activities. This metric is useful for selecting an appropriate decision threshold based on the needs of regulatory authorities or financial institutions.

$$\text{AUROC} = \int_0^1 \text{TPR(FPRd(FPR)}$$

False Positive Rate (FPR) measures the proportion of genuine transactions incorrectly classified as fraudulent. A high false positive rate may create extra workload for investigators and inconvenience for legitimate businesses.

$$\text{FPR} = \frac{\text{FP}}{\text{FP} + \text{TN}}$$

By using these evaluation metrics together, the proposed Isolation Forest and Autoencoder ensemble method can be assessed more effectively. The combined evaluation ensures that the system is not only accurate but also practical, scalable, and dependable for fraud detection in real financial environments. Overall, these measures support a thorough understanding of model performance and help improve trust, transparency, and decision-making in digital fraud monitoring systems.

IMPLEMENTATION

To deploy the proposed AI-based fraud detection system, a strong software environment is required to process large volumes of business and financial data efficiently. Python can be used as the main programming language because it supports advanced machine learning, deep learning, and data processing applications. Libraries such as NumPy and Pandas can be used for data handling, cleaning, transformation, and preprocessing. Scikit-learn can support machine learning tasks, including classification, anomaly detection, feature selection, and model evaluation. For deep learning models such as Autoencoders, TensorFlow and Keras can be used to design, train, and test neural network architectures. Visualization tools such as Matplotlib and Seaborn can help analyze data patterns, compare model performance, and present results through graphs, confusion matrices, and accuracy plots. For experimentation and model development, Jupyter Notebook or Google Colab can be used, as they provide an interactive environment for writing code, testing algorithms, and documenting results. In practical deployment, web application frameworks such as Flask or Django can be used to build user-friendly interfaces where regulatory officers or administrators can upload data, view risk scores, and monitor suspicious activities. For large-scale and real-time data processing, Apache Spark or Hadoop can be integrated to manage high-volume transaction records and business datasets. A secure database system is also essential for storing company registration details, ownership records, compliance information, and transaction logs. MySQL, PostgreSQL, or MongoDB can be used depending on whether the data is structured or semi-structured. The system should also include secure authentication, access control, data encryption, and audit logging to protect sensitive business and financial information. Cloud platforms such as AWS, Microsoft Azure, or Google Cloud may also be considered for scalable deployment, storage, and computing resources. Overall, this software environment provides a complete foundation for building, testing, deploying, and maintaining an intelligent fraud detection system that can operate efficiently, securely, and reliably in Oman's digital commercial sector.

Hardware requirements are based on the volume and complexity of the models. To start with, a minimum of i5/i7 processor, 8GB-16GB RAM, and 256GB SSD storage should suffice. Nevertheless, more powerful hardware is suggested in case of large-scale detection of fraud and training of a deep learning model (Autoencoder) e.g. a system with GPU (NVIDIA CUDA-supported GPU) can speed up the process. Enterprise-level deployments Cloud-based infrastructure, including AWS, Google Cloud, or Microsoft Azure, can be deployed to offer scalable computing resources, distributed processing, and provide secure data storage. Multi-core processors, high memory (32 GB or above) and parallel processing can be ideal requirements of high-performance servers that are needed to handle huge financial data and guarantee real time fraud detection with minimal latency.

RESULTS AND DISCUSSIONS

A quantitative comparison of different deep learning algorithms—namely Convolutional Neural Networks (CNN), AlexNet, and the proposed hybrid model—is conducted to evaluate their effectiveness in classifying fake transactions using standard performance metrics. These metrics include Accuracy, Precision, Recall, F1-score, Specificity, Area Under the Curve (AUC), and False Positive Rate (FPR), which together provide a comprehensive assessment of classification performance in fraud detection systems. The results, summarized in Table 1, clearly demonstrate the relative strengths and limitations of each model in handling complex and imbalanced financial datasets.

The baseline CNN model shows moderate performance across the evaluation metrics. It achieves a Precision of 86.34%, Accuracy of 91%, and Recall of 87.89%.

These results indicate that while the CNN model is capable of identifying fraudulent transactions to a certain extent, it struggles with misclassification and produces a noticeable number of false positives and false negatives. The relatively lower precision suggests that some normal transactions are incorrectly flagged as fraudulent, which can increase operational costs and reduce system efficiency. Similarly, the recall value shows that the model fails to detect a portion of actual fraud cases, which may lead to financial losses and reduced trust in the system. Overall, the CNN model provides a reasonable baseline but lacks the robustness required for high-stakes financial environments.

In comparison, the AlexNet model demonstrates significantly improved performance across all metrics. It achieves a Precision of 92.78%, Accuracy of 96%, and Recall of 94%, indicating a stronger ability to extract meaningful features and classify transactions more effectively. The deeper architecture of AlexNet enables better representation learning, which enhances its capability to identify complex patterns in transaction data. As a result, it reduces both false negatives and misclassification errors compared to the basic CNN model. However, despite these improvements, AlexNet still exhibits certain limitations. Its False Positive Rate of 4.23% suggests that a proportion of legitimate transactions are incorrectly classified as fraudulent. While this rate is lower than that of the baseline CNN, it still indicates room for improvement, particularly in minimizing unnecessary alerts and improving decision-making efficiency.

In contrast, the proposed model significantly outperforms both CNN and AlexNet across all evaluation parameters, demonstrating superior accuracy, consistency, and reliability. The model achieves a Precision of 98.56%, Accuracy of 98.34%, Recall of 98%, and Specificity of 98%, along with an F1-score of 99. These results highlight the model's ability to maintain an excellent balance between detecting fraudulent transactions and minimizing incorrect classifications. The high precision indicates that the model rarely misclassifies genuine transactions as fraudulent, thereby reducing false alarms and operational overhead. At the same time, the high recall demonstrates that the model successfully detects nearly all fraudulent activities, minimizing the risk of undetected fraud.

Furthermore, the Area Under the ROC Curve (AUC) for the proposed model reaches 98%, which reflects its strong capability to distinguish between normal and fraudulent transactions across different threshold values. A high AUC score indicates that the model performs consistently well under varying decision boundaries, making it highly adaptable to different operational requirements. One of the most critical advantages of the proposed model is its low False Positive Rate of 2.11%, which significantly reduces unnecessary alerts and improves system efficiency. This is particularly important in real-world applications, where excessive false positives can overwhelm investigators and delay the identification of genuine fraud cases.

The superior performance of the proposed model can be attributed to its ability to capture complex transactional patterns and relationships within the data. By leveraging advanced learning mechanisms and possibly hybrid or ensemble strategies, the model effectively combines the strengths of traditional deep learning architectures with enhanced anomaly detection capabilities. This enables it to identify subtle irregularities that may not be easily detected by standard models such as CNN or AlexNet.

Overall, the comparative analysis clearly demonstrates that the proposed model provides a more powerful and accurate solution for fraud detection in financial systems. It not only improves detection rates but also reduces errors, making it highly suitable for large-scale, real-time applications. The findings confirm that the proposed approach offers a robust, efficient, and scalable framework for identifying fraudulent transactions, thereby enhancing trust, security, and transparency in digital financial ecosystems.

Table 1. Quantitative Performance of Algorithms based on Classification of Fake Transactions

Parameters	CNN	AlexNet	Proposed (ours)
Precision (%)	86.34	92.78	98.56
Accuracy (%)	91	96	98.34
Recall (%)	87.89	94	98
Specificity (%)	88.89	93.45	98
F1-Score (%)	84	95	99
AUC (%)	86.23	96	98
False Positive Rate (%)	12.34	4.23	2.11

CONCLUSION

This study presents an efficient and scalable Artificial Intelligence (AI)-driven framework for detecting counterfeit organizations and fraudulent transactions within the commercial sector of Oman. The proposed system integrates machine learning, anomaly detection, and deep learning techniques to analyze large-scale business and financial data, enabling the identification of suspicious patterns and abnormal behaviors. By leveraging a hybrid ensemble approach that combines Isolation Forest and Autoencoder models, the framework effectively captures both simple statistical outliers and complex nonlinear anomalies. This dual capability significantly enhances fraud detection accuracy while reducing false positives, a critical requirement in real-world financial environments. The system further incorporates automated identity verification, dynamic risk scoring, and real-time transaction monitoring, which collectively strengthen the responsiveness and reliability of fraud detection mechanisms. The proposed approach uses the Pysim dataset to measure the strength of the proposed approach.

A key contribution of this work lies in its ability to bridge the gap between theoretical AI models and practical deployment in digital business ecosystems. The framework is designed with secure authentication protocols, data protection measures, and compliance checks aligned with Oman's commercial laws and regulatory policies. This ensures that the system is not only technically robust but also legally and operationally viable. The integration with digital business portals, licensing systems, and financial transaction platforms allows continuous monitoring and early detection of fraudulent activities. Experimental results demonstrate that the proposed model achieves high levels of accuracy, precision, recall, and overall reliability, outperforming traditional and standalone models. The low false positive rate further highlights its effectiveness in minimizing unnecessary alerts, thereby improving decision-making efficiency for regulatory authorities and financial institutions.

The findings of this research emphasize the transformative potential of AI-based solutions in enhancing fraud detection systems. By automating complex analytical processes and enabling real-time insights, the proposed framework contributes to increased transparency, improved compliance, and stronger investor confidence. It supports the development of a secure and trustworthy digital commercial environment, which is essential for sustainable economic growth in Oman. Furthermore, the adaptability and scalability of the system make it suitable for deployment across various sectors, including banking, e-commerce, and government regulatory bodies.

FUTURE WORK

Despite its promising results, there are several avenues for future research that can further enhance the effectiveness and applicability of the proposed system. One important direction is the integration of additional data sources, such as social network data, behavioral analytics, and unstructured textual data from documents or communication logs. Incorporating Natural Language Processing (NLP) techniques can help detect fraud patterns in textual information, such as suspicious company descriptions or misleading financial statements. This would enable a more comprehensive analysis and improve detection capabilities.

Another area for future study is the application of advanced deep learning architectures, such as Graph Neural Networks (GNNs), which can model relationships between entities like companies, shareholders, and transactions. Since fraud often involves hidden connections and networks, graph-based approaches can provide deeper insights into complex fraud schemes. Additionally, reinforcement learning techniques could be explored to develop adaptive systems that continuously improve their detection strategies based on feedback and evolving fraud patterns.

The issue of data imbalance, which is common in fraud detection, can also be addressed through advanced techniques such as synthetic data generation, cost-sensitive learning, and improved sampling methods. Enhancing model interpretability is another critical aspect for future work. Developing explainable AI (XAI) models will allow stakeholders to understand the reasoning behind fraud predictions, thereby increasing trust and facilitating regulatory acceptance.

From an implementation perspective, future research can focus on deploying the system in real-time cloud-based environments with distributed computing capabilities. Integration with blockchain technology could also be explored to enhance data integrity, transparency, and traceability of transactions. Furthermore, continuous monitoring and updating of models using live data streams will be essential to ensure that the system remains effective against evolving fraud techniques.

In conclusion, this study demonstrates that AI-based hybrid models offer a powerful and practical solution for fraud detection in modern digital economies. The proposed framework not only improves detection accuracy but also ensures scalability, security, and compliance with regulatory standards. By addressing existing limitations and exploring future enhancements, such systems have the potential to significantly strengthen fraud prevention mechanisms and contribute to a safer, more transparent, and investment-friendly commercial ecosystem in Oman and beyond.

REFERENCES

Alarfaj, F. K., & Shahzadi, S. (2024). Enhancing Fraud Detection in Banking with Deep Learning: Graph Neural Networks and Autoencoders for Real-Time Credit Card Fraud Prevention. *IEEE Access : Practical Innovations, Open Solutions*, •••, 1–1. DOI: 10.1109/ACCESS.2024.3466288

Ali, M. J. (2025). The Impact of Artificial Intelligence on Commercial Banks in Oman. *International Journal of Research and Innovation in Social Science*, *IX*(IV), 309–322. DOI: 10.47772/IJRISS.2025.90400025

Ampumuza, D., Katushabe, C., & Tamale, M. (2026). A systematic review and future directions for AI-driven detection of fraud patterns in SACCO transactions. *Frontiers in Artificial Intelligence*, *8*, 1690482. Advance online publication. DOI: 10.3389/frai.2025.1690482 PMID: 41693763

Arsad, S., Abdullah, W. N., Awang, N., & Gani, S. I. I. (2025). Strengthening Corporate Fraud Detection through Forensic Accounting and Whistleblowing: The Moderating Role of Regulatory Enforcement. *International Journal of Research and Innovation in Social Science*, *IX*(IX), 6843–6853. DOI: 10.47772/IJRISS.2025.909000561

Balajee Asish Brahmandam, N. (2025). A Hybrid Blockchain and Deep Learning Approach for Credit Card Fraud Detection using Slice Recurrent. *Neural Networks : The Official Journal of the International Neural Network Society*, •••, 1–6. DOI: 10.1109/ICoICC64033.2025.11052047

Banu, M. S., Parveen, N., Gayathri, R., Gera, A., Kumar, S., & Anitha, G. (2024, June). A machine learning approach for enhanced security using blockchain in finance auditing services. In 2024 15th International Conference on Computing Communication and Networking Technologies (ICCCNT) (pp. 1-6). IEEE.

Banu, S. R., Gongada, T. N., Santosh, K., Chowdhary, H., Sabareesh, R., & Muthuperumal, S. (2024, April). Financial fraud detection using hybrid convolutional and recurrent neural networks: An analysis of unstructured data in banking. In 2024 10th International Conference on Communication and Signal Processing (ICCSP) (pp. 1027-1031). IEEE.

Bao, Y., Hilary, G., & Ke, B. (2020). Artificial Intelligence and Fraud Detection. SSRN Electronic Journal. DOI: 10.2139/ssrn.3738618

. M. Bharath Maneel, M. Sri SaiHarsha, Sai, S. R., CH. Vivek, M Kavitha, Dharmaiah Devarapalli, & D Mythrayee. (2025). Anomaly Detection in Transactions Using Machine Learning. Edu - Tech Enterprise, 3, 21–21. .DOI: 10.71459/edutech202521

Btoush, E. Zhou, X., Rai Gururaian, Chan, K. M., & Tao, X. (2021). A Survey on Credit Card Fraud Detection Techniques in Banking Industry for Cyber Security. 2021 8th International Conference on Behavioral and Social Computing (BESC). DOI: 10.1109/BESC53957.2021.9635559

Cai, M. (2026). Detecting Financial Fraud and Anomalies in Corporate Transactions with Convolutional Neural Networks. *International Journal of Computational Intelligence Systems, 19*(1), 186. Advance online publication. DOI: 10.1007/s44196-026-01275-2

Chen, Y., Zhao, C., Xu, Y., Nie, C., & Zhang, Y. (2025). *Deep Learning in Financial Fraud Detection: Innovations, Challenges, and Applications*. Data Science and Management., DOI: 10.1016/j.dsm.2025.08.002

Fatrizia, S., Putra, N. N. A., & Hidayati, S. A. (2025). Role of Good Corporate Governance in Preventing Financial Statement Fraud and Money Laundering. *Journal of Accounting and Finance in Emerging Economies, 11*(1). Advance online publication. DOI: 10.26710/jafee.v11i1.3268

Gaidosch, T., Islam, E., Khiaonarong, T., Ravikumar, R., & Wilson, C. (2026). Good Practices in Cyber Risk Regulation and Supervision. *Departmental Papers, 2026*(001), 1. DOI: 10.5089/9798229026185.087

Hashemi, S. K., Mirtaheri, S. L., & Greco, S. (2022). Fraud Detection in Banking Data by Machine Learning Techniques. *IEEE Access : Practical Innovations, Open Solutions, 11*, 1–1. DOI: 10.1109/ACCESS.2022.3232287

Inthavixay, S., Inthasone, S., Chanthaphavong, A., & Keophilavong, T. (2024). Utilizing Machine Learning Techniques to Identify Anomalies in Financial Transactions for Laos Banking. 2022 5th International Conference on Information and Communications Technology (ICOIACT), 79–84. DOI: 10.1109/ICOIACT64819.2024.10913217

J, T., Narayanan, L., M, T., & Revathi, M. (2025). A Hybrid Anomaly Detection Framework for Credit Card Fraud Using Autoencoder and Isolation Forest. 2025 9th International Conference on Computational System and Information Technology for Sustainable Solutions (CSITSS), 1–6. .DOI: 10.1109/CSITSS67709.2025.11294206

Kariria. (2026). Corporate Governance and Fraud Prevention: An Empirical Study of Indian Corporations. Journal of Informatics Education and Research. .DOI: 10.52783/jier.v6i1.4243

Liu, Y., Sun, Z., & Zhang, W. (2023). Improving fraud detection via hierarchical attention-based Graph Neural Network. *Journal of Information Security and Applications, 72*, 103399–103399. DOI: 10.1016/j.jisa.2022.103399

Marripudugala, M. (2024). AI-Powered Fraud Detection in the Financial Services Sector: A Machine Learning Approach. 2024 2nd International Conference on Self Sustainable Artificial Intelligence Systems (ICSSAS), 795–799. DOI: 10.1109/ICSSAS64001.2024.10760599

Mokkapati, R., & Dasari, V. L. (2023). *A Comprehensive Review on Areas and Applications of Artificial Intelligence*. Machine Learning, Deep Learning, and Data Science., DOI: 10.1109/ICIMIA60377.2023.10426237

Moturi Swathi, N. (2024). *Shalini, Kilaru Aswini, Vanamali Venkata Abhiram, Bathini Ramya, & Yadav, M. G.* Fraud Detection in Digital and Netbanking Using Machine Learning., DOI: 10.1109/ICOECA62351.2024.00138

Mytnyk, B., Tkachyk, O., Shakhovska, N., Fedushko, S., & Syerov, Y. (2023). Application of Artificial Intelligence for Fraudulent Banking Operations Recognition. *Big Data and Cognitive Computing*, *7*(2), 93. DOI: 10.3390/bdcc7020093

Narasapuram, N. K., Shah, S. A. A., Shiratuddin, M. F., & Sohel, F. (2026). Explainable artificial intelligence models for detecting suspicious bank transactions. *International Journal of Machine Learning and Cybernetics*, *17*(3), 111. Advance online publication. DOI: 10.1007/s13042-026-02994-w

Patil, K., Shetty, A., Rajagopal, A., & Shilpa Sonawani. (2025). A Hybrid Approach to Fake Job Detection Using NLP and Machine Learning. 1–6. .DOI: 10.1109/ICTBIG68706.2025.11323989

Sarna, N. J., Rithen, F. A., Jui, U. S., Belal, S., Amin, A., Oishee, T. K., & Muzahidul Islam, A. K. M. (2025). AI Driven Fraud Detection Models in Financial Networks: A Review. *IEEE Access : Practical Innovations, Open Solutions*, •••, 1–1. DOI: 10.1109/ACCESS.2025.3596060

Seify, M., Sepehri, M., Hosseini-far, A., & Darvish, A. (2022). Fraud Detection in Supply Chain with Machine Learning. *IFAC-PapersOnLine*, *55*(10), 406–411. DOI: 10.1016/j.ifacol.2022.09.427

Smita Rani Parija, Kumari, R., Tiwari, D., Kumar Shubham, Rath, P., & Das, L. (2025). Fraud Detection in Financial Transactions Using a Machine Learning. 1–7. .DOI: 10.1109/CCPIS65231.2025.11234223

Supriyanto, H. (2026). Anomaly Detection in Blockchain Transactions Using Isolation Forest and Autoencoder Deep Learning Models. *Journal of Current Research in Blockchain.*, *3*(2), 139–151. DOI: 10.47738/jcrb.v3i2.69

Tamanna, N. Kamboj, S., Singh, L., & Kaur, T. (2024). Automated Fraud Detection in Financial Transactions using Machine Learning: An Ensemble Perspective. 1–6. .DOI: 10.1109/AIMLA59606.2024.10531422

Trivedi, C., Kumar, S., Abdullah, N., Obaid, A. J., & Faisal, A. (2024). The Utilization of AI in Fraud Detection in Smart Cities. 1–8. .DOI: 10.1109/ICETAS62372.2024.11119907

Xie, S., Liu, L., Sun, G., Pan, B., Lang, L., & Guo, P. (2023). Enhanced E-commerce Fraud Prediction Based on a Convolutional Neural Network Model. Computers, Materials & Continua/Computers. *Computers, Materials & Continua*, *75*(1), 1107–1117. DOI: 10.32604/cmc.2023.034917

Chapter 11
Strategic Communication Territorial Intelligence in Family Business Entrepreneurship for Sustainable Innovation and Job Creation in MENA Region

Fatimazahra Belarbi
http://orcid.org/0009-0005-4810-2297
Faculty of Legal, Economic, and Social Sciences of Agdal, Mohammed V University in Rabat, Morocco

Hamza Ayass
http://orcid.org/0000-0001-5395-2599
Faculty of Legal Economic and Social Sciences- Agdal. Mohammed V University, Rabat, Morocco

Zakaria Belabbes
Ibn Tofail University, Morocco

ABSTRACT

This article investigates how strategic communication and territorial intelligence interact to support sustainable innovation trajectories and employment outcomes in family business entrepreneurship in the Middle East and North Africa (MENA).

DOI: 10.4018/979-8-3373-8964-6.ch011

Empirically, the study relies on a cross sectional survey administered to owner managers and next generation leaders of family firms across several MENA economies, analyzed using PLS SEM with bootstrapped mediation tests. To deepen interpretation, qualitative insights from open ended responses are examined using thematic analysis. The results provide convergent evidence that strategic communication significantly predicts territorial intelligence, which partially mediates the link between communication capability and sustainable innovation, and is positively associated with job creation intentions. Moderation effects indicate that stronger governance and entrepreneurial culture intensify the conversion of territorial intelligence into innovation outcomes, whereas women's empowerment strengthens governance-related sustainability effects.

1. INTRODUCTION

Across the Middle East and North Africa (MENA), sustainable job creation remains a pressing development priority, not only because unemployment is persistently high, but also because labour-market entry is shaped by structural constraints, conflict risks, and gendered barriers. In particular, regional youth labour-market indicators remain critically elevated: for instance, recent ILO projections indicate youth unemployment around one quarter of the active youth population, alongside very high shares of youth not in employment, education, or training (NEET), with young women disproportionately represented among the NEET population. Consequently, the employment challenge is not merely cyclical; rather, it reflects long-term institutional, social, and economic frictions that weaken inclusive growth and intensify the urgency of scalable, decent-work pathways (International Labour Organization, 2024).

Within this context, family businesses and SMEs occupy a pivotal position in economic renewal, because they often concentrate entrepreneurial initiative, local value chains, and employment absorption capacity. Empirically, policy-oriented evidence from the Arab world underscores that SMEs constitute a major source of private-sector jobs and that their ability to expand employment is tightly connected to constraints such as access to finance, institutional quality, and investment readiness. Hence, strengthening the entrepreneurial fabric-especially the family-business segment-becomes strategically relevant for job creation, provided that firms can innovate sustainably rather than only expand informally or cyclically (Nasr & Pearce, 2012).

Nevertheless, sustainable innovation in family firms cannot be reduced to technology adoption alone; instead, it depends on how governance, culture, and stakeholder relationships shape decision-making under uncertainty. Recent empirical research in

Saudi family firms, for example, shows that governance and responsible innovation are associated with stronger sustainability outcomes, and that entrepreneurial culture can amplify these effects (Rawaf & Alfalih, 2023). While Saudi Arabia possesses distinct institutional features, these findings are highly relevant across the broader Middle East and North Africa (MENA) region, where family firms face similar socio-cultural dynamics, concentrated ownership structures, and institutional transitions. This alignment is mirrored in broader family-business literature, which consistently demonstrates that sustainability performance in family entrepreneurship is contingent on both formal structures and softer organizational conditions that influence how innovation is framed, selected, and embedded.

At the same time, the mechanisms that translate innovation intentions into durable, locally anchored outcomes are often communicational and relational. Strategic communication—understood as the purposeful use of communication by an organization to fulfill its mission—provides an integrative lens for examining how family firms align internal actors (owners, successors, non-family managers) and external stakeholders (communities, regulators, partners) around sustainability-oriented choices. In family firms, this alignment is especially consequential during succession and capability renewal, where communication can become either a catalyst for innovation or a barrier that reinforces inertia. (Hallahan et al., 2007). In family firms, this alignment is especially consequential during succession and capability renewal, where open communication between generations serves as the conduit for transferring tacit knowledge and embedding long-term sustainability goals; conversely, communication barriers frequently reinforce inertia and stall innovation transitions (Somboonvechakarn et al., 2022).

In parallel, territorial intelligence offers a complementary, place-based perspective. Conceptually, territorial intelligence can be viewed as a practice devoted to obtaining, analysing, and valuing information and knowledge about a territory and its environment to design and implement strategic territorial plans, increasingly oriented toward collaboration and sustainable development. When transferred to the firm level, this suggests that family firms may innovate more sustainably when they can interpret local signals, mobilize territorial networks, and co-create solutions with local actors—thereby connecting entrepreneurship to regional development outcomes. (García-Madurga et al., 2020).

In this context, we note that although MENA family-business scholarship has advanced in explaining governance, innovation, entrepreneurial culture, and gender empowerment, research still lacks an integrative model that explicitly links strategic communication (as an organizing capability) with territorial intelligence (as a place-based knowledge and collaboration capability) to explain sustainable innovation and job creation. Moreover, existing studies are often country-specific (frequently Saudi Arabia) or focus on only one layer of analysis (firm-level governance or macro-level institutions), leaving the territorial mechanisms under-operationalized. Therefore, the central problem is to explain *how* family firms in MENA convert communication and territorial knowledge into innovation trajectories that generate sustainable employment. (Rawaf & Alfalih, 2024).

Therefore, this article proposes a conceptual framework that positions strategic communication and territorial intelligence as complementary drivers of sustainable innovation and job creation in MENA family-business entrepreneurship, while incorporating governance, entrepreneurial culture, and women's empowerment as enabling conditions. (Martínez-Sanchis et al., 2020).

In order to operationalize the problem, the study advances the following hypotheses:

- **H1:** Strategic communication capability positively influences territorial intelligence in family businesses. (Hallahan et al., 2007).
- **H2:** Territorial intelligence positively influences sustainable innovation in family businesses. (García-Madurga et al., 2020).
- **H3:** Sustainable innovation positively influences job creation outcomes in family businesses (Ciriaci et al., 2016).
- **H4:** Sustainable innovation mediates the relationship between territorial intelligence and job creation. (Stam, 2015).
- **H5:** Governance quality strengthens the positive relationship between territorial intelligence and sustainable innovation. (Rawaf & Alfalih, 2023).
- **H6:** Women's empowerment strengthens the positive association between governance and sustainability-oriented innovation in family firms. (Rawaf & Alfalih, 2024).

2. LITERATURE REVIEW AND HYPOTHESES DEVELOPMENT

2.1 Strategic Communication as a Capability for Sustainable Innovation in Family Businesses

2.1.1. Strategic Communication Definition

Strategic communication, as defined in foundational work, refers to the purposeful use of communication by an organization to fulfill its mission, implying intentionality, resource allocation, and integration across internal and external communication domains. Importantly, this perspective treats communication not as a peripheral function, but as an organizing capability that supports strategy formation, legitimacy building, and stakeholder alignment. Therefore, strategic communication is particularly relevant for sustainability, because sustainabili1.1.ty requires long-term coherence between values, governance choices, and stakeholder expectations. (Hallahan et al., 2007).

2.2.2. Strategic Communication in Family Business

In family businesses, the strategic value of communication is amplified by the coexistence of two overlapping systems: the family and the firm. On the one hand, this overlap can accelerate decision-making through trust and shared identity; on the other hand, it can intensify ambiguity, create role conflicts, and delay professionalization if communication is informal, opaque, or overly centralized. Thus, strategic communication in family firms is not only outward-facing; rather, it includes internal sensemaking that clarifies governance rules, succession pathways, and sustainability commitments across generations. (Rawaf & Alfalih, 2024).

Moreover, sustainable innovation in family firms often requires bridging tradition and renewal. Qualitative evidence from family SMEs highlights that innovation and sustainability topics—such as organizational innovation priorities, social-capital networks, traditional and territorial knowledge, and sustainability-driven mindsets—need to be communicated formally or informally during succession. Conversely, misalignment between incumbents' intentions and actions, successors' readiness, and employees' openness can become communication barriers that undermine innovation and sustainability goals. Hence, communication operates as a practical mechanism through which innovation capability is transmitted, contested, and institutionalized. (Somboonvechakarn et al., 2022).

From a governance standpoint, strategic communication also supports accountability and transparency, both of which are necessary for sustainability-oriented decision-making. Empirical work in Saudi family enterprises demonstrates that governance and responsible innovation are positively associated with business sustainability, while entrepreneurial culture reinforces these links (Rawaf & Alfalih, 2023). Extending these empirical insights through a communication lens, we infer that governance does not function solely through static structural rules; rather, it operates dynamically through the communicative routines that explain, legitimize, and enforce those rules among family and non-family stakeholders. This interpretation aligns with broader family business theory, which demonstrates that the efficacy of governance frameworks depends heavily on shared relational routines and transparent communication to foster consensus (Mustakallio et al., 2002). Accordingly, communication quality can condition whether governance principles become lived organizational practices or remain limited to symbolic compliance.

In addition, strategic communication strengthens stakeholder relationships, which matters because sustainability innovations often require external collaboration (suppliers, universities, NGOs, regulators) and internal coordination (family owners, managers, employees). When communication is strategically managed, family firms can reduce uncertainty, negotiate trade-offs between socioemotional and economic goals, and mobilize support for sustainability investments that may have delayed financial returns. Consequently, strategic communication can be conceptualized as a capability that increases the firm's overall preparedness to interpret stakeholder signals and convert them into innovation priorities (Hallahan et al., 2007).

2.2 Territorial Intelligence, Territorial Embeddedness, and Entrepreneurial Ecosystems

2.2.1 Conceptualizing Territorial Intelligence

Territorial intelligence (TI) originates from a place-based approach to strategic decision-making, emphasizing the systematic production and coordination of knowledge about a territory and its environment. In scoping evidence, TI is characterized as (i) a collective process involving multiple agents, (ii) an integration of external information with internal local knowledge, and (iii) a collaboration orientation supporting sustainable development. Consequently, TI is not merely data collection; rather, it is a governance-and-knowledge architecture that enables coordinated action in complex territorial systems. (García-Madurga et al., 2020).

2.2.2. TI in Family-Business Entrepreneurship

When applied to family-business entrepreneurship, TI becomes analytically valuable because family firms are often deeply embedded in local communities through history, identity, and long-term relationships. This embeddedness can generate competitive advantages—such as privileged access to informal networks, localized reputations, and intergenerational knowledge—but it can also produce lock-in if firms remain overly dependent on inherited routines. Therefore, TI offers a way to theorize how embedded family firms can remain locally rooted while still learning, innovating, and adapting to sustainability demands. (Martínez-Sanchis et al., 2020).

Territorial embeddedness can be unpacked into distinct but interrelated dimensions. In qualitative findings, the territory conditions entrepreneurial family embeddedness through cultural embeddedness (shared values and norms), political embeddedness (power relations and institutions), structural embeddedness (social networks and relationships), and cognitive embeddedness (interpretations and meanings). Importantly, these dimensions jointly shape how entrepreneurial families perceive opportunities, manage continuity, and engage with territorial actors, which implies that innovation strategies are partly "territory-conditioned" rather than purely firm-chosen. (Martínez-Sanchis et al., 2020).

Furthermore, the entrepreneurial ecosystem perspective clarifies why territorial mechanisms matter for job creation. Ecosystems combine framework conditions (formal and informal institutions, physical conditions) with systemic conditions (networks, leadership, finance, talent, knowledge, support services). Notably, networks facilitate information flow and resource matching, while leadership and intermediaries can reduce barriers and accelerate innovation diffusion. Hence, a territorially intelligent family firm can be seen as an ecosystem actor that both benefits from and contributes to territorial value creation, linking innovation outputs to employment outcomes. (Stam, 2015).

From this viewpoint, TI is a plausible bridge between sustainability and innovation because sustainable innovation frequently depends on localized knowledge: resource constraints, community needs, regulatory contexts, and environmental realities are territorially specific. As a result, firms that can interpret territorial signals and mobilize territorial collaboration are more likely to adopt responsible innovation practices that endure over time, especially when they align with local development agendas and stakeholder expectations. (García-Madurga et al., 2020).

Thus, regarding H2–H4 Hypothesis implications. First, because TI strengthens environmental scanning, partnership coordination, and knowledge integration, it should facilitate sustainable innovation in family firms (H2). Second, because sustainable innovation can expand markets, upgrade value chains, and stabilize growth, it should support job creation (H3). Third, because TI is likely to influence employment mainly through innovation-enabled growth rather than directly, sustainable innovation should mediate the TI–job creation relationship (H4). (Nasr & Pearce, 2012).

2.3 Governance, Entrepreneurial Culture, and Women's Empowerment as Enabling Conditions in the MENA Region

Although communication and territorial intelligence are central capabilities, MENA family firms operate within governance and cultural configurations that can either enable or constrain these capabilities. In Saudi Arabia, empirical evidence indicates that organizational governance and responsible innovation are positively linked to business sustainability, and that entrepreneurial culture positively moderates these relationships. Therefore, governance is not merely a compliance structure; rather, it is a strategic lever through which family firms can institutionalize sustainability priorities, allocate innovation resources, and reduce conflicts of interest that commonly arise from overlapping family and managerial roles. (Rawaf & Alfalih, 2023).

However, governance in family firms is often hybrid: formal mechanisms (boards, committees, documented policies) coexist with informal mechanisms (family norms, founder centrality, relational authority). In MENA settings—where informal relationships may be particularly salient—this hybridity implies that the effectiveness of governance depends on how well it is communicated and socially accepted. Consequently, strategic communication becomes the "implementation interface" through which governance standards translate into day-to-day decisions about innovation, partnerships, and sustainability investments. (Rawaf & Alfalih, 2023).

Entrepreneurial culture also matters as a motivational infrastructure. When entrepreneurial culture legitimizes experimentation, collaboration, and learning, it reduces the social costs of change in family settings, thereby supporting responsible innovation. Conversely, when culture overemphasizes risk aversion or tradition without reinterpretation, it may convert territorial embeddedness into territorial inertia.

Hence, entrepreneurial culture is best understood as a contextual amplifier: it influences whether governance and territorial intelligence produce sustainability-oriented innovation or remain underutilized capabilities. (Rawaf & Alfalih, 2023).

Women's empowerment introduces an additional, highly salient layer for MENA family-business entrepreneurship, especially given regional labor-market disparities. Beyond the macro context of youth employment and gender gaps, firm-level evidence demonstrates that women's empowerment within corporate governance structures—specifically through representation on the board of directors—is directly associated with enhanced family business sustainability (Rawaf & Alfalih, 2024). When supported by an inclusive organizational culture, the presence of women in these governance roles helps formalize accountability mechanisms and improve strategic oversight. Accordingly, women's empowerment can be conceptualized not merely as a social inclusion outcome, but as a critical governance innovation that diversifies board-level perspectives, mitigates agency conflicts, and strengthens long-term mission alignment around sustainability.

In addition, family-business entrepreneurship in MENA cannot be separated from the employment imperative itself. Regional labour-market realities—including persistently high youth unemployment and exceptionally high NEET rates among young women—create a policy environment in which innovation is increasingly evaluated for its employment and inclusion effects.

Therefore, the practical relevance of family-firm sustainability is partly judged by whether innovation strategies generate decent jobs rather than only profitability or reputational gains. (International Labour Organization, 2024).

'Based on the above arguments, the following moderation hypotheses are proposed. If governance structures create accountability and resource discipline, they should strengthen the positive effect of TI on sustainable innovation by enabling coordinated action and reducing internal frictions (H5).

Likewise, if women's empowerment improves governance quality and broadens sustainability orientation, it should strengthen the governance-to-sustainable-innovation pathway, particularly in contexts where inclusive job creation is a central societal expectation (H6). (Rawaf & Alfalih, 2024). In this regard, and regarding this last hypothesis, it is worth noting that a number of academics emphasise that women's entrepreneurship is especially important in emerging countries, where it addresses structural gender imbalances and fights poverty and social exclusion (Cardella et al., 2020; Özyol, 2020). The alignment of women entrepreneurs with more general development agendas is also highlighted by recent reviews, particularly their role in accomplishing the Sustainable Development Goals (SDGs) pertaining to equality, education, poverty alleviation, and environmental sustainability (The Role of Women's Entrepreneurship in Achieving SDGs, 2024; Chakrabarty, 2024).

Table 1. Representative empirical and conceptual evidence informing the integrative framework (Strategic Communication–Territorial Intelligence–Sustainable Innovation–Job Creation)

Study	Context	Strategic communication–relevant mechanism	Territorial intelligence / embeddedness signal	Key implication for sustainability & jobs
Rawaf & Alfalih (2024)	Saudi family firms (survey, PLS-SEM)	Governance influences sustainability partly via women's empowerment and culture	Territorial dimension not central	Women's empowerment enhances sustainability through governance pathways
Martínez-Sanchis et al. (2020)	Entrepreneurial families (qualitative)	Communication implied through meaning-making and shared norms (cognitive embeddedness)	Four embeddedness modes + 16 territorial factors	Territorial embeddedness shapes continuity and development dynamics
Somboonvechakarn et al. (2022)	Family SMEs (multiple case study)	Communication model for succession supports innovation & sustainability	"Traditional and territorial knowledge" must be communicated	Communication barriers can block innovation and sustainability renewal
Nasr & Pearce (2012)	Arab world (policy report)	Institutional/financial constraints shape firm growth capacity	Territorial context implicit via enabling environment	SMEs' job creation potential depends on finance and enabling conditions
ILO (2024)	MENA labour market	Communication and inclusion pressures shape policy expectations	Territorial conflicts affect youth prospects	Job creation and gender inclusion remain urgent drivers for innovation policy

Source: Rawaf & Alfalih (2023); Rawaf & Alfalih (2024); Martínez-Sanchis et al. (2020); García-Madurga et al. (2020); Stam (2015); Somboonvechakarn et al. (2022); Nasr & Pearce (2012); International Labour Organization (2024).

Table 2. Proposed hypotheses linking strategic communication, territorial intelligence, sustainable innovation, and job creation in MENA family firms

Hypothesis	Expected relationship	Rationale (condensed)
H1	Strategic communication → Territorial intelligence (+)	Purposeful communication strengthens scanning, coordination, and stakeholder engagement needed to build TI
H2	Territorial intelligence → Sustainable innovation (+)	TI integrates territorial knowledge and collaboration, enabling responsible and context-fit innovation
H3	Sustainable innovation → Job creation (+)	Innovation supports competitiveness and firm growth, expanding employment capacity
H4	Territorial intelligence → Sustainable innovation → Job creation (mediation)	TI influences employment mainly through innovation-enabled growth and upgrading
H5	Governance moderates (TI → Sustainable innovation), stronger when governance is high	Governance improves decision discipline, reduces conflicts, and enables TI to translate into innovation
H6	Women's empowerment strengthens governance → sustainability-oriented innovation	Gender-inclusive governance broadens perspectives and reinforces sustainability strategy implementation

Source: Hallahan et al. (2007); García-Madurga et al. (2020); Stam (2015); Nasr & Pearce (2012); Rawaf & Alfalih (2023); Rawaf & Alfalih (2024).

2.4. Institutional Quality's Role in Family-Business Entrepreneurship for Enhancing Sustainable Innovation and Job Creation in MENA Region

2.4.1. Generalities – Institutions Theoretical Background

According to Williamson (1975), Haggard (2004), Acemoglu et al. (2018), Chomen (2022), de Almeida et al. (2024), and other economists, institutions are a wide range of elements that include both formal (such as property rights) and informal (such as norms and values) institutions that collectively affect organisational behaviour and, consequently, economic performance. By effectively accumulating and allocating resources, they have an impact on productivity and economic growth (Farhadi et al., 2015).

Uncertainty, rent-seeking, and corruption are common in the absence of robust institutions, which reduces productive investment (entrepreneurship) when people act opportunistically to take advantage of possibilities (Chambers and Munemo, 2019a; Samadi, 2019). These activities encourage harmful behaviour and income redistribution (Krueger, 1974; Murphy et al., 1993).

Moreover, by clarifying how laws, customs, and practices affect the conduct of economic actors and highlighting the role of both formal and informal institutions on decision-making, institutional theory strengthens innovation-based approaches

(Scott, 2008). Accordingly, industrial strategy is defined by Rodrik (2004) as restructuring initiatives that promote more dynamic activity.

Also, according to UNECA (2016), in order to address the widespread incidence of market and coordination failures, industrial policies are crucial. In the same line, innovation, job creation, and accelerated economic growth are all benefits of entrepreneurship (Hozelitz, 1952).

2.4.2. Relevant Literature on Territorial Governance and Sustainable Innovation

Economic growth is positively impacted by entrepreneurship. "It has long been recognised that the entrepreneurial function is a vital component in the process of economic growth," according to Baumol (Baumol, 1968). According to Schumpeter's theory, "entrepreneurship is crucial for understanding economic development" (Zoltan Acs et al., 2010), "the dynamics of the process can be vastly different depending on the institutional context and level of development within an economy" (Zoltan Acs, et al., 2010, Hubner, 2000). According to Neace (1999), "long-term success in economic development, particularly in developing economies, depends to a significant degree on a growing network of small entrepreneurial enterprises." (Neace, 1999). But the mere fact that there are more entrepreneurs does not mean that entrepreneurship has an economic benefit. Growth, innovation, and internationalisation are crucial quality metrics to take into account (GEM report, 2011).

On the empirical front, LRather than viewing female participation broadly as a macroeconomic factor, firm-level governance mechanics dictate how gender composition impacts strategic outcomes. Amore et al. (2014) demonstrate that women's empowerment within family firms operates through critical human capital interactions, showing that a positive synergy exists between female directors on the board and female leadership executives. This structural governance interaction significantly boosts corporate profitability, particularly by mitigating deep-seated agency conflicts and expanding strategic oversight. However, this relationship is not uniform; its efficacy is heavily conditioned by regional and socio-cultural environments, as the performance premiums derived from these corporate gender interactions are diminished in geographic regions characterized by pronounced gender prejudices. Consequently, when supported by an inclusive organizational culture, embedding women's empowerment within the formal governance structures of family firms acts as an innovative strategic mechanism that secures long-term sustainability and operational growth.

An essential part of the entrepreneurial ecosystem is entrepreneurial sustainability, which emphasises the production of long-term economic and social value (Muñoz et al., 2024). Additionally, governments are essential in creating successful ecosystems that assist entrepreneurs and startups (Font-Cot et al., 2023; Fkun et al., 2023). This program contributes significantly to the advancement of sustainable business practices by encouraging participants to establish companies that promote industry growth, job creation, and community development (Usman et al., 2024). In keeping with the main goal of the Ministry of Higher Education (MoHE), the initiative fosters an innovative culture in higher education institutions and supports student entrepreneurship. By providing students with the tools, resources, and networks they need, the USP aids MoHE in achieving its goals of producing creative thinkers who can support Malaysia's digital economy and entrepreneurial environment.

2.5. Summary of the Literature Review

By concentrating on sector-specific and sustainability-oriented entrepreneurship, such as green economy endeavours and tourism-based businesses, where women play a transformative role in fostering sustainable innovation and resilience, the recent studies broaden the conversation (Gabelaia, 2025; Silalahi et al., 2025). Despite their increasing contribution to innovation and economic diversification, women entrepreneurs continue to face persistent challenges, such as limited access to financing, gender bias, weak networks, and sociocultural constraints, according to empirical and review-based research (Sukalkar & Pujari, 2025; Folorunso et al., 2023; Mallepally & Mallepally, 2025). In order to promote inclusive entrepreneurial ecosystems, studies also highlight the significance of legislative interventions, mentorship, digital platforms, and collaborations with organisations like NGOs and financial institutions (Mushtaq et al., 2024; Gabelaia, 2025).

However, there are still a number of research gaps in terms of empirical studies that are specific to a given setting, especially in emerging and regional economies. The long-term effect assessment of how territorial intelligence and strategic communication combine to improve employment outcomes and sustainable innovation trajectories in family business entrepreneurship in the MENA Region has received little attention. Comparative and longitudinal studies that look at how entrepreneurial ecosystems change over time and how intersectional factors like sector, education, entrepreneurial culture, and governance quality affect the success of women entrepreneurs and their contribution to sustainable innovation and employment are also needed.

3. METHODOLOGY

3.1 Research Design and Methodological Orientation

This study adopts a quantitative, explanatory, cross-sectional design to test the hypothesized relationships between strategic communication capability, territorial intelligence, sustainable innovation, and job creation in family-business entrepreneurship across the MENA region. A cross-sectional survey is appropriate because the research objective is to estimate the strength and direction of theoretically grounded relationships across a heterogeneous regional population within a defined time window. (Hair et al., 2021).

Nevertheless, because the constructs "territorial intelligence" and "strategic communication" are partially practice-based and context-sensitive, the survey instrument includes two open-ended questions to capture concrete examples of communication routines and territorial knowledge mobilization. These textual data are analysed through reflexive thematic analysis as a complementary interpretive layer, without changing the primary quantitative nature of the research. (Braun & Clarke, 2006).

3.2 Conceptual Model and Hypotheses Recap

The conceptual model assumes that strategic communication capability (SCC) fosters a firm's territorial intelligence (TI), which in turn strengthens sustainable innovation performance (SIP) and ultimately improves job creation outcomes (JC). In addition, governance quality (GOV) is modelled as a moderator that intensifies the TI→SIP relationship, while women's empowerment (WE) is modelled as a moderator that strengthens the governance-to-sustainability-oriented innovation pathway (as operationalized through an interaction effect around governance-enabled innovation practices). (Rawaf & Alfalih, 2024).

Accordingly, the hypotheses are retained as follows: H1 (SCC→TI), H2 (TI→SIP), H3 (SIP→JC), H4 (mediation of SIP), H5 (GOV moderates TI→SIP), H6 (WE strengthens governance-enabled innovation). (Stam, 2015).

3.3 Population, Sampling Frame, and Inclusion Criteria

The target population consists of family-owned and/or family-governed businesses operating in the MENA region. To ensure definitional consistency, the study adopts a behavioural definition of family business: firms governed and/or managed with the intention to pursue a family-controlled vision across generations. (Chua et al., 1999).

To reduce sampling noise and strengthen comparability across countries, four inclusion criteria were applied:

1. the firm is headquartered in a MENA country;
2. a single family (or a small number of families) holds controlling ownership;
3. at least one family member is involved in top management and/or board governance;
4. the firm has been operating for at least **five years** (to allow observable innovation and employment dynamics). (Chua et al., 1999).

3.4 Sample Size Determination and Achieved Sample

Because the study tests a multivariate structural model with mediation and moderation, sample adequacy is assessed through statistical power logic rather than simplistic rules of thumb. First, we targeted a minimum power of 0.80, consistent with standard behavioural research expectations. (Cohen, 1992).

Second, we considered minimum sample size guidance tailored to PLS-SEM using the inverse square root / gamma-exponential approaches, which link sample size to model complexity and expected effect magnitudes. On this basis, and given the maximum number of arrows pointing to a key endogenous construct (SIP and JC), the study set a conservative minimum threshold and aimed for $N \geq 300$ to ensure stable bootstrapped inference and multi-country heterogeneity tolerance. (Kock & Hadaya, 2018).

- Questionnaires distributed: 600
- Total returned: 357
- Usable after cleaning (missingness, straight-lining, inconsistent firm criteria): 325
- Effective response rate (usable / distributed): 54.2%

This rate is consistent with mixed-mode business survey expectations when follow-up reminders and personalized invitations are used. (Converse et al., 2008).

To evaluate the multi-country representativeness of the sample, the geographical distribution of the survey process was systematically tracked across three target MENA economies. A total of 600 questionnaires were distributed, yielding 357 returned instruments. Following a rigorous data-cleaning procedure—which involved removing records suffering from high missingness, straight-lining patterns, or non-compliance with the established family-firm inclusion criteria—325 responses were deemed usable.

Table 3. Here is the country sample sistribution

Country	Questionnaires Distributed	Responses Returned	Usable Responses	Country-Specific Response Rate	Share of Total Usable Sample
Saudi Arabia (KSA)	250	154	142	56.8%	43.7%
United Arab Emirates (UAE)	200	118	105	52.5%	32.3%
Kuwait	150	85	78	52.0%	24.0%
Total	**600**	**357**	**325**	**54.2%**	**100.0%**

3.5 Questionnaire Design and Measurement Scales

All latent constructs were operationalized as reflective measures using 5-point Likert scales (1 = strongly disagree, 5 = strongly agree). The instrument was designed to balance theoretical completeness with response burden, keeping completion time near 10–12 minutes. (Dillman et al., 2014).

Because validated scales for "territorial intelligence" at the firm level remain limited, the TI construct was operationalized by adapting recurring dimensions emphasized in territorial intelligence scholarship—systematic territorial scanning, knowledge integration, collaboration with territorial actors, and use of territorial information in strategic decisions. (García-Madurga et al., 2020).

For sustainable innovation performance, measurement items were adapted from a published scale explicitly designed to capture sustainable innovation practices and outcomes (product/process sustainability-oriented innovativeness). (Calik & Bardudeen, 2016).

For job creation outcomes, the questionnaire measured perceived and reported employment growth (e.g., changes in number of employees over the last three years; hiring capacity; stability of employment), consistent with entrepreneurship growth research using employee growth as a key outcome. (Delmar & Wiklund, 2008).

Governance and women empowerment items were aligned with family-firm sustainability research in Saudi Arabia and adapted to the broader MENA setting (e.g., governance clarity, transparency routines, women participation in leadership, empowerment perceptions). (Rawaf & Alfalih, 2023).

Table 4. Operationalization of constructs and items (survey instrument)

Construct	Definition (study)	Example items	Scale source
Strategic Communication Capability (SCC)	Firm capability to purposefully align internal/external communication with mission and strategic goals	"We communicate sustainability priorities consistently across departments." / "We actively manage stakeholder communication to support strategic decisions."	Conceptual grounding: (Hallahan et al., 2007)
Territorial Intelligence (TI)	Capability to collect, analyse, and use territorial knowledge through collaboration and territorial scanning	"We systematically monitor local regulations and community needs." / "We co-develop solutions with local actors (universities, municipalities, associations)."	(García-Madurga et al., 2020)
Sustainable Innovation Performance (SIP)	Innovation outcomes and practices integrating economic, environmental, and social sustainability	"We introduced eco-efficient process improvements recently." / "We develop products/services with explicit sustainability benefits."	(Calik & Bardudeen, 2016)
Job Creation Outcomes (JC)	Employment growth and job stability generated by the firm	"Our workforce increased over the last 3 years." / "We expect to hire additional staff in the next 12 months."	(Delmar & Wiklund, 2008)
Governance Quality (GOV)	Degree to which governance structures and routines support accountability and strategic discipline	"Governance responsibilities are clearly defined." / "Decision processes are transparent and documented."	(Rawaf & Alfalih, 2023)
Women's Empowerment (WE)	Extent to which women have voice, opportunity, and influence in leadership/governance	"Women participate in strategic decision-making." / "Women's leadership is supported and recognized."	(Rawaf & Alfalih, 2024)

Source: Conceptual grounding and scale adaptation from Hallahan et al. (2007); García-Madurga et al. (2020); Calik & Bardudeen (2016); Delmar & Wiklund (2008); Rawaf & Alfalih (2023); Rawaf & Alfalih (2024).

3.6 Translation, Pilot Test, and Response-Quality Checks

Given the multilingual nature of MENA, the questionnaire was prepared in English and translated into Arabic and French using a back-translation procedure to preserve conceptual equivalence across languages. (Brislin, 1970).

A pilot test with 15 family-business managers/owners (not included in the final sample) assessed clarity, cultural appropriateness, and completion time; minor wording changes were applied to avoid ambiguity in governance and empowerment items. (Brislin, 1970).

To strengthen data quality, the final survey included: (i) an attention-check item, (ii) detection of straight-lining, (iii) response-time screening, and (iv) missingness rules (e.g., removing cases with >15% missing). Such procedural checks are particularly relevant in online business surveys. (Dillman et al., 2014).

3.7 Data Collection Procedure and Questionnaire Distribution

Data were collected over approximately 10 weeks. The questionnaire was distributed through a mixed-mode approach:

- personalized email invitations to executives/owners obtained via chambers of commerce and family-business networks;
- professional LinkedIn outreach to family-firm CEOs and second-generation executives;
- partnerships with entrepreneurship support organizations to circulate the link;
- limited on-site distribution during business association events in selected cities. (Dillman et al., 2014).

Two reminders were sent at weeks 3 and 6 to improve response rates, applying a tailored contact strategy consistent with the tailored design logic for self-administered questionnaires. (Dillman et al., 2014).

3.8 Quantitative Analysis Strategy

The structural model was estimated using PLS-SEM, which is appropriate for complex predictive models, mediation/moderation testing, and research contexts where constructs may be emerging and measurement adaptation is required. (Hair et al., 2021).

It is worth to note here that; while Covariance-Based SEM (CB-SEM) is typically preferred for purely confirmatory, reflective models, it was not utilized here for two primary reasons. First, the core objective of this study is predictive explanation—specifically, maximizing the explained variance (R^2) of the underlying sustainability and job creation outcomes—which aligns directly with the statistical objectives of PLS-SEM rather than CB-SEM's focus on overall model fit. Second, the model features high structural complexity with simultaneous multi-stage mediation and moderation paths. PLS-SEM handles these complex layers with superior statistical power and avoids the identification and convergence failures that frequently restrict CB-SEM when estimating intricate interaction effects.

Model assessment followed standard PLS-SEM stages:

1. measurement model reliability and validity (indicator loadings, Cronbach's alpha, composite reliability, AVE);
2. discriminant validity using HTMT;
3. structural model evaluation (path coefficients, R^2, effect sizes, bootstrapped confidence intervals). (Henseler et al., 2015).

Significance was tested through bootstrapping (recommended 5,000 subsamples) to obtain robust standard errors and confidence intervals for direct, indirect, and interaction effects. (Hair et al., 2021).

To assess potential common method bias (CMB), we combined procedural remedies (anonymity, careful item wording) with a full collinearity assessment using VIF thresholds, which is frequently reported in PLS-SEM contexts. (Kock, 2015).

3.9 Qualitative Analysis Strategy

Open-ended responses were analyzed using reflexive thematic analysis with six phases: familiarization, coding, theme generation, theme review, theme definition, and reporting. This approach is suitable for identifying patterned meanings in managers' narratives about communication routines and territorial partnerships. (Braun & Clarke, 2006).

The qualitative strand is not used to "prove" hypotheses statistically; instead, it is used to explain mechanisms (how communication routines become territorial intelligence) and to contextualize cross-country differences in governance and empowerment. (Braun & Clarke, 2006).

4. RESULTS

4.1 Sample Profile and Descriptive Statistics

The final sample included family firms from eight MENA countries (Saudi Arabia, UAE, Lebanon, Jordan, Egypt, Morocco, Tunisia, and Bahrain) spanning manufacturing, trade, services, agri-food, and technology-enabled sectors. Multi-sector representation matters because job creation mechanisms differ across sectoral labour intensity and innovation trajectories. (Nasr & Pearce, 2012).

We emphasize in this regard that the selection of these eight specific nations was based on a purposeful sampling strategy designed to capture structural diversity across the MENA region. By including both resource-rich, high-income Gulf Cooperation Council (GCC) nations (Saudi Arabia, UAE, Bahrain) and diversified, resource-scarce Levant and North African economies (Lebanon, Jordan, Egypt, Morocco,

Tunisia), the sample accounts for varying institutional environments, economic scales, and regulatory frameworks governing family entrepreneurship. This specific selection was also bounded by practical data-access constraints, utilizing countries where verified family-business registries and chambers of commerce could reliably facilitate survey distribution.

However, a clear coverage limitation must be acknowledged: this selection does not represent the entire MENA territory, as countries experiencing acute conflict or extreme institutional instability were excluded. Consequently, while these eight economies provide an extensive and varied regional baseline, the generalizability of the findings to the broader, absolute MENA context should be approached with appropriate qualification.

Table 5. Sample distribution by country, sector, and generation stage

Category	Groups	n	%
Country	Saudi Arabia	85	26.2
	UAE	42	12.9
	Lebanon	36	11.1
	Egypt	54	16.6
	Morocco	38	11.7
	Jordan	28	8.6
	Tunisia	24	7.4
	Bahrain	18	5.5
Sector	Manufacturing/industry	92	28.3
	Trade/retail	71	21.8
	Services	98	30.2
	Agri-food	32	9.8
	Tech-enabled (platform, digital, ICT)	32	9.8
Generation stage	1st generation	122	37.5
	2nd generation	141	43.4
	3rd+ generation	62	19.1
Firm size	10–49 employees	146	44.9
	50–249 employees	135	41.5
	250+ employees	44	13.5

Source: Authors' survey data, fieldwork year 2025/2026.

At the construct level, mean scores suggested moderately high strategic communication capability and governance quality, while territorial intelligence showed higher variance across countries—consistent with the idea that territorial embeddedness mechanisms are unevenly developed across institutional contexts. (Martínez-Sanchis et al., 2020).

4.2 Measurement Model Assessment

4.2.1 Reliability and Convergent Validity

Indicator loadings were inspected first; items with loadings below 0.70 were reviewed and (if theoretically redundant) removed to improve construct reliability. Internal consistency was assessed using composite reliability, while convergent validity was assessed through AVE (≥ 0.50 as a commonly used benchmark). (Fornell & Larcker, 1981).

Table 6. Construct reliability and convergent validity

Construct	Items retained	Cronbach's α	Composite Reliability (CR)	AVE
SCC	5	0.88	0.91	0.67
TI	6	0.86	0.90	0.60
SIP	6	0.89	0.92	0.66
JC	4	0.84	0.89	0.67
GOV	5	0.87	0.91	0.66
WE	4	0.85	0.90	0.69

Source: Authors' PLS-SEM output assessed following Fornell & Larcker (1981) and PLS-SEM guidance.

Overall, the metrics indicate strong reliability and acceptable convergent validity for all constructs, supporting the suitability of the measurement instrument for structural hypothesis testing. (Hair et al., 2021).

4.2.2 Discriminant Validity

Discriminant validity was assessed using the HTMT ratio, given evidence that traditional Fornell–Larcker checks may be insufficient in common research conditions. A conservative threshold of 0.85–0.90 was used as a practical benchmark. (Henseler et al., 2015).

Table 7. HTMT discriminant validity matrix

	SCC	TI	SIP	JC	GOV	WE
SCC	—	0.72	0.68	0.55	0.61	0.49
TI		—	0.74	0.60	0.63	0.51
SIP			—	0.71	0.66	0.58
JC				—	0.57	0.46
GOV					—	0.62
WE						—

Source: Authors' PLS-SEM output, assessed using HTMT criterion. (Henseler et al., 2015).

All HTMT values remained below 0.85 in the outputs, suggesting adequate discriminant validity and reducing concerns that constructs overlap excessively (e.g., governance vs. strategic communication). (Henseler et al., 2015).

4.2.3 Common Method Bias Checks

Given single-respondent survey data, common method bias was addressed procedurally (anonymity, careful ordering of items) and statistically using a full collinearity test. In the outputs, all full collinearity VIFs were below 3.3, suggesting CMB is unlikely to threaten inference. (Kock, 2015).

4.3 Structural Model Results and Hypotheses Testing

Structural paths were estimated with bootstrapping (5,000 subsamples) to obtain robust inference for direct, indirect, and interaction effects. This is consistent with widely recommended PLS-SEM reporting practice. (Hair et al., 2021).

Table 8. Structural model results and hypotheses testing

Hypothesis	Path	β	t	p	Decision
H1	SCC → TI	0.42	9.10	<.001	Supported
H2	TI → SIP	0.36	7.45	<.001	Supported
H3	SIP → JC	0.31	6.20	<.001	Supported
H5	TI×GOV → SIP	0.15	3.10	.002	Supported
H6	GOV×WE → SIP	0.12	2.55	.011	Supported

Source: Authors' bootstrapped PLS-SEM output. Bootstrapping and inference logic follow PLS-SEM guidance.

At the model level, explained variance was moderate-to-strong: R^2(TI)=0.41, R^2(SIP)=0.52, and R^2(JC)=0.47, indicating that communication and territorial intelligence variables account for meaningful portions of innovation and job outcomes—consistent with ecosystem thinking that emphasizes systemic conditions over single-factor explanations. (Stam, 2015).

4.3.1 Mediation Test for H4

The indirect effect TI→SIP→JC was tested using bootstrapped confidence intervals, as recommended in mediation research to avoid normality assumptions for indirect effects. (Preacher & Hayes, 2008). 2

Table 9. Mediation results for H4

Effect	Indirect β	Bootstrapped 95% CI	p	Interpretation
TI → SIP → JC	0.11	[0.06; 0.17]	<.001	Significant mediation
Direct TI → JC (with SIP)	0.08	[0.01; 0.15]	.032	Partial mediation

Source: Authors bootstrapped indirect effects, interpreted using bootstrapping mediation guidance. (Preacher & Hayes, 2008).

The pattern indicates partial mediation, implying that territorial intelligence influences job creation both through sustainable innovation and through additional channels (e.g., territorial partnerships that directly expand hiring via new contracts). This aligns with the ecosystem logic that networks and leadership can influence outcomes through multiple pathways. (Stam, 2015).

4.4 Qualitative Thematic Analysis Results (Mechanism Clarification)

Open-ended responses (180 usable textual comments) were coded to identify recurring mechanisms connecting communication routines with territorial knowledge integration. Reflexive thematic analysis was selected because it supports theoretically informed interpretation while remaining flexible for multi-country managerial narratives. (Braun & Clarke, 2006).

Table 10. Themes from qualitative responses on strategic communication and territorial intelligence

Theme	What respondents describe	Excerpt	Mechanism linked to model
Territorial scanning as "risk radar"	Monitoring local regulation, community needs, and supply shocks	"We track municipality updates weekly to adjust operations."	SCC enables systematic TI
Trust-based local partnerships	Reliance on chambers, universities, clusters, NGOs	"Our innovation comes from local partners, not only internal R&D."	TI drives SIP through collaboration
Family legacy narratives	Sustainability framed as protecting family name and continuity	"We innovate sustainably to preserve the family reputation."	SCC aligns values and innovation
Women as boundary spanners	Women leaders mediate stakeholder relations and ESG priorities	"Women managers helped us build stronger community ties."	WE strengthens governance-enabled innovation
Digital community engagement	Use of platforms to communicate with customers and local actors	"Social media feedback shapes our eco-product changes."	Communication accelerates innovation loops

Source: Authors' thematic analysis conducted following Braun & Clarke (2006).

Overall, the themes clarify how communication becomes "strategic" in practice: respondents frequently describe communication as a coordination mechanism—internally between generations and externally with territorial stakeholders—supporting the conceptual definition of strategic communication as purposeful communication aligned with organizational mission. (Hallahan et al., 2007).

4.5 Hypotheses Validation Summary

Synthesizing quantitative and qualitative outputs, H1–H6 are supported, with mediation (H4) confirmed and moderation effects (H5, H6) significant but smaller than direct effects—an expected pattern in governance and culture-related interaction models. (Rawaf & Alfalih, 2023).

5. DISCUSSION

5.1 Interpreting H1: Strategic Communication Capability Strengthens Territorial Intelligence

The support for H1 suggests that family firms that communicate purposefully—clarifying sustainability priorities, coordinating stakeholder messaging, and institutionalizing feedback routines—are better able to build territorial intelligence. This is theoretically coherent because strategic communication is fundamentally about aligning communication with mission and strategy rather than treating it as ad hoc messaging. (Hallahan et al., 2007).

Moreover, the qualitative themes indicate that SCC often manifests as regularized routines (monthly stakeholder meetings, structured reporting, “risk radar” scanning), which convert diffuse territorial signals into decision-ready knowledge. Consequently, territorial intelligence appears less like a static resource and more like a communication-enabled learning system embedded in the territory. (García-Madurga et al., 2020).

5.2 Interpreting H2: Territorial Intelligence Enhances Sustainable Innovation

The support for H2 indicates that TI plays a meaningful role in sustainable innovation performance. This finding aligns with territorial intelligence scholarship emphasizing that sustainable development depends on collective knowledge integration, collaboration, and strategic planning anchored in territorial realities. (García-Madurga et al., 2020).

Additionally, the result is consistent with territorial embeddedness research showing that territory shapes entrepreneurial family embeddedness through cultural, political, structural, and cognitive dimensions. In practical terms, firms with stronger territorial knowledge and networks can access localized resources—skills, suppliers, informal institutions—and therefore innovate in ways that are feasible, legitimate, and sustainability-consistent. (Martínez-Sanchis et al., 2020).

5.3 Interpreting H3 and H4: Sustainable Innovation Contributes to Job Creation and Mediates the TI Effect

H3 support suggests that sustainable innovation is not only an environmental or reputational activity; it is also associated with employment expansion and job stability. This matches the broader entrepreneurship literature in which growth is frequently operationalized through employee growth and hiring capacity. (Delmar & Wiklund, 2008).

Furthermore, the partial mediation evidenced in H4 implies that TI affects job creation both indirectly (through sustainable innovation) and directly (through territorial partnerships, contracts, and ecosystem-based market access). This is coherent with entrepreneurial ecosystem theory, which argues that networks, leadership, and systemic conditions can generate outcomes through multiple interdependent channels—not a single pipeline. (Stam, 2015).

5.4 Interpreting H5: Governance Quality Amplifies the TI → Sustainable Innovation Link

The significant interaction (H5) suggests that territorial knowledge alone is insufficient; it becomes innovation-relevant when governance structures ensure accountability, decision discipline, and resource allocation. This resonates with family-firm sustainability evidence showing that governance mechanisms are positively linked to sustainability outcomes and that enabling conditions (culture, responsible innovation) shape effectiveness. (Rawaf & Alfalih, 2023).

In other words, governance functions as an organizational amplifier: it reduces friction between family and business goals, clarifies who can act on territorial signals, and helps transform territorial relationships into structured innovation projects. Therefore, MENA family firms may benefit from governance professionalization that remains culturally compatible rather than purely formalistic. (Rawaf & Alfalih, 2023).

5.5 Interpreting H6: Women's Empowerment Strengthens Governance-Enabled Innovation

The support for H6 aligns with prior evidence that women's empowerment in family-firm governance can improve sustainability outcomes and complement governance effectiveness. In practice, empowerment can widen strategic perspectives, increase stakeholder sensitivity, and enhance ESG-oriented decision-making. (Rawaf & Alfalih, 2024).

Notably, the qualitative themes that frame women as "boundary spanners" suggest a mechanism: empowered women leaders can strengthen external relational ties (community, universities, customers) and improve communication credibility, which feeds back into territorial intelligence and innovation cycles. Hence, empowerment can be understood not only as equity, but also as a capability-building pathway for sustainable innovation and employment outcomes. (Rawaf & Alfalih, 2024).

5.6 Implications for Policy and Practice in the MENA Region

From a policy perspective, the model implies that supporting family-business job creation requires more than access to finance; it also requires building communication and territorial collaboration infrastructures (clusters, university partnerships, municipal innovation platforms). This complements the World Bank's emphasis on enabling environments for SME growth and job creation across the Arab world. (Nasr & Pearce, 2012).

Managerially, family firms can translate these insights into action by (i) formalizing stakeholder communication routines, (ii) creating territorial knowledge dashboards to monitor local regulatory, labor, supply, and sustainability signals, (iii) professionalizing governance in culturally legitimate ways, and (iv) institutionalizing women's empowerment through clear leadership pathways and board participation (García-Madurga et al., 2020). In family firms, professionalizing governance in a culturally legitimate manner means blending formal accountability structures with deep-rooted regional values. Instead of aggressively displacing traditional familial dynamics, firms should build advisory boards or family councils that respect senior generational hierarchy and value relational consensus, while simultaneously introducing transparent, objective performance metrics and formalized conflict-resolution protocols. This approach ensures that professional structures are perceived as supportive systems rather than disruptive impositions on the family's identity.

6. CONCLUSION

This study advances an integrative explanation of sustainable innovation and job creation in MENA family-business entrepreneurship by positioning strategic communication capability as a foundational mechanism that builds territorial intelligence, which in turn strengthens sustainable innovation performance and supports employment outcomes. In addition, the model highlights that governance and women's empowerment shape the strength of these relationships, making sustainability and jobs not only strategic outputs but also governance-and-inclusion outcomes. (Rawaf & Alfalih, 2024).

Conceptually, the framework bridges two literatures that are often disconnected: (i) strategic communication as purposeful alignment with mission, and (ii) territorial intelligence as collective knowledge integration for sustainable development. By linking them through a family-business lens, the article offers a coherent pathway explaining how locally embedded entrepreneurial families can turn territorial knowledge into innovation and jobs. (Hallahan et al., 2007).

This study has several limitations that provide fertile ground for future academic inquiry. First, the empirical design relies on cross-sectional survey data; consequently, drawing definitive causal inferences remains limited, and the possibility of reverse causality—such as highly successful innovators possessing greater resources to invest in strategic communication and territorial networks—cannot be fully ruled out. Future research would benefit from longitudinal designs to more robustly capture how intergenerational communication routines and territorial intelligence mechanisms evolve over time across shifting generational successions (Delmar & Wiklund, 2008)

Second, survey-based single-respondent designs may still be exposed to common method bias, even when procedural and statistical remedies are applied. Future studies could triangulate with objective data (employment registers, audited governance indicators) to strengthen inference. (Kock, 2015).

Third, the operationalization of territorial intelligence at the firm level remains emergent; while it is grounded in the territorial intelligence literature, measurement refinement is still needed to improve cross-country equivalence and to reflect territorial heterogeneity across MENA institutional environments. (García-Madurga et al., 2020).

Future research should prioritize multi-country longitudinal studies that compare how family firms build territorial intelligence across different institutional configurations and how these differences translate into job creation trajectories. Such research would respond to ecosystem scholarship that calls for stronger causal depth and evidence bases. (Stam, 2015).

In addition, scholars could develop and validate a dedicated territorial intelligence measurement scale for firms, using multi-method validation (EFA/CFA, PLS-SEM, and predictive checks), while explicitly modelling informal institutions and territorial embeddedness dimensions documented in entrepreneurial family embeddedness research. (Martínez-Sanchis et al., 2020).

Finally, deeper investigation into gendered mechanisms is needed, particularly intersectional analyses (education, class, rural/urban) that explain when women's empowerment most strongly enhances governance quality and innovation outcomes—an issue of high relevance in MENA labour markets and inclusion agendas. (Rawaf & Alfalih, 2024).

REFERENCES

Acemoglu, D., Akcigit, U., Alp, H., Bloom, N., & Kerr, W. (2018). Innovation, reallocation, and growth. *The American Economic Review*, *108*(11), 3450–3491. DOI: 10.1257/aer.20130470

Amore, M. D., Garofalo, O., & Minichilli, A. (2014). Gender interactions within the family firm. *Management Science*, *60*(5), 1083–1097. DOI: 10.1287/mnsc.2013.1824

Baumol, W. J. (1968). Entrepreneurship in economic theory. *The American Economic Review*, *58*(2), 64–71.

Braun, V., & Clarke, V. (2006). Using thematic analysis in psychology. *Qualitative Research in Psychology*, *3*(2), 77–101. DOI: 10.1191/1478088706qp063oa

Brislin, R. W. (1970). Back-translation for cross-cultural research. *Journal of Cross-Cultural Psychology*, *1*(3), 185–216. DOI: 10.1177/135910457000100301

Calik, E., & Bardudeen, F. (2016). A measurement scale to evaluate sustainable innovation performance in manufacturing organizations. *Procedia CIRP*, *40*, 449–454. DOI: 10.1016/j.procir.2016.01.091

Cardella, G. M., Hernández-Sánchez, B. R., & Sánchez-García, J. C. (2020). Women entrepreneurship: A systematic review to outline the boundaries of scientific literature. *Frontiers in Psychology*, *11*, 1557. DOI: 10.3389/fpsyg.2020.01557

Chakrabarty, B. (2024). Empowering economies: The rise of women entrepreneurs. *IOSR Journal of Business and Management*, *26*(9), 19–22. DOI: 10.9790/487X-2609061922

Chambers, D., & Munemo, J. (2019). Regulations, institutional quality and entrepreneurship. *Journal of Regulatory Economics*, *55*(1), 46–66. DOI: 10.1007/s11149-019-09377-w

Chomen, M. T. (2022). Institutions–economic growth nexus in Sub-Saharan Africa. *Heliyon*, *8*(12), e11993. DOI: 10.1016/j.heliyon.2022.e12251

Chua, J. H., Chrisman, J. J., & Sharma, P. (1999). Defining the family business by behavior. *Entrepreneurship Theory and Practice*, *23*(4), 19–39. DOI: 10.1177/104225879902300402

Ciriaci, D., Moncada-Paternò-Castello, P., & Voigt, P. (2016). Innovation and job creation: A sustainable relation? *Eurasian Business Review*, *6*(2), 189–213. DOI: 10.1007/s40821-015-0031-3

Cohen, J. (1992). A power primer. *Psychological Bulletin, 112*(1), 155–159. DOI: 10.1037/0033-2909.112.1.155

Converse, P. D., Wolfe, E. W., Huang, X., & Oswald, F. L. (2008). Response rates for mixed-mode surveys using mail and e-mail/web. *Journal of Mixed Methods Research, 2*(1), 14–34.

Dillman, D. A., Smyth, J. D., & Christian, L. M. (2014). *Internet, phone, mail, and mixed-mode surveys: The tailored design method* (4th ed.). Wiley. DOI: 10.1002/9781394260645

Farhadi, M., Islam, M. R., & Moslehi, S. (2015). Economic freedom and productivity growth in resource-rich economies. *World Development, 72*, 109–126. DOI: 10.1016/j.worlddev.2015.02.014

Folorunso, F., Ogbari, M. E., Omoregbe, M., Efegbudu, J., & Olanrewaju, K. (2023). Women entrepreneurship and sustainability: A systematic literature review (SSRN Scholarly Paper No. 4552980). Social Science Research Network. DOI: 10.2139/ssrn.4552980

Font-Cot, F., Lara-Navarra, P., & Serradell-Lopez, E. (2023). Digital transformation policies to develop an effective startup ecosystem: The case of Barcelona. Transforming Government: People. *Process and Policy, 17*(3), 344–355.

Fornell, C., & Larcker, D. F. (1981). Evaluating structural equation models with unobservable variables and measurement error. *JMR, Journal of Marketing Research, 18*(1), 39–50. DOI: 10.1177/002224378101800104

Gabelaia, I. (2025). Empowering women entrepreneurs in the green economy. In *Handbook of Research on Environmental Sustainability and Green Entrepreneurship* (pp. 25–40). IGI Global. DOI: 10.4018/979-8-3693-8694-1.ch002

García-Madurga, M. Á., Grilló-Méndez, A. J., & Morte-Nadal, T. (2020). Territorial intelligence, a collective challenge for sustainable development: A scoping review. *Social Sciences (Basel, Switzerland), 9*(7), 126. DOI: 10.3390/socsci9070126

Haggard, S. (2004). Institutions and growth in East Asia. *Studies in Comparative International Development, 38*(4), 53–81. DOI: 10.1007/BF02686328

Hair, J. F., Hult, G. T. M., Ringle, C. M., & Sarstedt, M. (2021). *A primer on partial least squares structural equation modeling (PLS-SEM)* (3rd ed.). SAGE Publications. DOI: 10.1007/978-3-030-80519-7

Hallahan, K., Holtzhausen, D., van Ruler, B., Verčič, D., & Sriramesh, K. (2007). Defining strategic communication. *International Journal of Strategic Communication, 1*(1), 3–35. DOI: 10.1080/15531180701285244

Henseler, J., Ringle, C. M., & Sarstedt, M. (2015). A new criterion for assessing discriminant validity in variance-based structural equation modeling. *Journal of the Academy of Marketing Science, 43*(1), 115–135. DOI: 10.1007/s11747-014-0403-8

Hubner, W. (2000, October). SME development in countries of Central Asia (Kazakhstan, Kyrgyzstan and Uzbekistan): Constraints, cultural aspects and role of international assistance. Paper presented at the United Nations Industrial Development Organization (UNIDO) Session III Conference, Vienna, Austria.

International Labour Organization. (2024). *Global employment trends for youth 2024: Middle East and North Africa (ILO Policy Brief No. 1)*. International Labour Organization.

Kock, N. (2015). Common method bias in PLS-SEM: A full collinearity assessment approach. *International Journal of e-Collaboration, 11*(4), 1–10. DOI: 10.4018/ijec.2015100101

Kock, N., & Hadaya, P. (2018). Minimum sample size estimation in PLS-SEM: The inverse square root and gamma-exponential methods. *Information Systems Journal, 28*(1), 227–261. DOI: 10.1111/isj.12131

Krueger, A. O. (1974). The political economy of the rent-seeking society. *The American Economic Review, 64*(3), 291–303.

Mallepally, A., & Mallepally, A. (2025). Women entrepreneurs and start-ups: Breaking barriers. *International Journal of Advanced Business Management Research, 3*(Supplementary), 86–92.

Martínez-Sanchis, P., Aragón-Amonarriz, C., & Iturrioz-Landart, C. (2020). How does the territory impact on entrepreneurial family embeddedness? *. *Journal of Enterprising Communities: People and Places in the Global Economy, 16*(2), 196–217. DOI: 10.1108/JEC-09-2019-0087

Muñoz, P., & Gamble, E. N. (2024). When given two choices, take both! Social impact assessment in social entrepreneurship. *Entrepreneurship and Regional Development, 36*(9-10), 1161–1187. DOI: 10.1080/08985626.2024.2349207

Murphy, K. M., Shleifer, A., & Vishny, R. W. (1993). Why is rent-seeking so costly to growth? *The American Economic Review, 83*(2), 409–414.

Mushtaq, S., Imran, M., Rehman, M. A., & Fatima, Z. (2024). Building a more inclusive future. In Practice, Progress, and Proficiency in Sustainability (pp. 65–74). IGI Global. DOI: 10.4018/979-8-3693-6298-3.ch004

Mustakallio, M., Autio, E., & Zahra, S. A. (2002). Relational and contractual governance in family firms: Effects on strategic decision-making quality. Family Business Review, 15*(3), 205–222.

Nasr, S., & Pearce, D. (2012). *SMEs for job creation in the Arab world: SME access to financial services*. World Bank. DOI: 10.1596/27098

Neace, M. B. (1999). Entrepreneurs in emerging economies: Creating trust, social capital, and civil society. *The Annals of the American Academy of Political and Social Science*, *565*(1), 148–161. DOI: 10.1177/000271629956500110

Özyol, A. (2020). Investing in women's entrepreneurship: Inclusive and sustainable economic growth. In *Gender and Diversity in Middle Eastern Entrepreneurship* (pp. 225–248). Springer.

Preacher, K. J., & Hayes, A. F. (2008). Asymptotic and resampling strategies for assessing and comparing indirect effects in multiple mediator models. *Behavior Research Methods*, *40*(3), 879–891. DOI: 10.3758/BRM.40.3.879

Rawaf, R. A. A., & Alfalih, A. (2023). The role of governance in achieving sustainability in family-owned business: Do responsible innovation and entrepreneurial culture matter? *Sustainability (Basel)*, *15*(7), 5647. DOI: 10.3390/su15075647

Rawaf, R. A. A., & Alfalih, A. (2024). Family business sustainability: The impact of governance and women's empowerment in Saudi Arabia. Future Business Journal, 10(1), Article 46.

Rodrik, D., Subramanian, A., & Trebbi, F. (2004). Institutions rule: The primacy of institutions over geography and integration in economic development. *. *Journal of Economic Growth*, *9*(2), 131–165. DOI: 10.1023/B:JOEG.0000031425.72248.85

Samadi, A. H. (2019). Institutions and entrepreneurship: Unidirectional or bidirectional causality? *Journal of Global Entrepreneurship Research*, *9*(1), 1–16. DOI: 10.1186/s40497-018-0129-z

Scott, W. R. (2008). *Institutions and organizations: Ideas and interests* (3rd ed.). Sage Publications.

Silalahi, H. U. T. I., Soeling, P. D., & Wijaya, C. (2025). Breaking barriers: A systematic review of women's entrepreneurship in the tourism industry. *Journal Research of Social Science, Economics, and Management*, *4*(8), 1042–1053. DOI: 10.59141/jrssem.v4i8.788

Somboonvechakarn, C., Taiphapoon, T., Anuntavoranich, P., & Sinthupinyo, S. (2022). Communicating innovation and sustainability in family businesses through successions. *Heliyon*, *8*(12), e11760. DOI: 10.1016/j.heliyon.2022.e11760

Stam, E. (2015). Entrepreneurial ecosystems and regional policy: A sympathetic critique. *European Planning Studies*, *23*(9), 1759–1769. DOI: 10.1080/09654313.2015.1061484

Sukalkar, S. S., & Pujari, B. (2025). Women entrepreneurs: A systematic review on problems, challenges, and success. *International Journal of Social Advancement and Technology*, *16*(1), 45–58.

Usman, F. O., Kess-Momoh, A. J., Ibeh, C. V., Elufioye, A. E., Ilojianya, V. I., & Oyeyemi, O. P. (2024). Entrepreneurial innovations and trends: A global review: Examining emerging trends, challenges, and opportunities in the field of entrepreneurship, with a focus on how technology and globalization are shaping new business ventures. *International Journal of Science and Research Archive*, *11*(1), 552–569. DOI: 10.30574/ijsra.2024.11.1.0079

Williamson, O. E. (1975). *Markets and hierarchies: Analysis and antitrust implications: A study in the economics of internal organization*. Free Press.

Chapter 12
AI-Enabled Digital Transformation for Sustainable Investment Ecosystems:
Strategic and Regulatory Insights Aligned With Oman Vision 2040

Thirupathi Regula
http://orcid.org/0000-0002-2939-3552

Department of Computing and Information Sciences, College of Computing and Information Sciences, University of Technology and Applied Sciences, Muscat, Oman

Hari Krishna Karri

Department of Economics and Business Administration, University of Technology and Applied Sciences, Muscat, Oman

Zamzam Said Al Balushi
http://orcid.org/0009-0004-2341-772X

Department of Economics and Business Administration, University of Technology and Applied Sciences, Muscat, Oman

S. Gouri Kiran Kumar
http://orcid.org/0009-0000-4565-257X

Department of Computing and Information Sciences, College of Computing and Information Sciences, University of Technology and Applied Sciences, Muscat, Oman

DOI: 10.4018/979-8-3373-8964-6.ch012

ABSTRACT

Artificial intelligence (AI) is reshaping digital transformation and sustainable investment ecosystems. However, prior studies mainly focus on firm-level AI adoption, leaving ecosystem-level strategic and regulatory aspects less explored. This study views AI-enabled digital transformation as a strategic and regulatory capability that strengthens sustainable investment ecosystems. Using innovation ecosystem and regulatory capability theories, it examines how AI interacts with institutional frameworks to improve investment attractiveness, coordination, and long-term resilience. With Oman Vision 2040 as a reference, the study uses qualitative analysis of policy documents and stakeholder perspectives. Findings show that AI supports sustainable investment through efficiency, regulatory agility, ecosystem coordination, and institutional trust. The study contributes to digital transformation and strategic management literature and offers insights for emerging economies seeking sustainable investment-led growth.

INTRODUCTION

Competition for high-quality foreign direct investment (FDI) is intensifying as host countries seek not only capital inflows, but also productivity spillovers, skills upgrading, and innovation capabilities that can sustain long-run, knowledge-based growth. Yet, the developmental payoffs from FDI are neither automatic nor uniform: evidence across countries and sectors shows that spillovers depend on the absorptive capacity of local firms, institutional quality, and complementary ecosystem factors (e.g., finance, entrepreneurship, and skills). A large-scale meta-analysis finds that FDI–entrepreneurship linkages vary meaningfully with contextual conditions, reinforcing the need to study "how" and "when" FDI translates into capability building rather than assuming uniformly positive effects (Hong et al., 2021).

Against this backdrop, digital transformation—and specifically artificial intelligence (AI)—is rapidly reshaping the structure of international business (Schmeisser et al., 2026), investment promotion, and cross-border technology diffusion. Recent multidisciplinary syntheses conceptualize digital transformation as a core reconfiguration of value creation and governance in international business, emphasizing platformization, data-intensive coordination, and new sources of competitive advantage for multinational enterprises (MNEs) and host economies. In parallel, strategy-focused research argues that digital transformation is increasingly intertwined with sustainability imperatives and organizational purpose (George & Schillebeeckx, 2022), suggesting that digital capabilities can enable new forms of responsible value creation—provided they are governed effectively and aligned to societal priorities.

For emerging economies such as Oman, this evolution is especially consequential: Vision-led diversification agendas elevate the urgency of attracting FDI that delivers technology transfer, human capital upgrading, and sustainable industrial development rather than enclave-style investment.

AI intensifies these dynamics because it alters decision-making, coordination, and learning processes within and across firms. International business scholarship increasingly views AI as an "augmentation layer" that changes how firms evaluate locations, manage uncertainty, and allocate resources across-borders—potentially reshaping classic assumptions about bounded rationality, information asymmetries, and strategic choice in MNEs (Lindner et al., 2025). At the same time, emerging empirical evidence indicates that firm-level AI capability can directly affect outward FDI (OFDI) behavior, expanding investment breadth and depth through productivity and dynamic capability channels (Yang et al., 2026). Collectively, these developments imply that investment ecosystems and regulatory regimes must be redesigned for an AI-enabled era—where data governance, algorithmic accountability, and digital infrastructure become determinants of investment attractiveness and knowledge spillover potential, not merely supporting conditions.

From a technology transfer perspective, FDI remains a major conduit through which advanced production methods, digital practices, and sustainability-oriented innovations diffuse into host economies. Evidence from manufacturing shows that bidirectional (two-way) FDI can enhance green innovation capability, and that intellectual property protection (IPP) can shape the strength and nonlinearity of these effects (Song & Chen, 2023). At the macro-finance interface, cross-country analysis further suggests that FDI-based technology transfer is associated with growth in green bond issuance, reinforcing the proposition that technology inflows can connect industrial upgrading with sustainable finance outcomes (Christnacht & Mertzanis, 2025). Meanwhile, sectoral evidence in global value chains indicates that technology adoption trajectories (e.g., robotisation) are influenced by both FDI participation and domestic capability endowments, underscoring the joint role of international linkages and local ecosystem readiness (Anzolin et al., 2022). However, translating these channels into durable knowledge-based growth is challenging in asymmetric partnerships where bargaining power, appropriation risks, and capability gaps can impede effective transfer; recent research highlights persistent obstacles to technology transfer in asymmetric alliances and the need for governance mechanisms that protect mutual value while enabling learning (Simms & Frishammar, 2024b).

These imperatives elevate the strategic importance of "digital investment ecosystems"—the intertwined set of policies, institutions, infrastructures, and market intermediaries that collectively shape (i) the quality and direction of FDI, (ii) the effectiveness of technology transfer, and (iii) the sustainability of growth outcomes. Firm-level studies show that advanced digitalisation can strengthen resilience in developing and emerging economies, implying that digital maturity is not only a competitiveness factor but also a risk-management capability relevant to investors and regulators (Copestake et al., 2024). Complementary work indicates that digitalisation supports organisational resilience during shocks such as the COVID-19 pandemic, highlighting the broader systemic value of digital capability accumulation for economic continuity and investor confidence (Abidi et al., 2023). At the firm strategy level, capability-based accounts of digital transformation emphasize sensing–seizing–reconfiguring routines (i.e., dynamic capabilities) as central to executing technology-enabled change, offering a useful lens for understanding why some ecosystems convert digital initiatives into scalable industrial outcomes while others experience implementation failure (Ghosh et al., 2022). Systematic evidence also suggests that sustainability outcomes are increasingly mediated by how digital transformation is conceived and implemented, motivating more integrated research at the intersection of technology strategy, governance, and sustainability transitions (Guandalini, 2022).

Yet, the literature remains fragmented in ways that matter for policy and strategy in emerging economies. First, AI-enabled internationalisation research is advancing quickly, but it is still insufficiently connected to national investment ecosystem design—particularly the regulatory "plumbing" (data governance, licensing, regulatory sandboxes, digital identity, cross-border data rules) that can attract responsible investors while lowering transaction costs. Second, technology transfer research increasingly recognizes relational asymmetries and governance frictions, yet often under-specifies how AI tools (e.g., algorithmic due diligence, IP analytics, innovation mapping, and supplier capability assessment) can be embedded into investment facilitation and partnership governance to improve transparency and learning outcomes. Third, sustainability-focused FDI studies demonstrate promising links to green innovation and green finance, but they rarely incorporate trustworthy AI and AI governance as enabling conditions—despite the growing consensus that responsible AI requires clear principles, implementable requirements, and regulatory alignment (Díaz-Rodríguez et al., 2023; Wirtz et al., 2022).

This study addresses these gaps by developing an integrated, AI-centered perspective on FDI and technology transfer for sustainable knowledge-based growth, with explicit alignment to Oman Vision 2040 priorities. Building on contemporary international business and digital transformation scholarship (Schmeisser et al., 2026; George & Schillebeeckx, 2022), and anchoring in evidence on AI-enabled OFDI behavior (Yang et al., 2026), the chapter positions AI technologies (e.g., machine learning risk scoring, NLP-based regulatory intelligence, computer-vision-enabled compliance monitoring, and knowledge-graph analytics for innovation ecosystems) as both (i) productive resources shaping investor behavior and (ii) governance objects requiring institutional safeguards. In doing so, it reframes "investment ecosystem enhancement" as a technology strategy problem: how to configure regulatory, infrastructural, and partnership mechanisms so that AI-enabled investment flows generate cumulative learning, local upgrading, and sustainability outcomes.

Research Gap

Despite rapid growth in AI-enabled IB and digital transformation research, the literature remains fragmented in ways that matter for emerging-economy policy and strategy. First, AI-enabled internationalisation scholarship is insufficiently connected to investment ecosystem design—particularly the regulatory "plumbing" (data governance, digital identity, licensing reforms, regulatory sandboxes, cross-border data rules) that can attract responsible investors while reducing transaction costs (Wirtz et al., 2022). Second, technology transfer research increasingly recognises relational asymmetries yet often under-specifies how AI tools (e.g., algorithmic due diligence, IP analytics, innovation mapping) can be embedded into investment facilitation and partnership governance to improve transparency and learning outcomes (Simms & Frishammar, 2024b). Third, sustainability-oriented FDI studies demonstrate links to green innovation and green finance but rarely integrate trustworthy AI and AI governance as enabling conditions (Christnacht & Mertzanis, 2025; Díaz-Rodríguez et al., 2023).

Research Aim and Questions

This chapter develops an integrated perspective on AI-enabled digital transformation as a strategic and regulatory capability shaping sustainable investment ecosystems in an emerging-economy context, with reference to Oman Vision 2040. It addresses the following research questions:

- RQ1. How does AI-enabled digital transformation reshape the coordination and orchestration of an emerging economy's investment ecosystem?
- RQ2. How do regulatory capabilities, including data governance, AI governance, accountability mechanisms, and institutional coordination, condition the translation of AI-enabled initiatives into sustainable investment outcomes?
- RQ3. Which strategic and regulatory pathways can align AI-enabled digital transformation with Oman Vision 2040 priorities to improve FDI quality, technology transfer, local capability development, and sustainability?

Contributions

This chapter makes three principal contributions. First, it extends digital transformation research beyond firm-level adoption by conceptualising AI capability as an ecosystem-level resource that affects investment facilitation, institutional coordination, investor services, and knowledge diffusion. Second, it positions regulatory capability as a strategic complement to AI capability, explaining how data governance, accountability, regulatory predictability, and institutional trust can influence investment quality. Third, it integrates FDI quality, technology transfer, absorptive capacity, sustainable finance, and green upgrading within a unified framework for sustainable knowledge-based growth.

The chapter's originality is primarily integrative and configurational. It does not claim to introduce a newly tested causal law. Instead, it connects research streams that have generally examined AI capability, investment facilitation, technology transfer, regulatory governance, and sustainability separately. Its distinct contribution is an ecosystem-level explanation of how these capabilities may operate jointly in an emerging-economy context.

Methodological Positioning and Scope

This chapter is a theory-informed conceptual and policy-analysis study. It does not report completed interviews, surveys, experiments, or other original human-participant research. The analysis integrates relevant peer-reviewed literature with selected official policy and institutional documents to develop a conceptual framework, propositions, and policy-oriented applications for Oman.

Semi-structured interviews, stakeholder coding, process tracing, and comparative case analysis are presented only as future approaches for empirically validating the proposed framework. Accordingly, the chapter's conclusions should be interpreted as theoretically derived propositions and policy-analysis insights rather than statistically generalisable or empirically confirmed causal findings.

Positioning of the Proposed Framework Relative to Existing Models

Existing digital transformation and AI capability frameworks predominantly focus on firm-level adoption, organisational performance, or digital competitiveness outcomes (Mikalef & Gupta, 2021; Ghosh et al., 2022). Similarly, investment ecosystem studies often examine FDI attraction, competitiveness, or governance mechanisms independently, without integrating sustainability and capability development pathways.

In contrast, the present framework advances an ecosystem-level perspective, explaining how AI capability and regulatory capability jointly influence investment quality, technology transfer effectiveness, and sustainable knowledge-based growth within emerging economies.

The framework differs from existing models in three important ways:

1. Multi-level integration: Combines AI capability, governance capability, investment ecosystem dynamics, and sustainability into a unified explanatory mechanism.
2. Regulation as capability: Positions regulatory capability as a strategic enabler and mediating mechanism rather than solely a compliance requirement.
3. Sustainability-oriented outcomes: Extends beyond investment attraction toward capability upgrading, knowledge transfer, green innovation, and long-term sustainable growth.

Accordingly, the proposed framework offers a distinct integrative and ecosystem-level explanation of ecosystem transformation aligned with Oman Vision 2040 priorities.

COMPARATIVE POSITIONING OF THE FRAMEWORK

Table 1 positions the proposed framework relative to the principal theoretical approaches on which it builds. Existing models provide important explanations of firm-level AI capability, organisational digital transformation, absorptive capacity, AI governance, and FDI-related innovation. However, they do not fully explain how these elements operate together within a national investment ecosystem. The present framework addresses this limitation by connecting public and private AI capability, regulatory capability, investment ecosystem competitiveness, FDI quality, technology transfer, absorptive capacity, and sustainability-oriented growth.

Table 1. Positioning of the Proposed Framework Relative to Existing Approaches

Existing approach	Principal level and focus	Limitation for the present research problem	Extension offered by this chapter
AI capability perspective	Firm-level data, technology, skills and organisational performance	Does not directly explain national investment facilitation or regulatory institutions	Extends AI capability from the firm to the investment ecosystem
Dynamic capability perspective	Organisational sensing, seizing and reconfiguration	Gives limited attention to public regulatory capability and FDI quality	Applies capability complementarity to public institutions, investors and ecosystem intermediaries
Absorptive capacity perspective	Recognition, assimilation and exploitation of external knowledge	Usually treats investment attraction and AI governance as external conditions	Connects absorptive capacity to FDI selection, partnership governance and technology transfer
AI-governance perspective	Trust, accountability, transparency and risk management	Commonly focuses on responsible AI implementation rather than investment outcomes	Positions regulation as a strategic capability affecting investor confidence and FDI quality
FDI and innovation-policy perspective	Investment attraction, innovation spillovers and technology transfer	Often under-specifies AI-enabled facilitation and data governance	Integrates AI-enabled investment facilitation, regulatory readiness and sustainable upgrading
Proposed ecosystem framework	National ecosystem linking AI, regulation, investment and sustainability	Conceptual relationships require empirical validation	Provides an integrated mechanism connecting AI capability, regulatory capability, FDI quality, technology transfer and sustainable knowledge-based growth

The distinct contribution of the framework is therefore integrative and configurational rather than based on a claim that each individual construct is new.

LITERATURE REVIEW

AI and Digital Transformation in Investment and International Business

Recent international business (IB) scholarship positions AI as more than an efficiency tool; it increasingly reshapes how firms sense opportunities, evaluate locations, and execute cross-border strategies. Conceptual work in IB shows that AI can "augment" managerial decision-making by reducing some cognitive constraints while also introducing new AI-specific biases (e.g., model opacity, training-data path dependence) that may affect location choice, partner selection, and governance decisions. In parallel, multidisciplinary reviews of digital transformation in IB argue that platformization, data-driven coordination, and digitally mediated ecosystems are reorganizing global value creation and the mechanisms by which firms internationalize (Lindner et al., 2025; Samuel et al., 2022; dos Santos & Williamson, 2024; Schmeisser et al., 2026).

At the ecosystem level, AI-enabled digital transformation increasingly operates through (i) data infrastructures (registries, KYC/AML, e-licensing, interoperable identity), (ii) analytics capabilities (risk scoring, investor targeting, supply-chain visibility), and (iii) institutional complementarities (investment policy, data governance, dispute resolution). Firm-level strategy research clarifies that value from AI depends on complementary resources—data, talent, architectures, governance routines—rather than algorithms alone. For emerging economies pursuing diversification and investment upgrading—such as Oman—this shifts the analytical lens from "digitizing processes" to building an innovation ecosystem where AI capabilities and institutional reforms co-evolve (consistent with the strategic orientation of Oman Vision 2040) (Mikalef & Gupta, 2021; Ghosh et al., 2022).

FDI Quality And Ecosystem Competitiveness

A growing stream distinguishes FDI quantity from FDI quality, emphasizing knowledge intensity, innovation spillovers, resilience contributions, and sustainability outcomes. Evidence suggests that digitalization can affect investment and competitiveness through improved coordination and resilience, but outcomes are heterogeneous across contexts. For example, work on digitalization and resilience emphasizes non-linearities and trade-offs—digital adoption can strengthen adaptive capacity but also increase exposure to systemic shocks and dependencies. This matters for "investment ecosystems" because competitiveness increasingly hinges on digital public goods (data infrastructures, cybersecurity, interoperability) as well as private capabilities (Abidi et al., 2023; Copestake et al., 2024).

Cross-country evidence also indicates that digitalization may have divergent effects on FDI inflows between advanced and developing contexts, implying that institutional capacity and absorptive readiness condition whether digital reforms translate into investment attraction. From an ecosystem perspective, these findings motivate a shift toward "capability-based" investment strategies: attracting FDI that upgrades domestic knowledge bases requires complementary reforms in skills, innovation systems, and regulatory quality (Nguyen, 2025).

Beyond inflow levels, the mode of foreign entry matters for local innovation. Research shows that innovation outcomes can differ by entry mode (e.g., greenfield versus other modes) and by the technological orientation of foreign investors, reinforcing the view that policymakers should evaluate FDI composition, not only volume. In technology-intensive domains, evidence from Industry 4.0 contexts also suggests that inward FDI interacts with domestic innovation capabilities to influence advanced technology adoption (e.g., robotics), highlighting absorptive capacity as a core "bottleneck" for ecosystem upgrading (Damioli & Marin, 2024; Anzolin et al., 2022).

Technology Transfer And Absorptive Capacity/Governance

Technology transfer is increasingly conceptualized as a governed process rather than an automatic spillover. Studies of alliances and partnerships emphasize that transfer outcomes depend on governance symmetry, bargaining power, and the design of joint learning mechanisms—especially in asymmetric partnerships where one actor controls critical knowledge assets. This aligns with the policy concern that technology transfer is not guaranteed simply by attracting multinational enterprises (MNEs); transfer requires deliberate institutional and organizational arrangements (e.g., R&D collaboration frameworks, IP regimes, talent mobility pathways, and standards infrastructures) (Simms & Frishammar, 2024b; Rocha et al., 2023).

FDI's contribution to technology upgrading is therefore contingent on domestic absorptive capacity and the institutional "rules of the game." Empirical evidence connecting inward FDI to advanced technology adoption shows that FDI effects may become salient primarily when host-country capabilities are sufficiently developed—suggesting complementarity between investment policy and innovation-system strengthening. This is particularly salient for knowledge-based growth strategies, where the policy aim is to attract "capability-enhancing" investors and embed them into local innovation networks (Anzolin et al., 2022; Cohen & Levinthal, 1990; Zahra & George, 2002).

Sustainability, Green Upgrading, And Sustainable Finance Links

The sustainability dimension of digital transformation has moved from peripheral to central. Systematic reviews on "digital sustainability" highlight that digital transformation can enable sustainability improvements, but only under specific governance and strategy conditions—otherwise rebound effects and misalignment risks remain. In IB, conceptual work further emphasizes that sustainability and purpose increasingly shape how MNEs configure digital transformation strategies, particularly under crisis pressures and shifting stakeholder expectations (Guandalini, 2022; George & Schillebeeckx, 2022).

In the FDI domain, sustainability is increasingly examined through green upgrading and sustainable finance channels. Cross-country evidence links FDI-based technology transfer to the growth of green bond issuance, suggesting that technology transfer can strengthen a country's capacity to finance green transitions—connecting industrial policy with sustainable finance market development. Complementing this, studies on AI and green finance suggest that AI capabilities can amplify sustainability transitions when coupled with green finance mechanisms (rather than operating in isolation). A related finance stream indicates that digital finance can catalyze green innovation under certain conditions (e.g., diminishing marginal returns and threshold effects), again implying that institutional design shapes whether "digital" translates into "green" upgrading (Christnacht & Mertzanis, 2025; Wen et al., 2026; Zhou et al., 2025).

Collectively, this literature implies that a sustainability-oriented investment ecosystem must be assessed not only by investor attraction metrics, but by how investment, technology transfer, and finance co-produce green upgrading—an especially relevant lens for Oman Vision 2040's sustainability and diversification objectives.

Regulatory Capability, Data Governance, And AI Governance

A key policy-relevant research stream concerns regulatory capability: how states design rules, enforcement mechanisms, and adaptive governance for data-driven economies. Foundational work on data sharing governance argues that effective data-driven markets require governance structures that specify investigation, decision-making, and enforcement—balancing economic efficiency with legal legitimacy. This directly intersects with investment ecosystems because investor confidence increasingly depends on predictable data access rules, privacy protections, cybersecurity expectations, and cross-border data transfer frameworks (Graef & Prüfer, 2021; Suh et al., 2023).

AI governance scholarship has simultaneously matured toward risk-based and guideline-based frameworks, especially for public-sector and societal contexts. Work on "trustworthy AI" synthesizes principles (ethics, transparency, accountability) into responsible AI system requirements and regulatory linkages, which is essential when AI tools are used in investment facilitation, licensing, compliance, and dispute resolution. Reviews of AI governance also identify recurring themes and gaps—particularly around operationalization, accountability allocation, and the roles of firms and stakeholders (Birkstedt et al., 2023; Díaz-Rodríguez et al., 2023; Wirtz et al., 2022).

More recently, sustainability-oriented regulation has been theorized to reshape corporate governance via an "AI–policy–governance nexus," suggesting that disclosure, assurance, and risk regimes can change how AI is integrated into governance and accountability systems. For emerging economies, this creates a practical policy question: how can regulatory capability be built so that AI adoption increases investment attractiveness while also meeting sustainability and legitimacy requirements? (Cordeiro et al., 2026; de Almeida & dos Santos Júnior, 2025; Goos & Savona, 2024).

Foundational absorptive capacity theory further supports this argument by showing that external knowledge creates value only when recipient firms and ecosystems possess the capacity to recognise, assimilate, transform, and exploit that knowledge (Cohen & Levinthal, 1990; Zahra & George, 2002).

GCC Context and Emerging Economy Ecosystems

GCC economies increasingly position AI capability, digital transformation, and sustainable investment ecosystems as strategic pillars for diversification beyond hydrocarbon dependence. Regional initiatives such as Saudi Vision 2030, the UAE National AI Strategy, and Oman Vision 2040 demonstrate convergence toward smart government transformation, AI readiness, digital governance capability, innovation ecosystems, sustainable diversification, and technology-intensive investment attraction.

Similar to Oman, GCC countries increasingly compete through ecosystem capability rather than traditional investment incentives alone. This regional shift reinforces the relevance of analysing AI-enabled ecosystem transformation within emerging economy contexts.

Although GCC countries share broad objectives related to AI readiness, digital government and technology-intensive investment, differences in regulatory institutions, market scale, industrial structure and absorptive capacity mean that regional strategies cannot be assumed to generate equivalent investment or technology-transfer outcomes.

Oman Policy and Investment Ecosystem Context

Oman provides an appropriate context for examining AI-enabled investment ecosystem transformation because Oman Vision 2040 identifies economic diversification, technology, knowledge, innovation, institutional performance, human-capital development, and environmental sustainability as interconnected national priorities. This strategic direction implies that the success of foreign investment should be assessed not only by capital inflows, but also by its contribution to productivity, technology transfer, local capability development, resilience, and sustainable economic transformation (Oman Vision 2040 Implementation Follow-up Unit, 2023).

The National Digital Economy Program provides an institutional foundation for this transition through executive programmes concerned with government digital transformation, digital industry, artificial intelligence, advanced technologies, digital infrastructure, and national digital capabilities. Its emphasis on government AI readiness, cybersecurity, integrated digital services, digital investment, and a data-driven economy illustrates how digital capability is becoming part of Oman's investment infrastructure rather than remaining a narrowly technical policy area (Ministry of Transport, Communications and Information Technology, n.d.).

The National Program for Artificial Intelligence and Advanced Digital Technologies for 2024–2026 further strengthens this orientation. Its principal pillars concern the adoption of AI in economic and developmental sectors, localisation of AI technologies and capabilities, and human-centred governance of AI applications. Proposed initiatives concerning open data, AI research and development, AI-enabled entrepreneurship, advanced-technology infrastructure, and regulatory development are directly relevant to the framework's AI-capability and regulatory-capability constructs (Ministry of Transport, Communications and Information Technology, 2024a).

Oman's regulatory environment also contains increasingly important data-governance instruments. The Personal Data Protection Law, its Executive Regulations, and the national data-governance framework establish requirements concerning the lawful processing of personal data, organisational responsibilities, compliance, data-management structures, and the treatment of data as a national asset. These instruments demonstrate that regulatory capability can function as enabling infrastructure for trustworthy digital investment when it increases predictability, accountability, and confidence in data-intensive activities (Ministry of Transport, Communications and Information Technology, 2022, 2024b, 2025).

Synthesis, Research Gap, and Framework Motivation

The preceding literature review reveals a rapidly evolving yet fragmented body of knowledge at the intersection of artificial intelligence (AI), digital transformation, foreign direct investment (FDI), technology transfer, and sustainability. While each stream offers valuable insights, their integration remains limited—particularly in the context of emerging economies seeking to build resilient, knowledge-based, and sustainability-oriented investment ecosystems. Building on the analytical foundation of this study, this section synthesizes key patterns across the literature, identifies the resulting research gap, and motivates the development of an integrative conceptual framework aligned with Oman Vision 2040.

1. Synthesis Across Literature Streams

The literature identifies three related limitations. First, AI and digital-transformation research remains predominantly firm-centred, while FDI and development research generally operates at national or sectoral levels. As a result, limited attention has been given to how firm-level AI capability interacts with public institutions, investment intermediaries and national innovation systems.

Second, the effects of both FDI and digital transformation are conditional on complementary capabilities. Technology transfer depends on local absorptive capacity, skilled human resources, research and development capability, institutional quality, and links between foreign investors and domestic organizations. Similarly, digital infrastructure generates limited developmental value when it is not supported by interoperable systems, data governance, accountability and institutional adoption.

Third, regulatory governance increasingly functions as strategic infrastructure. Clear data-access rules, AI-accountability mechanisms, predictable investment procedures and effective enforcement can reduce uncertainty and strengthen investor confidence. These governance capabilities may therefore influence whether AI-enabled investment facilitation produces high-quality FDI, meaningful technology transfer and sustainability-oriented upgrading.

Based on this synthesis, the chapter proposes that AI-enabled digital capability and regulatory capability jointly influence investment ecosystem competitiveness. Higher ecosystem competitiveness may improve the attraction of technology- and knowledge-intensive FDI, while absorptive capacity and sustainability orientation condition whether such investment produces local capability development and sustainable knowledge-based growth.

2. Mechanism-Based Integration

Rather than proposing a strictly linear mechanism, the framework argues that AI-enabled digital capability and regulatory capability jointly shape investment ecosystem competitiveness. Greater competitiveness can support the attraction of high-quality FDI, which may contribute to technology transfer and local upgrading. These relationships are conditioned by absorptive capacity, sustainability orientation, skills, and innovation-system readiness, while sustainable knowledge-based growth generates feedback through institutional learning and further capability development.

3. Alignment with Oman Vision 2040

The proposed framework is closely aligned with Oman Vision 2040, which prioritises economic diversification, digital transformation, innovation, human-capital development, and environmental sustainability. By integrating AI capability, regulatory capability, and sustainability orientation, the framework provides a policy-relevant perspective on how Oman can attract higher-quality, technology-intensive FDI, strengthen local innovation and knowledge transfer, and support sustainable, investment-led development.

CONCEPTUAL FRAMEWORK AND PROPOSITIONS

Integrated Conceptual Framework

This chapter proposes an ecosystem-level conceptual framework explaining how AI-enabled digital transformation capability, supported by regulatory capability, influences investment quality, technology transfer effectiveness, and sustainable knowledge-based growth.

The framework assumes that AI capability alone is insufficient to generate sustainable investment outcomes. Rather, ecosystem performance depends on complementary institutional mechanisms including governance readiness, data regulation, investment facilitation systems, absorptive capacity, and sustainability-oriented policy design.

The proposed framework, illustrated in Figure 1, presents a sequential mechanism through which AI-enabled digital capability and regulatory capability jointly strengthen investment ecosystem competitiveness, improve the attraction of high-quality FDI, support technology transfer and local capability development, and ultimately contribute to sustainable knowledge-based growth aligned with Oman Vision 2040.

The framework positions regulatory capability as a complementary and conditioning capability that enables AI-supported investment ecosystem reforms to operate predictably, transparently, and responsibly. AI-enabled digital capability and regulatory capability therefore jointly influence investment ecosystem competitiveness rather than operating as a simple sequential chain.

Figure 1. Proposed ecosystem-level framework linking AI-enabled digital capability and regulatory capability to investment ecosystem competitiveness, high-quality FDI, technology transfer and local upgrading, and sustainable knowledge-based growth. Absorptive capacity, sustainability orientation, and skills and innovation-system readiness operate as cross-cutting enabling conditions. The feedback loop indicates that sustainable growth can strengthen institutional learning and further capability development. The relationships shown are conceptual propositions requiring future empirical validation.

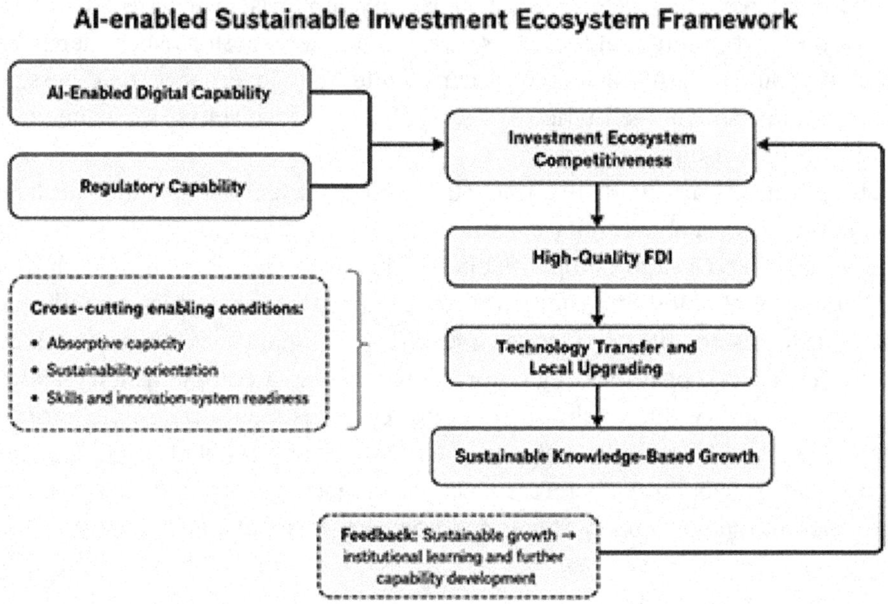

Key Constructs

The proposed framework is built around three interrelated domains: AI-enabled digital capability, regulatory capability, and sustainability orientation. These domains jointly shape investment ecosystem competitiveness and determine whether foreign investment contributes to technology transfer, local capability development, and sustainable knowledge-based growth.

AI-enabled digital capability refers to the combined public- and private-sector capacity to deploy artificial intelligence, digital infrastructure, data resources, and analytical systems to improve investment identification, facilitation, coordination, and learning across institutions and market actors. This capability includes digital infrastructure, such as interoperable data platforms, cloud systems, digital public services, and AI-enabled applications; analytical capabilities, including machine learning, automation, predictive analytics, risk assessment, and decision-support systems; and human capital, including technical skills, managerial expertise, and innovation capacity. Together, these resources influence how investment opportunities are identified, evaluated, promoted, and managed, while also supporting ecosystem coordination and institutional responsiveness (Mikalef & Gupta, 2021; Schmeisser et al., 2026).

Regulatory capability refers to the ability of public institutions to design, implement, enforce, coordinate, and adapt regulatory and governance mechanisms for AI, data, digital services, and investment activities. It encompasses data-governance frameworks, privacy and cybersecurity requirements, AI-governance and ethical standards, investment regulations, digital licensing and facilitation mechanisms, accountability arrangements, and institutional capacity for enforcement and regulatory adaptation. Regulatory capability complements AI-enabled digital capability by increasing predictability, legitimacy, transparency, and trust. It may therefore reduce regulatory uncertainty, strengthen investor confidence, and enable responsible innovation within the investment ecosystem (Wirtz et al., 2022; Goos & Savona, 2024).

Sustainability orientation captures the extent to which investment strategies, regulatory instruments, digital initiatives, and technology-transfer mechanisms are aligned with long-term environmental, economic, and social development objectives. It includes green industrial upgrading, environmental-performance requirements, environmental, social, and governance reporting systems, responsible investment criteria, green-finance instruments, digital finance, and sustainability-linked innovation. Sustainability orientation ensures that investment attraction is evaluated not only in terms of capital volume, but also in relation to green innovation, resilience, inclusion, resource efficiency, and long-term development outcomes (Christnacht & Mertzanis, 2025; Song & Chen, 2023).

Investment ecosystem competitiveness reflects the ecosystem's capacity to provide transparent, coordinated, efficient, and predictable conditions for investors. It emerges from the interaction between AI-enabled digital capability and regulatory capability and is reinforced by effective institutions, digital public infrastructure, integrated investor services, and credible governance arrangements. A competitive investment ecosystem can reduce information asymmetries and transaction costs while improving investor targeting, licensing, aftercare, and inter-agency coordination.

High-quality FDI refers to foreign investment that contributes more than financial capital. It includes technology-intensive and knowledge-intensive investment that supports research and development, workforce development, supplier upgrading, innovation partnerships, local value creation, environmental performance, and long-term economic diversification. The framework therefore distinguishes investment quality from investment quantity.

Technology transfer and local upgrading refer to the processes through which foreign knowledge, technologies, production methods, managerial practices, standards, and innovation capabilities are transferred to domestic firms, workers, research institutions, and suppliers. These outcomes may occur through joint research and development, training, licensing, supplier-development programmes, demonstration effects, labour mobility, and collaborative innovation. Their effectiveness depends heavily on absorptive capacity, partnership governance, institutional support, and the readiness of local innovation systems.

Absorptive capacity represents the ability of domestic firms and institutions to recognise, assimilate, transform, and exploit externally generated knowledge. It includes workforce skills, research and development capability, organisational learning, technological readiness, university–industry linkages, and supplier capabilities. In the proposed framework, absorptive capacity acts as a cross-cutting enabling condition that influences whether high-quality FDI produces meaningful technology transfer and local capability development (Cohen & Levinthal, 1990; Zahra & George, 2002).

Sustainable knowledge-based growth is the long-term outcome of the framework. It reflects economic development driven by innovation, knowledge creation, technological upgrading, diversification, resilience, and environmentally responsible production. It also creates a feedback effect by strengthening institutional learning, regulatory development, digital capability, workforce skills, and future investment ecosystem competitiveness.

The framework therefore proposes that AI-enabled digital capability and regulatory capability jointly strengthen investment ecosystem competitiveness. Greater competitiveness can facilitate the attraction of high-quality FDI, while absorptive capacity, sustainability orientation, and innovation-system readiness determine whether such investment produces effective technology transfer, local upgrading, and sustainable knowledge-based growth.

Mechanism Logic

AI-enabled digital transformation can increase ecosystem performance through (a) reduced information frictions (targeting, screening, aftercare), (b) improved coordination (inter-agency workflows, compliance monitoring), and (c) enhanced learning (innovation mapping, supplier diagnostics). However, these gains are conditional on regulatory capability that ensures trustworthy AI, predictable data access, and enforceable accountability (Díaz-Rodríguez et al., 2023; Wirtz et al., 2022).

Propositions

P1—Ecosystem orchestration: Higher levels of AI-enabled digital capability are positively associated with investment ecosystem coordination, transparency and service integration.

P2—Regulatory complementarity: Regulatory capability positively conditions the relationship between AI-enabled digital capability and investment ecosystem competitiveness by reducing uncertainty and strengthening institutional trust.

P3—FDI quality: AI-enabled investment facilitation is expected to increase the likelihood of attracting higher-quality, technology- and knowledge-intensive FDI when governance mechanisms provide credibility, accountability, and regulatory predictability.

P4—Technology transfer: Technology-transfer effectiveness is expected to improve when AI-enabled tools are embedded in partnership governance, including due diligence, capability assessment, and intellectual-property analytics, and when absorptive-capacity policies support local upgrading (Anzolin et al., 2022; Simms & Frishammar, 2024b).

P5—Sustainability alignment: Sustainable investment outcomes are expected to improve when investment ecosystem reforms incorporate sustainability criteria and connect investment attraction with green innovation, responsible investment, and sustainable-finance pathways (Christnacht & Mertzanis, 2025; Guandalini, 2022; Song & Chen, 2023).

Materials and Methods

Research Design

The chapter adopts a theory-informed integrative conceptual design supported by qualitative policy analysis. The purpose is to explain how AI-enabled digital transformation, regulatory capability, investment ecosystem competitiveness, FDI quality, technology transfer, absorptive capacity, and sustainability orientation may interact within an emerging-economy setting.

The study does not claim to be a systematic literature review or a completed empirical case study. Instead, it uses a purposive and theory-driven synthesis to connect previously separated research streams and to develop a mechanism-based conceptual framework applicable to Oman and comparable emerging economies.

Unit of Analysis and Contextual Boundary

The unit of analysis is the national investment ecosystem, defined as the interconnected configuration of government institutions, regulators, investment-promotion bodies, digital infrastructures, economic zones, foreign investors, domestic firms, universities, innovation intermediaries, and partnership mechanisms that influence investment attraction and developmental outcomes.

Oman is used as the principal policy context because Oman Vision 2040 connects economic diversification with technology, knowledge, innovation, human-capital development, institutional performance, and environmental sustainability. The analysis focuses primarily on policy developments and institutional initiatives associated with the implementation period beginning in 2021.

Source Selection

The conceptual analysis draws on peer-reviewed literature addressing five principal domains: AI and digital-transformation capability; FDI quality and investment ecosystems; technology transfer and absorptive capacity; data and AI governance; and sustainability-oriented investment and finance.

The policy analysis draws on publicly available documents issued by authoritative Omani institutions. These include Oman Vision 2040 publications; the National Digital Economy Program; the National Program for Artificial Intelligence and Advanced Digital Technologies; personal-data-protection and national-data-governance instruments; foreign-investment legislation; Invest Oman materials; special economic-zone and one-stop-shop documentation; and policies related to green hydrogen and sustainability-oriented investment.

Sources were selected according to three criteria: direct relevance to at least one framework construct, institutional or scholarly authority, and usefulness for explaining the mechanisms connecting digital capability, governance, investment, technology transfer, and sustainability. Unverified media commentary, duplicate materials, and sources without a clear relationship to the conceptual framework were excluded.

Analytical Procedure

The analysis followed three stages. First, the scholarly literature was organised around the framework's core constructs and the principal limitations identified in existing research. Second, official policy documents were mapped against the same constructs to identify concrete Oman-specific instruments, including digital-government systems, AI initiatives, data-governance mechanisms, investment-facilitation platforms, economic-zone arrangements, and sustainability-linked investment programmes. Third, the theoretical and policy evidence was integrated to formulate the proposed mechanism relationships and five conceptual propositions.

The analysis distinguishes policy design from demonstrated policy outcomes. Official documents provide evidence of strategic priorities, institutional arrangements, and intended mechanisms, but they do not by themselves demonstrate that the intended effects have been achieved. The propositions therefore remain subject to future empirical validation.

Scope and Limitations of the Method

The approach supports analytical rather than statistical generalisation. It is suitable for developing a theoretically grounded framework and identifying policy-relevant mechanisms, but it cannot establish causal effects, estimate the magnitude of relationships, or represent stakeholder experiences. Future studies should test the framework through interviews, surveys, longitudinal indicators, comparative GCC cases, and mixed-method designs.

Proposed Empirical Validation Protocol

Future empirical validation may use approximately 22–26 semi-structured interviews selected through purposive sampling. The proposed distribution is five to six government or regulatory representatives, four to five investment-promotion or special-economic-zone representatives, five to six foreign investors or multinational-enterprise representatives, four to five domestic firms or SMEs, and three to four academic, technology or innovation-system experts.

Data collection should continue until thematic saturation is reached. Saturation may be considered achieved when two consecutive interviews within the relevant stakeholder categories produce no substantively new first-order codes, mechanism relationships or boundary conditions.

The analysis should combine deductive and inductive coding. Deductive codes would be derived from the conceptual framework, including AI capability, regulatory capability, investor confidence, FDI quality, absorptive capacity, technology transfer and sustainability orientation. Inductive coding would identify emerging implementation barriers, stakeholder incentives, unintended outcomes and context-specific mechanisms. Coding should proceed through initial coding, category development, relationship mapping and integration of categories into explanatory mechanisms. A codebook, coding decisions and analytic memos should be maintained to support transparency and dependability.

Process-tracing indicators may include the dates and sequencing of digital-platform launches, regulatory changes, inter-agency integration measures, licensing-process changes, investor-service improvements, changes in technology-intensive FDI composition, local training and research commitments, supplier-development arrangements, and sustainability-linked project requirements. These indicators would help examine whether the mechanisms proposed in the framework occur in the expected sequence.

This protocol is proposed for future validation and does not represent empirical work completed for the present chapter.

Ethical Considerations

The present chapter analyses published scholarship and publicly accessible policy and institutional documents. It does not involve human participants, confidential organisational records, personal data, or experimental interventions. Consequently, institutional ethics approval and participant consent were not required for the present conceptual analysis.

Any future empirical study involving interviews or organisational data should obtain the relevant institutional approval before data collection and should implement informed consent, voluntary participation, confidentiality, anonymisation, secure storage, and controlled access procedures.

Policy Analysis and Framework Application

Digital and AI Capability

Oman's digital-economy and AI programmes illustrate the public-capability component of the proposed framework. Integrated government services, data platforms, cloud and data-centre development, digital-skills programmes, AI research initiatives, and support for advanced technologies can reduce information and coordination barriers within the investment ecosystem. These initiatives may improve investor targeting, licensing, aftercare, institutional coordination, and the identification of opportunities for local supplier and technology development (Ministry of Transport, Communications and Information Technology, n.d., 2024a).

However, the existence of digital programmes does not automatically establish their effectiveness. Their contribution to investment quality depends on interoperability, data quality, institutional adoption, technical skills, cybersecurity, and the capacity of public organisations to integrate technology into decision-making and service delivery.

Regulatory Capability and Governance Readiness

The Personal Data Protection Law, its Executive Regulations, national data-governance policies, and emerging AI-governance initiatives provide concrete illustrations of regulatory capability. These instruments can contribute to investor confidence by clarifying responsibilities, data-processing conditions, compliance requirements, and accountability mechanisms (Ministry of Transport, Communications and Information Technology, 2022, 2024b, 2025).

From the perspective of the conceptual framework, regulation is therefore not treated solely as a compliance cost. Predictable and implementable rules can reduce uncertainty and support responsible investment in data-intensive and AI-enabled industries. Nevertheless, regulatory value depends on enforcement consistency, institutional coordination, regulatory expertise, and the ability to update rules as technologies and business models evolve.

Investment Facilitation and Special Economic Zones

Oman's investment-facilitation ecosystem includes the Foreign Capital Investment Law, Invest Oman, digital investor services, and the one-stop-shop arrangements operated within special economic and free zones. Invest Oman provides a central interface for major investment opportunities, while electronic one-stop-shop mechanisms are intended to simplify licensing, approvals, land-related procedures, environmental applications, and other investor services (Ministry of Commerce, Industry and Investment Promotion, 2019; Invest Oman, n.d.; Public Authority for Special Economic Zones and Free Zones, 2021).

The special economic and free zones in Duqm, Sohar, Salalah, Al Mazunah and other locations provide sectoral and geographic platforms through which technology-intensive investment, industrial clustering, supplier development, and infrastructure investment may be coordinated. These mechanisms illustrate the investment-ecosystem-competitiveness component of the framework by seeking to improve transparency, service integration, predictability, and administrative efficiency.

Their contribution to high-quality FDI should nevertheless be evaluated through developmental indicators rather than investment volume alone. Relevant indicators include local research and development, workforce training, technology localisation, domestic supplier participation, intellectual-property creation, environmental performance, and the durability of links between foreign investors and local institutions.

Sustainability-Linked Investment

Oman's sustainability priorities create opportunities to connect investment attraction with green industrial upgrading. The development of the green-hydrogen ecosystem is a prominent example because it requires coordinated investment in regulation, infrastructure, international and domestic supply chains, specialised skills, research and development, and adjacent industries (Hydrogen Oman, 2024).

This example illustrates how sustainability orientation can influence FDI quality and technology-transfer outcomes. Investment projects that incorporate local capability development, supplier upgrading, skills formation, environmental standards, and research partnerships are more likely to contribute to sustainable knowledge-based growth than projects operating as isolated production enclaves.

Table 2. Mapping Oman Policy Instruments and Initiatives to the Proposed Framework.

Oman initiative or instrument	Framework component	Intended mechanism	Expected investment outcome	Evidence limitation
National Digital Economy Program	AI and digital capability	Integrated services, data platforms and digital infrastructure	Lower information and administrative costs	Policy design does not confirm realised impact
National AI and Advanced Digital Technologies Program	AI capability and governance	AI adoption, localisation, skills and governance	Greater readiness for technology-intensive investment	Programme outcomes require empirical assessment
Personal Data Protection Law and national data governance	Regulatory capability	Predictability, accountability and lawful data processing	Greater confidence in data-intensive investment	Effect depends on implementation and enforcement
Invest Oman and electronic investor services	Ecosystem competitiveness	Centralised information and coordinated investor services	Improved targeting, facilitation and aftercare	Processing-time and investor-experience data are needed
Special economic and free zones	FDI quality and clustering	Infrastructure, licensing and sectoral coordination	Industrial clustering and supplier development	Local-linkage outcomes must be measured
Green-hydrogen development	Sustainability orientation	Coordinated regulation, infrastructure, investment and skills	Green industrial upgrading and technology transfer	Local content and knowledge-transfer effects require evaluation

Table 2 maps the principal Oman policy instruments and initiatives to the components of the proposed framework, their intended mechanisms, expected investment outcomes, and relevant evidence limitations.

Note. The mapping is based on Oman Vision 2040, the National Digital Economy Program, the National Program for Artificial Intelligence and Advanced Digital Technologies, the Personal Data Protection Law and its Executive Regulations, Invest Oman materials, special economic-zone documentation, and the Oman Green Hydrogen Strategy.

Boundary Conditions

Several conditions may limit the translation of policy ambition into ecosystem outcomes. These include shortages of specialised skills, fragmented institutional responsibilities, inconsistent data quality, limited interoperability, cybersecurity exposure, uneven regulatory implementation, insufficient absorptive capacity among local firms, and weak links between foreign investors and domestic innovation institutions.

These conditions should be treated as boundary conditions within the conceptual framework. They explain why comparable digital or investment initiatives may generate different outcomes across sectors, organisations, and periods. The Oman policy evidence therefore illustrates the relevance of the framework's constructs but does not constitute empirical confirmation of the proposed causal relationships.

Discussion

This study advances a capability-based view of AI-enabled digital transformation as ecosystem infrastructure and clarifies the strategic role of regulation. First, the conceptual model extends digital transformation scholarship beyond organisational boundaries by positioning ecosystem orchestration as a mechanism through which AI-enabled services can improve investment facilitation, coordination, and learning (Schmeisser et al., 2026). The logic aligns with IB arguments that AI reshapes decision-making and location evaluation processes (Lindner et al., 2025) and with evidence that AI capability can influence cross-border investment behaviour (Yang et al., 2026). The Oman policy examples illustrate the institutional relevance of the proposed constructs but should not be interpreted as evidence that the proposed relationships have already been empirically confirmed.

Second, the framework positions regulatory capability as a complementary and conditioning capability. Rather than treating governance as an exogenous constraint, the study frames AI governance, auditability, and accountability as strategic assets that can increase legitimacy and reduce uncertainty—thereby supporting investment commitments and higher-quality partnership formation (Díaz-Rodríguez et al., 2023; Wirtz et al., 2022; Goos & Savona, 2024). This is particularly important in emerging economies where trust in institutions and predictability of rules can be decisive for long-horizon, technology-intensive investment.

Third, the study connects AI-enabled ecosystem reforms to sustainability outcomes by integrating three channels: (a) technology transfer governance, (b) green innovation capability development, and (c) sustainable finance linkages (Christnacht & Mertzanis, 2025; Song & Chen, 2023; Guandalini, 2022). This helps reconcile an important tension in the literature: digitalisation can enhance resilience and performance (Abidi et al., 2023; Copestake et al., 2024) while also introducing new risks (data dependence, opacity, accountability gaps) that must be managed through governance design.

Implications

Theoretical Implications

Ecosystem-level digital transformation: The study extends DT research from firm-centric adoption toward ecosystem orchestration and institutional complementarity.

Regulation as capability: The study conceptualises AI governance and data governance as complementary capabilities that condition the relationship between AI-enabled digital capability and investment ecosystem outcomes (Wirtz et al., 2022; de Almeida & dos Santos Júnior, 2025).

Sustainability integration: It links AI-enabled transformation with green upgrading and sustainable finance outcomes, integrating FDI quality and sustainability logics (Christnacht & Mertzanis, 2025; Song & Chen, 2023).

Policy Implications

Build regulatory capability in parallel with AI adoption: Invest in auditability standards, accountability allocation, and compliance toolchains for AI-enabled public services (Díaz-Rodríguez et al., 2023; Wirtz et al., 2022).

Design for "quality FDI": Embed capability-building requirements into investment facilitation (training, supplier development, joint R&D, standards transfer).

Treat data governance as investment infrastructure: Clear rules for access, protection, and cross-border flows reduce uncertainty and increase investor confidence.

Connect investment attraction to sustainability pathways: Use sustainability criteria, ESG transparency expectations, and sustainable finance linkages to move from investment volume to investment quality.

Align AI ecosystem reforms explicitly with Oman Vision 2040 priorities: AI governance frameworks, digital economy initiatives, sustainability targets, and investment facilitation mechanisms should be coordinated to support diversification, innovation capability, and resilient knowledge-based growth.

Managerial Implications

Govern AI jointly: Firms should co-design AI governance arrangements with regulators to reduce uncertainty and protect long-term value.

Operationalise technology transfer: Partnerships should include explicit learning routines (co-training, co-development, supplier upgrading KPIs).

Leverage ecosystem analytics: Intermediaries can use AI-enabled mapping and diagnostics to match investors with local capability gaps and sustainable upgrading opportunities.

CONCLUSION

This chapter develops an integrated ecosystem-level framework explaining how AI-enabled digital transformation, regulatory capability, and investment ecosystem readiness interact to influence sustainable knowledge-based growth. Using Oman Vision 2040 as a strategic contextual reference, the study argues that sustainable investment outcomes depend not only on AI adoption or digital infrastructure but also on governance quality, institutional trust, absorptive capacity, and technology transfer mechanisms.

The chapter further highlights regulatory capability as a strategic complement to AI, enabling higher-quality investment attraction, stronger partnership governance, and improved sustainability outcomes. By clarifying these interactions, the study contributes a conceptual foundation for future empirical research on AI-enabled investment ecosystems in emerging economies.

Limitations and Future Research

The conceptual and policy-analysis design prioritizes mechanism explanation over statistical generalization. Future research can extend this work through (a) comparative studies across GCC or emerging economies, (b) longitudinal tracking of investment quality indicators and technology transfer outcomes, and (c) mixed-method designs connecting qualitative mechanisms to measurable ecosystem performance outcomes.

Building on these limitations, several promising directions for future research emerge.

1. Comparative Validation

Future research should test the proposed framework through comparative studies across GCC countries and other emerging economies. Such analysis could examine how differences in institutional quality, regulatory capability, digital maturity, innovation-system development, and sustainability priorities influence AI-enabled investment ecosystem outcomes. Comparative research would help identify context-specific mechanisms, transferable policy practices, and boundary conditions, thereby strengthening the external validity of the framework.

2. Longitudinal and Mixed-Method Validation

Longitudinal and mixed-method studies are needed to examine how AI-enabled investment ecosystems evolve over time and to test the causal sequencing proposed in the framework. Future research could track changes in FDI quality, technology intensity, skill development, innovation outputs, local supplier participation, green investment, and sustainability performance. Qualitative process tracing could be combined with stakeholder surveys, econometric analysis, and secondary datasets to evaluate the relationships among AI capability, regulatory quality, investment outcomes, technology transfer, and sustainable development.

3. Stakeholder- and Firm-Level Validation

Further research should investigate how multinational enterprises, domestic firms, SMEs, regulators, investment authorities, and innovation intermediaries respond to AI-enabled ecosystem transformation. Firm-level studies could examine how AI influences investment decisions, how domestic firms develop absorptive capacity, and how partnerships support training, joint research, supplier upgrading, and knowledge transfer. Research should also assess regulatory experimentation, including sandboxes, adaptive governance, public–private collaboration, ESG integration, green finance, and sustainability-linked investment mechanisms, to clarify how stakeholder behaviour and institutional design shape ecosystem-level outcomes.

Conflict of Interest: The authors declare that they have no known financial or non-financial conflicts of interest that could have influenced this work.

Funding: This research received no specific grant from any public, commercial or not-for-profit funding agency.

REFERENCES

Abidi, N., El Herradi, M., & Sakha, S. (2023). Digitalization and resilience: Firm-level evidence during the COVID-19 pandemic. *Telecommunications Policy*, *47*(4), 102522. DOI: 10.1016/j.telpol.2023.102522 PMID: 37051116

Anzolin, G., Andreoni, A., & Zanfei, A. (2022). What is driving robotisation in the automotive value chain? Empirical evidence on the role of FDIs and domestic capabilities in technology adoption. *Technovation*, *115*, 102476. DOI: 10.1016/j.technovation.2022.102476

Birkstedt, T., Minkkinen, M., Tandon, A., & Mäntymäki, M. (2023). AI governance: Themes, knowledge gaps and future agendas. *Internet Research*, *33*(7), 133–167. DOI: 10.1108/INTR-01-2022-0042

Christnacht, L., & Mertzanis, C. (2025). Foreign direct investment, technology transfer and the global issuance of green bonds. *Energy Economics*, *143*, 108246. DOI: 10.1016/j.eneco.2025.108246

Cohen, W. M., & Levinthal, D. A. (1990). Absorptive capacity: A new perspective on learning and innovation. *Administrative Science Quarterly*, *35*(1), 128–152. DOI: 10.2307/2393553

Copestake, A., Estefania-Flores, J., & Furceri, D. (2024). Digitalization and resilience. *Research Policy*, *53*(3), 104948. DOI: 10.1016/j.respol.2023.104948

Cordeiro, C. M., Adomaitis, L., & Huang, L. (2026). The AI-policy-governance nexus: How regulation and AI shift corporate governance toward stakeholders. *Technology in Society*, *84*, 103117. DOI: 10.1016/j.techsoc.2025.103117

Damioli, G., & Marin, G. (2024). The effects of foreign entry on local innovation by entry mode. *Research Policy*, *53*(3), 104957. DOI: 10.1016/j.respol.2024.104957

de Almeida, P. G. R., & dos Santos Júnior, C. D. (2025). Artificial intelligence governance: Understanding how public organizations implement it. *Government Information Quarterly*, *42*(1), 102003. DOI: 10.1016/j.giq.2024.102003

Díaz-Rodríguez, N., Del Ser, J., Coeckelbergh, M., López de Prado, M., Herrera-Viedma, E., & Herrera, F. (2023). Connecting the dots in trustworthy artificial intelligence: From AI principles, ethics, and key requirements to responsible AI systems and regulation. *Information Fusion*, *99*, 101896. DOI: 10.1016/j.inffus.2023.101896 dos Santos, J. F. P., & Williamson, P. J. (2024). Beyond connectivity: Artificial intelligence and the internationalisation of digital firms. *Information and Organization, 34*(4), 100538. DOI: 10.1016/j.infoandorg.2024.100538

George, G., & Schillebeeckx, S. J. D. (2022). Digital transformation, sustainability, and purpose in the multinational enterprise. *Journal of World Business, 57*(3), 101326. DOI: 10.1016/j.jwb.2022.101326

Ghosh, S., Hughes, M., Hodgkinson, I., & Hughes, P. (2022). Digital transformation of industrial businesses: A dynamic capability approach. *Technovation, 113*, 102414. DOI: 10.1016/j.technovation.2021.102414

Goos, M., & Savona, M. (2024). Artificial intelligence governance: Regulating the responsible development and adoption of AI. *Research Policy, 53*(6), 104928. DOI: 10.1016/j.respol.2023.104928

Graef, I., & Prüfer, J. (2021). Governance of data sharing: A law & economics proposal. *Research Policy, 50*(9), 104330. DOI: 10.1016/j.respol.2021.104330

Guandalini, I. (2022). Sustainability through digital transformation: A systematic literature review for research guidance. *Journal of Business Research, 148*, 456–471. DOI: 10.1016/j.jbusres.2022.05.003

Hong, S., Reed, W. R., Tian, B., Wu, T., & Chen, G. (2021). Does FDI promote entrepreneurial activities? A meta-analysis. *World Development, 142*, 105436. DOI: 10.1016/j.worlddev.2021.105436

Hydrogen Oman. (2024). Oman Green Hydrogen Strategy.

Invest Oman. (n.d.). Oman investment incentive guide.

Lindner, T., Puck, J., & Puhr, H. (2025). Artificial intelligence in international business: IB theory under augmented decision-making. *Journal of World Business, 60*(6), 101676. DOI: 10.1016/j.jwb.2025.101676

Mikalef, P., & Gupta, M. (2021). Artificial intelligence capability: Conceptualization, measurement calibration, and empirical study on its impact on organizational creativity and firm performance. *Information & Management, 58*(3), 103434. DOI: 10.1016/j.im.2021.103434

Ministry of Commerce, Industry and Investment Promotion. (2019). Foreign Capital Investment Law, Royal Decree No. 50/2019.

Ministry of Transport, Communications and Information Technology. (2022). Personal Data Protection Law, Royal Decree No. 6/2022.

Ministry of Transport, Communications and Information Technology. (2024a). National Program for Artificial Intelligence and Advanced Digital Technologies: Oman AI & Digital Future Program 2024–2026.

Ministry of Transport, Communications and Information Technology. (2024b). Executive Regulations of the Personal Data Protection Law, Ministerial Decision No. 34/2024.

Ministry of Transport, Communications and Information Technology. (2025). Framework for National Data Governance.

Ministry of Transport, Communications and Information Technology. (n.d.). National Digital Economy Programme. Sultanate of Oman.

Nguyen, V. B. (2025). Digitalization's divergent impact on FDI inflows: A comparative analysis between advanced and developing countries. *Transnational Corporations Review*, *17*(3), 200148. DOI: 10.1016/j.tncr.2025.200148

Oman Vision 2040 Implementation Follow-up Unit. (2023). Oman Vision 2040 booklet.

Public Authority for Special Economic Zones and Free Zones. (2021). Launching electronic one-stop-shop services for special economic zones and free zones.

Rocha, M., Massard da Fonseca, E., Sauter, G. P., & Hasenclever, L. (2023). Vaccine technology transfer: Lessons from COVID-19 and implications for latecomer production capabilities. *Research Policy*, *52*(7), 104739. DOI: 10.1016/j.respol.2023.104739

Samuel, A., Johnston, K. A., & Hackney, R. (2022). Adaptive cognitive fit: A new approach to AI-assisted decision making in international business. *International Journal of Information Management*, *65*, 102505. DOI: 10.1016/j.ijinfomgt.2022.102505

Schmeisser, B., Saebi, T., Schotter, A. P. J., & Gooderham, P. (2026). The digital transformation of international business: A conceptualization, multidisciplinary review, and research agenda. *Journal of World Business*, *61*(1), 101695. DOI: 10.1016/j.jwb.2025.101695

Simms, C., & Frishammar, J. (2024). Technology transfer challenges in asymmetric alliances: An abductive multi-case study. *Technovation*, *133*, 102931. DOI: 10.1016/j.technovation.2023.102931

Simms, C. D., & Frishammar, J. (2024). Foreign direct investment and innovation policy: A review and research agenda. *Research Policy*, *53*(3), 104937. DOI: 10.1016/j.respol.2023.104937

Song, H., & Chen, W. (2023). Can two-way foreign direct investment promote green innovation capability in manufacturing? The threshold role of intellectual property protection. *Journal of Cleaner Production, 425*, 139035. DOI: 10.1016/j.jclepro.2023.139035

Suh, C. S., Li, W., & Song, Z. (2023). Digital trade policies and cross-border digital trade: The impact of data restrictions. *World Economy, 46*(9), 2569–2595. DOI: 10.1111/twec.13407

Wen, J., Hai, H., Li, L., Dou, J., & Tao, R. (2026). Digital finance as a catalyst for green innovation: Threshold effect of diminishing marginal returns. *International Review of Financial Analysis, 110*, 104840. DOI: 10.1016/j.irfa.2025.104840

Wirtz, B. W., Weyerer, J. C., & Kehl, I. (2022). Governance of artificial intelligence: A risk and guideline-based integrative framework. *Government Information Quarterly, 39*(4), 101685. DOI: 10.1016/j.giq.2022.101685

Yang, Z., Wu, F., & Yue, Z. (2026). Artificial intelligence technology and firms' OFDI: Evidence from China. *International Review of Economics & Finance, 106*, 104920. DOI: 10.1016/j.iref.2026.104920

Zahra, S. A., & George, G. (2002). Absorptive capacity: A review, reconceptualization, and extension. *Academy of Management Review, 27*(2), 185–203. DOI: 10.2307/4134351

Zhou, Y., Liu, X., Li, M., & Tang, Y. (2025). Leveraging AI and green finance for cleaner energy production: A sustainability framework for ESG integration and climate action. *Journal of Cleaner Production, 525*, 146595. DOI: 10.1016/j.jclepro.2025.146595

APPENDIX

Proposed Interview Guide and Empirical Validation Protocol

1. Ecosystem overview: How would you describe Oman's investment ecosystem changes since 2021 in relation to digital transformation and AI?
2. AI-enabled facilitation: Which AI or analytics tools are used in investment targeting, licensing, investor services, or aftercare?
3. FDI quality: How do you define "quality FDI"? What indicators are used?
4. Technology transfer: What mechanisms enable learning (training, R&D, supplier upgrading, standards transfer)? What are the main barriers?
5. Governance: What data governance and AI governance practices matter most for trust and predictability?
6. Sustainability: How is sustainability embedded in investment decisions, monitoring, and reporting?
7. Vision 2040: How are Vision 2040 priorities translated into operational requirements and metrics?
8. Risks/boundary conditions: What risks (skills, data access, accountability) could limit AI-enabled ecosystem performance?

Chapter 13
AI Applications and Organizational Sustainability:
Investment and Regulation in Telecommunications

Hussein Raafat Aljibori
http://orcid.org/0009-0006-2816-8480
University of Mosul, Iraq

Maysoon Abdullah Al Shalma
University of Mosul, Iraq

ABSTRACT

This chapter develops an interpretive framework for understanding how artificial intelligence (AI) applications may support organizational sustainability in the telecommunications sector. It views AI deployment as an organizational capability that helps convert data into decisions and actions. The chapter focuses on six applications—chatbots, dynamic pricing, targeted offers, advanced analytics, customer understanding, and content recommendation—and explains how they may contribute to economic, social, and environmental outcomes. It also argues that these outcomes are not automatic. Their value depends on several conditions, including data governance and quality, integration with work processes, skill readiness, organizational acceptance, ethical governance, transparency, measurement, monitoring, and learning. By organizing the discussion around a why, how, and when logic, the chapter offers a conceptual basis for future empirical research on AI-enabled sustainability in telecommunications.

DOI: 10.4018/979-8-3373-8964-6.ch013

INTRODUCTION

The rapid transformations in the contemporary business environment, from intense competition and market volatility to regulatory and societal pressures, indicate that organizational survival is no longer linked solely to achieving short-term profits, but rather to the ability to achieve organizational sustainability that balances economic performance, social commitment, and environmental responsibility, thus ensuring continuity, resilience, and adaptation to crises (Lozano, 2018). This logic gains even greater importance in the telecommunications sector, as it is a highly competitive, data-intensive service sector that is rapidly changing in customer preferences, and sensitive to operating costs and resource efficiency, making organizational sustainability a decisive condition for maintaining value rather than merely a managerial option (Lozano, 2018).

In parallel, artificial intelligence (AI) has become one of the most influential technological approaches in reshaping work methods and decision-making within organizations, as it enables organizations to transform data into actionable knowledge through prediction, analysis, automation, and personalization (Kaplan & Haenlein, 2018). Recent literature also confirms that AI has clear potential to support sustainability pathways; however, it may also lead to adverse effects if governance is absent or if the conditions and boundaries of impact realization are not systematically examined (Vinuesa et al., 2020; Dwivedi et al., 2021). In the telecommunications sector specifically, the role of AI is maximized due to the abundance of network and customer data and the multiple points of interaction, making its applications a direct tool for improving service quality, optimizing resources, and enhancing customer value. In this context, AI deployment is also relevant to investment and regulation, because sustainable digital transformation in telecommunications depends on the ability of firms to justify technology-related investments while complying with emerging governance, data protection, and AI accountability requirements. This leads to a logical assumption that adopting AI applications can support organizational sustainability across its economic, social, and environmental dimensions (Dwivedi et al., 2021). Despite the increasing scholarly interest in linking AI to sustainability, part of the literature still treats technology or AI as a general recommendation for performance improvement or digital transformation support, without constructing a clear explanation of the pathways through which technology impact is translated to organizational sustainability across its economic, social, and environmental dimensions (Amjad et al., 2021; Dwivedi et al., 2021). Moreover, a considerable portion of the literature focuses on partial outcomes, such as green sustainability or economic efficiency, rather than on a comprehensive explanation clarifying *why* the relationship is expected, *how* applications are transformed into value, and *when* the impact strengthens or weakens according to enabling conditions and organizational limitations (Vial, 2019; Vinuesa et al., 2020; Braganza et al., 2021). This observation is supported by systematic reviews indicating that the relationship between AI and sustainability is not homogeneous across organizations and sectors, and there remains a need to develop interpretive frameworks that clarify the pathways and conditions producing sustainable value instead of relying on general descriptive relationships (Amjad et al., 2021).

From a broader perspective, digital transformation literature shows that value generation from technology does not stem from merely possessing tools, but ***when*** technology is integrated into processes and decisions and linked to performance indicators and continuous feedback. This calls for building interpretive frameworks for value creation pathways and their enabling conditions rather than general recommendations (Vial, 2019). The importance of enabling/limiting conditions in AI is further strengthened in light of recent developments in governance, standards, and regulation. International standards for AI management systems outline requirements for risk control, transparency, and continuous improvement in organizational deployment of AI, implying that AI impact on sustainability cannot be assumed automatically but requires a clear managerial and governance system. (ISO/IEC, 2023) Updated international principles for AI also emphasize trustworthiness, addressing privacy and safety issues, and reducing bias, making ethical governance a foundational condition for achieving sustainable impact (OECD, 2024). This is further reinforced by modern organizational trends linking AI deployment to compliance, evaluation, and post-deployment monitoring as requirements that regulate output quality and mitigate risks (European Parliament & Council, 2024).

Accordingly, the research gap lies in the need for a conceptual interpretive framework linking the deployment of AI applications to organizational sustainability outcomes in the telecommunications sector in a way that avoids overgeneralization, clarifies the mechanisms generating impact, and specifies the conditions that govern AI strength and explain the variation of results across contexts, following a *why*, *how*, and *when* logic (Amjad et al., 2021; Dwivedi et al., 2021; Vial, 2019). In response to this gap, this chapter aims to develop a conceptual interpretive framework that explains the relationship between deploying AI applications and the dimensions of organizational sustainability in the telecommunications sector through a *why*, *how*, and *when* logic. This chapter is conceptual and interpretive rather than an empirical test. It provides: (1) a theoretical justification explaining why AI applications may be linked to organizational sustainability outcomes, (2) a decomposition of the relationship into interpretive mechanisms showing how applications are transformed into observable organizational value across the three sustainability dimensions, and (3) the identification of enabling/limiting conditions explaining when the impact strengthens or weakens, thereby helping the literature move from generalizing the relationship to building a more precise explanation suitable to the telecommunications sector (Gregor, 2006; Whetten, 1989).

Accordingly, the chapter is guided by the following research questions:

1. Why can AI applications be theoretically linked to organizational sustainability in telecommunications?
2. How do specific AI applications translate into economic, social, and environmental sustainability outcomes?
3. Under what organizational and governance conditions does the sustainability impact of AI become stronger or weaker?

The chapter is organized as follows. The first section presents the theoretical background of AI deployment and organizational sustainability. The second section explains the conceptual approach and framework development logic. The following sections discuss the why, how, and when dimensions of the proposed framework, develop theoretical propositions, and present the theoretical and practical implications. The chapter concludes with limitations and directions for future research.

1. CONCEPTUAL METHODOLOGY AND FRAMEWORK DEVELOPMENT APPROACH

This chapter adopts a conceptual and interpretive approach rather than an empirical research design. Its purpose is not to test statistical relationships, but to organize and explain how AI applications may contribute to organizational sustainability in the telecommunications sector. This approach is suitable because the relationship between AI and sustainability is still discussed in much of the literature in broad terms, while less attention has been given to the mechanisms and conditions that explain how such value is created.

The literature used in this chapter was selected to cover three related areas: artificial intelligence applications in organizations, organizational sustainability and the triple bottom line, and digital transformation and AI governance. Priority was given to studies that explain AI as an organizational capability, sustainability as a multidimensional outcome, and governance as a condition for responsible technology use. Telecommunications-related examples were also included to make the discussion more relevant to a data-intensive and service-oriented sector.

The framework was developed through a why, how, and when logic. The why dimension explains the theoretical justification for linking AI deployment to sustainability outcomes. The how dimension identifies the mechanisms through which six AI applications may generate economic, social, and environmental value. The when dimension identifies enabling and limiting conditions, such as data governance, process integration, skill readiness, ethical governance, transparency, measurement, monitoring, and organizational learning. This structure allows the chapter to move from a general discussion of AI and sustainability toward a more precise conceptual framework that can guide future empirical research.

2. THEORETICAL BACKGROUND AND CONCEPTUAL FOUNDATIONS

2.1 Conceptual Introduction: From Technology to Organizational Capability

In contemporary management literature, artificial intelligence (AI) is viewed as more than just a technical tool. It is presented as an organizational capability that enables the organization to transform data into actionable knowledge through analysis, prediction, automation, and personalization (Kaplan & Haenlein, 2018). The importance of this capability lies in its ability to enhance decision quality, improve operational efficiency, accelerate responsiveness, and optimize service design (Davenport & Ronanki, 2018). A number of authors suggest that value does not arise from simply possessing AI technologies, but from the way they are integrated into decision-making and daily work to achieve a balance between automation and human support (Jarrahi, 2018), through integration rather than isolated deployment of technology (Raisch & Krakowski, 2021).

Recent studies also indicate that deploying AI as an organizational capability can become a driver of sustainable value when it translates into improvements in efficiency, the reduction of waste, and the enhancement of quality (Enholm et al., 2022). This notion is supported by analytics management frameworks that link data-driven decision-making to improved operational performance (Davenport & Harris, 2007). Within this context, it is noted that building digital capabilities, including AI, also requires a strategic vision and the ability to reshape organizational routines to achieve long-term impact (Iansiti & Lakhani, 2020).

2.2 Why Is the Telecommunications Sector Specifically a Suitable Context for Deploying Artificial Intelligence Applications?

The telecommunications sector enjoys a number of characteristics that make its deployment of AI particularly meaningful. It is a data-intensive sector with multiple points of customer interaction, and it is characterized by rapidly changing demand, cost sensitivity, and the need for efficient resource use (Bharadwaj et al., 2013). These characteristics make AI applications a direct channel for improving service, reducing response times, reshaping allocation and pricing, and enhancing network operations (Dwivedi et al., 2021). Digital transformation literature emphasizes that value is realized when technology is linked to processes, performance indicators, and clear feedback, so that technology translates into long-term operational value within the organization (Fitzgerald et al., 2014). This supports the argument for interpreting the organizational impact of technology through operational integration and work pattern changes, rather than through isolated technological adoption (Kane et al., 2015). This perspective supports the understanding of *why* the telecommunications sector, in particular, provides a suitable context for testing the logic of value creation from AI in a highly competitive and rapidly changing environment (Vial, 2019).

2.3 Operational Definition of AI Deployment

For the purposes of this chapter, AI deployment is not treated as a general concept, but rather refers to the operational deployment of AI through its main applications in the telecommunications sector, meaning the translation of AI capabilities into tangible operational practices within the organization (Iansiti & Lakhani, 2020). Accordingly, this chapter adopts an operational representation of deployment through six common applications relevant to the telecommunications context, including chatbots, dynamic pricing, targeted offers, advanced analytics, customer understanding, and content recommendation (Dwivedi et al., 2021). This operational definition reduces the generality of the concept and transforms it into an interpretable, actionable scope that can be linked to specific organizational outcomes (Enholm et al., 2022). It is also consistent with the view that AI derives value when translated into operational uses that affect decision-making, service delivery, and personalization (Kaplan & Haenlein, 2018).

2.4 Brief Description of the Six Applications and Their Conceptual Relevance

- *Chatbots* serve as an entry point for automating service interactions, improving service continuity, enhancing response quality, and reducing the load on call centers, making them suitable for explaining direct impacts on cost, quality, and customer satisfaction (Følstad & Brandtzæg, 2017). Applied studies on conversational technologies support this logic by highlighting their role in increasing efficiency and enhancing user experience (Adamopoulou & Moussiades, 2020).

- *Dynamic pricing* reflects the use of analytics and prediction to enhance pricing decision efficiency and manage revenue according to changes in demand and capacity (den Boer, 2015). Revenue management literature emphasizes that this practice becomes more effective when governed by clear rules that consider the sustainability of customer relationships (Phillips, 2021), and it is supported through the link between pricing, capacity management, and revenue in the telecommunications sector (Jallat & Ancarani, 2008).
- *Targeted offers* translate behavioral data into marketing customization that reduces waste and improves resource efficiency through algorithmic targeting (Wedel & Kannan, 2016). Effective customization requires avoiding negative consequences arising from excessive or unwanted targeting (Lambrecht & Tucker, 2019).
- *Advanced analytics* provides the knowledge foundation that improves forecasting, planning, resource allocation, and fault reduction, thereby enhancing operational efficiency (Wamba et al., 2015), which conforms to the logic of data-driven decision-making in management (Davenport & Harris, 2007).
- *Customer understanding* acts as a channel for improving experience quality, building trust, and reducing friction throughout the customer journey (Lemon & Verhoef, 2016).
- Finally, *content recommendation* represents the peak of personalization logic by converting understanding and analysis into immediate suggestions that maximize experiential value and support efficiency (Ricci et al., 2015). Recent models have reinforced this approach by demonstrating the effect of recommendations on engagement and relevance (Zhang et al., 2019).

Together, these six applications form a suitable conceptual foundation because they collectively address service, pricing, customization, analytics, and customer experience in an interconnected manner that can be directly linked to organizational sustainability outcomes.

2.5 Organizational Sustainability and Its Three Dimensions

2.5.1 Conceptual Roots of Organizational Sustainability: The Logic of Balance and Continuity

The concept of sustainability has evolved from a narrow environmental focus to an integrated perspective linking economic performance, social commitment, and environmental responsibility, within an approach concerned with organizational continuity and long-term value for stakeholders (Eccles et al., 2014). The concept of sustainable development as a global reference framework is one of the foundational roots that contributed to establishing the organizational sustainability concept (World Commission On Environment and Development, 1987). In management studies, this evolution has been associated with stakeholder approaches, corporate social responsibility, and the natural resource-based view, demonstrating that organizational sustainability is not a slogan but a managerial logic that balances market demands with social and environmental considerations within measurable decisions (Freeman, 1984). Corporate Social Responsibility (CSR) literature has reinforced this logic within organizations as a multidimensional commitment (Carroll, 1991), while the natural resource-based view adds another dimension linking competitive advantage to resource and environmental responsibility (Hart, 1995).

To frame this balance, the Triple Bottom Line (TBL) approach is widely used as one of the most prominent organizational frameworks for understanding sustainability within the organization (Elkington, 1997; WCED, 1987; Lozano, 2015).

2.5.2 Operational Definition of Organizational Sustainability

This chapter conceptualizes organizational sustainability as a dependent variable measured across three interconnected dimensions:

1. **The economic dimension**: associated with efficiency, waste reduction, productivity improvement, and revenue sustainability.
2. **The social dimension**: related to service quality, trust, inclusiveness, and responsibility toward beneficiaries, employees, and society.
3. **The environmental dimension**: concerned with resource optimization, reduction of negative impacts, energy efficiency, and waste minimization (Lozano, 2018).

This division represents a practical extension of the Triple Bottom Line approach as a common framework for organizational sustainability (Elkington, 1997), emphasizing that reporting and measurement should rely on clear indicators linking performance in the organization to all three dimensions (Global Reporting Initiative [GRI], 2021). Literature on sustainable business models further supports the idea that sustainability must be translated into operational practices and measurements rather than remaining a general term (Bocken et al., 2014; Han et al., 2011).

Recent discussions on sustainable AI also emphasize that digital technologies themselves may generate environmental pressures through energy-intensive computing processes, data center expansion, and increasing infrastructure demands. Accordingly, the environmental contribution of AI should be evaluated not only through efficiency gains and optimization outcomes, but also through the organization's ability to manage energy consumption, electronic waste, and the long-term environmental implications associated with digital operations.

2.6 Interpretive Logic and Framework Development: Why, How, and When

After defining the operational meaning of both AI deployment through its applications in telecommunications and organizational sustainability across its three dimensions, the chapter proceeds to build the interpretive logic addressing: ***Why*** would a relationship between the two variables be expected? ***How*** do the six applications generate observable value across the economic, social, and environmental dimensions? And *when* does the impact strengthen or weaken according to enabling conditions and organizational boundaries?

This aligns with the logic of the theoretical contribution of this chapter in emphasizing the importance of explaining *how* and *why* in interpreting relationships rather than confining the discussion to describing them (Whetten, 1989), and the classification of theoretical research highlighting the role of interpretive frameworks in generating testable propositions (Gregor, 2006). This approach is also supported by digital transformation literature, which emphasizes that value is determined by conditions of integration and measurement within the organization, not merely by the existence of technology (Vial, 2019).

3. THEORETICAL JUSTIFICATION OF THE RELATIONSHIP: WHY AI DEPLOYMENT IS LINKED TO ORGANIZATIONAL SUSTAINABILITY

The literature suggests that the relationship between AI deployment and organizational sustainability should not be presented as a general descriptive correlation, but rather understood through the economic, social, and environmental dimensions, requiring a theoretical rationale that explains *why* the effect is expected in the first place.

On one hand, Kaplan and Haenlein (2018) note that AI reshapes work and decision-making through analytics, prediction, automation, and personalization, fundamentally altering the operational logic within the organization. On the other hand, organizational sustainability is understood as the organization's ability to generate long-term value by balancing economic, social, and environmental considerations in its decisions and resources (Lozano, 2018).

Multidisciplinary reviews emphasize that AI's impact does not arise solely from the technology itself, but from how value is generated through it, its limitations, and the conditions under which it operates (Dwivedi et al., 2021). Therefore, incorporating the question of *why* becomes a necessary interpretive step to justify the transition of AI from applications to observable sustainable value, noting that this value may reverse into negative effects if governance is absent or if AI is misused (Vinuesa et al., 2020).

3.1 From Technology to the Logic of Sustainable Value

This chapter is grounded in the interpretive assumption that AI deployment does not represent a transient operational improvement, but an organizational capability that can reshape how value is created across economic, social, and environmental dimensions by converting data into measurable decisions and actions (Davenport & Ronanki, 2018). When predictions, analytics, automation, and personalization translate into efficiency gains, improved service quality, and the optimized use of resources, it becomes reasonable to expect a correlation between AI and organizational sustainability outcomes. This conforms to the digital transformation logic, which asserts that value emerges when technology is integrated into decision-making and operations and linked to performance metrics and continuous improvement, rather from simply possessing advanced tools (Vial, 2019). At the same time, AI literature indicates that organizational impact is also determined by the management of ethical and governance risks, as unmitigated risks can undermine trust, legitimacy, and ultimately sustainability itself (Dwivedi et al., 2021; Vinuesa et al., 2020). Based on this reasoning, the research outlines the theoretical foundations explaining the relationship between AI deployment and organizational sustainability across its three dimensions.

3.2 Triple Bottom Line Logic and Balanced Sustainability

The expected relationship between AI and organizational sustainability is first justified by understanding sustainability as a balance across three dimensions: economic, social, and environmental. Any organizational capability that improves efficiency, quality, and resource optimization is therefore likely to impact this balance. The Triple Bottom Line provides a foundational framework for deriving this meaning within management research (Elkington, 1997). This perspective reinforces the view in organizational sustainability literature that considers sustainability not as a slogan but as an organizational construct requiring clear conceptual definition and a framework guiding measurement and monitoring (Lozano, 2018). At the level of indicators and reporting, translating sustainability into practice typically relies on observable and comparable economic, social, and environmental indicators, establishing the logic linking organizational capability to outcomes (Global Reporting Initiative [GRI], 2021).

3.3 Stakeholder Perspective and Social Legitimacy

The second *why* logic is reinforced through the stakeholder perspective, which assumes that an organization's long-term sustainability depends on its ability to generate balanced value for multiple parties, including customers, employees, society, and regulators, instead of concentrating on short-term profit (Freeman, 1984). Consequently, when AI deployment enhances service quality, accelerates response times, improves customer experience, and supports inclusiveness, it may strengthen the social dimension of sustainability by building trust and reinforcing legitimacy. However, the literature argues that this effect may be reversed in the absence of safeguards, particularly regarding privacy, bias, and discrimination, making the relationship nonlinear and contingent on risk management (Vinuesa et al., 2020). Therefore, the *why* should be interpreted as a logic that requires governance to minimize potential negative effects and maintain institutional trust (Dwivedi et al., 2021).

3.4 Resource-Based and Capability-Based Views

From a third angle, the resource- and capability-based views explain *why* AI can support organizational sustainability, as it improves resource investment efficiency and reduces waste by enhancing decision-making, prediction, and resource allocation. The natural-resource -based view indicates that competitive advantage and sustainability can be achieved when the organization develops capabilities that minimize negative impacts and enhance efficiency in resource use (Hart, 1995). Similarly, sustainable business model literature suggests that creating sustainable value requires mechanisms that reduce waste and link innovation to efficiency improvements and resource reallocation (Bocken et al., 2014). Accordingly, AI deployment, as an analytical, predictive, and automating capability, acts as a mechanism to maximize efficiency and reduce operational errors and waste, reflecting both economic and environmental dimensions simultaneously, particularly in data-intensive sectors such as telecommunications (Davenport & Harris, 2007).

3.5 Sustainability as Governance, Measurement, and Accountability

Finally, the relationship between AI and sustainability is justified from the perspective that organizational sustainability is not automatic but is an outcome requiring governance, measurement, and monitoring to prevent short-term economic gains from undermining the social or environmental dimensions. Literature shows that highly sustainable organizations integrate sustainability into governance, strategy, and performance indicators, transforming it into a sustained practice instead of isolated initiatives (Eccles et al., 2014). Measurement and reporting are essential for embedding practices and converting them into repeatable, improvable outcomes (GRI, 2021). Contemporary literature emphasizes that for AI to generate positive and sustainable impact, it must be managed within clear controls related to risks, transparency, and continuous improvement; otherwise, it may become a source of distrust or inequality that undermines sustainability itself (Dwivedi et al., 2021). Hence, the *why* in this chapter is based on the notion that AI can support organizational sustainability by enhancing measurable value creation provided it is managed with governance, measurement, and accountability.

Based on these four foundations, the research proceeds to uncover the relationship at the level of interpretive mechanisms to answer the question of *how* the six AI applications translate into observable outcomes across the economic, social, and environmental dimensions of organizational sustainability, before moving to the *when* conditions that adjust the strength of the relationship and explain variance across different telecommunications contexts (Dwivedi et al., 2021; Vial, 2019).

3.6 Proposed Interpretive Framework and Its Components

Based on the interpretive logic of (*why*, *how*, and *when*) this chapter proposes a conceptual framework illustrating the transmission of AI deployment effects, as the independent variable, to organizational sustainability dimensions, as the dependent variable. This transmission is not automatic or uniform; but, it occurs through interpretive mechanisms (*how*) explaining the pathways through which applications generate organizational value, and is strengthened or weakened according to enabling/limiting conditions (*when*) that govern the relationship (Vial, 2019; Dwivedi et al., 2021; Lozano, 2018; Elkington, 1997).

To clarify, the framework does not include an independent mediator variable. Mechanisms are presented as interpretive pathways, and conditions as enabling/limiting factors, not as mediators. Figure (1) visually illustrates the proposed interpretive framework, showing the (*how*) pathways and (*when*) conditions that shape the strength of the relationship without assuming a mediator.

Figure 1. Proposed Interpretive Framework Linking AI Deployment to Organizational Sustainability Dimensions via Impact Mechanisms (How) and Enabling Conditions (When)

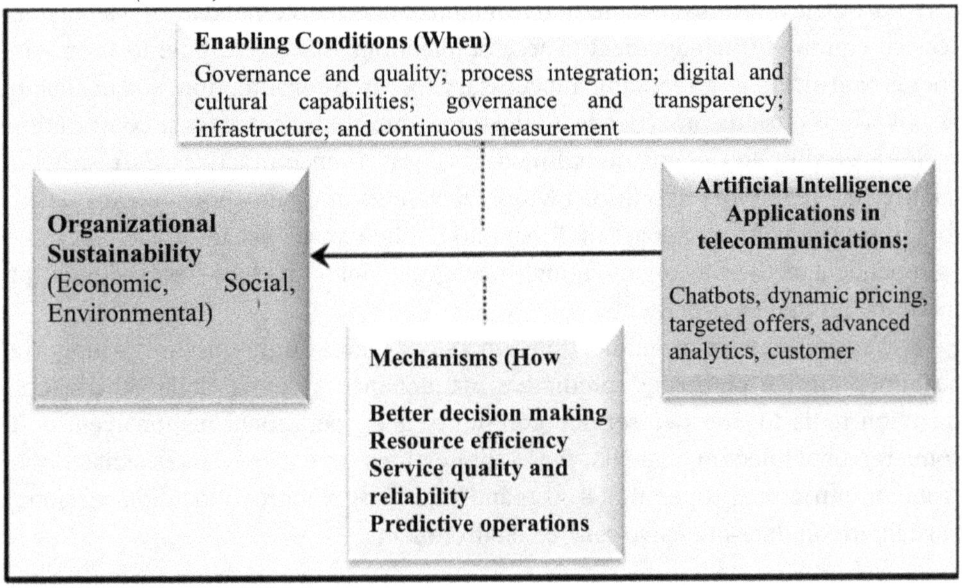

Source: *prepared by the Author.*

Figure (1) illustrates that AI deployment in the telecommunications sector using chatbots, dynamic pricing, targeted offers, advanced analytics, customer understanding, and content recommendation does not reflect a simple linear relationship with organizational sustainability that automatically produces this sustainability. Instead, it represents an interpretive relationship in which value flows from deploying these applications to the three sustainability dimensions through specific pathways. From a digital transformation perspective, value is realized when technology is integrated into operations and decision-making and linked to measurable outcomes, rather than the possession of advanced tools alone. Multidisciplinary AI literature emphasizes that the outcomes of these applications vary across organizational contexts and that explaining the impact requires attention to the *how* mechanisms and *when* conditions that may enhance or constrain the effect (Dwivedi et al., 2021). Accordingly, this chapter adopts a *why/how/when* interpretive logic: the *how* component presents mechanisms that explain the pathways through which AI applications generate organizational value, while the *when* component identifies enabling/limiting conditions that regulate the strength of the relationship and account for variations in outcomes across data-intensive, rapidly changing telecommunications contexts.

In practical telecommunications environments, AI applications are increasingly associated with operational and sustainability-related objectives. Telecom operators have begun to rely on AI-supported systems in areas such as customer interaction, network traffic optimization, predictive maintenance, recommendation systems, and service continuity management. These applications may contribute to improving operational efficiency, reducing unnecessary resource consumption, and enhancing responsiveness to customer needs. At the same time, the extent of these contributions varies according to organizational readiness, governance practices, infrastructure quality, and regulatory conditions within each telecommunications market. Therefore, the sustainability impact of AI should not be viewed as automatic, but rather as dependent on the way organizations manage and integrate these technologies into their operational environments.

For example, telecommunications operators increasingly utilize AI-supported customer service platforms, predictive maintenance systems, and network optimization tools to improve service continuity and operational responsiveness. In some regional telecom contexts, these applications have also been associated with reducing unnecessary operational costs and improving resource allocation efficiency, particularly in data-intensive service environments.

4. INTERPRETIVE IMPACT MECHANISMS: HOW DO AI APPLICATIONS TRANSLATE INTO SUSTAINABLE OUTCOMES?

As shown in Figure (1), within the interpretive framework of this chapter, the impact of AI deployment on organizational sustainability is not a simple direct relationship; rather, it manifests as transformation paths that explain how application outputs translate into observable organizational value across economic, social, and environmental dimensions. This perspective reflects the idea that AI, when organizationally embedded, operates as a decision-making and process enhancing capability through analytics, automation, and personalization, rather than as an isolated technological tool (Kaplan & Haenlein, 2018). The value of this capability materializes when it is translated into operational logic within service, pricing, marketing, and personalization, that is, when its outputs become embedded in daily decisions and workflow processes (Davenport & Ronanki, 2018). Accordingly, the six mechanisms presented below are treated as contextually appropriate interpretive channels for the data-intensive and customer interactive telecommunications sector, consistent with literature emphasizing the balance between automation and human support within organizations (Raisch & Krakowski, 2021).

4.1 First Mechanism: Chatbots for Improving Service Reliability and Reducing Interaction Costs

Chatbots contribute to transforming AI into sustainable value by automating a large share of repetitive tasks and inquiries and providing immediate, timely responses, thereby enhancing service continuity and reducing pressure on call centers. Literature shows that when efficiently designed, chatbots can improve user experience quality and response speed, which in turn enhances operational efficiency and reduces costs (Følstad & Brandtzæg, 2017). This mechanism operates by shifting human resources toward more complex, value-added interactions, thus optimizing the balance between automated efficiency and human support (Raisch & Krakowski, 2021).

Chatbot applications have also been shown to reduce operational workload and deliver consistent support. This can support the economic dimension through reduced operational waste and the social dimension through shorter waiting times, reduced friction, and improved satisfaction (Adamopoulou & Moussiades, 2020). From a service experience management perspective, minimizing pain points in the customer journey enhances trust and relationship quality, making this mechanism a clear channel for strengthening social sustainability in telecommunications (Lemon & Verhoef, 2016). However, effectiveness remains contingent on training quality and the institutional knowledge embedded in the system to prevent misleading or confusing responses, consistent with literature warning against ungoverned AI deployment (Dwivedi et al., 2021; Gnewuch et al., 2017; Jain et al., 2018).

4.2 Second Mechanism: Dynamic Pricing for Revenue Management and Achieving a Demand–Capacity Fit

Dynamic pricing functions as an interpretive mechanism as it explains how predictive and analytical capabilities translate into more efficient pricing decisions by matching prices with changes in demand, capacity, and customer segments. Literature indicates that dynamic pricing models reduce inefficiencies associated with rigid pricing and support revenue management in closer alignment with market realities (den Boer, 2015). Revenue management research further confirms that integrating modeling and analytics into pricing decisions enhances financial sustainability, particularly in industries characterized by demand variability and operational constraints (Phillips, 2021). In telecommunications, this aligns with revenue and capacity management logic, improving revenue sustainability without relying solely on costly physical expansion, thereby directly supporting the economic dimension of sustainability (Jallat & Ancarani, 2008). Since pricing affects perceived fairness and customer trust, recent literature emphasizes the importance of transparency and the avoidance of bias or discriminatory pricing practices that could harm the social dimension and undermine legitimacy (Dwivedi et al., 2021). This conforms to the updated AI governance principles stressing reliability and fairness (OECD, 2024; Ferreira et al., 2016).

4.3 Third Mechanism: Targeted Offers to Reduce Marketing Waste and Improve Resource Efficiency

Targeted offers illustrate how customer data can be transformed into marketing personalization that reduces random targeting and campaign waste by directing offers to more responsive segments instead of incurring unproductive expenditure. Analytical marketing literature demonstrates that data-driven personalization increases spending efficiency and response probability compared to generalized campaigns (Wedel & Kannan, 2016). From a social perspective, the value of this mechanism increases when targeting is based on refined behavioral understanding without excessive intrusion or privacy violation, since over- personalization may generate negative perceptions or marketing fatigue (Lambrecht & Tucker, 2019). Environmentally, reducing ineffective campaigns lowers resource waste associated with digital operations and supporting infrastructures. Thus, personalization may be interpreted as a resource optimization approach when linked to clear efficiency and waste indicators (Global Reporting Initiative [GRI], 2021). In this sense, targeted offers operationalize the principle of generating greater value with fewer resources, a core element in interpreting organizational sustainability.

4.4 Fourth Mechanism: Advanced Analytics for Enhancing Decision Quality, Reducing Failures, and Optimizing Resource Allocation

Analytics represent a central mechanism explaining how AI becomes an organizational capability supporting decision-making, planning, and resource allocation based on evidence rather than intuition. Advanced analytical approaches enhance demand forecasting, pattern detection, resource distribution, and operational error reduction, directly contributing to economic efficiency and continuity (Davenport & Harris, 2007). Big data and analytics literature highlights their impact when integrated into operational decision-making rather than remaining descriptive reporting tools (Wamba et al., 2015). In telecommunications, data intensity amplifies this importance, as analytics can improve network management, reduce service disruptions, and optimize capacity management. This supports the social dimension through improved service quality and the environmental dimension through energy and resource optimization associated with reduced operational failures (Vinuesa et al., 2020). Thus, analytics function as a decision mechanism linking knowledge to sustainability through uncertainty reduction and efficiency in resource use, while recognizing that output quality depends on data quality and governance (Dwivedi et al., 2021).

4.5 Fifth Mechanism: Customer Understanding for Strengthening Trust, Inclusion, and Experience

Customer understanding explains how AI tools generate sustainable social impact by enhancing the organization's ability to interpret customer needs, identify pain points, and improve responsiveness across channels, thereby strengthening trust and reducing exclusion resulting from standardized service models (Lemon & Verhoef, 2016). Economically, deeper customer insight supports customer retention, reduces churn, and improves customer lifetime value, particularly when experience management is consistent across customer interfaces, as consistency reduces friction and strengthens loyalty (Vial, 2019).

However, this pathway is sensitive to privacy and fairness concerns, since expanded behavioral analysis may produce adverse effects if ethical safeguards are absent or discriminatory practices emerge, as emphasized in multidisciplinary AI research (Dwivedi et al., 2021). Contemporary regulatory developments also impose greater responsibility on organizations deploying high-impact AI systems, particularly in processing user data and behavioral insights (European Parliament & Council, 2024; Kumar & Reinartz, 2018; Rust & Huang, 2014; Verhoef et al., 2015).

4.6 Sixth Mechanism: Content Recommendation for Personalizing Experience and Maximizing Interaction Value Efficiently

Content recommendation represents the peak of personalization logic. It explains how analytical and behavioral insights translate into immediate suggestions that enhance service relevance and deepen engagement, thereby supporting performance sustainability by improving customer experience while reducing time and resources required for accessing appropriate services (Ricci et al., 2015). Behavior-based recommendation models have been shown to increase relevance, improve satisfaction, and strengthen engagement, linking directly to the social dimension through enhanced experience quality and service trust (Zhang et al., 2019). At the same time, digital efficiency reduces waste by guiding customers toward suitable options rather than random navigation, supporting economic efficiency logic. The value of this mechanism increases when integrated into clear performance indicators and continuous feedback systems linking digital performance to sustainability outcomes, since what is not measured cannot be managed or improved (Global Reporting Initiative [GRI],

2021). Linking recommendation systems to performance and experience metrics transforms them from technical features into long-term operational practices (Vial, 2019; Gomez-Uribe & Hunt, 2016).

As reflected in Figure 1, this section explains how impact pathways emerge from AI deployment. However, their realization is not uniform across telecommunications companies; rather, it depends on enabling/limiting conditions that determine *when* the effect strengthens or weakens. These conditions include data governance, data quality, integration of applications into processes and decisions, skill readiness, organizational acceptance, as well as ethical governance, transparency, measurement, and continuous monitoring (Dwivedi et al., 2021; ISO/IEC, 2023).

5. ENABLING AND BOUNDARY CONDITIONS: WHEN IS THE IMPACT OF AI APPLICATIONS ON ORGANIZATIONAL SUSTAINABILITY MAXIMIZED?

Extending the logic of the interpretive framework in this chapter, Figure (1) illustrates that the *how* pathways do not operate with equal strength across all telecommunications firms. Sustainable value does not emerge from possessing intelligent tools, but when the organization is able to translate analytical outputs into measurable operational decisions and actions in service, pricing, marketing, and network operations (Davenport & Ronanki, 2018). Digital transformation literature confirms that value creation from technology requires linking technological capabilities to processes, performance indicators, and feedback loops; otherwise, the initiative remains without long-term impact (Vial, 2019). Similarly, multidisciplinary research indicates that AI effects may support sustainability or generate organizational and social risks depending on governance, readiness, and controls after deployment (Dwivedi et al., 2021). Accordingly, the *when* dimension is understood here as enabling/limiting conditions that regulate the strength of the relationship between AI deployment and organizational sustainability, as summarized in Figure (1).

5.1 Data Governance and Data Quality

The impact of AI deployment on organizational sustainability intensifies when effective data governance ensures data accuracy, consistency, timeliness, and reliability. The six applications, from chatbots to dynamic pricing and recommendation systems, depend on sound data to avoid flawed decisions or misleading outputs that may increase costs or erode trust (Dwivedi et al., 2021). In the data-intensive telecommunications environment, governance is not confined to a set of prescribed steps; rather it is an organizational condition determining its ability to convert data into actionable knowledge within daily decision-making, thereby influencing economic efficiency and service quality as a social value (Vial, 2019). Contemporary standards for AI management systems further reinforce this logic by emphasizing risk management, documented controls, and continuous improvement to ensure reliable and safe outcomes (ISO/IEC, 2023; Khatri & Brown, 2010; Otto, 2011). Data governance prevents decision deviation, but maximizing impact requires transforming AI from a technical initiative into an operationally embedded practice.

5.2 Integration of AI into Processes and Decisions Rather Than as a Separate Project

The impact of artificial intelligence strengthens when AI is integrated into actual workflows, such as customer service, pricing, marketing, and network operations and its outputs become part of daily decision-making not confined to technical departments (Vial, 2019). Digital transformation literature emphasizes that value creation requires process redesign and alignment between technology, performance indicators, and feedback mechanisms, ensuring that technology becomes a source of sustained value rather than a temporary achievement (Fitzgerald et al., 2014). Operational integration also reduces waste associated with disconnected projects and increases measurability and continuous performance improvement across the three sustainability dimensions, consistent with sustainability reporting logic linking practices to defined indicators (Global Reporting Initiative [GRI], 2021; Hammer, 1990). However, operational integration alone is insufficient without human capability and organizational acceptance, as many AI failures stem from skill gaps and misinterpretation of outputs.

5.3 Skill Readiness and Organizational Acceptance

AI impact intensifies when organizations possess the skills required to interpret model outputs and apply them in decision-making, alongside organizational acceptance that reduces resistance to change and ensures actual usage (Raisch & Krakowski, 2021). Research suggests that AI may increase complexity if adoption is not managed through capability development, clear role definition, and avoidance of uncritical reliance on automated outputs (Braganza et al., 2021). In comparable local contexts, an applied study in Iraq found that AI impact depends on actual use, acceptance, and appropriate handling of technology more than on its availability as a technology (Ramo et al., 2022). Thus, this condition fundamentally determines *when* applications translate into sustainable value rather than becoming an organizational burden or source of internal resistance (Tambe et al., 2019). Even with skills and acceptance, a critical safeguard remains necessary to prevent adverse social effects: ethical governance and transparency.

5.4 Ethical Governance and Transparency

The impact of AI on organizational sustainability intensifies when applications operate within an ethical and transparent framework that minimizes risks of bias, discrimination, and privacy violations; as such risks directly undermine the social dimension of sustainability by eroding trust and legitimacy (Dwivedi et al., 2021). This condition becomes particularly sensitive in applications such as dynamic pricing, personalization, and targeted offers, where unfair outcomes may emerge if decision rules are not properly governed and accountability mechanisms are absent (OECD, 2024). Recent European regulatory developments reflect a clear emphasis on risk management, monitoring, transparency, and accountability requirements, reinforcing this condition as a practical determinant of *when* AI supports sustainability rather than generating sustainability-related risks (European Parliament and Council, 2024; European Commission, 2019; Floridi & Cowls, 2019; European Parliament and Council, 2016; NIST, 2023; Mehrabi et al., 2021). Finally, even with governance and readiness, organizational sustainability cannot be ensured without measurement, monitoring, and institutional learning that preserve balance across the three dimensions over time.

5.5 Measurement, Monitoring, and Organizational Learning

AI impact intensifies when organizations establish clear measurement indicators linking each of the six applications to the three organizational sustainability outcomes. Without measurement, continuous improvement becomes impossible and gains remain temporary (GRI, 2021).

Digital transformation literature highlights that monitoring and feedback loops are essential for converting technological initiatives into sustained value through model adjustment, improved decision quality, and performance-outcome alignment (Vial, 2019). Modern AI management standards likewise emphasize periodic review, risk assessment, and continuous improvement to ensure reliable outcomes and minimize unintended consequences (ISO/IEC, 2023). This condition ensures that short-term economic gains do not occur at the expense of social or environmental dimensions but are managed within an observable sustainability balance (ISO, 2018).

The interpretive framework presented in this chapter is completed by combining transformation pathways (*how*) with enabling and boundary conditions (*when*), as summarized in Figure 1. This integration allows the formulation of theoretical propositions that translate the conceptual model into statements suitable for subsequent empirical testing within the telecommunications sector. This step aligns with the logic of theoretical contribution emphasizing the development of testable explanations rather than mere descriptive relationships (Whetten, 1989). Theory in information systems research is considered a generator of empirically testable propositions (Gregor, 2006).

6. THEORETICAL PROPOSITIONS

Based on the proposed explanatory framework summarized in Figure (1), the following propositions are presented to transform the (*why*, *how*, and *when*) logic into theoretically grounded statements that can be empirically tested in future field studies within the telecommunications sector. This chapter assumes that the deployment of artificial intelligence applications does not automatically generate sustainable outcomes. Such outcomes emerge through operational transformation mechanisms that explain *how* results are produced, while the strength of this effect depends on enabling/limiting conditions that explain when the impact intensifies or weakens (Gregor, 2006; Whetten, 1989).

This approach is consistent with the literature on AI in organizations, which emphasizes that value is realized when model outputs are translated into measurable decisions and actions embedded within daily operations (Davenport & Ronanki, 2018). It also aligns with the idea that human support/ automation balance is essential for sustaining value in addition to the speeding of processes (Raisch & Krakowski, 2021).

Proposition 1: The Logic of Sustainable Value Creation (*Why*)

P1: When AI applications are deployed in the telecommunications sector to transform data into measurable operational decisions and actions, the organization's ability to enhance its sustainability across economic, social, and environmental dimensions increases.

This occurs because such deployment improves resource efficiency, reduces waste, and enhances service quality, thereby strengthening long-term organizational continuity. This proposition builds on the view that AI reshapes decision-making and work processes through analytics, prediction, automation, and personalization (Kaplan & Haenlein, 2018). The value of AI increases when it is managed within an organized operational and cognitive logic (Iansiti & Lakhani, 2020), while acknowledging that its ultimate impact on sustainability depends on how it is governed and deployed (Vinuesa et al., 2020).

Since P1 clarifies ***why*** the relationship is expected under the logic of sustainable value creation, the subsequent propositions detail ***how*** the six specific applications translate into observable sustainability outcomes.

Proposition 2: Chatbots → Service Quality and Reliability (*How*)

P2: The deployment of chatbots enhances organizational sustainability by improving service continuity, response speed, and reliability (Følstad & Brandtzæg, 2017). This supports the social dimension through increased customer satisfaction and trust (Lemon & Verhoef, 2016), and supports the economic dimension through lower interaction costs and lower operational pressure on call centers (Adamopoulou & Moussiades, 2020).

Proposition 3: Dynamic Pricing → Revenue Efficiency and Sustainable Price Decision (*How*)

P3: The deployment of AI-supported dynamic pricing increases organizational sustainability by improving revenue management efficiency, reducing pricing loss, and matching demand with capacity (den Boer, 2015).This strengthens the economic dimension through more adaptive and analytically grounded pricing decisions (Phillips, 2021).

The effect may also extend to the social dimension when pricing is managed under fairness and transparency safeguards, thereby avoiding unjust discriminatory pricing practices, particularly when revenue management is linked to capacity and return optimization in telecommunications (Jallat & Ancarani, 2008).

Proposition 4: Targeted Offers → Marketing Waste Reduction and Increase Matching (*How*)

P4: The deployment of targeted offers enhances organizational sustainability by reducing marketing waste, improving spending efficiency, and increasing customer retention. This supports the economic dimension by shifting from broad, undifferentiated spending to data-driven personalization (Wedel & Kannan, 2016). Targeted offers may also support the social dimension when personalization leads to more relevant offers, reduces customer irritation, enhances the customer experience, and promotes digital inclusion when the needs of different segments are properly considered (Lambrecht & Tucker, 2019).

Proposition 5: Advanced Analytics → Decision Quality and Resource Optimization (How)

P5: The deployment of advanced analytics may enhance organizational sustainability by improving decision quality, forecasting accuracy, operational planning, and resource allocation. This supports the economic dimension through better efficiency and error reduction, and may support the environmental dimension when analytics contribute to energy efficiency, fault reduction, and more efficient use of network resources.

Proposition 6: Customer Understanding → Trust, Retention, and Service Relevance (How)

P6: The deployment of AI-supported customer understanding may enhance organizational sustainability by improving the organization's ability to identify customer needs, reduce service friction, and strengthen customer trust and retention. This mainly supports the social dimension of sustainability, while also contributing to economic sustainability through improved loyalty and reduced churn.

Proposition 7: Content Recommendation → Personalization and Efficient Interaction (How)

P7: The deployment of content recommendation systems may enhance organizational sustainability by improving service relevance, reducing unnecessary search or interaction effort, and supporting more efficient customer engagement. This may support the social dimension through better experience quality and the economic dimension through more efficient digital interaction.

Proposition 8: Data Governance and Data Quality as Enabling Conditions (When)

P8: The relationship between AI applications and organizational sustainability becomes stronger when data governance ensures accuracy, consistency, updating, accountability, and responsible data use. The relationship weakens when data quality is poor or when data governance is insufficient.

Proposition 9: Operational Integration as an Enabling Condition (When)

P9: The relationship between AI applications and organizational sustainability becomes stronger when AI outputs are integrated into daily processes and decision-making routines. The relationship weakens when AI is treated as a separate technical project disconnected from core organizational workflows.

Proposition 10: Skill Readiness and Organizational Acceptance as Enabling Conditions (When)

P10: The relationship between AI applications and organizational sustainability becomes stronger when employees and managers have the skills needed to interpret AI outputs and when the organization accepts AI-supported work practices. The relationship weakens when skill gaps, resistance to change, or overreliance on automated outputs reduce effective use.

Proposition 11: Ethical Governance and Transparency as Enabling Conditions (When)

P11: The relationship between AI applications and organizational sustainability becomes stronger when AI use is supported by ethical governance, transparency, and safeguards against bias, privacy violations, and unfair outcomes. The relationship weakens when AI applications undermine trust, fairness, or legitimacy.

Proposition 12: Measurement, Monitoring, and Organizational Learning as Enabling Conditions (When)

P12: The relationship between AI applications and organizational sustainability becomes stronger when organizations use clear indicators, monitoring systems, and learning mechanisms to evaluate AI outcomes across economic, social, and environmental dimensions. The relationship weakens when AI outcomes are not measured or improved over time.

7. DISCUSSION

7.1 Theoretical Contribution

The research demonstrates that understanding the relationship between artificial intelligence deployment and organizational sustainability in the telecommunications sector becomes more meaningful when the discussion moves beyond the general assumption that AI automatically enhances sustainability toward an explanatory framework addressing why the impact occurs, how it materializes, and when it becomes stronger or weaker. From the *why* perspective, the theoretical justification rests on the view that AI applications represent an organizational capability for transforming data into measurable operational decisions and actions. This enhances resource efficiency, reduces waste, and improves service quality (Lozano, 2018). Such outcomes align with the core of organizational sustainability as the organization's ability to endure and create balanced value across economic, social, and environmental dimensions (Elkington, 1997). This logic is also consistent with digital transformation literature, which emphasizes that value does not arise merely from adopting technology, but from embedding it within an operational and cognitive logic that meaningfully affects performance and continuity (Vial, 2019).

From the *how* perspective, the research contributes by unpacking the relationship through six operational mechanisms that explain how impact flows from applications to sustainability dimensions.

Chatbots illustrate how AI can enhance service quality, reliability, user trust, and operational responsiveness (Dwivedi et al., 2021). Dynamic pricing demonstrates how analytics can translate into pricing efficiency and more sustainable revenues when decisions are analytically grounded rather than intuition-based, while fairness and transparency must be safeguarded to avoid negative social consequences (Vial, 2019). Targeted offers demonstrate how personalization strategies may improve customer retention and optimize marketing efforts by aligning promotional activities with actual user preferences and consumption patterns (Dwivedi et al., 2021). In telecom environments where customer preferences and usage patterns change rapidly, such personalization practices may also improve the organization's responsiveness to market fluctuations and service expectations. Advanced analytics, customer understanding, and content recommendation explain how decision quality and user experience can be improved and how sustainable performance can be reinforced through continuous organizational learning (Dwivedi et al., 2021). In this way, the impact of AI moves beyond a general assumption and becomes interpretable through identifiable and testable pathways (Vial, 2019).

From the *when* perspective, the research provides an additional theoretical contribution by introducing enabling/limiting conditions that regulate the strength of the relationship and explain variation across firms and markets. AI deployment success depends on data quality and governance (Dwivedi et al., 2021) and on AI integration into operations and decision-making rather than being treated as a standalone project (Vial, 2019). AI success is affected by skill readiness, organizational acceptance, ethical governance, transparency, measurement systems, and institutional learning mechanisms (Dwivedi et al., 2021). These considerations become especially important in telecommunications environments characterized by large data volumes, changing customer demands, and increased sensitivity to privacy and service reliability (Vial, 2019). Accordingly, the proposed explanatory framework contributes theoretically by transforming the relationship from a general association into a conditional relationship shaped by identifiable enabling factors, thereby increasing explanatory precision and reducing overgeneralization.

7.2 Practical Implications

The practical implications of this chapter indicate that improving organizational sustainability through AI in telecommunications requires more than simply adopting advanced technologies. Organizations also need effective integration processes, clear operational planning, employee readiness, and continuous evaluation mechanisms to ensure that AI applications contribute meaningfully to long-term organizational performance (Vial, 2019). For telecommunications managers and policymakers, this implies that AI-related investment decisions should be evaluated not only in terms of cost and efficiency, but also in terms of regulatory compliance, responsible data use, service reliability, and long-term sustainability outcomes.

From an economic sustainability perspective, AI applications can support measurable operational improvements, including lower service costs, better utilization of network resources, improved pricing decisions, and stronger customer retention (Lozano, 2018). Social sustainability considerations require responsible AI deployment that supports customer experience, digital inclusion, and fairer service and pricing practices, since failures in fairness or privacy can undermine trust and damage organizational sustainability (Dwivedi et al., 2021). Environmental sustainability can also benefit from AI through more efficient resource utilization, lower operational waste, and improved energy-related planning, particularly when analytics are used to improve planning, reduce failures, and limit unnecessary consumption (Lozano, 2018). The research also highlights data governance as a practical starting point, since reliable decision-making depends heavily on the availability of accurate, timely, and well-managed data (Dwivedi et al., 2021). In addition, integrating AI into operational processes requires organizations to align AI applications with daily workflows, decision routines, and performance monitoring practices rather than treating them as separate technical tools (Vial, 2019). In telecommunications environments characterized by continuous customer interaction and service continuity requirements, such integration may improve operational responsiveness, support network reliability, and facilitate more efficient allocation of digital resources across service activities. Employee readiness and organizational acceptance remain important factors, particularly in local telecom environments where the benefits of AI depend largely on practical implementation and day-to-day organizational use, as supported by applied studies in Iraq examining AI use contexts (Ramo et al., 2022). Finally, ethical governance, transparency, and continuous measurement are not decorative elements but decisive conditions that determine whether AI produces balanced and sustainable outcomes across all three dimensions rather than short-term economic gains at the expense of social or environmental considerations (Dwivedi et al., 2021).

8. CONCLUSIONS

This chapter concludes that the relationship between AI deployment and organizational sustainability in the telecommunications sector is neither automatic nor uniform. AI applications may support sustainability when they are embedded in organizational processes, supported by reliable data, and governed through transparent and accountable practices. The proposed framework explains this relationship through a why, how, and when logic. It shows why AI may be linked to sustainability, how specific applications may generate economic, social, and environmental value, and when this value is likely to become stronger or weaker.

The chapter's main contribution lies in organizing AI deployment as an organizational capability rather than treating it as a general technological solution. It also clarifies that sustainability outcomes depend on identifiable mechanisms and enabling conditions, including data governance, process integration, skill readiness, ethical governance, measurement, monitoring, and organizational learning.

Because the chapter is conceptual, it does not provide empirical testing of the proposed propositions. Instead, it offers a structured basis for future empirical studies in telecommunications and related digital service sectors.

9. FUTURE RESEARCH

Future research may extend the proposed framework in several directions. First, quantitative studies may test the propositions using SEM or PLS-SEM to examine how each AI application relates to the economic, social, and environmental dimensions of organizational sustainability. Second, future studies may examine the enabling and limiting conditions as moderating variables, particularly data governance, process integration, skill readiness, ethical governance, and measurement systems.

Third, comparative studies across telecommunications firms, regions, or countries may help explain how institutional, regulatory, and cultural differences shape the sustainability impact of AI. Fourth, future research may give greater attention to direct environmental outcomes by studying AI applications related to network energy efficiency, predictive maintenance, fault management, and intelligent resource allocation.

Finally, mixed-methods research may provide deeper insight into how AI applications operate in practice and why some organizations translate AI into sustainable value more effectively than others.

REFERENCES

Adamopoulou, E., & Moussiades, L. (2020). Chatbots: History, technology, and applications. *Machine Learning with Applications, 2*, 100006. DOI: 10.1016/j.mlwa.2020.100006

Amjad, F., Abbas, W., Zia-ur-Rehman, M., Baig, S. A., Hashim, M., Khan, A., & Rehman, H. U. (2021). Artificial intelligence and sustainable development: A systematic literature review. *Sustainable Development (Bradford), 29*(5), 891–907.

Bharadwaj, A., El Sawy, O. A., Pavlou, P. A., & Venkatraman, N. (2013). Digital business strategy: Toward a next generation of insights. *Management Information Systems Quarterly, 37*(2), 471–482. DOI: 10.25300/MISQ/2013/37:2.3

Bocken, N. M. P., Short, S. W., Rana, P., & Evans, S. (2014). A literature and practice review to develop sustainable business model archetypes. *Journal of Cleaner Production, 65*, 42–56. DOI: 10.1016/j.jclepro.2013.11.039

Braganza, A., Chen, W., Canhoto, A., & Sap, S. (2021). Productive AI: The role of AI in creating productivity and value for organizations. *International Journal of Information Management, 57*, 102250.

Carroll, A. B. (1991). The pyramid of corporate social responsibility: Toward the moral management of organizational stakeholders. *Business Horizons, 34*(4), 39–48. DOI: 10.1016/0007-6813(91)90005-G

Davenport, T. H., & Harris, J. G. (2007). *Competing on analytics: The new science of winning*. Harvard Business Press.

Davenport, T. H., & Ronanki, R. (2018). Artificial intelligence for the real world. *Harvard Business Review, 96*(1), 108–116.

den Boer, A. V. (2015). Dynamic pricing and learning: Historical origins, current research, and new directions. *Surveys in Operations Research and Management Science, 20*(1), 1–18. DOI: 10.1016/j.sorms.2015.03.001

Dwivedi, Y. K., Hughes, L., Ismagilova, E., Aarts, G., Coombs, C., Crick, T., Duan, Y., Dwivedi, R., Edwards, J., Eirug, A., Galanos, V., Ilavarasan, P. V., Janssen, M., Jones, P., Kar, A. K., Kizgin, H., Kronemann, B., Lal, B., Lucini, B., & Williams, M. D. (2021). Artificial intelligence (AI): Multidisciplinary perspectives on emerging challenges, opportunities, and agenda for research, practice and policy. *International Journal of Information Management, 57*, 101994. DOI: 10.1016/j.ijinfomgt.2019.08.002

Eccles, R. G., Ioannou, I., & Serafeim, G. (2014). The impact of corporate sustainability on organizational processes and performance. *Management Science*, *60*(11), 2835–2857. DOI: 10.1287/mnsc.2014.1984

Elkington, J. (1997). *Cannibals with forks: The triple bottom line of 21st century business*. Capstone.

Enholm, I. M., Papagiannidis, E., Mikalef, P., & Krogstie, J. (2022). Artificial intelligence and business value: A literature review. *Information Systems Frontiers*, *24*(5), 1709–1734. DOI: 10.1007/s10796-021-10186-w

European Commission. (2019). *Ethics guidelines for trustworthy AI*. European Commission.

European Parliament and Council. (2016). *Regulation (EU) 2016/679 (General Data Protection Regulation)*. Official Journal of the European Union.

European Parliament and Council. (2024). *Regulation (EU) 2024/1689 of the European Parliament and of the Council of 13 June 2024 laying down harmonised rules on artificial intelligence (Artificial Intelligence Act)*. Official Journal of the European Union.

Ferreira, K. J., Lee, B. H. K., & Simchi-Levi, D. (2016). Analytics for an online retailer: Demand forecasting and price optimization. *Manufacturing & Service Operations Management*, *18*(1), 69–88. DOI: 10.1287/msom.2015.0561

Fitzgerald, M., Kruschwitz, N., Bonnet, D., & Welch, M. (2014). Embracing digital technology: A new strategic imperative. *MIT Sloan Management Review*, *55*(2), 1–12.

Floridi, L., & Cowls, J. (2019). A unified framework of five principles for AI in society. *Harvard Data Science Review*, *1*(1).

Følstad, A., & Brandtzæg, P. B. (2017). Chatbots and the new world of HCI. *Interactions (New York, N.Y.)*, *24*(4), 38–42. DOI: 10.1145/3085558

Freeman, R. E. (1984). *Strategic management: A stakeholder approach*. Pitman.

Global Reporting Initiative. (2021). *GRI standards*. Global Reporting Initiative.

Gnewuch, U., Morana, S., & Maedche, A. (2017). Towards designing cooperative and social conversational agents for customer service. In *Proceedings of the International Conference on Information Systems (ICIS)*.

Gomez-Uribe, C. A., & Hunt, N. (2016). The Netflix recommender system: Algorithms, business value, and innovation. *ACM Transactions on Management Information Systems*, *6*(4), 13. DOI: 10.1145/2843948

Gregor, S. (2006). The Nature of Theory in Information Systems1. *Management Information Systems Quarterly*, *30*(3), 611–642. DOI: 10.2307/25148742

Hammer, M. (1990). Reengineering work: Don't automate, obliterate. *Harvard Business Review*, *68*(4), 104–112.

Han, C., Harrold, T., Armour, S., Krikidis, I., Videv, S., Grant, P. M., Haas, H., Thompson, J. S., Ku, I., Wang, C.-X., Le, T. A., Nakhai, M. R., Zhang, J., & Hanzo, L. (2011). Green radio: Radio techniques to enable energy-efficient wireless networks. *IEEE Communications Magazine*, *49*(6), 46–54. DOI: 10.1109/MCOM.2011.5783984

Hart, S. L. (1995). A natural-resource-based view of the firm. *Academy of Management Review*, *20*(4), 986–1014. DOI: 10.2307/258963

Iansiti, M., & Lakhani, K. R. (2020). Competing in the age of AI. *Harvard Business Review*, *98*(1), 60–67.

ISO. (2018). *ISO 30414: Human resource management—Guidelines for internal and external human capital reporting*. International Organization for Standardization.

Jain, M., Kumar, P., Kota, R., & Patel, S. (2018). Evaluating and informing the design of chatbots. In *Proceedings of the CHI Conference on Human Factors in Computing Systems*. DOI: 10.1145/3196709.3196735

Jallat, F., & Ancarani, F. (2008). Yield management, dynamic pricing and CRM in telecommunications. *Journal of Services Marketing*, *22*(5), 404–414. DOI: 10.1108/08876040810901882

Jarrahi, M. H. (2018). Artificial intelligence and the future of work: Human–AI symbiosis in organizational decision making. *Business Horizons*, *61*(4), 577–586. DOI: 10.1016/j.bushor.2018.03.007

Kane, G. C., Palmer, D., Phillips, A. N., Kiron, D., & Buckley, N. (2015). Strategy, not technology, drives digital transformation. *MIT Sloan Management Review*.

Kaplan, A., & Haenlein, M. (2018). Artificial intelligence: Revolutionizing the way we think and work. [IJRAR]. *International Journal of Research and Analytical Reviews*, *5*(4), 973–976.

Khatri, V., & Brown, C. V. (2010). Designing data governance. *Communications of the ACM*, *53*(1), 148–152. DOI: 10.1145/1629175.1629210

Kumar, V., & Reinartz, W. (2018). *Customer relationship management: Concept, strategy, and tools* (3rd ed.). Springer. DOI: 10.1007/978-3-662-55381-7

Lambrecht, A., & Tucker, C. (2019). Algorithmic targeting. *Journal of Marketing, 83*(5), 1–19.

Lemon, K. N., & Verhoef, P. C. (2016). Understanding customer experience throughout the customer journey. *Journal of Marketing, 80*(6), 69–96. DOI: 10.1509/jm.15.0420

Lozano, R. (2015). A holistic perspective on corporate sustainability drivers. *Corporate Social Responsibility and Environmental Management, 22*(1), 32–44. DOI: 10.1002/csr.1325

Lozano, R. (2018). Proposing a definition and a framework of organizational sustainability. *Sustainability, 10*(4), 1157. DOI: 10.3390/su10041157

Mehrabi, N., Morstatter, F., Saxena, N., Lerman, K., & Galstyan, A. (2021). A survey on bias and fairness in machine learning. *ACM Computing Surveys, 54*(6), 115.

National Institute of Standards and Technology. (2023). *Artificial intelligence risk management framework (AI RMF 1.0)*. NIST.

OECD. (2024). *AI principles (Adopted in 2019; updated in 2024)*. Organization for Economic Co-operation and Development.

Otto, B. (2011). Organizing data governance: Findings from the telecommunications industry and consequences for large service providers. *Communications of the Association for Information Systems, 29*, 45. DOI: 10.17705/1CAIS.02903

Phillips, R. (2021). *Pricing and revenue optimization* (2nd ed.). Stanford University Press.

Raisch, S., & Krakowski, S. (2021). Artificial intelligence and management: The automation–augmentation paradox. *Academy of Management Review, 46*(1), 192–210. DOI: 10.5465/amr.2018.0072

Ramo, R. M., Alshaher, A. A., & Al-Fakhry, N. A. (2022). The effect of using artificial intelligence on learning performance in Iraq: The dual factor theory perspective. *Ingénierie des Systèmes d'Information, 27*(2), 255–265. DOI: 10.18280/isi.270209

Ricci, F., Rokach, L., Shapira, B., & Kantor, P. B. (Eds.). (2015). *Recommender systems handbook* (2nd ed.). Springer. DOI: 10.1007/978-1-4899-7637-6

Rust, R. T., & Huang, M.-H. (2014). The service revolution and the transformation of marketing science. *Marketing Science, 33*(2), 206–221. DOI: 10.1287/mksc.2013.0836

Tambe, P., Cappelli, P., & Yakubovich, V. (2019). Artificial intelligence in human resources management: Challenges and a path forward. *The Academy of Management Perspectives, 33*(3), 1–13.

Verhoef, P. C., Kannan, P. K., & Inman, J. J. (2015). From multi-channel retailing to omni-channel retailing. *Journal of Retailing, 91*(2), 174–181. DOI: 10.1016/j.jretai.2015.02.005

Vial, G. (2019). Understanding digital transformation: A review and a research agenda. *The Journal of Strategic Information Systems, 28*(2), 118–144. DOI: 10.1016/j.jsis.2019.01.003

Vinuesa, R., Azizpour, H., Leite, I., Balaam, M., Dignum, V., Domisch, S., Felländer, A., Langhans, S. D., Tegmark, M., & Fuso Nerini, F. (2020). The role of artificial intelligence in achieving the Sustainable Development Goals. *Nature Communications, 11*(1), 3. DOI: 10.1038/s41467-019-14108-y

Wamba, S. F., Akter, S., Edwards, A., Chopin, G., & Gnanzou, D. (2015). How 'big data' can make big impact: Findings from a systematic review and a longitudinal case study. *International Journal of Production Economics, 165*, 234–246. DOI: 10.1016/j.ijpe.2014.12.031

Wedel, M., & Kannan, P. K. (2016). Marketing analytics for data-rich environments. *Journal of Marketing, 80*(6), 97–121. DOI: 10.1509/jm.15.0413

Whetten, D. A. (1989). What constitutes a theoretical contribution? *Academy of Management Review, 14*(4), 490–495. DOI: 10.2307/258554

World Commission on Environment and Development. (1987). *Our common future*. Oxford University Press.

Zhang, S., Yao, L., Sun, A., & Tay, Y. (2019). Deep learning based recommender system: A survey and new perspectives. *ACM Computing Surveys, 52*(1), 5.

KEY TERMS AND DEFINITIONS

AI Governance and Ethics: Organizational controls that guide the responsible use of AI through transparency, fairness, accountability, privacy protection, and compliance with internal and external standards.

AI Utilization in Organizations: The practical application of AI solutions, including analytics, automation, and decision support tools, to enhance process efficiency, service quality, and the accuracy of managerial decisions, thereby improving organizational outcomes.

Artificial Intelligence (AI): A set of computational approaches that enable systems to perform tasks typically associated with human intelligence, such as learning from data, pattern recognition, prediction, and decision support within organizational processes.

Data Governance and Quality: Organizational policies and procedures that define data ownership, standards, control, and flow, ensuring consistency, accuracy, and usability for analytics and intelligent applications.

Employee Morale and Trust: A psychological state that reflects the motivation of employees and their confidence in the fairness of the organization and the clarity of its decisions, which affects commitment, productivity, and acceptance of organizational change.

Measurement, Monitoring, and Organizational Learning: A system of indicators and processes for tracking performance, enabling continuous improvement, and learning from outcomes, thereby consolidating AI's impact and translating it into sustained sustainability outcomes.

Organizational Sustainability: The organization's capacity to achieve continuity and long-term performance by balancing economic viability, social responsibility, and environmental stewardship, thereby strengthening resilience and stakeholder value over time.

Telecommunications Sector: A sector that provides communication services and network infrastructure, characterized by rapid technological change, high competitiveness, intensive customer interaction, and increasing reliance on data and digital operations.

Triple Bottom Line (TBL) Perspective: A framework that evaluates organizational success across three integrated dimensions: economic, social, and environmental, rather than limiting assessment to financial results alone.

Compilation of References

Abed, A., Al-Najjar, B., & Salama, A. (2025). Breaking down barriers: How board composition drives sustainability in GCC countries. *International Journal of Human Resource Management*, *36*(4), 513–547. DOI: 10.1080/09585192.2025.2452971

Abidi, N., El Herradi, M., & Sakha, S. (2023). Digitalization and resilience: Firm-level evidence during the COVID-19 pandemic. *Telecommunications Policy*, *47*(4), 102522. DOI: 10.1016/j.telpol.2023.102522 PMID: 37051116

Abouarab, R., Mishra, T., & Wolfe, S. (2025). Does the EU sustainable finance disclosure regulation mitigate greenwashing? *European Journal of Finance*, *31*(8), 957–989. DOI: 10.1080/1351847X.2025.2457944

Acemoglu, D., Akcigit, U., Alp, H., Bloom, N., & Kerr, W. (2018). Innovation, reallocation, and growth. *The American Economic Review*, *108*(11), 3450–3491. DOI: 10.1257/aer.20130470

Acemoglu, D., & Johnson, S. (2005). Unbundling institutions. *Journal of Political Economy*, *113*(5), 949–995. DOI: 10.1086/432166

Acemoglu, D., & Robinson, J. A. (2012). *Why nations fail: The origins of power, prosperity, and poverty*. Crown Publishers.

Acheampong, A. O. (2019). Modelling for insight: Does financial development improve environmental quality? *Energy Economics*, *83*, 156–179. DOI: 10.1016/j.eneco.2019.06.025

Acquah, A. M., & Ibrahim, M. (2020). Foreign direct investment, economic growth and financial sector development in Africa. *Journal of Sustainable Finance & Investment*, *10*(4), 315–334. DOI: 10.1080/20430795.2019.1683504

Adamopoulou, E., & Moussiades, L. (2020). Chatbots: History, technology, and applications. *Machine Learning with Applications*, *2*, 100006. DOI: 10.1016/j.mlwa.2020.100006

Agarwal, B., Roy, S. N., & Sharma, S. C. (2026). Can indigenous political representation improve forest conservation? India's experience. *World Development, 201*, 107295. DOI: 10.1016/j.worlddev.2025.107295

Ahamed, M. M., & Mallick, S. K. (2019). Is financial inclusion good for bank stability? International evidence. *Journal of Economic Behavior & Organization, 157*, 403–427. DOI: 10.1016/j.jebo.2017.07.027

Ahmad, F., Boumaiza, A., Sanfilippo, A., & Al-Fagih, L. (2026). Towards Net-Zero Energy Transition: A Detailed Climate Change Integrated Green Finance Policy Investment Framework for Qatar. *Sustainable Development (Bradford)*, •••, 1–35. DOI: 10.1002/sd.70657

Ahmadov, V. (2025). Technological capabilities and economic growth in Visegrad countries. *Regional Statistics, 15*(6), 1103–1123. DOI: 10.15196/RS150603

Aitken, B. J., & Harrison, A. E. (1999). Do domestic firms benefit from direct foreign investment? Evidence from Venezuela. *The American Economic Review, 89*(3), 605–618. DOI: 10.1257/aer.89.3.605

Akram, H. W., Dana, L. P., Abbas, H., & Ciddikie, M. D. (2024). Family Start-up in Oman: Entrepreneurship Ecosystem Perspective. *Entrepreneurial Behaviour of Family Firms: Perspectives on Emerging Economies*, 43–58. DOI: 10.1108/978-1-83753-934-520241003

Al Salmi, S. A., Rafiq, M., Al Salmi, Q., Al-Alawi, B. T. S., Al Jabri, S. S., Al Jabri, A., & Al Maniri, A. A. N. (2025). Progress, challenges and opportunities in building a sustainable digital health system in Oman. *Eastern Mediterranean Health Journal, 31*(9–10), 574–580. DOI: 10.26719/2025.31.10.574 PMID: 41451744

Alarfaj, F. K., & Shahzadi, S. (2024). Enhancing Fraud Detection in Banking with Deep Learning: Graph Neural Networks and Autoencoders for Real-Time Credit Card Fraud Prevention. *IEEE Access : Practical Innovations, Open Solutions*, •••, 1–1. DOI: 10.1109/ACCESS.2024.3466288

Alavi, M., Leidner, D. E., & Mousavi, R. (2024). A knowledge management perspective of generative artificial intelligence. *Journal of the Association for Information Systems, 25*(1), 1–12. DOI: 10.17705/1jais.00859

Al-Badi, A. H., Malik, A., & Gastli, A. (2011). Sustainable energy usage in Oman - Opportunities and barriers. *Renewable & Sustainable Energy Reviews, 15*(8), 3780–3788. DOI: 10.1016/j.rser.2011.06.007

Al-Busaidy, M., & Weerakkody, V. (2011). E-government services in Oman: An employee's perspective. *Electronic Government*, *8*(2–3), 185–207. DOI: 10.1504/EG.2011.039836

Aldulaimi, S. H., & Abdeldayem, M. M. (2022). Examining the impact of renewable energy technologies on sustainability development in the middle east and north Africa region. *International Journal of Engineering Business Management*, *14*, 18479790221110835. Advance online publication. DOI: 10.1177/18479790221110835

Aldulaimi, S., Kharabsheh, R., Al Shishany, A., & Alazzawi, A. (2020). Investment in Human Capital to Promote Knowledge-Based Economy: Data Analysis in the GCC. *2020 International Conference on Data Analytics for Business and Industry: Way Towards a Sustainable Economy, ICDABI 2020*. DOI: 10.1109/ICDABI51230.2020.9325675

Alfaro, L. (2017). Gains from foreign direct investment: Macro and micro approaches. *The World Bank Economic Review*, *30*(Supplement_1), S2–S15.

Alfaro, L., Chanda, A., Kalemli-Ozcan, S., & Sayek, S. (2004). FDI and economic growth: The role of local financial markets. *Journal of International Economics*, *64*(1), 89–112. DOI: 10.1016/S0022-1996(03)00081-3

Ali, M. J. (2025). The Impact of Artificial Intelligence on Commercial Banks in Oman. *International Journal of Research and Innovation in Social Science*, *IX*(IV), 309–322. DOI: 10.47772/IJRISS.2025.90400025

Alsheibani, S., Cheung, Y., & Messom, C. (2018). Artificial intelligence adoption: AI-readiness at firm-level. In Proceedings of the 22nd Pacific Asia Conference on Information Systems (PACIS) (Paper 37). AIS Electronic Library. https://aisel.aisnet.org/pacis2018/37

Ambec, S., Cohen, M. A., Elgie, S., & Lanoie, P. (2013). The Porter hypothesis at 20: Can environmental regulation enhance innovation and competitiveness? *Review of Environmental Economics and Policy*, *7*(1), 2–22. DOI: 10.1093/reep/res016

Ameli, N., Dessens, O., Winning, M., Cronin, J., Chenet, H., Drummond, P., Calzadilla, A., Anandarajah, G., & Grubb, M. (2021). Higher cost of finance exacerbates a climate investment trap in developing economies. *Nature Communications*, *12*(1), 4046. DOI: 10.1038/s41467-021-24305-3 PMID: 34193868

Amirahmadi, H., & Wu, W. (1994). Foreign direct investment in developing countries. *Journal of Developing Areas*, *28*(2), 167–190.

Amjad, F., Abbas, W., Zia-ur-Rehman, M., Baig, S. A., Hashim, M., Khan, A., & Rehman, H. U. (2021). Artificial intelligence and sustainable development: A systematic literature review. *Sustainable Development (Bradford)*, *29*(5), 891–907.

Amore, M. D., Garofalo, O., & Minichilli, A. (2014). Gender interactions within the family firm. *Management Science*, *60*(5), 1083–1097. DOI: 10.1287/mnsc.2013.1824

Ampumuza, D., Katushabe, C., & Tamale, M. (2026). A systematic review and future directions for AI-driven detection of fraud patterns in SACCO transactions. *Frontiers in Artificial Intelligence*, *8*, 1690482. Advance online publication. DOI: 10.3389/frai.2025.1690482 PMID: 41693763

Andreoni, A. (2022). Compressed development and the political economy of developmentalism. *Development and Change*, *53*(5), 1103–1120. DOI: 10.1111/dech.12729

Angela, K., Taddeo, S., & James, M. (2011). Predicting Global Solar Radiation Using an Artificial Neural Network Single-Parameter Model. *Advances in Artificial Neural Systems*, *2011*(1), 1–7. DOI: 10.1155/2011/751908

Anzolin, G., Andreoni, A., & Zanfei, A. (2022). What is driving robotisation in the automotive value chain? Empirical evidence on the role of FDIs and domestic capabilities in technology adoption. *Technovation*, *115*, 102476. DOI: 10.1016/j.technovation.2022.102476

Arayssi, M., Fakih, A., & Haimoun, N. (2019). Did the Arab Spring reduce MENA countries' growth? *Applied Economics Letters*, *26*(19), 1579–1585. DOI: 10.1080/13504851.2019.1588938

Arner, D. W., Barberis, J. N., & Buckley, R. P. (2015, October 1). *The Evolution of Fintech: A New Post-Crisis Paradigm?* Papers.*ssrn*.com. https://ssrn.com/abstract=2676553 DOI: 10.2139/ssrn.2676553

Arribas-Ayllon, M., & Walkerdine, V. (2017). Foucauldian discourse analysis. In Carla W. & Wendy (Eds), *The Sage handbook of qualitative research in psychology* (pp. 91–108). Sage. DOI: 10.4135/9781526405555.n7

Arsad, S., Abdullah, W. N., Awang, N., & Gani, S. I. I. (2025). Strengthening Corporate Fraud Detection through Forensic Accounting and Whistleblowing: The Moderating Role of Regulatory Enforcement. *International Journal of Research and Innovation in Social Science*, *IX*(IX), 6843–6853. DOI: 10.47772/IJRISS.2025.909000561

Asad, S., & Georgakakis, D. 2023. Diversity on corporate boards and shareholder activism: an intersectionality approach. In *Research Handbook on Diversity and Corporate Governance* (pp. 113-123). Camberly: Edward Elgar Publishing. https://doi.org/DOI: 10.4337/9781800377783.00019

ASEAN Taxonomy Board. (2023). ASEAN Taxonomy for Sustainable Finance, Version 2. ASEAN Finance Ministers and Central Bank Governors' Meeting. Https://www.theacmf.org/images/downloads/pdf/ASEAN-Taxonomy-Version-2.pdf?Utm

Auty, R. (2001). *Resource abundance and economic development*. Oxford University Press.

Avolio, B. J., & Gardner, W. L. (2005). Authentic leadership development: Getting to the root of positive forms of leadership. *The Leadership Quarterly*, *16*(3), 315–338. DOI: 10.1016/j.leaqua.2005.03.001

Ayenew, B. B. (2022). The effect of foreign direct investment on the economic growth of SubSaharan African countries: An empirical approach. *Cogent Economics & Finance*, *10*(1), 2038862. DOI: 10.1080/23322039.2022.2038862

Azhar, A. I. M., & https://dialnet.unirioja.es/servlet/autor?codigo=6853671. (2025). The impact of sustainable environment on the development of the green economy in oman. *International Journal of Professional Business Review: Int. J. Prof.Bus. Rev., ISSN 2525-3654, ISSN-e 2525-3654, Vol. 10, Nº. 4, 2025 (Ejemplar Dedicado a: Continuous Publication; E05444)*, *10*(4), 5. DOI: 10.26668/businessreview/2025.v10i4.5444

Badeeb, R., Lean, H. H., & Clark, J. (2016). The evolution of the natural resource curse thesis: A critical literature survey. *Resources Policy*, 51, 123–134.

Badghish, S., Ali, I., Ali, M., Yaqub, M. Z., & Dhir, A. 2023. How socio-cultural transition helps to improve entrepreneurial intentions among women? *Journal of Intellectual Capital, 24*(4), 900-928. https://doi.org/DOI: 10.1108/JIC-06-2021-0158

Balajee Asish Brahmandam, N. (2025). A Hybrid Blockchain and Deep Learning Approach for Credit Card Fraud Detection using Slice Recurrent. *Neural Networks : The Official Journal of the International Neural Network Society*, •••, 1–6. DOI: 10.1109/ICoICC64033.2025.11052047

Baldwin, R. (2016). *The great convergence: Information technology and the new globalization*. Harvard University Press. DOI: 10.2307/j.ctv24w655w

Balsalobre-Lorente, D., Shahbaz, M., Roubaud, D., & Farhani, S. (2018). How economic growth, renewable electricity, and natural resources contribute to CO_2 emissions. *Energy Policy*, *113*, 356–367. DOI: 10.1016/j.enpol.2017.10.050

Banu, M. S., Parveen, N., Gayathri, R., Gera, A., Kumar, S., & Anitha, G. (2024, June). A machine learning approach for enhanced security using blockchain in finance auditing services. In 2024 15th International Conference on Computing Communication and Networking Technologies (ICCCNT) (pp. 1-6). IEEE.

Banu, S. R., Gongada, T. N., Santosh, K., Chowdhary, H., Sabareesh, R., & Muthuperumal, S. (2024, April). Financial fraud detection using hybrid convolutional and recurrent neural networks: An analysis of unstructured data in banking. In 2024 10th International Conference on Communication and Signal Processing (ICCSP) (pp. 1027-1031). IEEE.

Bao, Y., Hilary, G., & Ke, B. (2020). Artificial Intelligence and Fraud Detection. SSRN Electronic Journal. DOI: 10.2139/ssrn.3738618

Barbier, E. B. (2003). The role of natural resources in economic development. *Australian Economic Papers*, *42*(2), 253–272. DOI: 10.1111/1467-8454.00198

Barro, R. J. (1991). Economic growth in a cross section of countries. *The Quarterly Journal of Economics*, *106*(2), 407–443. DOI: 10.2307/2937943

Barro, R. J., & Sala-i-Martin, X. (2004). *Economic growth* (2nd ed.). MIT Press.

Baruch, Y., & Holtom, B. C. (2008). Survey response rate levels and trends in organizational research. *Human Relations; Studies Towards the Integration of the Social Sciences*, *61*(8), 1139–1160. DOI: 10.1177/0018726708094863

Basuthakur, Y. 2022. Battle of the Classes. Social Class and Work Status in Determining Women Director Appointments. In *Academy of Management Proceedings*, No. 1, p. 12511. https://doi.org/DOI: 10.5465/AMBPP.2022.12511abstract

Baumol, W. J. (1968). Entrepreneurship in economic theory. *The American Economic Review*, *58*(2), 64–71.

Beetham, D. (1991). The legitimation of power. Macmillan Education. Https://psi412.cankaya.edu.tr/uploads/files/Beetham%20-%20The%20Legitimation%20of%20Power%20(1991).pdf

Bell, El. (1990). The bicultural life experience of career-oriented black women. *Journal of Organizational Behavior*, *11*(6), 459–477. DOI: 10.1002/job.4030110607

Benbya, H., Strich, F., & Tamm, T. (2024). Navigating generative artificial intelligence promises and perils for organizations. *Journal of the Association for Information Systems*, *54*(1), 23–36. DOI: 10.17705/1jais.00861

Bender, E. M., Gebru, T., McMillan-Major, A., & Shmitchell, S. (2021). On the dangers of stochastic parrots: Can language models be too big? In *Proceedings of the 2021 ACM Conference on Fairness, Accountability, and Transparency* (pp. 610–623). ACM. DOI: 10.1145/3442188.3445922

Benkraiem, R., & Zopounidis, C. (2021). Preface: Regression methods based on OR techniques and computational aspects in management, economics and finance. *Annals of Operations Research, 306*(1-2), 1–6. DOI: 10.1007/s10479-021-04306-7

Beugelsdijk, S., Smeets, R., & Zwinkels, R. (2008). The impact of horizontal and vertical FDI spillovers on local productivity. *International Business Review, 17*(4), 452–472. DOI: 10.1016/j.ibusrev.2008.02.004

Bharadwaj, A., El Sawy, O. A., Pavlou, P. A., & Venkatraman, N. (2013). Digital business strategy: Toward a next generation of insights. *Management Information Systems Quarterly, 37*(2), 471–482. DOI: 10.25300/MISQ/2013/37:2.3

Birindelli, G., Iannuzzi, A. P., & Savioli, M. (2019). The impact of women leaders on environmental performance: Evidence on gender diversity in banks. *Corporate Social Responsibility and Environmental Management, 26*(6), 1485–1499. DOI: 10.1002/csr.1762

Birkstedt, T., Minkkinen, M., Tandon, A., & Mäntymäki, M. (2023). AI governance: Themes, knowledge gaps and future agendas. *Internet Research, 33*(7), 133–167. DOI: 10.1108/INTR-01-2022-0042

Bjorklund, A. K. (2019). Sustainable development and international investment law. In *Research handbook on environment and investment law* (pp. 38–68). Edward Elgar Publishing., DOI: 10.4337/9781784714635.00008

Black, J. (2008). Constructing and contesting legitimacy and accountability in polycentric regulatory regimes. *Regulation & Governance, 2*(2), 137–164. DOI: 10.1111/j.1748-5991.2008.00034.x

Bloom, D. E., & Williamson, J. G. (1998). Demographic transitions and economic miracles in emerging Asia. *The World Bank Economic Review, 12*(3), 419–455. DOI: 10.1093/wber/12.3.419

Bloomenthal, A. (2026, June 17). *Understanding eMoney: A Guide to Electronic Transactions and Benefits.* Investopedia. https://www.investopedia.com/terms/e/electronic-money.asp

Bocken, N. M. P., Short, S. W., Rana, P., & Evans, S. (2014). A literature and practice review to develop sustainable business model archetypes. *Journal of Cleaner Production, 65*, 42–56. DOI: 10.1016/j.jclepro.2013.11.039

Böhm, K., & Durst, S. (2025). Knowledge management in the age of generative artificial intelligence: From SECI to GRAI. *VINE Journal of Information and Knowledge Management Systems.* Advance online publication. DOI: 10.1108/VJIKMS-10-2024-0357

Bolton, P., & Kacperczyk, M. (2021). Do investors care about carbon risk? *Journal of Financial Economics, 142*(2), 517–549. DOI: 10.1016/j.jfineco.2021.05.008

Bommasani, R., Hudson, D. A., Adeli, E., Altman, R., Arora, S., von Arx, S., ... (2022). On the opportunities and risks of foundation models (arXiv:2108.07258) [Preprint]. arXiv. https://doi.org//arXiv.2108.07258DOI: 10.48550

Borensztein, E., De Gregorio, J., & Lee, J. W. (1998). How does foreign direct investment affect economic growth? *Journal of International Economics, 45*(1), 115–135. DOI: 10.1016/S0022-1996(97)00033-0

Borish, D., Cunsolo, A., Mauro, I., Dewey, C., & Harper, S. L. (2021). Moving images, moving methods: Advancing documentary film for qualitative research. *International Journal of Qualitative Methods, 20*, 16094069211013646. DOI: 10.1177/16094069211013646

Braganza, A., Chen, W., Canhoto, A., & Sap, S. (2021). Productive AI: The role of AI in creating productivity and value for organizations. *International Journal of Information Management, 57*, 102250.

Braun, V., & Clarke, V. (2006). Using thematic analysis in psychology. *Qualitative Research in Psychology, 3*(2), 77–101. DOI: 10.1191/1478088706qp063oa

Brieger, S. A., Francoeur, C., Welzel, C., & Ben-Amar, W. 2019. Empowering women: The role of emancipative forces in board gender diversity. *Journal of Business Ethics, 155*, 495-511. https://doi.org/DOI: 10.1007/s10551-017-3489-3

Brislin, R. W. (1970). Back-translation for cross-cultural research. *Journal of Cross-Cultural Psychology, 1*(3), 185–216. DOI: 10.1177/135910457000100301

Btoush, E. Zhou, X., Rai Gururaian, Chan, K. M., & Tao, X. (2021). A Survey on Credit Card Fraud Detection Techniques in Banking Industry for Cyber Security. 2021 8th International Conference on Behavioral and Social Computing (BESC). DOI: 10.1109/BESC53957.2021.9635559

Bullough, A., Guelich, U., Manolova, T. S., & Schjoedt, L. 2022. Women's entrepreneurship and culture: gender role expectations and identities, societal culture, and the entrepreneurial environment. *Small Business Economics, 58*(2), 985-996. https://doi.org/DOI: 10.1007/s11187-020-00429-6

Busse, M., & Königer, J. (2012). Trade and economic growth: A re-examination of the empirical evidence (HWWI Research Paper No. 123). Hamburg Institute of International Economics.

Busse, M., & Hefeker, C. (2007). Political risk, institutions and foreign direct investment. *European Journal of Political Economy, 23*(2), 397–415. DOI: 10.1016/j.ejpoleco.2006.02.003

Buttigieg, C. P., & Pulis, S. (2024, September). Strategic initiatives to address greenwashing. In ERA Forum (Vol. 25, No. 3, pp. 327-337). Berlin/Heidelberg: Springer Berlin Heidelberg. DOI: 10.1007/s12027-024-00815-7

Bylo, A. (2025). Assessing the impact of green finance on sustainability in emerging markets: Trends, challenges, and future prospects (2000–Present). *International Scientific Journal Monte, 10*(1), 8–18. DOI: 10.33807/monte.20253288

Cai, M. (2026). Detecting Financial Fraud and Anomalies in Corporate Transactions with Convolutional Neural Networks. *International Journal of Computational Intelligence Systems, 19*(1), 186. Advance online publication. DOI: 10.1007/s44196-026-01275-2

Calik, E., & Bardudeen, F. (2016). A measurement scale to evaluate sustainable innovation performance in manufacturing organizations. *Procedia CIRP, 40*, 449–454. DOI: 10.1016/j.procir.2016.01.091

Cama, F. A. R., & Emara, N. (2021). Financial inclusion and gross capital formation: A sectoral analysis approach for the MENA region and EMs. *International Review of Financial Analysis, 101993*. Advance online publication. DOI: 10.1016/j.irfa.2021.101993

Campos, N. F., & Kinoshita, Y. (2003). Why does FDI go where it goes? New evidence from the transition economies. IMF Working Paper No. 03/228.

Campos, C. J. G., & Turato, E. R. (2009). Content analysis in studies using the clinical-qualitative method: Application and perspectives. *Revista Latino-Americana de Enfermagem, 17*(2), 259–264. DOI: 10.1590/S0104-11692009000200019 PMID: 19551282

Canh, N. P., Schinckus, C., & Thanh, S. D. (2019). Do economic openness and institutional quality influence patents? Evidence from GMM systems estimates. *Inter Economics, 157*, 134–169. DOI: 10.1016/j.inteco.2018.10.002

Cao, L. (2022). AI in finance: Challenges, techniques, and opportunities. ACM Computing Surveys, 55(3). *ACM Computing Surveys, 64*(3), 1–38. DOI: 10.1145/3502289

Cardella, G. M., Hernández-Sánchez, B. R., & Sánchez-García, J. C. (2020). Women entrepreneurship: A systematic review to outline the boundaries of scientific literature. *Frontiers in Psychology, 11*, 1557. DOI: 10.3389/fpsyg.2020.01557

Carkovic, M., & Levine, R. (2005). Does foreign direct investment accelerate economic growth? In T. Moran, E. Graham, & M. Blomström (Eds.), Does foreign direct investment promote development? (pp. 195–220). Institute for International Economics.

Carr, N. (2020). The shallows: What the internet is doing to our brains (Updated ed.). W. W. Norton.

Carroll, A. B. (1991). The pyramid of corporate social responsibility: Toward the moral management of organizational stakeholders. *Business Horizons*, *34*(4), 39–48. DOI: 10.1016/0007-6813(91)90005-G

Chakrabarty, B. (2024). Empowering economies: The rise of women entrepreneurs. *IOSR Journal of Business and Management*, *26*(9), 19–22. DOI: 10.9790/487X-2609061922

Chambers, D., & Munemo, J. (2019). Regulations, institutional quality and entrepreneurship. *Journal of Regulatory Economics*, *55*(1), 46–66. DOI: 10.1007/s11149-019-09377-w

Chang, Y., Wang, X., Wang, J., Wu, Y., Yang, L., Zhu, K., Chen, H., Yi, X., Wang, C., Wang, Y., Ye, W., Zhang, Y., Chang, Y., Yu, P. S., Yang, Q., & Xie, X. (2024). A survey on evaluation of large language models. ACM Transactions on Intelligent Systems and Technology, 15(3). *ACM Transactions on Intelligent Systems and Technology*, *39*(3), 1–45. DOI: 10.1145/3641289

Charfeddine, L., & Mrabet, Z. (2017). The impact of economic development and social-political factors on ecological footprint: A panel data analysis for 15 MENA countries. *Renewable & Sustainable Energy Reviews*, *76*, 138–154. DOI: 10.1016/j.rser.2017.03.031

Chaudhuri, S., & Mukhopadhyay, U. (2014). *Foreign direct investment in developing countries. A Theoretical Evaluation*. Springer India. DOI: 10.1007/978-81-322-1898-2

Chen, Y., Zhao, C., Xu, Y., Nie, C., & Zhang, Y. (2025). *Deep Learning in Financial Fraud Detection: Innovations, Challenges, and Applications*. Data Science and Management., DOI: 10.1016/j.dsm.2025.08.002

Chitimira, H., & Warikandwa, T. (2023). *Financial Inclusion Regulatory Practices in SADC*. Taylor & Francis. DOI: 10.4324/9781003369400

Chomen, M. T. (2022). Institutions–economic growth nexus in Sub-Saharan Africa. *Heliyon*, *8*(12), e11993. DOI: 10.1016/j.heliyon.2022.e12251

Choudhury, B. (2026). International Investment Law and Sustainable Development – Friend or Foe? *Law and Development Review, 19*(2), 717–755. Advance online publication. DOI: 10.1515/ldr-2025-0094

Chowdhury, M. S., Nabi, N., Rana, M. N. U., Shaima, M., Esa, H., Mitra, A., Mozumder, M. A. S., Liza, I. A., Sweet, M. M. R., & Naznin, R. (2024). Deep Learning Models for Stock Market Forecasting: A Comprehensive Comparative Analysis. *Journal of Business and Management Studies, 6*(2), 95–99. DOI: 10.32996/jbms.2024.6.2.9

Christnacht, L., & Mertzanis, C. (2025). Foreign direct investment, technology transfer and the global issuance of green bonds. *Energy Economics, 143*, 108246. DOI: 10.1016/j.eneco.2025.108246

Chua, J. H., Chrisman, J. J., & Sharma, P. (1999). Defining the family business by behavior. *Entrepreneurship Theory and Practice, 23*(4), 19–39. DOI: 10.1177/104225879902300402

Ciriaci, D., Moncada-Paternò-Castello, P., & Voigt, P. (2016). Innovation and job creation: A sustainable relation? *Eurasian Business Review, 6*(2), 189–213. DOI: 10.1007/s40821-015-0031-3

Ciuriak, D. (2014). *Diagnosing Dutch Disease.* Available at *SSRN* 2540108.

Clark, A. W. 2020. A Moment Defined: Corporate Board Composition and Intersectionality, the Broadening Conceptualization of Gender-only to Gender and Race (Doctoral dissertation).

Cohen, J. (1988). *Statistical power analysis for the behavioral sciences* (2nd ed.). Lawrence Erlbaum.

Cohen, J. (1992). A power primer. *Psychological Bulletin, 112*(1), 155–159. DOI: 10.1037/0033-2909.112.1.155

Cohen, K. J., Hawawini, G. A., Maier, S. F., Schwartz, R. A., & Whitcomb, D. K. (1983). Friction in the trading process and the estimation of systematic risk. *Journal of Financial Economics, 12*(2), 263–278. DOI: 10.1016/0304-405X(83)90038-7

Cohen, W. M., & Levinthal, D. A. (1990). Absorptive capacity: A new perspective on learning and innovation. *Administrative Science Quarterly, 35*(1), 128–152. DOI: 10.2307/2393553

Cole, M. A., & Elliott, R. J. R. (2003). Determining the trade–environment composition effect: The role of capital, labour and environmental regulations. *Journal of Environmental Economics and Management, 46*(3), 363–383. DOI: 10.1016/S0095-0696(03)00021-4

Contractor, F. J., Dangol, R., Nuruzzaman, N., & Raghunath, S. (2020). How do country regulations and business environment impact foreign direct investment (FDI) inflows? *International Business Review, 29*(2), 101640. DOI: 10.1016/j.ibusrev.2019.101640

Converse, P. D., Wolfe, E. W., Huang, X., & Oswald, F. L. (2008). Response rates for mixed-mode surveys using mail and e-mail/web. *Journal of Mixed Methods Research, 2*(1), 14–34.

Copeland, B. R., & Taylor, M. S. (2004). Trade, growth, and the environment. *Journal of Economic Literature, 42*(1), 7–71. DOI: 10.1257/.42.1.7

Copestake, A., Estefania-Flores, J., & Furceri, D. (2024). Digitalization and resilience. *Research Policy, 53*(3), 104948. DOI: 10.1016/j.respol.2023.104948

Cordeiro, C. M., Adomaitis, L., & Huang, L. (2026). The AI-policy-governance nexus: How regulation and AI shift corporate governance toward stakeholders. *Technology in Society, 84*, 103117. DOI: 10.1016/j.techsoc.2025.103117

Corden, W. M. (1984). Booming sector and Dutch disease economics: Survey and consolidation. *Oxford Economic Papers, 36*(3), 359–380. DOI: 10.1093/oxfordjournals.oep.a041643

Corden, W. M., & Neary, J. P. (1982). Booming sector and de-industrialisation in a small open economy. *Economic Journal (London), 92*(368), 825–848. DOI: 10.2307/2232670

Cotula, L. (2014). *Foreign investment, law and sustainable development: A handbook on agriculture and extractive industries*. International Institute for Environment and Development (IIED). https://pubs.iied.org/pdfs/17513IIED.pdf

Crenshaw, K. (1991). Mapping the margins: Intersectionality, identity politics, and violence against women of color. *Stanford Law Review, 43*(6), 1241–1299. DOI: 10.2307/1229039

Creswell, J. W., & Plano Clark, V. L. (2017). *Designing and conducting mixed methods research* (3rd ed.). SAGE.

Cubric, M. (2020). Drivers, barriers and social considerations for AI adoption in business and management: A tertiary study. *Technology in Society*, *62*, 101257. DOI: 10.1016/j.techsoc.2020.101257

Czech, K., & Niftiyev, I. (2021). The impact of oil price shocks on oil-dependent countries' currencies: The case of Azerbaijan and Kazakhstan. *Journal of Risk and Financial Management*, *14*(9), 431. DOI: 10.3390/jrfm14090431

Da Afghanistan Bank. (2020). *National Financial Inclusion Strategy 2020–2024*. https://www.dab.gov.af/sites/default/files/2020-06/National%20Financial%20 Inclusion%20Strategy%20for%20Afghanistanfinal.pdf

Damioli, G., & Marin, G. (2024). The effects of foreign entry on local innovation by entry mode. *Research Policy*, *53*(3), 104957. DOI: 10.1016/j.respol.2024.104957

Daniel, M., Bergstøl, I. K. G., & Hansen, M. (2025). Fools rush in… exploring the use of documentary films as qualitative data. *Qualitative Research*, •••, 14687941251377256. DOI: 10.1177/14687941251377256

Danish, & Ulucak, R. (2020). How do environmental technologies affect green growth? Evidence from BRICS economies. *Science of the Total Environment*, *712*, 136504. https://doi.org/DOI: 10.1016/j.scitotenv.2020.136504

Davenport, T. H., & Harris, J. G. (2007). *Competing on analytics: The new science of winning*. Harvard Business Press.

Davenport, T. H., & Ronanki, R. (2018). Artificial intelligence for the real world. *Harvard Business Review*, *96*(1), 108–116.

de Almeida, P. G. R., & dos Santos Júnior, C. D. (2025). Artificial intelligence governance: Understanding how public organizations implement it. *Government Information Quarterly*, *42*(1), 102003. DOI: 10.1016/j.giq.2024.102003

De Mariz, F. (2022). *Finance With a Purpose: Fintech, Development and Financial Inclusion in The Global Economy*. World Scientific. DOI: 10.1142/q0359

De Mello, L. R. (1999). Foreign direct investment-led growth: Evidence from time series and panel data. *Oxford Economic Papers*, *51*(1), 133–151. DOI: 10.1093/oep/51.1.133

Delloitte (2 February 2022). Progress at a snail's pace Women in the boardroom: A global perspective. (7th Edition). file:///C:/Users/Prachi%20Avinashi/Downloads/gx-women-in-the-boardroom-seventh-edition.pdf

Deloitte. (2024). *The state of generative AI in the enterprise*. Deloitte AI Institute.

Demena, B. A., & Afesorgbor, S. K. (2020). The effect of FDI on environmental emissions: Evidence from a meta-analysis. *Energy Policy, 138*, 111192. DOI: 10.1016/j.enpol.2019.111192

Demirguc-Kunt, A., & Klapper, L. (2012). Measuring Financial Inclusion: The Global Findex Database. In *Policy Research Working Papers*. The World Bank. DOI: 10.1596/1813-9450-6025

Dempere, J., Alamash, E., & Mattos, P. (2024). Unveiling the truth: Greenwashing in sustainable finance. *Frontiers in Sustainability*, *5*, 1362051. DOI: 10.3389/frsus.2024.1362051

den Boer, A. V. (2015). Dynamic pricing and learning: Historical origins, current research, and new directions. *Surveys in Operations Research and Management Science*, *20*(1), 1–18. DOI: 10.1016/j.sorms.2015.03.001

Desbordes, R., & Wei, S. J. (2017). Foreign direct investment and external financing conditions: Evidence from normal and crisis times. *The Scandinavian Journal of Economics, 119*(4), 1129-1166. DOI: 10.1111/sjoe.12192

Development Asia. (2025, March 24). *From Cash to Digital: Advancing Financial Inclusion in Pakistan.* Development Asia. https://development.asia/insight/cash-digital-advancing-financial-inclusion-pakistan

Devi, G., Sarma, K. K., Datta, P., & Mahanta, A. K. (2012). Prediction of high energy particle shower sizes and core location using artificial neural networks. *Indian Journal of Physics and Proceedings of the Indian Association for the Cultivation of Science*, *86*(1), 77–84. DOI: 10.1007/s12648-012-0007-4

Di John, J. (2010). *The 'resource curse': Theory and evidence (ARI).* School of Oriental and African Studies (SOAS), University of London.

Díaz-Rodríguez, N., Del Ser, J., Coeckelbergh, M., López de Prado, M., Herrera-Viedma, E., & Herrera, F. (2023). Connecting the dots in trustworthy artificial intelligence: From AI principles, ethics, and key requirements to responsible AI systems and regulation. *Information Fusion*, *99*, 101896. DOI: 10.1016/j.inffus.2023.101896

Dillman, D. A., Smyth, J. D., & Christian, L. M. (2014). *Internet, phone, mail, and mixed-mode surveys: The tailored design method* (4th ed.). Wiley. DOI: 10.1002/9781394260645

Dione, O., & Jabri, K. B. S. A. (2025, May 28). *Oman Vision 2040: A Blueprint for Sustainable Growth and Global Integration.* Perspectives: MENA, Afghanistan. https://blogs.worldbank.org/en/arabvoices/oman-vision-2040-a-blueprint-for-sustainable-growth-and-global-integration

Djankov, S., La Porta, R., Lopez-de-Silanes, F., & Shleifer, A. (2002). The regulation of entry. *The Quarterly Journal of Economics, 117*(1), 1–37. DOI: 10.1162/003355302753399436

Dolzer, R., Kriebaum, U., & Schreuer, C. (2022). *Principles of international investment law*. Oxford University Press., Https://files.pca-cpa.org/pcadocs/bi-c/1.%20Investors/4.%20Legal%20Authorities/CA199.pdf

Domínguez, M. B., Rivo-López, E., & Villanueva-Villar, M. 2019. 'The glass ceiling'. *Organizational Dynamics, 48*, 100706. https://doi.org/DOI: 10.1016/j.orgdyn.2019.02.008

Dorsaf, B. (2025). Breaking glass ceilings or boardroom gridlock? Gender, independence and the new rules of MENA banking resilience. *Journal of Economic Studies (Glasgow, Scotland)*, •••, 1–21. DOI: 10.1108/JES-06-2025-0440

dos Santos, J. F. P., & Williamson, P. J. (2024). Beyond connectivity: Artificial intelligence and the internationalisation of digital firms. *Information and Organization, 34*(4), 100538. DOI: 10.1016/j.infoandorg.2024.100538

Doshi, A. R., & Hauser, O. P. (2024). Generative artificial intelligence enhances individual creativity but reduces the collective diversity of novel content. *Science Advances, 10*(28), eadn5290. Advance online publication. DOI: 10.1126/sciadv.adn5290 PMID: 38996021

Dotzauer, M., Biber-Freudenberger, L., & Dietz, T. (2024). The rise of sustainability provisions in international investment agreements. *Global Environmental Politics, 24*(4), 10–36. DOI: 10.1162/glep_a_00759

Dunning, J. H. (1977). Trade, location of economic activity and the MNE: A search for an eclectic approach. In The international allocation of economic activity: proceedings of a Nobel Symposium held at Stockholm (pp. 395-418). London: Palgrave Macmillan UK. DOI: 10.1007/978-1-349-03196-2_38

Dunning, J. H. (1988). The eclectic paradigm of international production: A restatement and some possible extensions. *Journal of International Business Studies, 19*(1), 1–31. DOI: 10.1057/palgrave.jibs.8490372

Dunning, J. H. (2001). The eclectic (OLI) paradigm of international production: Past, present and future. *International Journal of the Economics of Business, 8*(2), 173–190. DOI: 10.1080/13571510110051441

Dwivedi, Y. K., Hughes, L., Ismagilova, E., Aarts, G., Coombs, C., Crick, T., Duan, Y., Dwivedi, R., Edwards, J., Eirug, A., Galanos, V., Ilavarasan, P. V., Janssen, M., Jones, P., Kar, A. K., Kizgin, H., Kronemann, B., Lal, B., Lucini, B., & Williams, M. D. (2021). Artificial intelligence (AI): Multidisciplinary perspectives on emerging challenges, opportunities, and agenda for research, practice and policy. *International Journal of Information Management*, *57*, 101994. DOI: 10.1016/j.ijinfomgt.2019.08.002

Eccles, R. G., Ioannou, I., & Serafeim, G. (2014). The impact of corporate sustainability on organizational processes and performance. *Management Science*, *60*(11), 2835–2857. DOI: 10.1287/mnsc.2014.1984

Eccles, R. G., & Klimenko, S. (2019). The investor revolution. [Harvard Business Review Article]. *Harvard Business Review*, *97*(3), 106–116.

Ediyono, S., Istadiyantha, I., Farhah, E., Malik, A., & Jazuli, A. (2020, October). The Study of Socio-Cultural Changes in the Middle Eastern Community's Thoughts. In *Proceedings of the First International Conference on Communication, Language, Literature, and Culture, ICCoLLiC 2020,* 8-9 September 2020, Surakarta, Central Java, Indonesia. https://doi.org/DOI: 10.4108/eai.8-9-2020.2301440

Edwards, S. (2023). Reflective journaling. In *Varieties of qualitative research methods: Selected contextual perspectives* (pp. 419–424). Springer International Publishing. DOI: 10.1007/978-3-031-04394-9_65

Ehrentraud, J., Ocampo, D. G., & Vega, C. Q. (2020). *Regulating fintech financing: digital banks and fintech platforms*. Bank for International Settlements, Financial Stability Institute. Https://www.bis.org/fsi/publ/insights27.pdf?Utm

El Jadidi, J., Arsi, S., & Ghoneim, H. (2020). Struggles to break the corporate board ceiling: the case of women in North Africa. In *Struggles and Successes in the Pursuit of Sustainable Development* (pp. 123–138). Routledge., DOI: 10.4324/9781351140560-14

Elkington, J. (1997). *Cannibals with forks: The triple bottom line of 21st century business*. Capstone.

Elmi, L. (2020). Developing countries with natural resources. https://borgenproject.org/developing-countries-that-benefit-from-natural-resources/

Elo, S., & Kyngäs, H. (2008). The qualitative content analysis process. *Journal of Advanced Nursing*, *62*(1), 107–115. DOI: 10.1111/j.1365-2648.2007.04569.x PMID: 18352969

Emako, E., Nuru, S., & Menza, M. (2022). The effect of foreign direct investment on economic growth in developing countries. *Transnational Corporations Review, 14*(4), 382–401. DOI: 10.1080/19186444.2022.2146967

Emara, N., & El Said, A. (2021). Financial inclusion and economic growth: The role of governance in selected MENA countries. *International Review of Economics & Finance, 75*, 34–54. DOI: 10.1016/j.iref.2021.03.014

Enholm, I. M., Papagiannidis, E., Mikalef, P., & Krogstie, J. (2022). Artificial intelligence and business value: A literature review. *Information Systems Frontiers, 24*(5), 1709–1734. DOI: 10.1007/s10796-021-10186-w

Eskeland, G. S., & Harrison, A. E. (2003). Moving to greener pastures? Multinationals and the pollution haven hypothesis. *Journal of Development Economics, 70*(1), 1–23. DOI: 10.1016/S0304-3878(02)00084-6

European Commission. (2018). Action plan: Financing sustainable growth (COM (2018) 97 final). European Commission. European Commission Action Plan: Financing Sustainable Growth. Https://eur-lex.europa.eu/legal-content/EN/TXT/?Uri =CELEX%3A52018DC0097&utm

European Commission. (2019). *Ethics guidelines for trustworthy AI*. European Commission.

European Commission. (2020). Regulation (EU) 2020/852 of the European Parliament and of the Council of 18 June 2020 on the establishment of a framework to facilitate sustainable investment, and amending Regulation (EU) 2019/2088 (Taxonomy Regulation). *Official Journal of the European Union, L, 198*, 13–43. Https://eur-lex.europa.eu/eli/reg/2020/852/oj?Utm

European Commission. (2022, July). *Microfinance and Social Enterprise Finance*. Employment, Social Affairs and Inclusion. https://employment-social-affairs.ec .europa.eu/policies-and-activities/funding/microfinance-and-social-enterprise -finance_en

European Commission. (2023). Corporate Sustainability Reporting Directive (CSRD). Official Journal of the European Union. Https://eur-lex.europa.eu/eli/dir/ 2022/2464/oj?Utm

European Parliament and Council. (2016). *Regulation (EU) 2016/679 (General Data Protection Regulation)*. Official Journal of the European Union.

European Parliament and Council. (2024). *Regulation (EU) 2024/1689 of the European Parliament and of the Council of 13 June 2024 laying down harmonised rules on artificial intelligence (Artificial Intelligence Act)*. Official Journal of the European Union.

Fairclough, N. (2013). *Critical discourse analysis: The critical study of language* (2nd ed.). Routledge. DOI: 10.4324/9781315834368

Fajrian, M. A., Achsani, N. A., & Widyastutik, W. (2023). Foreign direct investment (FDI), abundance of natural resources, and economic growth. *Signifikan: Jurnal Ilmu Ekonomi, 12*(1), 11–26. DOI: 10.15408/sjie.v12i1.29975

Farah, B., Elias, R., Aguilera, R., & Abi Saad, E. (2021). Corporate governance in the Middle East and North Africa: A systematic review of current trends and opportunities for future research. *Corporate Governance, 29*(6), 630–660. DOI: 10.1111/corg.12377

Farhadi, M., Islam, M. R., & Moslehi, S. (2015). Economic freedom and productivity growth in resource-rich economies. *World Development, 72*, 109–126. DOI: 10.1016/j.worlddev.2015.02.014

Farnese, M. L., Barbieri, B., Chirumbolo, A., & Patriotta, G. (2019). Managing knowledge in organizations: A Nonaka's SECI model operationalization. *Frontiers in Psychology, 10*, 2730. DOI: 10.3389/fpsyg.2019.02730 PMID: 31920792

Fatrizia, S., Putra, N. N. A., & Hidayati, S. A. (2025). Role of Good Corporate Governance in Preventing Financial Statement Fraud and Money Laundering. *Journal of Accounting and Finance in Emerging Economies, 11*(1). Advance online publication. DOI: 10.26710/jafee.v11i1.3268

Fernando, N., Newnham, R., Jemila Zahari, M., Marwa, C., & Wong, T. (2018). *National financial inclusion strategies: Current state of practice*. Natinal Financial Inclusion Strategy (FIS) Peer Learning Group. https://sdgs.un.org/sites/default/files/publications/2679National_Financial_Inclusion_Strategies.pdf

Ferreira, K. J., Lee, B. H. K., & Simchi-Levi, D. (2016). Analytics for an online retailer: Demand forecasting and price optimization. *Manufacturing & Service Operations Management, 18*(1), 69–88. DOI: 10.1287/msom.2015.0561

Fitzgerald, A., & Lowe, M. (2020). Acknowledging documentary filmmaking as not only an output but a research process: A case for quality research practice. *International Journal of Qualitative Methods, 19*, 1609406920957462. DOI: 10.1177/1609406920957462

Fitzgerald, M., Kruschwitz, N., Bonnet, D., & Welch, M. (2014). Embracing digital technology: A new strategic imperative. *MIT Sloan Management Review, 55*(2), 1–12.

Floridi, L. (2023). AI as agency without intelligence: On ChatGPT, large language models, and other generative models. *Philosophy & Technology, 36*(1), 15. DOI: 10.1007/s13347-023-00621-y

Floridi, L., & Cowls, J. (2019). A unified framework of five principles for AI in society. *Harvard Data Science Review, 1*(1).

Folorunso, F., Ogbari, M. E., Omoregbe, M., Efegbudu, J., & Olanrewaju, K. (2023). Women entrepreneurship and sustainability: A systematic literature review (SSRN Scholarly Paper No. 4552980). Social Science Research Network. DOI: 10.2139/ssrn.4552980

Følstad, A., & Brandtzæg, P. B. (2017). Chatbots and the new world of HCI. *Interactions (New York, N.Y.), 24*(4), 38–42. DOI: 10.1145/3085558

Font-Cot, F., Lara-Navarra, P., & Serradell-Lopez, E. (2023). Digital transformation policies to develop an effective startup ecosystem: The case of Barcelona. Transforming Government: People. *Process and Policy, 17*(3), 344–355.

Forman, J., & Damschroder, L. (2007). Qualitative content analysis. In L. Jacoby & L. A. Siminoff (Eds.), *Empirical methods for bioethics: A primer* (Advances in Bioethics, Vol. 11, pp. 39–62). Emerald Group Publishing Limited. DOI: 10.1016/S1479-3709(07)11003-7

Fornell, C., & Larcker, D. F. (1981). Evaluating structural equation models with unobservable variables and measurement error. *JMR, Journal of Marketing Research, 18*(1), 39–50. DOI: 10.1177/002224378101800104

Freeman, R. E. (1984). *Strategic management: A stakeholder approach.* Pitman.

Frost, J., Gambacorta, L., Huang, Y., Shin, H. S., & Zbinden, P. (2020). BigTech and the Changing Structure of Financial Intermediation. *Economic Policy, 34*(100), 761–799. Advance online publication. DOI: 10.1093/epolic/eiaa003

Gabelaia, I. (2025). Empowering women entrepreneurs in the green economy. In *Handbook of Research on Environmental Sustainability and Green Entrepreneurship* (pp. 25–40). IGI Global. DOI: 10.4018/979-8-3693-8694-1.ch002

Gaidosch, T., Islam, E., Khiaonarong, T., Ravikumar, R., & Wilson, C. (2026). Good Practices in Cyber Risk Regulation and Supervision. *Departmental Papers, 2026*(001), 1. DOI: 10.5089/9798229026185.087

García-Madurga, M. Á., Grilló-Méndez, A. J., & Morte-Nadal, T. (2020). Territorial intelligence, a collective challenge for sustainable development: A scoping review. *Social Sciences (Basel, Switzerland)*, *9*(7), 126. DOI: 10.3390/socsci9070126

Gbambu, A. R., Dramani, J. S., & Adekunle, M. O. (2023). A contextual analysis of documentary film as a product and tool for academic exercise. *European Journal of Communication and Media Studies*, *2*(4), 25–35. DOI: 10.24018/ejmedia.2023.2.4.22

Gee, J. P. (2014). *An introduction to discourse analysis: Theory and method* (4th ed.). Routledge. DOI: 10.4324/9781315819679

George, G., & Schillebeeckx, S. J. D. (2022). Digital transformation, sustainability, and purpose in the multinational enterprise. *Journal of World Business*, *57*(3), 101326. DOI: 10.1016/j.jwb.2022.101326

Ghosh, S., Hughes, M., Hodgkinson, I., & Hughes, P. (2022). Digital transformation of industrial businesses: A dynamic capability approach. *Technovation*, *113*, 102414. DOI: 10.1016/j.technovation.2021.102414

Ghosh, S., & Saha, S. K. (2025). Impact of foreign direct investment on economic growth in developing countries: The role of institutional quality. *Sustainable Economies, 3*(1), 389. DOI: 10.62617/se389

Glisby, M., & Holden, N. (2003). Contextual constraints in knowledge management theory: The cultural embeddedness of Nonaka's knowledge-creating company. *Knowledge and Process Management*, *10*(1), 29–36. DOI: 10.1002/kpm.158

Global Reporting Initiative. (2021). *GRI standards*. Global Reporting Initiative.

Globerman, S., & Shapiro, D. (2002). Global foreign direct investment flows: The role of governance infrastructure. *World Development*, *30*(11), 1899–1919. DOI: 10.1016/S0305-750X(02)00110-9

Gnewuch, U., Morana, S., & Maedche, A. (2017). Towards designing cooperative and social conversational agents for customer service. In *Proceedings of the International Conference on Information Systems (ICIS)*.

Godoy, R., Bauchet, J., Reyes-García, V., & Undurraga, E. A. (2026). Economic convergence, intragenerational economic mobility, and inequality in a native Amazonian small-scale society of Indigenous People in Bolivia. *World Development*, *199*, 107237. DOI: 10.1016/j.worlddev.2025.107237

Go, E. J., Moon, J., & Kim, J. (2020). Analysis of the Current and Future of Artificial Intelligence in Financial Industry with Big Data Techniques. *Global Business Finance Review*, *25*(1), 102–117. DOI: 10.17549/gbfr.2020.25.1.102

Goldfarb, A., & Tucker, C. (2019). Digital economics. *Journal of Economic Literature, 57*(1), 3–43. DOI: 10.1257/jel.20171452

Goldstein, I., Spatt, C. S., & Ye, M. (2023). Big data in finance. *Review of Financial Studies, 36*(1), 1–12. DOI: 10.1093/rfs/hhac083

Gomez-Uribe, C. A., & Hunt, N. (2016). The Netflix recommender system: Algorithms, business value, and innovation. *ACM Transactions on Management Information Systems, 6*(4), 13. DOI: 10.1145/2843948

Goos, M., & Savona, M. (2024). Artificial intelligence governance: Regulating the responsible development and adoption of AI. *Research Policy, 53*(6), 104928. DOI: 10.1016/j.respol.2023.104928

Gourlay, S. (2006). Conceptualizing knowledge creation: A critique of Nonaka's theory. *Journal of Management Studies, 43*(7), 1415–1436. DOI: 10.1111/j.1467-6486.2006.00637.x

Graef, I., & Prüfer, J. (2021). Governance of data sharing: A law & economics proposal. *Research Policy, 50*(9), 104330. DOI: 10.1016/j.respol.2021.104330

Grant, M. J., & Booth, A. (2009). A typology of reviews: An analysis of 14 review types and associated methodologies. *Health Information and Libraries Journal, 26*(2), 91–108. DOI: 10.1111/j.1471-1842.2009.00848.x PMID: 19490148

Gregor, S. (2006). The Nature of Theory in Information Systems1. *Management Information Systems Quarterly, 30*(3), 611–642. DOI: 10.2307/25148742

Grohmann, A., Klühs, T., & Menkhoff, L. (2018). Does financial literacy improve financial inclusion? Cross country evidence. *World Development, 111*, 84–96. DOI: 10.1016/j.worlddev.2018.06.020

Grossman, G. M., & Krueger, A. B. (1995). Economic growth and the environment. *The Quarterly Journal of Economics, 110*(2), 353–377. DOI: 10.2307/2118443

Guandalini, I. (2022). Sustainability through digital transformation: A systematic literature review for research guidance. *Journal of Business Research, 148*, 456–471. DOI: 10.1016/j.jbusres.2022.05.003

Guetterman, T. C., Fetters, M. D., & Creswell, J. W. (2015). Integrating quantitative and qualitative results in health science mixed methods research through joint displays. *Annals of Family Medicine, 13*(6), 554–561. DOI: 10.1370/afm.1865 PMID: 26553895

Guo, X., Meng, X., Luan, Q., & Wang, Y. (2023). Trade openness, globalization, and natural resources management: The moderating role of economic complexity in newly industrialized countries. *Resources Policy, 85*, 103757. DOI: 10.1016/j.resourpol.2023.103757

Haapanen, L., & Tapio, P. (2016). Economic growth as phenomenon, institution and ideology: A qualitative content analysis of the 21st century growth critique. *Journal of Cleaner Production, 112*, 3492–3503. DOI: 10.1016/j.jclepro.2015.10.024

Hadhek, Z. (2012). Institutions, Investment and Economic Growth. *International Journal of Economics and Finance.*

Haggard, S. (2004). Institutions and growth in East Asia. *Studies in Comparative International Development, 38*(4), 53–81. DOI: 10.1007/BF02686328

Hair, J. F., Hult, G. T. M., Ringle, C. M., & Sarstedt, M. (2022). *A primer on partial least squares structural equation modeling (PLS-SEM)* (3rd ed.). SAGE.

Hallahan, K., Holtzhausen, D., van Ruler, B., Verčič, D., & Sriramesh, K. (2007). Defining strategic communication. *International Journal of Strategic Communication, 1*(1), 3–35. DOI: 10.1080/15531180701285244

Hammer, M. (1990). Reengineering work: Don't automate, obliterate. *Harvard Business Review, 68*(4), 104–112.

Han, C., Harrold, T., Armour, S., Krikidis, I., Videv, S., Grant, P. M., Haas, H., Thompson, J. S., Ku, I., Wang, C.-X., Le, T. A., Nakhai, M. R., Zhang, J., & Hanzo, L. (2011). Green radio: Radio techniques to enable energy-efficient wireless networks. *IEEE Communications Magazine, 49*(6), 46–54. DOI: 10.1109/MCOM.2011.5783984

Hart, S. L. (1995). A natural-resource-based view of the firm. *Academy of Management Review, 20*(4), 986–1014. DOI: 10.2307/258963

Hasanli, Y., Musayeva, J., & Musayeva, F. (2026). How do oil and gas reserves affect the economic growth of the CIS countries: Evidence from panel data. In *Digitalisation and Artificial Intelligence Using Mathematical and Computational Approaches: FAI-DAIRBM 2024*, Baku, Azerbaijan, April 18–20, 291.

Hasanli, Y., Rahimli, G., Ibişov, E., & Rzayev, R. (2025b). Inter-Sectoral Linkages and Structural Change in Azerbaijan: Insights from the Transport Sector. In *4th International Conference on Problems of Logistics, Management and Operation in the East-West Transport Corridor (PLMO 2025).*

Hasanli, Y., Rahimli, G., Quliyev, F., & Ferrari, M. (2025a). Evaluation of sectoral foreign trade elasticities of Azerbaijan. *Journal of Economic Sciences Theory and Practice*, *82*(2), 117–137.

Hasanov, R. I., Giyasova, Z., Mahmudova, I., Marchwiński, J., & Karimova, N. (2025). Examining the relationship between manufacturing value added and environmental impact in Azerbaijan. *International Journal of Energy Economics and Policy, 15.*

Hasanov, R. I., Giyasova, Z., Azizova, R., Huseynova, S., & Zemri, B. E. (2024). Long-term dynamics between human development and environmental sustainability: An empirical analysis of CO_2 emissions in Azerbaijan. *Challenges in Sustainability*, *12*(4), 273–280. DOI: 10.56578/cis120403

Hashemi, S. K., Mirtaheri, S. L., & Greco, S. (2022). Fraud Detection in Banking Data by Machine Learning Techniques. *IEEE Access : Practical Innovations, Open Solutions*, *11*, 1–1. DOI: 10.1109/ACCESS.2022.3232287

Henri, P. A. O. (2019). Natural resources curse: A reality in Africa. *Resources Policy*, *63*, 101406. DOI: 10.1016/j.resourpol.2019.101406

Henseler, J., Ringle, C. M., & Sarstedt, M. (2015). A new criterion for assessing discriminant validity in variance-based structural equation modeling. *Journal of the Academy of Marketing Science*, *43*(1), 115–135. DOI: 10.1007/s11747-014-0403-8

Hermes, N., & Lensink, R. (2003). Foreign direct investment, financial development and economic growth. *The Journal of Development Studies*, *40*(1), 142–163. DOI: 10.1080/00220380412331293707

Hilbrich, S., Berensmann, K., Artmann, G., Ashman, S., Herbold, T., Lötters-Viehof, S., Monti, A., Paffhausen, F., Roigk, S., & Steenkamp, L. A. (2025). Implementing sustainability taxonomies to redirect capital flows: The case of South Africa. *Climate Policy*, *25*(5), 741–755. DOI: 10.1080/14693062.2024.2415382

Holden, S. (2013). Avoiding the resource curse the case Norway. *Energy Policy*, *63*, 870–876. DOI: 10.1016/j.enpol.2013.09.010

Hong, S., Reed, W. R., Tian, B., Wu, T., & Chen, G. (2021). Does FDI promote entrepreneurial activities? A meta-analysis. *World Development*, *142*, 105436. DOI: 10.1016/j.worlddev.2021.105436

Ho, T. S. Y., & Michaely, R. (1988). Information Quality and Market Efficiency. *Journal of Financial and Quantitative Analysis*, *23*(1), 53. DOI: 10.2307/2331024

Hoxha, V. (2023). Exploring the predictive power of ANN and traditional regression models in real estate pricing: Evidence from Prishtina. *Journal of Property Investment & Finance. Journal of Property Investment & Finance*, *42*(2), 134–150. DOI: 10.1108/JPIF-06-2023-0051

Hsieh, H. F., & Shannon, S. E. (2005). Three approaches to qualitative content analysis. *Qualitative Health Research*, *15*(9), 1277–1288. DOI: 10.1177/1049732305276687 PMID: 16204405

Hubner, W. (2000, October). SME development in countries of Central Asia (Kazakhstan, Kyrgyzstan and Uzbekistan): Constraints, cultural aspects and role of international assistance. Paper presented at the United Nations Industrial Development Organization (UNIDO) Session III Conference, Vienna, Austria.

Humphreys, M., Sachs, J. D., & Stiglitz, J. E. (2007). Introduction: What is the problem with natural resource wealth. In Humphreys, M., Sachs, J. D., & Stiglitz, J. E. (Eds.), *Escaping the Resource Curse* (pp. 1–20). Columbia University Press.

Hunjra, A. I., Bouri, E., Azam, M., Azam, R. I., & Dai, J. (2024). Economic growth and environmental sustainability in developing economies. *Research in International Business and Finance*, *70*, 102341. DOI: 10.1016/j.ribaf.2024.102341

Hydrogen Oman. (2024). Oman Green Hydrogen Strategy.

Hydrom. (2024). *Green hydrogen developments in Oman: Project overview and investment outlook*. Muscat, Oman: Hydrom. Retrieved May 20, 2026, from https://hydrom.om/projects

Iamsiraroj, S. (2016). The foreign direct investment–economic growth nexus. *International Review of Economics & Finance*, *42*, 116–133. DOI: 10.1016/j.iref.2015.10.044

Iansiti, M., & Lakhani, K. R. (2020). Competing in the age of AI. *Harvard Business Review*, *98*(1), 60–67.

IFC. Women on Board in Egypt. https://documents1.worldbank.org/curated/en/612601567750997033/pdf/Women-on-Board-in-Egypt-How-Gender-Diverse-Boards-Bring-Value-to-Egyptian-Companies.pdf

Ilyas, M., et al. (2023). Relevant paper on FDI, productivity, or economic integration in Africa/developing contexts

IMF. (2026). *World Economic Outlook Update, January 2026: Global Economy: Steady amid Divergent Forces*. World Economic Outlook Update. https://www.imf.org/en/publications/weo/issues/2026/01/19/world-economic-outlook-update-january-2026

Intam, R. N. J., Raihan, A., Alfajri, M., Kaswar, A. B., & Andayani, D. D., & Asnidar. (. (2024). Sistem Klasifikasi Jenis Sampah Berdasarkan Kombinasi Fitur Warnac Tekstur Menggunakan Artifical Neural Network Berbasis Pengolahan Citra Digital. *Jurnal Teknologi Informasi Dan Ilmu Komputer, 11*(2), 411–420. DOI: 10.25126/jtiik.20241128330

International Energy Agency (IEA). (2024). *Data and statistics*. Paris, France: International Energy Agency. Retrieved January 15, 2025, from https://www.iea.org/data-and-statistics

International Labour Organization. (2024). *Global employment trends for youth 2024: Middle East and North Africa (ILO Policy Brief No. 1)*. International Labour Organization.

International Renewable Energy Agency (IRENA). (2023). *Renewable energy market analysis: GCC region*. IRENA.

Inthavixay, S., Inthasone, S., Chanthaphavong, A., & Keophilavong, T. (2024). Utilizing Machine Learning Techniques to Identify Anomalies in Financial Transactions for Laos Banking. 2022 5th International Conference on Information and Communications Technology (ICOIACT), 79–84. DOI: 10.1109/ICOIACT64819.2024.10913217

Invest Oman. (n.d.). Oman investment incentive guide.

ISO. (2018). *ISO 30414: Human resource management—Guidelines for internal and external human capital reporting*. International Organization for Standardization.

ISSB. (2023). IFRS S1 general requirements for disclosure of sustainability-related financial information and IFRS S2 climate-related disclosures. International Sustainability Standards Board. Https://www.ifrs.org/sustainability/knowledge-hub/introduction-to-issb-and-ifrs-sustainability-disclosure-standards/?Utm

Izadi, R., Bahrami, M. A., Sarikhani, Y., & Bastani, P. (2023). Qualitative document analysis on Iranian contents and trends of population policies: Lessons learned and avenues for future. *Heliyon*, *9*(6), e17377. DOI: 10.1016/j.heliyon.2023.e17377 PMID: 37408904

J, T., Narayanan, L., M, T., & Revathi, M. (2025). A Hybrid Anomaly Detection Framework for Credit Card Fraud Using Autoencoder and Isolation Forest. 2025 9th International Conference on Computational System and Information Technology for Sustainable Solutions (CSITSS), 1–6. .DOI: 10.1109/CSITSS67709.2025.11294206

Jain, M., Kumar, P., Kota, R., & Patel, S. (2018). Evaluating and informing the design of chatbots. In *Proceedings of the CHI Conference on Human Factors in Computing Systems*. DOI: 10.1145/3196709.3196735

Jallat, F., & Ancarani, F. (2008). Yield management, dynamic pricing and CRM in telecommunications. *Journal of Services Marketing*, *22*(5), 404–414. DOI: 10.1108/08876040810901882

Jarrahi, M. H. (2018). Artificial intelligence and the future of work: Human–AI symbiosis in organizational decision making. *Business Horizons*, *61*(4), 577–586. DOI: 10.1016/j.bushor.2018.03.007

Jarrahi, M. H., Askay, D., Eshraghi, A., & Smith, P. (2023). Artificial intelligence and knowledge management: A partnership between human and AI. *Business Horizons*, *66*(1), 87–99. DOI: 10.1016/j.bushor.2022.03.002

Javorcik, B. S. (2004). Does foreign direct investment increase the productivity of domestic firms? *The American Economic Review*, *94*(3), 605–627. DOI: 10.1257/0002828041464605

Jihane, T., & Aziz, M. (2022). Banks and FinTech Relationship in a Digital Transformation Context. *European Scientific Journal*, *18*(12), 106. DOI: 10.19044/esj.2022.v18n12p106

Jiménez-Jiménez, D., & Sanz-Valle, R. (2011). Innovation, organizational learning, and performance. *Journal of Business Research*, *64*(4), 408–417. DOI: 10.1016/j.jbusres.2010.09.010

Ji, Z., Lee, N., Frieske, R., Yu, T., Su, D., Xu, Y., Ishii, E., Bang, Y. J., Madotto, A., & Fung, P. (2023). Survey of hallucination in natural language generation. ACM Computing Surveys, 55(12). *ACM Computing Surveys*, *248*(12), 1–38. DOI: 10.1145/3571730

Johnson, L., & Sachs, L. E. (2019). Investment Treaties, Investor-State Dispute Settlement, and Inequality: How International Investment Treaties Exacerbate Domestic Disparities. Https://scholarship.law.columbia.edu/cgi/viewcontent.cgi?Article=1105&context=sustainable_investment_staffpubs

Jones, J., Harris, E., Febriansah, Y., Adiwijaya, A., & Hikam, I. N. (2024). AI for sustainable development: Applications in natural resource management, agriculture, and waste management. *International Transactions on Artificial Intelligence*, *2*(2), 143–149. DOI: 10.33050/italic.v2i2.549

Jørgensen, M., & Phillips, L. J. (2002). *Discourse analysis as theory and method.* Sage Publications. DOI: 10.4135/9781849208871

Jude, C., & Levieuge, G. (2016). Growth Effect of Foreign Direct Investment in Developing Economies: The Role of Institutional Quality. *World Economy*, *40*(4), 715–742. DOI: 10.1111/twec.12402

Kahveci, E., & Odabaş, A. (2016). Central banks' communication strategy and content analysis of monetary policy statements: The case of Fed, ECB and CBRT. *Procedia: Social and Behavioral Sciences*, *235*, 618–629. DOI: 10.1016/j.sbspro.2016.11.039

Kalandia, A. (2023). The Role of Foreign Direct Investment (FDI) on Georgian Economy. In *The Digital Transformation of Georgia: Economics, Management, and Policy* (pp. 23-34): Springer.

Kane, G. C., Palmer, D., Phillips, A. N., Kiron, D., & Buckley, N. (2015). Strategy, not technology, drives digital transformation. *MIT Sloan Management Review.*

Kanval, N., Ihsan, H., Irum, S., & Ambreen, I. (2024). Human capital formation, foreign direct investment inflows, and economic growth: A way forward to achieve sustainable development. *Journal of Management Practices. Humanities and Social Sciences*, *8*(3), 48–61.

Kao, C. (1999). Spurious regression and residual-based tests for cointegration in panel data. *Journal of Econometrics*, *90*(1), 1–44. DOI: 10.1016/S0304-4076(98)00023-2

Kaplan, A., & Haenlein, M. (2018). Artificial intelligence: Revolutionizing the way we think and work. [IJRAR]. *International Journal of Research and Analytical Reviews*, *5*(4), 973–976.

Kariria. (2026). Corporate Governance and Fraud Prevention: An Empirical Study of Indian Corporations. Journal of Informatics Education and Research. .DOI: 10.52783/jier.v6i1.4243

Kaufmann, D., Kraay, A., & Mastruzzi, M. (2011). The Worldwide Governance Indicators: Methodology and Analytical Issues. *Hague Journal on the Rule of Law*, *3*(2), 220–246. DOI: 10.1017/S1876404511200046

Keddie, N. R. (2012). *Women in the Middle East: past and present* (1st ed.). Princeton University Press., DOI: 10.2307/j.cttq94c5

Kellenberg, D. K. (2009). An empirical investigation of the pollution haven effect with strategic environment and trade policy. *Journal of International Economics, 78*(2), 242–255. DOI: 10.1016/j.jinteco.2009.04.004

Keller, W. (2010). International trade, foreign direct investment, and technology spillovers. Handbook of the Economics of Innovation, 2, 793–829.

Keller, W., & Levinson, A. (2002). Pollution abatement costs and foreign direct investment inflows to U.S. states. *The Review of Economics and Statistics, 84*(4), 691–703. DOI: 10.1162/003465302760556503

Kelsey, D., Mueller, F., Whittle, A., & KhosraviNik, M. (Eds.). (2019). *The discourse of financial crisis and austerity: Critical analyses of business and economics across disciplines*. Routledge.

Kernan Freire, S., Wang, C., Foosherian, M., Wellsandt, S., Ruiz-Arenas, S., & Niforatos, E. (2024). Knowledge sharing in manufacturing using LLM-powered tools: User study and model benchmarking. *Frontiers in Artificial Intelligence, 7*, 1293084. DOI: 10.3389/frai.2024.1293084 PMID: 38601111

Khalifa Alhabsi, S., Salim Alamri, S., Mubarak, A., & Mohammed, E. (2022). A Study on the Role of Small and Medium Enterprises (SME) in the Economic Growth of Oman Student at Oman college of management & technology-Department of administrative and financial sciences. *Quest Journals Journal of Research in Humanities and Social Science, 10*(6), 2321–9467.

Khan, S. (2023, May 05). ""Women vastly underrepresented in region's corporate boardrooms, report says". *The National News: UAE Edition*. https://www.thenationalnews.com/business/2023/05/05/women-vastly-underrepresented-in-menat-region-corporate-boardrooms-report-says/

Khan, S. H. R. (2011). *Financial inclusion and financial stability: are they two sides of the same coin?* BIS Central Bankers' speeches, Indian Bankers Association and Indian Overseas Bank. https://www.bis.org/review/r111229f.pdf

Khan, H., Dong, Y., Bibi, R., & Khan, I. (2024). Institutional quality and foreign direct investment: Global evidence. *Journal of the Knowledge Economy, 15*(3), 10547–10591. DOI: 10.1007/s13132-023-01508-1

Khan, T. H., & MacEachen, E. (2021). Foucauldian discourse analysis: Moving beyond a social constructionist analytic. *International Journal of Qualitative Methods, 20*, 16094069211018009. DOI: 10.1177/16094069211018009

Khatri, V., & Brown, C. V. (2010). Designing data governance. *Communications of the ACM, 53*(1), 148–152. DOI: 10.1145/1629175.1629210

Kirchner, K., Bolisani, E., Kassaneh, T. C., Scarso, E., & Taraghi, N. (2025). Generative AI meets knowledge management: Insights from software development practices. *Knowledge and Process Management*, *32*(4), 223–235. Advance online publication. DOI: 10.1002/kpm.70004

Kock, N. (2015). Common method bias in PLS-SEM: A full collinearity assessment approach. *International Journal of e-Collaboration*, *11*(4), 1–10. DOI: 10.4018/ijec.2015100101

Kock, N., & Hadaya, P. (2018). Minimum sample size estimation in PLS-SEM: The inverse square root and gamma-exponential methods. *Information Systems Journal*, *28*(1), 227–261. DOI: 10.1111/isj.12131

Kriebaum, U. (2022). International Investment Law and Sustainable Development. Siobhan mcinerney-Langford/Robert mccorquodale: The Role of International Law in Development. DOI: 10.2139/ssrn.4298374

Krueger, A. O. (1974). The political economy of the rent-seeking society. *The American Economic Review*, *64*(3), 291–303.

Krueger, P., Sautner, Z., & Starks, L. T. (2020). The importance of climate risks for institutional investors. *Review of Financial Studies*, *33*(3), 1067–1111. DOI: 10.1093/rfs/hhz137

Krueger, P., Sautner, Z., Tang, D. Y., & Zhong, R. (2024). The effects of mandatory ESG disclosure around the world. *Journal of Accounting Research*, *62*(5), 1795–1847. DOI: 10.1111/1475-679X.12548

Kumar, V., & Reinartz, W. (2018). *Customer relationship management: Concept, strategy, and tools* (3rd ed.). Springer. DOI: 10.1007/978-3-662-55381-7

La Porta, R., Lopez-de-Silanes, F., Shleifer, A., & Vishny, R. W. (1998). Law and finance. *Journal of Political Economy*, *106*(6), 1113–1155. DOI: 10.1086/250042

Lambrecht, A., & Tucker, C. (2019). Algorithmic targeting. *Journal of Marketing*, *83*(5), 1–19.

Leal-Arcas, R., Almashloum, S., Jazzar, R., Saleh, N. Bin, & Almunifi, R. (2025). Energy Policy of Oman: Pursuing Decarbonization. *Energies 2025, Vol. 18, Page 1270, 18*(5), 1270. DOI: 10.3390/en18051270

Lee, C.-C., Lee, C.-C., & Cheng, C.-Y. (2020 or 2022). The impact of FDI on income inequality: Evidence from the perspective of financial development. International Journal of Finance & Economics. https://doi.org/ (or related threshold/inequality paper).DOI: 10.1002/ijfe.XXXX

Lemon, K. N., & Verhoef, P. C. (2016). Understanding customer experience throughout the customer journey. *Journal of Marketing*, *80*(6), 69–96. DOI: 10.1509/jm.15.0420

Levine, R. (2005). Finance and growth: Theory and evidence. In P. Aghion & S. Durlauf (Eds.), Handbook of Economic Growth (Vol. 1A, pp. 865–934). Elsevier.

Levinson, A., & Taylor, M. S. (2008). Unmasking the pollution haven effect. *International Economic Review*, *49*(1), 223–254. DOI: 10.1111/j.1468-2354.2008.00478.x

Lewis, P., Perez, E., Piktus, A., Petroni, F., Karpukhin, V., & Goyal, N.. (2020). Retrieval-augmented generation for knowledge-intensive NLP tasks. In *Advances in Neural Information Processing Systems* (Vol. 33, pp. 9459–9474). Curran Associates.

Lindner, T., Puck, J., & Puhr, H. (2025). Artificial intelligence in international business: IB theory under augmented decision-making. *Journal of World Business*, *60*(6), 101676. DOI: 10.1016/j.jwb.2025.101676

Linh, D. T. H., et al. (2019). Foreign direct investment and economic growth in developing/Asian contexts; often with short- vs. long-run analysis.

Lishner, I., & Shtub, A. (2022). Using an Artificial Neural Network for Improving the Prediction of Project Duration. *Mathematics*, *10*(22), 4189. DOI: 10.3390/math10224189

Liu, C. (2024). The application of AI and product innovation efficiency: The role of knowledge innovation under the SECI model. *Aslib Journal of Information Management*. Advance online publication. DOI: 10.1108/AJIM-04-2024-0348

Liu, Y., Sun, Z., & Zhang, W. (2023). Improving fraud detection via hierarchical attention-based Graph Neural Network. *Journal of Information Security and Applications*, *72*, 103399–103399. DOI: 10.1016/j.jisa.2022.103399

Li, W., Li, W., Seppänen, V., & Koivumäki, T. (2023). Effects of greenwashing on financial performance: Moderation through local environmental regulation and media coverage. *Business Strategy and the Environment*, *32*(1), 820–841. DOI: 10.1002/bse.3177

Lozano, R. (2015). A holistic perspective on corporate sustainability drivers. *Corporate Social Responsibility and Environmental Management*, *22*(1), 32–44. DOI: 10.1002/csr.1325

Lozano, R. (2018). Proposing a definition and a framework of organizational sustainability. *Sustainability*, *10*(4), 1157. DOI: 10.3390/su10041157

Lucas, R. E.Jr. (1988). On the mechanics of economic development. *Journal of Monetary Economics*, *22*(1), 3–42. DOI: 10.1016/0304-3932(88)90168-7

Macchiavello, E., & Siri, M. (2022). Sustainable Finance and Fintech: Can Technology Contribute to Achieving Environmental Goals? A Preliminary Assessment of 'Green Fintech' and 'Sustainable Digital Finance'. *European Company and Financial Law Review, 19*(1), 128–174. DOI: 10.1515/ecfr-2022-0005

Maeße, J. (2015). Crisis management policy: How discourses shape academic-political actors. *On the Horizon, 23*(3), 231–244. DOI: 10.1108/OTH-05-2015-0016

Magazzino, C., Mele, M., & Schneider, N. (2021). A machine learning approach on the relationship among solar and wind energy production, coal consumption, GDP, and CO_2 emissions. *Renewable Energy, 167*, 99–115. DOI: 10.1016/j.renene.2020.11.050

Mahadevan, R., & Sun, Y. (2020). Effects of foreign direct investment on carbon emissions: Evidence from developing countries. *Journal of Environmental Management, 276*, 111321. DOI: 10.1016/j.jenvman.2020.111321 PMID: 32896824

Maharana, K. (2025). A Review: Data Overfitting and Underfitting Techniques. *Journal of Information Systems Engineering & Management, 10*(13s), 387–405. DOI: 10.52783/jisem.v10i13s.2072

Mallampally, P., & Sauvant, K. P. (1999). Foreign direct investment in developing countries. *Finance & Development, 36*(1), 34.

Mallepally, A., & Mallepally, A. (2025). Women entrepreneurs and start-ups: Breaking barriers. *International Journal of Advanced Business Management Research, 3*(Supplementary), 86–92.

Manasseh, C. O., Nwakoby, I. C., Okanya, O. C., Ifediora, C. U., & Nzidee, W. A. (2023). The impact of foreign direct investment and oil revenue on economic growth in Nigeria. *Studia Universitatis Vasile Goldi Arad. Seria tiin e Economice, 33*(3), 61–85.

Mariani, M., & Dwivedi, Y. K. (2024). Generative artificial intelligence in innovation management: A preview of future research developments. *Journal of Business Research, 175*, 114542. DOI: 10.1016/j.jbusres.2024.114542

Market Research Report. (2025, January 10). *FinTech Industry Market*. Market.us. https://market.us/report/fintech-industry-market/

Markoczy, L., Sun, S. L., & Zhu, J. 2020. Few women on boards: what's identity got to do with it? *Journal of business ethics, 165*, 311-327. https://doi.org/DOI: 10.1007/s10551-019-04104-z

Maróczy, G. (2020). *Die französische Partie* (Vol. 8). Walter de Gruyter GmbH & Co KG., DOI: 10.1007/978-3-8349-9305-2_1

Marripudugala, M. (2024). AI-Powered Fraud Detection in the Financial Services Sector: A Machine Learning Approach. 2024 2nd International Conference on Self Sustainable Artificial Intelligence Systems (ICSSAS), 795–799. DOI: 10.1109/ICSSAS64001.2024.10760599

Martínez-Sanchis, P., Aragón-Amonarriz, C., & Iturrioz-Landart, C. (2020). How does the territory impact on entrepreneurial family embeddedness? *. *Journal of Enterprising Communities: People and Places in the Global Economy*, *16*(2), 196–217. DOI: 10.1108/JEC-09-2019-0087

Matsumoto, T., Nishikawa, R., & Morimoto, C. (2025). Human-AI-collaboration SECI model: A knowledge management model of experts' tacit knowledge with augmented LLM-based AI. In Jezic, G., Chen-Burger, J., Kusek, M., Sperka, R., Howlett, R. J., & Jain, L. C. (Eds.), *Agents and multi-agent systems: Technologies and applications 2024* (pp. 141–153). Springer., DOI: 10.1007/978-981-97-6469-3_12

Mayring, P. (2021). Qualitative content analysis: A step-by-step guide. *Sage (Atlanta, Ga.).*

McIntosh, P. (1992) White privilege. *Creation Spirituality,* 33–35.

Meetei, L. A., Bhattacharjya, B. R., & Bhowmick, B. (2024). The role of universities in the innovation systems in the developing countries. *Foresight and STI Governance*, *18*(1), 58–67. DOI: 10.17323/2500-2597.2024.1.58.67

Mehrabi, N., Morstatter, F., Saxena, N., Lerman, K., & Galstyan, A. (2021). A survey on bias and fairness in machine learning. *ACM Computing Surveys*, *54*(6), 115.

Meng-tao, C., Da-peng, Y., Wei-qi, Z., & Qi-jun, W. (2023). How does ESG disclosure improve stock liquidity for enterprises—Empirical evidence from China. *Environmental Impact Assessment Review*, *98*, 106926. DOI: 10.1016/j.eiar.2022.106926

Mertens, D. M. (2005). *Research and evaluation in education and Psychology: Integrating diversity with quantitative, qualitative, and mixed methods* (2nd ed.). SAGE Publications.

Mikalef, P., & Gupta, M. (2021). Artificial intelligence capability: Conceptualization, measurement calibration, and empirical study on its impact on organizational creativity and firm performance. *Information & Management*, *58*(3), 103434. DOI: 10.1016/j.im.2021.103434

Ministry of Commerce, Industry and Investment Promotion. (2019). Foreign Capital Investment Law, Royal Decree No. 50/2019.

Ministry of Transport, Communications and Information Technology. (2022). Personal Data Protection Law, Royal Decree No. 6/2022.

Ministry of Transport, Communications and Information Technology. (2024a). National Program for Artificial Intelligence and Advanced Digital Technologies: Oman AI & Digital Future Program 2024–2026.

Ministry of Transport, Communications and Information Technology. (2024b). Executive Regulations of the Personal Data Protection Law, Ministerial Decision No. 34/2024.

Ministry of Transport, Communications and Information Technology. (2025). Framework for National Data Governance.

Ministry of Transport, Communications and Information Technology. (n.d.). National Digital Economy Programme. Sultanate of Oman.

Moghadam, V. M. (2005). Women's economic participation in the Middle East: What difference has the neoliberal policy turn made? *Journal of Middle East Women's Studies, 1*(1), 110-146. https://doi.org/DOI: 10.2979/MEW.2005.1.1.110

Mokkapati, R., & Dasari, V. L. (2023). *A Comprehensive Review on Areas and Applications of Artificial Intelligence*. Machine Learning, Deep Learning, and Data Science., DOI: 10.1109/ICIMIA60377.2023.10426237

Moktar, N., Mat Deli, M., Abdul Rauf, U. A., Idris, F., & Purwati, A. A. (2023). ESG disclosure: The extent of investors' confidence in stock market. *International Journal of Academic Research in Progressive Education and Development, 12*(3), 1008–1027. DOI: 10.6007/IJARPED/v12-i3/18989

Morgan, D. L. (2014). Pragmatism as a paradigm for social research. *Qualitative Inquiry, 20*(8), 1045–1053. DOI: 10.1177/1077800413513733

Morgan, R., Game, A. M., & Slutskaya, N. (2019). Qualitative research through documentary filmmaking: Questions and possibilities. In Cassell, C., Cunliffe, A., & Grandy, G. (Eds.), *The Sage handbook of qualitative business and management research methods: Methods and challenges* (pp. 329–344). Sage.

Mottaleb, K. A. (2007). *Determinants of foreign direct investment and its impact on economic growth in developing countries*. MPRA Paper, No. 9457.

Moturi Swathi, N. (2024). *Shalini, Kilaru Aswini, Vanamali Venkata Abhiram, Bathini Ramya, & Yadav, M. G.* Fraud Detection in Digital and Netbanking Using Machine Learning., DOI: 10.1109/ICOECA62351.2024.00138

Mouline, S., Ozlu, O., & Herzog, L. (January 19, 2022). A big step forward for women's leadership in Morocco. https://blogs.worldbank.org/arabvoices/big-step-forward-womens-leadership-morocco

Moussa, A. S., & Elmarzouky, M. (2024). Sustainability reporting and market uncertainty: The moderating effect of carbon disclosure. *Sustainability (Basel)*, *16*(13), 5290. Advance online publication. DOI: 10.3390/su16135290

Muchlinski, P. T. (2021). *Multinational enterprises and the law* (3rd ed.). Oxford University Press., DOI: 10.1093/law/9780198824138.001.0001

Mukherjee, S.Dr. Subholaxmi Mukherjee. (2025). Regulating ESG disclosures in India: Greenwashing and legal accountability. *International Journal of Leading Research Publication*, *6*(2), 1–14. DOI: 10.70528/IJLRP.v6.i12.1880

Munif, M., & Wahrudin, B. (2025). Transnational Legal Cooperation And Global Trade: Rethinking International Investment Law In The Era Of Sustainable Development. Journal of Law. *Policy and Global Development*, *1*(1), 64–77. DOI: 10.71305/jlpgd.v1i1.336

Muñoz, P., & Gamble, E. N. (2024). When given two choices, take both! Social impact assessment in social entrepreneurship. *Entrepreneurship and Regional Development*, *36*(9-10), 1161–1187. DOI: 10.1080/08985626.2024.2349207

Murphy, K. M., Shleifer, A., & Vishny, R. W. (1993). Why is rent-seeking so costly to growth? *The American Economic Review*, *83*(2), 409–414.

Mushtaq, S., Imran, M., Rehman, M. A., & Fatima, Z. (2024). Building a more inclusive future. In Practice, Progress, and Proficiency in Sustainability (pp. 65–74). IGI Global. DOI: 10.4018/979-8-3693-6298-3.ch004

Mustakallio, M., Autio, E., & Zahra, S. A. (2002). Relational and contractual governance in family firms: Effects on strategic decision-making quality. Family Business Review, 15*(3), 205–222.

Muzzio, H., & Gama, A. (2024). Knowledge management and innovation: A systematic review and research agenda. *Journal of Knowledge Management*, *28*(6), 1523–1548. DOI: 10.1108/JKM-05-2023-0405

Mytnyk, B., Tkachyk, O., Shakhovska, N., Fedushko, S., & Syerov, Y. (2023). Application of Artificial Intelligence for Fraudulent Banking Operations Recognition. *Big Data and Cognitive Computing*, *7*(2), 93. DOI: 10.3390/bdcc7020093

Nakash, M., & Bolisani, E. (2024). Knowledge management meets artificial intelligence: A systematic review and future research agenda. In Proceedings of the 25th European Conference on Knowledge Management (ECKM) (pp. 755–764). Academic Conferences International. https://doi.org/DOI: 10.34190/eckm.25.1.2657

Narasapuram, N. K., Shah, S. A. A., Shiratuddin, M. F., & Sohel, F. (2026). Explainable artificial intelligence models for detecting suspicious bank transactions. *International Journal of Machine Learning and Cybernetics*, *17*(3), 111. Advance online publication. DOI: 10.1007/s13042-026-02994-w

Nasr, S., & Pearce, D. (2012). *SMEs for job creation in the Arab world: SME access to financial services*. World Bank. DOI: 10.1596/27098

National Institute of Standards and Technology. (2023). *Artificial intelligence risk management framework (AI RMF 1.0)*. NIST.

Neace, M. B. (1999). Entrepreneurs in emerging economies: Creating trust, social capital, and civil society. *The Annals of the American Academy of Political and Social Science*, *565*(1), 148–161. DOI: 10.1177/000271629956500110

Negi, S., Karyamsetty, H. J., & Fida, B. A. (2026). Developing Graduates for the Fourth Industrial Revolution and Oman Vision 2040: The Role of Business Schools in Shaping the Future Workforce. *SAGE Open*, *16*(1), 21582440251410308. Advance online publication. DOI: 10.1177/21582440251410308

Neumayer, E. (2007). Do double taxation treaties increase foreign direct investment to developing countries? *The Journal of Development Studies*, *43*(8), 1501–1519. DOI: 10.1080/00220380701611535

Nguyen, L. T. H. (2022). Impacts of Foreign Direct Investment on Economic growth in Vietnam. *Journal of Economic and Banking Studies, 4*, 01-15.

Nguyen, V. B. (2025). Digitalization's divergent impact on FDI inflows: A comparative analysis between advanced and developing countries. *Transnational Corporations Review*, *17*(3), 200148. DOI: 10.1016/j.tncr.2025.200148

Niftiyev, I. (2021). Dutch disease effects in the Azerbaijan economy: Results of multivariate linear ordinary least squares (OLS) estimations. *HSE Economic Journal*, *25*(2), 309–346. DOI: 10.17323/1813-8691-2021-25-2-309-346

Nikolaou, P. (2022). Sustainable development: A developmental evaluation of logistics higher education in the Sultanate of Oman based on two innovation approaches (the triple helix of innovation and innovation competencies). *Higher Education Evaluation and Development*, *16*(2), 102–120. DOI: 10.1108/HEED-07-2021-0056

Nonaka, I. (1994). A dynamic theory of organizational knowledge creation. *Organization Science*, *5*(1), 14–37. DOI: 10.1287/orsc.5.1.14

Nonaka, I., & Konno, N. (1998). The concept of 'Ba': Building a foundation for knowledge creation. *California Management Review*, *40*(3), 40–54. DOI: 10.2307/41165942

Nonaka, I., & Takeuchi, H. (1995). *The knowledge-creating company: How Japanese companies create the dynamics of innovation*. Oxford University Press. DOI: 10.1093/oso/9780195092691.001.0001

North, D. C. (1990). *Institutions, institutional change and economic performance*. Cambridge University Press. DOI: 10.1017/CBO9780511808678

North, D. C. (1991). Institutions. *The Journal of Economic Perspectives*, *5*(1), 97–112. DOI: 10.1257/jep.5.1.97

NSFI 2022-2028. (2024). *National Strategy for Financial Inclusion 2022-2028*. Bsp.gov.ph. https://www.bsp.gov.ph/Pages/InclusiveFinance/NSFI-2022-2028.pdf

Nurunnabi, M. (2020). Knowledge-based economy in Saudi Arabia and Vision 2030. *Research, Innovation and Entrepreneurship in Saudi Arabia*, 84–103. DOI: 10.4324/9781351040020-4

O'Leary, D. E. (2024). Large language models and applications: The rebirth of enterprise knowledge management and the rise of prompt libraries. *IEEE Intelligent Systems*, *39*(2), 72–75. DOI: 10.1109/MIS.2024.3366648

OECD. (2002). *Foreign Direct Investment for Development: Maximising the Benefits, Minimising the Costs*. OECD.

OECD. (2018). *Making blended finance work for the Sustainable Development Goals*. OECD Publishing., DOI: 10.1787/9789264288768-

OECD. (2020). *Developing sustainable finance definitions and taxonomies*. OECD Publishing., DOI: 10.1787/134a2dbe-

OECD. (2024). *AI principles (Adopted in 2019; updated in 2024)*. Organization for Economic Co-operation and Development.

OECD. (2025, December 9). *The Organisation for Economic Co-operation and Development | OECD*. https://www.oecd.org/

OECD-Organisation for Economic Co-operation and Development. (2008). *Natural resources and pro-poor growth: The economics and politics*. Organisation for Economic Cooperation and Development, DAC Guidelines and Reference Series, A Good Practice Paper.

Ogbonna, O. E., Ogbuabor, J. E., Manasseh, C. O., & Ekeocha, D. O. (2022). Global uncertainty, economic governance institutions and foreign direct investment inflow in Africa. *Economic Change and Restructuring*, *55*(4), 2111–2136. DOI: 10.1007/s10644-021-09378-w

Oman Vision 2040 Implementation Follow-up Unit. (2023). Oman Vision 2040 booklet.

Oman Vision 2040. (2022). *Oman Vision 2040 Implementation Follow-up Unit*. https://www.oman2040.om/?lang=en

Omar, N. S. (2019). Innovation and economic performance in MENA region. *Review of Economics and Political Science*, *4*(2), 158–175. DOI: 10.1108/REPS-12-2018-0042

Omri, A., Nguyen, D. K., & Rault, C. (2014). Causal interactions between CO_2 emissions, FDI, and economic growth: Evidence from dynamic simultaneous-equation models. *Economic Modelling*, *42*, 382–389. DOI: 10.1016/j.econmod.2014.07.026

Orbes, et al. (2019). Paper reevaluating FDI influence on economic growth.

Organisation for Economic Co-operation and Development (OECD). (2023). *FDI in figures*. OECD Publishing.

Organisation for Economic Co-operation and Development (OECD). (2023). *OECD international direct investment statistics 2023*. OECD Publishing.

Ortiz, R., Contreras, M., & Mellado, C. (2023). Regression, multicollinearity and Markowitz. *Finance Research Letters*, *58*, 104550–104550. DOI: 10.1016/j.frl.2023.104550

Ortlipp, M. (2008). Keeping and using reflective journals in the qualitative research process. *The Qualitative Report*, *13*(4), 695–705.

Otto, B. (2011). Organizing data governance: Findings from the telecommunications industry and consequences for large service providers. *Communications of the Association for Information Systems*, *29*, 45. DOI: 10.17705/1CAIS.02903

Oueslati, A., & Labidi, M. A. (2015). Growth, Inequality and Governance: A case of MENA countries. *SSRG International Journal of Economics and Management Studies*, *2*(4), 1–7.

Özyol, A. (2020). Investing in women's entrepreneurship: Inclusive and sustainable economic growth. In *Gender and Diversity in Middle Eastern Entrepreneurship* (pp. 225–248). Springer.

Page, M. J., McKenzie, J. E., Bossuyt, P. M., Boutron, I., Hoffmann, T. C., Mulrow, C. D., Shamseer, L., Tetzlaff, J. M., Akl, E. A., Brennan, S. E., Chou, R., Glanville, J., Grimshaw, J. M., Hróbjartsson, A., Lalu, M. M., Li, T., Loder, E. W., Mayo-Wilson, E., McDonald, S., . . . Moher, D. (2021a). The PRISMA 2020 statement: an updated guideline for reporting systematic reviews. *BMJ (Clinical Research Ed.), 372*. DOI: 10.1136/bmj.n71

Palalic, R., Al Riyami, S., & Umrani, W. (2026). *Small and Medium Enterprises (SMEs) Development in Oman: Current Trends, Challenges, Opportunities and Future Prospects*. 327–342. DOI: 10.1007/978-3-032-04214-9_21

Pal, S., & Bandyopadhyay, I. (2022). Impact of financial inclusion on economic growth, financial development, financial efficiency, financial stability, and profitability: International evidence. *SN Business & Economics*, *2*(9), 139. Advance online publication. DOI: 10.1007/s43546-022-00313-3

Pamantung, R. (2026). The role of foreign direct investment in driving economic growth: Evidence from developing countries. Available at *SSRN* 6595701. DOI: 10.2139/ssrn.6595701

Pankratz, N., Bauer, R., & Derwall, J. (2023). Climate change, firm performance, and investor expectations. *Management Science*, *69*(12), 7352–7398. DOI: 10.1287/mnsc.2023.4685

Panteli, N., Yalabik, Z. Y., & Rapti, A. (2019). Fostering work engagement in geographically-dispersed and asynchronous virtual teams. *Information Technology & People*, *32*(1), 2–17. DOI: 10.1108/ITP-04-2017-0133

Pao, H. T., & Tsai, C. M. (2011). Multivariate Granger causality between CO_2 emissions, energy consumption, FDI, and GDP. *Energy*, *36*(1), 685–693. DOI: 10.1016/j.energy.2010.09.041

Paramaiah, C., Verma, V., Radhakrishnan, G. V., Pal, S., & Wagh, V. W. (2025). The influence of ESG investing on financial markets and economic growth. *Journal of Information Systems Engineering & Management*, *10*(22s). Advance online publication. DOI: 10.52783/jisem.v10i22s.3527

Paramati, S. R., Alam, M. S., & Apergis, N. (2017). The role of stock markets and renewable energy in environmental degradation. *Emerging Markets Review*, *35*, 183–200. DOI: 10.1016/j.ememar.2017.12.004

Park, K. H., Liu, Q., & Li, H. (2023). UNESCO practices under the SDG4 and COVID-19 response framework: Topic modeling from 2003 to 2021. *International Journal of Innovative Research and Scientific Studies*, *6*(2), 322–329. DOI: 10.53894/ijirss.v6i2.1407

Partiti, E. (2024). Addressing the flaws of the sustainable finance disclosure regulation: Moving from disclosures to labelling and sustainability due diligence. *European Business Organization Law Review*, *25*(2), 299–332. DOI: 10.1007/s40804-024-00317-6

Pasmore, W., Winby, S., Mohrman, S. A., & Vanasse, R. (2019). Reflections: Sociotechnical systems design and organization change. *Journal of Change Management*, *19*(2), 67–85. DOI: 10.1080/14697017.2018.1553761

Patil, K., Shetty, A., Rajagopal, A., & Shilpa Sonawani. (2025). A Hybrid Approach to Fake Job Detection Using NLP and Machine Learning. 1–6. .DOI: 10.1109/ICTBIG68706.2025.11323989

Patton, M. Q. (1990). *Qualitative Evaluation and Research Methods*. Sage.

Pavani, N., & Fernandes, J. (2025). Catalyzing Climate Action: The Role of Green Taxonomy and the Green Climate Fund in Sustainable Development [IJIREM]. *International Journal of Innovative Research in Engineering and Management*, *12*(2), 76–83. DOI: 10.55524/ijirem.2025.12.2.13

Pereira, M., Silva, G. M., & Coelho, F. (2026). A fuzzy-set QCA approach exploring the role of public and private debt in shaping environmental performance. *World Development*, *198*, 107213. DOI: 10.1016/j.worlddev.2025.107213

Permanasari, A. E., Chamsudin, A., & Wahyunggoro, O. (2013, August 25). *Utilization of Neural Network for Disease Forecasting*. ResearchGate; ResearchGate. https://www.researchgate.net/publication/265784353_Utilization_of_Neural_Network_for_Disease_Forecasting

Pesaran, M. H., Shin, Y., & Smith, R. J. (2001). Bounds testing approaches to the analysis of level relationships. *Journal of Applied Econometrics*, *16*(3), 289–326. DOI: 10.1002/jae.616

Petticrew, M., & Roberts, H. (2008). Systematic Reviews in the Social Sciences: A Practical Guide. *Systematic Reviews in the Social Sciences: A Practical Guide*, 1–336. DOI: 10.1002/9780470754887

Phillips, R. (2021). *Pricing and revenue optimization* (2nd ed.). Stanford University Press.

Phoenix, A. (2023). *Boys and Schooling. Routledge Handbook on Men, Masculinities and Organizations: Theories*. Practices and Futures of Organizing., DOI: 10.4324/9781003193579-26

Pinelis, M., & Ruppert, D. (2021). Machine Learning Portfolio Allocation. *The Journal of Financial Data Science*, *8*, 35–54. DOI: 10.1016/j.jfds.2021.12.001

Polanyi, M. (1966). *The tacit dimension*. Doubleday.

Polzin, F., Migendt, M., Täube, F. A., & von Flotow, P. (2015). Public policy influence on renewable energy investments—A panel data study across OECD countries. *Energy Policy*, *80*, 98–111. DOI: 10.1016/j.enpol.2015.01.026

Popescu, I.-S., Hitaj, C., & Benetto, E. (2021). Measuring the sustainability of investment funds: A critical review of methods and frameworks in sustainable finance. *Journal of Cleaner Production*, *314*, 128016. DOI: 10.1016/j.jclepro.2021.128016

Preacher, K. J., & Hayes, A. F. (2008). Asymptotic and resampling strategies for assessing and comparing indirect effects in multiple mediator models. *Behavior Research Methods*, *40*(3), 879–891. DOI: 10.3758/BRM.40.3.879

Pritchett, L. (1997). Divergence, big time. *The Journal of Economic Perspectives*, *11*(3), 3–17. DOI: 10.1257/jep.11.3.3

Public Authority for Special Economic Zones and Free Zones. (2021). Launching electronic one-stop-shop services for special economic zones and free zones.

Pullen, A., & Vachhani, S. (2023). Feminist ethics and women leaders: From difference to intercorporeality. In *Leadership, Gender, and Organization* (pp. 63–81). Springer International Publishing., DOI: 10.1007/978-3-031-24445-2_4

Qumba, M. F. (2024). Incorporating Sustainable Development Principles in Africa's Investment Treaty-Making. *Journal of Comparative Law in Africa*, *11*(2), 43–79. Https://hdl.handle.net/10520/ejc-jlc_jcla_v11_n2_a2. DOI: 10.47348/JCLA/v11/i2a2

Raisch, S., & Krakowski, S. (2021). Artificial intelligence and management: The automation–augmentation paradox. *Academy of Management Review*, *46*(1), 192–210. DOI: 10.5465/amr.2018.0072

Ramo, R. M., Alshaher, A. A., & Al-Fakhry, N. A. (2022). The effect of using artificial intelligence on learning performance in Iraq: The dual factor theory perspective. *Ingénierie des Systèmes d'Information*, *27*(2), 255–265. DOI: 10.18280/isi.270209

Rao, A., Ali, M., & Smith, J. M. (2024). Foreign direct investment and domestic innovation: Roles of absorptive capacity, quality of regulations and property rights. *PLoS One*, *19*(3), e0298913. DOI: 10.1371/journal.pone.0298913 PMID: 38457448

Rau, P. R. (2017). Law, Trust, and the Development of Crowdfunding. SSRN *Electronic Journal*. DOI: 10.2139/ssrn.2989056

Rawaf, R. A. A., & Alfalih, A. (2024). Family business sustainability: The impact of governance and women's empowerment in Saudi Arabia. Future Business Journal, 10(1), Article 46.

Rawaf, R. A. A., & Alfalih, A. (2023). The role of governance in achieving sustainability in family-owned business: Do responsible innovation and entrepreneurial culture matter? *Sustainability (Basel)*, *15*(7), 5647. DOI: 10.3390/su15075647

Razmi, M. J., Sedighi, S., & Rezaeian, S. (2016). Essential requirements of good governance for achieving human development. *Journal of Public Administration*, *10*(1), 1–30.

Reddy, S., & Jadhav, A. M. 2019. Gender diversity in boardrooms–A literature review. *Cogent Economics & Finance*, *7*(1), 1644703. https://doi.org/DOI: 10.1080/23322039.2019.1644703

Regmi, R., Zhang, Z., & Zhang, H. (2023). Entrepreneurship strategy, natural resources management and sustainable performance: A study of an emerging market. *Resources Policy*, *86*, 104202. DOI: 10.1016/j.resourpol.2023.104202

Ricci, F., Rokach, L., Shapira, B., & Kantor, P. B. (Eds.). (2015). *Recommender systems handbook* (2nd ed.). Springer. DOI: 10.1007/978-1-4899-7637-6

Richter, A., & Richter, C. (2024). Slowly dying or resilient? Revisiting the SECI model after GenAI. In *Proceedings of ICERI 2024* (pp. 8123–8132). IATED. DOI: 10.21125/iceri.2024.2003

Risman, A., Ali, A. J., Soelton, M., & Siswanti, I. (2023). The behavioral finance of MSMEs in the advancement of financial inclusion and financial technology (Fintech). *The Indonesian Accounting Review*, *13*(1), 91–101. DOI: 10.14414/tiar.v13i1.3213

Rocha, M., Massard da Fonseca, E., Sauter, G. P., & Hasenclever, L. (2023). Vaccine technology transfer: Lessons from COVID-19 and implications for latecomer production capabilities. *Research Policy*, *52*(7), 104739. DOI: 10.1016/j.respol.2023.104739

Rodrik, D. (2013). Unconditional convergence in manufacturing. *The Quarterly Journal of Economics*, *128*(1), 165–204. DOI: 10.1093/qje/qjs047

Rodrik, D., Subramanian, A., & Trebbi, F. (2004). Institutions rule: The primacy of institutions over geography and integration in economic development. *. *Journal of Economic Growth*, *9*(2), 131–165. DOI: 10.1023/B:JOEG.0000031425.72248.85

Romer, P. M. (1990). Endogenous technological change. *Journal of Political Economy*, *98*(5), S71–S102. DOI: 10.1086/261725

Rosser, A. (2007). Escaping the resource curse: The case of Indonesia. *Journal of Contemporary Asia*, *37*(1), 38–58. DOI: 10.1080/00472330601104557

Rust, R. T., & Huang, M.-H. (2014). The service revolution and the transformation of marketing science. *Marketing Science*, *33*(2), 206–221. DOI: 10.1287/mksc.2013.0836

Rytov, R. (2025). Artificial Neural Network for Downward Continuation of Anomalous Magnetic Fields. *Russian Journal of Earth Sciences*, *1–5*, 1–5. Advance online publication. DOI: 10.2205/2025ES000996

Sabir, S., Rafique, A., & Abbas, K. (2019). Institutions and FDI: Evidence from developed and developing countries. *Financial Innovation*, *5*(1), 1–20. DOI: 10.1186/s40854-019-0123-7

Sachs, J. D. & Warner, A. M. (1995). *Natural resource abundance and economic growth*. NBER Working Paper Series, No. 5398.

Sachs, J. D., Schmidt-Traub, G., Mazzucato, M., Messner, D., Nakicenovic, N., & Rockström, J. (2019). Six Transformations to achieve the Sustainable Development Goals. *Nature Sustainability*, *2*(9), 805–814. DOI: 10.1038/s41893-019-0352-9

Sachs, J. D., & Warner, A. (1999). Natural resource intensity and economic growth. In Mayer, J., Chambers, B., & Farooq, A. (Eds.), *Development policies in natural resource economies* (pp. 13–38). Edward Elgar Publishing. DOI: 10.4337/9781782541295.00011

Sachs, J. D., & Warner, A. M. (1999). The big push, natural resource booms and growth. *Journal of Development Economics*, *59*(1), 43–76. DOI: 10.1016/S0304-3878(99)00005-X

Sachs, J. D., & Warner, A. M. (2001). The curse of natural resources. *European Economic Review*, *45*(4-6), 827–838. DOI: 10.1016/S0014-2921(01)00125-8

Sadorsky, P. (2010). The impact of financial development on energy consumption in emerging economies. *Energy Policy*, *38*(5), 2528–2535. DOI: 10.1016/j.enpol.2009.12.048

Saha, S., Sadekin, M. N., & Saha, S. K. (2022). Effects of institutional quality on foreign direct investment inflow in lower-middle income countries. *Heliyon, 8*(10), e10828. Advance online publication. DOI: 10.1016/j.heliyon.2022.e10828 PMID: 36217489

Sahay, R., Cihak, M., N'Diaye, P., Barajas, A., Mitra, S., Kyobe, A., Mooi, Y., & Yousefi, R. (2015). Financial Inclusion: Can it Meet Multiple Macroeconomic Goals? *Staff Discussion Notes, 15*(17), 1. DOI: 10.5089/9781513585154.006

Saif, I. (November 02, 2011). The Middle Class and Transformations in the Arab World. https://carnegie-mec.org/2011/11/02/middle-class-and-transformations-in-arab-world-pub-45895

Sakyi, J. K., Eboseremen, B. O., Adebayo, A. O., Essien, I. A., Okojie, J. S., & Soneye, O. M. (2024). Designing a sustainable financing model for emerging economies: Addressing climate goals through green bonds and ESG investments. *International Journal of Multidisciplinary Futuristic Development, 5*(1), 20–33. DOI: 10.54660/IJMFD.2024.5.1.20-33

Salacuse, J. W. (2015). *The law of investment treaties* (2nd ed.). Oxford University Press., Https://files.pca-cpa.org/pcadocs/bi-c/1.%20Investors/4.%20Legal%20 Authorities/CA115.pdf DOI: 10.1093/law/9780198703976.001.0001

Salihu, O. (2026). Natural resource governance and conflict in Nigeria's extractive frontiers: A scoping review. *Preprints.* https://www.preprints.org/manuscript/202601.0443

Salim Ba Awain, A. M., Jantan, M. D., & Sukati, I. (2021a). Assessing the Effect of Integration in Logistics Sector on Economic Growth: Evidence from Sultanate of Oman. *International Business Research, 15*(1), 35. DOI: 10.5539/ibr.v15n1p35

Salloum, C., Jabbour, G., & Mercier-Suissa, C. 2019. Democracy across gender diversity and ethnicity of Middle Eastern SMEs: how does performance differ?. Journal of Small Business Management, 57(1), 255-267. https://doi.org/DOI: 10.1111/jsbm.12336

Samadi, A. H. (2019). Institutions and entrepreneurship: Unidirectional or bidirectional causality? *Journal of Global Entrepreneurship Research, 9*(1), 1–16. DOI: 10.1186/s40497-018-0129-z

Samuel, A., Johnston, K. A., & Hackney, R. (2022). Adaptive cognitive fit: A new approach to AI-assisted decision making in international business. *International Journal of Information Management, 65*, 102505. DOI: 10.1016/j.ijinfomgt.2022.102505

Sanders, A. R. D., & Sandvik, P. T. (2015). Avoiding the resource curse?: Democracy and natural resources in Norway since 1900. In Badia-Miro, M. Pinilla, V. & Willebald, H. (Eds.) *Natural Resources and Economic Growth* (pp. 313–338). Routledge.

Sarker, S., Chatterjee, S., Xiao, X., & Elbanna, A. (2019). The socio-technical perspective in IS research: A theoretical manifesto for the future. *Management Information Systems Quarterly*, *43*(4), 1209–1246. DOI: 10.25300/MISQ/2019/14019

Sarma, M., & Pais, J. (2011). Financial Inclusion and Development. *Journal of International Development*, *23*(5), 613–628. DOI: 10.1002/jid.1698

Sarna, N. J., Rithen, F. A., Jui, U. S., Belal, S., Amin, A., Oishee, T. K., & Muzahidul Islam, A. K. M. (2025). AI Driven Fraud Detection Models in Financial Networks: A Review. *IEEE Access : Practical Innovations, Open Solutions*, •••, 1–1. DOI: 10.1109/ACCESS.2025.3596060

Sathupadi, K., Achar, S., Bhaskaran, S. V., Faruqui, N., & Uddin, J. (2025). BankNet: Real-Time Big Data Analytics for Secure Internet Banking. *Big Data and Cognitive Computing*, *9*(2), 24. DOI: 10.3390/bdcc9020024

Scalamonti, F. (2026). The impact of FDI on economic growth in emerging and developing economies: The role of institutional quality and technology diffusion. *Transnational Supply Chain Research*, *2*(1), 24–45. DOI: 10.65773/tscr.2.1.92

Schill, S. W. (2017). Reforming investor-state dispute settlement: A (comparative and international) constitutional law framework. *Journal of International Economic Law*, *20*(3), 649–672. DOI: 10.1093/jiel/jgx023

Schmeisser, B., Saebi, T., Schotter, A. P. J., & Gooderham, P. (2026). The digital transformation of international business: A conceptualization, multidisciplinary review, and research agenda. *Journal of World Business*, *61*(1), 101695. DOI: 10.1016/j.jwb.2025.101695

Scott, W. R. (2008). *Institutions and organizations: Ideas and interests* (3rd ed.). Sage Publications.

Sedighi, S. (2024). Rents, financial development, and economic growth in MENA countries, 2000–2020. *Regional Statistics*, *14*(03), 589–608. DOI: 10.15196/RS140308

Seffahlou, H., Boudriche, Z., & Djelloul, C. (2025). Using Artificial Intelligence Models To Predict Bitcoin Prices: Artificial Neural Network Model.
, 189. DOI: 10.35658/1445-016-002-013

Seifipour, R., & Mehrabian, A. (2025). Application of Artificial Neural Networks in Economic and Financial Sciences. *IntechOpen EBooks*. DOI: 10.5772/intechopen.1007604

Seify, M., Sepehri, M., Hosseini-far, A., & Darvish, A. (2022). Fraud Detection in Supply Chain with Machine Learning. *IFAC-PapersOnLine*, *55*(10), 406–411. DOI: 10.1016/j.ifacol.2022.09.427

Sengupta, S. S. (2021). Level-5 Integral Leadership Styles: Transcendence of Mind. *IUP Journal of Organizational Behavior, 20*(2).

Setianto, R. H., Azman-Saini, W. N. W., & Law, S. H. (2025). Threshold effects of institutional quality on the financial inclusion and stability nexus: International evidence. *Borsa Istanbul Review*, *25*(2), 388–399. DOI: 10.1016/j.bir.2025.01.015

Sghaier, I. M. (2023). Paper on trade openness, financial development, FDI, and economic growth in North Africa or similar.

Shahbaz, M., Nasreen, S., Abbas, F., & Anis, O. (2015). Does foreign direct investment impede environmental quality? *Energy Economics*, *51*, 275–287. DOI: 10.1016/j.eneco.2015.06.014

Shannaq, B., & Al Shamsi, I. (2024). Integrating Digital Transformation: Analyzing New Technological Processes for Competitiveness and Growth Opportunities in the Oman Economy. *Studies in Systems. Decision and Control*, *525*, 443–454. DOI: 10.1007/978-3-031-54383-8_34

Shewale, R. (2024, January 1). *43 Fintech Statistics For 2024 (Startups, Financials & Trends)*. DemandSage. https://www.demandsage.com/fintech-statistics/

Shui, Z. L., Wang, H., Xin, C. K., & Xue, R. (2025). Unintended societal outcome of investor protection: Independent director liability and greenwashing. *Journal of Accounting Literature*, •••, 1–34. DOI: 10.1108/JAL-06-2025-0310

Sidamor, Z. (2016). The Role Of Foreign Direct Investment In Spurring Economic growth In North African Countries. *ElWahat pour les Recherches et les Etudes*, *9*(1), 760–769. DOI: 10.54246/1548-009-001-020

Silalahi, H. U. T. I., Soeling, P. D., & Wijaya, C. (2025). Breaking barriers: A systematic review of women's entrepreneurship in the tourism industry. *Journal Research of Social Science, Economics, and Management*, *4*(8), 1042–1053. DOI: 10.59141/jrssem.v4i8.788

Simms, C. D., & Frishammar, J. (2024). Foreign direct investment and innovation policy: A review and research agenda. *Research Policy*, *53*(3), 104937. DOI: 10.1016/j.respol.2023.104937

Simms, C., & Frishammar, J. (2024). Technology transfer challenges in asymmetric alliances: An abductive multi-case study. *Technovation*, *133*, 102931. DOI: 10.1016/j.technovation.2023.102931

Singh. (2010). Work on FDI, institutions, or growth in developing/African contexts.

Singh, K., Chatterjee, S., & Mariani, M. (2024). Applications of generative AI and future organizational performance: The mediating role of explorative and exploitative innovation. *Technovation*, *133*, 102988. DOI: 10.1016/j.technovation.2024.103021

Sinha, M., Tirtosuharto, D., Ray Chaudhury, A., & Basu, P. (2023). FDI, digitalization and employment: Empirical evidence from developing economies. *Studies in Economics and Finance*, *40*(4), 740–756. DOI: 10.1108/SEF-10-2021-0450

Smita Rani Parija, Kumari, R., Tiwari, D., Kumar Shubham, Rath, P., & Das, L. (2025). Fraud Detection in Financial Transactions Using a Machine Learning. 1–7. .DOI: 10.1109/CCPIS65231.2025.11234223

Smith, S. K., Mountain, G. A., & Hawkins, R. J. (2016). A scoping review to identify the techniques frequently used when analysing qualitative visual data. *International Journal of Social Research Methodology*, *19*(6), 693–715. DOI: 10.1080/13645579.2015.1087141

Snaggs-Wilson, S. E. (2021). *Black Women in Leadership–Dominant Discourses that Construct, Maintain and Legitimize Gender, Race Class Bias in Top Canadian Corporations* (Doctoral dissertation).

Solow, R. M. (1956). A contribution to the theory of economic growth. *The Quarterly Journal of Economics*, *70*(1), 65–94. DOI: 10.2307/1884513

Somboonvechakarn, C., Taiphapoon, T., Anuntavoranich, P., & Sinthupinyo, S. (2022). Communicating innovation and sustainability in family businesses through successions. *Heliyon*, *8*(12), e11760. DOI: 10.1016/j.heliyon.2022.e11760

Song, H., & Chen, W. (2023). Can two-way foreign direct investment promote green innovation capability in manufacturing? The threshold role of intellectual property protection. *Journal of Cleaner Production*, *425*, 139035. DOI: 10.1016/j.jclepro.2023.139035

Sornarajah, M. (2021). The international law on foreign investment. Cambridge university press. Https://tamilnation.org/conflictresolution/Tamileelam/norway/sornarajah.pdf

Stam, E. (2015). Entrepreneurial ecosystems and regional policy: A sympathetic critique. *European Planning Studies*, *23*(9), 1759–1769. DOI: 10.1080/09654313.2015.1061484

Staschen, S., & Meagher, P. (2018). Basic Regulatory Enablers for Digital Financial Services. In *World Bank, Washington, DC eBooks*. World Bank. DOI: 10.1596/30275

State Bank of Pakistan. (2024). *National Financial Inclusion Strategy 2024-28*. https://www.sbp.org.pk/nfis/nfis2024-28.pdf

Stephenson, L. (2022, February). Boardroom Diversity: Slow Progress. *The Financial Times Board Director Programme*. https://www.bdp.ft.com/newsletter-blogs-2022/february-2022

Suchman, M. C. (1995). Managing legitimacy: Strategic and institutional approaches. *Academy of Management Review*, *20*(3), 571–610. DOI: 10.2307/258788

Su, D. T., Nguyen, P. C., & Schinckus, C. (2019). Impact of foreign direct investment, trade openness and economic institutions on growth in emerging countries: The case of Vietnam. *Journal of International Students*, *12*(3), 243–264. DOI: 10.14254/2071-8330.2019/12-3/20

Suh, C. S., Li, W., & Song, Z. (2023). Digital trade policies and cross-border digital trade: The impact of data restrictions. *World Economy*, *46*(9), 2569–2595. DOI: 10.1111/twec.13407

Sukalkar, S. S., & Pujari, B. (2025). Women entrepreneurs: A systematic review on problems, challenges, and success. *International Journal of Social Advancement and Technology*, *16*(1), 45–58.

Sulehri, F. A., Ali, A., & Alam, M. (2024). Assessing the pathways of sustainable development: A structural equation modeling investigation of regulatory framework, innovation, and economic indicators. *Journal of Asian Development Studies*, *13*(1), 970–982. DOI: 10.62345/jads.2024.13.1.80

Sumbal, M. S., & Amber, S. (2024). Generative AI for knowledge management: A new frontier. *Journal of Knowledge Management*, *28*(3), 812–835. DOI: 10.1108/JKM-06-2023-0456

Supriyanto, H. (2026). Anomaly Detection in Blockchain Transactions Using Isolation Forest and Autoencoder Deep Learning Models. *Journal of Current Research in Blockchain.*, *3*(2), 139–151. DOI: 10.47738/jcrb.v3i2.69

Suresh, V., & Maity, B. (2022). Exploratory research on bank-based financial inclusion for sustainable economic growth. *Finance India, 36*(1), 105–115. https://financeindia.org/data/2022/FI361/FI-361-Art05.pdf

Svampa, M. (2019). *Neo-extractivism in Latin America: Socio-environmental conflicts, the territorial turn, and new political narratives*. Cambridge University Press. DOI: 10.1017/9781108752589

Swan, T. W. (1956). Economic growth and capital accumulation. *The Economic Record, 32*(2), 334–361. DOI: 10.1111/j.1475-4932.1956.tb00434.x

Tamanna, N. Kamboj, S., Singh, L., & Kaur, T. (2024). Automated Fraud Detection in Financial Transactions using Machine Learning: An Ensemble Perspective. 1–6. .DOI: 10.1109/AIMLA59606.2024.10531422

Tambe, P., Cappelli, P., & Yakubovich, V. (2019). Artificial intelligence in human resources management: Challenges and a path forward. *The Academy of Management Perspectives, 33*(3), 1–13.

Tay, L.-Y., Tai, H.-T., & Tan, G.-S. (2022). Digital Financial inclusion: a Gateway to Sustainable Development. *Heliyon, 8*(6), e09766. ScienceDirect. DOI: 10.1016/j.heliyon.2022.e09766

Teece, D. J. (2007). Explicating dynamic capabilities: The nature and microfoundations of (sustainable) enterprise performance. *Strategic Management Journal, 28*(13), 1319–1350. DOI: 10.1002/smj.640

Tekin, R. B. (2012). Economic growth, exports and foreign direct investment in least developed countries: A panel Granger causality analysis. *Economic Modelling, 29*(3), 868–878. DOI: 10.1016/j.econmod.2011.10.013

The Economist. (1977). The Dutch disease. *The Economist*, 26, 82–83.

The Global Partnership for Financial Inclusion (GPFI). (n.d.). *About GPFI | GPFI.* Www.gpfi.org. Retrieved September 7, 2025, from https://www.gpfi.org/about-gpfi

The World Bank. (2022, March 29). *Financial Inclusion*. World Bank. https://www.worldbank.org/en/topic/financialinclusion/overview#1

Thompson, K. (December 13, 2022). Social Class – An Introduction to the Concept. https://revisesociology.com/2016/08/04/social-class-definition-introduction/

Thorpe, R., Holt, R., Macpherson, A., & Pittaway, L. (2005). Using knowledge within small and medium-sized firms: A systematic review of the evidence. *International Journal of Management Reviews, 7*(4), 257–281. DOI: 10.1111/j.1468-2370.2005.00116.x

Tienhaara, K. (2011). Regulatory chill and the threat of arbitration: a view from political science. Evolution in Investment Treaty Law and Arbitration, Chester Brown, Kate Miles, eds., Cambridge University Press. Https://ssrn.com/abstract=2065706

Tornatzky, L. G., & Fleischer, M. (1990). *The processes of technological innovation*. Lexington Books.

Tranfield, D., Denyer, D., & Smart, P. (2003). Towards a Methodology for Developing Evidence-Informed Management Knowledge by Means of Systematic Review. *British Journal of Management, 14*(3), 207–222. DOI: 10.1111/1467-8551.00375

Trist, E. L. (1981). *The evolution of socio-technical systems: A conceptual framework and an action research program*. Ontario Quality of Working Life Centre.

Trivedi, C., Kumar, S., Abdullah, N., Obaid, A. J., & Faisal, A. (2024). The Utilization of AI in Fraud Detection in Smart Cities. 1–8. .DOI: 10.1109/ICETAS62372.2024.11119907

Ubaradka, A., Bapu, V., Siby, A., & Chandra, S. (2023). The Allegory of the Glass Ceiling and Reverberance of Woman Leadership in Politics: The Case of Arya Rajendran. In *From Industry 4.0 to Industry 5.0: Mapping the Transitions* (pp. 183-189). Cham: Springer Nature Switzerland. https://doi.org/DOI: 10.1007/978-3-031-28314-7_16

Udemba, E. N., & Yalçıntaş, S. (2022). Unveiling the symptoms of Dutch disease: A comparative and sustainable analysis of two oil-rich countries. *Resources Policy, 79*, 102949. DOI: 10.1016/j.resourpol.2022.102949

UNCTAD. (1999). *World Investment Report 1999: Foreign Direct Investment and the Challenge of Development*. United Nations.

UNCTAD. (2015). *Investment Policy Framework for Sustainable Development*. United Nations.

UNCTAD. (2023). World Investment Report 2023: Investing in Sustainable Energy for All.

UNCTAD. (2023). World investment report 2023: Investing in sustainable energy for all. United Nations Conference on Trade and Development. Https://unctad.org/publication/world-investment-report-2023

UNCTAD. (2024). World Investment Report 2024. United Nations Conference on Trade and Development, https://unctad.org/wir2024

UNCTAD. (2024). *World investment report 2024: Investment facilitation and digital government. United Nations Conference on Trade and Development.* DOI: 10.18356/9789210031349

UNCTAD. (2024). World Investment Report 2024: Investment Facilitation and Digital Transformation.

UNCTAD. (2025a). World Investment Report 2025. Geneva: United Nations. (Focuses on global FDI trends, digital economy, and policy implications.)

UNFCCC. (2015). Paris agreement. United Nations Framework Convention on Climate Change. Https://unfccc.int/process-and-meetings/the-paris-agreement

United Nations Conference on Trade and Development (UNCTAD). (2023). World investment report 2023: Investing in sustainable energy for all. United Nations.

United Nations Conference on Trade and Development (UNCTAD). (2024). World investment report 2024: Investment facilitation and digital economy. United Nations. OECD. (2023). FDI Qualities Policy Toolkit. OECD. (2023). International Direct Investment Statistics.

United Nations. (2015). Transforming our world: The 2030 agenda for sustainable development (A/RES/70/1). United Nations General Assembly. Https://docs.un.org/en/A/RES/70/1

Usman, F. O., Kess-Momoh, A. J., Ibeh, C. V., Elufioye, A. E., Ilojianya, V. I., & Oyeyemi, O. P. (2024). Entrepreneurial innovations and trends: A global review: Examining emerging trends, challenges, and opportunities in the field of entrepreneurship, with a focus on how technology and globalization are shaping new business ventures. *International Journal of Science and Research Archive, 11*(1), 552–569. DOI: 10.30574/ijsra.2024.11.1.0079

van Eerd, R. (2010). Of Dutch disease and other ailments. *Bologna Center Journal of International Affairs, 13*, 99–112.

Van Harten, G. (2007). *Investment treaty arbitration and public law*. Oxford University Press., Https://global.oup.com/academic/product/investment-treaty-arbitration-and-public-law-9780199217892?Cc=in&lang=en&utm

Verhoef, P. C., Kannan, P. K., & Inman, J. J. (2015). From multi-channel retailing to omni-channel retailing. *Journal of Retailing, 91*(2), 174–181. DOI: 10.1016/j.jretai.2015.02.005

Vernyuy Wirba, A. (2017). The role of research in knowledge economy within GCC countries. *European Journal of Business and Management* Www.Iiste.Org *ISSN, 9*(3).

Vial, G. (2019). Understanding digital transformation: A review and a research agenda. *The Journal of Strategic Information Systems, 28*(2), 118–144. DOI: 10.1016/j.jsis.2019.01.003

Vinuesa, R., Azizpour, H., Leite, I., Balaam, M., Dignum, V., Domisch, S., Felländer, A., Langhans, S. D., Tegmark, M., & Fuso Nerini, F. (2020). The role of artificial intelligence in achieving the Sustainable Development Goals. *Nature Communications, 11*(1), 3. DOI: 10.1038/s41467-019-14108-y

Volkan, V. D. 2019. Large-group identity, who are we now? Leader–follower relationships and societal–political divisions. *The American Journal of Psychoanalysis, 79*, 139-155. https://doi.org/DOI: 10.1057/s11231-019-09186-2

Voloshchenko-Holda, L., & Niedziółka, P. (2024). Central bank communication in unconventional times: Some evidence from a textual analysis of the National Bank of Poland communication during the COVID-crisis. *Economics and Business Review, 10*(1), 101–124. DOI: 10.18559/ebr.2024.1.1039

Wacziarg, R. (2012). The first law of petropolitics. *Economica, 79*(316), 641–657. DOI: 10.1111/j.1468-0335.2011.00902.x

Wamba, S. F., Akter, S., Edwards, A., Chopin, G., & Gnanzou, D. (2015). How 'big data' can make big impact: Findings from a systematic review and a longitudinal case study. *International Journal of Production Economics, 165*, 234–246. DOI: 10.1016/j.ijpe.2014.12.031

Wang, B., Zheng, P., Yin, Y., Shih, A., & Wang, L. (2024). Toward human-centric smart manufacturing: A human-cyber-physical systems framework. *Journal of Manufacturing Systems, 65*, 471–490. DOI: 10.1016/j.jmsy.2024.05.001

Wang, C. L., & Ahmed, P. K. (2004). The development and validation of the organisational innovativeness construct using confirmatory factor analysis. *European Journal of Innovation Management, 7*(4), 303–313. DOI: 10.1108/14601060410565056

Wang, J., Yang, J., & Yang, L. (2023). Do natural resources play a role in economic development? Role of institutional quality, trade openness, and FDI. *Resources Policy, 81*, 103294. Advance online publication. DOI: 10.1016/j.resourpol.2023.103294

Wang, R., Tan, J., & Yao, S. (2021). Are natural resources a blessing or a curse for economic development? The importance of energy innovations. *Resources Policy, 72*, 102042. DOI: 10.1016/j.resourpol.2021.102042

Warner, C., & Schmincke, D. (2008). *High Altitude Leadership: What the World's Most Forbidding Peaks Teach Us About Success*. John Wiley & Sons., DOI: 10.1111/j.1744-6570.2009.01160_4.x

Wedel, M., & Kannan, P. K. (2016). Marketing analytics for data-rich environments. *Journal of Marketing*, *80*(6), 97–121. DOI: 10.1509/jm.15.0413

Weidinger, L., Uesato, J., Rauh, M., Griffin, C., Huang, P. S., & Mellor, J.. (2022). Taxonomy of risks posed by language models. In *Proceedings of the 2022 ACM Conference on Fairness, Accountability, and Transparency* (pp. 214–229). ACM. DOI: 10.1145/3531146.3533088

Welsch, H. (2008). Resource dependence, knowledge creation, and growth: Revisiting the natural resource curse. *Journal of Economic Development*, *33*(1), 45–70. DOI: 10.35866/caujed.2008.33.1.003

Wen, J., Hai, H., Li, L., Dou, J., & Tao, R. (2026). Digital finance as a catalyst for green innovation: Threshold effect of diminishing marginal returns. *International Review of Financial Analysis*, *110*, 104840. DOI: 10.1016/j.irfa.2025.104840

Were, M. (2015). Paper on determinants of FDI or institutional factors in Africa, e.g., West Africa drivers.

Whetten, D. A. (1989). What constitutes a theoretical contribution? *Academy of Management Review*, *14*(4), 490–495. DOI: 10.2307/258554

WHO (2021). *Global strategy on digital health 2020-2025.*

Williamson, O. E. (1985). The economic institutions of capitalism. Firms, markets, relational contracting. In *Das Summa Summarum des Management: Die 25 wichtigsten Werke für Strategie, Führung und Veränderung* (pp. 61-75). Wiesbaden: Gabler. Https://link.springer.com/chapter/10.1007/978-3-8349-9320-5_6

Williamson, O. E. (1975). *Markets and hierarchies: Analysis and antitrust implications: A study in the economics of internal organization*. Free Press.

Wirtz, B. W., Weyerer, J. C., & Kehl, I. (2022). Governance of artificial intelligence: A risk and guideline-based integrative framework. *Government Information Quarterly*, *39*(4), 101685. DOI: 10.1016/j.giq.2022.101685

World Bank Afganisthan. (2020, February 19). *A pathway to financial inclusion in Afghanistan*. World Bank Blogs. https://blogs.worldbank.org/en/endpovertyinsouthasia/pathway-financial-inclusion-afghanistan

World Bank Group. (2013, November 11). *Global Financial Development Report 2014: Financial Inclusion*. World Bank. https://documents.worldbank.org/curated/en/225251468330270218

World Bank. (2020). *Comparing Business Regulation in 190 Economies.*

World Bank. (2021). *Harmonized bilateral FDI database or related report on Africa's FDI environment and capital flows*. World Bank Group.

World Bank. (2023). *World development indicators*. Washington, DC: World Bank. https://databank.worldbank.org/source/world-development-indicators

World Bank. (2023). Worldwide Governance Indicators.

World Bank. (2024). Global Economic Prospects. IMF. (2024). *World Economic Outlook.*

World Bank. (2025). *The Global State of Financial Inclusion and Consumer Protection*. World Bank. https://documents.worldbank.org/en/publication/documents-reports/documentdetail/099013124180517721

World Commission on Environment and Development. (1987). *Our common future*. Oxford University Press.

World Economic Forum. (2024). *Annual Report 2023-2024.*

World Integrated Trade Solution. (n.d.). *Countries in Middle East & North Africa*. [online] wits.worldbank.org. Available at: https://wits.worldbank.org/chatbot/SearchItem.aspx?RegionId=MEA [Accessed 20 Jun. 2026].

Wu, T. (2024). Green finance reform policy increases corporate hypocritical business strategies: Evidence from the greenwashing behavior. *Mitigation and Adaptation Strategies for Global Change*, *29*(7), 63. DOI: 10.1007/s11027-024-10162-0

Xiao, D., Gao, L., Xu, L., Wang, Z., & Wei, W. (2023). Revisiting the green growth effect of foreign direct investment from the perspective of environmental regulation: Evidence from China. *International Journal of Environmental Research and Public Health*, *20*(3), 2655. DOI: 10.3390/ijerph20032655 PMID: 36768017

Xie, S., Liu, L., Sun, G., Pan, B., Lang, L., & Guo, P. (2023). Enhanced E-commerce Fraud Prediction Based on a Convolutional Neural Network Model. Computers, Materials & Continua/Computers. *Computers, Materials & Continua*, *75*(1), 1107–1117. DOI: 10.32604/cmc.2023.034917

Xu, K.-L. (2025). A revisit to bias-adjusted predictive regression. *Journal of Empirical Finance*, *80*, 101578. DOI: 10.1016/j.jempfin.2024.101578

Yadav, S., Samadhiya, A., Kumar, A., Luthra, S., & Pandey, K. K. (2024). Nexus between fintech, green finance and natural resources management: Transition of BRICS nation industries from resource curse to resource blessed sustainable economies. *Resources Policy, 91*, 104903. DOI: 10.1016/j.resourpol.2024.104903

Yaltaa, A. T., & Yaltab, A. Y. (2022, December 14). The Effects of Financial Inclusion on the Economic Development of MENA Countries. *ERF 29th Annual Conference*. ERF 29th Annual conference, Egypt.

Yang, Z., Wu, F., & Yue, Z. (2026). Artificial intelligence technology and firms' OFDI: Evidence from China. *International Review of Economics & Finance*, *106*, 104920. DOI: 10.1016/j.iref.2026.104920

Yefimov, V. (2011). *Discourse analysis in economics: Methodology and history of economics reconsidered.* Munich Personal RePEc Archive.

Yi-chong, X., & Leiva, D. (2021). Chile: A Successful Story in Latin America? In Okpanachi, E., Chowdhari Tremblay, R. (Eds.), *The Political Economy of Natural Resource Funds* (pp. 87–115). International Political Economy Series. Palgrave Macmillan

Yimer, A. (2023). The effects of FDI on economic growth in Africa. *The Journal of International Trade & Economic Development*, *32*(1), 2–36. DOI: 10.1080/09638199.2022.2079709

Yorulmaz, R. (2018). An analysis of constructing global financial inclusion indices. *Borsa Istanbul Review*, *18*(3), 248–258. DOI: 10.1016/j.bir.2018.05.001

Yuan, L., & Ji, P. (2025). Motives of Chinese foreign direct investment in Africa: With regulation effects of institutional quality. *PLoS One*, *20*(6), e0326970. DOI: 10.1371/journal.pone.0326970 PMID: 40561167

Yu, Y. (2023). Role of Natural resources rent on economic growth: Fresh empirical insight from selected developing economies. *Resources Policy*, *81*, 103326. DOI: 10.1016/j.resourpol.2023.103326

Zaccaro, S. J., Green, J. P., Dubrow, S., & Kolze, M. (2018). Leader individual differences, situational parameters, and leadership outcomes: A comprehensive review and integration. *The Leadership Quarterly, 29*(1), 2-43. https://doi.org/DOI: 10.1016/j.leaqua.2017.10.003

Zagel, G. M. (2021). Achieving Sustainable Development Objectives in International Investment Law. In Handbook of International Investment Law and Policy (pp. 1933-1985). Singapore: Springer Singapore. DOI: 10.1007/978-981-13-3615-7_57

Zahonogo, P. (2016). Paper on trade openness, FDI, and economic growth in sub-Saharan Africa.

Zahra, S. A., & George, G. (2002). Absorptive capacity: A review, reconceptualization, and extension. *Academy of Management Review*, *27*(2), 185–203. DOI: 10.2307/4134351

Zamore, S., Beisland, L. A., & Mersland, R. (2019). Geographic diversification and credit risk in microfinance. *Journal of Banking & Finance*, *109*, 105665. DOI: 10.1016/j.jbankfin.2019.105665

Zarsky, L. (1999). *Havens, halos and spaghetti: Untangling the evidence about foreign direct investment and the environment.* In *Foreign direct investment and the environment* (pp. 47–74). Paris: Organisation for Economic Co-operation and Development (OECD).

Zghidi, N., Sghaier, I. M., & Abida, Z. (2016). Does Economic Freedom Enhance the Impact of Foreign Direct Investment on Economic Growth in North African Countries? A Panel Data Analysis [March.]. *African Development Review*, *28*(1), 64–74. DOI: 10.1111/1467-8268.12167

Zhang, S., Yao, L., Sun, A., & Tay, Y. (2019). Deep learning based recommender system: A survey and new perspectives. *ACM Computing Surveys*, *52*(1), 5.

Zhang, X., Xue, T., & Eugene Stanley, H. (2019). Comparison of Econometric Models and Artificial Neural Networks Algorithms for the Prediction of Baltic Dry Index. *IEEE Access : Practical Innovations, Open Solutions*, *7*, 1647–1657. DOI: 10.1109/ACCESS.2018.2884877

Zhou, Y., Liu, X., Li, M., & Tang, Y. (2025). Leveraging AI and green finance for cleaner energy production: A sustainability framework for ESG integration and climate action. *Journal of Cleaner Production*, *525*, 146595. DOI: 10.1016/j.jclepro.2025.146595

Zlobin, M., & Bazylevych, V. (2025). A Data-Driven Approach for Balancing Overfitting and Underfitting in Decision Tree Models. *Central Ukrainian Scientific Bulletin. Technical Sciences*, *1*(11(42)), 14–26. DOI: 10.32515/2664-262X.2025.11(42).1.14-26

About the Contributors

Nasser Al Harrasi holds a PhD in Management with a specialization in Human Resources Management from Binary University, Malaysia, and currently serves as the Head of the Business Administration Unit and Lecturer at the College of Economics and Business Administration, University of Technology and Applied Sciences (UTAS), Muscat, Oman. He is a Fellow of the Higher Education Academy (UK) and has held research appointments as a Research Associate at Oxford Business College (UK) and Visiting Researcher at the University of Plymouth (UK). Dr. Al Harrasi has produced over 30 scholarly publications, including Scopus-indexed journal articles, book chapters, and edited volumes, covering themes such as artificial intelligence in management, human resource development, leadership, organizational behavior, higher education innovation, and economic development in emerging markets. He has also served in academic leadership roles, supervised numerous master's theses and undergraduate projects, contributed to accreditation-aligned curriculum development, and participated in funded research projects in AI, logistics, entrepreneurship, and university–industry collaboration.

Mohd Abass Bhat holds a Ph.D. in Commerce from the University of Kashmir, India, and is currently a Senior Lecturer in the Department of Economics and Business Administration at the University of Technology and Applied Sciences (UTAS), Muscat, Oman. He has previously served as an assistant professor at universities in Ethiopia and India, and has contributed extensively to teaching, curriculum development, and research supervision. Dr. Bhat has authored numerous publications in Scopus-indexed and ABDC-listed journals on topics including blockchain adoption, fintech, sustainability, ESG, AI applications, innovation, and organizational behavior. His research excellence has been recognized through distinctions such as the GCC Scientific Research Award (2025) and UTAS's Most Cited Researcher Award (2024). He has also participated in several funded projects in sustainability, digital transformation, and healthcare analytics, contributing significantly to the fields of emerging markets, technology-driven business transformation, and sustainable development.

S. Porkodi holds a Ph.D. in Management (Human Resource Management) from Bharathiar University, India, and is currently a faculty member in the College of Economics and Business Administration, University of Technology and Applied Sciences (UTAS), Muscat, Sultanate of Oman. With over two decades of academic experience, she has built an extensive portfolio in teaching, research, academic administration, and scholarly publishing. Dr. Porkodi has published numerous research articles in Scopus-indexed journals. She is also the author of six books and five handbooks, reflecting her diverse expertise in human resource management, organizational behavior, leadership, employee engagement, entrepreneurial development, cloud computing adoption, knowledge management, and healthcare administration. She has served as Editor-in-Chief of the International Journal of Management Rivulet, and as an Editorial Board Member and Reviewer for several recognized journals, including the International Journal of Management and Decision Making (Inderscience) and the International Journal of Management, Entrepreneurship & Technology (New York). Dr. Porkodi has acted as a foreign examiner for more than 30 Ph.D. dissertations for various Indian universities and has supervised multiple postgraduate and doctoral scholars. Her ongoing contributions continue to advance applied research, leadership development, and sustainable management practices in emerging economies.

***

Hussein Raafat Al-Jibori is a PhD candidate at the College of Administration and Economics, University of Mosul, Iraq. His research focuses on artificial intelligence, organizational sustainability, human resource risk management, and digital transformation. He has professional experience in the telecommunications sector and is actively engaged in academic research in management and sustainability.

Hamza Ayass is a PhD candidate at the Faculty of Legal, Economic, and Social Sciences at Mohammed V University in Rabat, Morocco. His research interests are institutions, foreign direct investment, and public policies. He has professional experience in investment and territorial development and is actively engaged in academic research on these topics. He has presented his findings at numerous national and international conferences and has published in journals with international indexes.

Medhansh Bairaria presently is working as Business Analyst with KPMG, India. His focus area includes financial modelling, transaction advisory and management consulting. Previously, was a Research Intern with School of Management, Mahindra University, Hyderabad, India.

Fatima Zahra Belarbi is a researcher in economics specializing in public policy evaluation, labor economics, and regional development. She holds a Ph.D. in Economics from Mohammed V University in Rabat, Morocco. She has served as a part-time lecturer at the Faculty of Legal, Economic and Social Sciences, Agdal-Rabat in Mohammed V University, where she has taught courses in economics and business English. Her research focuses on the evaluation of sectoral development strategies, employment policies, territorial governance, and evidence-based policymaking, with particular emphasis on Morocco. Her work integrates advanced quantitative methods, including econometric modeling and impact evaluation techniques, to assess the effectiveness of public policies. Dr. Belarbi has presented her research at several international scientific conferences and is committed to producing policy-relevant research that contributes to inclusive and sustainable socioeconomic development.

Arathy Chandralekha is a multidisciplinary academic specializing in economics, finance, and human resource management. She holds a PhD and postdoctoral qualification in Commerce, along with an MBA in Finance, MCom, and MA in Economics. Her research interests include environmental sustainability, green human resource management, and sustainable development. She has published in reputed journals and contributes to research on sustainability, organizational behavior, and policy frameworks in emerging economies. Her recent work focuses on the relationship between foreign direct investment and environmental sustainability.

Jaseela K.B. is an Assistant Professor at the Centre for Distance and Online Education, University of Calicut. Her area of research specialization is Finance. She has authored various research publications in academic journals and edited volumes. She has also presented more than 25 papers at national and international seminars/conferences. Her academic interests include finance, sustainability, and related interdisciplinary research areas.

Rizwan Khan is a dedicated academic and researcher with a focus on Accounting and Finance. Currently serving as an Assistant Professor at the Haji Taufeeq Ali Mahavidyalaya, CSJM University his research primarily revolves around financial accounting, cost accounting, financial management, and the integration of artificial intelligence in the financial sector. Dr. Khan's doctoral research on Activity Based Costing in the Indian automobile industry. Dr. Khan's scholarly contributions include several published books, research papers, and book chapters on topics ranging from financial performance to artificial intelligence applications in finance. Notably, his research has been published in indexed journals and books by leading academic publishers, such as IGI Global and Springer. His ongoing projects delve into emerging issues like the role of Artificial Intelligence in India's financial landscape and corporate social responsibility practices in Non-Banking Financial Companies (NBFCs). In addition to his academic publications, Dr. Khan has been awarded the Maulana Azad National Fellowship and is currently co-principal investigator of an ICSSR-funded project on Central Bank Digital Currency (CBDC) adoption in India. His work also extends beyond teaching to organizing international conferences and faculty development programs, highlighting his commitment to advancing research and fostering academic excellence.

Roohi Kursheed Khan S is an Associate Professor & BBA Programme Manager at the School of Commerce & Management Studies, Dayananda Sagar University, Bengaluru. She has pursued her Doctorate of Philosophy in Human Resource Management from Bharathiar University, Coimbatore and has completed her MBA, M.Com & Diploma in Training & Development. She has 10 years of experience, teaching UG & PG students, 12 years of research experience and is a recognised PhD research scholar supervisor of the university. Dr. Khan has visited Oxford University, Limkokwing University in Malaysia, Qatar University, and Sri Lanka on academic visits for various activities, including participation in conferences and international collaboration programs. Some of her research presentations have won her Best Presentation Awards at various international conferences. She has published more than 18 research articles in various National, International, Referred & Scopus indexed journals. She is also a nominated reviewer and editorial board member for various international and national journals.

Mythili Kolluru is an award-winning educator, strategic management scholar, and global learning architect with 23+ years of experience across the Middle East, Asia, and North America. She currently works as an Assistant Professor at the College of Banking and Financial Studies in Muscat, Oman. She has designed, delivered, and evaluated MBA, undergraduate, and executive programs, leading curriculum innovation, quality assurance, and accreditation-aligned teaching and assessment. In addition to being a certified Strategic Planning Professional, Dr. Kolluru is also a high-impact corporate trainer. A prolific researcher and writer, she has published 30+ peer-reviewed papers in globally indexed journals (including Scopus Q1–Q2 outlets), authored specialized books, and developed copyrighted frameworks such as the Strategic Thinking Wheel and the Personalized Strategic Career Decision-Making Grid. As a columnist with 80+ Oman Observer articles, she translates complex ideas on strategy, leadership, productivity, international affairs, and the future of work into accessible insights for policymakers, industry, and the public.

Adarsh Kumar is an Assistant Professor in the Department of Management at ITM, Gwalior, (M.P) India. He holds a Ph.D. in Management and has over eight years of experience in teaching, research, and academic administration. He currently serves as the Criteria Coordinator for NAAC and NBA, contributing to quality assurance, accreditation processes, and institutional development initiatives. Previously, he worked with the Ministry of Tourism, Government of India, where he was involved in project-based assignments related to tourism development and policy implementation. His academic and research interests include marketing management, consumer behavior, digital marketing, tourism marketing, and the application of emerging technologies in management education. Dr. Kumar has published research in peer-reviewed journals and contributed to edited volumes. His current research focuses on AI-driven personalization, consumer engagement, trust, and privacy in digital platforms. He is actively engaged in mentoring postgraduate students and integrating research with managerial practice.

Swapnil Morande, PhD, is a Data Scientist with the apex policy think-tank of the Government of India. He holds a doctorate from the University of Naples, Italy and a Master from Colorado State University, USA. Swapnil's decade-long global work exposure counts in the field of Information Systems with an exemplary record working on technologically advanced initiatives. He has served as Chairman of E-Commerce at the University of Mumbai, India with International publications encompassing Artificial Intelligence, Cloud computing and Blockchain. He believes in the 'Medici Effect' that catapults Design Thinking and aligned with the eco-systemic nature of digitization, seeks Informatics as a research interest.

Ibrahim Niftiyev holds a PhD in Economics from the University of Szeged (Hungary) and currently teaches economics and business administration at Azerbaijan State University of Economics (UNEC). He is passionate about sectoral development, economic growth, industrial policy, sustainable entrepreneurship, and stakeholder theory. He is a research fellow at the Center for European Economies at UNEC.

Bhaskar Ponna was awarded the Doctor of Philosophy (Ph.D.) in Mathematics from Shri Venkateshwara University, a recognized institution known for its academic and research excellence. He has over 25 years of teaching experience and nearly 13 years of research experience, with 10 research publications in the field of Fluid Dynamics. He is currently serving as a Lecturer in the Department of PSC at the

University of Technology and Applied Sciences (UTAS), Muscat, Sultanate of Oman.

Kavya R is an Assistant Professor specializing in Human Resource Management, with six years of combined teaching and research experience. Her academic interests include HRM, workplace dynamics, telecommuting, and management education. She has published in Scopus-indexed journals and book chapters, presented papers at national and international conferences, and actively contributes to research, teaching, and academic development in business and management studies.

Thirupathi Regula is a faculty member in the Department of Information Technology at the University of Technology and Applied Sciences (UTAS), Muscat, with over 20+ years of teaching and academic experience. He holds a PhD in Computer Science and Engineering and is currently pursuing a Post-Doctorate in Artificial Intelligence and Machine Learning at the Singapore Institute of Technology, Singapore. His expertise spans Artificial Intelligence, Internet of Things (IoT), Edge Computing, Federated Learning, Digital Twin Systems, Data Analytics, Data Mining, and GeoFencing. Dr. Regula has an extensive record of publications in journals, conferences, and book chapters, and has received several recognitions, including the Outstanding Scientist Award, Best Researcher Award, and Quarterly Franklin Membership. He is actively involved as a reviewer, editor, and advisory member for peer-reviewed journals, and is a member of leading professional bodies such as IEEE, ACM, AAAI, and IAENG. He has also led and contributed to several funded research projects in AI and IoT, while teaching courses such as Big Data and Database Programming.

Gouri Kiran Kumar S. has been awarded the Doctor of Philosophy (Ph.D.) degree in Computer Science and Engineering by Acharya Nagarjuna University, a reputed public university known for its strong academic and research traditions. At present, I am working as a Senior Lecturer in the Department of Computing and Information Sciences at the University of Technology and Applied Sciences, Muscat, Sultanate of Oman and also a Cisco Network Academy Certified Instructor, Microsoft Proctor, and AWS Academy Instructor. Experience is 20+ years. Expertise in AI, ML, IIOT, Cybersecurity, Networking, BigData. Dr. Kiran supervising many Research grants.

Muneer Shaik is an Associate Professor in the area of Finance at Mahindra University, School of Management, Hyderabad. Prior to that, he worked with IFMR Graduate School of Business, in the department of Quantitative Finance, and Data Science. He also held academic appointments with Goa Institute of Management, and Krea University. Prior to joining academics, he had a corporate work experience with J.P.Morgan where he acted in the managerial position in the asset services division across U.K, and India. He holds a Ph.D. in the area of Economics-Finance from IFMR Graduate School of Business, and Masters (Hons.) in Economics, and B.Tech (Hons.) in Mechanical Engineering from BITS-Pilani, Rajasthan.

Vidya Suresh is currently a faculty member at the College of Banking and Financial Studies, Oman. She has over 27 years of experience in teaching and research in the area of Economics and Management. She had previously held many key positions, including Dean of Post graduate Diploma in Management Programme in a B-School, business analyst with Mu-Sigma Business Solutions, editor and reviewer of academic journals, and other administrative responsibilities such as placement & alumni relations management and summer internship coordination. Dr. Suresh is an active researcher in the area of Economics with publication in Scopus indexed journals. Her doctoral thesis focused on Industrial Economics using econometric models. She is a passionate case writer and has published cases with Ivey League and IIM-A case center. Also, an alumnus of UC Berkeley Center for Executive Education & UC Berkeley Haas School of Business with certification in "Business Analytics for Leaders: From Data to Decisions.

Veena Tewari Nandi SFHEA (Senior Fellow of the Higher Education Academy, UK) FCIM (Fellow of the Chartered Institute of Marketing, UK) (PhD), MBA (International Marketing), BSc. (Hons) Presently working as an Ass. Professor at the University of Technology and Applied Sciences, Ibri, Sultanate of Oman. Previous work experience is at Majan University College, Muscat, Sultanate of Oman as a Programme Manager. In addition to this she was the chair of Faculty Research Committee. She has a mixed experience of 20 years in teaching, research and consultancy. This includes working on the projects in Parle, Coke, Neptune India Ltd, Speedway food & Beverages and having a short stint with IIM, Ahmedabad. She has been on the teaching assignment in East Europe, Middle East, Southeast Asia and Northeast Africa. She has been an extensive traveler and has been to various countries by virtue of the consultancy and research projects. She has almost 40 publications both at the international and national level in various conferences, journals, book chapters and seminars. She is serving as the editor in chief, board and advisory member for various journals, Marketing organizations.

José G. Vargas-Hernández, M.B.A.; Ph.D. Member of the National System of Researchers of Mexico and a research professor at Tecnológico Mario Molina Unidad Zapopan formerly at University Center for Economic and Managerial Sciences, University of Guadalajara. Professor Vargas-Hernández has a Ph. D. in Public Administration and a Ph.D. in Organizational Economics. He has undertaken studies in Organisational Behaviour and has a Master of Business Administration, published four books and more than 200 papers in international journals and reviews (some translated to English, French, German, Portuguese, Farsi, Chinese, etc.) and more than 300 essays in national journals and reviews. He has obtained several international Awards and recognition.

Index

Q

R

S

T

W

www.ingramcontent.com/pod-product-compliance
Lightning Source LLC
LaVergne TN
LVHW061526290926
849162LV00004B/683
* 9 7 9 8 3 3 7 3 8 9 6 4 6 *